S0-CTK-758

1,300

Critical Evaluations

of

Selected Novels and Plays

1,300 Critical Evaluations of Selected Novels and Plays

OFFPRINTS OF ALL THE NEW MATERIAL FROM THE 12-VOLUME REVISED EDITION OF *MASTERPLOTS*

Edited by
FRANK N. MAGILL

Volume Two
Epi - Mac
653 - 1308

SALEM PRESS
Englewood Cliffs

For information address the publisher, Salem Press, Inc., Englewood Cliffs, New Jersey 07632.

LIBRARY OF CONGRESS CATALOG CARD NUMBER: 78-55387

Complete Set: ISBN 0-89356-043-X
Volume 2: ISBN 0-89356-045-6

Some of the material in this work also appears in *Masterplots*, Revised Edition (1976).

PRINTED IN THE UNITED STATES OF AMERICA

LIST OF TITLES IN VOLUME TWO

Epic of Gilgamesh, The—*Unknown* 653
Epitaph of a Small Winner—*Joaquim Maria Machado De Assis* 655
Erec and Enide—*Chrétien de Troyes* 658
Erewhon—*Samuel Butler* 661
Esther Waters—*George Moore* 662
Ethan Frome—*Edith Wharton* 664
Eugene Aram—*Edward George Earle Bulwer-Lytton* 665
Eugene Onegin—*Alexander Pushkin* 666
Eugenie Grandet—*Honoré de Balzac* 667
Eunuch, The—*Terence (Publius Terentius Afer)* 670
Euphues and His England—*John Lyly* 671
Euphues, the Anatomy of Wit—*John Lyly* 674
Evan Harrington—*George Meredith* 676
Evangeline—*Henry Wadsworth Longfellow* 677
Eve of St. Agnes, The—*John Keats* 679
Evelina—*Fanny Burney (Madame d' Arblay)* 682
Every Man in His Humour—*Ben Jonson* 685
Every Man out of His Humour—*Ben Jonson* 688
Everyman—*Unknown* 690
Exiles—*James Joyce* 693

Fable, A—*William Faulkner* 694
Faerie Queen, The—*Edmund Spenser* 698
Fair Maid of Perth, The—*Sir Walter Scott* 701
Faithful Shepherdess, The—*John Fletcher* 703
Fall of the House of Usher, The—*Edgar Allan Poe* 705
Family at Gilje, The—*Jonas Lie* 709
Family Reunion, The—*T. S. Eliot* 710
Far Away and Long Ago—*W. H. Hudson* 711
Far from the Madding Crowd—*Thomas Hardy* 713
Farewell to Arms, A—*Ernest Hemingway* 716
Father, The—*August Strindberg* 719
Father Goriot—*Honoré de Balzac* 724
Fathers and Sons—*Ivan Turgenev* 727
Faust—*Johann Wolfgang von Goethe* 730
Felix Holt, Radical—*George Eliot (Mary Ann Evans)* 733
Fellowship of the Ring, The—*J. R. R. Tolkien* 734
Fields, The—*Conrad Richter* 736
Fiesta in November—*Eduardo Mallea* 737
File No. 113—*Emile Gaboriau* 740
Filostrato, Il—*Giovanni Boccaccio* 742
Financier, The—*Theodore Dreiser* 745
Finn Cycle, The—*Unknown* 747

Fisher Maiden, The—*Björnsterne Björnson* 750
Five Women Who Loved Love—*Ibara Saikaku* 751
Foma Gordyeeff—*Maxim Gorky* 753
Fool of Quality, The—*Henry Brooke* 755
Fool's Errand, A—*Albion W. Tourgee* 756
For Whom the Bell Tolls—*Ernest Hemingway* 758
Forsyte Saga, The—*John Galsworthy* 761
Fortitude—*Hugh Walpole* 764
Fortress, The—*Hugh Walpole* 766
Fortunata and Jacinta—*Benito Pérez Galdós* 768
Fortunes of Nigel, The—*Sir Walter Scott* 771
Fortunes of Richard Mahony, The—*Henry Handel Richardson* (*Ethel Robertson Richardson*) 774
Forty Days of Musa Dagh, The—*Franz Werfel* 776
Framley Parsonage—*Anthony Trollope* 777
Frankenstein—*Mary Godwin Shelley* 778
Fraternity—*John Galsworthy* 780
Friar Bacon and Friar Bungay—*Robert Greene* 782
Frithiof's Saga—*Esaias Tegnér* 783
Frogs, The—*Aristophanes* 784
Fruit of the Tree, The—*Edith Wharton* 787
Funeral, The—*Sir Richard Steele* 788

Gambler, The—*Fyodor Mikhailovich Dostoevski* 790
Garden, The—*L. A. G. Strong* 793
Gardener's Dog, The—*Lope de Vega* 794
Gargantua and Pantagruel—*François Rabelais* 797
Gaucho: Martin Fierro, The—*José Hernández* 800
"Genius," The—*Theodore Dreiser* 803
Gentleman Dancing Master, The—*William Wycherley* 805
Gentleman Usher, The—*George Chapman* 807
Germinal—*Émile Zola* 808
Germinie Lacerteux—*Edmond* and *Jules de Goncourt* 809
Gettysburg—*Elsie Singmaster* 811
Ghosts—*Henrik Ibsen* 813
Giants in the Earth—*O. E. Rölvaag* 817
Gil Blas of Santillane—*Alain René Le Sage* 820
Gilded Age, The—*Mark Twain* and *Charles Dudley Warner* 822
Glass Key, The—*Dashiell Hammett* 823
Goat Song—*Franz Werfel* 825
Gods Are Athirst, The—*Anatole France* 826
Gold Bug, The—*Edgar Allan Poe* 828
Golden Asse of Lucius Apuleius, The—*Lucius Apuleius* 829
Golden Bowl, The—*Henry James* 831
Golden Boy—*Clifford Odets* 834
Gondoliers, The—*W. S. Gilbert* 836
Good Companions, The—*J. B. Priestley* 838
Good Earth, The—*Pearl S. Buck* 839
Good Soldier: Schweik, The—*Jaroslav Hašek* 842
Goodbye, Mr. Chips—*James Hilton* 844
Gorboduc—*Thomas Norton* and *Thomas Sackville* 846
Grand Hotel—*Vicki Baum* 848

Grandissimes, The—*George W. Cable* 849
Grandmothers, The—*Glenway Wescott* 851
Grapes of Wrath, The—*John Steinbeck* 853
Great Expectations—*Charles Dickens* 856
Great Galeoto, The—*José Echegaray* 859
Great Gatsby, The—*F. Scott Fitzgerald* 860
Great Meadow, The—*Elizabeth Madox Roberts* 863
Great Valley, The—*Mary Johnston* 865
Green Bay Tree, The—*Louis Bromfield* 866
Green Grow the Lilacs—*Lynn Riggs* 868
Green Mansions—*W. H. Hudson* 870
Green Mountain Boys, The—*Daniel Pierce Thompson* 871
Grettir the Strong—*Unknown* 873
Gringa, La—*Florencio Sánchez* 876
Growth of the Soil—*Knut Hamsun* 878
Grüne Heinrich, Der—*Gottfried Keller* 880
Guard of Honor—*James Gould Cozzens* 881
Gulliver's Travels—*Jonathan Swift* 884
Guy Mannering—*Sir Walter Scott* 887
Guy of Warwick—*Unknown* 888
Guzman de Alfarache—*Mateo Alemán* 890

Hajji Baba of Ispahan—*James Morier* 892
Hakluyt's Voyages—*Richard Hakluyt* 894
Hamlet, The—*William Faulkner* 896
Hamlet—*William Shakespeare* 897
Handful of Dust, A—*Evelyn Waugh* 900
Handley Cross—*Robert Smith Surtees* 901
Handy Andy—*Samuel Lover* 902
Hangman's House—*Donn Byrne* 903
Hard Times—*Charles Dickens* 904
Harp of a Thousand Strings—*H. L. Davis* 905
Havelok the Dane—*Unknown* 908
Hazard of New Fortunes, A—*William Dean Howells* 910
Headlong Hall—*Thomas Love Peacock* 911
Heart Is a Lonely Hunter, The—*Carson McCullers* 912
Heart of Darkness—*Joseph Conrad* 914
Heart of Midlothian, The—*Sir Walter Scott* 917
Heart of the Matter, The—*Grahame Greene* 920
Heat of the Day, The—*Elizabeth Bowen* 923
Heaven's My Destination—*Thornton Wilder* 926
Hedda Gabler—*Henrik Ibsen* 928
Heimskringla, The—*Snorri Sturluson* 931
Helen—*Euripides* 934
Henry Esmond—*William Makepeace Thackeray* 935
Henry the Eighth—*William Shakespeare* 938
Henry the Fifth—*William Shakespeare* 939
Henry the Fourth, Part One—*William Shakespeare* 942
Henry the Fourth, Part Two—*William Shakespeare* 945
Henry the Sixth, Part One—*William Shakespeare* 948
Henry the Sixth, Part Two—*William Shakespeare* 949
Henry the Sixth, Part Three—*William Shakespeare* 950

Herakles Mad—*Euripides* 952
Hercules and His Twelve Labors—*Unknown* 953
Hereward the Wake—*Charles Kingley* 956
Hero of Our Time, A—*Mikhail Yurievich Lermontov* 957
Herself Surprised—*Joyce Cary* 959
High Wind Rising, A—*Elsie Singmaster* 960
Hill of Dreams, The—*Arthur Machen* 961
Hillingdon Hall—*Robert Smith Surtees* 962
Hippolytus—*Euripides* 964
History of Colonel Jacque, The—*Daniel Defoe* 966
History of Mr. Polly, The—*H. G. Wells* 967
H. M. S. Pinafore—*W. S. Gilbert* 968
Holy Terrors, The—*Jean Cocteau* 970
Honest Whore, Part One, The—*Thomas Dekker* with *Thomas Middleton* 971
Honest Whore, Part Two, The—*Thomas Dekker* 973
Honey in the Horn—*H. L. Davis* 975
Hoosier Schoolmaster, The—*Edward Eggleston* 976
Horace—*Pierre Corneille* 978
Horse's Mouth, The—*Joyce Cary* 981
Horseshoe Robinson—*John P. Kennedy* 982
House by the Churchyard, The—*Joseph Sheridan Le Fanu* 983
House by the Medlar Tree, The—*Giovanni Verga* 985
House in Paris, The—*Elizabeth Bowen* 988
House of Atreus, The—*Aeschylus* 991
House of Gentlefolk, A—*Ivan Turgenev* 994
House of Mirth, The—*Edith Wharton* 997
House of the Seven Gables, The—*Nathaniel Hawthorne* 1000
House with the Green Shutters, The—*George Douglas* 1003
How Green Was My Valley—*Richard Llewellyn* 1005
Howards End—*E. M. Forster* 1006
Huasipungo—*Jorge Icaza* 1009
Huckleberry Finn—*Mark Twain* (*Samuel L. Clemens*) 1012
Hudibras—*Samuel Butler* 1015
Hugh Wynne, Free Quaker—*Silas Weir Mitchell* 1016
Human Comedy, The—*William Saroyan* 1017
Humphry Clinker—*Tobias Smollett* 1018
Hunchback of Notre Dame, The—*Victor Hugo* 1021
Hunger—*Knut Hamsun* 1024
Huon de Bordeaux—*Unknown* 1026
Hyde Park—*James Shirley* 1027
Hypatia—*Charles Kingsley* 1029
Hypochondriac, The—*Molière* (*Jean Baptiste Poquelin*) 1031

I, Claudius—*Robert Graves* 1034
I Speak for Thaddeus Stevens—*Elsie Singmaster* 1035
Iceland Fisherman, An—*Pierre Loti* 1036
Ides of March, The—*Thornton Wilder* 1037
Idiot, The—*Fyodor Mikhaĭlovich Dostoevski* 1039
Idylls of the King, The—*Alfred, Lord Tennyson* 1042
If Winter Comes—*A. S. M. Hutchinson* 1045
Iliad, The—*Homer* 1046

Importance of Being Earnest, The—*Oscar Wilde* 1049
In Dubious Battle—*John Steinbeck* 1050
In the Wilderness—*Sigrid Undset* 1051
Inazuma-byôshi—*Santô Kyôden* 1052
Independent People—*Halldór Laxness* 1053
Indian Summer—*William Dean Howells* 1056
Indiana—*George Sand* 1057
Inês de Castro—*António Ferreira* 1059
Informer, The—*Liam O'Flaherty* 1061
Innocent Voyage, The—*Richard Hughes* 1064
Inspector General, The—*Nikolai V. Gogol* 1065
Intruder in the Dust—*William Faulkner* 1067
Invisible Man, The—*H. G. Wells* 1070
Iolanthe—*W. S. Gilbert* 1072
Ion—*Euripides* 1074
Iphigenia in Aulis—*Euripides* 1975
Iphigenia in Tauris—*Euripides* 1076
Israel Potter—*Herman Melville* 1079
It Is Better than It Was—*Calderón de la Barca* 1081
It is Worse than It Was—*Calderón de la Barca* 1082
Italian, The—*Mrs. Ann Radcliffe* 1083
Itching Parrot, The—*Jose Joachín Fernandez de Lizardi* 1085
Ivanhoe—*Sir Walter Scott* 1087

Jack of Newberry—*Thomas Deloney* 1090
Jack Sheppard—*William Harrison Ainsworth* 1093
Jalna—*Mazo de la Roche* 1094
Jane Eyre—*Charlotte Brontë* 1095
Jason and the Golden Fleece—*Unknown* 1098
Java Head—*Joseph Hergesheimer* 1101
Jean-Christophe—*Romain Rolland* 1102
Jennie Gerhardt—*Theodore Dreiser* 1105
Jerusalem Delivered—*Torquato Tasso* 1107
Jew of Malta, The—*Christopher Marlowe* 1109
Jewess of Toledo, The—*Franz Grillparzer* 1112
Joanna Godden—*Sheila Kaye-Smith* 1113
John Brown's Body—*Stephen Vincent Benét* 1115
John Halifax, Gentleman—*Dinah Maria Mulock* 1117
John Inglesant—*Joseph Henry Shorthouse* 1119
Jonathan Wild—*Henry Fielding* 1121
Jorrocks' Jaunts and Jollities—*Robert Smith Surtees* 1123
Joseph Andrews—*Henry Fielding* 1124
Joseph Vance—*William De Morgan* 1127
Journey to the End of the Night—*Louis Ferdinand Céline* 1128
Journey's End—*Robert C. Sherriff* 1129
Jovial Crew, A—*Richard Brome* 1131
Jude the Obscure—*Thomas Hardy* 1133
Judith Paris—*Hugh Walpole* 1136
Julius Caesar—*William Shakespeare* 1139
Jungle, The—*Upton Sinclair* 1142
Jungle Books, The—*Rudyard Kipling* 1143
Juno and the Paycock—*Sean O'Casey* 1144

Jurgen—*James Branch Cabell* 1147
Justice—*John Galsworthy* 1148

Kalevala—*Elias Lönnrot* 1150
Kate Fennigate—*Booth Tarkington* 1151
Kenilworth—*Sir Walter Scott* 1152
Kidnapped—*Robert Louis Stevenson* 1154
Kim—*Rudyard Kipling* 1156
King and No King, A—*Francis Beaumont* and *John Fletcher* 1158
King John—*John Bale* 1160
King John—*William Shakespeare* 1162
King Lear—*William Shakespeare* 1163
King of the Golden River, The—*John Ruskin* 1166
King of the Mountains, The—*Edmond Francois About* 1167
King Paradox—*Pio Baroja* 1168
King Solomon's Mines—*H. Rider Haggard* 1169
King, the Greatest Alcalde, The—*Lope de Vega* 1171
Kingdom of God, The—*Gregorio Martínez Sierra* 1175
Kings in Exile—*Alphonse Daudet* 1176
King's Row—*Henry Bellamann* 1177
Kipps—*H. G. Wells* 1178
Knight of the Burning Pestle, The—*Francis Beaumont* 1179
Knights, The—*Aristophanes* 1180
Kreutzer Sonata, The—*Count Leo Tolstoy* 1183
Kristin Lavransdatter—*Sigrid Undset* 1185

Lady from the Sea—*Henrik Ibsen* 1188
Lady into Fox—*David Garnett* 1190
Lady of the Lake, The—*Sir Walter Scott* 1191
Lady Windermere's Fan—*Oscar Wilde* 1192
Lady's Not for Burning, The—*Christopher Fry* 1193
L'Aiglon—*Edmond Rostand* 1194
Lais of Marie de France, The—*Marie de France* 1196
Lalla Rookh—*Thomas Moore* 1197
L'Amorosa Fiammetta—*Giovanni Boccaccio* 1198
Last Athenian, The—*Viktor Rydberg* 1200
Last Chronicle of Barset, The—*Anthony Trollope* 1201
Last Days of Pompeii, The—*Edward George Earle Bulwer-Lytton* 1203
Last of Summer, The—*Kate O'Brien* 1205
Last of the Barons, The—*Edward George Earle Bulwer-Lytton* 1207
Last of the Mohicans, The—*James Fenimore Cooper* 1208
Last of the Vikings, The—*Johan Bojer* 1211
Last Puritan, The—*George Santayana* 1214
Last Tycoon, The—*F. Scott Fitzgerald* 1216
Late George Apley, The—*John P. Marquand* 1218
Late Mattia Pascal, The—*Luigi Pirandello* 1221
Lavengro—*George Henry Borrow* 1223
Lay of the Last Minstrel, The—*Sir Walter Scott* 1225
Lazarillo de Tormes—*Unknown* 1226
Legend of Sleepy Hollow, The—*Washington Irving* 1229
Legend of the Moor's Legacy—*Washington Irving* 1231
Legend of Tyl Ulenspiegel, The—*Charles de Coster* 1233

LIST OF TITLES

Letters from the Underworld—*Fyodor Mikhailovich Dostoevski* 1235
Lieh Kuo Chih—*Feng Meng-lung* 1238
Life and Death of Cardinal Wolsey, The—*George Cavendish* 1240
Life Is a Dream—*Calderón de la Barca* 1241
Life on the Mississippi—*Mark Twain (Samuel L. Clemens)* 1244
Life with Father—*Clarence Day* 1246
Ligeia—*Edgar Allan Poe* 1247
Light in August—*William Faulkner* 1250
Liliom—*Ferenc Molnar* 1253
Link, The—*August Strindberg* 1255
Lion of Flanders, The—*Hendrik Conscience* 1257
Little Clay Cart, The—*Shudraka* 1258
Little Dorrit—*Charles Dickens* 1260
Little Foxes, The—*Lillian Hellman* 1261
Little Minister, The—*James M. Barrie* 1263
Little Women—*Louisa May Alcott* 1264
Liza of Lambeth—*W. Somerset Maugham* 1266
Long Journey, The—*Johannes V. Jensen* 1268
Long Night, The—*Andrew Lytle* 1271
Longest Journey, The—*E. M. Forster* 1272
Look Homeward, Angel—*Thomas Wolfe* 1273
Looking Backward—*Edward Bellamy* 1274
Lord Jim—*Joseph Conrad* 1275
Lorna Doone—*R.D. Blackmore* 1278
Lost Horizon—*James Hilton* 1280
Lost Illusions—*Honoré de Balzac* 1284
Lost Lady, A—*Willa Cather* 1285
Lost Weekend, The—*Charles Jackson* 1286
Love for Love—*William Congreve* 1287
Love in a Wood—*William Wycherley* 1289
Love's Labour's Lost—*William Shakespeare* 1291
Loving—*Julian Green* 1292
Lower Depths, The—*Maxim Gorky* 1293
Loyalities—*John Galsworthy* 1295
Lucien Leuwen—*Stendhal (Marie-Henri Beyle)* 1297
Lusiads, The—*Luis Vaz de Camoëns* 1299
Lysistrata—*Aristophanes* 1301

Mabinogion, The—*Unknown* 1303
Macbeth—*William Shakespeare* 1306

THE EPIC OF GILGAMESH

Type of work: Poem
Author: Unknown
Type of plot: Heroic adventure
Time of plot: Remote antiquity
Locale: The ancient world
First transcribed: c. 2,000 B.C.

Written almost four thousand years ago, this epic contains many of the themes found in the later epic literary tradition of Achilles, Odysseus, Samson, Beowulf, Roland, and King Arthur. Although two-thirds god, Gilgamesh experiences from his human nature love and conflict, joy and sorrow, courage and fear, and ultimately the horror and mystery of death. Although of heroic stature, he is also a sympathetic human figure who must learn through his suffering and errors.

The Epic of Gilgamesh belongs to that group of Ancient Near Eastern myths which may be termed "societal." Each nation had its societal myth to justify and sustain its particular social system and to fulfill several crucial functions: to validate prevailing social patterns, to provide rules and acceptable models for living, to supply divine sanction of the existing power structure, and to prove to the individual that the laws and customs of his country were superior to those of other countries. Thus the myth served the purpose of preserving the *status quo*. Particularly in the case of hero tales like the Gilgamesh epic, the heroes were models of proper and improper behavior whose feats dramatized just what should or should not be attempted. Through the events narrated in this chronicle of the life of King Gilgamesh, therefore, one may make several assumptions concerning the Babylonian social system which the tale was intended to substantiate.

The action in *The Epic of Gilgamesh* falls into three major phases of the hero's development. In the first phase, King Gilgamesh is a proud tyrant who rejects the concept of the king as a loving and concerned shepherd of his people; instead, he drives his subjects so cruelly that they petition the god Anu for relief. Since Gilgamesh is two-thirds god himself, a powerful chastisement is necessary, and Anu commissions the king's mother, the goddess Aruru, to create a foe powerful enough to fight with Gilgamesh and thus redirect his energies and interests. This creation—in many ways the sophisticated king's uncivilized alter ego—is named Engidu. After Engidu and Gilgamesh engage in a colossal battle of strength and endurance, they become inseparable friends, and the hero embarks on the second phase of his career. In this phase Gilgamesh rises above the level of pure selfishness and brute force and goes in search of romantic adventures which will bring meaning to his life and lasting fame to himself and his accepted brother. During the course of his adventures, Gilgamesh mocks and insults the goddess of love, Ishtar, and scornfully rejects her offer to become his lover, but escapes death at her hands because of his own divinity and great strength. Soon after, however, Engidu dies a slow and painful death, thus precipitating Gilgamesh into the final stage of his travels. In this stage, the hero, horrified at the terrible death of his friend and fearing a similar end for himself, departs on a journey to find immortality. This search ultimately terminates in failure when a serpent eats the plant of everlasting life which the hero has located on the bottom of the sea. After an interview with the spirit of Engidu in which his friend reveals to him that nothing awaits man after death but worms and mud, Gilgamesh reaches the conclusion that the only course left open for him is to return to his city of Uruk and fulfill his role of king and shepherd to his people.

The message conveyed through this societal myth is clear: if a heroic demigod cannot acquire immortality and is led to accept his ordained role, there is nothing for the humble Babylonian citizen to do but acknowledge the inevitability of death and likewise embrace the role assigned to him by the social system, no matter how lowly. And while the myth reinforces the Near Eastern belief that there is no life after death, it also offers some practical advice, through the words of a barmaid whom Gilgamesh meets on his travels, on how to make the most of this life:

> Make every day a day of joy.
> Dance, play, day and night . . .
> Cherish the child who grasps your hand.
> Let your wife rejoice in your bosom
> For this is the fate of man.

EPITAPH OF A SMALL WINNER

Type of work: Novel
Author: Joaquim Maria Machado de Assis (1839-1908)
Type of plot: Philosophical realism
Time: of plot: 1805-1869
Locale: Rio de Janeiro, Brazil
First published: 1880

Although long enjoyed by readers of the original Portuguese and the Spanish translations, this Brazilian novel did not appear in English until seventy-two years after its first publication. Epitaph of a Small Winner *is a statement of thorough philosophical pessimism, the story of an ordinary man whose one small victory in life is that he fathers no children who will have to endure the misery of existence.*

Machado de Assis' ancestry is slightly mysterious. His father was supposedly a "son of free mulattos" and a house painter, and his mother an impoverished white washerwoman, but these versions of his background are open to question. Although John Nist, for example, wrote that Machado de Assis left the slums of Rio de Janeiro to found Brazil's Academy of Letters, after having conquered Brazil with the greatest outpouring of literary talent in that country's history, some persons question the tradition that he grew up in poverty in Rio's slums. While little is known of Machado de Assis until he reached fifteen years of age, he is known to have had only a primary-level education. It is also known that a French bakeshop owner taught him French and that he was an autodidact, acquiring his impressive culture by educating himself. Even though rather finely featured, he was spindly-legged, myopic, rachitic, a stammerer, endured alarming epileptic seizures, and suffered intestinal disorders. He was Caucasian in features, but his African blood was an added problem for him in nineteenth century Brazil. His white wife's brothers strongly opposed her marriage to Machado de Assis on racial grounds.

Machado de Assis has been awarded a unique place in Brazilian literature and is considered its most singular eminence. Brazilians have called him their sphinx, their enigma, their myth. His writings, including *Epitaph of a Small Winner,* have been contradictorily labeled brilliant, dry, rich, colorless, or ironic, refined, intuitive, pure, correct, limpid, balanced, boring and elegant. Some Brazilians smell the scent of Brazilianism exuding from his pages, or a literary nativism so strong as to comprise a natural emanation. But Pedro Calmon wrote that he did not seem Brazilian, and his works were once described as being psychologically French. Besides *Epitaph of a Small Winner* (in Portuguese as *Memórias Pósthumas de Braz Cubas*), three of his novels and fifteen of his other works have been translated into English, while his reading public in the Northern Hemisphere grows each year. Literary critics commonly eulogize him for stylistic purity, perfect linguistic knowledge, and a great inner richness. It was once said that he knew well all the secrets of the art of writing, and that his intuitive insight into man's intimate peculiarities was remarkable.

As is evident in *Epitaph of a Small Winner* and the three novels that chronologically followed it, Machado de Assis became steadily more disillusioned with human beings. It is said that these novels, plus his masterpiece, *Dom Casmurro,* published twenty-eight years after *Epitaph of a Small Winner,* supply the most convincing evidence for his ever-continuing disillusionment. In any event, each of Machado de Assis' most celebrated novels paint a wasted human life.

His disenchantment with human beings became universal, and his soul was ever more strained by inner turmoil. He liked to expose human egotism and believed that all nature revealed man's idiocy, that everything in the universe resented what it was and pined to be something else. He came to view man as always bouncing, ball-like, until his passions destroyed him. Sometimes compared to William Somerset Maugham for his inferiority complex, Machado de Assis deliberately withheld information about his personal life and hinted that it had little to do with his writing. In *Epitaph of a Small Winner,* however, Machado de Assis puts into Braz Cubas' mouth the statement that although many European novelists had made tours of one or more countries, he, Braz Cubas, had made a tour of life. In this tour, added Braz Cubas, he had seen human asininity, human evil, and the sorry vanity of all matter.

Machado de Assis strove for thirty years to master the art of narration. *Epitaph of a Small Winner* as well as his other early works, give a hint of the development to come, for he always experimented with his storytelling skills. He usually used short sentences, brief chapters, and deliberately interrupted narrative. He was eventually credited with brilliant manipulation of language and haunting character analysis through skilled use of symbols and metaphors. Machado de Assis has also been likened to a hard-rock miner delving into the earth to seek man's infernal image. He cautioned his readers to scrutinize his lines for an interlocking pattern that integrated the various parts. He tinged names of characters with significance and color, and derived inspiration from Shakespeare. He withdrew from the Romanticist movement that was literarily dominant during his youth and became a Realist. In 1907, shortly before his death, he noted that thirty years time had separated two editions of one of his works, and that these thirty years illustrated the difference in composition and temper of his writing.

Machado de Assis rarely left his native Rio de Janeiro, entwined in its granite mountains and curving bay, and never journeyed far when he did. He remained an autodidact in ideas and cultural values to the end of his life. He died as he lived, loathing the idea of being either a bore, spectacle, or hypocrite. As he was dying, attended by Brazil's most famous writers of the day, he wanted to call a priest, but then reflected that it would be hypocritical.

In any event, it can be said that despite Machado de Assis' celebrated pessimism and bleak insight into human nature, none of his novels alleges that it is impossible to view the world in a more cheerful light than he did; they merely state that it would be difficult.

William Freitas

EREC AND ENIDE

Type of work: Poem
Author: Chrétien de Troyes (c.1140-c.1190)
Type of plot: Chivalric romance
Time of plot: Sixth century
Locale: Arthurian England
First transcribed: Before 1164

Erec and Enide *is the first of four metrical romances which are the most idealized expression of the chivalric code available to the modern reader. Although it is the oldest extant romance in the vernacular based on Arthurian materials, this poem, written in eight-syllable rhyming couplets, reveals nothing of the primitive Celtic origins of the Arthurian legends; instead, it reflects the sophisticated and intricately detailed chivalric standards set by the French courts of love which flourished in the Middle Ages.*

Like *Yvain,* by the same author, *Erec and Enide* deals with the conflict between and the attempt to reconcile knightly and marital responsibilities. It is about many other things but this problem is its main theme.

Apparently Chrétien de Troyes himself thought much of the work: in the romance's first paragraph he tells us " . . . and now I shall begin the tale which will be remembered so long as Christendom endures. This is Chrétien's boast."

Perhaps his scarcely modest claim was well-founded, for this romance of Arthurian England in the sixth century, has outlived many other medieval romances. Even today it offers the reader riches of varied sorts. A mélange of real and unreal incidents, exact and exaggerated statistics, logical and implausible motivation, wildly supernatural events in close juxtaposition with homely, concrete ones, mark his poem.

But from all these seemingly warring elements, Chrétien de Troyes manages to devise a well-constructed plot. Perhaps to the casual reader, Erec's surviving all his ordeals, the various adventures that he and Enide, his wife, encounter in their wanderings, the apparently unconnected strangers they meet, as well as assorted dwarfs, giants, Morgan le Fay with a magic plaster —even a knight in "vermillion arms"—appear unlikely to say the least. But the author, in welding diverse and sometimes incongruous factors together, has a serious purpose. He was interested in problems of conscience within the individual: choices he had to make in the face of conflicting loyalties and personal emotions. He was definitely intrigued with how man solves these individually as a member of his social group. All the usual and contrived situations of medieval romance served Chrétien de Troyes as means of setting forth these problems—providing the complicating webs to entrap the protagonists.

Although Erec, a king's son, married the daughter of a poor vavasour, or country squire, Chrétien takes care to make them equal in beauty and gentilesse. However, when because of excessive love of his wife, reports circulate that Erec has permitted himself to desert the tourneys and quests, thus failing to prove his knighthood, the story takes up its serious purpose. For, after all, this is a tale of married love subjected to the pressures of a man's other obligations and duties: those to his code and to proving his own valor. It is also a story of a wife's patient endurance of her husband's eccentricities and abuse. In many respects Chrétien de Troyes intends *Erec and Enide*, for all its comic incidents and exaggerated postures, to be a sober narrative of love-testing. In this it is similar to Chaucer's "Clerk's Tale" on the familiar "patient Griselda" theme.

Enide's unquestioning obedience may disturb the modern reader, who still cannot fault Chrétien's logic of her reasoning and emotions. It is characteristic of the author that he proves himself an expert at love analysis, particularly within the minds of his heroines. Such subtleties of thought are rare in medieval romance, but Chrétien de Troyes' women in love keenly verbalize their considerations in matters of the heart. Enide, for example, reproaches herself for telling Erec that men say his reputation has suffered, that he is a recreant and that they blame her for it. In a soliloquy she upbraids herself for pride and says it is right she must suffer woe: "One does not know what good fortune is until he has made trial of evil." Enide knows, as her author comments: " . . . she had now made her bed, and must lie in it." Not until the fourteenth century in Chaucer's Criseyde does one find a romance heroine engaged in such subtle love analysis.

Chrétien manages to offer convincing characters, not stock types. In *Erec and Enide* that which he wants readers to concentrate on is not the battles or such farcical scenes as the one where Enide must marry the Count against her will, but Erec's gradual realization of the great love his wife has for him. More important perhaps for the story is Erec's own statement at the testing's end: " . . . for I love you now more than ever I did before." He has learned humility and what faithfulness involves.

In a time when *fin amour,* or courtly love, was supposed to be the reigning material for poets and romance writers—in other words, adulterous love—Chrétien de Troyes shows far more concern for love within the marriage bond. As a matter of fact, he seems to stress this kind of love as the ideal union. When he must deal with adulterous love as in his *Lancelot,* he seems ill at ease and handles both plot and characterization with less finesse. Most critics as a result conclude that in this latter work he wrote upon demand, not inclination. But in both *Yvain* and *Erec and Enide* he concentrates on the difficulties in marriage and their solution.

We feel that if it is true as Chrétien de Troyes also said at the beginning of this romance, that "jongleurs were accustomed to garble and mutilate" the story, he himself has ordered such material into a unified, coherent whole.

He does this well. And the reader feels Chrétien was not so interested in reviving customs and feats of valor characteristic of Arthurian knights in a time long past, but of involving his French audience in a tale they could understand and with which they could identify.

Chrétien de Troyes not only successfully develops the plot; he also shows progression in character development. He brings together the lavish ornamentation of watered silk, ivory, gold tapestries, red armor; ragged garments of a peasant girl in a poor household; hardships of wayfaring on roads infested with evils of all sorts; and finally a happy ending with the elevation of King Arthur in a brilliant coronation ceremony for the reconciled Erec and Enide. He has managed with consummate artistry to make it all entertaining and at the same time to pose comments upon problems of married love, not only as they might have existed in the sixth century, or in the twelfth, but perhaps always.

Muriel B. Ingham

EREWHON

Type of work: Novel
Author: Samuel Butler (1835-1902)
Type of plot: Utopian satire
Time of plot: 1870's
Locale: Erewhon and England
First published: 1872

"Erewhon" is an anagram of "nowhere," but the institutions satirized in this novel are unmistakably British. Much of its satire growing out of the ideas of Charles Darwin and Thomas Huxley, Erewhon *begins as an adventure story but develops into an elaborate allegory. Some of the targets of satire are psychologists ("straighteners" in Butler's utopia) and the system of criminal justice.*

Erewhon is Butler's attempt to work into novel form four philosophic papers written between 1860 and 1870; these appear as the chapters in the novel entitled "The Book of the Machines," "The World of the Unborn," "The Musical Banks," and "Some Erewhonian Trials." While apparently dissimilar, these pivotal chapters all treat the theme of free will, thus unifying the book.

In adapting to his environment, man constructs machines which threaten his survival. With prophetic insight, Butler examines this irony. He argues that the laws governing organic evolution also apply to machines and their development. Challenging the distinction between "organic" and "inorganic," Butler reduces all processes to their mechanical basis and shows how machines are evolving independently of human control. Like Marx, he sees man's nature as changing under the impact of a mechanized environment. But unlike Marx, he predicts man's ultimate enslavement by this environment.

Both comic and serious elements mingle in the Erewhonian myth of preexistence. Because the "unborn" *will* to become humans, they must bear the consequences of their choice. Thus the Erewhonians make babies sign "birth formulae" which absolve parents from responsibility for the deprivations and deficiencies which go with living. The unborn also elect to share man's essential fate: to be "fettered" to free will while knowing that its proper exercise requires such accidental advantages as innate talent and high social position.

In "The Musical Banks," Butler satirizes commercialism's corruption of religion; the Banks symbolize the existence of "a kingdom not of this world" whose laws measure and judge human laws. For Butler, there is a Divine Will which inhabits the subconscious and which all cultures tacitly acknowledge. In the trials of the unfortunate and sick, Butler uses absurdity to examine further the nature of freedom and responsibility. In Erewhon, crime is a disease and disease a crime; Butler accepts the first equation while mocking the second.

ESTHER WATERS

Type of work: Novel
Author: George Moore (1852-1933)
Type of plot: Naturalism
Time of plot: Late nineteenth century
Locale: England
First published: 1894

Realism, like beauty, is in the eye of the beholder. Still, Moore's narrative of an impoverished but richly principled servant girl successfully rearing her illegitimate child despite rigid social obstacles definitely can be classified as realism in one sense: it treats the subject matter with an explicitness hitherto taboo in the English novel. The strong influence of Zola and Balzac is evident.

English fiction in the nineteenth century maintained a delicate balance between realism and romanticism, with an often strong underlayer of sentimentality. George Moore, at the end of the century, led British fiction toward Flaubert and Zola and modern French realism. But he saw that the most carefully observed facts are insufficient unless they are seen through the glass of imagination and humanity. *Esther Waters* is the first English novel to reveal, and with a frankness previously unknown in the country, the pilgrimage through life of a human being as a physical creature. The novel caused a scandal almost as great as that caused by Hardy's *Jude the Obscure,* and was banned from circulating libraries; it had a tremendous influence on younger writers, such as Somerset Maugham in his *Liza of Lambeth.*

Moore deliberately took a mundane subject and wrote about it with much circumstantial realism and without melodrama; his simple prose style established place and setting with a surprisingly poetic impact. The heroine Esther is seen as a sensual young woman from her first entry into the story, when it is explained that she is fond of touching living creatures. But her physical desires are in conflict with her strict Christian background, and later with her duties as a mother. No scene in modern literature is more powerful than that of Esther confronting Mrs. Spires and the cradles of sickly babies, and refusing Mrs. Spires' offer to murder her baby for five pounds, so that she can be free from responsibility. The horror that Esther feels is transmitted to the reader, who sees the social importance of the terrible situation.

The book presents a vivid picture of life downstairs in large country houses and in lower-middle-class homes. The life of a servant at the end of the nineteenth century was grim, and the only alternatives for a girl like Esther were prostitution or suicide. The realities of such an existence are shown without exaggeration, but with great feeling. Always, Esther is absorbed by one central thought: how to save her child, raise him, and make him into a decent man. Her struggle is told in human terms, and she emerges as a heroine of majestic proportions, all the more magnificent because in her own eyes she is only a miserable creature doing the best she can with little hope and few expectations. Meanwhile, the narrowness and hypocrisy of the middle-class households through which Esther passes are exposed fully, illuminating the genuine goodness of Esther, Miss Rice, and a few other characters.

ETHAN FROME

Type of work: Novel
Author: Edith Wharton (1862-1937)
Type of plot: Domestic tragedy
Time of plot: Late nineteenth century
Locale: Starkfield, Massachusetts
First published: 1911

Unrepresentative though it is of Wharton's works, Ethan Frome *is the most critically acclaimed and most popular. Wharton's terse depiction of Ethan's wasted talents and passions becomes a cynical fable describing the triumph of a trivial, conventional society over the ambitious, creative individual.*

Ethan Frome is a compact novelette which etches with acid the existential tragedy of misspent lives and talent gone awry. In it, Edith Wharton depicts Ethan Frome and Mattie Silver as intelligent and fundamentally decent human beings whose souls—and finally, whose bodies—are crushed by meaningless but inexorable social conventions, represented by Zeena Frome.

Ethan in particular reflects Wharton's view that twentieth century America has repudiated the fine nineteenth century values which Wharton cherishes so deeply, for Ethan stands for all those bygone qualities which she admires. He has a good mind, commendable ambition, and strong integrity. A twentieth century Ethan might, for example, think of killing Zeena—and possibly even attempt it—but Wharton's nineteenth century man, living in an inhospitable twentieth century, is instead slowly destroyed by a society which has no use for him or his anachronistic values. In the end, he is tended by Zeena, who takes care of him much as a museum curator takes care of ancient artifacts entrusted to him.

Although *Ethan Frome* is unusual in the large corpus of Wharton's work for its revelations about the author's bitterness toward what she views as the shallowness of modern industrial society, it is by no means unique. Wharton earlie- treated a similar theme in *The House of Mirth* (1905), a novel frequently paired with *Ethan Frome* for purposes of comparison. And indeed the likenesses are there. Like Ethan, for instance, Lily Bart in *The House of Mirth* is meant for a better life than she has. But in her pursuit of what she clearly deserves, she is subjected to calumny, deceit, and fraud which finally drive her to a fatal overdose of sedatives. These two simple tragedies stand out from Wharton's other work, which concerned itself largely with complex socio-moral conflicts, but they are certainly not inferior, despite their apparently anomalous position. In fact, *Ethan Frome* is considered by many to be Wharton's finest work.

EUGENE ARAM

Type of work: Novel
Author: Edward George Earle Bulwer-Lytton (1803-1873)
Type of plot: Mystery romance
Time of plot: Mid-eighteenth century
Locale: England
First published: 1832

The actual facts of the crime and trial of Eugene Aram had long fascinated English writers before Bulwer-Lytton wrote a novel on the subject. Aram's case raised debate over such issues as, "Can a good man murder and can murder be justified on the ground that it benefits mankind?" Similar questions are dealt with in Crime and Punishment.

Although best known for his historical romance, *The Last Days of Pompeii,* Bulwer-Lytton achieved literary prominence in a variety of forms. His account of English manners, *England and the English* (1833), and his account of English dandyism, *Pelham* (1828), have gained an increasing number of appreciative readers. Bulwer stressed sensationalism in his romances in order to win readers away from Walter Scott's historical novels, but his own historical objectivity and almost clinical fascination with all kinds of psychological aberrations acted as a corrective to the vulgarizing tendencies of his lurid plots and occult themes.

In writing *The Last Days of Pompeii* Bulwer carefully examined the ancient site and read closely in recent studies of antiquity as well as in the works of Pliny, the diarist; Vitruvius, the architect; and Strabo, the geographer. Similarly, when writing *Eugene Aram,* Bulwer had access not only to the public records of the actual crime and trial but also could rely on his own family's association with the historical Aram. The Eugene Aram of real life had been engaged by Bulwer's grandfather as an occasional tutor to his daughters. Bulwer also established contact with Admiral Burney, who as a schoolboy had known Aram. The whole account of Aram's relations with the Lester family in the novel was taken "word for word, fact for fact," from Burney's notes.

What intrigued Bulwer was the opportunity of telling a story about a highly abnormal personality (Eugene Aram, the idealist scholar who could rationalize the act of murder; an anticipation of Dostoevski's Raskolnikov in *Crime and Punishment*) based almost entirely on actual records. Bulwer discovered the "dandy" as a literary type, and it is a short distance from social hedonism to a metaphysics of psychological superiority. Pelham and Eugene Aram, although such opposites in personality and character, provide a fascinating paradigm for the later theories of Oscar Wilde and Nietzsche on the superior or super man.

EUGENE ONEGIN

Type of work: Poem
Author: Alexander Pushkin (1799-1837)
Type of plot: Impressionistic romance
Time of plot: Nineteenth century
Locale: Russia
First published: 1833

Pushkin's lyric poem describing the eccentric life of Eugene Onegin reworks the Don Juan legend familiar to readers of Byron. Regarded as the inspiration for the great Russian novels of the nineteenth century, Pushkin's romantic lyric has the world-weary Onegin duel and kill his only friend and spurn the love of a worthy woman, only to fall in love with her after she has despaired of him and married another.

Eugene Onegin occupies a central place in the life work of Pushkin, as it does in the history of Russian literature. Its composition occupied eight years, between 1823 and 1831, a period during which most of Pushkin's other narrative poems were composed. Thus it reflects the growth and development of the poet, who appears in the poem as narrator, and through whose eyes the events of the poem are seen. Indeed, the chapters of the poem were originally published individually as they were finished, and they displayed some of the marks of a serialized novel. Pushkin described the work as "in the manner of [Byron's] *Don Juan,*" and the Byronic elements of the work are clear, beginning with the stanzaic form, the mixture of humor and seriousness in the narrator's tone, and the figure of the narrator himself, who tells the story in a conversational, highly personal way, including bits of autobiography, long digressions, and ironic comments on the work. Pushkin, however, never presses the irony as far as does Byron, who verges on bitterness at times; his work is more disciplined and classical in form, achieving a completeness and finality which made it impossible for Pushkin to continue the work beyond its conclusion, even though friends pressed him to compose a sequel.

Pushkin referred to the work as a novel in verse, and even called the cantos "chapters." His style blends lyric inspiration with realistic detail to parallel his cast of characters, who unite the mundane reality of Russian life with an artistic perception of life. All his main characters are strongly influenced by foreign literary models: Lensky, the poet who has absorbed German Romanticism at Göttingen; Tatyana, who spends her time reading the sentimental novels of Richardson; and Onegin, whose library shows him to be a fan of Byron. It is the interplay between these worlds—ironic, parodistic, at times humorous, but ultimately leading to tragedy and disillusionment—that gives the work its fascination and the power which made it the ancestor of so much of subsequent Russian fiction.

EUGÉNIE GRANDET

Type of work: Novel
Author: Honoré de Balzac (1799-1850)
Type of plot: Naturalism
Time of plot: Early nineteenth century
Locale: Saumur, France
First published: 1833

Considered one of Balzac's most powerful works, Eugénie Grandet *delineates the character of a miser whose calculating and inhumane parsimoniousness cripples the lives of his wife and his only child, Eugénie. The tale is told simply with an abundance of realistic detail characteristic of French naturalists such as Zola.*

Eugénie Grandet is part of Honoré de Balzac's grand design, *La Comédie Humaine.* Some say it is one of the best parts. Rather late in his prolific writing career, Balzac conceived the idea of arranging his novels, stories, and studies in a certain order. He described his plan in *Avant-Propos* (1842, although he claimed the idea originated in 1833), where he named the project *La Comédie Humaine, The Human Comedy.* Influenced by Georges Louis Leclerc de Buffon, Étienne Geoffroy Saint-Hilaire, and Jean Lamarck, all naturalists, Balzac sought to apply their scientific principles—especially the taxonomic system—to literature, particularly for the purpose of organizing information. Balzac firmly believed that "social species" could be classified just as "zoological species" were, and he attempted to classify his fifty-odd previously written works as well as his future writings to fit such a scheme. To accommodate his plan, he adopted eight major topic headings: Scenes from Private Life, Scenes from Provincial Life, Scenes from Parisian Life, Scenes from Political Life, Scenes from Military Life, Scenes from Rural Life, Philosophical Studies, and Analytical Studies. The works were arranged, re-arranged, and arranged again, *ad infinitum. Eugénie Grandet* was finally a Scene of Provincial Life. As a consequence of this ambitious organizational plan, Balzac exercised Procrustean prerogatives, tailoring his earlier output to his new standards. The results were predictably disastrous, but the literary qualities of the novels themselves—notably *Eugénie Grandet*—are irrefutable testimony to the triumph of art over science.

Balzac realized his goal of presenting typical human species in spite of, not because of, his "scientific" system of taxonomy. As the unsurpassed historian of the French middle class during the first half of the nineteenth century, he incarnated the stereotypes which were novel in the nineteenth century but are well known today: the snob, the provincial, the prude, the miser, the lecher, and a great many others. He did so on the strength of his artistic skill and not by virtue of scientific analysis, for Balzac was not a systematic philosopher or a scientist, but an artist. He wrote fine novels—even though they are often marred by his insensitivity to language and his proclivity for excessive details—which outlined the essential characteristics of the nineteenth century French middle class more clearly than anyone else has ever done. Matching Juvenal and Martial, Balzac satirized avarice, ambition, lust, vanity, and hypocrisy. Greed, however, was his *bête noire* and Monsieur Grandet his archetype. The author himself was something of a prototype.

Money is a pervasive theme in Balzac's novels, where its evil effects are resoundingly deplored. The figure of the greedy miser furnishes Balzac with one of his best characters, Grandet. Ironically, the novel, in fact, reflects Balzac's own preoccupation with money and his desire to earn vast sums of it. Like many of his characters, he wanted wealth and social position. Early in his career, he was poor and constantly in debt; but even after his novels began earning him sizable sums, he was still constantly in debt because he lived an extravagant life style well beyond his means. He never did learn how to manage money. When he was writing, he lived like a monk, working furiously for long hours with virtually no time out even for eating. When the novel was completed, however, Balzac devoted that same energy to nonstop revelry. His feasts were legendary, his capacity for fine foods gargantuan—one hundred oysters as an *hors d'oeuvre,* for example. His drinking and other debauches were no less excessive. He would agree with Monsieur Grandet that money is power and power is all that matters; therefore, money is the only important factor in life.

Balzac, however, wanted money for what it would buy, and Grandet wanted money for its own sake. Balzac cultivated the Dionysian life-style with the same single-minded dedication that Grandet cultivated abstemiousness. Therein lies the difference between author and character. The former enjoyed a grand style; the latter took pleasure from self-denial. Yet Grandet dominates the novel just as he dominates his family. To be sure, the novel is entitled *Eugénie Grandet,* and it depicts the sterility of provincial life. Balzac's neat categories notwithstanding, Grandet dominates the story. He is the overwhelming force that determines the destiny of his wife—who is ultimately killed by his penny-pinching vindictiveness—and his daughter—who is emotionally warped by his miserly indoctrination. The novel is thus as much about Grandet as it is about Eugénie.

Monsieur Grandet is what literary critics call an undeveloped or a "flat" character. He undergoes no change in the course of the novel. From start to finish, he is venal and miserly. He experiences no enlightenment. In fact, Eugénie is the only character who undergoes change as she moves from innocence to experience. The others remain as they were at the beginning. More importantly, the emotional power which Grandet exercises as his prerogative kills his wife and permanently damages Eugénie. Although Eugénie knows nothing of Grandet's machinations in accumulating his fortune, she is nonetheless shaped by her father's influence. Grandet thus exerts his wishes even beyond the grave since his training of Eugénie—implicit or explicit—is reflected in her behavior long after he is dead. She adopts his parsimonious living habits, even though she is publicly charitable. Seemingly without effort, she increases her fortune rather than depletes it. Her father taught her well. In this way, Grandet rivals Eugénie as the novel's protagonist.

Eugénie would not be what she is without having grown up with such a father. The cause-effect matrix of this interpersonal relationship illustrates one of Balzac's major premises (which was to become a tenet of late nineteenth century literary naturalism): that the combined effects of genetics and environment cannot be surmounted. This phenomenon is labeled "determinism"—more precisely, "mechanistic determinism," to distinguish it from its religious counterpart of predestination. Eugénie is born into a given social environment with a given genetic makeup. She is unable to change those factors, yet they are the twin determinants of her fate. The novel traces her development up to the time when she accepts that fate which was foreordained at the outset: she is very, very rich and very, very unhappy. The inescapable forces of determinism thus work through to their inevitable conclusion.

Eugénie Grandet is an unusually moving novel, for the reader can hardly fail to sympathize with Eugénie while despising her father. It comes as something of a shock, then, to realize that Eugénie bore her father no malice. Even her vengeance of Charles' betrayal is so subtle that it is untainted; Charles is oblivious to subtlety, and the reader does not begrudge Eugénie her one, lone exercise of financial power. Balzac's incredible prestidigitation is at work here, manipulating us, the readers, so that we accept the novel's point of view without imposing extraneous judgments. Truly, *Eugénie Grandet* is a tribute to the novelist's craft and art.

Joanne G. Kashdan

THE EUNUCH

Type of work: Drama
Author: Terence (Publius Terentius Afer, c. 190-159 B. C.)
Type of plot: Comedy of intrigue
Time of plot: Fourth century B. C.
Locale: Athens
First presented: 161 B. C.

The Eunuch *was the most popular of Terence's plays. In it, he gives an uncommon complexity to the personalities and roles of stereotypes common to Roman comedy: the insolent parasite, the rascally slave, and the braggart warrior. Like most Roman drama, its inspiration came from the Greek masters.*

Like all of Terence's comedies and Roman drama in general, *The Eunuch* had its origins in the plays of the Greek dramatists, and borrowings from the works of Menander are apparent. In fact, Terence openly admitted that he combined portions of *The Eunuch* and *The Flatterer* by Menander in adapting his play to the Roman stage. However, since neither of the two originals has survived, it is impossible to tell how extensively Terence depended on them.

Consistent with his dramatic practice, he uses a double plot, showing the courtships of two brothers. Their methods of attaining the women they love and the conditions under which they win them are contrasted, indicating the character of each brother. Phaedria, the eldest, has fallen in love with a mature and charming courtesan. Thais is intelligent, self-possessed, determined, and principled in some respects (seeking to free Pamphila, for instance); while Phaedria is something of a cipher, and an amoral cipher at that, since he finds living on his father's and Thraso's funds perfectly agreeable. He wins Thais, not through any effort of his own, but because Thais charms his father into supporting them both.

His youngest brother, Chaerea, is more appealing even though he rapes Pamphila. He has the pluck to take on the humiliating pose of a eunuch in order to be near her, and after he impulsively rapes her, he feels shame and tries to make amends for it through apology and marriage. Pamphila herself, in contrast to Thais, is without personality; while Chaerea has the character his brother lacks. Thraso and his parasite are brought into the play mainly for comic relief, but the skill with which Terence introduces them into the action shows the hand of an accomplished playwright.

EUPHUES AND HIS ENGLAND

Type of work: Novel
Author: John Lyly (c. 1554-1606)
Type of plot: Didactic romance
Time of plot: 1579-1580
Locale: England
First published: 1580

Concerning itself with an exploration of the many facets of love, and praise of England and Queen Elizabeth, Lyly's romance is most notable for its style. The rhetorical ornamentation, in similes and metaphors, which abound in the work are credited with inspiring greater talents to more freely explore the possibilities of English prose.

Euphues and His England is a sequel to the enormously popular *Euphues, the Anatomy of Wit* (1578). Both of these prose romances were widely acclaimed in the 1580's. Indeed, euphuism, the prose style named for the linguistic mannerisms of these works, was cultivated by contemporary ladies of the court. The style is, of course, excessive in its exaggerated use of certain rhetorical figures. It was attacked in its own time by Sir Philip Sidney for its violations of decorum, and its vogue was over before the end of Elizabeth's reign.

Lyly's elaborate prose style did not appear out of nowhere. Lyly combined and concentrated elements which had appeared in Lord Berner's translation of Froissart's *Chronicles* (1523, 1525), Sir Thomas North's translation of Guevara's *The Dial of Princes* (1557), and, most importantly, George Pettie's *A Petite Palace of Pettie His Pleasure* (1576). To a great extent the style seems to have been designed to attract female readers. Even if it was a short-lived phenomenon, it does seem to reflect many characteristics and concerns of its age. In a period that was increasingly self-conscious about the potentialities of English, as opposed to the classical languages for literary expression, it is a highly artful attempt to refine English prose.

The refinements are primarily in the repeated and extended use of a few decorative rhetorical figures. Balance and, in particular, antithesis are so omnipresent that they frequently overpower the flow of the plot and the dialogue. Narrative sequence and logical consistency are less important than parallel structures. The parallelisms are further embellished with consonance, assonance, alliteration, and other figures of speech which develop self-conscious rhythms and harmonies. The result is like the most ornate poetry of Spenser turned into prose and gone wild. Still, it does share the Elizabethan preoccupation with linguistic decoration.

The narrative is also adorned with proverbs and with allusions to classical antiquity and to the bizarre matter of Renaissance natural histories. The fondness for proverbial wisdom, which can be noticed even in Shakespeare's plays, is quite characteristic of the period, though it should be added that Shakespeare, in *Love's Labour's Lost,* did satirize Lyly's verbal excesses. The fanciful descriptions in the natural histories, some borrowed from Pliny and more fashioned out of the wild imaginations of the naturalists, are bizarre, but very much a part of the extravagant wit of the Elizabethan age. What is eccentric is the overwhelming repetition of the features. Like the figures of speech, the proverbs and allusions tend to smother the narrative and reduce the style to a clever curiosity. Paradoxically, the potential orderliness of the balanced style, with its frequent repetitions, is an apt medium for an age which saw an order in the cosmos and in the life of man, which it tried to recreate in the artful control of language. At its best, say in the poetry of Spenser, the style is a leisurely, pleasing and decorous elaboration of common themes. At its worst, in Lyly's prose, it becomes monstrous and sometimes even comic.

Euphues and His England is much less remembered as a narrative than as a stylistic fad. As a piece of fiction, it is a romance which gathers several essentially unrelated stories together and unites them only by means of a single central character and a few recurrent themes which punctuate the action. All characters in the work, including Euphues, are highly conventional. They do not come to any epiphanies or undergo moral evolutions. Rather they are stock figures who are put into standard situations and given the opportunity to expatiate at considerable length on a variety of time-honored themes. In speeches, dialogues, and letters, the characters deliver themselves of opinions on the prominent topics of the day—love, youthful excess, constancy, friendship, education. Although the loose structure of the plot owes much to the contemporarily popular Italian romances, the themes are strikingly those of Elizabethan England, topics repeatedly addressed in the lyric poetry of the sonneteers and in the popular books on behavior like Ascham's *The Schoolmaster* and Hoby's translation of Castiglione's *The Courtier.*

The two most frequent preoccupations of the narrative are (1) the combination of Platonism and Christian moralism which emanated from the writings of the humanists of the later Renaissance and (2) self-congratulatory reveling in the imperial glories of Elizabethan England. Events provide a pretext for philosophical debate. Thus, when Philautus becomes infatuated with Camilla and later when he falls in love with Frances, there is ample opportunity for extensive discussion of the levels of love and of the ultimate superiority of the divine over the human. Similarly, Fidus' advice on the principles of monarchy and Euphues' praise of English customs and governmental institutions are extensive presentations of the habitual themes of the courtesy books and of even so distinguished a work as *The Faerie Queene.*

Some critics have suggested that the Euphues romances are predecessors of the novel of manners and of the psychological novel. Yet they seem to contain too little plot or character development to assign them this seminal role in the history of fiction. Rather they seem to look to the past—to the combination and elaboration of conventional themes in the episodic Medieval romance. If Lyly had any influence, it was more probably on the history of style. For all his absurdities, he did much to loosen the rigidity of the Latinate rhetoric which had been superimposed on English. Certainly he influenced the earlier work of writers such as Robert Greene. However, even as a stylist, he has barely survived his age except as an oddity. Indeed, in his concentration of the conventional ideas of Platonism, Protestantism, and courtesy, and in his sometimes maniacal overuse of ornamentation, Lyly not only reflected his age, but unconsciously parodied it, and himself.

Edward E. Foster

EUPHUES, THE ANATOMY OF WIT

Type of work: Novel
Author: John Lyly (c. 1554-1606)
Type of plot: Didactic romance
Time of plot: Sixteenth century
Locale: Naples and Athens
First published: 1579

Lyly's place in the history of English prose rests entirely on his "euphuistic" style. His writing is characterized by numerous similes, constant allusion to nature and mythology, frequent rhetorical questions, balanced sentence construction, and alliteration. Extremely popular in Elizabethan England, the story is completely secondary to the exercise of a graceful and ornate prose style.

Although John Lyly wrote drama, poetry, and other prose, his major fame rests on his two prose romances, *Euphues, the Anatomy of Wit* and its sequel, *Euphues and His England* (1580). Both are more noted for their style than their substance. *Euphues, the Anatomy of Wit,* for instance, combines the Biblical parable of the Prodigal Son with a tale from Boccaccio's *Decameron* (Day 10, Story 8) creating the merest wisp of a story, which, in turn, serves mainly as a springboard for a series of moralistic treatises on such topics as love, friendship, women, education, and the like.

Style, however, is the key to *Euphues, the Anatomy of Wit.* To be sure, Lyly did not invent the ornate style which came to be known as "euphuistic," but the fame of *Euphues* lent it an influence which appeared as imitation in numerous other works. Lyly's intent was to adapt poetic devices to a prose medium in order to create poetic prose. To this end, Lyly wedded poetry and rhetoric in a rococo explosion of verbal contrivances. He utilized the imagery, rhythm, and meter of poetry; he incorporated conventions of animal personification—the dull, stupid ass, the ravenous wolf, the timorous hare, the courageous, magnanimous lion—among dozens of others; he drew upon the balanced sentence structure, the rhetorical question, the classical and historical allusion, and similar devices associated with oratory. The results were more spectacular than substantial, but Lyly set an important precedent which gave impetus to such later, and more successful, writers as De Quincey, Ruskin, and Pater.

Especially in its own time, *Euphues* was praised, condemned, and widely copied. Robert Greene and Thomas Lodge admired the style of *Euphues* and adopted it in their own writing. Sir Philip Sidney deplored euphuism in his treatise *The Defence of Poesie,* yet his own prose romance, *Arcadia,* is very nearly as ornately contrived as *Euphues*. Shakespeare ridiculed the euphuistic style in several of his plays, and in one play (*Love's Labour's Lost*) employed both ridicule and imitation. The influence of and the controversy over *Euphues* did not disappear with the passing of the Elizabethan era. As late as the nineteenth century, Sir Walter Scott mocked euphuism in one of his novels, while Charles Kingsley defended it in one of his. To the modern reader, this dispute over the merits of euphuism may seem trivial, since Lyly's style, judged by today's standards, is preposterously affected. But *Euphues* stands as a warning to any literary age, illustrating that the chic, extreme fashion of one era may appear as self-conscious and comical contrivance to a later time.

EVAN HARRINGTON

Type of work: Novel
Author: George Meredith (1828-1909)
Type of plot: Social satire
Time of plot: Nineteenth century
Locale: England
First published: 1861

Meredith's thesis in this novel is that a common tradesman can possess more innate refinement than individuals of the upper class. Although the plot has complications often difficult to follow, it is rich in social satire, smoothly maneuvered to reach its climax, and ironically amusing in its consistent characterizations. The characters are largely drawn from Meredith's own family.

Evan Harrington displays Meredith's keen irony and fine sense of distinctions, both social and human, while his sense of appropriate detail lends the book a density and richness of design. It is easy to see the influence of Meredith's friend and father-in-law Thomas Love Peacock in this early novel, especially in the witty dialogue. Epigrams stud the narrative, many of them truly witty, others too strained. For example, Meredith observes: "Most youths are like Pope's women; they have no character at all." But the narrative does not possess the extreme artificiality of Peacock; the story moves well, and many scenes are funny in themselves, without the embroidery of added "wit."

Meredith's genius for comedy is allowed full scope in *Evan Harrington's* almost farcical exposure of snobbery. What is a gentleman? The question is asked frequently, in different forms, throughout the book. The postillion thinks that he is a man with "a purse long and liberal," but the countess holds that he is indefinable. Evan seeks to become a gentleman safely and permanently, yet is not happy about denying his filial past. The deceptive nature of appearances also plays an important part in the story. Is a man what he appears? asks Meredith. How far do a fine figure and bearing and patrician features go toward making a person truly of the gentry? Are the qualities that make a gentleman hereditary, or can they be acquired? And how far can they be stretched without appearing absurd? Meredith poses the questions and then lets the reader draw his own conclusions from the events in the story. *Evan Harrington* is one of George Meredith's most readable novels, filled with delightful characterizations, such as the Cogglesby brothers and Evan's trio of snobbish sisters. Its comedy makes some shrewd points, but is no less fun for its serious intent.

EVANGELINE

Type of work: Poem
Author: Henry Wadsworth Longfellow (1807-1882)
Type of plot: Pastoral romance
Time of plot: Mid-eighteenth century
Locale: French Canada and the United States
First published: 1847

The note of gentleness on which Evangeline, A Tale of Acadie *begins never falters throughout. The description of a kindly, contented people who accept their exile as God's will, is followed by an account of Evangeline's patient wanderings throughout a lifetime of disappointment. The freshness, music and poetic imagery, as well as its story of thwarted young love, give the poem wide appeal.*

It is difficult in an unsentimental age to appreciate and understand the enormous appeal this poem had for readers in Longfellow's time. It was hailed from the beginning as a truly "American" poem and its success was virtually unlimited. This pastoral romance relates an odyssey of sorts and dwells on the idea of search, wandering, and Evangeline's constancy. Longfellow sought to imbue the poem with a classical flavor within the framework of the American landscape. It is enriched with elaborate descriptions of the historic American drive toward the west and the south. The rivers, forests, and prairies about which Longfellow writes are the imaginative product of his reading and research, for most of the places mentioned he had never seen.

The basic setting of the story revolves around the cruel displacement of the Acadians by the British. Longfellow does not elaborate on the inequities of the British mandate to drive people from their homes; he is more interested in achieving a melancholy emotional tone by concentrating on the reality of exile and the frustration of search. The mood is a tranquil one. Longfellow looks at his two lovers from a distance, creating a hazy image of things far away. Much of the poem's action takes place at night, or by moonlight, as if to shade the drama with some of the mystery of the prairie.

There is no doubt that the constancy and patience of Evangeline was appealing to Longfellow and his readers. Evangeline's loyalty and fidelity play a major role in the structuring of this romance. While Evangeline is the embodiment of feminine virtue, tenderness, and chastity, she does not have the dimension of a heroic figure. The poem suggests minor poetic form, certainly not of epic grandeur. Evangeline and Gabriel are not realistic lovers, but exponents of the romanticism of the times.

Longfellow felt that the English world was not sufficiently awakened to the beauty of the classical hexameter, so he decided from the beginning to employ this meter in *Evangeline*. There are difficulties with the use of this meter in English and Longfellow was aware of them; yet he painstakingly sought to adhere to this classical measure. The meter does add an intrinsic charm and appropriateness to the tale, despite the sometimes monotonous quality of the lines. Longfellow's use of hexameter triggered a new interest in the meter and inspired much critical evaluation of its use and value.

THE EVE OF ST. AGNES

Type of work: Poem
Author: John Keats (1795-1821)
Type of plot: Chivalric romance
Time of plot: Middle Ages
Locale: A castle
First published: 1820

The plot of Keats's poem is built around an ancient superstition that a maiden who retires to her bed on St. Agnes Eve after practising a particular ritual will be awakened in her dreams by her lover. An example of English Romanticism at its best, the poem is matchless in its musical verse and vivid in its descriptions of color, sight, and sound.

Keats wrote "The Eve of St. Agnes" in January and February of 1819, the first of an astonishing spate of masterpieces that belied his failing health and emotional turmoil, and which ended abruptly one year later when it became apparent that his illness was mortal. "La Belle Dame Sans Merci," "Lamia," and six great odes were all written before October of that year. The near circumstance of his death seems to throw into a kind of relief the luscious descriptions of physical reality in this and other poems. More striking still is the poet's refusal to take comfort in the simplistic assurances of any religious or philosophical system that denied either the complexity of mind or the reality and importance of sense. "The Eve of St. Agnes" manifests Keats's characteristic concern with the opposition and subtle connection of the sensual world to the interior life. He shared this preoccupation with other Romantic poets, notably Coleridge and Wordsworth, taking as his subject the web of an antithesis at the heart of human experience; like them, he cloaked his meditations in sensuous imagery.

In this and other ways, Keats and all the Romantics abandoned the poetic theory of the century before. Eighteenth century poetry was formal, didactic, and objective in stance. Its chief aim was to show to the world (that is, to mankind) a picture of itself for its own improvement and edification. Its chief ornament was art: puns, wordplay, satiric description, and so forth. In short, what eighteenth century poets saw as virtue in poetry was logic and rigid metrics. Nineteenth century poets wrote from a radically different philosophical base, due in part to the cataclysmic political changes surrounding the American and French Revolutions. Before these upheavals occurred, a belief in order and measure extended into all facets of life, from social relations to literature; extremes were shunned in all things as unnatural, dangerous, and perhaps blasphemous.

After 1789, when the social order in France turned upside down, an expectation of the millennium arose in England, especially in liberal intellectual circles; the old rules of poetry were thrown off with the outworn social strictures, and a new aesthetic bloomed in their place. Its ruling faculty was imagination. The world seemed made new, and poetry released from bondage. Romantic poets frequently stated that poems ought to be composed on the inspiration of the moment, thereby faithfully to record the purity of the emotion. In fact, Keats and his contemporaries labored hard over their creations; they exerted themselves not to smoothness of meter but to preserving the grace of spontaneity while achieving precision in observation of natural and psychological phenomena. Poets saw themselves as charting hitherto unexplored reaches of human experience, extremes of joy and dejection, guilt and redemption, pride and degradation. They wrote meditations, confessions, and conversations, in which natural things were seen to abet internal states. And they wrote ballads and narratives, such as "The Eve of St. Agnes," set in the past or in distant parts of the world and using archaic language and rhythms to make the events related seem even more strange and wonderful. And over and over they described epiphanous moments when the human consciousness becomes one with nature, when all is made new, when divinity animates the inanimate, and the lowest creature seems wondrous. This way of seeing was thought to be a return to an earlier consciousness lost in early childhood, and is the theme of Wordsworth's seminal "Ode: Intimations of Immortality."

In "The Eve of St. Agnes," Keats attempts, among other things, to maintain this elevated state of mind throughout the narrative. He sets the story in medieval times, so that the familiar Romeo-and-Juliet characters take on charm from their quaint surroundings, and from the archaic language in which they speak and are described. Its verse form is the Spenserian stanza, smooth yet free, with its slightly asymmetric rhyme scheme that avoids the monotony of couplet or quatrain, and the piquant extension of the ninth line which gives to the whole an irregularity echoing ordinary speech. The first five stanzas contrast the Beadsman, coldly at his prayers, with the "argent revelry" making gaudy the great hall. This imagery of cold and warmth, silver and scarlet, chastity and sensuality continues throughout the poem, a comment on the plot.

That the poem is named for a virgin martyr yet tells the story of an elopement is likewise significant; for the point of the poem, on the one hand, is that piety and passion are opposing but inseparable drives. Each without the other has no point of reference. Porphyro without Madeline becomes the gross Lord Maurice, the savage Hildebrand; Madeline without Porphyro becomes the Beadsman with his deathlike abrogation of sense. Instead, Porphyro is made to faint at the celestial beauty of Madeline at her prayers, Madeline to be wooed by songs and colors and things to eat. But what fruits! Not mere groceries, but the glowing essence of fruitfulness, tribute to a love match of the meditative and emotional faculties that, when accomplished in one individual, fulfills the whole human potential.

The other theme, or perhaps the other face of the same theme, is the relentless press of quotidian misery on the poetic personality, another favorite arena of reflection among the Romantics, and one that was poignantly near Keats's heart, menaced by tuberculosis as he was, and his younger brother having died of the disease the previous winter. The lovers are shown, unearthly fair, escaping from a house where wrath and drunkenness hold sway, bound for a dream-vision of happiness. But significantly the poet does not follow them to their southern sanctuary. Instead he relates the wretched end of Angela, who dies "palsy-twitched" in her sleep; the cold sleep of the Beadsman among the ashes; the drunken nightmares of the Baron and his guests. The ending, in short, is not unreservedly happy, but partakes of that bittersweet emotion which in the midst of joy acknowledges wretchedness, the mark of a mind that strives for aesthetic detachment while believing in its duty to the rest of human kind.

Edward E. Foster

EVELINA

Type of work: Novel
Author: Fanny Burney (Madame d'Arblay, 1752-1840)
Type of plot: Sentimental romance
Time of plot: Eighteenth century
Locale: England
First published: 1778

The theme and substance of Evelina *are clear from its subtitle "The History of a Young Lady's Entrance into the World." Written in an epistolary form, the work holds the reader's interest with its descriptions of English social life as seen through the eyes of a seventeen-year-old girl. Possibly difficult to accept is the character of the heroine herself. Like Melanie in* Gone with the Wind, *Evelina never so much as verges on an unkind thought from the narrative's beginning to its end.*

Evelina is Fanny Burney's first and most successful novel. When it was published in 1778, the book's appeal was attributed to its sentimental value, but it has held lasting interest because of the realistic portrayal of eighteenth century English life. Burney's attentiveness to the manners and pretentiousness of socialites enabled her to show in *Evelina* not only the culture, but its foibles. *Evelina* is particularly descriptive of the social position of women.

The heroine, Evelina, sensitively reared by the Rev. Mr. Villars, has become a kind, compassionate young woman. As she steps into the social life of London, her unblemished perception of society affords both delight at its marvels and disdain for its unscrupulousness and frivolity. Her letters to Mr. Villars convey clear images of London high society.

Evelina first writes with some amazement that London life begins so late that people spend the morning in bed. She adjusts, however, to the night life, and enjoys the opera, plays, and other events with which she and her company are entertained almost nightly. She is annoyed by audiences who are so talkative throughout the events that the artists cannot be heard, and quickly realizes that the purpose of the events is more for socializing than for the merit of the performances themselves.

Fanny Burney places her heroine with various guardians in a variety of situations in both city and country. Evelina's first awkward fortnight in London with the kind Mirvan ladies abruptly contrasts with her second visit in London in the company of Madam Duval and her relatives, the Braughtons, who are crude and ill-mannered, and who cause Evelina embarrassment by her forced association with them. In her third venture away from her benefactor, Mr. Villars, Evelina is again in cultured company under the guardianship of the aggressive Mrs. Selwyn.

In each group, regardless of its social position, Evelina finds individuals of sincerity and those who are masters of divisiveness and deception. Mrs. Mirvan and Maria are sincere and well-mannered. Captain Mirvan, though uncouth, cruel, and contemptuous, is, nevertheless, sincere. He is his own person, honest in his brutal way. Madam Duval shares with her tormentor, Captain Mirvan, the quality of being her own person, disagreeable as she, too, may be.

Evelina readily acknowledges the honorable qualities of Lord Orville and Mr. Macartney. She also quickly perceives the duplicity of Sir Clement, Mr. Lovel, Lord Merton, the Braughtons, Lady Louisa, and Mr. Smith. In lady or silversmith, airs and presumptuousness repel Evelina. Evelina is shocked at the insincerity of those whose honor and good manners directly relate to dress, immediate company, and situation. Lord Merton ignores Evelina while Lady Louisa is present, yet lavishes her with attention at Lady Louisa's absence. Sir Clement is a chameleon whose attention to Evelina is gained at any expense. Lady Louisa acts out roles constantly, purposely ignoring Evelina until she learns that Evelina is to become her brother's wife.

Evelina detects affectation and shows it as being as ridiculous as it truly is. She describes for Mr. Villars an episode from her first dance at which a young man approached her with comically stilted mannerisms and speech. "Allow me, Madam . . . the honour and happiness—if I am not so unhappy as to address you too late—to have the happiness and honour. . . . " She confesses that she had to turn away to conceal her laughter.

Evelina is bewildered by social etiquette which she has had no opportunity to learn at Berry Hill, but her sense of propriety causes her to suffer for her ignorance. She is always aware of her dependent position and constantly relies on her protectors, benefactors, or guardians.

Fanny Burney did not intend for Evelina's dependence to be read negatively. On the contrary, Evelina was idyllic in her feminine compliance and sensibility. She was a model lady for the times. It is interesting to note, however, how vastly the roles and rights of men and women in the novel differ. Mr. Lovel says, "I have an insuperable aversion to strength, either in body or mind, in a female." Lord Merton echoes a similar view, "for a woman wants nothing to recommend her but beauty and good nature; in everything else she is either impertinent or unnatural."

Burney comments on women's sensibility through her characters. Lady Louisa, whose feigned delicate nature corresponds with her posturing, seems to be the extreme of insincere sensibility. Mrs. Selwyn represents another extreme. She is powerful and aggressive and is disliked by both men and women for her outspokenness. Evelina wishes that Mrs. Selwyn were more sensitive to her needs in awkward situations, and finds her lacking in femininity. Evelina writes, "I have never been personally hurt by her want of gentleness, a virtue which nevertheless seems so essential a part of the female character." Lord Orville, the ideal male in the novel, is described by Evelina as "feminine," a compliment to his gentle character. Evelina's description of Mrs. Selwyn, however, as "masculine" is definitely a negative criticism.

Because of the impropriety of acting independently, Evelina and all gentlewomen must rely upon others for advice. Unfortunately, those counselors are likely to take advantage of women's dependency. Fortunately, Evelina's good sense alerts her to unreliable protectors, but her situation clearly indicates the powerless situation of women who are perpetually rescued or victimized.

Perhaps Mr. Villar's response to Evelina's interference in the attempted suicide of Mr. Macartney best expresses Burney's attitude toward women. "Though gentleness and modesty are the peculiar attributes of your sex, yet fortitude and firmness, when occasion demands them, are virtues as noble and as becoming in women as in men."

Evelina was first published without the name of the author, and was generally assumed to have been written by a man. Fanny Burney was indeed as dependent as her Evelina—in getting the book into publication, a male secret agent smuggled the manuscript to the publisher.

Mary Peace Finley

EVERY MAN IN HIS HUMOUR

Type of work: Drama
Author: Ben Jonson (1573?-1637)
Type of plot: Comedy of humors
Time of plot: Late sixteenth century
Locale: London
First presented: 1598; rewritten before 1616

In the play's title, the word "humour" refers to the medieval theory which explains an individual's temperament by the particular mixture of the four basic humours which compose each person's character: hot, dry, moist, and cold. Though all comedy is based on aberration from the normal, Jonson's technique of distinguishing each character by heightening his principal folly set a new pattern for subsequent dramas. It is believed that Shakespeare acted in this play, first produced at The Curtain Theater in the summer of 1598.

Jonson substantially revised *Every Man in His Humour* for his 1616 Folio publication and added a famous Prologue which defends his sort of comedy. He changed the setting of the play from exotic Italy to everyday London, renamed the characters, eliminated extraneous speeches, and particularized general and high-flown speeches of several characters. He writes in the Prologue that the play will not utilize the marvelous or the mechanistic (such as thunder machines), "But deeds and language such as men do use." He also explains that his comedy will "sport with human follies, not with crimes." *Every Man in His Humour* is thus a light-hearted portrayal of man's follies, and the medieval theory of the four humours is not very important here. For Jonson, the humours were simply the exaggerated and often caricatured manners of men, so that the comedy of humours is really a comedy of manners.

Perhaps more clearly than any other Jonson comedy, *Every Man in His Humour* demonstrates how much his is a comedy of noninteraction—in structure and plot, in character and language. By contrast, Shakespearean comedy thrives on close consequence; for example, the resolution of subplot and main plot always results in an organic merging. What resolution there is at the end of *Every Man in His Humour* is artificial, imposed by Justice Clement, but not strongly felt by the audience to be genuine. The traditional concluding symbols of judgment, marriage, and banquet are arbitrarily imposed on an ending which would otherwise seem hopelessly fragmentary.

Structurally, noninteraction is here very apparent, because the subplots that serve to make up plot seem to be accidental rather than mutually necessary. Meetings between members of different subplots are coincidental and suggest disorder rather than resolution; the meetings in Moorfields and outside Cob's house are good examples. Also, Jonson's characters are each extremely individualistic, almost solipsistic in their belief in the importance of their own existence. This subjectivism produces mazes of misapprehension and nonunderstanding when characters try to communicate. This condition is compounded by the disguises of Brainworm, who casts himself as manipulator of much of the action.

Most of the characters seem unable to practice directness; they resort to communication through go-betweens, thus increasing the possibilities of mistakes and misperceptions. Knowell deals with Edward through Brainworm, who also mediates for Edward with his father. Wellbred conducts Edward's courtship; Kitely tells Cash of his fears about his wife, and Cash then sends Cob with the message to Kitely. Bobadill insults Downright for Matthew, and Justice Clement even relates to a client who is standing before him by means of his assistant. A desire to avoid encounters motivates much of the action: Kitely and Dame Kitely do not speak their minds to each other; Knowell is worried about Edward's and Wellbred's friendship; Brainworm tries to keep apart those he is manipulating. Direct, emotion-filled conversation usually does not occur. Bridget and Edward utter not a single word to each other either before or after marriage, nor does Knowell congratulate Edward. Kitely's feeble remarks to his wife after their reconciliation suggest their essential estrangement. The only place for protestations of real feeling is in soliloquy; in person, the characters are incapable of genuine dialogue.

Noninteraction comes to its logical conclusion in the events which take place before Cob's house (Act IV). Instead of creating a recognition and discovery scene, the characters misunderstand both the action and one another because they refuse to go beyond their ossified solipsisms. Thus, Knowell "recognizes" Dame Kitely as Edward's lover; Kitely believes Knowell to be his wife's lover; and Knowell mistakes Kitely for Edward. Justice Clement's plea for reconciliation is not met by any real change in the characters.

In his early Jonson comedy, the debate about poetry which frames the play (Knowell's opening speech and Clement's closing one) does not provide the unity which similar debates do in later Jonson works. The ideal of poetry seems unlikly here to do more than achieve an arbitrary connection with the unity dictated by Clement; for although the characters often speak about poetry, they do not seem to be particularly concerned with it.

As in most Jonsonian comedy, characters' names—be they serious, satiric, or comic—disclose ideas about personality. Justice Clement, as his name suggests, tempers his justice with mercy, but Knowell usually acts the opposite of a knowledgeable father. Some of the characters are recognizable types deriving from Roman comedy, especially that of Plautus: Brainworm, the witty servant; Kitely, the jealous husband; Knowell, the strict father; Wellbred, the man-about-town; Bobadill, the *miles gloriosus,* or braggart soldier. Though he borrowed these typed characters, Jonson made them thoroughly English and assimilated them to his ideas of human follies.

The characters are often connected by contrasts, so that those who appear similar are shown to be different, while those who seem opposed are linked. Thus Matthew, the town gull, supposedly so different from Stephen, the country gull, is actually the same sort of person. Both ape fashions in sport (rapier dueling or hawking) and praise a particular fashion in dress; the difference is that the town gull is *in* style and the country gull *out* of style. Similarly, Edward is shown to be essentially different from his friend Wellbred—the one serious and temperate, the other frivolous and extreme. There are also sets of characters that seem to parody each other's behavior: Cob's jealousy burlesques Kitely's, and both reflect Knowell's spying on his son; the relationship of Edward to Wellbred is mimicked by that of Matthew to Bobadill. These contrasts and distorted mirrors help to give a structural balance to the play but do not change its nonrelational quality. Each character is set on a particular course by his personality, a course that is not altered by any collision with another person.

Like *Bartholomew Fair, Every Man in His Humour* portrays a multiplicity of human aberrations, though here they are more lighthearted follies. Jonson's favorite satiric targets can be found—man's illusions about education, love, poetry, social place—as a group of characters reiterates each issue. Justice Clement's plea "to put off all discontent" marks the necessary illusion of change and unity at the end. Only the later Ben Jonson (of *Bartholomew Fair*) can accept these follies and aberrations as part of man's nature.

Margaret McFadden-Gerber

EVERY MAN OUT OF HIS HUMOUR

Type of work: Drama
Author: Ben Jonson (1573?-1637)
Type of plot: Comedy of humors
Time of plot: Early seventeenth century
Locale: Not specified, but ostensibly London
First presented: 1599

Like many sequels to a success, this play, a companion to Every Man in His Humour, *does not succeed as well as its predecessor. The numerous characters are not integrated into its rambling plot. Further, the play is a product of the "War of the Theaters," a controversy in which playwrights used their play as vehicles to ridicule their competitors. As such, much of the play's topical satire no longer holds meaning for a modern audience.*

Although intended as a battle in the War of the Theaters, particularly as an attack upon Dekker and Marston, *Every Man Out of His Humour* is more than that. Jonson's comedy of humours conceived of stage personalities on the basis of a ruling trait or passion, much as Dickens later gave his fictional characters certain dominant traits or characteristics. By placing these typified traits in juxtaposition, the spark of comedy was struck in their conflict and contrast. The result, in *Every Man Out of His Humour,* is often funny. Jonson possessed an arrogant, self-righteous personality and he smarted under the satire of his competitors, seeking to get back at them with this play. But the satirical picture of contemporary manners, vivid caricatures, and the witty dialogue carry the play beyond any merely personal attacks. *Every Man Out of His Humour* not only satirizes individuals but also levels a general attack upon corruptions in the abstract.

Jonson could not resist lampooning his enemies, but he raised dramatic lampooning to an art. Marston probably was intended as the character Carlo Buffone, that "public, scurrilous, and profane jester." Asper is undoubtedly meant to be a comic idealization of Jonson himself—wholly admirable and just, "an ingenious and free spirit" and "one whom no servile hope of gain or frosty apprehension of danger, can make to be a parasite. . . ."

While Lyly and others were perfecting the filigree of their prose for courtly audiences, another kind of prose was beginning to be heard in the popular theater, a rough-and-tumble language based on the vernacular. Jonson was among the writers adopting a more abrupt, staccato language, truer to life than the oratorical speeches of most of his contemporaries. The speeches of Carlo Buffone and some of the other characters in *Every Man Out of His Humour* simulates live language much more closely than had been done before. Carlo's spiteful disposition is chiefly revealed in his penchant for coining scurrilous likenesses, and he leaps in a single speech from the figure of a starved dog to that of scalding oil and fire to that of gunpowder, all to describe Macilente. His speech rhythms trip, stumble, and flicker back and forth between metaphoric and literal abuse.

The characters in this play remain isolated, blocked off from one another, immobilized in their humours. The plot is a kaleidoscopic series of characteristic poses adopted by the personalities; each individual pursues his humour oblivious of everything else about him. For example, Fungoso, eyes greedily on Fastidious Brisk's suit, makes half-answers to his uncle, while privately calculating how much it will cost him to duplicate the suit. Sogliardo, at the same time, is too engrossed by the prospect of vulgar pleasures in London to notice Fungoso's inattention. Sordido, scarcely aware of the others, gazes into the sky for signs of rain that will raise the value of his wheat.

Jonson's characters rail at one another in a scorching indictment of folly; but they are not mere mouthpieces for their author. Even during the War of the Theaters, Jonson was too much of an artist to use the satiric speeches of his characters merely as clubs. Falling victim to their own imbalance of humours and distempered view of the world, they always have their place in a larger design.

EVERYMAN

Type of work: Drama
Author: Unknown
Type of plot: Moral allegory
Time of plot: Any time
Locale: Any place
Earliest extant version: 1508

Thanks to the preservation of four printed versions from the sixteenth century, this is one of the few morality plays to survive into the present. In addition, it has contemporary appeal, having been produced several times within the twentieth century. Written to teach moral lessons to the illiterate masses, the characters of the play are personifications of virtue and vice.

The morality play, of which *Everyman* is the best extant example, and the mystery play are the two principal kinds of Medieval drama. The mystery play is a dramatic recreation of a story from Scripture, and its aim is the elucidation of the revelation contained in the Bible. The morality play is an allegorical form, peopled by personified abstractions, such as Beauty, Justice, and Fortitude, and types such as Everyman, Priest, and King. In addition, the subject matter is admonitory, particularly concerning man's last end. As Albert Baugh has pointed out, it is difficult to discover precise sources for the subject matter or the dramatic method. There are, however, certain parallels in Medieval sermons, which often bolstered moral exhortations with allegorical examples. Indeed, allegory is pervasive in Medieval literature as is, for that matter, concern about a happy death, but how these evolved into the particular form of the morality play is hard to tell.

Few morality plays have survived and only *Everyman* is well enough thought of to be dignified with modern performance. One reason for the unpopularity of the genre is the limitation placed on dramatic complication by the static nature of the personifications. The characters are of necessity simple and there is no possibility of change except perhaps in a central type like Everyman. All characters are partially—and most characters are completely—frozen as what they are. As a result, there can be little psychological insight and little of the diverse movement that invigorates earlier and later drama.

Like all forms of allegory, the method is essentially intellectual. The active involvement of the spectator is not through emotion so much as it is in the discovery of the meanings of characters and the significance of the configurations in which they are arranged. Allegory engages the mind and *Everyman* succeeds well in representing a complex, highly specific, theological system, while generating, by juxtaposition and order, sufficient immediacy to give force to the moral exhortation. The structure is elegant and compact; there is no attempt to catalog the deficiencies of Everyman's past life. Rather the play focuses on the poignant hour of death and implies what Everyman is and what he ought to be at that critical moment.

Because of the allegorical method, it is easy to trivialize the significance of the play by reducing it to the identification of the personifications. But one thereby misses the awesome power of its abstractions and the complex view of life that is represented. A play about the reaction to imminent death, *Everyman,* in its configurations of characters, implies much about how life should be lived. When God initiates the action, we begin with the premise that all men are to be called to give an account of their actions. As the plot develops, it would perhaps be more accurate to refer to the central character as Anyman, but the use of the name Everyman implies that the experience is not random, not what might happen, but is paradigmatic of what will happen and how we ought to respond.

As Everyman turns to his valued, habitual companions for comfort on his difficult and dangerous journey, it is important that the playwright does not present a pageant of specific sins. Instead, in Fellowship, Kindred, and Goods, we have summary abstractions, which are not particular sins in themselves, but rather examples of the distractions which divert man away from positive direction towards God and salvation. Thus, Everyman's failures are represented not by a static series of vices, but by the vital enticements which have taken too much of his attention. The conception is a Dantescan analysis of sin as a turning away from God, the end towards Whom we ought to tend, towards the preoccupations of this world.

In the theology of the play, salvation obviously cannot come by faith alone, since it is imperative that Everyman be accompanied to judgment by Good Deeds. However, Good Deeds is so infirm, because of Everyman's prior misdirection, that a prior step is necessary: Everyman is entrusted to Knowledge for guidance. The implication is that knowledge of the institutional Church and its remedies is necessary for the successful living of the good life. Knowledge first directs Everyman to Confession, one of the tangible means of repentance and regeneration. When Confession has been completed, Good Deeds begins to revive since contrition and amendment free the accumulated merits of past virtuous actions.

Knowledge also summons other attainments which can travel at least part way with Everyman. Beauty, Strength, Discretion, and Five Wits are all auxiliary human accomplishments which can help and comfort men along their way, though none can persevere to the final moment of judgment. As they fall away, one by one, we are watching the process of death. Of course Beauty is the first to depart in this telescoped version of man's demise. Strength follows as life ebbs. The last of the attainments to leave is Five Wits, the sensual means through which man acquires whatever understanding he gains in life.

In the end, even Knowledge, the representative of the human intellect, which builds on sense and is a higher power than sense, cannot go the whole distance with Everyman. The respect for Knowledge in the play's implied theological system is enormous: Knowledge plays the pivotal role in informing Everyman of the way to salvation. Yet, in the final analysis, only Good Deeds can descend into the grave with Everyman because it is only the efficacious result of knowledge in right living that merits eternal reward.

An examination of the abstractions and of the arrangement of them reveals in *Everyman* the complex shape of Medieval Christianity. The play suggests a means to salvation everywhere consistent with the prescriptions of the Medieval Church: there is an ultimate accountability, but man has the capacity, through faith and reason, to direct himself towards God by using the institution of the Church to enable him to do the good which is required of all men.

Edward E. Foster

EXILES

Type of work: Drama
Author: James Joyce (1882-1941)
Type of plot: Naturalism
Time of plot: 1912
Locale: Merrion and Ranelagh, Dublin suburbs
First published: 1918

The theme of artist as hero began with the Romantic Movement, a movement which continues into this century. Instinctively feeling the tenuousness of his place in the present industrial world, the artist must protest. Two of the major characters, Robert and Beatrice, are forced into compromising with the world and with themselves. By contrast, the artist Richard is self-reliant, dependent only on his own intellectual and emotional values. As such, he alone finds fulfillment and is armored against sentimentality and the moral anarchy of the modern world. Exiles *falls within the period which saw Joyce finish* A Portrait of the Artist as a Young Man *and begin* Ulysses.

James Joyce's own exile from Dublin began when he was twenty years old and lasted for nearly forty years, during which time he only visited his homeland twice. Yet he never lost touch with Ireland, retaining a unique relationship with it. In his art he considered himself the "moral conscience of his race." To maintain that function and to protect the integrity of his art, however, Joyce—like Richard Rowan—believed that he must exist in a spiritual state of exile, if not in an actual physical one. Exile itself was for Joyce a state of integrity in which he could achieve wholeness, singularity, and objectivity, all necessary for the survival of his self and, therefore, his art.

The character of Robert Hand in *Exiles,* partly based on Joyce's brother, Stanislaus, is the image of the man the author feared he might have become if he had stayed in Dublin. Like Gabriel Conroy of Joyce's great short story, "The Dead," a man of talent who has sold himself to journalism and is no longer capable of autonomy, he has betrayed himself. Unable to stand alone, he seeks to attach himself to Richard Rowan through Bertha. Bertha herself is only attracted to Robert because she sees in him an opportunity to express her independence from Richard.

Finally the play should be seen as an attempt by Richard and Bertha—whose character was based on Joyce's wife, Nora—to work out their relationship, one based on mutual trust yet offering each of them independence. For his own sake, Richard realizes that not only must he sever all absolute attachments but that if he is to remain free, no one else can be allowed to attach themselves to him. *Exiles* is then a play about freedom and its nature and conditions—the major theme of all Joyce's work.

A FABLE

Type of work: Novel
Author: William Faulkner (1897-1962)
Type of plot: Religious allegory
Time of plot: 1918
Locale: The Western Front in France
First published: 1954

Like many of Faulkner's other novels, A Fable *is steeped in mythic allusions, both Biblical and pagan. Yet, the work still has a life of its own, a statement equally true for Faulkner's other works. Nine years in the writing, the novel obviously alludes to the events of Christ's passion and crucifixion; these elements are interwoven into a narrative set during World War I. The work departs, as does* The Wild Palms, *from Faulkner's ambitious and spectacularly successful development of his own mythic creation, Yoknapatawpha County.*

A Fable is probably the most ambitious, though not the most successful, work of one of the twentieth century's most ambitious novelists. By juxtaposing elements of the Passion of Christ against a story of trench mutiny in World War I, Faulkner attempts to combine two very different types of narrative: an allegorical "fable" based upon parallels between the events of his story and those of the original "myth" as well as a realistic narrative of war, politics, and personal relationships.

Most of the similarities to Christ's life and death are obvious. The Corporal, who was born in a stable and is thirty-three years old, leads a mutinous group of twelve followers and the events surrounding his capture and execution suggest the Passion: one disciple betrays him for money, another denies him three times; the followers have a "Last Supper"; the Corporal is executed between two thieves in a manner that suggests Christ's crucifixion; he acquires a crown of thorns; he is mourned by women who resemble Mary Magdalene and Mary; and his body vanishes three days after burial. But it is necessary to remember that *A Fable* is *not* the Passion retold in modern dress. Faulkner does not simply update or interpret Christian myth: he *uses* it. Therefore any attempt to come to terms with *A Fable* must consider the unique, personal vision that Faulkner presents in his book.

Some critics have faulted the novel on the grounds that the personality of the Corporal is insufficiently developed. It is true that he is not strongly individualized, but to present the character in greater detail would risk either the creation of a purely symbolic figure or one too humanized to maintain the Christ parallel. Instead, the Corporal remains a silent, mysterious embodiment of man's spiritual side; the concrete presentation of his "meaning" is entrusted to other characters. The most important thing is that, for all of the Biblical allusions, the Corporal is not the chosen Son of God, but is definitely a son of man—specifically of the Marshal—and the thematic center of the novel is dramatized in the conflict between the Corporal and his Father-Marshal antagonist.

In the single most powerful and important scene of the novel, the final confrontation between the two men, the Marshal defines their basic natures as

> . . . two articulations . . . not so much to defend as to test two inimical conditions which . . . must contend and one of them—perish: I champion of the mundane earth . . . while you champion of an esoteric realm of man's baseless and his infinite capacity—no passion—for unfact. . . .

Thus, *A Fable* is not really about man's relationship to God, or even to society, but to himself. Each of these men stands for one aspect of the human personality and the conflict between them can be seen in several ways: son versus father, youth versus age, idealist versus realist, common man versus authority, heart versus mind. In short, the major conflict of the book is, in the words of Faulkner's Nobel Prize Speech, "the human heart in conflict with itself"—*man's basic dualism*: the major theme of Faulkner's late fiction.

However, if the Corporal remains the shadowy incarnation of man's spiritual side, the Marshal, both in his symbolic and his realistic functions, is a much more vivid and complicated character. On the literal level, it is he, as the supreme commander of the Allied Armies in France, who masterminds the successful military counterstrategy; symbolically, as the primary representative of secular power, the Marshal represents everything in human society that denies personal autonomy and spiritual freedom to man.

But any attempt to pin down the Marshal's symbolic antecedents more precisely is very difficult. At times he suggests Satan, at times Pilate or Caesar, or simply Military Authority, but in the central confrontation scene his role seems to most closely resemble that of the "Grand Inquisitor" who appears in the greatest of earlier "Second Coming" fictions, Ivan Karamazov's parable in Fyodor Dostoevski's *The Brothers Karamazov*.

Like the Grand Inquisitor, the Marshal faces a Christ surrogate who poses a threat to the established order. Likewise, the Marshall makes an offer to his antagonist of life and freedom in return for betrayal which he knows in advance will be refused. The Marshal s background also resembles the Inquisitor's in that he, too, began life with a spiritual quest by renouncing the world in favor of the desert and the mountains. Like the Inqusitor—and Christ—the Marshal was tempted and, like the Inquisitor—*but unlike Christ*—he accepted the temptations and the view of life they represented in return for temporal power.

Thus, although he knows and understands man's duality, the Marshal rejects the spiritual and creative side of man and accepts him only as a mundane, earthbound creature who needs security and control rather than individual freedom and spiritual fulfillment. And, on the practical level, he commits himself to the human institution that fixes and formalizes this view of man. Like the Inquisitor, the Marshal justifies his actions on the grounds that they are what man needs and wants. He taunts his opponent with the notion that he, not the Corporal, is the true believer in man: "after the last ding dong of doom has rung and died there will still be one sound more; his voice, planning still to build something higher and faster and louder. . . . I don't fear man, I do better: I respect and admire him. . . . Because man and his folly—they will prevail."

These words echo the Nobel Prize Speech, but differ in one important respect from the novelist's own; in the address Faulkner went on to add: "He is immortal, not because he alone among creatures has an inexhaustible voice, but because he has a soul, a spirit capable of compassion and sacrifice and endurance." This statement defines the essence of the conflict between Marshal and the Corporal and their visions.

If the Marshal's view of mankind is correct, then the military hierarchy, the rituals and institutions it supports, and the war itself are things man creates for himself and needs for survival. The Corporal's mutiny is, therefore, not only foolish, but even destructive to man's well-being. On the other hand, if the Corporal's vision is true, such things are artificial, malevolent restraints on man's potential. The mutiny in this context becomes a necessary act in the struggle to cast off the life-denying lies and organizations imposed on him and to fulfill his own human and spiritual capacities by taking control of his own destiny. Because the immediate secular power belongs to the Marshal, the earthbound view seems to win, but the question Faulkner raises is whether the impact of the Corporal's actions and martyrdom does not postulate the ultimate triumph of the spiritual vision.

To answer that question Faulkner attempts to work out the implications of the Corporal's ethic in the actions of several other characters and especially in the attempt of the English Runner to ferment a second and wider mutiny. Here lies the primary critical problem of the book: do these secondary actions establish and elaborate the main thrust of the novel or do they obscure and finally bury it?

Although he borrows Christian symbolism, Faulkner is clearly not presenting a conventionally religious message. He affirms the human spirit, but his attitude toward its ultimate fate is ambiguous. If the Corporal dies a heroic martyrdom, the other witnesses to the human spirit—the English Runner, the Sentry, the Reverend Sutterfield, the Quartermaster General—suffer dubious or ignominious fates and even the Corporal's death has no clear effect beyond stimulating the Runner's Quixotic gestures. Faulkner postulates *hope* and *faith* as vital elements in man's fulfillment, but they are presented as ends in themselves; it is unclear as to what man should hope *for* or have faith *in*.

It seems likely that Faulkner began to write *A Fable* with a number of abstract concepts in mind, rather than a special set of human experiences. In his best works, however, the meanings grow out of the concrete situations; in *A Fable* he tries to impose his meanings on his character's actions. Consequently, the novel is not completely satisfying on either the realistic or the symbolic level.

But, even with these problems, *A Fable* is a powerful reading experience. If it fails to fulfill completely Faulkner's most ambitious intentions, it does present separate characters and scenes that are powerful and memorable, and if all of Faulkner's concepts are not completely clear, his dramatization of man's basic duality is stimulating and provocative.

Keith Neilson

THE FAERIE QUEENE

Type of work: Poem
Author: Edmund Spenser (1552?-1599)
Type of plot: Allegorical epic
Time of plot: The Arthurian Age
Locale: England
First published: Books I-III, 1590; Books IV-VI, 1596

The Faerie Queene *is the first sustained poetic creation in English after Chaucer. For this lengthy epic, Spenser created his own form, known as the Spenserian stanza: nine lines, eight of five feet, and one of six, rhyming ababbcbcc. The characters and plot are completely allegorical, representing such concepts as chastity and its trials, and lust and its conquests. Most importantly, however, the richness of characterization and detail of plot, as well as the beauty of its language, give* The Faeric Queene *much more than historical significance.*

Although Spenser completed only six books, and part of a seventh, of the twelve projected books of *The Faerie Queene,* the bulk of what he did finish is so great that *The Faerie Queene* is, sad to say, generally more honored than read. The grand conception and execution of the poem reflect both the life of the poet and his participation in the life and ideals of his age. Spenser was committed to public service in the expansive period of Elizabethan efflorescence. A gentleman poet and friend of the great, Spenser never received the preferment he hoped for, but he remained devoted to Elizabeth, to England, and to late sixteenth century optimism. Even during his lifetime, Spenser was honored as a poet by the court and by other men of letters. To the present, Spenser's allegorical imagination and his control of language have earned him a reputation as "the poet's poet."

Like other Elizabethan poets, Spenser produced ecologues and a sonnet sequence, but *The Faerie Queene* is his great accomplishment. In a famous letter to Sir Walter Raleigh, Spenser explained the ambitious structure and purpose of his poem. It was to be composed of twelve books, each treating one of Aristotle's moral virtues as represented in the figure of a knight. The whole was to be a consistent moral allegory and the twelve books taken together would describe the circumscribing Aristotelian virtue of magnanimity, which Spenser called Magnificence.

At some point Spenser apparently decided to modify this plan. By the fourth book the simple representation of one virtue in one hero has broken down, though each book still does define a dominant virtue. More significantly, virtues are included which are not in Aristotle. Spenser is true to Aristotle, however, in consistently viewing virtue as a mean between extremes, as a moderate path between many aberrations of excess and defect.

The poem owes many debts to other antecedents. It is filled with references to and echoes of the Bible and the Greek and Latin classics. It is suffused with the spirit and much of the idealized landscape and atmosphere of medieval romance. However, its greatest debts are to the writers of the Continental Renaissance, particularly Ariosto. Ariosto's loosely plotted *Orlando Furioso* was the most influential single model and Spenser borrows freely, but where Ariosto was ironic or skeptical, Spenser transforms the same material into a serious medium for his high ethical purposes. Moreover, while allegory is a dimension added to Ariosto by his critics, Spenser is motivated throughout by his allegorical purpose: "to fashion a gentleman or noble person in vertuous and gentle discipline." In this aim, he is within the Renaissance tradition of writing courtesy books, such as Castiglione's *The Courtier*, guides to conduct for the gentleman who would seek excellence in behavior and demeanor. *The Faerie Queene* is a courtesy book turned to the highest of purposes—the moral formation of the ideal Christian gentleman.

Book I, the story of Red Cross Knight, the Knight of Holiness, is the truest to the original structure intention. Red Cross is assigned to Una to relieve her kingdom of a menacing dragon. Through the book Red Cross's chivalric exploits gradually develop in him the virtue he represents, so that he can ultimately kill the dragon. Book II also makes its demonstration in a relatively straightforward way. Sir Guyon, the Knight of Temperance, despite temporary setbacks and failures, eventually gains the knowledge of what true temperance is by seeing how it is violated both by excess and defect, by self-indulgence and by inhuman austerity. Ultimately Guyon can reject the opulent pleasures of the sensuous Bower of Bliss.

In Book III the allegorical method begins to change, probably because the virtues represented are more sophisticated in concept and more difficult to define. This complexity is mirrored in plot as earlier characters reappear and subsequent characters make brief entries. The result is an elaborate suspense and an intricate definition of virtues by means of examples, comparisons, and contrasts.

Book III deals with Chastity, Book IV with Friendship; both incorporate Renaissance platonic notions of love. Chastity is infinitely more than sexual abstinence, because by the perception of beauty and experience of love man moves closer to divine perfection. The concept of mutuality is emphasized in Book III by the fact that Scudamour cannot accomplish his quest without Britomart's contribution to his development. Book IV further explores platonic love by defining true friendship through a series of examples and counter examples which culminate in the noblest kind of friendship, that between a man and a woman.

In Book V, the adventures of Artegall, Spenser develops a summary statement of his political philosophy. Justice is relentless and inexorable; it is not only a matter of abstract principle but also of wise governing. After the stringency of the Book of Justice, Book VI is a softer, more pastoral treatment of the chivalric ideal of Courtesy in the person of Sir Calidore.

Spenser's allegory is enlivened by the meanderings of plot as well as by the fullness and appeal of his personifications. In addition to the well-wrought moral allegory, there is sporadic political allegory, as Elizabeth occasionally becomes visible in Una or Britomart or Belphoebe, or as contemporary events are evoked by the plot. At every point Spenser's style is equal to his noble intentions. The verse-form, the Spenserian stanza, is an ingenious modification of the rhyme royal stanza, in which the last line breaks the decasyllabic monotony with a rhythmically flexible Alexandrine. The diction has often been called archaic, but is perhaps more a capitalizing on all the resources of Elizabethan English, even the obsolescent, in the service of the beauty of sound. Alliteration and assonance also contribute to a consummate aural beauty which not only reinforces sense but also provides a pervasive harmony which is distinctly Spenserian.

Edward E. Foster

THE FAIR MAID OF PERTH

Type of work: Novel
Author: Sir Walter Scott (1771-1832)
Type of plot: Historical romance
Time of plot: 1396
Locale: Scotland
First published: 1828

In this novel, Scott sets his numerous fictional and historical characters against the backdrop of the rise to power of the Earl of Douglas, the Scottish leader who fought against Percy at the battle of Chevy Chase. Not one of his more notable works, The Fair Maid of Perth *still shows Scott's ability to delineate finely his characters both as individuals and types. Good and bad exist among both the nobility and the citizenry and are present in each individual in varying degrees.*

The reputation of Sir Walter Scott has declined over the years. As critical standards have changed, emphasizing polished writing and careful literary construction, the faults of Scott's writing have become only too obvious. *The Fair Maid of Perth,* for example, shows evidence of the same hurried composition, unnecessarily Latinate style, and excessive verbiage that his earlier novels exhibit; it also contains the characteristic idealization of women and improbable plot.

When all this is said, however, there remain positive values in Scott's historical novels such as *The Fair Maid of Perth.* These values are most evident in the concrete historical life that Scott is able to evoke, in the themes that he chooses to treat, and in the historical insight he is able to bring to his fiction.

The life of fourteenth century Scotland, its houses, churches, streets, and businesses is described in the most complete detail. Methods of warfare, methods of trading, and methods of lovemaking are presented. Furthermore, Scott is able to integrate this vast complex of late medieval detail into a single, though loosely connected, structure. Scott is expert at painting a great variety of social strata on the same canvas; in *The Fair Maid of Perth* there are nobility, rising mercantilists, churchmen, peasants, and poor folk. Not only are all these groups given roles in the drama, but all of them are shown in dramatic relationship to one another. In this way Scott succeeds in creating an organically developed society.

But it is not a society at rest. The story of *The Fair Maid of Perth,* recounting the victory of middle-class citizens over the schemings and violence of aristocratic forces, might stand as an emblem for the general historic trends of the era. Medieval institutional structures and morality were crumbling. A new system, based on men such as Henry Gow, was developing and coming into conflict with the old. The drama of this conflict, as well as the thematic tension between pacifism and the need for arms (between Henry and Catherine) overshadow the plot as such. But the historical process, and the themes Scott raises through his characters, more than compensate for artificial plot lines and stylistic deficiencies.

THE FAITHFUL SHEPHERDESS

Type of work: Drama
Author: John Fletcher (1579-1625)
Type of plot: Pastoral tragi-comedy
Time of plot: Remote antiquity
Locale: Thessaly
First presented: c. 1609

In this play, Fletcher's characters are not rounded but merely static symbols representing various types of chaste and lascivious love. The intricate plot is a predictable vehicle which juxtaposes these characters and finally illustrates the triumph of chastity. Fletcher's verse is technically of a high order, but hardly powerful enough for a successful dramatic rendering.

John Fletcher's first complete play, *The Faithful Shepherdess* was published in an undated quarto probably in 1609, although it may have been performed by a company of boy actors as early as 1608. In his dedicatory verse to Sir Walter Aston, Fletcher acknowledges the failure of the drama upon the stage, but he defends its virtues as a poetic "interlude"; and in his Introduction to the reader, he remarks upon the originality of its concept. A "pastoral tragicomedy," the play is, according to the author's famous definition of the new type, "not so called in respect of mirth and killing, but in respect it wants deaths." While the play comes close to tragedy, "which is enough to make it no comedy," its conclusion for the characters concerned is sober but not dreadful. As a model of tragicomedy, *The Faithful Shepherdess* is the first in a line of Jacobean dramas that became popular after Beaumont and Fletcher's *Philaster* and Shakespeare's *Cymbeline,* both of 1609.

Moreover, from a historical point of view, the play is interesting as a forerunner of the courtly masque during the period of Caroline (Cavalier) verse drama, 1625-1642. Unlike the more robust Elizabethan masques, notable for their lavish entertainments, rambling forms, and splendid pageantry, Fletcher's play established a more nearly classical model, formally elegant, artificial, and finely structured. Based upon Guarini's *Pastor Fido* and Cinthio's *Egle, The Faithful Shepherdess* reduces many of the complicated subplots from the sources to a symmetry of design: the conflict between chaste love and lust.

To a modern audience, Fletcher's elaborate presentation of this conflict may appear strained, not to say offensive. His characters, either virtuous or lewd, become stereotypes of sexual restraint or license. Taken as a whole, the play celebrates the chief virtue of virginity. Clorin, who has renounced love to preserve her chastity, acts as the agent of redemption for the wanton Cloe and Amarillis, heals Amoret's wounds, teaches Perigot to recognize Amoret's fidelity, and pronounces sentence upon the unrepentant, lascivious Sullen Shepherd. She even tames the Satyr, so that he becomes her servant in the cause of sexual continence.

Fletcher's emphasis upon the theme of virginity as a test of moral conduct may be explained as a retrospective compliment to the cult of Elizabeth's chastity; or it may be understood historically as a defense against mounting Puritan attacks upon the lechery of the theater. But another, more satisfactory explanation is that the subject is treated with such exaggeration that it is intended, for sophisticated patrons of the stage, as a satire. As Helen C. Gilde has ably demonstrated in her studies on Elizabethan erotic verse romances, a tradition of that genre is, at least partly, satiric and comic. Read in this light, *The Faithful Shepherdess* is an elegant, static, but witty play that explores with sly delicacy the comedy of sexual pursuit.

THE FALL OF THE HOUSE OF USHER

Type of work: Short story
Author: Edgar Allan Poe (1809-1849)
Type of plot: Gothic romance
Time of plot: Nineteenth century
Locale: The House of Usher
First published: 1839

The twins Madeline and Roderick are the last of the Ushers and symbolic of two warring facets of the human character: sensuality and intellect. The story follows Roderick's descent into madness and culminates in his entombment of his still-living sister. As she fights her way from the premature grave, a final apocalypse occurs. Battered by an almost supernatural storm, the Usher Castle and its occupants literally crumble and sink into a miasmic swamp. Truly one of Poe's finest short stories, it also ranks with the best in the genre.

A full century and a quarter after his death, Edgar Allan Poe probably remains, both in his life and his work, America's most controversial writer. Numerous biographical and critical studies have not succeeded in rectifying the initially distorted "myth" of Poe, promulgated by his hostile first biographer, as a self-destructive, alcoholic, almost daemonic creature. Even today, after much serious research and analysis, the "true" Poe remains enigmatic and elusive. The same is true of his works. Experts as important and varied as D. H. Lawrence, Henry James, T. S. Eliot, Charles Baudelaire, and Aldous Huxley have differed greatly in assessing their merits, with opinions ranging from extravagant eulogy to total dismissal. And no work of his has excited more diverse opinion or been given more conflicting analyses than his short story "The Fall of the House of Usher."

The problem is that there are many completely different, yet seemingly "valid," interpretations of the tale; contradictory readings that can "explain" all of the story's numerous ambiguities. And yet, obviously, as one prominent Poe critic has lamented, "they cannot all be right." Is there any way of choosing between these views or of synthesizing the best of them into a single one? Perhaps the task is not impossible if two important facts about the author are remembered: he was an adroit, conscious craftsman and critic who worked out his ideas with mathematical precision, and yet he was essentially a lyric poet.

These diverse readings can be divided roughly into three primary types: "natural" or "psychological," "supernatural," and "symbolic." In the first approach, the analysis has usually focused on the "unreliable" narrator as he chronicles Roderick Usher's descent into madness. As an artist, intellectual, and introvert, Usher has become so lopsided that his prolonged isolation, coupled with the sickness of his sister, has driven him to the edge of madness; along with the narrator, the reader sees him go over the edge. Or perhaps the tale is simply a detective story minus a detective; Usher manipulates the narrator into helping him murder Madeline and then goes insane from the emotional strain. The crucial "fantastic" elements in the story—Madeline's return from the tomb and the collapse of the house into the tarn—are "logically" explained in terms of the narrator's mounting hysteria, the resulting hallucination, and the natural destructiveness of the storm.

According to the second general view, the actions of the characters can be explained only by postulating a supernatural agency: the Usher "curse" is working itself out; the house is "possessed" and is destroying the occupants; Roderick is a demon drawing vitality from his sister until, as a Nemesis figure, she returns to punish him; Madeline is a vampire claiming her victim.

In the third view, the story is seen as an allegory: Roderick as intellect is suppressing sensuality (Madeline) until it revolts; Madeline is a "Mother Figure" who returns from the grave to punish "Usher-Poe" for deserting her and for having incest desires; Roderick is the "artist" who must destroy himself in order to create; the entire story is a symbolic enactment of the Apocalypse according to Poe.

Both as a critic and a writer, Poe was thoroughly aware of the machinery of the Gothic Romance and "The Fall of the House of Usher" is a veritable catalog of devices from the genre—the "haunted mansion," the "artistic hero-villain," the "twins motif," suggestions of vampirism, and all of the physical paraphernalia—dank crypts, violent electrical storms. But it does not follow that because Poe utilizes the conventions of the form, that he is holding himself to the substance of them. It is precisely because he does not commit himself exclusively to either a "rational," "supernatural," or "symbolic" reading of the tale, that he is able to provoke emotional reactions by indirection and implication that would be impossible if he "fixed" his meaning more precisely. The technique is essentially that of the lyric poet who uses the power of image, atmosphere, and suggestion to evoke emotions and produce the desired "*single effect*" on the reader—which was Poe's stated aim as a short story writer.

"I feel that the period will sooner or later arrive," says Roderick Usher, "when I must abandon life and reason together, in some struggle with the grim phantasm, FEAR." Thus Poe underscores "fear" as the central emotion he wishes to provoke and the story can best be discussed in terms of how he develops this response.

The tale divides into five distinct parts: (1) the description of the house and the background of the narrator's relationship to Usher; (2) his meeting with Roderick Usher that ends with his glimpse of Lady Madeline; (3) the survey of Usher's "art"—music, painting, the recitation of the poem "The Haunted Palace," Roderick's theory of "sentience," and the description of the library; (4) Madeline's "death" and entombment; (5) her return from the crypt counterpointed against the narrator's reading of "The Mad Trist" story which culminates in the death of the twins, the narrator's flight, and the collapse of the house into the tarn. Each of these phases not only furthers the plot line, but also intensifies the emotions provoked in the reader by means of the narrator's progressive hysteria and the growing distortion of the atmosphere.

The narrator is quickly characterized as a skeptic, who attempts to explain everything rationally, but who is, at the same time, quite susceptible to unexplained anxieties and undefined premonitions. His first glimpse of the Usher mansion provokes "a sense of unsufferable gloom." As he describes it the house resembles a giant face or skull with "eye-like windows" and hair-like "minute fungi" that almost seems to hold the decayed building together, as well as a "barely perceptible fissure" that threatens to rip it apart. He is even more horrified when he looks into the tarn (a small, stagnant lake in front of the house) and sees its inverted reflection in the black water. Thus, in the first paragraph of the tale we are introduced to three crucial elements: the subjective reactions of the narrator, which begins with this furtive, general uneasiness and will end in complete hysteria; the central image of a huge, dead, decaying object that is, paradoxically, very alive; and the first of many "reflections" or "doubles" that reinforce and intensify the atmosphere and implications of the story.

When the narrator meets his old friend Roderick Usher, the other side of the death-life paradox is suggested. Whereas the dead objects seem "alive," the "live" things seem dead. All the peripheral characters—the two servants, the doctor, the "living" Madeline—are shadows. Roderick, with his "cadaverous" complexion, "large, liquid and luminous eye," "thin and very pallid" lips, and "hair of more than web-like softness," seems more zombie than human. Moreover, his description "mirrors" that of the house's exterior: his eyes are like the windows; his hair resembles the fungi.

And yet Roderick has a definable personality. For all of the spectral hints, Poe never abandons the possibility that Roderick's character and fate can be explained naturally. Although Usher's behavior is violent and erratic, perhaps "manic-depressive" by modern clinical standards, tenuous rationalizations are provided for everything he does.

Nor does Roderick's role as an artist resolve the questions about his character. The extended catalog of his artistic activities may seem digressive in terms of Poe's strict "single effect" theory, but it is, in fact, the necessary preparation for the story's harrowing finale. Each of Roderick's artistic ventures conforms to both his realistic personality and the otherworldliness of the situation; they can either signal his descent into psychosis or his ineffectual attempts to understand and withstand the incursion of supernatural forces. His "dirges" suggest death; his abstract painting of a vault-like structure previews Madeline's interment. When he recites "The Haunted Palace" poem he is either metaphorically recounting his own fall into madness or he is, literally, talking about "haunting." Roderick's statements about the sentience of all vegetable things—that is, the conscious life in all inanimate matter—brings a notion that has previously been latent in the reader's mind to the surface. And, finally, Roderick's exotic library, made up almost entirely of books about supernatural journeys, suggests either a perversely narrow and bizarre taste or an attempt to acquire the knowledge needed to defend against daemonic intruders.

But, for all of this mounting intensity of suggestion and atmosphere, the actual "story" does not begin until almost two thirds of the narrative has been completed. When Roderick announces that Lady Madeline is "no more," the story quickens. It is at this point that the narrator notices the "striking similitude between the brother and sister" and so emphasizes the "twin theme," the most important "reflection" or "double" in the tale. As they entomb her, the narrator takes note of the "mockery of a faint blush upon the bosom and the face." Does this suggest a trace of life and implicate Roderick, consciously or unconsciously, in her murder? Or does it hint at an "undead" specter who, knowing that she will return from the grave, mocks the attempt to inter her?

Nowhere is the value of indirection in the maximizing of suspense more evident than in the last sequence of the story. Having established the "literary" context of the narrative, Poe then counterpoints the reading of a rather trite medieval romance against Madeline's actual return from the crypt. At the simplest level the "Mad Trist" tale is a suspense-building device that magnifies the reader's excitement as he awaits Madeline's certain reappearance. Thematically, it suggests a parallel—either "straight" or "ironic," depending on one's interpretation—between the knight Ethelred's quest and Madeline's return from the tomb. Reinforced by the violent storm, the narrator's frenzy, and Usher's violence, Madeline's return, her mutually fatal embrace of her brother, the narrator's flight, and the disintegration of the house itself, all fuse into a shattering final effect, which is all that Poe claimed he wanted, and a provocative insight into—what? The collapse of a sick mind? The inevitable self-destruction of the hyper-introverted artistic temperament? The final end of aristocratic inbreeding? Or incest? Or vampirism? Or the end of the world?

Although the "meaning" of "The Fall of the House of Usher" remains elusive, the experience of the story is powerful, disturbing, and lasting. And that, in the final analysis, is where the greatness lies and why it must be considered one of the finest short stories of its kind ever written.

Keith Neilson

THE FAMILY AT GILJE

Type of work: Novel
Author: Jonas Lie (1833-1908)
Type of plot: Domestic realism
Time of plot: Nineteenth century
Locale: Norway
First published: 1883

A realistic exploration of the loves and hates between parent and child, this work earned Lie a place among such great Scandinavian writers as Ibsen and Bjørnson. Especially with the character of the favorite daughter, Inger-Johanna, Lie carefully explores one of the most universal problems of family life: the conflict between what the grown child comes to want for himself and the course of life a loving parent conceives to be in the child's best interest.

The Family at Gilje was the first of a dozen novels on family life produced by Jonas Lie in the 1880's. After an initial successful period in the early 1870's, followed by several years of poor literary output, Lie came to the most prolific and best period of his literary career with this series of family novels. The success of *The Family at Gilje* and the other novels of the series was due in part to the author's keen ability to portray through an impressionistic approach, the lives of the sophisticated upper-middle class as they were in Norway in the late nineteenth century. Lie, like the impressionistic painters of the era, was able to make his viewpoint known through a realistic, yet veiled, picture of his characters. The reader could see through the veil, yet he had to become deeply involved in the novel in order to be able to do so.

Once this veil was removed, the message of the plot was simple; Lie wanted to show the wasted energies of his characters in their pursuit of social and economic advantages while they neglected the most important aspect of life, human love. By making this message part of an engrossing and entertaining plot, Lie allowed the reader to draw his own conclusions without being forced into them.

At the point in his life when the family novels were produced, Lie was able to keep his views within the confines of his plots without overburdening his readers with a didactic message. As he grew older, however, his plots became increasingly less important in comparison to his message, and many critics have found them too heavily laden with psychological meanings to be considered great literature. The more serious and less enjoyable plots also decreased his popularity with the reading public and as a result his fame decreased as he grew into old age. It is for this reason that *The Family at Gilje* is commonly and critically regarded as the last of his great works.

THE FAMILY REUNION

Type of work: Drama
Author: T. S. Eliot (1888-1965)
Type of plot: Symbolic allegory
Time of plot: Twentieth century
Locale: England
First published: 1939

The impulse to murder and the actual deed itself are subtly explored in the incongruous setting of a family reunion called to celebrate the birthday of the family matriarch, Lady Monchensey. Murder comes to symbolize a means of awakening oneself from the insensitive conservatism of society. In this case, conservatism is represented by an English gentle family, crippled and decaying because of its worship of convention in both thought and deed.

The Family Reunion, Eliot's second play, while not as highly regarded as his earlier *Murder in the Cathedral,* contains many lines of fine poetry and is important as a further statement of his long concern with the theme of man's conscious recognition of evil and the burden such knowledge places upon him.

In *The Family Reunion,* Eliot returns to an idea formulated in his earlier work, *Sweeney Agonistes* (1932). Harry Monchensey is haunted by the realization of an impulse within himself toward murder; this realization leads to a knowledge of evil in the world generally. Such knowledge, however, proves to be uncommunicable, especially to those to whom, as Harry expresses it, "nothing has ever happened." These are the average kinds of men and women who have never been made to perceive the reality of evil nor had to face the agonizing consciousness of private guilt. Harry calls the knowledge he has brought to Wishwood "Untranslatable"; and to most of the others in the play, it remain just that; the only exceptions are Agatha and, to a lesser extent, Mary and Downing. The chorus of other characters in the play represents common humanity, those not selected to suffer the awareness of evil and therefore incapable of grasping the meaning of Harry's message or the reasons for his actions.

By the end of the play, however, Harry himself has perceived even further that there can be no meaningful understanding of good without an accompanying recognition of the nature and reality of its opposite. Though he did not actually push his wife overboard, Harry is, in Christian terms, as guilty for the thought as for the deed. But he comes to understand that the Eumenides are not the ancient Greek Furies of retribution, but rather the means toward the expiation of sin. It is they who bring about in men the conscious recognition of sin and evil, as well as the awareness of their role in man's salvation. Harry learns that it is only in the acknowledgment of evil that one can begin to atone for his sins, and in so doing consciously choose between good and evil.

FAR AWAY AND LONG AGO

Type of work: Autobiography
Author: W. H. Hudson (1841-1922)
Type of plot: Reminiscence and nature notes
Time of plot: Mid-nineteenth century
Locale: Argentina
First published: 1918

William Henry Hudson wrote his autobiography while battling for his life during a six-week illness. Between bouts of fever and sleep, he recorded the impressions of his childhood from ages three to sixteen. The product is a portrait of a child free to roam upon the Argentine pampas who interested himself deeply in all types of people and in every variety of animal life. The book reveals the source of the man Hudson became: a poet, naturalist, and mystic.

In his autobiography *Far Away and Long Ago,* W. H. Hudson details, with the practiced eye of a naturalist, the pungent but lyrical memories of his childhood and adolescence up to the age of sixteen. Although Hudson wrote most of the book when he was in his middle seventies, he recalled with nearly photographic precision the impressions of places, scenes in nature—above all, the living creatures—that were the meaningful parts of his youthful days in Argentina. Previously he had published in *Gentleman's Magazine* (1886) material from his first chapter, and much of the second and third chapters appeared earlier in *English Review* (1912); the rest of the book he composed during a six-week period while he was confined to a hospital bed. Yet his memories of "long ago" are not, as one might expect, the ruminations of an infirm old man; rather, they are presented with childlike freshness and wonder, the delight that comes from discovering the "root of things."

In spite of Hudson's remarkable powers of capturing the sharpest details of his past life, *Far Away and Long Ago* is not entirely reliable as autobiography. Because the author was unduly sensitive about revealing his true age, the book is purposefully vague about dates, including birthdates; Hudson alters the chronology of some historical events (for example, material concerning the tyrant Rosas); and he distorts some time-sequences, so that the reader has only a general, imprecise notion of time itself. In places, Hudson's evasive method works to his artistic advantage. Because the passage of time is made to seem unimportant, the action of the book is filtered through the author's consciousness, as though in dream or reverie. Events in his life are treated without concern for exact chronology, and thus are made to appear more significant than they should be, or more trivial. For example, Hudson's first memories are not those fixed on his parents or siblings, but on his dog Pechicho; reflecting upon another beloved dog from his early childhood, Caesar, he writes: "Nothing in the past I can remember so well." Hudson has little to say about his father, except that he was reputed to be an amiable man, and he discusses his mother at some length only in the last chapter, commenting on the subject of her death. Also in this final chapter, "Loss and Gain," he mentions for the first significant time his older brother, whose influence upon his scientific education must have been crucial. Other curious—and psychologically meaningful—attitudes become apparent from Hudson's distortion of chronology and his reticence about describing his family life. He remembers with astonishing precision natural phenomena: birds, snakes, trees, flowers, small and large animals, storms and other convulsions of the weather. But his descriptions of people tend to be caricatures: Constair "Lovair," indelibly recalled for his strangeness; the ferocious beggars of Buenos Aires; Mr. Trigg, who "didn't own a box"; the dandy Don Anastacio Buenavida; or the patriarch Don Evaristo Peñalva, who married six wives yet was "a virtuous man." Or Hudson remembers scenes of human violence: a young officer murdered by his soldiers, his throat cut; Mr. Royd, who commits suicide by slashing his throat; the image is repeated in scenes describing the slaughter of cattle, also with their throats cut by the sadistic gauchos.

Although the author treats people with scientific coolness or reclusion, remembering mostly their cruelties or foibles, he remembers nature with unaffected warmth. To the boy, the city is frightening, but the open grassland is beautiful and protective. With poetic luminosity Hudson describes the pampas, "level as a billiard-table"; the Ombú trees, Lombardy poplars, mulberries, and the peach trees in vivid bloom; the small creatures of the plains—rats, columbine snakes, vipers, *vizcachas* (rodents); flowers, especially those in early spring; and, above all, his beloved birds—the scarlet fly catchers, plovers, purple cow-birds, many others. Hudson is at one with nature, even with the least appealing creatures, such as the black snakes. In the most significant chapter of the book, "A Boy's Animism," he declares his faith, with almost religious fervor, in nature as a spiritual force. Like Wordsworth, Hudson sees in nature not only beauty but also a presence of the divine. Through his art he recaptures his childlike sense of awe in worship of this "far away" but remembered presence.

FAR FROM THE MADDING CROWD

Type of work: Novel
Author: Thomas Hardy (1840-1928)
Type of plot: Psychological realism
Time of plot: 1869-1873
Locale: "Wessex," England
First published: 1874

This novel explores the tragedies caused by the confrontation of four strong characters, Bathsheba Everdene, and the three men who loved her: Gabriel Oak, Sergeant Troy, and William Boldwood. Characteristic of Hardy, inescapable "accidents" such as a destructive storm or a late appointment are potent forces that determine the direction of the plot. Such chance happenings, however, still do not determine personal destiny as much as the personalities of the characters.

As the title indicates, Hardy's first major novel has an isolated setting, rural, remote from the world, and mainly centered upon Upper Weatherbury Farm in "Wessex." But unlike that in *Under the Greenwood Tree,* this secluded environment at times gives way to the town: the busy corn exchange in Casterbridge, the King's Arms Hotel, the Casterbridge workhouse, the cities of Bath and Budmouth, and the lively Buck's Head Inn on the Casterbridge Road.

Still the setting has a timeless quality, accentuated or perhaps engendered by the round of seasonal activities and the continuity of agricultural life. Major scenes in the novel focus around the sheep shearing, saving of hay ricks in the storm, spring sheep washing, and the autumn sheep fair at Greenhill.

Nature here, however, is not merely background or a constant factor informing characters' actions and proclivities; it is more powerful, a force vast and indifferent to man's thoughts and actions. This is the Nature which in later novels will evolve into inexorable fate, before which man is helpless and in opposing which he comes to destruction. The main characters in this novel who survive are those who succeed in adjusting themselves to nature's laws, and often hostile dominance: Gabriel Oak and Bathsheba Everdene.

Far from the Madding Crowd exhibits confident power throughout in its fully developed characters, the imperceptible movements in the various conflicts involving Bathsheba and her three lovers, and in the way these conflicts evolve from their varied personalities. The combination of the four personalities furnishes the most explosive potential for melodramatic situation: Bathsheba's capriciousness and attractiveness to men; Oak's stolid, patient, unswerving loyalty and love for her; Boldwood's composite character with its "enormous antagonistic forces" and "wild capabilities"; Sergeant Troy's impulsiveness, his living only for the present moment, dashing but totally irresponsible; and the simple nature of Fanny, unaffected and victimized.

Interactions of these intimately associated characters, in an almost closed environment, engender passionate, at times almost unbelievable, conflicts.

Further complicating the clashes and intricate relationships among these four are the unforeseen, relentless accidents of nature: the initial loss of Oak's sheep, the heavy storm with water which ruins Troy's flowers on Fanny's grave and which precipitates his disappearance, the loss of Boldwood's hayricks in a second storm. The novel progresses in turns, driven headlong by Bathsheba's careless whim of sending Boldwood an anonymous valentine, again by Troy's determination to possess her in spite of all odds. Even Gabriel Oak and Fanny, the two who outwardly seem driven by the impulsive actions of others, unconsciously complicate the plot by their very quiet and uncomplaining natures. Fanny, betrayed by Sergeant Troy, goes down before forces she has no means to combat, although she has a macabre revenge in the scene where Bathsheba opens her coffin to find Troy's child dead with its mother.

Gabriel, of stronger stuff, endures—like the nature he is so close to and of which he seems an integral part. Although he feels Bathsheba rules his life, and the reader may be swept into this illusion, it is the earth and all its creatures to which he is bound. Only when Bathsheba comes full circle through her marriage to the dissolute, unstable Troy, her half-acceptance of Boldwood's position and estate, back to an understanding of the land and its enduring qualities as embodied in Oak, can their marriage be possible. What Gabriel held to in Bathsheba and what she herself did not recognize was the same elemental belonging to the land and its eternal strength.

The very language of the novel is bound to the earth; the best example of this is the rural chorus, which is to figure in Hardy's later novels and which provides much of the humor. The habitués of Warren's Malthouse on the Casterbridge Road are intimately involved in the action and contribute to domestic scenes and rural atmosphere. They not only serve to comment on the various episodes, but also reinforce the setting, for they, too, belong to the earth. In fact, they form part of the novel's foundation; it is of importance that Gabriel Oak is at home with them and shares their social outlook. When the Malthouse crowd appears at the end of the book to serenade the newly married Gabriel and Bathsheba with their "venerable worm-eaten instruments," Gabriel invites them: "Com in, souls, and have something to eat and drink wi' me and my wife."

In this novel one finds the emerging role of nature, the typical romantic, dramatic situations which will even intensify in later novels, and devices such as the village chorus and rural activities to mark the continuity and coherence of man's existence. Also apparent are the chance encounters, series of coincidences, unforeseen accidents, overheard conversations, secretly observed actions—all of which make up the fabric of a typical Hardy narrative. His plots, because of these devices, share an improbability and sense of the miraculous found in folklore. The coffin scene where Bathsheba finds Fanny's and Troy's child is the stuff of which ballads are made. Too, the sword exercise, in its bold sexual symbolism, foreshadows such scenes as the fight between Henchard and Farfrae in *The Mayor of Casterbridge* and the entwined couples at the hay-trusser's dance in *Tess of the D'Urbervilles.*

If not so carefully structured as his later novels, this work shows Hardy's ability to penetrate the minds of his characters, especially that of a complicated woman. He boldly draws his theatrical scenes, exploits his evocative rural settings, and for the first time dares give his work amplitude and passion.

Not yet, however, does one find here the intense sense of gloom over a vanishing way of life—a depression that marked much of Hardy's later writing. Nor does the story embody man's defeat and tragedy that increasingly became his preoccupation.

Muriel B. Ingham

A FAREWELL TO ARMS

Type of work: Novel
Author: Ernest Hemingway (1899-1961)
Type of plot: Impressionistic realism
Time of plot: World War I
Locale: Northern Italy and Switzerland
First published: 1929

This story of a tragic love affair is set on the Italian front during World War I. Hemingway tells his tale with an abundance of realistic detail. Rather than a celebration of the "Triumph of victory and the agony of defeat," the author's vision is uncompromisingly disillusioned. Not only is war useless, but efforts to maintain any meaningful relationship with individuals in the modern world are equally doomed.

Ernest Hemingway once referred to *A Farewell to Arms* as his *Romeo and Juliet*. Without insisting on a qualitative comparison, several parallels are obvious. Both works are about "star-crossed" lovers; both show erotic flirtations that rapidly develop into serious, intense, mature love affairs; and both describe the romances against a backdrop of social and political turmoil. Whether or not *A Farewell to Arms* finally qualifies as "tragic" is a matter of personal opinion, but it certainly represents, for Hemingway, an attempt to broaden his concerns from the aimless tragicomic problems of the expatriates in *The Sun Also Rises* (1926) to the fundamental question of life's meaning in the face of human mortality.

Frederic Henry begins the affair as a routine wartime seduction, "a game, like bridge, in which you said things instead of playing cards." He feels mildly guilty, especially after learning about Catherine's vulnerability because of the loss of her lover in combat, but he still foresees no complications from the temporary arrangement. It is not until he is wounded and sent to her hospital in Milan that their affair deepens into love—and from that point on they struggle to free themselves in order to realize it. But they are constantly thwarted, first by the impersonal bureaucracy of the military effort, then by the physical separation imposed by the war itself, and, finally, by the biological "accident" that kills Catherine at the point where their "separate peace" at last seems possible.

As Henry's love for Catherine grows, his disillusionment with the war also increases. From the beginning of the book Henry views the military efforts with ironical detachment, but there is no suggestion that, prior to his meeting with her, he has had any deep reservations about his involvement. Hemingway's attitude toward war was always an ambiguous one. He questioned the rationales for fighting them and the slogans offered in their defense. Like Henry, he felt that "abstract words such as glory, honor, courage, or hallow were obscene." But for the individual, war could be the necessary test. Facing imminent death in combat, one either demonstrated "grace under pressure" and did the "one right thing" or one did not; one either emerged from the experience as a whole person with self-knowledge and control or one came out of it lost and broken.

But there is little heroism in this war as Henry describes it. The hero's disengagement from the fighting is made most vivid in the extended "retreat from Caporetto," generally considered one of the great sequences in modern fiction. The retreat begins in an orderly, disciplined, military manner. But as it progresses, authority breaks down, emotions of self-preservation supersede loyalties and the neat military procession gradually turns into a panicking mob. Henry is caught up in the momentum and carried along with the group in spite of his attempts to keep personal control and fidelity to the small band of survivors he travels with. Upon reaching the Tagliamento River, Henry is seized, along with all other identifiable officers, and held for execution. After he escapes by leaping into the river—an act of ritual purification as well as physical survival—he feels that his "trial" has freed him from any and all further loyalty to the Allied cause.

Henry then rejoins Catherine, and they complete the escape together. In Switzerland, they seem lucky and free at last. Up in the mountains they hike, ski, make love, prepare for the baby, and plan for their postwar life together. Yet even in their most idyllic times there are ominous hints; they worry about the baby; Catherine jokes about her narrow hips; she becomes frightened by a dream of herself "dead in the rain."

Throughout the novel Hemingway associates the "plains" and "rain" with death, disease, and sorrow; the "mountains" and the "snow" with life, health, and happiness. Catherine and Frederic are safe and happy in the mountains, but it is impossible to remain their indefinitely. Eventually everyone must return to the plains. When Catherine and Henry descend to the city it is, in fact, raining, and she does, in fact, die.

Like that of Romeo and Juliet, the love between Catherine and Henry is not destroyed by any moral defect in their own characters. Henry muses that Catherine's fate is the "price" paid for the "good nights" in Milan, but such a price is absurdly excessive. Nor, strictly speaking, is the war responsible for their fate, any more than the Montague-Capulet feud directly provokes the deaths of Shakespeare's lovers. Yet the war and the feud provide the backdrop of violence and the accumulation of pressures that coerce the lovers into actions that contribute to their doom. But, in the final analysis, both couples are defeated by bad luck—the illness that prevents the friar from delivering Juliet's note to Romeo, the accident of Catherine's anatomy that prevents normal childbearing. Thus, both couples are "star-crossed." But if a "purpose" can be vaguely ascertained in Shakespeare's version—the feud is ended by the tragedy—there is no metaphysical justification for Catherine's death; it is, in her own words, "a dirty trick"—and nothing more.

Hemingway does not insist that the old religious meanings are completely invalid, only that they do not work for his people. Henry would like to visit with the priest in his mountain village, but he cannot bring himself to do it. His friend Rinaldi, a combat surgeon, proclaims atheism, hedonism, and work as the only available meanings. Count Greffi, an old billiard player Henry meets in Switzerland, offers good taste, cynicism, and the fact of a long, pleasant life. Catherine and Henry have each other: "You are my religion," she tells him.

But all of these things fail in the end. Religion is only for others, patriotism is a sham, hedonism becomes boring, culture is a temporary distraction, work finally fails (the operation on Catherine was "successful"), even love cannot last (Catherine dies; they both know, although they won't admit it, that the memory of it will fade).

All that remains is a stoic acceptance of the above facts with dignity and without bitterness. Life, like war, is absurd. Henry survives because he is lucky; Catherine dies because she is unlucky. But there is no guarantee that the luck ever balances out and, since everyone ultimately dies, it probably does not matter. What does matter is the courage, dignity, and style with which one accepts these facts as a basis for life and, more importantly, in the face of death.

Keith Neilson

THE FATHER

Type of work: Drama
Author: August Strindberg (1849-1912)
Type of plot: Psychological realism
Time of plot: Mid-nineteenth century
Locale: Sweden
First presented: 1887

The antagonism between the sexes concerned Strindberg in all his works. In The Father, *the Captain is driven to insanity by his wife and rejected by his own daughter. In the beginning of their relationship, his love for his wife was as a son for his mother. When he became her lover, she rebelled and planted in his mind the fear that he was not the father of their daughter, Bertha. Falling into insanity and finally suffering a stroke, the Captain is rejected by wife, daughter, and mother.*

The plays of August Strindberg have exerted a powerful and pervasive influence on modern drama in both Europe and America. His insights into naturalism, in such early plays as *The Father* and *Miss Julie,* were central in the shaping of that dramatic movement, while his later experiments with expressionism, in works such as *The Ghost Sonata, A Dream Play* and the *To Damascus* trilogy, have profoundly effected nonrealistic approaches to the modern stage. It is virtually impossible to separate Strindberg's life from his works and this is particularly true in the case of *The Father.* Even Strindberg recognized the close alliance between the two when, on November 12, 1887, he wrote to Axel Lundegärd: "It is to me as if I were walking in my sleep—as if creation and life were mingled. I do not know whether *The Father* is a creative work, or whether that was my real life."

The relationship between Strindberg's reality and his writing becomes apparent in an examination of *A Madman's Defense,* an autobiographical novel that contains many references essential to an understanding of *The Father.* Written between 1887 and 1888, it chronicles fourteen years of Strindberg's life, including his fateful meeting and marriage to Siri Von Essen. Strindberg intended the work as an exposé of Siri's attempts to confine him for mental treatment, but, in reality, it presents a clear picture of developing paranoia and acute mental instability.

Strindberg's first-person narrator names his wife Maria and portrays her as suspicious of her husband's sanity from the beginning of their marriage. (Indeed, in 1886 Siri consulted a Swiss doctor about Strindberg's instability, confirming his suspicion that she suspected mental imbalance in him all along and desired to obtain his insurance money or marry again.) Based on her conviction, Maria attempts to provoke behavior from the narrator that can be used as evidence to justify confinement. When she sides with the critics of her husband's book, he calls her a traitor who is responsible for starting rumors about his sanity. When he escapes to Paris to seek comradeship with friends, she follows him and insists on a retreat in Switzerland. Once there, she convinces the doctor, guests, proprietor, and servants that their new guest is, indeed, insane.

Beginning to doubt his own sanity and feeling a persecution mania, the narrator turns his suspicions and hostility on his wife. He studies her behavior and comes to believe that she is an adultress trying to cover her wrongdoings and gain his insurance money and writings by proving him mentally incompetent. He then looks for evidence to prove his theory by rifling through her letters and making her face his strenuous cross-examinations. Neither her denials nor the confessions he believes he extracts provide him with convincing answers, but they intensify his agitation and instability. The reader of *A Madman's Defense* cannot help but see the parallels between this autobiographical account and the basic plot structure of *The Father,* as well as the similarity between the narrator in the novel and the Captain in the play. Thus, in actuality, *The Father* becomes almost an adaptation of *A Madman's Defense.*

Along with the fictionalization of this building paranoia in *A Madman's Defense,* Strindberg's account closely parallels the events which surrounded the publication and subsequent blasphemy trial of the first volume of *Married* (1884). This collection of short stories deals with the husband-wife relationship with some of the material being related to Strindberg's early married life and *The Father.* The most important contribution of the collection to *The Father* is in the portrayal of women that it develops. Strindberg is scornful toward the "emancipated" woman in marriage, feeling that such a woman wants not "equality" with her mate, but domination over him. The ideal role for the woman, Strindberg believes, is that of wife and mother—anything else can only be destructive.

This view of woman clearly had its origins in Strindberg's personal experience; from his own background, he had cause to believe in the evil nature of the bad mother. Having been unwanted at birth and rejected as a child, Strindberg grew up as a "stranger" in his own home. Thus, what Strindberg sought in a suitable mate (he went through three stormy marriages) was not only a wife, but also a substitute mother. Since this was an ideal, it was naturally shattered over and over again, leading to an absolute confusion of roles —his first marriage greatly acerbating this confusion. When Strindberg first met Siri, the ambiguity of female roles became visible immediately, for he described her as "a deliciously girlish mother." Even during their trial separation, Strindberg stated that he felt "like an embryo prematurely detached from the umbilical cord." This attitude is echoed by the characters in *The Father,* when Laura tells the Captain (II, v): "I loved you as if you were my child. But you know, you must have felt it, when your sexual desires were aroused, and you came forward as my lover, I was reluctant, and the joy I felt in your embrace was followed by such revulsion that my very blood knew shame. The son become the lover-oh!"

Strindberg's confusion and disillusion led him naturally into bitter anti-feminism. Actually, his philosophy paralleled that of many contemporaries, particularly those in France—a country he frequented during his "exile" periods. The literary atmosphere there in the 1870's was extremely misogynistic. The theater had become particularly receptive to the movement, which is especially evidenced in the character of the *femme fatale,* as popularized by such actresses as Sarah Bernhardt. It was felt at the time that people of talent and intellect were being exploited—particularly men, since they belonged to the more imaginative and talented sex. Thus, the female was seen as a parasitic being who lived off of the productivity of the male. As Laura states to the Captain (II, v): "The mother was your friend, look you, but the woman was your enemy,—for sexual love is strife; and don't imagine that I gave myself; I gave nothing, I only took—what I meant to have. . . ."

The source for the question of paternity that is so central to *The Father* is provided by yet another biographical reference—Strindberg's personal correspondence. When Strindberg married Siri she was pregnant and had, not long before their marriage, shared the company of her first husband, Baron Wrangel. After Strindberg became actively paranoid, his remembrance of that situation provoked him to harbor active doubts about the paternity of his children. That the suspicion was in his mind was confirmed by his reaction to Henrik Ibsen's play *The Wild Duck.* After its appearance, Strindberg considered suing Ibsen for slander on the grounds that Ibsen had used him as a model for Hjalmar Ekdal, the central character of the play, who doubts the paternity of his child. Strindberg and Siri were also at odds about the future occupations of their two daughters. Siri wished them to become actresses, while Strindberg wanted them to be trained as midwives. Both of these two personal conflicts became central issues in *The Father*: Laura raises doubts in the Captain's mind regarding the paternity of his daughter in order to drive him insane, and the motivating force for Laura's actions is an argument with her husband over the future education of their daughter, Bertha.

However, although Strindberg's own experiences provided the major inspiration for *The Father,* he was also deeply influenced by the literary and cultural milieu of his time. The novels of the Goncourt brothers, with their emphasis on the physiological and psychological approach in human character analysis, and particularly *Chérie* (1884) which was Edmond Goncourt's last novel, may have directly affected the play. A naturalistic play, *Thérèse Raquin* by Émile Zola, with the same analytical emphasis may also have provided Strindberg with some insight. In addition, it is a fact that, before he began writing *The Father,* he studied popular contemporary theories in psychiatric and hypnotic literature with emphasis on the French. After finishing *The Father,* he articulated the results of these researches in an essay series entitled *Vivisections.* From their titles alone, two of the essays reveal their influence on *The Father*: "The Battle of the Brains" and "Psychic Murder."

These influences, coupled with "the battle of the brains" and the "psychic murder," connect *The Father* with the school of naturalism. The battle of the brains between Laura and the Captain is actually a Darwinian struggle for power, with survival going to the "fittest"—a central concept in the naturalistic school of thought. The Captain states that the battle with his wife is "to eat or to be eaten." At one point, the discussion becomes overtly Darwinistic":

> *Captain*: I feel in this battle one of us must succumb.
> *Laura*: Who?
> *Captain*: The weaker, of course.
> *Laura*: And the stronger is right?
> *Captain*: He is always right because he has the power.
> *Laura*: Then I am right.

The "amorality" of action—with the end justifying the means—the detached scientific tone, the emphasis on the psychological, and the objectivity of the playwright strengthen the play's naturalistic tendencies.

It was Émile Zola, however, the father of naturalism in the novel, who saw the yet undeveloped aspect of Strindberg's attempt to bring naturalism into the drama. Despite his extremely adequate psychological emphasis and scientific attitude, Strindberg, as Zola pointed out, had failed to give the play a "social setting"—that is, he had failed to emphasize the importance of heredity and environment in his characterization. Although he had attributed the Captain's initial weakness to his feelings of being unwanted when born and to the upbringing given him by a "bad" mother, he had gone no further in demonstrating the power of environmental influences on his characters. In spite of this weakness, Zola apparently saw Strindberg as his potential dramatic counterpart and encouraged him in his pursuits. After his crucial beginning in *The Father,* Strindberg presented perhaps the first important naturalistic drama with his next play, *Miss Julie*. The vital naturalistic factors of "heredity" and "milieu" are even more explicitly emphasized in this powerful play that dramatizes the destruction of a willful aristocratic female by her father's brazen valet.

Thus, at the time he wrote *The Father* Strindberg was a man of mental and emotional complexity who stood on the brink of developing one of the most important movements in modern dramatic literature—naturalism. In the third section of his autobiography, covering the period around 1886, Strindberg expresses an awareness of his position in the development of the modern drama. He saw himself as spanning the gap between romanticism and naturalism and being "like the blindworm, which retains rudimentary lizard feet inside its skin." But this dependence on his background and his "rudimentary lizard feet" was no detriment to his dramatic career.

Rather than holding him back, these autobiographical reliances, controlled and polished, became the driving force in his naturalistic writings and, in a different way, were to become the substance of his later experiments with expressionism.

His influence was felt not only on the continent but also in the United States, for though never awarded the coveted Nobel prize, he was noted by Eugene O'Neill in his acceptance speech for the Nobel prize as one of O'Neill's foremost literary inspirations. Since that time, Strindberg's reputation has grown until he is generally regarded today to be, along with Henrik Ibsen and Anton Chekhov, one of the three giants most responsible for the shape, direction, and power of the modern theater.

Phyllis E. Allran

FATHER GORIOT

Type of work: Novel
Author: Honoré de Balzac (1799-1850)
Type of plot: Naturalism
Time of plot: c. 1819
Locale: Paris
First published: 1835

A gallery of fascinating characters, each with his own intriguing history, are assembled in Mme. Vauquer's boarding-house. Among them is Father Goriot. Gradually, he squanders away his ample retirement funds to pay the bills of his two ungrateful and profligate daughters. Finally, he is buried in a pauper's grave, and his children do not even attend the funeral. Other stories and characters interweave within this larger frame. Most effective is the history of Eugène de Rastignac, a poor law student who is subtly transformed from a naïve provincial into a Parisian gentleman.

Honoré de Balzac's writing career spanned thirty years, from the decisive point in 1819 when he elected to abandon the study of law, until his untimely death in 1850. His work up until 1829 consisted of novels, stories, and sketches on a variety of philosophical and social themes. They are, on the whole, undistinguished; Balzac later averred that the decade from 1819 until he began work on *The Chouans* in 1829 constituted his apprenticeship in the art of fiction. Certainly the works of the last twenty years of his life show the benefits of that long period of development, both in stylistic and tonal precision and in general weight and narrative direction.

Many critics contend that the generative idea for *The Human Comedy* came to Balzac as he was writing *Father Goriot,* because in the manuscript the name of the young student is Massiac, until, in the scene of the afternoon call at Madame de Beauséant's house, "Massiac" is abruptly scratched out and "Rastignac" inserted. The character Eugène de Rastignac had appeared in a minor role in *The Wild Ass's Skin* (1831), and the assumption is that the decision to reintroduce him at an earlier stage of his life in *Father Goriot* betokens a flash of creative light that revealed to the author a cycle of interconnected novels depicting every aspect of society, and having numerous characters in common—*The Human Comedy*. That the idea came to him quite so suddenly is doubtful, since, as Henry Reed has pointed out, he had already decided to ring in Mmes. de Langeais and de Beauséant and the moneylender Gobseck, all of whom appear in previous works. But it is certain that *Father Goriot* is the first work in which the device of repetition occurs, and in which the uncertain fates of two main characters, Eugène and Vautrin, point so obviously to other stories.

The novel began as a short story about parental obsession and filial ingratitude. Its title is most often translated into English as *Father Goriot,* losing the significance of the definite article. Its inclusion is not grammatically necessary in French, hence pointed; the sense is more truly rendered as *Goriot the Father*. The point is that the condition of fatherhood absorbs the whole life and personality of old Goriot. At one time both a husband and a businessman, he has lost or given up these roles; he lives only in the paternal relation, existing at other times, in the boarders' neat phrase, as "an anthropomorphous mollusc." He seems, at first, horribly victimized, so betrayed and ill-repaid by his harpy daughters that his situation excites the silent sympathy of even such hard gems of the *haute monde* as the Duchesse de Langeais and Madame de Beauséant. His gratitude to his offspring for their least notice, slightingly and ungraciously bestowed as it may be, and his joyful self-sacrifice and boundless self-delusion fill the reader with pity. Was there ever, Balzac seems to ask, a parent so ill-used?

But he is the author of his own distress. Balzac leaves us in no doubt that Goriot reared the two girls in such a way as to ensure that they would be stupid, vain, idle, and grasping women. "The upbringing he gave his daughters was of course preposterous." As he lies dying his outburst of impotent rage reminds us of Lear; their situations are similar in that each in the folly of his heart wreaks his own ruin. Lear's abasement leads to self-recognition and moral rebirth, but Goriot clings to his delusion to the end, clings to it with a mad tenacity, demanding of unfeeling reality that it conform to his dream of the rewards due faithful parenthood. Yet in fact he is properly rewarded, for he has been a bad father, the worst of fathers. Parenthood being both privilege and trust, Goriot has enjoyed the first and betrayed the last, as he himself recognizes in a brief interval of lucidity: "The finest nature, the best soul on earth would have succumbed to the corruption of such weakness on a father's part." Indulging himself in the warmth of their goodwill, he has failed in his duty to their moral sense; they are, as adults, mirror-images of his own monumental selfishness, made, as it were, of the very stuff of it: "It was I who made them, they belong to me."

To this "obscure but dreadful Parisian tragedy" is added the separate tales of Rastignac and Vautrin, each quite self-contained and yet bound to the other two by the most subtle bonds. One of these links is the recurrent reference to parenthood, good and bad. At every turn some facet of the parent-child relation is held up for our notice: the wretchedness of the cast-off child Victorine Taillefer, for example, so like Goriot's wretchedness; Madame de Langeais' disquisition on sons-in-law, later echoed by Goriot; the parental tone taken with Eugène both by Madame de Beauséant ("Why you poor simple child!" and in a different way, by Vautrin ("You're a good little lad . . .") in giving him wicked worldly advice in contrast to the good but dull counsel of his own mother; the filial relationship which develops between Eugène and Goriot; even Vautrin's enormously ironic nicknames for his landlady ("Mamma Vauquer") and the police ("Father Cop").

Another element linking the *haut monde,* the Maison Vauquer, and the underworld is the fact that they are all partners in crime. Goriot, for example, made his original fortune in criminal collusion with members of the de Langeais family. Vautrin neatly arranges the death of Mademoiselle Taillefer's brother for the benefit of the half-willing Rastignac. The Baron de Nucingen invests Delphine's dowry in an illegal building scheme. Vautrin, Goriot, and Anastasie all resort to "Papa Gobseck" the money lender. We hear a precept uttered by Madame de Beauséant (" . . . in Paris, success is everything, it's the key to power") enunciated a few pages later by Vautrin ("Succeed! . . . succeed at all costs."). We are clearly meant to see that whatever differences exist among the various levels of society, they are differences not of kind but of degree. Corruption is universal.

Jan Kennedy Foster

FATHERS AND SONS

Type of work: Novel
Author: Ivan Turgenev (1818-1883)
Type of plot: Social criticism
Time of plot: 1859
Locale: Russia
First published: 1862

Fathers and Sons *differs from most nineteenth century Russian novels in that the characters are simply drawn and the plot is straightforward. Still, the work operates on two levels. On the one hand, Turgenev dramatizes the universal conflicts which arise between any two generations. On the other, he vividly portrays the unsettled state of the Russian peasantry before the Revolution. His discussions of political anarchy make the work an important document in Russian political history.*

In *Fathers and Sons* Turgenev wished to examine the forces for change operating, for the most part in isolation and frustration, in mid-nineteenth century Russia. The storm of protest and outrage produced from the moment the novel appeared indicates that he had indeed touched a sensitive nerve in Russian society. In fact, Turgenev never really got over the abuse heaped upon him; his periods of exile in Germany, France, and Italy were all the more frequent and of longer duration after the publication of the novel. One wonders at the excitement occasioned by *Fathers and Sons,* for a cooler reading undertaken one hundred years later indicates that Turgenev clearly attempted and achieved a balanced portrait of conservative and revolutionary Russia—a triumphant achievement in political fiction, where the passions of the moment so often damage the artistic effort.

The subtlety and rightness of Turgenev's technique is most clearly seen in the central character Bazaroff. A pragmatist, scientist, and revolutionary idealogue, Bazaroff is a prefiguration of two mythical-historical figures of our own time: the astronaut and the Marxist revolutionary. Turgenev was writing prophecy as well as social realism. Bazaroff is put into relationship with every important character and it is from these relationships that we get to know him and to understand more about him than he understands. A master of literary impressionism, Turgenev liked to do an "atmospheric" treatment of his characters, vividly rendering visual, auditory and other sense impressions in a nicely selected setting. This technique admits all sorts of lively and contradictory details and prevents the novel—and Bazaroff—from flattening out into mere ideology and political polemic. Most of all, for all his roughness and bearishness, Turgenev really liked Bazaroff and sympathized with him ("with the exception of [his] views on art, I share almost all his convictions," he wrote).

Bazaroff's chief conflict is with Pavel Kirsanoff, a middle-aged bachelor with refined continental tastes and a highly developed sense of honor. Pavel stands for everything Bazaroff despises: an old-world emphasis upon culture, manners, and refinement, and an aristocratic and elitist view of life. He represents the traditions which Bazaroff vainly struggles to destroy in his efforts to bring a democratic, scientific, and utilitarian plan of action into widespread use. For Bazaroff "a good chemist is more useful than a score of poets," because the chemist attacks the central problem of poverty, disease, and ignorance. The old humanism represented by Pavel, is, for him, a manifestation of ignorance which perpetrates and countenances needless suffering, particularly for the lower classes. His rude and sneering treatment of Pavel is undercut by his participation in the duel, which is an absurd custom of the upper classes he despises. Bazaroff is the loser in the duel and he knows it. His passion, which he tries to cover up with a cold, clinical attitude, leads him into it.

His relationship with Madame Odintzoff shows that Bazaroff is at heart a romantic, though he would hardly admit it. This cool and cultured widow provokes the most ardent response from him—despite his contention that women are mere instruments of amusement and pleasure. But with Madame Odintzoff he has unfortunately chosen an inadequate object for his passion. She is lovely but cold and detached, and unable to respond to him.

Bazaroff's romanticism, however, is chiefly frustrated in social and political matters. He deeply believes that conditions can be changed and that he and others can work together to that end. When we look at these "others" we see how painful and tragic his situation is. Arkady, his schoolmate and friend, is a kindly fellow who imitates Bazaroff's revolutionary attitudes. He is in awe of his friend's rough manner but he does not understand that Bazaroff really intends to follow his ideas to the end. Rather, Arkady is not even dimly aware at first that he is incapable of supporting Bazaroff all the way. Like most men, Arkady is conventional and conforming out of natural adaptability. His marriage to Katya is a model of bourgeois comfort and serves to underline Bazaroff's loneliness and ineffectuality. Like his father before him, Arkady chooses domestic satisfactions and a life of small compromises over the absurd "heroism" of his schoolfellow. The Kirsanoff homestead remains on the whole ill-managed and unimproved. No revolution in land management has occurred even though the peasants are about to be freed. Life goes on in a muddle despite the passionate efforts of one or two enlightened persons to reform it.

Bazaroff's curious and potentially violent behavior to Arkady when they are lying in a haystack, suggests that he knows that Arkady cannot follow him. Moreover, this scene reveals that Bazaroff is full of violent distaste for those who pretend to be reformers. He cannot spare them ridicule and his frustrated energies burst forth in threatening gestures. He is a leader without followers, a general without an army. Nonetheless, he loves his parents, two kindly old representatives of the traditional way of life, for they do not pretend to be anything they are not.

Bazaroff's death is a form of suicide. His willingness to take no immediate steps to prevent the spread of infection after he has carelessly cut himself suggests that he has seen the absurdity of his position and, to some extent at least, given in to it. In his delirium he states that Russia needs a cobbler, a tailor, a butcher more than she needs him. Nevertheless, for Turgenev, Bazaroff was "the real hero of our time."

Benjamin Nyce

FAUST

Type of work: Dramatic poem
Author: Johann Wolfgang von Goethe (1749-1832)
Type of plot: Philosophical allegory
Time of plot: Timeless
Locale: The world
First published: 1790-1831

A seminal work in the Romantic Movement, Faust *dissects the philosophical problem of human damnation brought about by the desire for knowledge and personal happiness. A basically good man and a man of genius, Faust sells his soul to the Devil in a contract stipulating that only when he finds an experience so great that he wishes it to endure forever can the Devil take his soul. He finally reaches his goal, but the experience is one in which he helps his fellow man. Thus Mephistopheles loses depite his efforts.*

Faust, Goethe's masterwork, virtually summarizes his entire career, stretching from the passionate storm and stress of his youth through his classical phase in his middle years and ending with his mature philosophical style. Its composition occupied him from the time of his first works in the 1770's until his death in 1832, and each of its various sections reveals new interests and preoccupations, as well as different stylistic approaches. Yet the work as a whole possesses a unity that testifies to the continuing centrality of the Faust subject in Goethe's mind.

The first scenes composed, those of Faust in his study and the Gretchen scenes, embody the spirit of the twenty-three-year-old Goethe, full of university parodies on the one hand, derived from Goethe's student days, and titanic projects on the other, a desire to fathom the depths of knowledge, to pass beyond all limitations, typical of the brilliant young writers of this period. In fact, *Faust* was originally one of a planned series of dramas about heroic figures who transgress society's rules—Julius Caesar, Prometheus, and Götz von Berlichingen among them.

Goethe stresses the tragedy of the scholar whose emotional life is not fulfilled and who quests after limitless knowledge, only to find himself frustrated by mortal limitations. The scenes with Gretchen provide for an emotional release, but leave Faust with a sense of guilt for the destruction of purity. The theme of the unwed mother was a popular one among young poets of this period, and represented a revolt against traditional bourgeois values, giving occasion for much social criticism. In the Gretchen scenes, Goethe, who as a student himself had romances with simple small town girls, evokes great sympathy for Gretchen, who acts always out of sincere emotion and desires only the good. His theme of the corruption of all human questing because of the inherent imperfections of man's knowledge and will receives here its first expression, though with no philosophical elaboration. Neither Faust nor

Gretchen wills evil, yet evil comes through Mephistopheles who in his every utterance is the cynic, opposed to Faust's idealistic hopes and exposing the coarse reality that in his view is the sole aspect of man's life on earth. When *Faust* was first published as a fragment in 1790, these elements, dating back to the 1770's, were all there was.

Between 1797 and 1806, under Schiller's encouragement, Goethe returned to the work, and created the Prologue in Heaven and the pact with Mephistopheles, both of which are crucial to the philosophical aspect of the work. Mephistopheles is no longer the absolute opponent of God, but is included in the divine framework; he is a necessary force in creation, a gadfly. The *Faust* action now becomes a wager between God and Mephistopheles, which God necessarily must win. Thus the old blood contract between Faust and Mephistopheles is converted into a wager: Mephistopheles must make Faust deny his very nature by giving up his quest for ever higher satisfactions, by giving him a moment of absolute fulfillment. Damnation, for Goethe, is the cessation of man's striving toward the absolute, and this striving is good, no matter what mistakes man makes in his limited understanding. This is made clear in the Prologue: God recognizes that man will err as long as he strives, but He states that only by seeking after the absolute, however confusedly, can man fulfill his nature. Mephistopheles sees only the confusion, the futility of the results, and the coarseness of man's life. He is blind to the visionary, poetic quality of Faust, the quality which animates his quest. This relationship established in Part I will continue until the end of the play. In each episode, Faust begins with an idealistic vision of what he seeks, but he never attains it. Seen externally, Mephistopheles is always right—it is internally that Faust's quest has meaning.

In the original Faust story, Faust meets Helen of Troy, and this episode occupied Goethe in the period of his fascination with the classical world. The third act of Part II is the union of Faust, the northern, modern, Romantic quester, with Helen, representative of classical harmony and ideal beauty. In this act, Goethe imitates first the style of Greek tragedy, then brings Faust and Helen together in an idyllic realm of fantasy filled with music. This music —Goethe actually wanted an operatic interlude—underlines the purely aesthetic nature of this experience. Helen cannot be the end of Faust's seeking; their relationship can exist only in the mythical Arcadia, where reality, symbolized perhaps by Helen's husband, Menelaus, cannot intrude. The act was subtitled "Classic-Romantic Phantasmagoria" and Goethe followed it immediately with a scene in which Faust sees visions of both Helen and Gretchen, and is drawn toward the latter in spite of Helen's ideal perfection. Gretchen, however tragic, is real.

The final sections of *Faust* were composed between 1825 and 1831. In them, Faust's appearances at court are developed and the final scenes of Faust's redemption return to the framework established in the Prologue.

Faust's last days are still unsatisfied and his quest is as violent as ever—his merchant ships turn to piracy and a gentle old couple are killed to make room for his palace. But his final vision is that of all humanity, striving onward to turn chaos to order, seeking a dimly imagined goal which is represented in the final scene by an endless stairway. Here, on the path toward the Divine, Faust is to continue to strive, and his life is redeemed by divine love, represented by Gretchen, who in spite of her crimes is also here, a penitent, praying for Faust. On earth all is transitory and insufficient, only from the point of view of the Divine does all the confused striving attain meaning, meaning which was, in fact, implicit in the stanzas of the three archangels sung at the opening of the play, 12,000 lines earlier.

Steven C. Schaber

FELIX HOLT, RADICAL

Type of work: Novel
Author: George Eliot (Mary Ann Evans, 1819-1880)
Type of plot: Political realism
Time of plot: 1832-1833
Locale: Rural England
First published: 1866

Centered around a political election in rural England at the time of the 1832 Reform Bill, this novel gives a vivid picture of all classes of English society. Though the intricate plot pits Tories against radicals, the novel is still a love story. Felix and Esther, after many trials, unite in a relationship which transcends the turbulent political experiences that first brought them together.

Mid-nineteenth century readers demanded intricate plots from their authors; today, these plots often seem forced and contrived. In *Felix Holt, Radical,* the complicated storyline, with the sudden twists and surprises, means less to modern readers than the realistic treatment of characterization and the analysis of human motive at which George Eliot excelled. The background of early Victorian society is skillfully painted, and the election riot, drawn from a recollection of one that Eliot saw as a child at Nuneaton, is a powerful piece of writing. But such figures as Mrs. Transome and Felix Holt, and Esther Lyon and her father give the book its greatness. The tragic character of Mrs. Transome is one of Eliot's triumphs; from the opening scene in which she waits for Harold's return to the manor, through her disappointments and the subsequent revelations, her personality is subtly revealed, with many delicate and moving touches. Mrs. Transome well knows that "half the sorrows of women would be averted if they could repress the speech they know to be useless—the speech they have resolved not to utter." Faced with her son's blind egotism, she sees what her life has amounted to, and must silently accept the bitter fact.

Felix Holt is quite a different character, a man of ideals misunderstood by those around him. Rufus Lyon is portrayed with an especially authentic quality; George Eliot's observations of the life of the poor clergyman are precise and vivid—such an existence easily could have spoiled a lesser man than Rufus Lyon.

The role of the woman is a prominent theme in *Felix Holt, Radical.* Harold Transome sets the tone of the times when he states that women are incapable of changing their views, which they have inherited from their fathers. But Esther is too bright to accept such a dominated role. Felix is intelligent and sensitive enough not to demand that Esther pretend to be less than she is; their love establishes them as equals.

THE FELLOWSHIP OF THE RING

Type of work: Novel
Author: J. R. R. Tolkien (1892- 1973)
Type of plot: Epic romance
Time of plot: The Third Age in a remote legendary past
Locale: The Middle-Earth between the Northern Waste and Sutherland
First published: 1954

This work is part of an epic romantic trilogy which creates an intricate myth delineating the struggle between Good and Evil. Tolkien's mythical world sprawls over many centuries, is replete with maps of various kingdoms, and is populated with tribes of elves, hobbits, orcs, wizards, dwarfs, trolls, men, and other creatures. The most innocent and homey of creatures, the hobbit Frodo is charged with withstanding the evil ring of the dark lord Sauron. He must cast it into the fires of Mordor and thus bring about once more a good and rightful order to the world.

The Fellowship of the Ring introduces two tales that run side by side throughout the trilogy *The Lord of the Rings*. One is the high saga of the destruction of Sauron and the return of King Elessar to the throne of his fathers; the other is the story of the journey of the hobbits from jolly complacency to unexpected heights of self-knowledge and self-sacrifice. The former gives the work its quality of ancient romance, for the characters are larger than life and speak to one another in elevated language; natural descriptions and expressions of emotion tend to be more formal and ceremonious than realistic. The latter tale contains elements of realism; the most realistic, homey, and familiar characters are from Tolkien's invented race, the hobbits.

The major figure in Tolkien's "high saga" is Aragorn, later King Elessar. He is certainly the most heroic of the characters in the classical sense, but the very elevation of his character has led some critics to see him as inhuman, lifeless, or "too good to be true." But actually he is a character of considerable subtlety and complexity; he earns his credentials as a hero honestly. Initially, in his disguise as "Strider," Aragorn must use guile and indirection to win the confidence of the hobbits. On the one hand they understand neither the implications of their situation nor their own personal danger. At the same time, Aragorn realizes that he is as frightening to them as any of Sauron's agents. Therefore, he uses their apprehensions toward him to stimulate their sense of danger, then he ingratiates himself to them by his wit, and, finally, by Gandalf's letter of identification. When asked why he did not formally identify himself earlier, he replies that he wants to be accepted for *himself*. Once the quest begins Aragorn proves his mettle and worthiness for kingship, not primarily by brute strength or heroic posturing, but by his adroit handling of men and his subtle strategies. A special poignancy and humanity are further given to him by his prolonged and tender love affair with Lady Arwen. Although we may never feel close to Aragorn, we can understand and feel for him as a human being, while still admiring him as a heroic figure.

However, while Aragorn leads the troops to victory in battle, the primary task of the epic falls not to the most heroic of the men, but to the mildest of the hobbits, Frodo Baggins. The name of this little race suggests a hob, hobnobbing, a dobbin; it calls up visions of fireside comforts, companionship, patient steadfastness, and good sense. Descriptions of hobbits and hobbit life in the prologue outline the prototype: a steady, plain little person, none too clever.

But this impression is belied in the romance by the characters of Samwise and Frodo, for in developing the character of Sam, Tolkien begins with a collection of those homely virtues which most nations of men arrogate to their own peasant class, and then adds, without loss of credibility, a quirky intelligence that outstrips shrewdness, and a fancy for elfish lore. In Frodo he marries the homely world of the Shire with the high deeds of the Dunedain; in Frodo are combined the best things of both worlds: he is the wisest and most noble of the hobbits and the bravest of the heroes because he is the smallest and most afraid.

It is primarily because of Frodo's unpretentiousness that he is "chosen" for the crucial task of casting the ring into the fire of Mordor. All the "large" heroes of the book, Aragorn and Gandalf, refuse the task, not from fear of external dangers, but from the knowledge that they would not be able to resist the ring's effect on them—they are too worldly and versed in the ways of power to be able to withstand the awful temptation to use it. Only Frodo is small enough and humble enough to withstand its corrupting influence right up to the edge of the fire—where even he weakens and the ring is finally destroyed by powers beyond his control.

THE FIELDS

Type of work: Novel
Author: Conrad Richter (1890-1968)
Type of plot: Regional romance
Time of plot: Early nineteenth century
Locale: Northwest Territory, later Ohio
First published: 1946

The Fields *is the second novel in a trilogy beginning with* The Trees *and ending with* The Town. *The three works trace the growth of a pioneer settlement in Ohio. Bearing many children and losing not a few, Sayward Wheeler, a woods woman, steadfastly refuses to leave her settlement for an easier life. Eventually vindicated, the settlement becomes a town, and inspired by her, her husband Portius becomes the town lawyer and schoolteacher.*

The second novel in Richter's trilogy, *The Fields*, expresses how progress is made in the Ohio pioneer settlement in the cultivation of farm land that had been dense forest; in the maturing of Sayward, emotionally and mentally; and in the growth of the Wheeler family and the settlement near their cabin. The making of a settlement and town from wilderness is Richter's recurrent theme, and he has researched pioneer life thoroughly so that his descriptions are accurate. Sayward's remembrances of the forest land and her comparisons of it to the new settlement add a vivid and personal touch to the historical account of the town's evolution.

Character development is as important in this novel as in *The Trees*. The personalities of Sayward's children are described primarily through Sayward's inner thoughts as she compares each one to Portius, to one of her brothers or sisters, or to herself. She begins to see how family and community circumstances together shape the characters of children.

In the community Portius represents education, sharp wit, and political awareness. He is the humorist and the proponent of progress. In his own sly way, Portius ridicules the church, the people's ignorance, the sawmill, and sometimes even his own wife. His views add a new perspective to the events surrounding community expansion.

The marriage relationship between Sayward and Portius is based on mutual respect for the other's skills and intelligence. Each has an independent streak: Sayward reveals hers in stubbornness when her principles are threatened; Portius displays his physically by leaving home occasionally. He also manifests his independence in an episode of adultery, which results in the strongest conflict Sayward has had in her marriage. Without benefit of counsel, Sayward works out an understanding of Portius and of her own feelings that preserves her marriage and self-respect. This is one example of the many situations in this pioneer family that require strength, humility, and acceptance of circumstances. These situations help give the novel its warmth, realism, and vitality.

FIESTA IN NOVEMBER

Type of work: Novel
Author: Eduardo Mallea (1903-)
Type of plot: Social criticism
Time of plot: The mid-1930's
Locale: Buenos Aires, Argentina
First published: 1936

Two plots having no obvious connection interrupt each other in this novel about the moral shallowness of the modern world. The elite of Argentinian society are gathering for a party at the Ragues'. Their oldest daughter Marta is bored, but manages to meet a kindred spirit in the person of Lintas, an artist. Though both feel outrage at the emptiness and potential evil of this society, which among other topics discusses the extermination of the lower classes, neither Marta nor Lintas can really communicate with each other. Meanwhile, in the second plot, an unsuspecting poet is roused from his work by a military patrol which later executes him for no apparent reason.

In a graceful style, rich with vivid, precise images, neither pretentious nor overly decorated, Eduardo Mallea tells the moving story of two people struggling to communicate with each other while lost in the midst of a shallow, violent world. Although the painter Lintas and Marta Rague are the two most sympathetic characters in this short novel, both are held back by their pride from the honesty and openness which would liberate them and enable them to achieve an authentic relationship. But they are the only individuals in *Fiesta in November* who even care about moral concerns, except for the poet, unnamed and doomed, whose brief story alternates like an almost subliminal theme with the main body of the story, illuminating and commenting upon it.

The two fiestas, one social, the other of blood, are linked thematically by Lintas' account to Marta of the fatal beating of a Jewish book dealer in Buenos Aires by a group of Argentine fascists. An undercurrent of violence also lies behind the conversation and actions of the guests in the house of Marta's mother, Eugenia Rague. The fragments of the condemned poet's story are in italics, suggesting that in spite of its shorter length, this narrative is the more important of the two.

The opening arrest of the poet could be that of Joseph K in *The Trial*. There are more than casual similarities between the work of Kafka and this novel. The contrast between the scene with the poet and the luxurious setting of Eugenia Rague's home is shocking. Eugenia's is a vain, acquisitive character. Her only passions are for her collection of objects from the past, and for power. "Power is power," she thinks, "and damn all the rest." She detests sentiment and everything connected with it, so it is not surprising that she is completely alienated from her two daughters. Her husband George, despite his wealth, feels no peace or fulfillment.

A sultry, perfumed lushness pervades the novel, the heat of summer and passion—and of violence. Objects seem to have lives of their own. The opening picture of the dinner party is a devastating glimpse of empty lives and futile social ritual. The characters are struggling with an inner tyranny, a psychic trap more terrible than the cruelty of society, if they only realized it. "All art," thinks Lintas, "is a great and terrible demand for response." And this unusual novel demands a response from the reader.

Lintas appears on the scene like a breath of fresh air in the stale world of the Rague mansion. Mr. and Mrs. Rague and their guests would be lost without their ceremonies, but Lintas deliberately walks over their carefully plotted maneuvers. Marta and Lintas recognize each other from the beginning as two of a kind—exiles in a world they detest. Marta, at twenty-seven, still is filled with a passionate curiosity, still is eager to experience life. Human beings, she reflects, only seek their own private ends, only hope to satisfy their appetites. Marta hates the pretense of society, the constant betrayal of her own nature. A dream—unknown but tragic—burns in the depths of her spirit, stifled by daily compromises.

Mirrors and windows and polished surfaces constantly reflect faces, oblique views of people, staring eyes. The reflected images seem more real than many of the actual figures and faces. Mallea seems to be asking, What *is* the reality and what is false?

Brenda Rague, Marta's sister, is having an abortion while her mother's fiesta is in progress. This revelation causes Marta to think in a new way about their lives, and her meeting with Lintas continues to stimulate her chain of thoughts. Lintas himself was made suddenly aware by the episode of the brutal beating of the bookseller. Are there social castes, they ask, or only moral castes? Where is the moral answer? The word *serve* appears to Marta as she walks down the empty city streets before dawn. What does it mean? Could it be the answer for her? She realizes that each individual must, in his own way, be heroic, walk alone, bravely, honestly, into his fate.

The inner dramas of the novel are not resolved. They move from climax to climax, cumulatively, charged with great lyric tension. Seemingly insignificant individual lives are transformed by Mallea into the very essence of the human condition. *Fiesta in November* is an extraordinary novel by a great author. It is a book that haunts the reader, as Mallea intended, for the questions that it raises are not easily answered.

Mallea's view of life is religious and moral. His works often suggest the European existentialists, although most of his writing anticipated their novels and dramas. He was descended from an old Creole family, and attended an English school in Bahía Blanca, where the majority of his classmates were the sons of immigrants. (He has never lost sight of the fact that Argentina is a melting pot.) At the age of thirteen, he moved to Buenos Aires with his family. The city was a revelation for the withdrawn adolescent. His first published stories won immediate attention and he eventually became an acclaimed public figure. In the 1930's and 1940's he was director of some of the most influential literary publications in Latin America. He was a steadfast opponent of the Perón regime. After the revolution which overthrew the Perón dictatorship, he was named ambassador to UNESCO in Paris. Subsequently, he returned to private life to devote himself exclusively to writing. He has lectured in Europe and the United States.

Fiesta in November and other novels and stories such as *All Green Shall Perish* and *Chaves* have established Mallea as one of Latin America's greatest writers and one of the outstanding prose stylists and moral spokesmen in the world. His works are great art because they are born out of an intense experience of life; they convey vividly this experience to the reader.

Bruce D. Reeves

FILE NO. 113

Type of work: Novel
Author: Émile Gaboriau (1835-1873)
Type of plot: Mystery romance
Time of plot: 1866
Locale: Paris
First published: 1867

An enormously popular writer of mysteries, Gaboriau creates detectives who are always staunch individualists, and who catch their criminal by brilliant reasoning, theatrical tactics, and the use of numerous impenetrable disguises. File No. 113 *has an improbable, melodramatic, and complicated plot, often typical of the mystery genre.*

In his own day Émile Gaboriau was enormously popular and considered second only to Conan Doyle as a master of the detective story genre. Twenty years after his death his crime novels were still best sellers. Today, however, he is largely ignored and his books are mentioned, if at all, only as important footnotes in the history of detective fiction. Since *File No. 113* is a typical Gaboriau novel, it vividly demonstrates both the strengths and weaknesses of the author and helps to explain his popularity in his own time—and his relative obscurity in our own.

File No. 113 follows the pattern that is basic to all of Gaboriau's crime novels. The robbery is discovered and the police investigation commences. Led by Detective Fanferlot, who is erratic and overly eager, they immediately make false hypotheses, ignore important clues, and arrest Prosper Bertomy, the wrong suspect. After the preliminary investigation has been thoroughly bungled, Monsieur Lecoq enters the action disguised as the clownish Venduret. By the time his true identity is revealed and his procedures made overt, Lecoq is well on his way to solving the case and the story moves quickly to a preliminary revelation. He correctly identifies Louis de Clameran and Raoul de Lagors as the culprits—with well over half the book yet remaining.

Once the criminal is named, Gaboriau stops describing the investigation and shifts his narrative to chronicle the events leading up to the crime from the viewpoint of the participants. Invariably the crime of the moment turns out to be related to older concealed crimes and improprieties that center in a rich and famous family. Thus, personal scandal is added to felony crime, and the investigation threatens not only the culprits, but also the honor and fortune of an aristocratic name.

In *File No. 113* the hidden scandal revolves around the premarital affair between Gaston de Clameran and Valentine Verberie, later Monsieur Fauvel's wife, and the long time villainy of Gaston's brother Louis. Thus, the story contains all of the sensational, melodramatic, and sentimental elements that Gaboriau's readers desired—victimized aristocratic ladies, frustrated love affairs, secret scandals, familial betrayal, fraud, deception, and profligacy. When this family chronicle reaches the point where the investigatory narrative had been suspended, the two plot lines are joined, Lecoq explains his deductions, and the malefactors are brought to justice—or, as in the case of Louis de Clameran, are punished by divine retribution.

But, however satisfying this double plot structure may have been to nineteenth century readers, it is too cumbersome, digressive, melodramatic, and psychologically implausible for modern tastes. In his short seven year career, Émile Gaboriau introduced many of the elements that were to become essential parts of the modern detective novel, but it remained for better writers to combine them into unified, realized works of art.

IL FILOSTRATO

Type of work: Poetry
Author: Giovanni Boccaccio (1313-1375)
Type of plot: Medieval romance
Time of plot: c. 1200 B.C.
Locale: The battle of Troy
First transcribed: c. 1335-1340

This metrical romance describes the noble and anguished love of Troilo, a Trojan warrior, for Griseida, the daughter of a Trojan who deserted to the Greeks. Aided by his friend, Pandaro, Troilo finally possesses his beloved. After a brief romance, she is exchanged with the Greeks for a captured Trojan warrior, and though she knows she may not see him again for a long time, she refuses to elope with Troilo. Ultimately, she is unfaithful to Troilo with a Greek commander, Diomede. Betrayed, Troilo fights like a man who cares not for his own life and is slain in battle by Achilles.

Il Filostrato, a word coined by Boccaccio meaning "the one who is vanquished by love," contains many of the traditional courtly love elements found in medieval romance but already presupposes a new world view based upon new moral standards. It can thus be seen as a transitional work, bridging the medieval and Renaissance periods.

One factor distinguishing Boccaccio from earlier writers of medieval romance is that he represents the new, rising bourgeois class which was so decisive a force in the dissolution of the Middle Ages. His attitude toward courtly love is thus quite different from both the mystical orientation of such writers as Dante and the aristocratic tradition of the writers of French romances such as Chrétien de Troyes.

An indication of the new manner in which Boccaccio approaches courtly love can be found in the particular way in which he transforms the tale of Troilus and Cressida as originally found in the *Roman de Troie* of Benoît de Saint-Maure. The story as narrated by Benoît was within the tradition of the medieval epic *(chansons de geste)* and represents a masculine and military orientation in which the prowess of arms plays the primary role. Women and love, if they appear at all, are of only secondary importance. When Benoît treats of love, his emphasis is on Troilus and Diomede, and not on Cressida. Indeed his story appears to be that of Diomede rather than of Troilus. Boccaccio takes the basic plot of Benoît and transforms it for his own purpose.

This purpose is related in the Proem to *Il Filostrato* in which Boccaccio indicates that he will narrate the suffering of Troilus so that the lady to whom the poem is addressed will understand that Boccaccio himself is suffering as Troilus had suffered. This lady is generally acknowledged to have been Maria d'Aquino, the natural daughter of the King of Naples, who had absented herself from Naples where Boccaccio was then residing. *Il Filostrato* was designed to function as a "go-between." This may have been an extraliterary reason for Boccaccio's amplification of the role of Pandarus. The purpose of the work was to seduce Maria (and cause her to return to Naples) as Pandarus helped to seduce Cressida. The ultimate goal was sexual satisfaction.

Superficially, *Il Filostrato* appears to be a conventional tale of courtly love, and many familiar conceits associated with the tradition of courtly love are in evidence. The work opens in a courtly setting with the presentation of questions in a "court of love." Love enters through the eyes in "the fair season." Cressida is described as being "so fair and so like an angel." Troilus is depicted as being ennobled by love; he becomes a more fierce and vigorous fighter against the Greeks because of the love bestowed upon him by Cressida. Troilus suffers (in this respect Boccaccio exceeds himself for he is supposedly basing his descriptions of anguish upon his own experience); he is pale, lacks appetite, loses sleep, becomes weak.

Boccaccio places particular emphasis on the courtly love doctrine of nobility as residing, not in noble birth, but in a noble heart. Since Boccaccio was a member of the bourgeoisie attempting to make his way in the royal court of Naples, this view was of personal interest. Nobility is depicted as based upon virtue, not power. Although of a lower social rank than Troilus, Cressida is considered worthy of his love because of her "proud and noble bearing . . . high worth and courtly speech . . . manner more courteous than those of other ladies."

Despite the presence of these traditional courtly love elements, other aspects of the tradition are contradicted within the poem. For example, the purpose of love is not ennoblement but satisfaction of Troilus' "hot desire." Cressida understands (as Boccaccio hopes Maria will understand) the true purpose of the courtship. She is outside the courtly love tradition, not merely for her later betrayal, but because of her easy seduction. The danger and barriers that confronted the lover in the garden of the *Roman de la Rose* (a typical medieval romance) are missing. Troilus, unlike the heroes of the medieval romances of Chrétien de Troyes, does not have to prove himself by submitting himself to constant danger. His love is unearned and too easily won. Troilus recognizes this when he states that "what I crave has not been earned by my service."

However, as has been noted, Boccaccio is not concerned with ennobling Troilus, but with satisfying his own passion. He wishes Maria to understand from the tale "how great and of what sort my desires are, what is their goal, and what beyond all else they crave." Like Troilus, Boccaccio is concerned with making his love known to his lady and drawing her to him. If his lady should fail to understand, he addresses her directly in the invocation to Canto III and requests that she "refuse not my high desire; graciously grant that which I ask."

Not only is the noble purpose of courtly love lacking, but the moral lesson as well. Boccaccio makes no distinction between earthly love and heavenly love. Boccaccio's salvation will come from his lady and not from heaven. The song of Troilus, dedicated to Venus, reinforces one's recognition that Boccaccio is concerned solely with earthly love. He is not rejecting religious values; they merely have no place within the context of his work.

The lack of a palinode in *Il Filostrato* is thus not surprising. (The palinode was the recantation of earthly love and the reassertion of the supreme value of heavenly love found at the conclusion of many traditional medieval romances. Its purpose was to remind the reader that although courtly love may be supreme on this earth, heavenly love was always preferable. Courtly love was, therefore, generally placed within a framework of religious values.) Since Boccaccio's narrative is based solely upon worldly values, there is no need to recant. Boccaccio's only warning to the reader is presented, not as a moral lesson, but as a practical lesson, in keeping with the practical tone of his poem. He advises young men to place their love in ladies of true nobility; that is, ladies who will not betray them.

Although Boccaccio in *Il Filostrato* is utilizing the conventions of courtly love for a purely sensual end, this should not suggest that he could not write tales completely within a courtly tradition. One has only to turn to the fifth day of *The Decameron* to realize with what seriousness Boccaccio could write of courtly love. In *Il Filostrato,* however, Boccaccio can be seen as a transitional figure, already drawing away from the values of the Middle Ages, but not completely caught within the value structure of the Renaissance.

When Chaucer took up the tale of Troilus and Cressida at the end of the fourteenth century, he changed it in both matter and manner to conform to an earlier, medieval concept of courtly love.

Phyllis Mael

THE FINANCIER

Type of work: Novel
Author: Theodore Dreiser (1871-1945)
Type of plot: Naturalism
Time of plot: About 1850 to 1874
Locale: Philadelphia
First published: 1912

Frank Cowperwood is the model of the aggressive, realistic, and relentless capitalist. Though he rises quickly to become one of the financial powers in Philadelphia, there is never an end to such successes since he must constantly strive to thwart more powerful monopolists. This leads him into shady deals involving politicians. Such machinations, in addition to the fact he is keeping as a mistress the daughter of the powerful politician Butler, lead to his downfall and imprisonment. In the end, he reestablishes himself, gains a divorce from his wife, and settles down in Chicago with his mistress.

Two symbolic passages concerning sea predators, one early in the novel and one at the conclusion, provide important clues to understanding Dreiser's theme in *The Financier*. As a boy, Frank Cowperwood stoically observes an unequal contest in a large fish tank between a lobster and a squid. The lobster, certain of victory, bides his time and slowly devours the defenseless squid. In the context of Dreiser's social metaphor, the strong destroy the weak, whether with sudden terrible force or gradually, relentlessly, like the lobster sporting with his prey. The final symbolic passage, crudely added as an epilogue to the novel, treats the *Mycteroperca Bonaci* (or Black Grouper) which, chameleon-like, changes its colors to avoid danger or to strike out at a weaker adversary. From Dreiser's point of view, the *Mycteroperca Bonaci* represents an element of "subtlety, chicanery, trickery" that is also part of the human condition. The fish is no more responsible, in a Godless universe, for its trickery than man—the social animal—is morally responsible for using deception as a means of power. Cowperwood's rise to wealth and influence, an ascent which is determined by the laws of Social Darwinism, will be continued by the author in *The Titan* (1914), as will the story of his socially-conditioned fall from power. In *The Financier,* Dreiser details, with a naturalistic concern for inductive evidence, the causes both for Cowperwood's success and his eventual failure, just as a scientist might describe the behavior of a fish in an aquarium.

However, unlike a true scientist who observes phenomena objectively, dispassionately, Dreiser views the activities of his hero from the bias of his socialistic philosophy. From that bias Cowperwood, the ruthless financier, ought to serve as an object lesson on the corruption of the capitalistic system. Yet Dreiser, in spite of the Marxist determinism at the center of his economic philosophy, obviously admires Cowperwood as a man, if not as a social creature. He sympathizes with his hero's single-minded ambition to succeed; his contempt for intellectual inferiors; his violent sexual passions; his stubborn, egoistical will. Although Dreiser's early view of Cowperwood may have been satirical, he treats him ultimately as a Nietzschean superman, advanced beyond the conventional feelings of petty morality, beyond remorse, pity, or loyalty—except for Aileen Butler, whose iron will and courage matches his own. Yet even in his love for Aileen there is a measure of selfishness instead of romantic idealism: quite simply, she satisfies his needs. Unlike many of the protagonists of Dreiser's other novels—Carrie Meeber, Jennie Gerhardt, Clyde Griffiths, Eugene Witla—Frank Cowperwood is a strong, magnetic, self-assured character, in the author's symbolism more the predatory lobster than the pitiful squid. Because Dreiser's attitude toward Cowperwood is ambivalent—he admires the man but is contemptuous of his capitalistic endeavors—the message of the novel is correspondingly ambiguous. How can one despise an economic system that gives its chief rewards to those like Cowperwood, who are the most adept competitors in the survival-of-the-fittest social ethic?

Other weaknesses besides its ambiguous theme will trouble readers of *The Financier*. Never a master of prose style, Dreiser often describes Lillian as "lymphatic" when he probably means *phlegmatic*. Also, he describes "sensuously lymphatic" women who "dwelt" in a brothel. When Alfred Semple, Lillian's first husband, comes to an "untimely" death, Dreiser writes that the man's passing is "dramatic in a dull way." Shortly before Frank marries Lillian, his world is "of roseate hue." Later, Dreiser mentions that in Frank's North Front Street house some "pleasing appropriately colored rugs covered the floor." Much later in the novel, Aileen writes to her father a letter that Dreiser describes as a "defiant screed," although the word *screed* seems hardly correct. These and many other lapses in diction and rhetoric damage the novel. Worse still, Dreiser breaks into the narrative, often with ludicrous effect, at times to converse with the reader, at other times to expound his philosophy of life. Yet in the major scenes, Dreiser—as he commonly succeeds in his important fiction—sustains a sense of realism with powerful, honest emotion. The author is at his best in analyzing Cowperwood's tangled love affair with Aileen. The trial scene is masterly; so are the prison scenes. Without sentimentality, Dreiser touches life. In spite of its ambiguous theme and its many stylistic weaknesses, *The Financier* is a novel of massive integrity that still has force to move the reader's emotions.

THE FINN CYCLE

Type of work: Ballad cycle
Author: Unknown
Type of plot: Historical adventure
Time of plot: Third century
Locale: Ireland
First transcribed: **Reputed eleventh century manuscript**

This series of ballads celebrates the exploits of the third century Irish hero Finn and his band of noble warriors, the Fianna Erinn. Finn is larger-than-life, a courageous leader who inspires his men. Like Robin Hood and King Arthur, he is a bold hero, a capable leader, and a tender lover. Also like them, he lives to witness the passing of his strength and the dissolution of his band. All of these events signal the waning of a heroic era.

The audience for whom *The Finn Cycle* was composed was naïve, socially young, and intellectually credulous, although it had a definite protocol and a certain dignified etiquette. This audience demanded stirring words from the storyteller, and also that he have a stimulating imagination. Although these tales were very popular in the eleventh and twelfth centuries, the stories of Finn, Oisin, and the others had existed among the people for many centuries. There is in the stories a note of nostalgia for a past glory, a longing for a heroic period. There is perhaps a contrast between the old hierarchical society of the legends and the society telling them, a society facing a rapidly changing and hostile world. The old ballad system was breaking down by this time, and these tales were the beginnings of a new, popular literature in Ireland and Scotland. The ballads were easier, the meters drastically simplified, and the versification easier, as the literature passed into the hands of the people.

Most, although not all, of the ballads and prose of this period are concerned with the hero, Finn, and his war band, or fian (hence, the word "Fenian"). The original meaning of the word fian was "a driving, pursuing, hunting," although it came to apply to warfare. Eventually, it came to mean a band of warriors on the warpath. In a stricter sense, fian meant a band of roving warriors who had joined for the purpose of making war on their own account. They were not, however, mere robbers or marauders. They were often men expelled from their clan, or landless men, the sons of kings who had quarreled with their fathers, or men who seized this way of avenging some private wrong. They were the only professional soldiers in Ireland in the old times, apart from mercenaries, who often were foreigners. This was why the word fian was often used, especially in poetry, in a wider sense for any war band. The various fianna were held together by discipline, and had their own organization and customs; men who wished to join the ranks, as is shown in *The Finn Cycle,* had to pass a test of skill or bravery. The various fianna took their names from their leaders. It was natural that the various fianna and their chiefs, from their roving life and adventures and exploits, should early have become the subject of storytelling. Probably, many such stories and ballads have been lost.

In modern times, it has become usual to assume that the word fianna always refers to the war band headed by Finn, or Mac Cumhal, as he came to be called. The development of this legend overshadowed all of the others, so that the ordinary meaning of the word fian or fianna was forgotten. But even as late as the tenth century Finn and his fianna were only one among several well-known similar bands. The figure of Finn, who in popular imagination overpowered other heroes, attracted to itself, from century to century, exploits originally attributed to others. *The Finn Cycle* absorbed much of the legendary lore of the older cycles, until all of Ireland held up Finn as the supreme heroic leader.

The popular imagination blended the tales and made them into the kind of legend the people needed and wanted. They were close to the earth and nature, and this is reflected in the tales of Finn. This was a time when the wild wood was giving way to pasture and tillage, and men no longer had reason to consider every wild cry of the night, to ponder each call of the birds and beasts. For Finn, the battles were but interruptions in the lifetime of hunting. The ballads speak of him delighting in the cackling of ducks, in the bellowing of the oxen and the whistle of the eagle. Many metaphors and allusions in the tales draw upon nature and animals. For example, when sorrow comes to the women, they feel sympathy for the wild birds and beasts which are like themselves.

Finn himself seems to transcend the world of which he is a part; certainly he is larger than time, than the moment in history. When the Fianna are broken up, at last, after hundreds of years of hunting and fighting, it hardly seems that he dies. More likely, he comes back again and again, in different shapes, and his son, Oisin, is made king over a divine country. Finn is not an individual man, in these ballads, as much as a force of nature, a part of the universe like the clouds or the gods which shape and reshape the clouds. Seer and poet, king and Druid, Finn was a mortal who became immortal. He was a better fighter, a better hunter, than any other man, and was infinitely wiser than any other mortal. Quiet in peace, the ballads say, but angry in battle, Finn always was the perfect leader.

These men in the stories are warriors, men of action rather than thought. Their existence is devoted to love and companionship, and they can imagine no higher consideration. There is none of the philosophical worrying of Arthur and Merlin in these ballads. The men here do not speculate on eternity; they are sure of their simple values and fight to defend them. The brotherhood of the warrior is all. It is based on their hard and vigorous way of life, and on their few necessary possessions, for, running through the ballads, is a strong sense of material goods, of the things that men use to live. A feeling of the matter-of-factness of life colors the ballads and the attitudes of the characters.

The structure of *The Finn Cycle* is loose and rambling, without the tightly woven pattern of the great epics. The many incidents that compose the cycle are a succession of detached episodes, rather than a continuing story such as the *Iliad* or King Arthur's legends. The people who imagined the cycle were unsophisticated, one might even say childlike, and did not comprehend a large literary design. Their stories wander without aim, each adventure independent of the previous one and the one that will follow. But the ballads of the cycle tell vividly of the heroic life, of the strength necessary to survive in a young and hard world, and of the codes of honor and companionship that make survival worthwhile.

Bruce D. Reeves

THE FISHER MAIDEN

Type of work: Novel
Author: Björnstjerne Björnson (1832-1910)
Type of plot: Pastoral romance
Time of plot: Early nineteenth century
Locale: Norway
First published: 1868

The central character of the novel, Petra, is an illegitimate, rustic fisher maiden. Filled with a tempestuous yet simple love for man and nature, she is forced to flee her village to escape scandal: three young men each believe themselves engaged to her. Sailing to the home of a northern pastor, she studies drama, for she had been deeply attracted to the theater during a sojourn in Bergen. She is reunited with the suitor she loved; he forgives her, yet marries another. She begins her career on the stage, adding courage, experience, suffering, and knowledge to her natural talent.

This novel by Nobel Prize winner Björnson is both unusual and deeply moving. It begins as if it is to be a tale of peasant folk in a village, but changes dramatically into the story of a fiery young woman who decides to become an actress upon seeing her first play. The account of Petra and the people in her life is told with economy of words and with strongly evoked emotion. The characters, all vividly drawn individuals, seem unable to avoid becoming entangled in conflicting passions; innocently, they end by tormenting themselves and others. At times, the perverse energy of the story suggests Björnson's fellow countryman, Ibsen.

Guilt is the dominant and ruling emotion in the novel. Hans Ödegaard nurses guilt for his past tragedy and tries to redeem himself by "saving" Petra, but one individual cannot save another. Both of Petra's parents feel guilt about their past, and suffer accordingly. Finally, Pedro is able to help his daughter by aiding her escape from the village and by leaving her his money when he dies. The old priest comes to experience guilt in relation to his attitude to Petra and her art, but he learns to overcome both his attitude and the guilt it caused. And the villagers feel guilty for driving away Petra and hurting Gunlaug, and try to make it up to Gunlaug after Petra is gone. Only by transcending guilt can any of the characters, including Petra, find happiness.

The description of Petra's first experience in a theater is one of the highlights of the novel; her wonder and deeply stirred emotions are vividly and convincingly portrayed. Björnson's aim in this novel was to show how irresistible the power of natural talent could be, and to vindicate the theater as both a place of amusement and of moral instruction. Much of Björnson, himself, is in Petra's character, for he too had to struggle to win approval for his art. His struggle is also mirrored in the strange poem about the young Viking which Petra recites when she first demonstrates her power as an actress.

FIVE WOMEN WHO LOVED LOVE

Type of work: Novelettes
Author: Ibara Saikaku (c. 1642-1693)
Type of plots: Sentimental romances
Time of plots: Seventeenth century
Locale: Japan
First published: c. 1685

Kôshoku Gonin Onna, *translated as* Five Women Who Loved Love, *consists of five novelettes based upon actual incidents. With one exception these tales of love end unhappily. A feeling of tragedy is evoked not only by the unfortunate events, but also by the author's portrait of each female protagonist. These women are not helpless, weak creatures, but beings of character whose very strength seems to cause their downfall.*

In order to appreciate fully the prose fiction of Saikaku, it is necessary to understand the nature of Japanese society during the latter half of the seventeenth century. Although Edo (Tokyo) was still the feudal capital (the residence of the shogun and the source of the real power), and Kyoto was still the residence of the mikado (the nominal ruler), Osaka witnessed the rise of a merchant class; but because of the rigid class distinctions and feudal laws maintained by the shogun and samurai, the merchants were unable to convert their economic power into political or social power. The official religion was Confucianism and the ensuing laws ensured the maintenance of a rigidly stratified society with a hierarchy of classes, making it punishable by death to attempt to move from one class to another. The merchants thus sought an outlet for the frustration of their thwarted power and for their money in the ukiyo (floating world).

"Ukiyo" originally had a Buddhist meaning of the transitory life, death, and decay, and in the works of Saikaku always retained some of this original meaning. However, in the seventeenth century, the ukiyo became the term for the gay quarters or the theater (kabuki). The new heroes of this society were the actors and courtesans; the new values were love and money.

The prose fiction of Saikaku reflects the new merchant class, powerful yet without power, attempting to assert their individuality in the face of a stern and rigid social code. In his work we see the individual coming into conflict with the laws, and the result is usually punishment or death. Some criticism of the social code that supports an outdated hierarchy seems to be implicit in some of these stories. Yet there is an ambiguity that seems to direct some of the criticism to those who give up everything in order to sacrifice themselves to the new values of love and money.

The five stories of *Five Women Who Loved Love* are linked by a common theme: the transgression of the social code for love. Each tale is divided into five parts (perhaps because of the five-act division of the drama), and the third part depicts a journey (also borrowed from drama). Each tale is linked to a particular locale, three to the major cities of Edo, Kyoto, and Osaka, and two to outlying provinces. In the first four tales, the transgression of the feudal law leads to death; in the fifth tale, however, the lovers live because they are both of the same social class. Throughout the work, Saikaku seems to imply that there should be no conflict between love and society, especially one made along class lines. The conflict exists, however; the heroines choose love and accept the consequences without despair.

FOMA GORDYEEFF

Type of work: Novel
Author: Maxim Gorky (Aleksei Maksimovich Peshkov, 1868-1936)
Type of plot: Psychological realism
Time of plot: Late nineteenth century
Locale: Russia
First published: 1899

This novel is set during the era which saw the rise of the Russian merchant class and the radical intellectuals who were to fuel the Russian Revolution. Born to a rich merchant during these uncertain times, the youth Foma shows spirit, nobility, and business acumen. However, the impoverished plight of the peasants and the vulgar pursuits of his own class cause him, like Hamlet, to question too closely the meaning of the world's order. When he publically denounces the individuals of his wealthy merchant community, they react forcibly committing him to an asylum.

Gorky, the pseudonym of Aleksei Peshkov, means "bitterness" in Russian, and, as the early life of Gorky was filled with poverty and bitterness, so this first novel also is colored with bitterness. *Foma Gordyeeff* is an uneven novel, at times brilliant, but occasionally rambling and confusing. The most impressive sections are those dealing with Foma's father and Foma's childhood. Ignat Gordyeeff is a magnificent character, a giant of a man, successful because of his vast energy (which, like a Dreiser protagonist, even he cannot fully understand), violent, but instinctively fair. He admires energy in others—even in nature; he is capable of watching with pleasure and admiration as the Volga destroys his own new barge. His second wife, the somnambulant Natalya, and mother of Foma, is a marked contrast to his own vigorous personality. The boy is a strange mixture of his parents' traits, both impetuous and violent, and surprisingly lethargic. The chapters dealing with his childhood and youth are sensitively drawn; Gorky's genius shines through as he recounts the impressions of boyhood, the beauty of the "mother" Volga, broad-breasted and triumphant, the boy's first vision of death when he sees a drowned man, and the confusing first days at school. The account of the young man groping for a meaning, a goal in life, is also well-handled.

As Foma begins to encounter women and takes over his father's business, however, the narrative loses momentum. Sometimes Gorky strains for effect and piles up emotional adjectives until the style becomes shrill, and philosophical digressions weaken the narrative. Nevertheless, Gorky's eye for physical detail, his talent for making characters live, and the vitality of his prose outweigh the defects of the novel. Many of the women are well drawn, particularly Liuboff, Foma's godsister, who tries to rouse his intellect, his Aunt Anfisa, who rears him, and his first mistress, the long-suffering Pelagaya.

Foma is looking for the "meaning of life," but nobody seems to be able to help him; everyone seems to be too busy looking after his or her own interests.

Even Madame Medynsky, a philanthropist, is attracted by his good looks and attempts to seduce him. His godfather equates money and power, and his schoolboy friends grub after success in their different ways. He is very impressed when an old former colleague of his father tells him, "Without labor, a man is ruined," and "Through freedom, man perishes!"

As he searches for understanding of the world around him, all he learns with certainty is that people cover their nakedness with lies and false façades. He is proud of being a "simple man—a savage man," and, finally, at the end, he destroys himself by attempting to expose the fakery of the so-called respectable men in power. But the effort is futile, and he is treated as a madman. The conclusion of the novel is effective, but Gorky's message is not completely clear. The use of the word "prophet" to refer to Foma suggests that he is meant to be a Christ figure, but the analogy does not fit the character that Gorky has built up for nearly four hundred pages. However, this rewarding novel is filled with the intensity of youth and is rich with detailed observations of Russia at the beginning of the twentieth century.

THE FOOL OF QUALITY

Type of work: Novel
Author: Henry Brooke (1703?-1783)
Type of plot: Didactic romance
Time of plot: Eighteenth century
Locale: England
First published: 1766-1770

This is less a novel than a vehicle for the author to present numerous didactic treatises on every subject from politics to child-rearing. Mr. Fenton, drawn to the innate goodness of his brother's neglected youngest child, kidnaps the boy. Fenton then proceeds to bring him up to be the perfect gentleman: endlessly charitable, just, honorable, and wise. He succeeds.

The Irish poet and playwright Henry Brooke used *The Fool of Quality* to expound the Rousseauean virtues of the "natural man." The dangers of civilized life (overpowering man's inborn virtues and strengths) are made much of in this rambling story. The protagonist's older brother lives a dissolute life, a victim to the vices of civilization; conversely, the boy Henry strips off the fine new clothes that tie him to civilized society when he comes to believe that they will stifle his "natural" powers. Throughout the book, the "noble savage" concept is held up as the ideal to which man should aspire.

The long philosophical digressions in *The Fool of Quality* are, for the most part, dated and superficial; the narrator's profundities tend to be obvious and fashionable (to the mid-eighteenth century mind). But these speculations and ramblings are set down with charm and style enough to be diverting and entertaining, and of genuine historical interest. Brooke was not an original thinker or writer, but he presents a good picture of the popular ideas and techniques of his day.

A friend of Swift, Pope, and other literary figures of the time, Brooke attempted to copy their success and methods in his own work. Different parts of *The Fool of Quality* owe their form and content to various writers of the period; the sentimental parts certainly may be linked with Laurence Sterne's *Sentimental Journey* and some passages of *Tristram Shandy*. Some of the humor and digressions may have been influenced by Fielding. The book oscillates between hectic activity and long-winded reflection, between sentimentality and genuine humor, but the novel is a very human and humane work. The protagonist, Henry Clinton, is supposedly reared by his foster father to be an ideal nobleman, but he possesses more than a little Don Quixote in his personality.

A FOOL'S ERRAND

Type of work: Novel
Author: Albion W. Tourgée (1838-1905)
Type of plot: Polemical realism
Time of plot: 1865-1877
Locale: Rockford County in a Southern state
First published: 1879

Servosse, an ex-Yankee soldier, settles in the South during the period of Reconstruction. His attempt to make it his home is unsuccessful; he only manages to alienate the defeated whites. The rise of the Klan is vividly depicted and heralds the return to the Southern social order that prevailed prior to the Civil War. Servosse comes to understand that he was on a fool's errand in his attempt to rebuild the South in the image of the North. He foresees that the reunification of the nation will require the work of many generations.

In almost all literature dealing with the Reconstruction period in the South following the end of the American Civil War, the carpetbagger is depicted as a villain motivated by greed, vengeance, and opportunism. Albion Tourgée's novel *A Fool's Errand* is the exception; its plot revolves around the career of an idealistic humanitarian Northerner, Comfort Servosse, a retired Union soldier who buys land in the South after the war for the sole purpose of devoting himself to helping the blacks build their future. In its general outline, the plot is modeled on the postwar career of Tourgée himself, whose experiences closely paralleled those of his protagonist.

Ironically, both the strengths and the weaknesses of *A Fool's Errand* arise, in large part, from the fiery zeal and desire to impart a message which inspired it. Tourgée is at his best when he is simply narrating a gripping tale of terror and suspense. Yet the truly powerful narrative is constantly interrupted by the author, who uses the old devise of letters to insert discussions of history, eulogies in praise of black people, or diatribes against the South. Likewise, the earnestness of Tourgée's message inspires him to write some of the most realistic and horrifying scenes of mob violence in Southern fiction, and to depict with great effectiveness scenes of rabble-rousing and lynching, of conspiracy, secret meetings, and the inner workings of the Ku Klux Klan. At the same time, however, the author presents a one-sided view of the total Southern situation through his omission of equally important facts concerning the corruption and shortsightedness of many Northerners involved in the Reconstruction government. Similarly, the realism Tourgée achieves in describing the brutality of the Klansmen breaks down when he comes to write the love story of a Northern girl who redeems her Southern lover from his wrong ideas. The same novel that is starkly real and objective in some portions, suffers from sentimentality and nearly miraculous turns of plot in others.

The chief merit of *A Fool's Errand* lies, however, not in its plot construction or scenario, but in its astute appraisal of the total failure of Reconstruction politics. Servosse himself is a pure and noble idealist, but he comes to realize that the Northern system of which he is a part is misguided and blind, and that the program it enforces is doomed to failure. The only solution to the Southern problem, Tourgée concludes, must come not from politics, but from mass education: "Let the Nation educate the colored man and the poor-white *because* the Nation held them in bondage, and is responsible for their education; educate the voter *because* the Nation cannot afford that he should be ignorant."

FOR WHOM THE BELL TOLLS

Type of work: Novel
Author: Ernest Hemingway (1899-1961)
Type of plot: Impressionistic realism
Time of plot: 1937
Locale: Spain
First published: 1940

The novel's title, an allusion to lines from John Donne's poem, "No Man Is An Island," tells the story of a young American, fighting voluntarily against Franco's fascist forces in Spain, who leads a band of guerrillas in what turns out to be a totally useless military exploit. The entire novel encompasses only a seventy-two-hour time period during which Robert Jordan loses his comrades in battle, falls in love, is wounded too badly to continue, and finally prepares to make a suicidal stand for his cause.

In 1940 Ernest Hemingway published *For Whom the Bell Tolls* to wide critical and public acclaim. The novel became an immediate best seller, erasing his somewhat flawed performance in *To Have and Have Not* (1937). During the 1930's Hemingway enjoyed a decade of personal publicity that put most American authors in his shade. These were the years of his African safari which produced *Green Hills of Africa* (1935) and his *Esquire* column (1933-1936). Wherever he went he was news. In 1940 he was divorced by his second wife, Pauline Pfeiffer, and then married Martha Gellhorn. He set fishing records at Bimini in marlin tournaments. He hunted in Wyoming and fished at Key West where he bought a home. In 1937 when the Spanish Civil War broke out, Hemingway went to Spain as a correspondent with a passionate devotion to the Spain of his early years. Not content merely to report the war, he became actively involved with the Loyalist Army in its fight against Franco and the generals. He wrote the script for the propaganda film *The Spanish Earth* (1937) which was shown at the White House at a presidential dinner. The proceeds of the film were used to buy ambulances for the Loyalists. In 1939, with the war a lost cause, Hemingway wrote *For Whom the Bell Tolls* just as World War II was beginning to destroy Europe.

Even more than in *A Farewell to Arms,* Hemingway here has focused the conflict of war on a single man. Like Frederic Henry, Robert Jordan is an American in a European country fighting for a cause that is not his by birth. Frederic, however, just happened to be in Italy when World War I broke out; he had no ideological commitment to the war. Robert Jordan has come to Spain because he believes in the Loyalist cause. Although the Loyalists have communist backing, Jordan is not a communist. He believes in the land and the people, and ultimately this belief costs him his life. Jordan's death is an affirmation. One need only compare it with the earlier novels to see this novel as a clear political statement of what a man must do under pressure.

For Whom the Bell Tolls is a circular novel. It begins with Robert Jordan belly-down on a pine forest in Spain observing a bridge he has been assigned to destroy. At the conclusion, Jordan is once again belly-down against the Spanish earth; this time snow covers the pine needles and he has a broken leg. He is carefully sighting on an enemy officer approaching on horseback, and "he could feel his heart beating against the pine needle floor of the forest." Between the opening and closing paragraphs, two hundred thousand words have passed covering a time period of only seventy hours. At the center of all the action and meditation is the bridge. It is the focal point of the conflict to which the reader and the characters are drawn back again and again.

In what was his longest novel to that point, Hemingway forged a tightly unified plot: a single place, a single action, and a brief time—the old Greek unities. Jordan's military action takes on other epic qualities associated with the Greeks. His sacrifice is not unlike that of Leonidas at the crucial pass, Thermopylae, during the Persian Wars. There, too, heroic action was required to defend an entry point, and there, too, the leader died in an action which proved futile in military terms but became a standard measure of courage and commitment.

Abandoning somewhat the terse, clipped style of his earlier novels, Hemingway makes effective use of flashbacks to delineate the major characters. Earlier central characters seemed to exist without a past. But if Robert Jordan's death was to "diminish mankind," then the reader had to know more about him. This character development takes place almost within suspended time. Jordan and Maria try to condense an entire life into those seventy hours. The reader is never allowed to forget time altogether, for the days move, light changes, meals are eaten, snow falls. Everything moves toward the time when the bridge must be blown, but this time frame is significant only to Jordan and the gipsy group. It has little reference to the rest of the world. Life, love, and death are compressed into those seventy hours, and the novel becomes a compact cycle suspended in time.

The novel has more fully developed characters than the earlier Hemingway novels. In the gipsy camp each person becomes important. Pilar is often cited as one of Hemingway's better female characters, just as Maria is often criticized as being unbelievable. However, Maria's psychological scars are carefully developed. She has been raped by the Fascists, and has seen her parents and village butchered. She is just as mentally unstable as were Brett Ashley and Catherine Barkley. Jordan, too, is a wounded man. He lives with the suicide of his father and the killing of his fellow dynamiter. The love of Jordan and Maria makes each of them whole again.

The bridge is destroyed on schedule, but, through no fault of Jordan's, its destruction is meaningless in military terms. Seen in the context of the military and political absurdities, Jordan's courage and death were wasted. However, the bridge was more important for its effect upon the group. It gave them a purpose and a focal point; it forged them into a unity, a whole. They can take pride in their accomplishment in spite of its cost. Life is ultimately a defeat no matter how it is lived; what gives defeat meaning is the courage that a man is capable of forging in the face of death's certainty. One man's death does diminish the group, for they are involved together. Jordan's loss is balanced by the purpose he has given to the group.

Just as the mountains are no longer a safe place from the Fascists with their airplanes, Hemingway seems to be saying that no man and no place are any longer safe. It is no longer possible to make a separate peace as Frederic Henry did with his war. When fascist violence is loose in the world, a man must take a stand. Jordan does not believe in the communist ideology that supports the Loyalists, but he does believe in the earth and its people. He is essentially the nonpolitical man caught in a political conflict which he cannot avoid. He does the best he can with the weapons available to him.

Michael S. Reynolds

THE FORSYTE SAGA

Type of work: Novel
Author: John Galsworthy (1867-1933)
Type of plot: Social chronicle
Time of plot: 1886-1920
Locale: England
First published: 1906, 1920, 1921

Composed of three novels, this work traces the lives of an upper-middle-class English family. In a saga ranging over several generations, the central character is Soames Forsyte. Wanting wealth, status, love, respectability, and an heir, he is thwarted by his beautiful wife Irene, who loathes him and finally leaves him. He tries to continue, but the shifting values of a younger generation and a younger wife undermine his attempt to build a lasting empire.

The Forsyte Saga—which won for its author the Nobel Prize for literature in 1932—after its initial popularity had subsided, remained in a state of semi-dormance as far as the general reading public was concerned until the work was dramatized in twenty-six episodes on the BBC in 1969. The immense popularity of the series, which eventually reached the entire world, brought forth a burst of enthusiasm for the characters and the story which led to numerous reprintings of the original stories and a plethora of criticism on them.

The three novelettes which make up the trilogy, *A Man of Property, In Chancery,* and *To Let,* are actually sequences in the history of a well-to-do English family, the Forsytes. They are wealthy members of the middle class, conscious of their social position and eager to keep it intact. Their pettiness in matters of decorum was typical of the wealthy bourgeoisie of the times.

Comparing the early sections of the work with the later ones, the reader can see why differences arose among the various members of the Forsyte clan. The older members of the family, such as Uncle Swithin and Old Jolyon, were in different worlds from the youngest Forsytes, such as Fleur and Jolly, both chronologically and psychologically. In the middle stood people of both worlds such as Soames and Winifred. They were products of the tranquil Victorian period, but they had to live through changes in society which made them cling to the old familiar ways and fear acceptance of new ideas and new people. This transition from the old world into the new is one of the major strengths of the novel. Galsworthy draws the reader into the lives of the Forsytes so that he feels that he is actually living through this time of change.

Perhaps the greatest merit of *The Forsyte Saga* is the fact that while its overall aim is one of social criticism, the characters are not sacrificed to this end, but only further illuminate the comments. Though one could say that none of the characters is quite complete—sometimes the reader feels as if he were looking at the action through a screen—the mystery of the main characters, especially Irene and Bosinney, draws the reader deeper into their lives. At times, the novel can become so engrossing that one attempts to "read between the lines" of the story in an effort to discover what the various characters are thinking and feeling. It is particularly difficult at times to do this, however, because Galsworthy very often leaves the reader on the precipice of an insight and then abruptly changes the scene. The widespread appeal of the television series was owed in part to its ability to fill in these missing portions of the novel.

Though the novel is definitely a period piece, it can be appreciated by readers who are not historically or nostalgically minded. The situations of the story and the turns of fortune of the main characters could be appreciated if set in any age. There is a great deal of irony in the story which is timeless as well. The first episode of the story, the festive occasion of a party celebrating the engagement of young June to Philip Bosinney is a case in point. The setting of a large family gathering intended to evaluate the worthiness of a prospective new member of the family is something which would appeal to anyone who had been at such a gathering. The conversation may at times have been uniquely Victorian, but the mood was quite ageless.

The romantic situation which arose among the characters of June, Bosinney, Irene and Soames is another ironic one. While Irene hopes to help June obtain family acceptance for Bosinney, she falls in love with him herself. When Soames tries to gain Irene's love by having a beautiful house built for her, he only succeeds in forcing her to leave him because of her growing love for Bosinney and her disgust for her husband.

Further irony is found in the fact that Irene forces Soames into becoming even more of the distasteful "man of property" than he had been because of her rejection. This hardening of Soames's character is one of the things which makes him more of a tragic character than a bad one.

Of all of the good points of the trilogy, the most lasting is, of course, the social criticism. Galsworthy, despite his episodic approach, has managed to capture the essence of the era which he is describing, even beyond the milieu of the upper middle-class English family of his concern. It was for this aspect of the novel that the author was awarded the Nobel Prize. Galsworthy has managed to show the reader the thought and actions of an age which was a transition from the staid and superficially tranquil Victorian age to the bustling, confused era of the early twentieth century. With a large family as a base, the various marriages and births enable the author to bring in a large variety of events and people.

The mixture of characters enables Galsworthy to present representatives of many personality types: Soames, the lonely businessman; Young Jolyon, the man who renounces his family to pursue a career as an artist; Fleur, the archetypal "flapper" of the post-World War I era. These and others are important not just for their role in the progress of the story, but because their characterizations are representative of the times. It is for these characterizations and for the overall view of the period that this trilogy will retain its position in literature.

Patricia Ann King

FORTITUDE

Type of work: Novel
Author: Hugh Walpole (1884-1941)
Type of plot: Sentimental romance
Time of plot: Late nineteenth century
Locale: England
First published: 1913

Fortitude *is a* Bildüngsroman, *tracing a young man's initiation through experience into maturity. Constantly making mistakes in judgment concerning people and circumstances, Peter Westcott misplaces his affections, sees his son die, and watches his wife desert him. Finally he comes to the recognition that fortitude in the face of life is the only emotion that can give him control over his own destiny.*

Walpole wrote the first page of *Fortitude* in Edinburgh on December 24, 1910, a place and date he came to regard as lucky, because the book enjoyed considerable popularity when it was published in 1913. Thereafter, whenever possible, he had the habit of starting his other novels—thirteen of them—in the same city on Christmas Eve, even if he had to travel some distance for the occasion. The circumstance is worth remembering, for Walpole is best understood as an unabashed sentimentalist.

Although he counted as his close friends such masters of psychological realism as Henry James, Joseph Conrad, Arnold Bennett, and W. Somerset Maugham, among others, Walpole is curiously Victorian rather than modern in his approach to fiction. *Fortitude,* a sentimental romance that imitates the format of realistic "apprenticeship" (or "education") novels successful at the time—Forster's *The Longest Journey* (1907), Wells's *Tono-Bungay* (1908), Bennett's *Clayhanger* (1910), Compton Mackenzie's *Sinister Street* (1911), to mention a few examples—is different from representative books of this type. Subtitled "a True and Faithful Account of the Education of an Adventurer," *Fortitude* is neither true (that is to say, mostly autobiographical), nor is it an authentic "education" novel. To be sure, the early part of the book recalls the author's own miserable childhood; Peter Westcott's public school resembled Walpole's unhappy experiences at Marlow; and two minor characters are based upon real people: Mrs. Launce upon Mrs. Belloc Lowndes, and Henry Galleon upon Henry James. But the novel as a whole is not the story of Walpole's life. Moreover, the education theme is only fitfully developed. Peter, Walpole's protagonist, learns from life a single and rather simplistic lesson, that courage—fortitude—is necessary for success. Walpole states the theme, which is no more than a truism, in the opening sentences of the novel: " 'Tisn't Life that matters! 'Tis the courage you bring to it." As the book progresses, Peter comes to understand the importance of this advice in his education to maturity.

Yet, from the standpoint of a modern reader, it is Peter's lack of maturity, at all stages of his career, that weakens the force of the novel. He is sentimental and naïve to the point of foolishness. He falls hopelessly in love with the self-indulgent Clare Rossiter when their fingers happen to touch. Clare proves to be a cool wife and careless mother; bored with her marriage, she finally runs off with a lover, one of Peter's former schoolboy chums. Right after this scene, Walpole melodramatically writes: "Peter Westcott was dead." But the statement must be taken as hyperbole. Peter is by no means dead; he is only wretched. Because of his obvious immaturity, he continues to be wretched throughout most of the novel. Structurally, the three major crises of the book concern Peter's misery on the occasion of the deaths of his mother, of his son, and of his true friend Nora Monogue. Only with the last tragedy is he able to evidence some maturity. He decides that, because life is difficult, one must face it with courage. If Nora (whom he had once described, with typical infelicity, as "the nicest ugly woman to look at I've ever seen") is able to die with dignity, Peter resolves that he can live with fortitude.

Five years after he published his novel, Walpole wrote in his diary: "*Fortitude* seems to me now an incredibly childish and naïve affair." Yet the novel, in spite of its obvious faults—sentimentality that approaches mawkishness, melodramatic exaggeration, feeble psychology—once charmed readers in 1913 and continues to hold a dwindling but faithful audience. One reason for the survival of *Fortitude* is that the book is entirely sincere. Unlike other twentieth century sentimental romances that are written to produce calculated effects of pathos, Walpole's novel is obviously heartfelt. Peter's hatred of his father, his affection for Stephen Brant (a friendship which is closer to love than is his supposed adoration for Clare), his childhood terrors of punishment are episodes that are handled with fervor. Although Walpole is not, in any sense of the word, a realistic writer, he can simulate with realistic intensity the emotions that are close to his own feelings. Thus the reader, swept along by the author's emotionalism more than by his fiction, may finally be moved by Peter's trials as a child-man, vulnerable and alone, in a man's world.

THE FORTRESS

Type of work: Novel
Author: Hugh Walpole (1884-1941)
Type of plot: Historical chronicle
Time of plot: Nineteenth century
Locale: England
First published: 1932

This novel covers a fifty-year period and is only the third part of a work chronicling two hundred years of English social history. Dealing with restless times which saw the birth of many reform movements, such as the Chartists, the novel's main plot centers on a bitter family feud. The original founders of this rivalry see their children bear the fruits of such enmity: thwarted love and unmerited hatreds.

The Fortress, while presenting important events in the story of the Herries family, is probably the weakest segment of the Herries chronicle. Even though the action is intense in many spots, Walpole seems to feel the need to pad this novel with unnecessary descriptions of scenery and of social gatherings. Probably the strongest aspect of *The Fortress* is its predominant theme of the conflict between good and evil forces. This theme informs all of the novels in the Herries chronicle; hence, the present novel is, in spite of its weaknesses, an important link in the series.

The main impetus for the novel's action is the continuation of the "broken fan" feud begun in the preceding novel, *Judith Paris.* The feud itself is a rather tepid affair, but the events and consequences that spring from it comprise the most intense action. This feud and Walter Herries' egocentric greed for power and possessions lead to the death of Jennifer Herries, leaving Judith Paris to see the battle out to its conclusion, as well as providing the basis for the conflict between John and Uhland Herries, which ends in the tragic death of both. In the context of the events issuing from the feud, the thematic conflict of good versus evil is seen not so much in the senseless, petty indignation shown by one side of a family towards another, but, more importantly, in the abuse of wealth, power, and prestige when in the hands of one like Walter Herries. The Francis Herries side of the family and of the feud represents the moral, humane, positive elements in society. In the same fashion, the conflict between John and Uhland Herries does not merely involve the misfit's wrath toward the rest of the more normal world, but it demonstrates that jealousy, like that of Uhland's, if allowed to be fed and to go unchecked—as Walter allowed it—can lead to tragic consequences.

To complement and strengthen the thematic significance of the Herries feud, Walpole also presents a picture of the growing Chartist movement. By his involvement in the movement, we see Adam Paris as the vehicle by which it is made clear that the type of power and status that Walter seeks represents the same evil oppression of the innocent commoners by the upper classes throughout England. In terms of thematic content and continuity, therefore, *The Fortress,* like other novels in the chronicle, is largely a well-crafted work.

Though the action is intense at various times, the overall narrative pace is impeded by such digressions as "The Summer Fair" chapter and much of "Judith and Adam in London," both in Part I, as well as other instances throughout the novel. These indulgences in the description of scenery or social gatherings are somewhat enlightening as to the milieu of the novel, but otherwise they do little to advance thematic purpose. Furthermore, after the tragic murder-suicide scene in "Skiddaw Forest" (Part III), the novel loses a great deal of its force. The last two hundred pages do introduce Vanessa, the protagonist of the novel to follow, but the rest is largely trivial.

A further weakness in *The Fortress* is that it lacks a paramount character upon whom the author and reader can focus attention. Judith Paris is less a strong protagonist in the second novel than the "rogue" was in the first, but there is even less of a defined protagonist in this third novel. The characterization of Judith Paris is strong, but, with reference to the novel bearing her name, she is little changed. The characterization of John, Adam, and Uhland are fairly complete, but lack the thoroughness that would make any of them central figures. Walpole does go far enough with his major characters to be congratulated on making them memorable, but, as in the case of narrative pace, *The Fortress* suffers in the area of characterization as well.

The Fortress marks another stage in the momentous task Hugh Walpole attempted in his Herries chronicle. In spite of the third novel's weaknesses, much of it is still very much a credit to Walpole's craftsmanship, and an important link in the continuing story of the Herries family.

FORTUNATA AND JACINTA

Type of work: Novel
Author: Benito Pérez Galdós (1845-1920)
Type of plot: Social chronicle
Time of plot: 1869-1875
Locale: Madrid, Spain
First published: 1886-1887

Re-creating the life of shopkeepers and professionals during the restoration of the Bourbon regime to Spain, the novel's plot is structured around the eternal triangle: man, woman, and infidelity. The innocent and loyal wife Jacinta keeps a faithful heart through her husband's affair with a lower-class mistress, Fortunata, and in the end, takes over the care of her husband's illegitimate child. Having lost all of his wife's respect, Juanito Santa Cruz is forced to conclude that his philandering has brought him to an early and empty old age.

Benito Pérez Galdós was born in the Canary Islands, grew up there, and was educated in an English school. Pérez Galdós was the youngest of a bourgeois family, and led the sheltered, placid life of a well-to-do *señorito,* being a stranger to manual labor and money worries. He was also shy and timid, but so studious that he read all the books that came within his grasp.

In 1863, at eighteen years of age, Pérez Galdós sailed to mainland Spain to study law at the University of Madrid. Little is known of his character, for he was reserved and close-mouthed during his student days, even while in the company of carefree companions. He failed his law course through lack of interest, but familiarized himself with the urban life of the metropolitan Spanish capital with its broad, crowded avenues and bustling cafes. An inland city set amidst the high and cold Castilian meseta—a land of austere tints, climatic extremes, and social extremes ranging historically from saintly mystics to Grand Inquisitors—Madrid was the focal point of a formerly great nation approaching national crisis. Spain was about to enter its Second Carlist War (1870-1876), when fanatic, red-bereted Catholic youths from the valleys and mountains of the North fought proletarians and Liberals from the Central-South. Pérez Galdós himself was destined to write one day fierce sketches of fanatic, rural Spain, an area that was devoted to Spain's traditional mystique of Christianity, nationalism, and honor—in Pérez Galdós' eyes a reactionary traditionalism. A nineteenth century Liberal during his youth, Pérez Galdós was convinced during and after his student days that Spain needed socio-scientific progress. He regarded himself as an anti-clerical, and suspected that something was markedly askew with European bourgeois society. It is said that no weakness escaped Pérez Galdós' eye, and he scorned Madrid's upper classes for lack of purpose in life. Pérez Galdós also became increasingly left wing in the course of his political life, but maintained a grudging respect for the hardy, Northern nobility and mountaineers; he realized that Spain's vitality was in its physically tough "common" people. He decried traditionalism, viewing it as ossified and without life-giving force, and preferred a God of love to a wrathful God. He also felt that science and art were not necessarily antagonistic interests.

Pérez Galdós wrote for newspapers after his student days and published his first novel in 1870. Of aristocratic appearance, with pince-nez and expensive apparel, he did not concentrate on writing novels until 1873. He also traveled through Northern Spain in third-class train compartments with his servant and bags, amidst peasants and animals. Pérez Galdós spent the bulk of his life in his comfortable residences in Madrid and the Basque city of Santander, but, as a Canary Islander, never regarded himself as a regionalist or *costumbrista* writer. He became known as "the novelist of Madrid," nevertheless, and lamented the failure of avant-garde novels to gain a toehold in Spain, attributing this failure to bad translations of foreign novels and the incapacity of Spanish novelists to observe the reality that surrounded them. Pérez Galdós also believed that the rise of social psychology was the nineteenth century's key development, and sought to be a social historian and social psychologist as well as a novelist. He gradually formed his own theory of the novel as a social mirror that could create an illusion of life itself. He received much opposition and occasional support from contemporary Catholics and nationalists, although his criticisms of Spain were not considered unpatriotic.

Pérez Galdós is sometimes considered the greatest Spanish novelist after Cervantes. He wrote seventy-five novels, divided into two categories:

1. The National Episodes. These comprise forty-six historical novels drawing lively pictures of Spanish history between the Battle of Trafalgar (1805) and 1874.

2. Contemporary Novels. These constitute Pérez Galdós' most eminent contribution to world literature and include his masterpiece, *Fortunata and Jacinta.* They are all set in Spain, Madrid being the epicenter, and are rich in characterization.

It is said that Pérez Galdós' personal life lacks interest because he devoted himself, monk-like, to writing some four novels a year. He wrote *Doña Perfecta* in about two months in 1876, but took much longer for *Fortunata and Jacinta,* a massive, four-tome novel (1886-1887), which has been compared to *War and Peace.* Deeply soaked in Spanish ambience, *Fortunata and Jacinta* presents a wide-angle view of Madrileño life between 1870 and 1875. It has been compared to the best novels of Balzac, Dickens, and Dostoevski, and is a gallery of national types. Its focus is on the individual rather than the mass; although Pérez Galdós is regarded as the only Spanish novelist of his time who understood the masses. Volume One of *Fortunata and Jacinta* is introductory, giving the setting and introducing Fortunata as an uninhibited and beautiful woman of the people. Jacinta is a passive and upper-class product, but both women are skillfully drawn—Fortunata, for example, as a spontaneous and vital type, sucking a raw egg on the steps of her apartment. Many subsidiary characters are drawn in all four volumes, but environment is advanced as the chief molder of personality. Pérez Galdós believed in Hegel's theory of psychological evolution, hence Fortunata travels through sundry stages in her psychological development. An unmarried man, Pérez Galdós is not considered a good painter of love interest, while traditionalist Spaniards sometimes criticize his work as mundane and inferior to the thematic grandeur of Miguel de Cervantes, who also led a much more active life of struggle, travel, and suffering.

Pérez Galdós did not participate actively in the "Generation of '98," the group of writers who sought to identify the reasons for Spain's decadence. He also lost his eyesight in 1912 and spent his remaining years in genteel poverty. He died in 1920, still considered by many as Spain's most representative nineteenth century novelist. The prestige of *Fortunata and Jacinta* has grown rather than diminished since his death, increasing his stature as one of the more balanced thinkers of his heyday and as a more intellectual novelist than Émile Zola, whose naturalistic theories of fiction were similar to those of Pérez Galdós.

William Freitas

THE FORTUNES OF NIGEL

Type of work: Novel
Author: Sir Walter Scott (1771-1832)
Type of plot: Historical romance
Time of plot: Early seventeenth century
Locale: England
First published: 1822

In this novel peopled with literally dozens of characters, Scott creates one of his finest historical portraits in the person of James I, King of England and Scotland. The involved plot centers around the efforts of Nigel Olifaunt to redeem the threatened loss of his family's estate in Scotland. Despite the attempts of London sophisticates to steal his property and discredit him with the king, Nigel succeeds in his quest.

Since most of Scott's important work was completed in the first twenty-five years of the nineteenth century, he is often considered part of the romantic literary movement. This literary impulse, rebelling against the formalism of the eighteenth century, advocated the "natural" expression of feelings, the value of nature against artifice, and the possibilities of life beyond the strict confines of rationalism. The diverse trends, intellectual and literary, within the romantic movement make the classification of most authors problematic; but there was a coherent movement and it did stand for certain modes of expression and ideas.

Clearly, many of the features of Scott's novels, and of *The Fortunes of Nigel,* can be considered romantic. Although he did not always succeed, he was interested in preserving and presenting the rhythms of the natural speech of his countrymen. His willingness to portray all the ranks of society, the loosely knit structure of the novel, the use of the past, the idealization of women, the intense sentiments—all these can be taken as romantic features in Scott's work in general and in *The Fortunes of Nigel* in particular. At the same time, however, there are clearly rationalist, neoclassic principles and principles of literary realism apparent in *The Fortunes of Nigel.* First, in the "Introductory Epistle" Scott attached to his novel there is a defensive essay (written, significantly, in the form of a dialogue) that supports the didactic views of neoclassic literature.

In fact, Scott's work stands at one of those junctures in the history of literature where various traditions meet, in mixtures of unpredictable and varying quality, only to separate again as historical and literary circumstances change; and it can be said that both historical realists and historical romantics claim him with justification. Alexandre Dumas and James Fenimore Cooper were profoundly influenced by him, but so were Honoré de Balzac and Leo Tolstoy. In short, whatever the value of his novels (and there has been much disagreement on that score), Sir Walter Scott is a seminal figure in literary history. Thus, *The Fortunes of Nigel* can be judged not only as a historical novel but as a work influential in the history of the novel.

Scott's literary production may be divided into four parts: the early poetry, the initial group of the Waverley series, the later group of historical novels, and the novels after his financial collapse in 1826. It was during the middle period of the Waverley novels, and the years immediately following, that Scott did his best work. *The Fortunes of Nigel* falls into the late Waverley period. *The Fortunes of Nigel,* like the early Waverley novels, was highly successful. Although the book was priced out of the reach of the ordinary reader, it nevertheless sold ten thousand copies in the first printing. Of these, Scott's publisher assured him that seven thousand had been sold before 10:30 in the morning of the day they were first issued.

The Fortunes of Nigel, in a manner characteristic of the Waverley series, abounds in realistic detail. Often there is not the excess, and little of the abstraction, typical of the romantic novel. In *The Fortunes of Nigel,* for example, an enormous variety of social strata are presented, the details of the characters' lives revealed, and their connections with other social groupings and classes dramatized. This sort of description is more exemplary of the historical realist than of the historical romantic. What separates *The Fortunes of Nigel* from the earlier Waverley group is the setting, which Scott chose to move from Scotland and the Scottish border to England. Although earlier readers and critics seem to have preferred the original setting, Scott's portrait of James I won him a much expanded audience south of the border.

But if the setting differs, the substance of the novel is similar to Scott's other work. *The Fortunes of Nigel* is about history—the social, personal, and political forces that comprise history. But in addition, the plot in *The Fortunes of Nigel* is less vivid than the scenes of life, of social contrasts and collisions, which appear throughout the book. And since Nigel is exceedingly passive, more observer of the action surrounding him than an active principal in it, he shares the plot's comparative weakness. The weakness of this character, and the incidental nature of the plot, led some contemporary critics of Scott, in reviewing *The Fortunes of Nigel,* to summarize its stereotyped features. In 1822, the *Quarterly Review* remarked: "The poor passive hero is buffeted about in the usual manner, involved, as usual, in the chicaneries of civil process, and exposed to the dangers of a criminal execution, and rewarded by the hand of the heroine, such as she is, and the redemption of the mortgage on the family estate."

It is true, certainly, that Scott repeated himself from novel to novel. He wrote very rapidly, almost never reviewed or rewrote his own work, and was frequently guilty of poor and careless writing. At the same time, however, Scott was a master of describing social and historical clashes. Above all, he was concerned with the process of history—the confrontation between the old and the new. For example, in the opening pages of *The For-*

tunes of Nigel Scott draws a picture of the construction of a new palace by James I. As critics have remarked, the passage is designed to show the position of James I, a monarch poised between feudalism and mercantile capitalism, between Scotland and England, between the past and the present.

Scott was also highly sensitive—in some cases—to the English language and especially to the social and cultural contexts of dialect. In *The Fortunes of Nigel,* Scott was able, for example, to switch fluently from Scots to English. Heriot, who uses formal English in his business transactions, finds himself speaking Scots when another character reminds him of home. The king himself uses an ornate, Latinized form in one social setting and then, for purposes of political image, or personal satisfaction, returns to Scots, or part Scots and part ornamented English.

Careful, polished writing, unhurried composition, and strong major characters have become bywords of modern literary criticism. As a result the reputation of Sir Walter Scott has suffered an eclipse. (Scott himself, in his introduction to *The Fortunes of Nigel,* shows an awareness of such questions —raised even in his own day—and tries to defend himself and his method of composition.) Other critics, however, as the Marxist George Lukàcs, argue that Scott was a great novelist. The introduction of history into the writing of novels, the vivid portrayal of social types, and the depiction of profound social and historical conflict, outweighs the stylistic and compositional faults of the novels for Lukàcs. And indeed, in addition to Lukàcs' comments, Scott's undeniable influence on writers such as Dumas, Cooper, Balzac, Tolstoy only underscore his impact not only on his contemporaries but also on the history of fiction.

Howard Lee Hertz

THE FORTUNES OF RICHARD MAHONY

Type of work: Novel
Author: Henry Handel Richardson (Ethel Richardson Robertson, 1870-1946)
Type of plot: Social chronicle
Time of plot: Nineteenth century
Locale: Australia
First published: 1917, 1925, 1929

Uncompromisingly realistic, this novel is one of the most distinguished works of Australian fiction. Richard Mahony, a doctor, starts a humble practice and accumulates wealth through wise financial investments. Returning to England, he and his wife Mary are snubbed as Australian peasants. Going back home, they find Richard's fortune stolen by his fraudulent broker. This reversal and the death of his second child break Mahony; he dies insane. Mary's strength and fidelity through these trials make the novel a tribute to her patient and enduring spirit.

The publication of *Ultima Thule* in 1929 brought the first widespread popular success to Henry Handel Richardson, who had been known before that date to a small but dedicated group of admirers since her first novel, *Maurice Guest* (1908). In 1929 *Australia Felix* and *The Way Home,* by then out of print, were quickly revived, and the trilogy came out under the title of *The Fortunes of Richard Mahony.*

Set in Australia in the period of the gold rush and based upon the experiences of her own parents, Richardson's trilogy is a brilliant and unsentimental treatment of the plight of a sensitive intellectual in the harsh environment of the Australian frontier. In contrast to many romanticized tales of adventure in the gold mines or the bush, Richardson wanted to deal with the problem of those who failed, who were unable to adapt to the strange hard world. Richard Mahony's tragedy is a personal, not a social one. There is no indictment of society as the cause for his decline. Those who possessed vigor, resourcefulness, and a large measure of common sense could survive and even prosper in the new land. But Mahony is doomed ultimately by his own nature, the inherent instability which keeps him always unsatisfied. As an educated Englishman, a doctor turned storekeeper, he is uncomfortable and inefficient. He turns to medical practice on Mary's urging and succeeds as long as he relies upon her judgment. But restlessness seizes him and he insists upon returning to England. Here the irony of the title *The Way Home* is revealed: the colonial becomes alienated from both the old and the new environments. Neither his native Ireland nor the England of his former life is now truly home for Mahony; both climate and people seem cramped and cold. But neither can Australia be a home for him as it becomes for Mary. On their return, his sense of alienation is exacerbated by their financial ruin, and his restlessness keeps them moving from place to place in a tragic attempt to find security. In *Ultima Thule,* the harrowing account of Mahony's deterioration into mental illness and of Mary's heroic devotion to him until his death forms a powerful conclusion to this superb trilogy.

THE FORTY DAYS OF MUSA DAGH

Type of work: Novel
Author: Franz Werfel (1890-1945)
Type of plot: Historical romance
Time of plot: 1915
Locale: Near Antioch, Syria
First published: 1934

Part of the unsung drama of Turkey's attempt to "eliminate" its Armenian population, this narration follows the efforts of the Armenian patriot, Gabriel Bagradian to defend the stronghold of Musa Dagh. Losing his son and estranging his wife in the defense, he ultimately succeeds against all odds by arranging the rescue of many of the defenders. Staying behind, Gabriel returns for a last look at his son's grave and is felled by a Turkish bullet.

The Forty Days of Musa Dagh marked Franz Werfel's greatest popular success as a storyteller. From an episode of actual history—the defense of Musa Dagh in 1915, which is celebrated by the Armenians as a major anniversary—Franz Werfel has taken the heroic drama of a little band of people struggling against great odds to preserve their lives and their heritage and has made a universal story of courage, love, and sacrifice. Werfel was much concerned with the relationship between Judaism and Christianity, and although he repeatedly declared himself a Jew, Christian thought is traceable throughout this work and others. In a time characterized by the onrushing threat of Nazism, he presented in this book a concept of piety as a vital element of the human soul that has nothing to do with organized religion.

In this novel, historical incident is given complete reality; the analysis and portrayal of mass action are remarkable. *The Forty Days of Musa Dagh* is both an exciting story of an astonishing military operation and a detailed record of one of history's worst crimes. It is a tale of human heroism, with overtones of Old Testament character, and a subtle piece of political propaganda. The handling of individual characters and their private relationships is the weakest part of this otherwise impressive book. Gabriel is successful as a type, a symbol, a man between two worlds, but not as an individual with private emotions and concerns. Psychology has been sacrificed to historical pageantry and moral vision.

The sudden, irrational destruction brought on by race hatred is portrayed by Werfel in all of its frustrating madness and horror. The victims find it hard to believe in the danger because the pretext seems so illogical, but the facts sweep over them. Hatred, Werfel makes clear, is not rational. With heartbreaking power, he dramatizes this story of the suffering caused by hatred. At times, the narrative turns into impassioned rhetoric, but the horror of the tale seems to demand it. *The Forty Days of Musa Dagh* is an important human document and a reminder of the dangers of racial prejudice, as well as a gripping, well-crafted novel.

FRAMLEY PARSONAGE

Type of work: Novel
Author: Anthony Trollope (1815-1882)
Type of plot: Domestic romance
Time of plot: 1850's
Locale: "Barsetshire" and London
First published: 1861

A novel lacking either villains or heroes, Framley Parsonage *ironically and fondly records the "goings-on" of the English middle class. Young Mark Robarts is innocently taken in by the impecunious scoundrel Sowerby. He signs a note for Sowerby which ruins the young man's chances for any romantic or financial success. He honorably takes full responsibility for his mistake, and his fortunes are happily reversed at the novel's conclusion.*

This novel, the fourth of the Barsetshire series, was brought out in the newly launched *Cornhill* magazine, edited by Thackeray, and was an immense popular success. Trollope's focus is on the social milieu and on the moral choices which confront his characters. Two clergymen are juxtaposed in the novel; both are good men, but one is too easily lured by worldly ambition and the other is too proud to accept help. Mark Robarts learns painfully that he is essentially too naïve to cope with the accomplished chicanery of people like Sowerby and to engage in the political sophistries of the circle surrounding the Duke of Omnium. He ultimately retreats to the security of Lady Lufton's patronage and the knowledge that his brush with the vultures of the larger world enables him to appreciate the felicities of his position at Framley Court. It is Trollope's particular genius that this resolution is made to seem fulfilling rather than defeatist. The Reverend Josiah Crawley, on the other hand, is unworldly to the point of excess. His selfless dedication to the ministry represents a type of clergyman which Trollope sees as becoming regrettably obsolete in the increasingly materialistic society of the nineteenth century; nevertheless, Crawley's asceticism, and his refusal to seek worldly advancement or even to accept it when offered, brings needless suffering to his poverty stricken family.

The women in the novel similary confront moral choices. Lucy Robarts is no meek ingenue, but a young lady of spirit who loves young Lord Lufton but is willing to give up both love and social position rather than be accused by his mother of social climbing. Griselda Grantly, on the other hand, has no such scruples. She coldly sets about using her great beauty and imposing manner to capture Lord Dumbello, and succeeds despite the absence of real affection between them. Lady Lufton represents the kind of mixed character that is Trollope's special accomplishment: she is both domineering and kind hearted, both arrogant and willing at last to bend. She most nearly illustrates Trollope's thesis, that those are happiest who can adapt to social change.

FRANKENSTEIN

Type of work: Novel
Author: Mary Godwin Shelley (1797-1851)
Type of plot: Gothic romance
Time of plot: Eighteenth century
Locale: Europe
First published: 1817

Victor Frankenstein, a brilliant inventor, actually succeeds in creating life. His creature, animate but lacking all human graces, is alone and scorned by mankind. Bitterly he accuses his creator and threatens to murder at will unless Victor creates a mate for him. Victor does, but in a moment of conscience, he destroys her. The monster avenges himself by strangling Victor's bride. Following the creature in an attempt to destroy him, Victor dies of exposure at the North Pole. The story hints in part at the possible dangers inherent in the pursuit of pure science; it also portrays the injustice of a society which persecutes such outcasts as Victor's creature.

The best remembered novel of "Gothic Terror," *Frankenstein* superficially resembles Ann Radcliffe's *The Mysteries of Udolpho* (1794), Matthew Gregory Lewis' *The Monk* (1796), and Charles Robert Maturin's *Melmoth the Wanderer* (1820). Like these romances of suggested or actual physical horror, Mary Shelley's novel is steeped in sentimental melancholy. Unlike most Gothic novels, however, *Frankenstein: or, The Modern Prometheus* is at least partially philosophical and offers a scientific rather than supernatural explanation for the horror.

Indeed, for its serious ideas the novel more closely resembles *St. Leon* (1799) by Mary Shelley's father, William Godwin. As an illustration of the humanitarian philosophy of Jean Jacques Rousseau, *Frankenstein* shows the destructive results of undeveloped affection. The Creature (who is at the time of his composition a "monster" only to the fearful and ignorant) craves but is denied ordinary human tenderness. Rejected as a man, he becomes a vengeful monster. Although he is given vital existence by science, he is never fully alive. Victor Frankenstein's science (or rather pseudo-science of vitalism, a belief in the "vital spark") is unable to produce a creature capable of attracting love. Instead, his scientific genius creates death—a theme that appears rarely in nineteenth century literature, but is a major one in the twentieth century.

Readers familiar with the motion picture adaptations of *Frankenstein* popular during the 1930's—or, indeed, with the more accurate version produced by Christopher Isherwood and Don Bachardy for television in the 1970's—are likely to be surprised when they come upon Mary Shelley's novel. Not only is the book considerably richer in details, fuller in its development of minor characters, and more complicated in plot structure than later adaptations and parodies; it also treats the Creature from a significantly different point of view. Contrary to the popular stereotypes of the Frankenstein monster, he is articulate and, at least in the beginning, quite sympathetic. His revenge, though excessive, is motivated. From a modern reader's assessment, he is a monster too sentimental to be wholly frightening. Yet *Frankenstein,* for all its appeal to modern readers, represents the culmination of a tradition of nineteenth century Gothic horror on the one hand, and sentimentalism on the other. Given a different philosophical orientation, much of that horror is bound to be misunderstood. What is remarkable, to be sure, is that so much survives.

FRATERNITY

Type of work: Novel
Author: John Galsworthy (1867-1933)
Type of plot: Social criticism
Time of plot: Early twentieth century
Locale: London
First published: 1909

In Fraternity, *Galsworthy exposes the complacency of the well-to-do intellectuals and their insensitivity to the plight of the lower classes. The plot centers on a couple who have long since agreed not to live as man and wife yet still manage to undergo the agonies of jealousy and infidelity. This situation is brought about by the introduction of an attractive, lower-class girl into their household. The girl is totally innocent, but is nonetheless a victim of her complacently superior employers who, despite their airs, are clearly unenlightened.*

Fraternity, the third of a four-volume series satirizing well-to-do society—in the words of the author, "my long four volume image of England's upper crust"—takes for its subject the cultured aesthetic intellectuals of London. They are filled with idealism, but their self-consciousness and complacency prevent them from acting in any substantial manner.

The novel's earlier, rejected title, *Shadows,* and the later title that became affixed to it are both appropriate, for Galsworthy presents two levels of society, the artistic intellectuals and the wretched slum-dwellers, each of which are "shadows" of the other, as revealed throughout the novel by the shifting point of view. At the same time, the upper-class Dallison family is going through the superficial motions of conceptualizing a "fraternity" of all men, much like the supposed vision in Mr. Stone's apocalyptic "Book of Universal Brotherhood."

All of the Dallisons' altruistic notions remain in the abstract, however, for the family represents "a section of society . . . who speculated on ideas," and their self-consciousness and fidelity to convention paralyze them from taking any affirmative action. While most of the family flatter themselves by simply thinking about equality in society, yet shrinking in fear from the thought that it might ever happen, three characters make a move forward but suffer for their transgression.

Hilary Dallison's attraction to and sympathy for Ivy Barton overtly manifests itself as a gesture to lift her out of her poor existence. Beyond this, though, Hilary is also paradoxically attracted by her sexuality while repulsed with fear at the risk to his own status in actually bringing about any union of the two levels of society. In response to this dilemma, he relies upon the expediency of a monetary gift to her and flees from the impending necessity to make a decision and commit himself to action. And just as fear motivates Hilary's behavior, so too does it defeat Thyme's attempt at unification with the lower strata of society. When she goes among them, she feels the strength and security of her station drain off and flow into them, and she fears the transformation that creates the "unreality of her intruding presence." As for the elder Mr. Stone, finally, fear was not his defeat as it was for the other two; rather, his over-zealous commitment to the idea of a universal brotherhood and his agonized efforts to put into concrete terms the essence and elements of that concept drove him to defeat in madness, perhaps because we are meant to feel that the consummation of his plan is an impossibility.

While *Fraternity* most clearly exposes the moral paralysis among the cultured upper classes, the slum-dwellers are also paralyzed by their immersion in dreams, never to be fulfilled, and resignation to a poverty stricken existence. Joshua Creed typifies the character of the slum-dweller; while he ekes out a living selling newspapers in the slum, his thoughts are directed to the far off, more attractive Mayfair. His one expectation is death and his only ambition to be "respectable," both during his life and at the end of it.

Galsworthy supplies no answers or solutions to the dilemma he has presented in *Fraternity*. It seems that his main purpose was to show, through the Dallisons' frustrations, complacency, sensitivity, and self-consciousness, how the intellectual segment of the country had been paralyzed by too many years of money and ease; they are unable to act in any decisive manner for the real benefit of anyone, or even to resolve their own moral questions and dilemmas.

FRIAR BACON AND FRIAR BUNGAY

Type of work: Drama
Author: Robert Greene (1558-1592)
Type of plot: Pseudo-historical chronicle
Time of plot: Thirteenth century
Locale: England
First presented: c. 1589

At least three main plots unconvincingly interweave in what is actually a series of dramatic scenes. In one, a humble girl inspires the love of both Edward, the English prince, and Lacy, the Earl of Lincoln. After many complications, she marries Lacy. Another plot has three scientist-magicians pitted against one another in a competition to determine which is the most skillful. In the meanwhile, Friar Bacon, one of the magicians, is attempting to build magically a brass wall around England. Because of the inattention of his servant, the project fails.

One of the earliest and most famous prototypes of the "Bohemian" artist who lives dissolutely, works furiously, and burns out early, Robert Greene was characteristically Elizabethan, with many contrasting elements composing his character. A scholar and a vagabond, a sinner and a puritan, he wrote in many forms, from the famous essays on conny-catching to graceful songs and sonnets, and to rough-and-ready dramas such as *Friar Bacon and Friar Bungay*. By temperament and inclination, he was a realist, but he wrote excellent romances, and in his dramas realism and romanticism are intermingled.

Friar Bacon and Friar Bungay bears a relationship in certain passages to Christopher Marlowe's *Doctor Faustus*. It is likely that it was written in order to compete with the popularity of Marlowe's play by showing an English sorcerer who defeats his German rival. Greene also was catering in this play to the widespread interest in magic and witchcraft during the last years of Elizabeth's reign. There is little doubt that the play was written—or pieced together—to appeal to specific interests and popular tastes. The emphasis on the establishment of peace in Queen Elizabeth's reign in Bacon's last speech, for example, was probably written after the defeat of the Spanish Armada in 1588. The play was performed at a special appearance of the troop before the queen, and it was revived many times; but because of its loose structure scenes frequently were added and subtracted according to the mood of the moment.

It is possible that *Friar Bacon and Friar Bungay* had a direct influence on Shakespeare's work; certainly, the character of Ralph Simnell suggests Falstaff, as Prince Edward suggests Prince Hal. Greene used every popular device of stagecraft he could force into the work: the appeal of court comedy, the popularity of historical characters, and even the appeal of morality plays that hung on from previous decades. Along with these elements, the rags-to-riches theme and the suggestion of forbidden scholarship guaranteed the play's success.

FRITHIOF'S SAGA

Type of work: Poem
Author: Esaias Tegnér (1782-1846)
Type of plot: Heroic epic
Time of plot: Eleventh century
Locale: Scandinavia
First published: 1825

A tale from ancient Scandinavian myth is here retold in an epic narrative poem of twenty-four cantos. Frithiof, in love with Ingeborg, is not acceptable to her two brothers, Helge and Halfdan. After much conflict, Frithiof wins Ingeborg, but only after killing one brother in battle and defeating the other.

Esaias Tegnér's long narrative poem displays an odd sort of virtuosity: the poem remains faithful to its ancestor, *Frithiof the Bold,* in theme and narrative detail, yet it is made up of a curious blend of Scandinavian and English images and rhetorical devices, in twenty-four different meters.

Frithiof's estranged love for Ingeborg bears resemblance to the legend of Tristan and Iseult. Through forces beyond his control, Frithiof's beloved marries another, King Hring. Yet, the hero gallantly respects the marriage, and the king to whom his beloved is married, by maintaining the proper courtly distance. However, *Frithiof's Saga* does not end tragically. Through Hring's benevolence, Frithiof and Ingeborg are reunited and Frithiof satisfies his vengeance of pride against the brother-kings. The magnificent Reconciliation Canto, rendered by Tegnér in blank verse, evokes the grandeur of Norse mythology and the theme of atonement for the "Wolf-in-Sanctuary."

Frithiof's Saga provided Tegnér with the opportunity to make a pastiche of images and rhetorical devices. His rendering of each canto in a different meter demonstrates both virtuosity and preoccupation with the surfaces of poetry. Virtuosity for its own sake is no virtue, and it is regrettable that Tegnér did not choose to render his poem in a less obtrusive and more unified manner, for he elevates style at the expense of content. Tegnér's use of imagery raises further concerns. For example, we find the Norse "Wolf-in-Sanctuary" amid Elizabethan roses and the lilies, nightingale, and vanished dreams of the English Romantics. One scholar, C. D. Locock, found two or three obvious plagiarisms from Shakespeare, and perhaps another from Shelley. It may be, however, that the Swedish poet, whose work "The Children of the Lord's Supper" was translated by Longfellow, wished to align his narrative poem with the English literary tradition.

THE FROGS

Type of work: Drama
Author: Aristophanes (c. 448-385 B.C.)
Type of plot: Humorous satire
Time of plot: Fifth century B.C.
Locale: Underworld
First presented: 405 B.C.

This vigorous and still humorous satire tells of the visit of Bacchus to the underworld. He wishes to go so that he might talk to the great playwrights of the past. After several adventures, he arrives in Pluto's realm to find Euripides and Aeschylus fighting over who is the better artist. Bacchus offers to judge, ultimately choosing Aeschylus.

The Frogs is deservedly one of the best-known plays of Aristophanes. It took the first prize for comedy on its initial presentation in 405 B.C., and it still retains much of its freshness and exuberance today. As a depiction of the foibles and follies of men and gods alike, the play is great satirical fun. But the high point of the comedy is the witty debate between Aeschylus and Euripides as to which of them produced the better tragedies. This *agon,* or contest, is the most humorous piece of literary criticism ever written. Yet to fully comprehend this play we need some knowledge of Aristophanes' opinions, the times in which he lived, the Athenian crisis at the end of the Peloponnesian War, and an understanding of Aeschylus and Euripides.

The play starts with an absurdity, for Bacchus braves the terrors of the Underworld to bring Euripides back to life. On this conceit Aristophanes builds a farcical sequence of situations that defies reason or probability. It is important here that Euripides' last play, *The Bacchae,* was produced shortly before Aristophanes wrote *The Frogs*. Euripides portrayed Bacchus (Dionysus) as a powerful, mysterious, fearless, and vengeful being. The joke, of course, is that Aristophanes shows him as a weak, pedestrian, cowardly, and pacific god who is obviously flattered by Euripides and wants him brought back to life to continue the praise. Thus, the humor of the first half of *The Frogs* is devoted to exposing Bacchus as a fraud, and by implication Euripides himself. *The Bacchae* was awarded first prize, posthumously; and the chorus of frogs in Aristophanes' comedy represents the popular clamor that greeted Euripides' play. Bacchus, incidentally, was both the god of wine and the god of the theater.

Having thoroughly deflated Bacchus, Aristophanes brings Euripides and Aeschylus on stage to engage in comic debate. Euripides is shown as an upstart in Hades. Recently dead, he tries to wrest the chair of honor from Aeschylus. Obviously, Aristophanes regarded Euripides as a base-born upstart in life as well, for the tragedian appeared as a farcical character in *The Acharnians* and *The Thesmophoriazusae* too, and was the butt of numerous jokes in other plays. The antagonism was largely due to Aristophanes' snobbery and conservatism, for the comic dramatist came from landed gentry.

Aristophanes thought that Euripides was partly responsible for the decline in Athenian politics and morality. There is no question that Euripides used tragedy to turn a light on current social issues and effect changes. This is the heart of the matter: the comic poet propagandized for conservatism, while the tragic poet urged reform. It is hard to grasp the importance of drama in Athenian life. Today we are plagued with distractions, but public oratory and the theater were the only media then—the only means of conveying propaganda to large audiences. We tend to dismiss Aristophanes' comments against Euripides as either pure fun or the prejudices of a clever conservative, but in actuality they were part of a battle to control public opinion.

Some of the charges Aristophanes makes against Euripides in *The Frogs* could be leveled at himself as well. Impiety, near-colloquial verse, sordid passions, and characters who reasoned sophistically without any sincerity are all a part of his comic art. What Euripides had done in essence was to lessen the difference between tragedy and comedy; but what Aristophanes could not forgive was that Euripides tended to be a left-wing social reformer, tearing away at established institutions.

The truth is that Athenian politics and life did degenerate during Euripides' long career, but it would be as foolish to blame it on him as on Aristophanes. The real villains were the demagogues who initiated the Peloponnesian War and kept it going for twenty-seven years.

The Frogs can be read as a literary, a social, or a political tract by a very amusing dramatist. On the literary level, Euripides pokes fun at Aeschylus' bombast and theatricality, while Aeschylus ridicules Euripides' commonness of diction. When Aeschylus' lines of poetry are weighed against those of Euripides in the funniest scene in the play, Euripides is shown quite literally to be a lightweight talent.

Socially, Aeschylus is made to represent the old, heroic, patriotic virtues of Athens, whereas Euripides stands for the degenerate contemporary society. Aristophanes hints that the latter comes of lower-class people, and states openly that his audience in Hades consists of felons, who love his sophistries.

But it is on the political plane that Aristophanes really indicts him, suggesting that the demagogues learned their twisting logic from Euripides. In fact, the contest between Aeschylus and Euripides is finally settled on the basis of which offers the best advice politically, and Aeschylus wins hands down, to be taken back to earth by Bacchus to teach the Athenians virtue. Aristophanes had no intention of playing fair. To him Euripides represented everything corrupt in Athenian society.

However, we should remember that *The Frogs* was written in a time of crisis, when it was clear to many that Athens had better make peace with Sparta or be ruled by her. The Peloponnesian War had one year to go. In the middle of the play Aristophanes makes a direct political plea to the audience, trying to set Athens straight in a last-ditch effort to avoid the inevitable defeat. The wonder is that, with such bias and in such a time, *The Frogs* is one of the most delightful comedies of any age.

James Weigel, Jr.

THE FRUIT OF THE TREE

Type of work: Novel
Author: Edith Wharton (1862-1937)
Type of plot: Social criticism
Time of plot: Late nineteenth century
Locale: The United States
First published: 1907

Wharton centers her theme in the character of Amherst, who wants to use his upper-class intelligence and sophistication to alleviate the problems of the lower classes. He is, of course, misunderstood on all sides. Through such a figure, Wharton is able to dissect a frivolous aristocracy where women are pampered and men sheltered from the realities of life.

The Fruit of the Tree, Edith Wharton's only novel of reform, is concerned with the fundamental differences, financial as well as social, between the lower and upper classes, and with the squalid factory conditions of the late 1800's. The focus of the novel is the cloth mill and the posture each character assumes concerning it. The issue unites and subsequently divides John and Bessy Amherst as they struggle to cope with their opposing ideals.

Wharton portrays both of these characters as unaware of their blind spots. John Amherst's social commitment is maintained at the expense of his other relationships and is untempered by sensitivity to his wife's needs. She, in turn, is whimsical and bored by the continuous unpleasant intrusion of the factory's problems into their life; sacrifice is unknown to her. At the same time, for John to give in to Bessy's lifestyle would necessitate for him the end to a meaningful existence. Wharton succeeds in setting these characters in the most elemental and crucial way, each against the other.

The third major character, Justine, is Bessy's friend and comforter and Amherst's confessor. Although no longer having family or wealth, she has the genteel manner of the rich plus the sensitivity and humility developed by her commitment to nursing. Those attributes which divide Bessy and John Amherst are united in Justine. She is a person who is aware of the power of money, but who does not assume as John does, that it can mend the problems of society or that it will create a humanistic environment. Edith Wharton has created in Justine a rounded human being who participates sensitively in the human drama. Justine and John share what Bessy does not comprehend, a sense of commitment.

In this novel Wharton has treated two of the major issues of her age: the problem of class and the effects of industrialization. She precedes Theodore Dreiser in the novel of reform, and she concerns herself with those issues typically avoided by her class.

THE FUNERAL

Type of work: Drama
Author: Sir Richard Steele (1672-1729)
Type of plot: Comedy of manners
Time of plot: Early eighteenth century
Locale: London
First presented: 1701

The play's subtitle, "Grief à la Mode," refers to a young hypocritical widow who is only too delighted at the demise of her wealthy, elderly husband. Her scheming goes so far as to cause the husband's son to be disinherited. For all its sincere social criticism and serious moral overtones, the play is a comedy of manners and is written with a tone of innocent freshness which sets it apart from the atmosphere of intrigue prevalent in similar Restoration dramas.

The Funeral opens on a scene with all the hallmarks of high Restoration comedy: two gentlemen discourse with an undertaker on the economics of grief, while the playwright applies numerous satirical needles to the balloons of hypocrisy and social pretension. But the courtier audience of the reign of Charles II would not have been satisfied for long with Steele's wit or his dramatic concerns. This is post-Jeremy Collier drama; written only twenty-five years after Etherege's *Man of Mode,* it seems closer in spirit to the good-natured comedy of Goldsmith, well over half a century later.

To be sure, many features of the older comedy remain. As Steele points out in his preface, his purpose is to level ridicule "at a set of people who live in impatient hopes to see us out of the world." There is considerable witty exposure of the topsy-turvy values of wives, undertakers, and lawyers, whose fortunes and happiness are made by the deaths of their spouses or clients. Some of the Restoration types strut pompously across the stage, such as the female fop, Mademoiselle Epingle, who affects a French accent to make herself more genteel; and the battle of the sexes continues with the women, as usual, winning through their wiles and "affections" over the "brutal power" of the men.

But the future cofounder (with Joseph Addison) of the *Tatler* and the *Spectator* has new concerns; he has already begun his attempt to refine the manners and sensibilities of his audiences. His heroes are not licentious rakes, but men of the highest honor and generosity. Ensign Campley, in a characteristic gesture, unobtrusively slips his straitened friend Lord Hardy three hundred pounds through Trim, his witty but good-natured and honest servant. The loyal and wise old steward Trusty works day and night for the best interests of his master, finally extricating him from a hopeless marriage. While the villains retreat in confusion, truth and virtue trumph at the conclusion in a paroxysm of sentiment that would have reduced a Restoration audience to gales of laughter: "O my children—oh, oh! These passions are too strong for my old frame—oh the sweet torture! My son, my son! I shall expire in the too mighty pleasure! my boy!" Even the sprightly heroine, Lady Harriot, who begins the play with a temperament as contrary as Congreve's Millamant, very early abandons her feminine haughtiness and affectations after a straight talking-to by her lover.

In addition to the elements of sentiment and sensibilty, there is a new, earnest note of morality and social consciousness. When Campley asks a soldier why he has been treated so badly by superiors, the soldier replies, "I was found guilty of being poor." The idle life of a gentleman is roundly condemned; and in the final scene, Lord Brumpton delivers a Polonius-like lecture (in verse) to his son on the duties and responsibilities of leadership for a "worthy lord." Finally, there is a timely note of seriousness at the close, as the men prepare to go off to war and to die, if necessary. Much comedy of this period ends with a song; it is indicative of Steele's dual concerns that he ends with two songs: the first, a conventional marriage hymn, the second, a martial air, urging the patriotic British on "to glorious death, or comely wounds."

THE GAMBLER

Type of work: Novel
Author: Fyodor Mikhailovich Dostoevski (1821-1881)
Type of plot: Psychological realism
Time of plot: Mid-nineteenth century
Locale: German watering places
First published: 1866

Set against the backdrop of a fashionable German spa, Dostoevski authoritatively describes the fatal attractions of gambling. At first using gambling merely as a means of impressing his beloved, Alexey finally loses heart and soul to the gaming compulsion. Besides Alexey, many other characters, from professional adventurers to venerable retired generals, fall victim to this passion.

Fyodor Dostoevski was, in his personal life, every bit as erratic, volatile, irresponsible, and contradictory as any of his fictional characters. He created most of his works in the face of extreme pressures and adversities which were, more often than not, the product of his own actions. *The Gambler,* a novel he probably never wanted to write, resulted from such a self-created pressure, a situation as pathetic and comic as the book itself.

In 1865, in severe financial difficulties (a frequent condition), Dostoevski signed a contract with Stellovsky, an unscrupulous publisher, in which he agreed to furnish a new novel by November 1, 1866, or else grant Stellovsky the right to publish all of his works royalty-free for nine years. As of October 1, Dostoevski had nothing on paper. In desperation he hired a stenography student and began to dictate. It was one of the most important decisions of his life. Prodded by the shy, awed, but firm and sensible young lady, Anna Grigorievna Snitkina, Dostoevski completed the novel in less than a month and salvaged his financial future. He also acquired, in Anna, a second wife who put an efficiency and order into his life that considerably eased his last years and freed him to concentrate on the writing of his greatest works.

The intense pressure under which *The Gambler* was composed is no doubt one reason why, except for *Notes from the House of the Dead,* it is the most directly personal, even autobiographical, of his fictions. The primary motifs in *The Gambler* are frustrated love and compulsive gambling, two conditions that dominated Dostoevski's life in the years immediately preceding its writing. The book's narrator, Alexey Ivanovitch, resembles the Dostoevski of that period in many ways and Polina Alexandrovna is a thinly disguised recreation of Polina Suslova (note the same names), a student half his age, whom he met in 1862 while on his first European visit. It was on this same tour that he also began to gamble. Thus, Alexey's experiences in Roulettenburg are loosely based on a confused and traumatic trip the novelist took with Polina Suslova in 1863. Consequently, the passions of love and gambling were inextricably bound in Dostoevski's mind and, in *The Gambler,* he renders them in all of their complexity.

But these motifs do not actually become central until quite late in the book. The first two-thirds of the novelette concentrates on the serio-comic machinations of the General's party as they vie with one another and with old "Granny" Antonida Tarasevitcheva. Except for the narrator and Polina, the characters, even the colorful old lady, are one-dimensional, almost caricatures. The General is a sophisticated Russian quasi-aristocrat who, cut off from his native roots, is the easy, pathetic victim of all West European temptations. De Grieux is the stock French adventurer: stylish, cultivated, shallow, and corrupt. The Englishman, Astley, is likewise a national type: stolid, laconic, honest, and dull. Mlle. Blanche is the French seductress: beautiful, coaxing, playful, free with sex and other people's money, but essentially selfish and shrewd (it is she who finally ends up with Granny's money). Even Antonida is a stereotype: the headstrong, obstinate, outspoken, outrageous old woman.

However, if individually the characters are little more than clichés, collectively they provoke a colorful sequence of comic situations that make the first two-thirds of the novelette exciting and amusing. Then, as Dostoevski comes to focus the book more intensely on Alexey and Polina, they retreat into the background, but continue to provide a grotesque comic counterpoint to the more serious antics of the principals.

The association of Alexey's love for Polina with his addiction to gambling is made early in the novel when she asks him to play roulette for her. Thus, from the beginning, Polina shows a dependence on Alexey, but, at that point in the novel, there is little he can do to help her. One of the most important, if subtle, movements in the book is the way Alexey gradually ascends from the position of a disdained inferior to that of a sought-after superior who gains powers over the others—the General, de Grieux, and finally Polina—and then rapidly loses it all.

Ostensibly, his power derives initially from his role as Granny's "adviser" and then from the fortune he wins gambling. But the real source of it probably lies in his lack of identity and commitment; because he has little interest in appearances and social postures, he has a great advantage over the others. As they strive to protect and enhance their social, financial, and romantic positions in the group, Alexey moves around freely and unobtrusively, capitalizing on his associates' failures and weaknesses. However, because he becomes progressively absorbed by his two passions, Polina and gambling, he cannot translate his advantages into permanent victory, but must ultimately destroy himself pursuing these addictions.

Polina is a fascinating mixture of *femme fatale* and passionate victim. She loves Alexey yet she feels a need to demean him. When he seriously expresses a willingness to kill himself for her, she reduces it to the comic by suggesting that he insult a German Baron. She mocks his vow to "kill her," but is excited by it. She fears being in his power, but comes to him in her hour of need. In the novel's enigmatic climax, when she offers herself to him, her behavior is erratic, volatile, almost hysterical; she rapidly alternates between abjectly demeaning herself, stridently justifying her behavior, belittling and berating Alexey, and proclaiming her lasting love for him. And then, after spending the night with him, she flings the money into his face and flees.

Alexey is perhaps even more puzzling. He both loves and hates Polina. He abjectly submits to her every whim, yet he also wants dominance—perhaps both at the same time. And his feelings for her are inevitably bound up with his gambling compulsions. At the point when she offers herself to him, he feels the need to rush out to the gaming table. As he feverishly plays, he forgets about her. After he wins, he hurries back and empties his pockets before her almost as an integral part of the lovemaking ritual. But, when she leaves him, he casually enters into an unexpected affair with Mlle. Blanche and gives her free reign to dissipate his modest fortune, which she quickly does. Many critics have seen this sudden shift in his character as unlikely and, after considering the pressures on the author, have dismissed it as a quick and easy resolution to the story.

But, if we remember Dostoevski's association of Alexey's compulsive gambling with his love for Polina, the ending makes definite psychological sense. Rationally, the hero's love for Polina has as its object the consummation of the affair; the gambling is a way of quickly procuring the money necessary to support the romance. Alexey is not, however, essentially a rational creature, but one driven by needs and emotions that he does not fully comprehend. It is the intensity of the experience of pursuing Polina, not the physical actuality of the woman, that really enraptures Alexey and, likewise, it is the excitement and danger of gambling, and not the monetary outcome, that captivates him. It is even possible that, given his taste for self-humiliation, Alexey gambles to lose rather than to win. Having "won" Polina, he casts money at her to provoke her rejection of him; having won the fortune, he subconsciously wants it taken from him.

Thus, in *The Gambler,* Dostoevski not only explores frustrated love and compulsive gambling, but he also analyzes the dynamics of psychological self-destruction, creating in Alexey a character type that was to become central in his most powerful novels.

Keith Neilson

THE GARDEN

Type of work: Novel
Author: L. A. G. Strong (1896-1958)
Type of plot: Impressionistic realism
Time of plot: Early twentieth century
Locale: Ireland
First published: 1931

Traveling from staid England to spend each summer in the more careless company of his Irish grandparents and cousins, Strong's autobiographical novel is first of all a reminiscence of the delightful childhood world of a young boy. In addition, there is a subtle contrast between social backgrounds which makes a quiet comment on the temperamental differences brought about by race and culture.

The Garden is a tender tale of the development of a boy, Dermot, into a young man. During most of his holidays, from a time he can barely remember to his last one in 1914, the English lad visits his grandparents and cousins in Ireland, "the dearest and loveliest place in the world," where you can see for "one hundred and ten miles." Eventually he grows up, and he and his cousin go off to die in the war. The story is beautifully told. L. A. G. Strong displays the narrative qualities of a gifted raconteur; his style is crisp and expressive and his humor is gentle and without malice as he unfolds the life of Dermot. The author obviously has great empathy with his characters; he is sometimes sentimental, but the book is saved by the simplicity of its development. The novel is rich in dialogue, and most of his characterizations are clear.

One of the most important decisions Dermot must make while growing up is whether to choose the matter-of-fact religion of his mother or the simple, demonstrative faith of his cousins. The latter faith makes life easier to live; it impresses him so much that he appreciates the sense of it, even while his intellect tells him that it has not been fully explained. Dermot loves the ritual of his grandparents' church during his earlier childhood, and the stained glass window with Christ walking on the water is one of his delights. His favorite scripture, "Heaviness may endure for the night; but joy cometh in the morning" is his epitaph.

In the epilogue, after the deaths of Dermot and his cousin, Dermot's sister tells their cousin, Eileen, that she likes to think of them together, happy and laughing at her confusion about the faith of which her aunt said, "seems easy enough to me. It's the living of it that's hard."

THE GARDENER'S DOG

Type of work: Drama
Author: Lope de Vega (Lope Félix de Vega Carpio, 1562-1635)
Type of plot: Comedy of manners
Time of plot: Late sixteenth century
Locale: Naples
First presented: c. 1615

Based on the old tale of the dog who would not eat his food, yet selfishly refused to let any other dog have it, this play tells of Diana, a countess who thwarts the romance between her secretary Teodoro and a lady-in-waiting, although she cares nothing about Teodoro. The technical perfection of this comedy of manners is especially to be appreciated in view of Lope de Vega's prolific career of eight hundred plays.

The Gardener's Dog has often been called Shakespearean in the style and manner of its serio-comic treatment of love. And indeed this play is, perhaps, Lope de Vega's *A Midsummer Night's Dream.* A dreamlike quality suffuses the action; before our very eyes, love turns into hate and back into love, affection turns to scorn, indifference turns to desire, sweet heroines turn vindictive, courtly lovers turn would-be murderers, lovers change partners, and confusion reigns supreme, as both audience and characters wonder: what happens next?

But if the treatment of love is Shakespearean, the treatment of illusion versus reality is close to Pirandello. Does Teodoro become a *de facto* count because everyone believes him to be one? The situation is an interesting reversal from Pirandello's Henry IV, who in his madness believes he is a king, while everyone else, knowing him for what he really is, simply humors his belief. In Lope's play, only Teodoro, Tristan, and Diana know the facts of the matter, while the rest of the world believes it is paying court to a true count. The practical result in both cases is of course the same. Lope is thereby suggesting, perhaps, that "nobility" is nothing more than a social convention, and has no other basis than that of people agreeing to honor its credentials, no matter how spurious they are.

This proposition may be self-evident to today's democratically-reared audiences, but in early seventeenth century Spain, it was an assumption that struck at the heart of the social order, though admittedly, in not quite so revolutionary a manner as Lope's *The Sheep Well.* And in fact, Teodoro's instant pedigree may have been less a social statement than simply a convenient dramatic device to bring Diana, the Countess of Belflor, and her secretary together at last. For centuries writers of comedy and romance have solved the problem of love between high-born and low-born by having the low-born hero or heroine turn out to be actually high-born (having been, like the baby in Tristan's story, stolen in childhood by pirates, or else, inadvertently mixed up with another baby). Lope's dramatic resolution is an interesting variation of this theme; nevertheless, he seems to accept the underlying premise that high-born and low-born must not defy convention and marry despite the prohibitions.

But for all the intriguing questions of appearance-reality that are raised, the main focus of this play is on the nature of love. Just what is this universal yet incomprehensible phenomenon? Love causes one to mount as if to heaven, Marcella sighs, in the first act. But in the second, she calls love, "god of envy, god of hate!" How does love originate? How is it affected by jealousy? How does it cause one to behave toward the loved one? How is it affected by absence? What happens when it is frustrated by power or by social convention? How does it affect a person's natural temperament? These and many other questions are dramatized as the play progresses.

The air of questioning and confusion that pervades the work is set at the very beginning of the first act. (The second line of the play, "Who's there?" echoes the first line of *Hamlet,* a play also suffused with doubt and ambiguity of motive.) Roused in the middle of the night by a mysterious noise, Diana and her ladies-in-waiting dash in and out and scurry around the stage, with only shadows and feathers as solid evidence of intruders. Was the disturbance a dream? We have indeed seen two figures on some unknown mission at the outset, but they disappeared after breathlessly delivering only four short lines.

As the action progresses, more questions press for answers. Is it possible that Diana had no inclination at all toward Teodoro until she learned that he loved and was loved by Marcella? How much of Teodoro's love for Diana is based on true passion, and how much on his greed for wealth and station? If the latter is his predominant motivation, then how much of our sympathy does he deserve? Teodoro complains at great length of the extremities to which Diana's passions run, and of her cruelty to him; and yet his own treatment of Marcella is crass and heartless in the extreme. He adores her at the beginning, instantly shifts his love to Diana when the countess suggests her interest in him, comes whining back to his first love when Diana's attitude seems to change, and then unfeelingly spurns Marcella a second time when the wind of love once more blows his way. When, at the conclusion, Diana expresses some concern that her former secretary may have some lingering feelings for Marcella, the "count" loftily assures her, "Noblemen know no maidservants."

To help him develop his ideas on the range of love, Lope uses an unconventional dramatic device: a series of sonnets interspersed through the action, and spoken by either Diana, Teodoro, or Marcella. Each sonnet develops a different aspect of love: Diana's first sonnet deals with the passion, the jealousy, and frustration of love; Teodoro's deals with the nature of new love, and with the conflicting feelings of affection, ambition, conscience, and cynicism it arouses; Marcella's deals with the constancy and permanency of love, despite all barriers and reverses. Other sonnets treat love's violence and cruelty, its cautions and terrors, and its black moments of despair. Counter-pointed to these sonnets are other set speeches on love. In the Marquis Riccardo's speech to Diana, for instance, we hear the conventional high-flown rhetoric of courtly love, as spendid as it is artificial: "Did I command gold . . . or the frozen tears of heaven . . . or mines of oriental gems whose gleam has ploughed a furrow through the heaving hillocks of the sun, I would lay them at your feet, and delve beyond the confines of the light. . . . " And earlier in the play, Teodoro reveals that his love for Marcella is based on an idealized view of woman: "pure serenely crystallized, transparent like glass." Tristan, who often acts like Lear's fool in throwing the cold water of common sense on these romantic illusions, responds with a more realistic picture of women that emphasizes their defects instead of their glories. (Like many a fool, Tristan is resourceful, shrewd, and basically decent—he rebukes Teodoro for his treatment of Marcella—though he ultimately lacks the nobility that elevates his master at the end.)

In its overall conception, *The Gardener's Dog* is a highly mature example of dramatic art. Unlike the majority of contemporary plays, including Lope's own, it does not rely on villainous antagonists for its plot complications, but rather on the vagaries of love and the effects of this ennobling and exasperating passion. All of the important characters are drawn with a high degree of sympathy, though the playwright is not afraid to look unflinchingly at their defects. And as long as the focus remains on love, the play remains a work of art. Unfortunately, the quality begins to decline markedly in the third and final act when character development begins to slacken and the standard mechanics of plot contrivance take over: the erstwhile suitors of Diana devise a plot to have Teodoro murdered, unknowingly choosing his lackey Tristan as the assassin (thereby creating a running gag for the remainder of the act), and Tristan, in turn, devises a highly successful plot to make Count Lodovico believe that Tristan is his long-lost son. But it would be charitable to forgive the prolific Lope for the absurdities of his dramatic resolution; for seldom, on the stage, have the many faces of love been presented so subtly and at the same time, so entertainingly.

Laurence Behrens

GARGANTUA AND PANTAGRUEL

Type of work: Mock-heroic chronicle
Author: François Rabelais (1490?-1553)
Type of plot: Burlesque romance
Time of plot: Renaissance
Locale: France
First published: Begun 1533; first complete edition, 1567

The Lives, Heroic Deeds and Sayings of Gargantua and His Son Pantagruel *is a vast mock-heroic panorama about an amiable dynasty of giants who are prodigious eaters and drinkers, gay and earthy. Discursive and monumental, the work demonstrates the theme that the real purpose of life is to expand the soul by exploring the sources of varied experience.*

Partly because France's greatest comic prose-writer was a legend even in his own lifetime, most of the facts of Rabelais' life remain hazy. A monk, doctor of medicine, and writer, Rabelais transferred from the Franciscan to the Benedictine order with the Pope's express permission, because the latter order was both more tolerant and more scholarly. The year 1532 found him in Lyons, at that time the intellectual center of France, where he published his first creative work, Book II (*Pantagruel*). As a satirist and humanist, Rabelais labored between the two religious extremes of Roman Catholicism and Genevan Protestantism; he had the mixed blessings of being attacked, alike, by Scaliger, St. Francis de Sales, and Calvin. All of them warned against his heretical impiety; he was, first and last, an iconoclast. Yet, like Erasmus, he attempted to steer a middle course—the attitude that led Thomas More to his death in the same period. This may have made Rabelais unpopular with his more radical contemporaries, such as Martin Luther and Ignatius Loyola; but it also made him one of the most durable, most human, comic writers of his century—and of all time.

In Rabelais the spirit of comedy blends with the spirit of epic to produce a novel work without parallel or close precedent. The chronicles are universally inclusive, expressing the Renaissance ambition to explore and chart all realms of human experience and thought. And the mood of the narrator matches the scope of the narration. Rabelais, as Alcofibras, attributes his infinite exuberance to his literal and symbolic inebriation, which he invites his readers to share. His curiosity, realism, joy, and unpredictability are all things to all men—as long as the reader, whoever he may be, is willing to be intoxicated by a distillation of strong wit and language. As a genre, the chronicles may be compared to the "institute" so popular during the Renaissance (such as Machiavelli's *The Prince,* Castiglione's *The Courtier,* Ascham's *The Scholemaster*); they have also been considered a parody of medieval adventure romances. But, in the end, Rabelais' work beggars generic typology. Its narrative includes, history, fable, myth, drama, lyric, comedy, burlesque, novel, and epic; just as its sources include sculpture, jurisprudence, pedagogy, architecture, painting, medicine, physics, mathematics, astronomy, chemistry, theology, religion, music, aeronautics, agriculture, botany, athletics, and psychological counseling. All these elements are thrown together, with characteristic flair and mad abandon, into a savory stew.

It is a consistency of flavor, of authorial mood, that holds together this diverse and variegated work. That flavor is not one of thought, for Rabelais is no great thinker. As his translator Jacques LeClerq says, "his ideas are primitive, fundamental and eternal in their simplicity." The unifying idea is the philosophy of Pantagruelism: "Do As Thou Wilt." The world of Pantagruel is a world in which no restrictions on sensual or intellectual exploration can be tolerated; excessive discipline is regarded as evil and inhuman. In true epicurean fashion, Rabelais has no patience for inhibitions; man lives for too brief a time to allow himself the luxury of denial. The Abbey of Thélème is thematic center of the work, with its credo that instinct forms the only valid basis for morality and social structure. Rabelais ignores the dangers of the anarchy this credo implies; he is talking about the mind, not the body politic. And the dullest thing imaginable is the unimaginative, conforming mind. His satirical pen is lifted against all who affect *freedom* of any kind in any fashion: against the hypocrites (Book II, Chapter 34), militarists (I.26-49), abusers of justice (III.39-43), pedants (II.18-20), and medieval scholastics (II.5-8).

The reader of these gigantic chronicles, then, must not expect a plot. Anything so regular is anathema to Pantagruelism. Nor are the characters themselves the focus of the author's art; they are, in fact, largely indistinguishable. One of the funniest things in the book is that they are also indistinguishably large; Pantagruel's mouth, described in one of the finest chapters in European literature (II.32), is, at times, large enough to contain kingdoms and mountain ranges, at other times, no larger than a dovecote. The exception is the normal-size man, Panurge. He is an unforgettable character who makes so strong an impression, even on the author, that he cannot be forgotten. The third, fourth, and fifth books, in fact, are based on his adventures—just as Shakespeare wrote *The Merry Wives of Windsor* to exploit the beloved character of Falstaff. Panurge is the heroic companion of Pantagruel, in the best epic tradition; he also has the cunning of Ulysses, the drunken mirth of Falstaff, the roguishness of Jack Wilton and Tyl Ulenspiegel (his numerous pockets filled with innumerable tricks), the cynical but light-hearted opportunism of Chaucer's Pardoner, the magic powers of Shakespeare's Puck or Ariel. He is the wise fool of Erasmus and King Lear, and a Socratic gadfly who bursts the pretensions and illusions of all he encounters. "How Panurge Non-plussed the Englishman Who Argued by Signs" (II.19) is a literary tour-de-force, concentrating into one vivid, raucous chapter the comic spirit forever to be known as rabelaisian. Important in other ways are "How Pantagruel Met a Limousin Who Spoke Spurious French" (II.6), for its attack on unfounded affectation; and Gargantua's letter to Pantagruel, expressing the entire range of Renaissance learning, juxtaposed with the chapter introducing Panurge, who personifies Renaissance wit.

Rabelais' chaotically inventive style, filled with puns, word-plays, and synonyms, as well as with neologisms of his own creation, makes him one of the most difficult of all writers to translate accurately. His language reflects the rich variety of sixteenth century French and he was the first to observe invariable rules in the writing of French prose—called, by Pasquier, "the father of our idiom." His syntax is flexible, supple, expansive, sparkling with vitality and the harmony of an ebullient character, complex and original. Rabelais does for French vocabulary what Chaucer did for English, fortifying it with ecclectically selected terms of the soil, mill, tavern, and market, as well as scholarly terms and phrases gleaned from nearly all languages. As his comic theme reflects the universal as well as the particular, Rabelais' language combines the provincial with the popular—in a stew fit for the mouths of giants. A gargantuan appetite has nothing to do with gluttony.

Kenneth John Atchity

THE GAUCHO: MARTIN FIERRO

Type of work: Poem
Author: José Hernández (1834-1886)
Type of plot: Adventure romance
Time of plot: Nineteenth century
Locale: Argentina
First published: Part the First, 1872
Part the Second, 1879

The poem's central character, Martín Fierro, has become an Argentinian legend. Similar to the American frontiersman and individualist, he is unjustly persecuted in turn by a rapacious government and the savage Indians. Finally reunited with sons he thought dead, he gives them this advice: "Be true to your friends, obey the law and do not cheat. If a woman wins your heart, you should treat her well and be true." The group parts, each to lead his own life.

Martín Fierro is the poetic epic of the gaucho race that settled the rich Argentine pampa. An "ocean of land," pancake flat, the pampa has fertile brown soil and is perhaps the only area on earth where one could yoke oxen to a plow and slice a furrow for 600 miles without turning up a stone. Before the Spaniards arrived it was peopled by warlike, nomadic Indians. Its deep grass supported birds and ostriches, its only tree was the rugged ombú, later sung about by Argentine poets, including the author of *Martín Fierro*. Cattle and horses introduced by the first Spaniards increased at an amazing rate around the port town of Buenos Aires, on the ocean's edge, and a cowboy type known as gaucho began to ride the plains near the town. Slowly, the first gauchos pushed inland, rolling back the Indians, thus starting what was to be their historic role of settling Argentina, "the silvery land" by the Plato (Silver) River. Gauchos also settled the "purple land" of Uruguay and the extensive Brazilian pampa of Rio Grande do Sul, but in Argentina they built a nation.

Usually of Spanish or mestizo blood, the gaucho lived on horseback in his sea of grass. He ate only meat, sometimes killing a steer simply to eat its tongue or to have a seat. He was nervous, restless, and almost always in motion. His weapons were a huge knife and the "bolas" that he twirled to capture steers or ostriches. His games were rough and on horseback; he was tough, ignorant, and despised city folk. He drank "Paraguay Tea," or yerba mate, and danced the tango. His literature was the so-called gaucho poetry, redolent of the pampa, that was sung around campfires at night by illiterate minstrels known as payadores. The payador was simply a medieval European minstrel, of Spanish origin, transplanted to the New World, his songs comprising a new, regional literature describing the various types of gaucho, such as the outlaw, the tracker, the tamer of horses, the lover, or the storyteller. This literary genre was to tinge all Argentine literature centuries later, even the drama, and from it came *Martín Fierro*.

A dichotomized Argentina grew during three centuries of colonialism under Spain. White bread was eaten only in "the Port," Buenos Aires, where an urban class dressed in European style and had more contact with Europe than with the semi-civilized gaucho of their own country's interior. After Argentina became independent early in the nineteenth century, an army of gauchos under their leader, Juan Manuel de Rosas, captured Buenos Aires. To symbolize the capture of the city by the country, Rosas' gauchos tied their horses in front of the Pink House, Argentina's presidential palace. For twenty-three years Rosas dominated Buenos Aires, persecuting the intellectual class and forcing everyone to wear red, his favorite color. One young intellectual, Domingo Sarmiento, went into exile and wrote a book titled "Facundo," or "Civilisation or Barbarism," in which the gaucho was criticized as Argentina's barbaric drawback. The title of "Facundo," today considered Argentina's literary masterpiece, was taken from one Facundo Quiroga, a gaucho tyrant who ruled La Rioja Province at the head of a gaucho army flying a black death's-head flag of skull and crossbones. Sarmiento included a blueprint, however, for a new Argentina, in which the gaucho would be tamed or replaced by European immigrants, the pampa fenced, railroads built, wheat planted, and higher bred livestock introduced. Rosas finally fell in 1852, and Sarmiento and others lived to carry out his blueprint for a modernized Argentina.

José Hernández was born on an Argentine estancia, or large ranch, in Rosas' day. He grew up among gauchos and Indians and loved their free way of life. He knew the gaucho thoroughly—his speech, folklore, psychology, heart, and soul. He also knew the pampa—its beauty, silence, climate, grass, sunrises, and sunsets. As the day of the gaucho began to wane, and Hernández realized that the anti-gaucho intellectuals were creating a new Argentina, he decided to tell the dying gaucho's story, to portray his manly virtues and his once-happy way of life.

Martín Fierro tells, thus, of the gaucho's passing. This took place after the 1850's when the last wild Indian tribes were being pushed up against the setting sun and the Andes foothills. And at the same time the gaucho was being supplanted by progress in the form of barbed wire, railroads, immigrants,, wheat, and the herds of purebred cattle and sheep and thoroughbred horses that have made Argentina famous. In telling the tragic story of *Martín Fierro* and his lost family and lost home, the poem includes many epic themes—the fight against injustice, against governmental power over individuals, man's struggle against nature, the yearning for lost freedom and lost loved ones during bitter years of exile in strange country. Present also are such themes as a temporary flight to the land of a hated enemy and the rescue of a maiden in distress. Drenched with the pampa's earthiness, *Martín Fierro* gives pictures of the land and sky, grass, birds, and creatures of the pampa, as well as of the gaucho himself as symbolized by the redoubtable but bigoted Martín. The poem gives us the life cycle of a race, and is as representative of Argentina as, say, the Mississippi is of the United States. The poetic style is brisk and clear, even though the language is replete with gaucho vocabulary and flavor of speech. Martín Fierro's character projects itself over the poem: we feel with him for the Job-like loss of his home and family, and all the lonely bitterness of his cruel military years fighting the raiding Indian hordes on the far frontier. We feel with him when he finally returns home to find his familiar little cabin abandoned, his wife and children gone, and only one familiar figure, his old cat prowling unhappily around the well. *Martín Fierro* holds one's interest throughout most of its stanzas, and is today at the summit of Argentine gaucho literature. It has thus attracted attention in Spanish America, Brazil, and Spain, where the noted Miguel de Unamuno often read it aloud to his classes in the halls of the Spanish Oxford, Salamanca University.

Gauchos no longer roam the unfenced pampa's grassy sea. They are often only peons on a mechanized estancia, but still have nostalgic yearnings for the past. At night, around camp fires, they often produce old copies of *Martín Fierro,* bound in calfskin. And the gauchos speak of Martín himself as if he still lives, and might, at any moment, flip open the cowhide door flap and walk in to sip yerba mate and sing his sorrows.

William Freitas

THE "GENIUS"

Type of work: Novel
Author: Theodore Dreiser (1871-1945)
Type of plot: Naturalism
Time of plot: 1889-1914
Locale: Alexandria, Illinois, Chicago, and New York
First published: 1915

Eugene Witla is the "genius," a painter obsessed with the search for beauty. Falling in love with many women, he finds that none of the affairs gives him peace or an enduring sense of value. Thus the artist is no better off than other human beings; he is just as unable to control his own destiny. Besides disappointing romances, Witla's search for beauty is further corrupted by his financial success in the advertising business. He gives up painting. Having failed in his search, he incorrigibly sets about projecting romantic dreams onto the life of his daughter Angela.

The "Genius" is generally conceded to be the weakest of Theodore Dreiser's major novels, but critical opinion differs over whether it is a magnificent failure or simply a big, bad look. The usual reason for its relative impotence is that Dreiser was too subjectively involved with the material to objectify his feelings and clarify his ideas about his artistic protagonist, Eugene Witla. Although all of Dreiser's writings contain many transcriptions of direct experience, *The "Genius"* chronicles traumatic events that were recent personal history. Witla's career as an artist closely parallels Dreiser's own—impoverished youth, odd jobs, modest artistic success, nervous breakdown, restoration, financial success, monetary and professional collapse, and, finally, serious artistic endeavors. More important, in terms of Dreiser's emotional identification with the story, is the fact that Witla's marriage to Angela Blue and all of its consequent disappointments, frustrations, hostilities, and psychic damage is a thinly disguised rendering of his own drawn out, agonized marriage to Sallie White.

But if the extreme subjectivity of *The "Genius"* hurts it artistically, it also makes the book a vital document to anyone interested in Dreiser's life and works. The novel is basically about the tensions between three fundamental elements: the urge to artistic creation, the unbridled sexual drive, and the corrupting influence of material success. For all of the complexity, inconsistency, redundancy, and confusion of *The "Genius,"* at the center—and the thing that gives the novel its redeeming strength—is Eugene Witla's prolonged and agonized attempt to reconcile these three diverse, powerful, contending forces.

In the opening segment of the book, Eugene is introduced to creative activity and sexuality at almost the same time. His artistic impulses, like Dreiser's, are to portray "life" as realistically and graphically as possible.

His vision of woman, however, is idealistic: the perfect woman is beautiful, sensual, and "always eighteen." Thus, his sexual impulses are intensified by the fact that he seeks an impossibility and, becoming increasingly frustrated, is driven from woman to woman in an effort to find that ideal—which gets progressively farther away as he ages.

This is made more complicated and painful by his foolish marriage to Angela Blue, the one woman for whom he feels, at best, a lukewarm sexual attraction. Initially, Angela represents America's small-town, conservative, hypocritical morality, especially in sexual matters. Her narrowness, provinciality, possessiveness, and domineering attitude toward Eugene frustrate both his artistic development and his personal fulfillment. Later, as he begins to drift to other women, Angela becomes fiercely aggressive sexually in an attempt to keep the marriage going. Then, in the novel's most absurd hypothesis, Dreiser ascribes Eugene's nervous breakdown to this "excessive" sexual activity provoked by Angela. She is damned if she doesn't and damned if she does.

Angela is also blamed for Eugene's turn from artistic creativity to crass commercialism. At her prompting, Witla puts his painting aside and becomes an advertising executive. Thus, a curious alliance of sex, materialism, and middle class morality combine to suppress temporarily Eugene's creativity. And his return to serious painting results not from any repudiation of materialism, but is the consequence, once again, of his rampant sexual adventuring. Witla's affair with eighteen-year-old Suzanne Dale, the daughter of a rich and powerful socialite, costs him his job, his fortune, and his social standing and forces him back to the easel where he quickly—much too quickly—regains all of his creative powers.

Thus Dreiser demonstrates that even the strong-willed and talented are ultimately buffeted by forces over which they have little control. In spite of his remarkable abilities and powerful drive, Eugene Witla's major decisions—to be an artist, to marry, to become a businessman, to return to painting—are all made for him by outside circumstances and internal impulses over which he has little conscious control. At the end of the book there are hopeful hints—his painting, his "forgiveness" of Angela, his feelings for his daughter—but the final image is that of an aged and unreconciled artist who feels neither personal satisfaction, nor social identification, nor even a conviction that his own life and art have real value and meaning.

THE GENTLEMAN DANCING MASTER

Type of work: Drama
Author: William Wycherley (1640-1716)
Type of plot: Satiric comedy
Time of plot: Seventeenth century
Locale: London
First presented: 1672

This play has as its comic premise a young suitor who gulls the father of his beloved by pretending to be a dancing master. In such a role, the father allows them to meet, inasmuch as this "teacher" is preparing his daughter with the graces to attract a suitable mate. Wycherley's style is in the manner of Molière and through him harks back to the commedia dell'arte*, with its criticism of affectation and its elaboration of such stereotypes as the gulled father, the saucy maid, the languorous lovers, and similar farcical types.*

To the modern reader Restoration comedies sometimes seem like snowflakes: each one is different, but viewed from a distance, they are difficult to tell apart. There are a limited and recurring number of types to act their parts (the witty heroine, the dashing hero, the Frenchified fop, and the obstinate parent), and a limited and recurring number of dramatic jobs to be done (expose affectation and folly, distinguish true love from lust or powerplays, and restore the natural order of things). The trick is to devise and expertly complicate fresh situations through which these conventional elements are driven to their inevitable conclusion. In the fiercely competitive world of Restoration theater, wit and novelty are the chief qualities which distinguish the efforts of a master craftsman like Wycherley from those of his competitors.

The Gentleman Dancing Master is not one of Wycherley's best plays, but it has sufficient wit and novelty to be worth reading today. Its strength lies not in its strained plot, at once hectic and thin, but in Wycherley's sharp characterizations, especially of the ludicrously affected Monsieur de Paris, and the sprightly and resourceful Hippolita who, despite her mask of innocence and simplicity, knows exactly what she wants and how she intends to get it. Paris and Don Diego (James Formal) form a perfect dramatic opposition: the precious pseudo-Frenchman and the stiff, gullible pseudo-Spaniard; and the scene in which Formal forces Paris to strip off his French dress and speech, and to substitute the Spanish *golilia* (collar-band) for his cravat makes for splendid theater.

The saucy servant, Prue, in the tradition of *commedia* saucy servants, is a sparkling example of her kind. Prue's speech on the "unfortunate conditions of us poor chambermaids," who must "shift for our mistresses, and not for ourselves," is strangely affecting (for a cynical Restoration comedy); and her subsequent clumsy attempt to lure Paris into her bed by telling him of an erotic dream she has supposedly had about him is both comic and pathetic.

Wycherley plays up the standard Restoration character virtues: wit, youth, good looks, self-knowledge, and plain dealing; but those who come off best, ultimately, are those who can most successfully manipulate others, with or without their knowledge and approval. Hippolita is the most admirable in this regard. She manipulates her fiancé, Paris, into procuring Gerrard for her in the first place and then into validating the dancing-master scheme, thereby allowing the courtship to progress. She manipulates Gerrard into becoming her husband after having manipulated him into revealing his true love (his willingness to take her without her dowry). Finally, she manipulates her father into believing the ruse, and even into leaving the couple his estate, in order to avoid looking like a fool. Don Diego himself manipulates his sister, Mrs. Caution, into conceding his own perspicacity and her gullibility (when in fact, she has seen through Gerrard from the beginning). And Mistress Flirt, the prostitute, manipulates Paris into agreeing to a highly advantageous financial settlement.

As in many other Restoration comedies, it is the women—Hippolita, Mrs. Flirt, Mrs. Caution—who are the wisest, strongest, and most resourceful characters; the men spend most of their time and energy trying to keep up with them. True love and devotion may be the ostensible ideal, but the play's real center of gravity lies in the caustic cynicism through which the playwright views the relationships between people, the follies that undo them, and the motives and strategies that impel them.

THE GENTLEMAN USHER

Type of work: Drama
Author: George Chapman (c. 1559-1634)
Type of plot: Romantic comedy
Time of plot: Seventeenth century
Locale: Italy
First presented: c. 1602

This comedy verges on tragedy, dealing as it does with a father and son enamored of the same woman. The intrigue of his son discovered by the father, he orders his son hunted down. Finally, seeing the tragic consequences of his actions, the Duke forgives all, and his son, though seriously wounded, recovers to marry his beloved. The play contains a wide range of effectively drawn characters; among them Bassiolo, the self-satisfied and gullible usher to the Count, is especially fine.

The Gentleman Usher is in many ways typical of the comedies of Renaissance England; it includes such stock characters from Italian comedy as the young lovers, the old man who impedes the consummation of young love, the old woman who perversely impells it, and the scheming servant who aids in its details.

The play combines romance with comic satire in the story of Vincentio and Margaret. This ideal relationship is threatened from the start by the boy's own father, Alphonso, who desires the girl for his own wife. As Duke, Alphonso has nearly absolute sway over every person in the play, thus giving occasion for satire upon cruel despotism as practiced by a man who does not deserve his position of power. The Duke is a lecher, desiring Margaret, evidently, solely for purposes of erotic pleasure; in this he contrasts with his son who proves the completeness of his love by continuing to love Margaret even after she has deformed her beautiful face. As an illustration of what Vincentio and Margaret's marriage presumably will become, Chapman presents the happy marriage of Strozza and Cynanche. Cynanche epitomizes the ideal Elizabethan wife, whose virtues are summarized in Strozza's eloquent appraisal (IV, iii, 2-37).

Once he has resigned himself to living with the extreme pain of the arrow in his side, Strozza displays the ability of the virtuous man to rise above the pains (and lusts) of the body and to exist upon a more spiritual plane. It is this ability which allows him his supernatural knowledge and his power, in the final scene, to unmask Medice and to dare the Duke's wrath by forcefully and logically revealing the evil in the Duke's lust. In doing so, he aids the young lovers in their movement toward marriage, the end of all romantic comedies.

GERMINAL

Type of work: Novel
Author: Ėmile Zola (1840-1902)
Type of plot: Naturalism
Time of plot: Nineteenth century
Locale: France
First published: 1885

One of the first novels dealing with the conflict between capital and labor, the book is still a work of fiction and not a manifesto. The events of the novel are based on an actual strike which occurred in France in 1884. Most notable about the work is Zola's ability to portray mob scenes; the emotions and movements of masses of people are so successfully rendered that the characters become believable results of the events which mold them.

Germinal depicts in a clear and concise fashion Zola's social and philosophical orientations. Zola's unquestionable sympathies for the French working class are as evident in this work as they are in his other volumes. In *Germinal,* as elsewhere, Zola championed a social group that stood estranged from political power and untouched by modern French social legislation. In fact, the work was a favorite with literate socialists of the age. It is ironic that France, which had ushered the modern age into European life with the Revolution of 1789, by the mid-nineteenth century had less social legislation than any major country in Europe. Zola was appalled by this condition and made it his life's work to bring to the attention of the French public the misery and squalor of its newest and most rapidly growing class of citizenry. Despite the grim living conditions and sordid lives described in *Germinal,* Zola remained optimistic about the prospects for reform. The title gives evidence of his sanguine nature; germinal means rebirth or germination.

Germinal, then, reveals Zola's social prejudices; it also documents his literary and intellectual methods. The novel is representative of the degree to which the scientific method and Social Darwinism influenced all areas of European thought in the late nineteenth century. Zola wrote this novel and all others as if he were conducting an experiment in a test tube. Zola tossed his characters like so many chemicals into a beaker and observed the results and changes each element underwent. Zola maintained that his novels were the social "lab reports" of his scientific observations.

In his methodology, then, Zola indicates his debt to the scientific community by incorporating the conclusions of Darwin. Darwin's biological theories are unmistakably present in all of the author's work. Zola describes all his characters in animal terms, and he further emphasizes the biological nature of man by stressing the genetically inherited qualities of each character; environment assumes immense importance as a socially determining factor.

GERMINIE LACERTEUX

Type of work: Novel
Authors: Edmond (1822-1896) and Jules (1830-1870) de Goncourt
Type of plot: Naturalism
Time of plot: Nineteenth century
Locale: Paris
First published: 1865

According to Zola, an admirer of the Goncourt brothers, the study of the lower classes in works of fiction began with this novel. Germinie is a servant girl. Left an orphan at four, her life is a series of disappointments, since neither her love affairs nor other strong attachments such as she has for her young niece are ever requited. The story is presented with clinical detatchment. Germinie's joys and pains are painstakingly analyzed in realistic detail.

The fourth of six novels written together by the Goncourt brothers, *Germinie Lacerteux* had its genesis in a discovery made by the Goncourts after the death of a servant who had been with them for a quarter-century. As revealed in *Le Journal des Goncourt* (1887-1896), after the servant's funeral they learned that for years she had lived two lives. Seemingly trustworthy and devoted to them in their home, she had debauched herself while away from it; she had been a drunkard and had stolen from them. Learning the facts of her miserable life, they decided upon a fictional representation of it which would nevertheless be faithful to these facts. They announced in a Preface to *Germinie Lacerteux*: "This is a true novel. . . . This is a clinical study of Love." The story was written, they said, not to shock or insult the public but to show that the so-called "lower orders" in society were entitled to a place in fiction.

Germinie's unhappy story, although often unpleasant and for some readers even nauseating at times, is saved by the Goncourts' style which has been called both "impressionistic" and "écriture artiste." They are not mere reporters but writers who transform through their art the sordid reality of Germinie's obsessive love for Jupillon. Her compulsive seeking out of the calculating, cruel man who brings her so much misery would be called masochistic today. The Goncourts were, however, in their sympathetic, penetrating, and convincing study of Germinie's sexual abnormality, several years ahead of the German novelist Leopold von Sacher-Masoch (1836-1895) from whose name the term "masochism" is derived.

Germinie's gradual but inevitable decline is as pathetic as it is masochistic. Paris is even more abnormal than poor Germinie, for the city is totally heartless whereas she sacrifices herself to the needs of the heart. The Goncourts balance pathos and objectivity in such a way that their work forms a clear link between the sentiment and feeling of Romanticism and the scientific objectivity of Zola's naturalism. Although Germinie is wasted by alcohol, she is not depicted in terms of total decay at the novel's end; although she is buried in an unmarked grave, her life of sacrifice and pathetic love is given an aura of sublimity in the closing chapter.

GETTYSBURG

Type of work: Short stories
Author: Elsie Singmaster (Mrs. E. S. Lewars, 1879-1958)
Types of plots: Historical chronicle and regional realism
Times of plots: 1863-1913
Locale: Gettysburg, Pennsylvania
First published: 1913

Living in Gettysburg, the writer heard at firsthand the stories of many men and women who remembered the events of those three successive days of July 1, 2, and 3, 1863. The book opens with a picture of the town when news comes that a battle will be fought there. The narrative continues with an account of the battle and the Confederate retreat, and closes with a group of stories dealing with characters whose experiences in the battle are told in retrospect: the blind Gunner Criswell, whose name was overlooked when a monument to the veterans was inscribed; Daggett, a substitute who was cheated of both honor and pay; and Mary Bowman, widowed during the battle.

Elsie Singmaster was a regional historical novelist whose fiction, both juvenile and adult, was devoted to presenting a realistic picture of two phases of American life: the quiet and isolated rural communities of German descent in Pennsylvania, where she grew up; and the scenes of crucial battles during America's Revolutionary and Civil Wars. As sources for novels and short stories dealing with the latter, the author relied upon personal conversations with people who had lived through the Civil War, as well as upon her own experience with the land and its geography; Singmaster made her home, from 1915 until her death, in Gettysburg, on a site overlooking Seminary Ridge, a pivotal landmark in her stories.

Gettysburg, a series of nine short stories, was the author's first published book and one of her finest. Chronologically, the stories fall into three groups: those set immediately prior to the battle; those depicting the Confederate retreat; and those concerning the reminiscences, told generations later, of people who were here. A unifying thread is provided in the character of Mary Bowman, who witnesses the inception of the battle; loses her husband in the fighting; cares for the wounded; hears Abraham Lincoln's dedication of the battleground three days later; and lives to see the fiftieth anniversary of the event. All the stories have a remarkable ring of truth about them; the reader senses immediately that the characters are based on real people who experienced the famous battle at firsthand, rather than on mere historical data.

Singmaster's style reflects her Pennsylvania German background in its economical prose, in its simple, straightforward language. Her handling of dialogue is particularly effective in establishing verisimilitude, while it allows her to probe deeply into the hopes and fears of persons involved in situations of intense emotional stress. Battle scenes are never presented directly, but rather recalled through the minds of soldiers, mothers, wives, and friends; the sense of irreparable loss brought on by war is omnipresent. Not only are the people drawn convincingly, but the land is brought vividly before the reader's eyes through descriptions that bear the mark of the author's personal involvement with the place.

GHOSTS

Type of work: Drama
Author: Henrik Ibsen (1828-1906)
Type of plot: Social criticism
Time of plot: Nineteenth century
Locale: Rosenvold, Norway
First presented: 1881

In Ghosts, *Ibsen substitutes the scientific concept of heredity for the Greek idea of fate. The plot hinges on a son who has inherited the nerve disease of his father, and like him, is doomed to a slow disintegration of mind and body. Yet, the play is more than a study of degenerative heredity; it is a mordant attack upon the standards of contemporary society. What rationale is there for convincing a wife that her social and moral duty is to stay with a husband who, besides being diseased, is a cruel and hopeless philanderer?*

Frequently called the "father of modern drama," Henrik Ibsen, like Picasso in painting and Stravinsky in music, was a dynamic innovator whose far-ranging experiments have had a pervasive, continuing influence on Western theater and culture. *Ghosts,* Ibsen's most celebrated—even notorious—play, was the key document in his "social-realistic" period (the 1870's and 1880's) and has obscured the fact that he was a protean writer whose "social-realistic" phase occupied only two decades of a career that spanned half a century (1849-1899) and explored a large number of social, psychological, and metaphysical problems in a wide range of theatrical styles.

In the 1880's, however, *Ghosts* was a red flag to the conventional theater audience and a defiant banner for the avant-garde. Ibsen's earlier social play, *A Doll's House* (1879), in which a woman leaves her husband in order to achieve maturity, found stout defenders but also excited denunciation—in fact, the playwright was forced to produce a "happy ending" (Nora stays home) for German consumption. This controversy was in large part responsible for the play's commercial success on stage and, even more emphatically, in book form. But *Ghosts,* which deals with a woman who stayed home, was another matter, for this time the reading public concluded that the play was entirely too shocking, especially for its open treatment of venereal disease and its defense of unmarried cohabitation. Even the sales of Ibsen's earlier plays dropped off. One newspaper crystalized the general opinion: "The book has no place on the Christmas table of any Christian home." Needless to say, once the dust raised by its attackers and defenders cleared, the play revealed itself to be one of the pillars of modern literature.

There are two basic themes in *Ghosts.* In the first place, it is a violent attack on conventional morality. Pastor Manders embodies everything Ibsen hated in those conventions; therefore, whatever we are told about Manders and his relations with the world around him applies to the conventions—the "ghosts" of the title. Manders is, for example, an unconscious hypocrite. Though he sees himself as a moral and ethical leader, he is motivated almost exclusively by fear of what others think of him. When he discusses the question of insuring the new orphanage, he makes it clear that he is not opposed to the principle of insurance: he is himself insured; his parishioners insure themselves and their businesses; Mrs. Alving carries insurance. But the pastor fears that if the orphanage is insured, his wealthier patrons may insist that he is showing less reliance than he should on divine providence. The decision not to insure the orphanage is, then, based neither on an interpretation of God's will nor on a concern for the orphans, but on a fear of public opinion. To Ibsen, therefore, the conventional moral code is itself hypocritical, and those who adhere to it are neither morally nor spiritually motivated.

In the closing act, fear of what others may think proves to be Manders' undoing. After the orphanage has burned to the ground, the unscrupulous, consciously hypocritical Engstrand convinces the pastor that he, Manders, caused the fire. Since Manders' sole concern is with his reputation, when Engstrand "accepts" the blame for the fire (and it is clear that he set it), the greatly relieved Manders agrees to provide financial support for Engstrand's "Sailors' Home"—a "home" that will clearly be little more than a brothel. To save his own skin, the spiritual mentor agrees to underwrite immorality.

Hypocrisy and opportunism, in fact, pervade the moral landscape of the play. Engstrand is an obvious and open hypocrite, a confidenceman who has persuaded Manders that he is a worthy soul. Regina sets her cap for Oswald, not because she loves him but because she wants to be taken to Paris, and, as a second string to her bow, makes advances to Pastor Manders. And, though Mrs. Alving is a thoroughly sympathetic character, she too has played the hypocrite in the past, hiding the lifelong philanderings of her husband behind a wall of public respectability: the last stone in that wall was to have been the orphanage named in Captain Alving's honor, but, ironically, his real, and more fitting, memorial is to be Engstrand's "Sailor's Home."

To Ibsen, the moral code enforces hypocrisy, and it ranges far beyond the reach of Mrs. Alving's house. When Manders suggests that men of means might object to insuring the orphanage, he suggests also (without himself understanding the implications of his statement) that these men, while speaking in spiritual terms, are interested in the orphanage solely for financial reasons; it will reduce the taxes they pay for charitable purposes. In an intense confrontation with Oswald (one of the scenes the audience of Ibsen's time found objectionable because Oswald defends unmarried cohabitation), Manders accuses Oswald of having moved in openly immoral circles in Paris, only to be told that Oswald has indeed seen a good deal of immorality abroad—when some of Manders' respectable parishioners have come to Paris to have their fling: "Then we had a chance of learning something, I can tell you."

The exposure of the conventional code in itself might have created a comedy—Engstrand and Manders are in many ways comic figures. Or it might have led to a serious problem play. But there is a second, more subtly stated theme, and in it lies the play's tragic momentum. For an understanding and exposure of the conventions does not destroy them or their power to harm; the truth does not make one free in Ibsen's worst of all possible worlds.

Mrs. Alving is quite contemptuous of the conventional code. She sees herself as an emancipated woman who has freed herself of her past and, by recalling Oswald from Paris, ensured her future happiness. In Act I, she seems in complete control of the situation; she is tranquil, confident, certain of herself. "And from tomorrow on," she tells Manders, "I shall be free at last. . . . I shall forget that such a person as Alving ever lived in this house—there'll be no one here but my son and me." But at that point, the conclusion of Act I, she and Manders hear Oswald running after the servant (and, unknown to him, his half-sister) Regina, an echo of the affair between Captain Alving and the servant who was Regina's mother. In the sad and bitter discussion that opens Act II, Mrs. Alving, no longer certain that the past can be shunted aside, states the second theme of the play explicitly: "We're all haunted in this world . . . by the ghosts of innumerable old prejudices and beliefs—half-forgotten cruelties and betrayals . . . and we can't get rid of them."

She does, however, make several more efforts to "get rid of them." When Oswald, telling her guiltily that he has acquired a venereal disease, speaks of the "joy of life" and the "joy of work," Mrs. Alving sees a pattern in the past that she had not discerned before. To Oswald and to Regina, both of whom have been kept in the dark, she reveals the full truth about Captain Alving—that he was a drunkard and a philanderer all his life. But at long last she manages to understand and excuse him, insisting that he had a "joy of life" in him for which his conventional environment could provide no outlet. The Captain's wasted life, she goes on to declare, was her own responsibility, because, instead of offering him "joy," she judged him by society's standards, thus driving him elsewhere—to one of the servants, among others. Mrs. Alving's final effort to face and, hopefully, undo the past, fails. Regina, learning that she should have been a daughter, not a servant, in Mrs. Alving's house, reacts with bitterness, and leaves. Oswald, facing mental oblivion, is more alone than ever. And, as the curtain comes down, Captain Alving's legacy to Oswald, the last stage of venereal disease, strikes the boy as Mrs. Alving stares at the horror that is her life. Physically, as well as spiritually, the past has destroyed both present and future.

Ghosts is a richly orchestrated play and remains one of the most complex and significant realistic dramas of the century. Its symbols—the rain that beats darkly on the large parlor window and represents the moral ghosts of the play, the sun that rises at the close to shine on Oswald's darkness—mesh closely with the action and the themes of the play. Its structure, a gradual revelation of the past that is fully disclosed only at the final catastrophe, is clearly and firmly joined to the idea that the past enters into and destroys the present. This form, developed and perfected by Ibsen, was to be employed over and over again as his influence merged with the dramatic streams pouring into the twentieth century.

Max Halperen

GIANTS IN THE EARTH

Type of work: Novel
Author: O. E. Rölvaag (1876-1931)
Type of plot: Regional romance
Time of plot: Late nineteenth century
Locale: The Dakotas
First published: 1924-1925

A significant saga of American pioneer life, the novel's theme is man's struggle to wrench an existence from the land and establish a culture despite the antagonism of the stubborn earth. It is the story of Per Hansa, a Norwegian who becomes the founder of a settlement in the bleak Dakota territory. Remorselessly fighting Indians, his wife, the weather, claim jumpers, and the despondency of his fellow settlers, Hansa is a study in human fortitude.

Ole Rölvaag was born in the Helgoland district of Norway and lived there until he was twenty years of age. He attended school irregularly; his ambition to become a poet, once broached in the family circle, brought a discouraging barrage of ridicule. At fourteen he left school entirely and went out with the Lofoten fishing fleet. He seemed destined to pursue this hard vocation all his life, and the prospect brought him little contentment. Though considered by his family as too stupid to learn, he read voraciously, both Norwegian and foreign authors. His reading gave him a view of the possibilities of life that made the existence to which he was bound seem intolerably circumscribed. When he had been a fisherman for five years, something occurred which forced him to a decision. The master of his boat, whom he greatly admired, offered to stake him to a boat of his own. Ole realized that if he accepted the offer, he would never be anything but a fisherman, so he declined it and emigrated to America.

For three years he farmed for an uncle in South Dakota; then at the age of twenty-three, with great trepidation, he entered a preparatory school in Canton, South Dakota. Six years later he was graduated *cum laude* from St. Olaf College. After a year of postgraduate study in Oslo, he took the chair of Norwegian literature at St. Olaf, which he held until his death.

By the time Rölvaag began work on *Giants in the Earth* at age forty-seven, he had already written five novels, of which four had been published. All were written in Norwegian, published in Minneapolis, and read exclusively by the Norwegian-speaking population of the Midwest. All the works deal with aspects of the Norwegian settlement, and so appealed strongly to an audience of immigrants. *Giants in the Earth* and its sequel *Peder Victorious* are his only works either to be translated into English or to be published in Scandinavia. Springing from a European artistic tradition, but treating matters utterly American, they are perhaps unique in both American and foreign literatures.

The European and specifically Norwegian elements that distinguish *Giants in the Earth* are its orientation toward the psychology rather than the adventures of its characters, and its strain of Nordic pessimism. The characters of Beret and Per Hansa illustrate two complementary facets in the psychology of the Norwegian settlers. In Per Hansa the desire to own and work his own land, to "found a new kingdom," seems to feed on the hazards he encounters. The brute resistance of the soil, the violence of the weather, the plagues of grasshoppers, the danger from Indians, the dispute over the claim-stakes only spur him on to greater feats of daring, endurance, and ingenuity. Every victory over misfortune makes him feel more lucky, and fuels his dream of a prosperous freehold for himself and his children. Freed from the cramped spaces and conventions of an old culture, he embraces the necessities of the new life joyfully, trusting in his instinct for the fitness of things to help him establish a new order. Beret, on the other hand, takes no joy in pioneer life and is instead deeply disturbed at having to leave an established way of life to confront the vast, unpeopled plains: uprooted, she feels morally cast adrift, as if her ethical sense, indeed her very identity, were attached to some physical place. Beret sees Per Hansa's exultant adaptability to pioneer life as evidence of the family's reversion to savagery. For a man to shelter with his livestock, to change his name or give his child a strange name, to parley with Indians, to christen in the absence of a minister—all these things indicate to her a failure of conscience, a giving up of the hallmarks of civilization.

Yet she, like Per, has brought her worst troubles with her from home. Her growing despondency about Per's and her neighbor's spiritual condition springs from her own sense of sin in having borne Ole out of wedlock. She sees herself as the deserving object of divine retribution; in her deranged state she takes every escape from disaster as a sign that God has marked her for some still more awful punishment. The very openness that thrills Per Hansa with its endless potentialities fills her with dread: "Here, far off in the great stillness, where there was nothing to hide behind—here the punishment would fall!" And Per, bearing her in his heart, is drawn down in the vortex of her despair.

Ironically, it is only after Beret regains her courage and her faith through religious ministration and ceases to expect calamity from minute to minute, that Per Hansa dies. It even seems as if she sends him out to die. But from an aesthetic point of view, his death is necessary to the work itself. For all its realism and modernity of tone, *Giants in the Earth* is a saga, and as sagas must, it ends with the death of heroes. Per Hansa and Hans Olsa are heroes of epic stature and like the heroes of old legend they complement each other's virtues. They have loved each other from their youth, and in their prime their strength and wit combine to carve a new home out of the wilderness. And like Beowulf braving the dragon, they sacrifice themselves in a last great struggle with the prairie before it succumbs to the plow and the fence. Thus "the great plain drinks the blood of Christian men and is satisfied." The deaths of Hans Olsa and Per Hansa signal the passing of the time of legend, when giants walked the earth, and one man could do the work of ten; they signal as well the beginning of a more comfortable time of clapboard houses and coffee hot and plentiful, and of heroes of a wholly different kind.

Jan Kennedy Foster

GIL BLAS OF SANTILLANE

Type of work: Novel
Author: Alain René Le Sage (1668-1747)
Type of plot: Picaresque romance
Time of plot: Seventeenth century
Locale: Spain
First published: 1715, 1724, 1735

Following the rogue-hero Gil Blas through numerous adventures, this work is an episodic romance. It is one of the first works to introduce thieves, vagabonds, and vulgar peasants into fiction. The work's appeal arises from the author's skillful narration of exciting tales and his more than superficial exploration of character motivation.

The picaroon or rogue hero originated at least as far back as Petronius, but it found its ultimate form in the picaresque novel of the Spanish Renaissance. The picaresque hero in *Gil Blas of Santillane* both looks back at his historical predecessors and extends the boundaries of the type. The scheming valet or servant with the roving instinct never was more charming or more deceitful than in Le Sage's novel. Part of the amusement of the genre was always the fact that the lowly born hero aspired to conditions above his station and stopped at nothing to reach his goal; his effrontery and daring made useful tools for the satirist attempting to expose the social structure. In *Gil Blas of Santillane,* Le Sage shows more dexterity even than the Spanish originators of the genre in manipulating both the satirical elements of the plot and the roving of the hero from one milieu to another. Le Sage possesses a sharp eye for the ridiculous and is reminiscent of Molière in his treatment of doctors, fops, vain authors, amorous spinsters, worldly priests, and other social types. But perhaps the pace of his style and the ironical overtones of the narrative are closer to Voltaire. Gil Blas himself is clearly a product of the French spirit, despite his Spanish pretensions. It is likely that *Gil Blas of Santillane* is more to be credited with making the picaresque novel a popular form than are the Spanish originals.

Le Sage borrowed episodes from Spanish and Italian sources and used Spanish local color, but the work is essentially a product of the imagination, a fanciful and extravagant work that seldom bothers to adhere too closely to reality. Most traditional picaresque heroes are coarse fellows, but thanks to the vitality of the narration, Gil Blas's relative refinement does not detract from the verisimilitude of the tale. The narrator-hero sees humor in his own actions as well as in those of the people he encounters in his travels.

Gil Blas of Santillane is the finest picaresque novel written in French. Le Sage's knowledge of the form came from his Spanish studies, but his mastery of the form took him beyond his Spanish masters; the book is no mere imitation of the Spanish episodic novel, but a unique fusion of humor and satire.

Although French society was the prime target for Le Sage's satire, the work possesses a universality that transcends nationalistic emphasis. The author shrewdly analyzes human nature and human foibles, even within the context of traditional types and traditional plot. The bite and style of the work falls off in the last volume, which was written some time after the rest of the book, and there is a certain amount of repetition as Gil Blas again faces the perils of court life. But the hero does redeem his moral character in this final section and witnesses poetic justice dispensed to some of the chief rogues of the story.

THE GILDED AGE

Type of work: Novel
Authors: Mark Twain (Samuel L. Clemens, 1835-1910) and Charles Dudley Warner (1829-1900)
Type of plot: Social satire
Time of plot: Nineteenth century
Locale: United States
First published: 1873

The misfortunes visited upon the innocent members of an "all-American" family become the vehicle for this satire. Originally conceived as an attack on virtually every aspect of society, special targets are graft, corruption, and the hypocrisy of established institutions. The coauthorship of the novel proves to be its major weakness; the tone strikes an uncertain balance between sober reality and sheer hilarity. The most memorable creation in the novel is the character of Colonel Beriah Sellers, a cherry optimist convinced that success is just around the corner. Needless to say, he never rounds the right corner.

Editor-critic E. L. Godkin described America during the 1870's as a "chromo civilization." Reflecting on the slovenly reality beneath the gaudy exterior of society, Twain dubbed the era the Gilded Age. In this period, society had become more fluid, and many of those individuals of humble origins who made it to the top proclaimed their achievements to the world in boisterous tones, and by wearing extravagant apparel and living in grotesque mansions. That treacherous, not always successful path from rags to riches fascinated Mark Twain and Charles Dudley Warner. The cost of attaining a pew in the church of the newly rich, while portrayed in a humorous and touching style, was their primary concern.

A crude frontier spirit invaded the realm of the genteel. Twain had seen this phase of the economic process work itself out, and felt that its real victims were the environment, and American traditions, ideals, and common sense. Washington was swarming with scoundrels, coal mine operators were scarring the once beautiful frontier, and people were selling themselves to the highest bidders. The characters in this novel were pulled from the life of a nation suffering from moral bankruptcy.

Twain especially hated graft, and to get to the root of this evil he attacked the sacred cows of his generation: organized religion, government, political parties, and flashy entrepreneurs. Colonel Sellers represented all that was naïve and forgivable in that age, and Senator Dilworthy the opposite. In true patriotic spirit, Sellers believed that prosperity would come from a congressional bill, but Dilworthy typified the unscrupulous residents of Capitol Hill.

The satire of this book was not appreciated at the time; people did not want to be ridiculed. When Twain wrote what his audience wanted to read, his fame increased; yet Twain, himself a product of the Gilded Age, would never be free of the cynicism that surfaced in this book.

THE GLASS KEY

Type of work: Novel
Author: Dashiell Hammett (1894-1961)
Type of plot: Mystery romance
Time of plot: 1930's
Locale: New York area
First published: 1931

This novel is an excellent example of the school of hard-boiled realism. In the course of tracking down a murderer, the detective-hero also breaks up a bootlegging operation and finds himself embroiled in a bitter political power play. As in most good detective novels, the culprit turns out to be the least suspected character; and since this is a modern form of the genre, the hero has a love interest.

The Glass Key was Dashiell Hammett's personal favorite among his novels and may well be, in the words of critic-novelist Julian Symons, "the peak of Hammett's achievement, which is to say, the peak of the crime writer's art in the twentieth century."

Although Ned Beaumont has much in common with Hammett's other "hard-boiled" heroes, Sam Spade and Continental Op, he is not simply a professional detective hired to solve a crime but a man involuntarily thrust into the center of a violent and puzzling situation. The fate of his employer and best friend, Paul Madvig—and ultimately of himself—is dependent on his ability to solve the murder of Henry Taylor. Beaumont's search for the murderer becomes, moreover, not only a problem in detection but also an exploration of the social mores and political forces operative in the America of 1931. And as Ned pursues his quest, he also comes to understand his own relationship to that social and political system.

Hammett's picture of big-city politics has little to do with electoral niceties. Favors are bought and sold. Survival and power go to the fittest; that is, to those most willing and able to manipulate the power factions as they vie to maintain and expand their own self interests. Paul Madvig is no more honest than his rival Shad O'Rory, only a bit more adroit and likeable. Holding on to power is a matter of keeping a delicate balance of contending factions; the slightest mistake can topple one from the pinnacle all the way down. Those not at the center of the struggle, from District Attorney Farr down to the bartender at the speakeasy where O'Rory is murdered, are loyal only to themselves and switch sides at the slightest indication that power relationships are changing. Thus, to everyone except his sister Janet, the murder of Henry Taylor matters only as a dangerous variable in this struggle for political dominance. The most "respectable" member of the establishment, old Senator Henry, turns out to be the most corrupt. He kills his own son in a fit of temper and is willing to kill again to keep the truth concealed.

Ned Beaumont accepts and even participates in this system of institutionalized corruption. But his loyalty to Paul, to Janet, and to the "job" he has to do, suggests another possible "morality" in the book based on personal relationships rather than on adherence to particular institutions or abstract principles. Although Beaumont fights with Madvig, leaves him at one point, and finally goes off with his girl, he maintains throughout the book a dogged loyalty to his boss and friend, even in the face of nearly fatal tortures and beatings. If the system is corrupt, Hammett seems to be saying, it is still possible for a man to retain his moral integrity by holding fast to his own sense of self, his personal "code," and those commitments, to self and others, that are the product of that "code."

The book ends on an optimistisc note. Ned and Janet are about to leave together. Paul accepts the new arrangement with equanimity and promises to use his expertise and power to do a "housecleaning." But this final optimism is unconvincing. The image of the "American Dream" that remains in the mind is that of Janet's dream which gives the book its title: a delicious banquet apparently free for the taking, but guarded by hidden snakes that swarm over the unwary who dare to unlock the door with a glass key.

GOAT SONG

Type of work: Drama
Author: Franz Werfel (1890-1945)
Type of plot: Symbolic allegory
Time of plot: Late eighteenth century
Locale: A Slavic countryside
First presented: 1921

The brutishness lurking beneath the civilized veneer of mankind is symbolized by the birth of a human monster to Milic, a farmer. The child is allowed to grow up but is kept hidden from the world. During a bloody feud between peasants and gipsies, the monster escapes and is found by the gipsies. Both warring factions view him as some sort of supernatural sign. In their zeal to find a scapegoat for their sins, they sacrifice a young girl to the strange god.

Goat Song belongs to a period of modern dramatic history when dramatists were struggling with new forms and symbols. O'Neill probed his characters' real attitudes and emotions with interior monologues, gave life to inanimate objects, and explored the forces of nature and time in his plays. Elmer Rice created a powerful symbol of modern life in *The Adding Machine*. Brecht strove to work past the audience's emotions and grip their intellects with his attacks on capitalism and modern corruption. Franz Werfel's *Goat Song* was part of this great experimental ferment which dominated European and American drama for two decades. Werfel was also influenced by his native Czechoslovakia and by the middle-European legends and attitudes, much as was his contemporary and fellow countryman, Franz Kafka. Utilizing the ancient character of the scapegoat, Werfel attempted in this play to create a modern myth.

Like Eve and Pandora, the girl Stanja begins the sequence of events by asking questions and urging her man to explore mysteries best left alone; and the doctor, with the arrogance of science, meddles foolishly and impotently in the affair. But it is the student, Juvan, the intellectual leader of the gipsies, who precipitates the action that leads to the violence and the ultimate destruction of the human "monster." The drama vividly illustrates the tendency human beings have toward irrational violence. Not only the ignorant are capable of cruelty and unreasoning acts of violence; not only the poor and hungry, are caught up in the passion of bloodletting. In retrospect, *Goat Song* seems almost a foreshadowing of the events which were to occur in Europe in the decades following its creation.

The hair-raising conclusion of the drama, when Stanja announces that she is carrying the monster's child, suggests that the seed of the perverse, the cause of evil, will always be with humanity, however men try to eradicate it. The evil lurks within them, not in outside forces or unseen and feared demons.

THE GODS ARE ATHIRST

Type of work: Novel
Author: Anatole France (Jacques Anatole Thibault, 1844-1924)
Type of plot: Historical satire
Time of plot: 1793-1794
Locale: Paris
First published: 1912

Set during the Reign of Terror which followed the French Revolution, The Gods Are Athirst *satirizes the excesses of the period. These excesses are caused not by events, but by the brutal, self-deceiving, self-glorifying nature of man himself. In particular the author castigates the brutality generated by a mind blindly committed to a political cause. Évariste Gamelin, a romantic artist, feels a sincere need to commit himself to the Jacobeans and ends by ordering the execution of his dearest friend.*

Anatole France was born in the revolutionary era just before the mid-nineteenth century, and lived through World War I. His generation saw the rising and unending conflict between religion and science; the rapid growth of industrial capitalism, with its early promise and later disillusionment; the brutalization of workers which led to proletarian revolutionary movements; and the optimism about man's future which displayed itself in world fairs. Literary experimentalism was active, with new forms and new approaches to subject matter more the rule than the exception. Through all of this, Anatole France was a man of perspective and therefore a satirist. Although his literary forms, in poetry, essay, and novel, were traditional, his satirical wit could be sharp, as when he defined justice as "the preservation for each of what is his own—for the rich his wealth, for the poor his poverty." Like Voltaire, his great eighteenth century predecessor, he was skeptical of organized religion and the sincerity of human motives.

In *The Gods Are Athirst (Les Dieux ont Soif),* a novel of the Revolution, France condemns the violence and extremism of the jurors on the Revolutionary Tribunal. Although the painter Évariste Gamelin is the central character in the novel, it is the aristocrat Brotteaux who acts as mouthpiece for the author's ideals. France treats Gamelin's romantic notion that men are innately virtuous with complete scorn, ascribing instead to Brotteaux' more cynical evaluation that virtue is instilled in children through their parents' beatings. Nevertheless, with his characteristic complexity and insight, France does not condemn the struggling idealist Gamelin outright. He is able to sympathize with his fanaticism even while he indicts it; while he bitterly attacks the atrocities perpetrated by the men on the Tribunal, he can still defend them in terms of his skeptical view of mankind: ". . . whoever might have agreed to put himself in their places would have acted as they did. . . ."

France is a critic of man; not a misanthrope by any means, but a critic with the capacity to make us simultaneously laugh and squirm. *The Gods Are Athirst* is not anti-French, nor, indeed, anti-revolutionary. Like the short story "The Procurator of Judea," it is content to show us as we are—doing the things men have done throughout history—to make us realize that we must somehow learn to do better.

THE GOLD BUG

Type of work: Short story
Author: Edgar Allan Poe (1809-1849)
Type of plot: Mystery romance
Time of plot: Early nineteenth century
Locale: South Carolina
First published: 1843

This short story has the eternal fascination of a plot which is the slow unraveling of a seemingly impenetrable puzzle. Once deciphered, a fortuitously found map drawn in invisible ink and complete with coded instructions leads the three protagonists to Captain Kidd's fabled treasure.

The Gold Bug, Poe's most famous story, belongs to the small group which he called "tales of ratiocination," that is, tales in which logical reasoning is employed to solve a puzzle. Other Poe stories of this type are *The Murders in the Rue Morgue*, *The Mystery of Marie Roget,* and *The Purloined Letter*—a series of three in which the protagonist is Monsieur C. Auguste Dupin, an amateur detective, whose unnamed friend tells the stories. A. Conan Doyle's Sherlock Holmes stories were admittedly inspired by the Dupin tales, and Poe has often been called the father of the modern detective story.

Poe's ratiocinative tales differ from his others in several ways. The vocabulary of several of his tales of terror not only reveals a nervous or fearful state of mind of the narrator but it is also intended to arouse in the reader an emotional response. The vocabulary of the ratiocinative tales, however, is consciously unemotional to stress the analytical nature of the tales. The structure of these tales also differs from that in the tales of terror. A representative terror tale builds up to a climax of action, often violent, as in *The Fall of the House of Usher* or *The Pit and the Pendulum.* The limited action of a ratiocinative tale occurs mainly in the first half of the story; most of the latter half is devoted to the explication of the mystery or puzzle given earlier. In *The Gold Bug* the action centers upon locating, digging up, and transporting the treasure, and this action is completed almost exactly halfway through the story. Nearly all of the remaining half is made up of the narrator's questions and Legrand's detailed answers or explanations concerning the parchment map and the translation of the cryptic message contained in the numbers and other characters or symbols on it.

In *The Gold Bug,* then, Poe has combined the romance of finding buried treasure with the mental excitement of unraveling a mystery. Critics have pointed out inaccuracies in geography and topography, defects in character portrayal, and weak attempts at humor in Jupiter's speech; but the reader forgets or ignores these as Poe carries him along in the search first for immense wealth and then for a meaning in an enigma.

THE GOLDEN ASS OF LUCIUS APULEIUS

Type of work: Tale
Author: Lucius Apuleius (125?-?)
Type of plot: Picaresque romance
Time of plot: Early second century
Locale: Greece
First transcribed: Second century manuscript

A repository of fantastic anecdotes, The Golden Ass of Lucius Apuleius *has a bawdy, realistic tone. An allegory describing the maturing of man runs loosely through the work. Two major portions of the narrative concern the metamorphosis of the hero into an ass and a lengthy retelling of the story of Cupid and Psyche.*

The Transformation of Lucius Apuleius of Madaura is the original title of the picaresque romance popularly known, through William Adlington's celebrated sixteenth century English translation, as *The Golden Asse.* From antiquity, the word *golden* has been added to the title, because a common custom for Roman storytellers was to demand payment for a "golden" story. In his "Address to the Reader," Apuleius describes the literary conventions of his tale as Egyptian, but the major sources for the book—which may be called a prototype of the novel—are Lucius of Patra's *The Ass,* of which no copy survives, or Lucian of Samosata's *Lucius, or the Ass,* a bawdy and comparatively crude tale that is still extant. Apuleius' novel is much longer, richer in invention, and more fully detailed than Lucian's. Moreover, it contains many stories left out of the source, including the splendid ironical tale "Cupid and Psyche"; the stories of Aristomenes, Thelyphron, and others; the episode concerning the Festival of Laughter; and the conclusion, written in an elevated, religious manner, instead of the farcical version of the original. The tone of Apuleius' Latin, for the most part intentionally archaic and odd, has been reproduced for generations of English readers in Adlington's translation; among modern English translations, Robert Graves's version has effectively captured the vigor, sly humor, and spontaneity of the author's language.

Because *The Golden Ass of Lucius Apuleius,* taken as a whole, is robustly comical and satirical, many readers may not fully appreciate the serious, religious parts of the novel. Yet the troubles of Lucius spring from his carelessness—if not impiety—towards the gods. He is guilty of two crimes: meddling with the powers of the supernatural, and associating with people who have bad luck. Through his dangerous curiosity about witchcraft, he brings upon himself the troubles resulting from his transformation; and through his sexual dalliance with the household slave girl Fotis, he invites all sorts of disasters, not the least of which is falling from the respectable class of well-born freeman to a level even beneath that of a slave, to the subhuman condition of the ass. Moreover, his extreme punishment is, from the standpoint of the cult of Isis and Osiris, fully deserved. The ass, which to the cultists represents lust, wickedness, and cruelty, rather than stubbornness or indolence, is the perfect agent of Lucius' metamorphosis. He must endure twelve months of suffering in the ass's skin, until he is redeemed at last—through the benevolent intercession of the Goddess Isis—as a human being. Thus his transformation is a spiritual autobiography, in which the hero's conversion from ass to man is shown symbolically as a religious rebirth.

In his condition as an ass, however, Lucius is powerless either to help himself or others. Indeed, the bad luck that plagues him passes over to those who merely come to possess him. Even those who befriend the ass or are otherwise guiltless in their association with him, such as the innocent Charites and her intrepid lover Thrasillus, come to a tragic end. As for the wicked tormenters of the ass—the bandits, the bailiff, the boy at the stud farm, the eunuch priests, the baker and his Christian wife—all suffer terrible fates. Ill-luck, Apuleius implies, is catching; and he does not spare the reader's sensibilities in his grisly accounts of cruelty. The author skillfully counterpoints scenes of mirth with others of terror, and his effects often resemble those of modern "black comedy." The comedy verges upon the horrific; and the horrors—for example, the robbers' plan to sew up Charites in the skin of the flayed ass—are so outrageous that they become comic. Above all, however, Apuleius keeps sight of his religious message. Erring humanity must be chastened, whether through terror or folly, until each penitent discovers the true path of salvation, as does the transformed ass. By the end of the tale, Lucius has not only redeemed himself from the indignity of his subhuman condition; he has become a prosperous lawyer, a priest in the cult of Isis, and is once again a freeborn citizen of Rome.

THE GOLDEN BOWL

Type of work: Novel
Author: Henry James (1843-1916)
Type of plot: Psychological realism
Time of plot: c. 1900
Locale: England and the Continent
First published: 1904

The Golden Bowl *is a meticulous, involved, and incredibly detailed exploration of the subtleties of thought and nuances of emotion of a small circle of wealthy, cultured Americans living in Europe. James's collection of psychological shades and discriminations are at times almost overwhelming to the reader. A forerunner of psychological expressionism, the novel describes characters who live in a world shut off from homely realities, a world that will not tolerate crudities.*

The Golden Bowl, along with *The Ambassadors* and *The Wings of the Dove*, is one of the novels of the triad of works upon which the high reputation of James's "major phase" rests. In these novels, James's already complex style reaches new levels of sophistication as, increasingly, the writing becomes more and more intricate and convoluted as it tends toward ever-increasingly subtle levels of analysis of character and event. Gradually the "center of consciousness" in the mind of a character, which had been essential to James's earlier works, gives way to an omniscient narrative point of view, and a narrative voice which is James's own. Though it hardly appears so to the eye, James's style of this period is essentially oral—he had developed the habit of dictating his material to a secretary—and reflects his characteristically ponderous manner of speech. Seeming to move endlessly to circle or enfold a subject or an idea without ever touching it directly, James's language and technique in these late novels has been admired highly by critics who place a premium on style, while frequently being disparaged by those who stress content and clarity of thought. For James himself, the art of the novel was everything in writing, and there is little doubt that in *The Golden Bowl* his artistry reached a peak.

With this novel, James continues the subject matter of the "international theme" which had characterized his work from its beginning by dealing with a group of Americans in Europe. Adam Verver, in particular, can be seen as an avatar of the American Adam who recurs in James's fiction, often, as here, in search of European culture which he will take back to his culturally barren homeland. Prince Amerigo is linked by his name to the historic connection between America and Europe, and, by his marriage to Maggie, might be seen as dramatizing a new dependence of the Old World upon the New. Yet, *The Golden Bowl* ultimately is less an international novel than such works as *The American, Daisy Miller,* or *The Ambassadors* because its concerns are finally more with individuals than with cultures. Though the Ververs begin in

America and Adam returns there at the novel's end, neither his experience nor that of Maggie or Charlotte is essentially contingent upon the sort of conflict of cultural values which is at the heart of James's international novels and stories. Rather, the problems of love and marriage at the heart of *The Golden Bowl* are truly universal, neither their nature nor their solution dependent upon an American perspective.

Like many of James's works, *The Golden Bowl* began in his notebooks with the recording of an anecdote he had heard concerning a young woman and her widower father, each of whom had taken spouses, who learned their partners were engaged in an affair. From this scant beginning, James crafted his longest and most elaborate novel not by greatly complicating the essential material of this simple plot, but by scrupulous elaboration of the conflicts and resolutions resulting from the complex relations among his four central characters. By making his characters members of the wealthy leisure class, James frees them from the mundane worries of the world so he can focus his, and their, entire attention on the one particular problem without regard to external complications. Ultimately, the novel seeks to pose moral and philosophical questions which transcend either the psychological or social levels of the work to confront the basic question of Maggie's adjustment to a less-than-perfect world.

The golden bowl is James's metaphor for the marriage between Amerigo and Maggie, and perhaps, in its larger implications, for life itself. The bowl, not really "golden" at all, but crystal gilded with gold leaf, has the superficial appearance of perfection, but is, in fact, cracked. As a symbol of Maggie's "perfect" marriage, the bowl very clearly illustrates the flaw at the heart of the relationship—a flaw which no doubt existed even before the Prince and Charlotte resume their old love affair, and which represents a potential threat to the marriage. Both Maggie and her father are guilty of treating the Prince as nothing more than one of the valuable objects they have come to Europe to purchase—they have bought the perfect marriage for Maggie. Unlike art, however, human relationships are not subject to purchase, nor can they, as in the case of Adam's marriage to Charlotte, be arranged for convenience without regard to the human factors concerned. In fact, both Maggie and her father tend to live in a small, supremely selfish world. Insulated by their money from the actuality of life, they isolate themselves from the real complexities of daily existence. Their world is, in effect, itself more "art" than "life."

The resolution of the novel turns around Maggie's positive act, but in the earlier parts of the novel she is more passive than active. The marriage itself, for example, seems more of an arrangement between the Prince and Adam Verver than a particular choice of Maggie's—Adam wants the perfect marriage for his daughter, and Prince Amerigo wants access to the Verver millions, so they come to an agreement between themselves. Maggie apparently has little to say about it, and even, judging from her relationship to the Prince throughout most of the novel, no very great interest in the marriage. Her real desire seems to be to continue life with her father pretty much as always, rather than to begin an independent life with her husband. Only when confronted with the Prince's infidelity does Maggie recognize that she must confront this reality for all their sakes. In choosing to separate from her father in order to begin making the best of her imperfect marriage, Maggie discovers a latent ability to confront the world as it really is, and to rise above the romantic idealism which had characterized her life with Adam Verver.

William E. Grant

GOLDEN BOY

Type of work: Drama
Author: Clifford Odets (1906-1963)
Type of plot: Social allegory
Time of plot: 1930's
Locale: New York
First presented: 1937

The play's plot concerns a young Italian violinist who becomes a prizefighter in order to gain money and fame. Odets himself described the work as an allegory reflecting the struggle of every individual to gain a place in the sun. Paradoxically, success as measured by society's terms can prove disastrous to the individual, emotionally and mentally. The play has been praised as good entertainment as well as denounced for its episodic, movie-like construction.

Clifford Odets is generally regarded as the most talented playwright to emerge from the depression generation. In his mid-twenties he became one of the founders of the Group Theatre, the most exciting and innovative American theater of the period, and its dominating playwright. In the spirit of the times, Odets quickly established himself as a volatile political dramatist with such intense theatrical statements as *Waiting for Lefty* (1935), *Till the Day I Die* (1935), *Awake and Sing!* (1935), and *Paradise Lost* (1935). Although admitting that *Golden Boy* was consciously written "to be a hit" and shore up the sagging finances of the Group Theatre, Odets insisted that it, too, was an anti-capitalistic social play. To a modern audience, however, the personal tragedy of Joe Bonaparte is the most important concern of the drama.

In essence *Golden Boy* is a variation on the old Faust theme of the man who sells himself for success and discovers, too late, that he has made a bad bargain. A poor Italian youth coming of age in the middle of the Depression, Joe knows that he can find personal satisfaction playing the violin, but the bitterness in his feelings of poverty, coupled with a desire for revenge against people who have scorned him for years, drives him into opting for the fist instead of the fiddle.

At first he boxes gingerly, trying to protect his hands for his music, but by the end of the first act he no longer cares. The balance of the play is devoted to showing how this decision corrupts and destroys him. The question of whether it is a social or a personal play probably depends on whether one interprets Joe's decision as resulting from indvidual weakness or social pressure. But once he makes it there is no doubt that the ethics of success which he embraces are totally self-destructive.

In the earliest version of the play Odets subtitled it an allegory, and, as such, it almost resembles a morality play. Embodiments of Good and Evil contend for Joe's "soul," although these other characters are, for the most part, also the victims of conflicting needs and values.

The positive moral forces in the story are represented by old Mr. Bonaparte, a fruit peddler, who encourages Joe's violin playing and is horrified by what he sees in the boxing business; Joe's brother, Frank, a labor organizer, who represents the right kind of militant, one who fights for the things he believes in; and Joe's trainer, Tokio, who, although a part of the fighting business, is a sensitive man who understand's Joe's needs and tries to help him find himself.

But Joe cannot take good advice. He must find things out for himself and, when he does, he has gone too far and it is too late. He rejects his real father and accepts Eddie Fuseli, the gangster-gambler, as his model. Joe emulates Fuseli's taste in clothing, goals, and values, and, only at the end of the play, realizes that Fuseli owns him, literally as well as professionally.

Success has done nothing to soften the hatred in Joe and it is this unleashed hostility that destroys him. He hits his last opponent, the Chocolate Drop, with all his might and kills him. In doing so, Joe finally realizes that he killed himself too. No longer able to fight, ruined for the violin, he commits suicide, either consciously or unconsciously, in the most appropriate way, by crashing his Dusenberg, symbol of materialism and speed, in the company of Lorna Moon, the good-bad girl who shares his confusion of values.

THE GONDOLIERS

Type of work: Comic opera
Author: W. S. Gilbert (1836-1911)
Type of plot: Humorous romance
Time of plot: 1750
Locale: Venice and Barataria
First presented: 1889

By a fluke, two gondoliers become monarchs, at least until the childhood nurse of the real prince can be found to identify which of the two is the rightful heir. Meantime, the two "monarchs" have wives, yet one must marry the lawful queen who is herself in love with Luiz, an attendant. Finally, cases of multiple bigamy are avoided because Luiz is discovered to be the true prince and all ends happily. This lighthearted operetta pokes gentle fun at the institution of monarchy.

William S. Gilbert wisely set the story of *The Gondoliers* in Italy rather than in England, so that he would have ample scope to satirize a topic otherwise unapproachable even for his genial talents: the institution of monarchy. However uncomfortable certain liberal spirits like Gilbert might have been with Queen Victoria, he could scarcely criticize upon the stage either her person or her prosperous reign; his was an audience which delighted, rather, in reading mischievous accounts about the vulgarity of American democracy, for which English travelers such as Mrs. Trollope gratified the public taste. But at the same time, Gilbert had to avoid offending American feelings, for his works were also popular in the United States. Consequently, he established his monarchy in the never-never land of Barataria and selected Venetians for his republican protagonists

Marco and Giuseppe, Gilbert's two would-be kings, are simple gondoliers who have been reared to respect liberty; they cannot understand the pomp and pretensions of courtly life, and they cherish their freedom. At the Court of Barataria, garbed in their kingly robes, they clean their own crowns and scepters, while around them their servants and ministers-of-state fuss over games of chance and petty gossip. Unlike the drones at court, they work (as they explain in the brisk duet "Rising Early in the Morning") only for the good of their subjects. Obviously, such egalitarian kings are unsuited to the monarchy. And with relief they learn that they are not kings, after all, but lowly gondoliers as before. Thus, with unobtrusive satire, Gilbert makes his point: the truly free are those who owe allegiance neither to king nor to the claims of ceremony.

Yet Gilbert is not so liberal that he neglects to expose, as well, the follies of republican government. Complete democracy, he shows, not only levels the privileges of caste but also suppresses the talents of great people to the condition of mediocrity. In Don Alhambra's patter song "There Lived a King," the author argues that the elite class should not, simply for the sake of a sentimental gesture, share power or wealth with the masses. The generous king who "wished all men rich as he," advanced everyone "to the top of the tree." But the result of his generosity—when "Chancellors were cheap as sprats / And Bishops . . . were plentiful as tabby cats"—was a bland communism in which all classes were reduced to the same state of meanness. Gilbert's message, quite as pleasing to the aristocracy as his satire on the monarchy must have been to socialists, is that so long as the ruling class ceases to care "for cloth of gold," up will go "the price of shoddy." So Gilbert hedges his bets, offends neither class, but amuses his whole audience—which objective, after all, is his intention.

THE GOOD COMPANIONS

Type of work: Novel
Author: J. B. Priestley (1894-)
Type of plot: Picaresque romance
Time of plot: The 1920's
Locale: England
First published: 1929

Jess Oakroyd, a stolid proper Yorkshireman, leaves behind a nagging wife to travel and seek adventure throughout England. Held together by Oakroyd's picaresque travels, the novel is filled with numerous characters drawn from every section of the social spectrum. In some ways, this comic novel is reminiscent of Charles Dickens, both in characterization and atmosphere. Oakroyd himself is an English version of the American Yankee: He says little, thinks much, and finally proves more astute than the sophisticated people around him.

J. B. Priestley had his first success at the age of thirty-five with *The Good Companions*. Other novels and plays and criticism followed, establishing him as one of the major literary figures of his time. Set in the 1920's, *The Good Companions* is a tale of a group of wandering English men and women from different classes and professions which reminds one of Chaucer, and which possesses a scope that suggests the Victorian novelists. The story moves briskly, and both plot and characters maintain reader interest to the last page. If the coincidences of plot (Jimmy Nunn encountering his old wife at the train station, or Miss Trant discovering her former lover, Dr. Mc Farlane, in the hospital, for example) strain credulity, the force of the narration, the freshness of the prose, and the richness of the characterizations prevent these coincidences from looming too importantly.

The characters set this book above commonplace novels. The pages are crowded with fascinating figures, of whom some soon disappear, while others stay and become old friends. All of them, from the little dressmaker, Miss Thong, who comes and goes with breathless speed, to the banjo-playing Morton Mitcham, who roars and tells his tall-tales to the very end, are given the touch of life by Priestley's skill. Priestley portrays an amazingly broad spectrum of humanity, ranging from the aristocratic Miss Trant to the workman Jess Oakroyd to the small-time entertainers and the faculty at the third-rate boys' school. Often he pokes gentle fun at people or attitudes, but the satire is never severe. Above all, Priestley succeeded in his comic purpose; *The Good Companions* is a comic masterpiece.

THE GOOD EARTH

Type of work: Novel
Author: Pearl S. Buck (1892-1973)
Type of plot: Social chronicle
Time of plot: Early twentieth century
Locale: Northern China
First published: 1931

With a detached, pastoral style, this novel follows the cycles of birth, marriage, and death in the Chinese peasant family of Wang Lung. The good years of plentiful harvest, marriage, and healthy children are balanced by the times of near starvation and stillborn progeny. Wang Lung finally finds himself a wealthy man, but his grown sons for whom he has worked so hard have no respect for their father's love of the good earth; they plan to sell his hardearned property as soon as he dies.

Pearl Sydenstricker Buck referred to herself as "mentally bifocal" with respect to her American and Chinese ways of looking at things. The daughter of American missionaries in China, Pearl Buck came to know that land better than any other. She spent her early formative years in China and that time was extremely significant in developing her ideas, viewpoints, and philosophy. She attended schools both in China and the United States and made several trips back and forth, some unwillingly as when she and her parents were expelled from China during the Boxer Rebellion of 1900.

Pearl Buck began her writing as a girl in China with articles and short stories. There is no doubt that she had a gift for making the strange, unknown, and distant appear familiar. Until the time of her first published success, *East Wind, West Wind,* very little had been written about simple Chinese life although China was becoming of increasing interest to businessmen, diplomats, and missionaries. Nevertheless, the general public thought of the Chinese in rather strange terms, not as people with whom they could easily identify. Buck's feeling for the fundamental truths of life transcended any preconceived notions that the reading public may have had about China, and portrayed her people as understandable human beings who struggled for happiness and success like anyone else.

The Good Earth was published in 1931 and is probably Buck's most popular and widely read novel. It depicts a simple picture, the cycle of life from early years until death. Some Americans who first read the book thought the simple detailed descriptions of everyday Chinese life were "too Chinese" and, therefore, unappealing. Then, too, some Chinese felt that the author's portrayal of their people was inaccurate and incomplete. Most Chinese intellectuals objected to her choice of the peasant farmer as a worthy subject of a novel. They preferred to have the Western world see the intellectual and philosophical Chinese, even though that group was (and is) definitely in the minority. Buck's only answer to such criticism was that she wrote about what she knew best and these were the people whom she saw and came to know and love during her years in the interior of China.

The theme of *The Good Earth* is an uncomplicated one with universal appeal. The author tries to show how man can rise from poverty and relative insignificance to a position of importance and wealth. In some ways, the story is the proverbial Horatio Alger tale that so many Americans know and admire. The difference with this novel and the feature which makes it unique is its setting. Wang Lung, the main character around whom the action in the novel resolves, is a poor man who knows very little apart from the fact that land is valuable and solid and worth owning. Therefore, he spends his entire life trying to acquire as much land as he can in order to insure his own security as well as that of his family and descendants for generations to come. Ironically, he becomes like the rich he at first holds in awe. He has allowed himself to follow in their path and separate himself from the land and live above toil and dirt. The earth theme appears repeatedly throughout the book. Wang Lung's greatest joy is to look out over his land, to hold it in his fingers and to work it for his survival. Even at the end of the novel he returns to the old quarters he occupied on his first plot of land so that he can find the peace he knows his kinship with the land can bring him.

Buck's style is that of a simple direct narrative. There are no complicated literary techniques such as foreshadowing, flashbacks, or stream of consciousness. Neither are there any involved subplots to detract from the main story line. Wang Lung is, as has been noted, the central character and all the other characters and their actions relate in one way or another to him. *The Good Earth* is structured upon characterization, and it is a book of dramatic episodes which are projected through the sensitivities and experiences of those characters. It may be said that a strength of the author's characterization is her consistency, that is to say, all of her characters act and react in keeping with their personalities. None are stereotypes, as their motives are too complex. O-lan is typically good, but there are aspects of her personality which give her depth, dimension, and originality. When she does some seemingly dishonest thing such as steal the jewels she found at the home of the plundered rich, or kill the small baby girl born to her in ill health, she is consistent with her character in the context of these situations. She is realistic and sees both acts as producing more good than evil. O-lan is courageous and faithful and throughout the novel she maintains a beautiful dignity which gives her a special identity of her own, even if she is an unpretty common slave.

One of the most obvious and significant Chinese customs which appears repeatedly in the novel is the submission of the wife in all things to the will of the man. Girl children were born only to be reared for someone else's house as slaves, while men were born to carry on family names, traditions, and property. This situation is based on the Chinese position that women are inferior to men. The reader cannot help but be struck by this attitude as it manifests itself in the lives of the men and women in *The Good Earth*.

The novel may be criticized as having no high point or climax. True enough, there is no point of great and significant decision. There is no one who causes Wang Lung any serious struggle. His only antagonists are the adversity of the elements and the occasional arguments he has with his lazy uncle and his worthless nephew. Dramatic interest is sustained in the novel by well placed turning points which give the story new direction. The first is Wang Lung's marriage to O-lan and their first satisfying years together. Then, in the face of poverty, destitution, and little hope of recovery, Wang Lung demands and receives the handful of gold from the rich man and is thus able to get back to his land. At this point we see how very much Wang Lung's land means to him and what he is willing to do to have it back. In the closing pages of the novel, the quiet servitude and devotion of Pear Blossom, his slave, brings him the only peace and contentment he is to know in his late years. While there is no moralizing as such, Pear Blossom and her relationship to her master leads one to reflect on the fruits of such hard labor and sacrifice. A simple slave girl in a house full of discord—this is all Wang Lung has.

The success of *The Good Earth* is apparent. Pearl Buck won the Pulitzer Prize for it and it has been dramatized as well as made into a motion picture. It is widely read in many languages, undoubtedly because of its universal appeal as a clear and to the point portrayal of one man's struggle for survival, success, and ultimate happiness.

Constance A. Cutler

THE GOOD SOLDIER: SCHWEIK

Type of work: Novel
Author: Jaroslav Hašek (1883-1923)
Type of plot: Military satire
Time of plot: World War I
Locale: Bohemia, Austria
First published: 1920-1923

The feeble-minded but irrepressibly cheerful Schweik is perhaps the strangest character to emerge from any fiction inspired by World War I. A former dog-trader, Schweik was discharged from compulsory military service for "feeble-mindedness." When war breaks out, he is recalled nonetheless and manages innocently to wreak havoc wherever he is sent, be it a military prison or the Russian front. Schweik is the antithesis of all which Prussian militarism stands for.

In *The Good Soldier: Schweik,* Jaroslav Hašek created a comic soldier for all time, a character of consuming ineptness, ingratiating naïveté, and childlike honesty. A bumbling nonwarrior, Schweik is condemned like Sisyphus to push his bulky boulder of honesty into the weighty, contervailing gravity of bureaucratic obesity. Schweik is at once the product of his society and a satirical threat to it.

Although a timeless soldier, Schweik was also of a time and place, a man with an unmistakable country. The country was Austria-Hungary, the now extinct brontosaur-like state ruled by the Habsburg family. At the time Hašek wrote his novel, this multi-national state comprised more than a dozen diverse nationalities recognizing no common unifying *raison d'état* except the lugubrious and all-encompassing Austrian bureaucracy. While centered in Vienna, the tentacles of the American imperial bureaucracy reached into all regions of the Habsburg domain and into all areas of life. In Prague, where Hašek lived, the presence of the bureaucracy was evident everywhere. Like his contemporary countryman, Franz Kafka, Hašek knew from firsthand experience the dehumanizing effects of the Austrian state machinery. But, whereas Kafka in *The Trial* wrote a horrifyingly spare and sober account of bureaucracy at work, Hašek chose to ridicule the institution.

Ironically, Hašek's satirical treatment of Schweik's relationship to the German-speaking Austrian bureaucracy written through the eyes of a Czech, linked him to a common Austrian literary portrayal of the institution. However, while many Austrian writers chose to point up the slovenliness or *Schlamperei* of the Austrian bureaucrat, they did so with affection and a certain paternalism which is completely lacking in Hašek's work. Adjustment, not ridicule, was the common prescription. Hašek was a writer with a strong sense of patriotism for Czech culture, not Austrian. It would have been impossible for Hašek to romanticize the ineptness of an institution which, as depicted through Schweik's eyes, acted—if at all—with arbitrary, automatic, and callous disregard for the needs of the individual. Unable to deal with honesty, the Austrian bureaucracy in *The Good Soldier: Schweik,* labels Schweik insane. The author, however, makes it clear that it is the institution which has gone mad because it has proven itself incapable of responding to the needs of those it purports to serve.

GOODBYE, MR. CHIPS

Type of work: Novelette
Author: James Hilton (1900-1954)
Type of plot: Sentimental romance
Time:of plot: 1870-1933
Locale: An English boys' school
First published: 1933

The genesis of this charming and instantly popular novel occurred when a young journalist, James Hilton, was given an assignment to write a Christmas story for an English newspaper. The novel consists of the reminiscence of the old schoolmaster, Mr. Chips. Sitting before a fire lit against the drear November weather, his mind wanders back over the many incidents and individuals who entered into his life over his long career as a teacher at Brookfield, an English prep school. Though a common man, Chips, through honesty, perseverance, and love, had become an esteemed legend at Brookfield.

It was not until the American publication of *Goodbye, Mr. Chips* in June, 1934, that James Hilton became a popular, successful, and critically admired author. Prior to that time he had written eight full-length novels, along with a large body of topical commentary and literary criticism, but he was still relatively unknown and unappreciated. Even *Lost Horizon,* which was later to become one of the best selling books of its time, was largely ignored when first issued in 1933. The spectacular success of *Goodbye, Mr. Chips* surprised all of the critics, including the author, and even today it is difficult to account for the book's enormous and continuing popularity.

Since *Goodbye, Mr. Chips* is presented as the reminiscence of an old man, the dominant mood is that of sentimental, nostalgic reverie. Hilton adroitly maintains a fine balance between the gentle humor characteristic of Chips' everyday life and the pathos of a few sad incidents (the death of Chips' wife in childbirth, of his students in combat, and, finally, of the old man himself). Thus, the book is neither overly cheerful nor maudlin, although it comes close, at times, to both.

Basing Chips on a synthesis of his own father and his favorite Latin teacher, Hilton created a character many readers recognized in their own experience. But it is doubtful that simple reader identification or the fact that Chips (Chipping, actually—Chips is a nickname) is a clearly defined, amiable, slightly eccentric, modestly humorous man is enough to account for the novel's enormous popularity. There must be something in this character of unexceptional ability, living an ordinary life, that struck a deeply responsive chord in the mid-1930's.

Chips' life covers the second half of the nineteenth century and the first third of the twentieth (1848-1933). The historically crucial events in the book, however, are World War I and, vaguely in the background, the Great

Depression. Chips' appeal can be fully understood only by seeing his uneventful life in the context of the very eventful historical epoch it passed through, with special emphasis on the time of publication: 1934.

Chips is, above all, a "common man." He admits to being an ordinary teacher at a good, but essentially second-class preparatory school. He gives up his early headmaster ambitions, because he decides that he is not good enough for the job. When he courts and marries Kathy Bridges, he cannot understand what she sees in him.

But, as an ordinary man, he demonstrates in moments of crisis an essential strength and resourcefulness, the outstanding example being the Latin lesson he conducts in the midst of an air raid. Thus, however frantic and chaotic the modern world becomes, Hilton assures us, the common man can find the needed inner strength and will to survive with dignity.

Chips is not just an ordinary man, however; he is also the embodiment of a tradition. Brookfield is not a great school, but it is a school rooted in the British tradition of greatness. As its exemplar, Chips stands for honor, dignity, continuity, and a strong organic connection to the past. And yet, primarily because of his marriage to Kathy, he has a sense of social movement and a compassion for the disadvantaged.

Thus, Chips balances the best of the old and the new, with the emphasis on the old. He clashes with the modern headmaster over the issue and it almost costs him his job. During World War I, he defies popular prejudice to publicly commemorate an ex-German teacher who died fighting for the enemy.

Accurately labeled "pre-war" by his students, Chips represents the traditional values and disciplined life style that existed prior to World War I. And, through him, Hilton suggests that they remain valid and can survive even in the frenetic modern world.

GORBODUC

Type of work: **Drama**
Authors: **Thomas Norton (1532-1584) and Thomas Sackville (1536-1608)**
Type of plot: **Romantic tragedy**
Time of plot: **Before the Saxon invasion of England**
Locale: **England**
First presented: **1562**

In the mythical history of Gorboduc, King of Britain and the last of his line, the dramatists embodied the concern of Elizabethans about their Queen's lack of an heir. With the deaths of Gorboduc, his queen, and their two sons, England is thrown into bloody civil unrest. The work is important in the history of English literature, being the first play written in blank verse and one of the first English tragedies to employ a domestic theme.

Thomas Sackville and Thomas Norton, at the time of composing *Gorboduc,* were law students of the Inner Temple in London and presented their play as an experimental attempt at handling British legend as subject matter for classical drama. The young men, like many university students and courtiers of the mid-sixteenth century, scorned the crudities of native drama and wished to infuse the homemade product with elegance of diction and more elaborate staging in the manner of Seneca.

They therefore used blank verse, which in *Gorboduc* has an unexpected sureness and skill of technique. However, they neglected story line and characterization in favor of innumerable epic passages, long soliloquies and philosophic tirades. As a result, their play has a static and mechanical quality.

Sackville and Norton relied heavily on well-known Senecan devices, such as the chorus, which is composed of "Four ancient and sage men of Britain." This chorus declaims in rhymed verse at the end of each of the first four acts, either foreshadowing events or summarizing past action. Together with the dumb shows, which precede each act, main incidents are described; the rest of the dramatic action is reported by the Senecan-derived *nuntius,* various counselors, Marcella, a Lady of the Queen's privy chamber, and in one instance, by the Duke of Cornwall. The murders of all main protagonists (Ferrex, Porrex, King Gorboduc, and Queen Videna) take place offstage, as is typical of Senecan-based models.

The authors make extensive use of myth; for example, one finds allusions to Phaeton, Apollo, the fall of Troy, and the Furies. Sackville and Norton read their Ovid and added classical mythology to their play to provide dignity and demonstrate deity's ineluctable control. The play also abounds in rhetorical devices such as exclamation, apostrophe, lamentation, and invocation. In fact, *Gorboduc's* rhetoric far exceeds that of classical drama. Nevertheless, in the hands of these young law students, the attempt to start a new trend in English drama succeeded not only because of its novelty, but because the play has some good lyric passages, exhibits coherence, and at times achieves the solid tone of classical tragedy.

Gorboduc has significance beyond its importance as the first English play in blank verse on a domestic theme utilizing the five-act structure; it influenced Ben Jonson to take up the line of development in a later Renaissance effort to continue classical drama based upon plays of Seneca and Plautus.

GRAND HOTEL

Type of work: Novel
Author: Vicki Baum (1888-1960)
Type of plot: Social chronicle
Time of plot: 1920's
Locale: Berlin
First published: 1930

Through the revolving doors of Berlin's Grand Hotel come people from all walks of life, each with his own obsessions and problems. The novel which emerges is a description of the way these divergent individuals influence and react to one another at this particular time and place. In addition to the inherent interest in such characters as an aging prima ballerina and a nobleman who is actually a con artist, the novel presents a composite picture of European society in the period between World War I and World War II.

Grand Hotel is one of the most perfectly constructed popular novels in modern literature. Skillfully and with notable artistry, the author blends the various ingredients required in her story. She includes the mechanics of running a great cosmopolitan hotel in the Berlin of the 1920's and integrates the subtle class differences which were so important in such an establishment. The guests of the hotel are presented briskly, with precise character sketches, and then put through their paces with professional skill. The author writes with a servicable, plain style, unpretentious and entertaining, neither overly poetic nor condescending. Vicki Baum's greatest gift was that of keeping a narrative moving, of simultaneously taking many stories forward and never sacrificing pace to detail. Yet she understood the value of knowing details and used them to breathe life into her setting and characters. Her craftsmanship is everywhere evident in *Grand Hotel*.

The characters of the novel are not always original, but they are often fascinating. The author seems to believe in her creations so intensely that she makes the reader believe in them, however improbable they might seem at first. It is impossible for the reader not to sympathize with Otto Kringelein, the little bookkeeper from Fredersdorf. The romantic and glamorous ballerina emerges almost as a tragic figure, as the Baron Gaigern becomes, by the end of the tale, a surprisingly noble one. In the milieu of postwar Berlin, corruption was commonplace, as evidenced in the character of Herr Generaldirektor Preysing, but Baum managed to collect in her story a number of worthy and admirable individuals, people imperfect but sympathetic perhaps because of their flaws. Although *Grand Hotel* is not of the highest order of fiction, it is a well-crafted and entertaining popular novel, and probably will endure as such.

THE GRANDISSIMES

Type of work: Novel
Author: George W. Cable (1844-1925)
Type of plot: Regional romance
Time of plot: 1804
Locale: New Orleans
First published: 1880

A story of love, honor, intrigue, and tragedy set in the Creole society of New Orleans, the novel re-creates a part of American life now gone. The villains of the piece are not so much the actors in the drama, but rather the institutions of slavery and the caste system. Because of these, lovers cannot marry each other, and the quadroon son of a wealthy nobleman must lead a life of humiliation. It has been said that the tragedy of the American black is more effectively and truthfully presented here than in many modern novels on the subject.

George Washington Cable has been best known as an early regionalist who evoked a picturesque society with an amusing variety of quaint dialects, but his best work was serious in its social and moral penetration. New Orleans gave him a fascinating stage for the interaction and conflict of cultures and values as well as dialects, and his approach was that of a linguist, sociologist, and moralist, rather than an entertainer. *The Grandissimes* is based on the true story of an African prince, Bras Coupé, captured by slavers and transported to Louisiana, a story Cable had been unable to publish separately because his publishers found it "unmitigatedly distressful." Cable, who felt that fiction should "teach without telling," therefore embodied his social criticism within a romantic plot, and succeeded in mitigating the distress sufficiently for a wide public; at the same time, he was able to convey a detailed and sweeping picture of New Orleans society that served as an indictment of race and caste prejudice. He later noted that any parallels his readers might find between the situation in the novel, that of the new American supremacy in 1803, and that of the Reconstruction period of seventy-five years later, were fully intended. Indignant reaction in New Orleans testified to the accuracy of his depiction, and his message still holds truth for modern readers.

The author analyzes in *The Grandissimes* with skill and a light although penetrating touch a complicated, if narrow, society. Each class or caste illustrated in the novel thinks itself above the others; from the African slave Prince to the Creoles and the pure whites, each refuses to bow before the others and submits only bitterly to physical, economic, or political domination. But the individuals in the book also possess a witty pride combined with a shrewd sense of self-appraisal; they know their worth and do not need to pretend to be more or less than they are. They cling to a long-standing sense of pride in family and clan as tenaciously as they cling to their old superstitions, many of which were taken from the slaves.

Cable neatly weaves a sly humor into the rich texture of his narrative, a humor that is even present in the intense discussion of deliberately narrow-minded and parochial attitudes and prejudices. Cable writes with an exquisite, graceful prose style, at once poetic and witty, realistic and fanciful. The novel introduced a new realism and breadth of vision into the literature of the South, as well as a new and highly professional standard of craftsmanship. The novel is important not only for its place in American and Southern literary history, but because it is a superbly written and deeply felt document and a work of fiction of the highest quality.

THE GRANDMOTHERS

Type of work: Novel
Author: Glenway Wescott (1901-)
Type of plot: Regional chronicle
Time of plot: 1830-1925
Locale: Wisconsin
First published: 1927

During his childhood, Alwyn Tower spent hours pouring over family albums. He begged his grandmother to tell him stories of her childhood, her children, and her relatives. Piece by piece, from grandmother, parents, aunts, uncles, and family records, young Alwyn learned of his roots. His heritage is a disordered one: a war deserter, an insane woman, a husband and wife who loathed each other, an uncle who lived off his mother-in-law's money. Alwyn knows that his character will be a rearrangement of his various progenitors who were, after all, one of the last pioneer families to settle the land.

In *The Grandmothers,* the author reveals the unknown and unseen tragedies that lie behind each person, making him what he has become. With tenderness and compassion, Wescott lays bare the hidden memories that necessarily remain unspoken between these inhibited and unintrospective characters. The tough and austere people who march through the pages of this novel, as they did across the untamed land, accept their grim fates with a sense of fatalism not far removed from classical tragedy. They all began their lives with great hopes and dreams, but soon learned that life plays cruel tricks, often destroying those who seem to hold the greatest promise, the most beautiful and the most clever, and letting the others live out their empty, long lives. Through all of the stories, Wescott shows a gift for bringing people to life through the use of authentic and touching period details, such as Serena Tower's hair albums and hair wreaths or Grandfather Tower's flute and deafness.

In an important sense, Alwyn Tower's quest to find his past is the quest of America; in his search to learn about his antecedents, Alwyn Tower stands for the nation looking back to the vital and strenuous days of its growth. It is clear that the author feels that only by understanding its traditions and past hardships can the country comprehend its present and future and surmount any future difficulties. The novel was an ambitious one, for it was meant to represent in one family the entire pioneer history of the United States. Yet, Wescott did not sacrifice individual characterization to his ambition for scope and symbolic representation. In fact, it is because his human beings are so filled with life and human passions that they can successfully merge into a legendary historical view. The plot is subordinated to the search for a meaning in the past; the individual stories are woven and interwoven, gradually filling in the intricate and always fascinating picture of the Tower family's often tragic history and the history of the growing American nation.

THE GRAPES OF WRATH

Type of work: **Novel**
Author: John Steinbeck (1902-)
Type of plot: Social criticism
Time of plot: 1930's
Locale: **Southwest United States and California**
First published: 1939

A bitter chronicle of the exodus of farm families from the Dust Bowl during the 1930's, this work is a harsh indictment of our capitalistic economy. Searching for work in California, the Joads begin their long journey. Treated like enemies by the businessmen along their path, the older members of the family die, and those remaining are herded into migrant camps where the poor help one another to survive.

The publication of John Steinbeck's *The Grapes of Wrath* caused a nationwide stir in 1939. This account of the predicament of migrant workers was taken more as social document than as fiction. Some saw it as an exposé of capitalist excesses; others, as a distorted call to revolution. Frequently compared to *Uncle Tom's Cabin,* it was awarded the Pulitzer Prize for 1940.

Recent literary critics, taking a second look at the novel, have often lumped it with a number of other dated books of the 1930's as "proletarian fiction." A careful reader, however, recognizes that beneath this outraged account of an outrageous social situation lies a dynamic, carefully structured story which applies not just to one era or society, but to the universal human predicament.

As a social document, the novel presents such a vivid picture of oppression and misery that one tends to doubt its authenticity. Steinbeck, however, had done more than academic research. He had journeyed from Oklahoma to California, lived in a migrant camp, and worked alongside the migrants. (Peter Lisca reports that after the novel appeared, the workers sent Steinbeck a patchwork dog sewn from scraps of their clothing and wearing a tag labeled "Migrant John.") Before making the motion picture, which still stands as one of the great films of the era, Darryl F. Zanuck hired private detectives to verify Steinbeck's story; they reported that conditions were even worse than those depicted in the book. The political situation was a powder keg; Freeman Champney has remarked that "it looked as if nothing could avert an all-out battle between revolution and fascism in California's great valleys."

Social injustice was depicted so sharply that Steinbeck himself was accused of being a revolutionary. Certainly he painted the oppressive economic system in bleak colors. Warren French argues convincingly, however, that Steinbeck was basically reformer, not revolutionary; that he wanted to change the attitudes and behavior of people—both migrants and economic barons—not overturn the private enterprise system. Indeed, Steinbeck observes that ownership of land is morally edifying to a man.

Steinbeck once declared that the writer must "set down his time as nearly as he can understand it," and that he should "serve as the watchdog of society . . . to satirize its silliness, to attack its injustices, to stigmatize its faults." In *The Grapes of Wrath,* he does all these things, then goes further to interpret events from a distinctly American point of view. Like Whitman, he expresses love for all men and respect for manual labor. Like Jefferson, he asserts a preference for agrarian society in which men retain a close, nourishing tie to the soil: his farmers dwindle psychologically as they are separated from their land, and the California owners become oppressors as they substitute ledgers for direct contact with the soil. Like Emerson, Steinbeck demonstrates faith in the common man and in the ideal of self-reliance. He also develops the Emersonian religious concept of an oversoul. The preacher, Jim Casy, muses " . . . maybe that's the Holy Sperit—the human sperit—the whole shebang. Maybe all men got one big soul ever'body's a part of it." Later Tom Joad reassures Ma that even if he isn't physically with her, "Wherever they's a fight so hungry people can eat, I'll be there. Wherever they's a cop beatin' up a guy, I'll be there. . . . I'll be in the way kids laugh when they're hungry an' they know supper's ready. . . . "

This theme, that all men essentially belong together, are a part of one another and of a greater whole that transcends momentary reality, is what removes *The Grapes of Wrath* from the genre of timely proletarian fiction and makes it an allegory for all men in all circumstances. Warren French notes that the real story of this novel is not the Joads' search for economic security, but their education, which transforms them from self-concern to a recognition of their bond with the whole human race. At first, Tom Joad is intensely individualistic, interested mainly in making his own way; Pa's primary concern is keeping bread on his table; Rosasharn dreams only of traditional middle-class success; and Ma, an Earth-Mother with a spine of steel, concentrates fiercely upon keeping the "fambly" together. At the end, Tom follows Casy's example in fighting for human rights; Pa, in building the dike, sees the necessity for all men to work together; Rosasharn forgets her grief over her stillborn child and unhesitatingly lifts a starving man to her milk-filled breast; and Ma can say, "Use' ta be the fambly was fust. It ain't so now. It's anybody. Worse off we get, the more we got to do." Thus the Joads have overcome that separation which Paul Tillich equates with sin, that alienation from others which existentialists are so fond of describing as the inescapable human condition.

It is interesting to note how much *The Grapes of Wrath,* which sometimes satirizes, sometimes attacks organized Christian religion, reflects the Bible. In structure, as critics have been quick to notice, it parallels the story of the Exodus to a "promised land." Symbolically, as Peter Lisca observes, the initials of Jim Casy are those of Jesus Christ, another itinerant preacher who rebelled against traditional religion, went into the wilderness, discovered his own gospel, and eventually gave his life in service to others.

Language, too, is frequently Biblical, especially in the interchapters which, like a Greek chorus, restate, reinforce, and generalize from the specific happenings of the narrative. The cadences, repetitions, and parallel lines all echo the patterns of the Psalms—Ma Joad's favorite book.

Even the title of the novel is Biblical; the exact phrase is Julia Ward Howe's, but the reference is to Jeremiah and Revelation. The grapes have been a central symbol throughout the book: first of promise, representing the fertile California valleys, but finally of bitter rage as the Midwesterners realize they have been lured West with false bait, that they will not partake of this fertility. The wrath grows, a fearsome, terrible wrath; but, as several interchapters make clear, better wrath than despair, because wrath moves to action. And Steinbeck would have his people act, in concert and in concern for one another—and finally prevail over all forms of injustice.

Sally Buckner

GREAT EXPECTATIONS

Type of work: Novel
Author: Charles Dickens (1812-1870)
Type of plot: Mystery romance
Time of plot: Nineteenth century
Locale: England
First published: 1860-1861

From two events, Miss Havisham's desertion by her fiancé on her wedding day, and the youngster Pip's aid to an escaped prisoner, Dickens weaves a story of vindictiveness on the one hand and gratitude on the other. The motives combine to affect the life of young Pip, for Miss Havisham has marked him as an object of her vindictiveness, while the prisoner has sworn to reward the boy. The novel, though resolved on a hopeful note, is primarily gloomy in tone, focusing on the constant pressures placed on the orphan boy, Pip.

G. K. Chesterton once observed that all of Dickens' novels could be titled "Great Expectations," for they are full of an unsubstantial yet ardent expectation of everything. Yet, as Chesterton pointed out with irony, the only book to which Dickens gave the actual title was one in which most of the expectations were never realized. To the Victorians, the word *expectations* meant legacy as well as anticipations. In that closed society, one of the few means by which a person born of the lower or lower-middle class could rise dramatically to wealth and high status was through the inheritance of valuables. Consequently, a major theme of the Victorian social novel involved the hero's movement through the class structure. And often the vehicle for that movement was money, either bestowed before death or inherited. Unlike many nineteenth century novels that rely upon the stale plot device of a surprise legacy to enrich the fortunate protagonists, *Great Expectations* probes deeply into the ethical and psychological dangers of advancing through the class system by means of wealth acquired from the toil of others.

Although the story of Pip's expectations dominates the bulk of the novel, he is not the only person who waits to benefit from another's money. His beloved Estella, the ward of Miss Havisham, is wholly dependent upon the caprices of the unstable old woman. Moreover, other characters are the mysterious instrumentalities of legacies. The solicitor Jaggers, who acts as the legal agent for both Miss Havisham and Abel Magwitch, richly benefits from his services. Even his lackey Mr. Wemmick, a mild soul who changes his personality from lamb to wolf to please his employer, earns his living from the legal machinery of the courts. Just as the source of Pip's money is revealed at last to be socially corrupted, so the uses of tainted wealth inevitably bring about corruption.

In *Bleak House* (1852-1853) Dickens had already explored with great skill the ruthless precincts of the law courts. But his next three novels—

Hard Times (1854), *Little Dorrit* (1855-1857), and *A Tale of Two Cities* (1859)—were not so well sustained and, in spite of memorable scenes, were less popular with the critics and public alike. *Great Expectations* (1860-1861, first published serially in *All the Year Round*) recovered for the author his supremacy with his vast reading audience. Serious, controlled, nearly as complex structurally as *Bleak House,* the novel also reminded Victorian readers of *David Copperfield* (1849-1850). Both are apprenticeship novels that treat the life-education of a hero. *Great Expectations* is somewhat less autobiographical than *David Copperfield,* but it repeats the basic formula of the genre, that of an honest, rather ingenuous but surely likeable young man who, through a series of often painful experiences, learns important lessons about life and himself. These lessons are always designed to reveal the hero's limitations. As he casts off his own weaknesses and better understands the dangers of the world, he succeeds—that is to say, he advances through the class system—and ends up less brash, a chastened but wiser man.

Great Expectations differs from *David Copperfield,* however, in the ways that the hero matures to self-knowledge. Both David and Pip are, in the beginning, young snobs (Pip more than David). Both suffer the traumas of a shattered childhood and troubled adolescence. But David's childhood suffering is fully motivated on the basis of his separation from loved ones. An innocent, he is the victim of evil which he does not cause. Pip, on the other hand, suffers from a childhood nightmare that forms a pattern of his later experience. An orphan like David, he lives with his brutal sister and her husband, the gentle blacksmith Joe Gargery. For whatever abuse he endures from Mrs. Joe, he more than compensates in the brotherly affection of this simple, generous man. Also he wins the loving sympathy of Biddy, another loyal friend. But he is not satisfied. And when he comes upon the convicts in the fog and is terrified, he feels a sense of guilt—misplaced but psychologically necessary—as much for his crimes against his protectors as for the theft of a pork pie. Thereafter, his motives, cloudy as the scene of his childhood terror, are weighted with secret apprehension and guilt. To regain his lost innocence, he must purge himself of the causes of this guilt.

Pip's life-apprenticeship, then, involves his fullest understanding of "crimes" against his loved ones and the ways to redeem himself. The causes of his guilt are, from lesser to greater, his snobbish pride, his betrayal of friends and protectors, and finally his participation in the machinery of corruption.

As a snob, he not only breaks the social mold into which he has been cast, but lords it over the underlings and unfortunates of the class system. Because of his presumed great expectations, he believes himself to be superior to the humbler Joe and Biddy. He makes such a pompous fool of himself that Trabb's boy—that brilliant comic invention, at once naughty boy and honest philosopher—parodies his absurd airs and pretensions. But his snobbery costs him a dearer price than humiliation by an urchin. He falls in love with Estella, like himself a pretender to high social class, only to be rejected in place of a worthless cad, Bentley Drummle. Finally, his fanciful dreams of social distinction are shattered forever when he learns the bitter truth about his benefactor, who is not the highborn Miss Havisham but the escaped convict Magwitch, the wretched stranger of his terror in the fog.

As Pip comes to understand the rotten foundations for his social position, he also learns terrible truths about his own weaknesses. Out of foolish pride he has betrayed his most loyal friends, Joe and Biddy. In a sense, he has even betrayed Miss Havisham. He has mistaken her insanity for mere eccentricity and allowed her to act out her fantasies of romantic revenge. When he tries to confront her with the reality of her life, he is too late. She expires in flames. He is almost too late, in fact, to come to the service of his real benefactor, Magwitch. So disturbed is he with the realization of the convict's sacrifice, that he nearly flees from the old man, now disguised as "Provis," when he is in danger. At best, he can return to Magwitch gratitude, not love. And his sense of guilt grows from his understanding that he cannot ever repay his debt to a man he secretly loathes.

Pip's final lesson is that, no matter how pure might be his motives, he has been one of the instruments of social corruption. In a sense, he is the counterpart to the malcontent Dolge Orlick. Like Orlick, as a youth he had been an apprentice at the forge. But whereas he was fortunate to move upward into society, Orlick, consumed by hatred, failed in every enterprise. In Chapter 53, a climactic scene of the novel, Orlick confronts his enemy and lays to Pip the blame for all of his failures. He even accuses Pip of responsibility for the death of Mrs. Joe. The charge, of course, is paranoiac and false: Orlick is the murderer. Yet, psychologically, Pip can—in his almost hallucinatory terror—accept Orlick's reasoning. As a child, Pip had hated his sister. If he had not been the active instrument of her death, nevertheless he profited from it. Similarly, Pip profited from the hard-earned toil of Magwitch. Indeed, most of the success he had enjoyed, thanks to the astute protection of Mr. Jaggers, had come not as his due but for a price, the payment of corrupted money. Since he had been the ignorant recipient of the fruits of corruption, his psychological guilt is all the greater.

Nevertheless, Pip, though chastened, is not overwhelmed by guilt. During the course of his apprenticeship to life he has learned something about himself, some valuable truths about his limitations. By the end of his career, when his apprenticeship is over and he is a responsible, mature being, he has cast off petty pride, snobbery, and the vexations of corrupted wealth. Although he has lost his innocence forever, he can truly appreciate Herbert Pocket, Joe, and Biddy, who have retained their integrity. When he turns to Estella, also chastened by her wretched marriage to the sadistic Drummle, he has atleast the hope of beginning a new life with her, one founded upon an accurate understanding of himself and the dangers of the world.

Leslie B. Mittleman

THE GREAT GALEOTO

Type of work: Drama
Author: José Echegaray y Eizaguirre (1832-1916)
Type of plot: Social satire
Time of plot: Nineteenth century
Locale: Madrid, Spain
First presented: 1881

The Great Galeoto *is a conscious rebellion against the limitations drama places on reality. Echegaray wants to place all of society on stage, showing as motivations not the personal impulses of individual characters but the nebulous mob-like motivations arising out of the interactions of groups of people within the social framework. Thus the play shows how the scandalous gossip of "the town" can force innocent individuals into scandalous behavior and even cause their deaths.*

The Great Galeoto is one of literature's most graphic representations of the frightful power of slander. José Echegaray thus administered a salutary admonition not only to Madrid society with the first representation of his play in 1881, but subsequently to the societies of Spanish America, where it was also represented. Echegaray has thus given effective dramatic treatment to a deadly, insidious social plague that has long been rampant in human history. For this reason, among others, *The Great Galeoto* has often cast almost a hypnotic spell on its audiences in Spain and in the eighteen republics of Spanish America. Severely condemned by the Bible as a deadly sin, slander, as so clearly shown in *The Great Galeoto,* is like acid because the denial often does not overtake the lie. And, as Echegaray so pungently demonstrates, the lie can eventually become a truth. Although Ernesto and Mercedes failed to react as vigorously against falsehood as they might have, the fact that they were finally forced into doing precisely what wagging tongues had so falsely accused them of doing is the play's most arresting theme.

Echegaray's dramatic skill enhanced the impact of his theme, but *The Great Galeoto* has been a traditional success in the Spanish-speaking world partially because historians have shown that certain segments of Hispanic and Hispanic-American society, like certain other ethnic groups, have changed their behavior patterns and acted as they have been taught to act by propaganda. Comparisons of this propaganda technique can be drawn with the modern example of "The Big Lie," a technique attributed by some scholars to Nikolai Lenin; also attributed by Adolf Hitler in *Mein Kampf* to his political enemies; and eventually attributed by Allied propaganda during World War II to Hitler's propaganda minister, Dr. Joseph Paul Goebbels.

Directly and indirectly, slander kills in *The Great Galeoto,* causing the death of Viscount Nebreda, the death of Julián, and the terror and ruination of Ernesto and Teodora.

THE GREAT GATSBY

Type of work: Novel
Author: F. Scott Fitzgerald (1896-1940)
Type of plot: Social criticism
Time of plot: 1922
Locale: New York City and Long Island
First published: 1925

Jay Gatz changes his name to Gatsby and amasses great wealth by dubious means solely to please Daisy, a socialite. Wooed earlier by the penniless Gatsby, Daisy had rejected him for her social equal, Tom Buchanan. Yet no matter how high Gatsby rises, he is doomed, for the wealthy Buchanans are not worthy of Gatsby's sincerity and innocence. Though Gatsby plans to take the blame for a hit-and-run murder committed by Daisy, Tom Buchanan tells the victim's husband that Gatsby was driving, and the husband murders Gatsby. The Buchanans retreat into the irresponsibility their wealth allows them.

F. Scott Fitzgerald, the prophet of the jazz age, was born in St. Paul, Minnesota, to the daughter of a self-made Irish immigrant millionaire. His father was a ne'er-do-well salesman who had married above his social position. From his mother, Fitzgerald inherited the dream that was America—the promise that any young man could become anything he chose through hard work. From his father he inherited the propensity for failure. This antithesis pervaded his own life and most of his fiction. Educated in the East, Fitzgerald was overcome with the glamour of New York and Long Island. To him it was the "stuff of old romance," "the source of infinite possibilities." His fiction focused primarily on the lives of the rich. With the family fortune depleted by his father, Fitzgerald found himself in his early twenties an army officer in love with a southern belle, Zelda Sayre, who was socially above him. She refused his first proposal of marriage because he was too poor. Fitzgerald was determined to have her. He wrote and published *This Side of Paradise* (1920), on the basis of which Zelda married him.

Their public life for the next ten years epitomized the dizzy spiral of the 1920's—wild parties, wild spending, and wild cars—and following the national pattern, they crashed just as spectacularly in the 1930's. Zelda went mad and was committed finally to a sanitarium. Fitzgerald became a functional alcoholic. From his pinnacle in the publishing field during the 1920's when his short stories commanded as much as $1500, he fell in the 1930's to writing luke-warm Hollywood scripts. He died in Hollywood in 1940, mostly forgotten and with most of his work out of print. Now back in academic vogue, Fitzgerald's place in American letters has been affirmed by a single novel—*The Great Gatsby*.

Fitzgerald once said, "America's great promise is that something's going to happen, but it never does. America is the moon that never rose." This indictment of the American Dream could well serve as an epigraph for *The Great Gatsby*. Jay Gatsby pursues his dream of romantic success without ever understanding that it has escaped him. He fails to understand that he cannot recapture the past (his fresh, new love for Daisy Buchanan) no matter how much money he makes, no matter how much wealth he displays.

The character of Gatsby was never intended by Fitzgerald to be a realistic portrayal; he is a romantic hero, always somewhat unreal, bogus and absurd. No matter the corrupt sources of his wealth such as bootlegging and gambling (and these are only hinted at) he stands for hope, for romantic belief—for innocence. He expects more from life than the other characters who are all more or less cynical. He is an eternal juvenile in a brutal and corrupt world.

To underscore the corruption of the Dream, Fitzgerald's characters all are finally seen as liars. Buchanan's mistress lies to her husband. Jordan Baker is a pathological liar who cheats in golf tournaments. Tom Buchanan's lie to his mistress Myrtle's husband results in the murder of Gatsby. Daisy, herself, is basically insincere; she lets Gatsby take the blame for her hit-and-run accident. Gatsby's whole life is a lie: he lies about his past and his present. He lies to himself. Nick Carraway, the Midwestern narrator, tells us that he is the only completely honest person he knows. However, he panders for Gatsby, and in the end he turns away from Tom Buchanan, unable to force the truth into the open. He knows the truth about Gatsby but is unable to tell the police. His affirmation of Gatsby at the end is complex; he envies Gatsby's romantic selflessness and innocence at the same time that he abhors his lack of self-knowledge.

The Great Gatsby incorporates a number of themes and motifs that unify the novel and contribute to its impact. The initiation theme governs the narrator Nick Carraway, who is a young man come East to make his fortune in stocks and bonds and who returns to the Midwest sadly disillusioned. The frontier theme is also present. Gatsby believes in the "green light," the ever-accessible future in which one can achieve what one has missed in the past. The final paragraphs of the novel state this important theme as well as it has ever been stated. Class issues are very well presented. Tom and Daisy seem accessible but when their position is threatened they close the doors, retreating into their wealth and carelessness, letting others like Gatsby pay the vicious price in hurt and suffering. The carelessness of the rich and their followers is seen in the recurring motif of the bad driver.

Automobile accidents are ubiquitous. At Gatsby's first party there is a smash-up with drunk drivers. Jordan Baker has a near accident after which Nick calls her "a rotten driver." Gatsby is stopped for speeding but is able to fix the ticket by showing the cop a card from the mayor of New York. Finally, Myrtle Wilson is killed by Daisy, driving Gatsby's car. Bad driving becomes a moral statement in the novel.

Settings in the novel are used very well by Fitzgerald, from the splendid mansions of Long Island through the wasteland of the valley of ashes presided over by the eyes of Dr. T. J. Eckleburg (where the Wilsons live) to the New York of the Plaza Hotel or Tom and Myrtle Wilson's apartment. In each case a variety of texture and social class is presented to the reader. Most important, however, is Fitzgerald's use of Nick as a narrator. Like Conrad before him—and from whom he learned his craft—Fitzgerald had a romantic sensibility which controlled fictional material best through the lens of a narrator. As with Marlow in Conrad's *Heart of Darkness,* Nick relates the story of an exceptional man who fails in his dream. He is both attracted and repelled by a forceful man who dares to lead a life he could not sustain. Like Marlow, he pays tribute to his hero who is also his alter-ego. Gatsby's tragedy is Nick's education. His return to the Midwest is a moral return to the safer, more solid values of the heartland. Fitzgerald himself was unable to follow such a conservative path but he clearly felt that the American Dream should be pursued with less frantic, orgiastic, prideful convulsions of energy and spirit. It is a lesson we are still learning.

Michael S. Reynolds

THE GREAT MEADOW

Type of work: Novel
Author: Elizabeth Madox Roberts (1886-1941)
Type of plot: Historical romance
Time of plot: 1774-1781
Locale: Western Virginia and Kentucky
First published: 1930

Though the young Diony Hall dreams of a life of fancy balls, carriages, and fine houses, she rejects the suitor who could provide these amenities. Instead, she marries the adventurous Jarvis and the couple set off for the frontier settlements of Kentucky. The historical settlement of the Kentucky country is only a background to the novel's real focus: the place of women in the wilderness. Roberts attempted to give the reader an insight into Diony's mind by the heavy use of images and symbols.

Though it was her fourth published novel, *The Great Meadow* had been slowly developing in Elizabeth Madox Roberts' mind for many years. She was descended from pioneers who had settled in the Kentucky wilderness, and she wished to commemorate the part such settlers had played in transforming the great meadowland beyond the mountains into homes for themselves. She carefully considered theme, characters, style, and form. The result is a novel laid in the period of the American Revolution and the settlement of land west of the southern Appalachians, with such historical personages as Daniel Boone, James Harrod, and George Rogers Clark playing subsidiary roles. The progress of the war was briefly reported from time to time as something happening far away, except for Indian raids, and skirmishes between white settlers and red men urged into battle by the British.

The dominant theme of the evolution of order out of chaos is developed in two movements: Diony Hall, an introspective but physically active young girl, seeks to control the welter of emotions and thoughts within herself as she matures into a young woman, and to find and understand the part she was intended to play in life by the great Author of Nature. She becomes a part of the other movement, that of the settlers who brought order and civilization into what had been raw wilderness. Diony is the only fully developed character in the novel, the only one seen from within as well as without. The two movements are intermeshed as the author alternately reveals Diony's thoughts and feelings and then shifts to the physical action of the story which involves Diony with the many other characters.

In style, the novel blends poetry and prose. Music abounds in ballads, hymns, the sounds of Thomas Hall's anvil, bird songs, the bells on horses' necks, and fiddle music for dancing. Images of weaving suggest the making of a historical tapestry ("the words and the wool were spun together"). Archaic locutions and dialectal words ("blowth," "frighted") give an eighteenth century folk flavor.

The principal weakness of *The Great Meadow* is the use of the Enoch Arden theme at the end when Berk returns after his long absence. For most readers, however, this ending may seem acceptable, particularly since Berk saved himself from being eaten by his captors through a convincing argument that his "thinking part" gave him his strength. This is a corollary of Diony's belief in "the power of reason over the wild life of the earth."

THE GREAT VALLEY

Type of work: Novel
Author: Mary Johnston (1870-1936)
Type of plot: Historical romance
Time of plot: 1735-1760
Locale: Virginia and Ohio
First published: 1926

This saga of an immigrant Scottish family in America is a historical romance, a genre which has long enjoyed tremendous popularity with American readers, but lacked much critical attention. The Selkirk family pushes westward, constantly in conflict with the Indians. Many of the clan are slain, some taken captive, and some reunited with their family after years of captivity. Though the novel deals with such grim realities, its tone is basically optimistic, celebrating the beauty of the land.

Mary Johnston intended *The Great Valley* as an epic of the opening of the American frontier, and in some respects she succeeded. It is a well-crafted and enjoyable novel, if not overly profound. An optimistic book, it does not avoid describing the hardships of the settlers' lives, but stresses the positive aspects of their adventure. The beauty of the virgin land comes to symbolize in the minds of John Selkirk and his family its promise for the future.

The characters are virtuous, indomitable, and almost too noble; yet the reader feels that such people must have existed to build up the country. For Mary Johnston's idealistic novel, at least, they are artistically right. The inner lives of the characters are not dealt with at all; Mary Johnston pays only the most superficial attention to the psychology of her people. Their lives are entirely composed of physical acts and of desires, of hopes for the future and of hard work, and, occasionally, of memories of past life in Scotland. They are not soft people; they are capable of meeting every adversity in their paths. "Crying's good too, sometimes," says Jean Selkirk. "But I don't cry much." And this is the key to her character and to most of the characters in the novel.

There is no complicated plot in *The Great Valley;* the story is that of the efforts of the Selkirk clan to establish themselves in the wilds of America. Some family members die, others marry and have children, and life moves on. The spare writing avoids melodrama. Johnston respects her characters, as they respect one another. John Selkirk respects all men, black and red as well as white, as long as they deserve respect; he refuses to countenance slavery, although his son differs from him on the issue. But even here there is no violent disagreement. The lives of the family move forward, and its members establish a base for their descendants, which was their dream when they first sailed on the *Prudence*.

THE GREEN BAY TREE

Type of work: Novel
Author: Louis Bromfield (1896-1956)
Type of plot: Social chronicle
Time of plot: Early twentieth century
Locale: Middle West
First published: 1924

The frontier may be gone, but this does not stop future generations of Americans from exercising the pioneer energy of their heritage in other directions. Thus young Lily Shane has an illegitimate child, refuses to marry the father, and goes abroad. She consistently decides not to choose the status quo. *Meanwhile the drab midwestern town she left goes through the upheavals of industrialization: violent strikes by mill workers, the rise of labor leaders, and ultimately the destruction of the family mansion. Lily loses her lover during World War I and her son is badly wounded. Though she has suffered, she still feels vindicated in choosing to be an individual.*

Louis Bromfield's first novel, *The Green Bay Tree,* along with *Possession* (1925), which continues the subplot of Ellen Tolliver, established for the author a popular reputation while he was still in his twenties. For its harsh treatment of small-town America, critics at the time compared the novel with Sherwood Anderson's *Winesburg, Ohio* (1919) and Sinclair Lewis' *Main Street* (1920). Yet the comparison is forced. Although Bromfield's Town—given no other name but certainly based upon the writer's hometown of Mansfield, Ohio—is described as vulgar, gossip-ridden, and provincial, it is treated, ambivalently, also as the heartland of people of strong, defiant character. Although Lily Shane is in "revolt" against the roots of her past, she occasionally returns from France to her home at Cypress Hill, always carrying with her the conviction that the rest of the world suffers from the same destructive forces that she has left behind in America. *The Green Bay Tree,* then, is not wholly a satire upon the sterility of American culture; it reaches outward in an attempt to understand the malaise that thrust many nations into the barbarism of World War I. At the same time, the book is a psychological study concerning the disintegration of people of violent, fixed temperament: John Shane, his wife Julia, and above all his strong-willed daughters Irene and Lily.

As a novel of psychological realism, indeed, *The Green Bay Tree* resembles Arnold Bennett's *The Old Wives' Tale* (1908). As in Bennett's novel, the main protagonists are two sisters, one conventional-minded and the other adventurous, whose lives are detailed from youth to old age or beyond, to death. Lily Shane, like Sophia Baines in Bennett's novel, leaves her provincial hometown to live most of her life in France. Although both heroines become sophisticated and—in a worldly sense, successful—both are shaped more by the forces of their heredity and early environment than by their later experiences. But the comparison is not complete: the Baines sisters live in a time of relative tranquility; even the Franco-Prussian War scarcely touches Sophia, although she lives through the seige of Paris. However, Lily and Irene live through times of violent social upheaval, as well as war. The Town, once the comfortable fiefdom of privileged older American stock—the wealthy established families like the Shanes, Harrisons, and Tollivers—is becoming a "melting pot" of many nations and races. The wretched mill workers of the flats struggle to unionize and overturn the power structure of capitalists and their political minions, like Judge Weissman. Men such as Stepan Krylenko represent the new breed of aggressive workers who will level the old aristocracy to their own vulgar but energetic commonality. To their struggle the neurotic Irene devotes her resources; and even the aristocratic Lily protects Krylenko from the police, thus betraying her social class. Although the Shane sisters at first seem strong enough to control their destinies, eventually social forces overtake them. Irene, dispirited, sexually repressed, dies in a convent; Lily learns not only to weep but also to submit to more powerful restraints.

Just as Bromfield's treatment of the Town is ambivalent, so is his concept of social change. On the one hand he sympathizes with the factory workers (in one terrible scene, reminding the reader of Upton Sinclair's *The Jungle,* 1906, an Italian immigrant falls into a vat of molten iron); on the other, he derides them, using the crude language of religious and national bigotry. Similarly, Bromfield is ambivalent in his treatment of the psychology of women. Without question, the female characters—the Shane women, Hattie and Ellen Tolliver, Madame Blaise and Madame Gigon—are more forceful than the men. The Governor, a willful but empty egoist, cannot win Lily's entire affection. Neither can her French lover Césaire. In her old age Lily chooses for a mate René de Cyon, a polite but surely anemic man, compared to her own wild father, the creator of Shane's Castle. So Lily's independence seems, in retrospect, to have been only moderately successful. Because Bromfield cannot resolve the contradictory elements in his novel, the conclusion of *The Green Bay Tree* is especially disappointing. The author's real sympathy seems to lie with William Harrison rather than Lily. When Harrison decides to sell his stock in the mill and buy a farm, he achieves a measure of permanent independence. Previously he had appeared to be weak-spirited compared to Lily, but now that he returns to the land he finds, as does Bromfield, the only refuge against the shattering forces of social revolution or psychological disintegration.

GREEN GROW THE LILACS

Type of work: Drama
Author: Lynn Riggs (1899-1954)
Type of plot: Regional romance
Time of plot: 1900
Locale: Indian Territory (later Oklahoma)
First presented: 1931

This play is an example of American folk drama at its best. The story seems almost an expansion of mountain folk ballads, and in fact the play includes many folk songs. Rogers and Hammerstein adapted the work, producing the musical "Oklahoma," which centers on the traditional feud between the pragmatic farmers and the romantic but penniless cowboys. In this case, the farmer's daughter Laurey domesticates her cowboy.

The great success and popularity of *Oklahoma!* has probably obscured the quality of the play upon which it is based, Lynn Riggs's *Green Grow the Lilacs*. Without slighting the creative and musical abilities of either Richard Rodgers or Oscar Hammerstein II, it is only fair to state that *Oklahoma!,* in essence, is *Green Grow the Lilacs*; the color, vitality, charm, and even many of the musical ideas are present in the original, as Hammerstein himself was the first to admit in the New York *Times* (September 5, 1943): "Mr. Riggs' play is the wellspring of almost all that is good in *Oklahoma!* . . . Lynn Riggs and *Green Grow the Lilacs* are the very soul of *Oklahoma!*"

But, while *Oklahoma!* made fortunes for most of those connected with the production, Riggs, a U.S. Army draftee at the time, collected a royalty of $250 per week. That fact is almost symbolic of Riggs's whole career. From his first play, *Knives from Syria* (1925), to his last, *Toward the Western Sky* (1951), Riggs was a prolific playwright who "flirted" for a lifetime with the New York theater, frequently appearing to be on the brink of success. But because of the caprices of commercial taste and his own uncompromising refusal to popularize his plays, he was never able to establish himself as a Broadway playwright. Out of the twenty-seven plays he authored during his lifetime, only four were ever produced on Broadway, and of those, only two, *Green Grow the Lilacs* and *Russet Mantle,* could be called even modest commercial successes. One of the final ironies of Riggs's career is that this authentic regional artist did his most profitable work in Hollywood, that most artificial of American environments, writing such screenplays as *The Garden of Allah* and *Sherlock Holmes Goes to Washington.*

Green Grow the Lilacs is a kind of rollicking, larger-than-life folktale with some serious undertones. From Curly's singing entrance to the final curtain, the play moves with unflagging zest and color, punctuated by much music and dancing, extravagant gestures and speeches, and rowdy humor, with occasional moments of suspense and violence.

The plot is simple and functional: boy meets girl, overcomes rival, defies the law for the sake of love, and wins out. The characters are broad and simple, but also quite energetic and colorful. Curly McClain is the cowboy braggart, a staple type in frontier humor, who is intelligent and sensitive beneath the braggadocio. Laurey Williams is the spoiled, spunky girl who flirts with all the men, but commits her affections freely at the right time, and who, for all of her apparent flightiness, demonstrates real strength and courage in moments of crisis. Jeeter Fry is the pure villain, a chronic misfit whose violence is only barely under control. Aunt Eller is the solid "earth mother" figure who appears to be the crusty, comical widowed aunt in the early scenes, but whose strong personality and common sense rescue the lovers at the play's climax.

Much of the play's charm and exuberance comes from Riggs's accurate and colorful use of the frontier milieu. Having grown up in the Indian Territory, Riggs could portray the customs, manners, and daily activities of these settlers with a sympathy and realism only slightly colored by nostalgic idealization. Two of the crucial scenes of the play occur as the result of popular local customs, the "hoe-down" where Curly proposes to Laurey, and the wedding night "shivoree" which leads to Jeeter's death and Curly's imprisonment.

And no small part of the atmosphere is due to Riggs's command of the local vernacular. The language goes from the homey, slangy diction of the farmers to the highly charged folk rhetoric of the principals. But the playwright insisted that there was no poetic exaggeration in his dialects.

Lynn Riggs was probably the finest playwright to come out of the American Southwest and one of the very few authentic "folk dramatists" that our country has produced. That so few of his works have received the attention they deserve is not so much a commentary on the plays as it is a judgment on the vagaries of the American commercial theater.

GREEN MANSIONS

Type of work: Novel
Author: W. H. Hudson (1841-1922)
Type of plot: Fantasy
Time of plot: Nineteenth century
Locale: South American jungles
First published: 1904

There have always been legends of animal-like humans, often children reared by wolves; but Hudson's legend has become a modern classic. The girl, Rima, haunts a rain forest. Luminous in appearance, she will kill no living creature and speaks most freely in a strange bird-like warbling. Her English is a halting, poetic language. The Indians in the vicinity believe her evil, but a young man named Abel, visiting the region, falls in love with her and seeks to help her find her origins. This fails, but Abel promises to stay with her always. The Indians kill her, and Abel, having loved her, carries an unshakable loneliness within him as he returns to civilization.

The subject matter and the narrative structure of W. H. Hudson's *Green Mansions* became popular and familiar during the late nineteenth century: a story of an exotic, foreign land told by a retired and lonely traveler. It seemed to satisfy the civilized reader's desire for adventure and his curiosity in a primitive way of life. It also fulfilled a certain wish for escape. Beside these matters, *Green Mansions*' popularity can also be traced to its loving, almost sacred treatment of nature; Hudson wrote of a new frontier, of particular interest to Americans who were gradually coming to the end of their own.

Yet Hudson did not imagine his frontier in a rough, masculine way, familiar to most Americans, but in both exotic and feminine terms. In the person of Rima, a rich and complex character, he presents his experience of the South American jungles. She embodies the playful, joyous spirit one sees in birds; she is also furtive, retiring, and vulnerable, speaking an inhuman language that seems to draw out man's hostility, superstition, and desire to destroy her. In one sense, she is a maternal figure protecting the creatures of the forest, such as the deadly snake that Mr. Abel is about to kill. After he is bitten, she also saves Abel's life. Rima is as well a forest creature, living among them, shy and elusive. In another and more complicated sense, she assumes the significance of man's spirit, alone and lost, seeking its home. Rima's frustrated desire to find her mother's people in the mountains, a yearning which sickens her to death, is finally what the narrator can identify with as he concludes his story, now that he is alone and old. It is also perhaps this spiritual theme which accounts for *Green Mansions*' popularity among its first as well as its contemporary readers.

THE GREEN MOUNTAIN BOYS

Type of work: Novel
Author: Daniel Pierce Thompson (1795-1868)
Type of plot: Historical romance
Time of plot: 1775-1776
Locale: Vermont
First published: 1839

This homespun work tells the story of Vermont's contribution to the Revolutionary effort: Ethan Allen and the Green Mountain Boys. The author was a lawyer, editor, and judge who spent much of his life in Montpelier, Vermont; his knowledge of frontier life was as extensive as J. Fenimore Cooper's. The author never strays far from historical facts and local scenery; Captain Warrington is a fictional version of Seth Warner. Mrs. Story, Munroe, Skene, Reed, McIntosh, Benedict Arnold, and Ethan Allen appear under their own names and are familiar figures in the early annals of the State of Vermont.

Thompson celebrates the independence of the early settlers of Vermont. His historical romance is very much a folk epic, complete with larger-than-life characters, humorous peasant types, and a series of loosely connected adventures that dramatize the birth of a regional consciousness. If at times the plotting seems too contrived, we must remember that the principal purpose of the book is not to tell a story but to embody the spirit of a group. In its humble and often sentimental way, *The Green Mountain Boys* is a rural *Iliad*: like Homer's heroes, Warrington (Seth Warner) and Ethan Allen outwit and outfight their lordly enemies.

Although the story alludes to the national struggle of the American Revolution and places its heroes in the service of the American cause, Thompson was not concerned primarily with the Revolution itself. In his introduction, he stresses the heroic independence of the few thousand Vermont settlers who successfully repelled the efforts of land grabbers from New York, a province possessing perhaps fifty times the population and resources of Vermont. The Green Mountain Boys form their defensive forces against New York, not Great Britain. It so happens that the New York authorities identify largely with the Tory cause when war breaks out. It was fortunate for the budding United States that the Green Mountain Boys turned out to be on its side.

Because it honors the rights of the little man, the independent yeoman, *The Green Mountain Boys* occupies an important and early place in the egalitarian tradition at the heart of the American novel, a tradition which includes *Huckleberry Finn* and *The Grapes of Wrath*.

The most stirring moment of Thompson's work is Ethan Allen's plea to the Vermonters to join him in the attack against the British at Ticonderoga. He convinces them of the justice of the cause by reminding them that the prize of the struggle will be Vermont's representation in a National Congress, where she will forever have the support of the entire United States against the predatory claims of her old enemy, New York.

GRETTIR THE STRONG

Type of work: Saga
Author: Unknown
Type of plot: Adventure romance
Time of plot: Eleventh century
Locale: Iceland, Norway, Constantinople
First transcribed: Thirteenth-century manuscr pt

One of the several memorable Norse sagas, this is the story of Grettir, a hero and an outlaw of medieval Iceland. Descended from Vikings who colonized Iceland in the second half of the ninth century, Grettir emerges as a larger-than-life outlaw and a tragic figure. Constantly using his strength, sometimes with provocation but often not, he cannot be subdued by any man. Finally, witchcraft is used to bring about his end. Grettir's story was handed down by word of mouth for more than two hundred years after the hero's death. It had by then absorbed the adventures of other folk heroes. In the main, the saga is true to the political and social history of the age.

Grettir the Strong is the saga of a brave man and his heroic deeds. Barely civilized, barely Christian, often childish in his behavior, careless of life and limb, this strong man of the north was formed by his homeland and by his heritage. Both good and evil are combined in the character of Grettir. He is proud and compulsive in his behavior and it sometimes appears that he is fighting the same battle over and over again though the antagonists are always different. His very strength is his weakness, yet he needs to prove this strength over and over again.

The Icelandic society into which Grettir is born in A.D. 997 was a stable one and except for the introduction of Christianity in 1000 and its ameliorating effects, the customs of the Norsemen remained much the same on into the eighteenth century. In this land of ice and bone-chilling cold, with its steep cliffs rising straight up from the sea and where only a small part of the land was arable, Grettir was born. It was a land of superstitions where trolls, who were demoniacal creatures, could possess a man's soul. The saga of Grettir invites the reader to speculate on the possibility that Grettir himself may have been possessed. He was certainly cursed.

Grettir's father did not like him and his mother doted on him. Psychologists of today could point to this fact alone and write a profile which would convince the reader that Grettir's daring and sometimes foolhardy deeds were all done in an effort to please his father.

Grettir was lazy. He did not want to work—this was partly the reason his father disliked him. When he was only ten years old, his father sent him to care for the geese. Because he did not want to work and considered this chore beneath him in any case, he wrung the gosling's necks and broke the wings of the geese—a senselessly cruel exercise in evil. Refusing to conform to the work ethic, even when he grew into a man, Grettir was never able to accept parental or social authority.

A descendant of Onund Treefoot, who had sailed the seas looting and exploring with his life constantly endangered by both the elements and his foes, Grettir came by his bravery honestly. The life of the sea was one of uncertainty and frustrations for all seamen, especially in the tenth and eleventh centuries. Supplies were often inadequate. Hunger was a constant companion. The murmur of the seas was often an accompaniment to the murmuring pangs of hunger for the old Norse seamen. And thus it was with Grettir in the uncharted seas of his life.

There were no family names in the Icelandic culture. Each person had one name and was further identified by his birthplace, a patronymic, or by a nickname such as "Grettir the Strong"—somewhat in the manner of the Shoshone and other Indians of the Americas. Perhaps it was necessary for Grettir to do some of the foolhardy things he did in order to maintain his identity.

William Morris, an Englishman, with the help of Eínekr Magnússon, was the first to translate Grettir's Saga into English in 1869. He offered a too literal translation which is strained and taxes the reader's patience. In 1878 Gudbrand Vigfusson noted some similarities between Grettir's Saga and *Beowulf*. Freidrich Panzer later pointed out some resemblances to the Strong John Fairy Tales and the Bear's Son. The consensus since then, however, is that the similarities were independently acquired and that *Grettir the Strong* was not patterned after *Beowulf*.

A later translation of Grettir's Saga by Denton Fox and Hermann Pálsson is straightforward and carries the reader through the prologue of Onund Treefoot, Grettir's great-grandfather, to Grettir's story, and on to the epilogue where the story of Grettir's half-brother, Thorsteinn, is told. Thorsteinn avenged his brother's death in Byzantium, and that is another claim to fame for Grettir. He is the only Icelander who was ever avenged there.

This latest translation of Grettir's Saga is excellent. The shape of the land, its creatures, and its customs are conveyed by the language used. The reader feels the despair of this sorely tried hero. He sees the bleak, cold country and shivers as Grettir swims across the channel to get fire for his shipwrecked companions and rises ice-encrusted from the sea.

In Norway, where Grettir fled when he was first outlawed, groups of robbers and outlaws, called berserks, often came charging out of the forests demanding a farmer's possessions or his women. One bloody episode involving the berserks is memorable because Grettir saves the farmer's daughter from them. Grettir runs toward a berserk, who is still on his horse, and kicks the end of his shield so hard that it is driven into the villain's mouth causing his lower jaw to dangle down to his chest; then Grettir cuts off his head.

Grettir was always a champion of the afflicted, particularly those assailed by trolls and other supernatural beings. Perhaps this was because Grettir was cursed by a troll-man whom he killed. After the curse Grettir said it was even harder than before to maintain his self-control. His fear of the dark and of being alone also dated from this ill-fated encounter. And the means of his death was brought about by witchcraft, which was later outlawed by the Althing, or General Assembly of Iceland, which met yearly to hear complaints. The chieftains were the members of the Althing and their consensus was that a man who ignobly killed a dying man through witchcraft was a coward. The man who killed Grettir was also outlawed by the Althing.

The saga ends with the beautiful story of Grettir's half-brother Thorsteinn, and Spes, the charming Byzantium woman who ransomed Thorsteinn from prison where he had been incarcerated for killing Grettir's murderer.

Grettir the Strong well deserves its place with other masterpieces of world literature. The reader is not left unmoved at the tragic life and death of this giant of a man who even as a child was mean enough to kill goslings, yet who risked his life to swim across a river so Steinvor and her daughter could go to Christmas Eve Mass.

Virginia Addington

LA GRINGA

Type of work: Drama
Author: Florencio Sánchez (1875-1910)
Type of plot: Social comedy
Time of plot: Early twentieth century
Locale: Pampas near Santa Fé, Argentina
First presented: 1904

Many early nineteenth century works of Argentine literature ridicule the foreign-born gringo. *In* La Gringa (The Foreign Girl), *the author sought to portray the foreigner's contributions to the nation. To this end, the character of the immigrant is sympathetic. Sánchez saw the hope of Argentina in a blending of the native spirit with the blood of ambitious, industrious immigrants such as Don Nicola.*

Florencio Sánchez underwent an impoverished and sickly youth. He lived in Bohemian style, dressed poorly, ate scantily, drank lustily, and labored for pittances. He worked for a time in a telegraph office and wrote his first plays on purloined telegraph pads. He suffered heart attacks and nervous seizures, and died of tuberculosis at thirty-five. Sánchez was thus unable to work systematically or attain intellectual discipline. He read socialist and anarchist tracts, but never broadened his political education. The pampa spirit tinges all of his works, both urban and rural, for his plots and themes flowed from gaucho life with its primitive passions, fatalism, and struggle for survival. His heroes are often gaucho individualists who resist social pressures, or reformers victimized by governmental and bureaucratic tyrannies while his villains are generally oppressors, parasites, rapscallions, bureaucrats, and hypocrites.

Sánchez helped bring European dramatic techniques to the Argentine stage, for he was influenced by Ibsen and Pérez-Galdós. Many Italian dramatic companies visited the River Plate area early in the twentieth century, further molding Sánchez, who was then writing the best current drama of Argentina and Uruguay. Sánchez's works usually contain dramatic intensity and poetic sentiment. They are often constructed laxly, and have predictable outcomes; but *La Gringa* is a comparatively hearty and optimistic work. Swollen with emotion, it is beautiful and realistic, with strong dialogue; it evokes famliar features of Argentina's hinterland, such as the estancia (ranch), the general store, and the immigrant farm home.

The play's theme is the emergence of a hardworking Italo-Creole people who blend the virtues of immigrant and creole-mestizo stock. The rugged and gnarled ombú tree, loved by Argentine poets and once the only tree of the billowing pampa, symbolizes the strength of the pure native, while European immigrant attributes are very visible and defended by Sánchez despite traditional Argentine resentment of "gringos." The clashing life styles, moreover, are not presented as hopelessly disharmonic. Sánchez's happy ending for *La Gringa* is actually the story of nineteenth century Argentina, where a new people evolved from a combination of Argentines with European immigrants.

GROWTH OF THE SOIL

Type of work: Novel
Author: Knut Hamsun (Knut Pedersen Hamsun, 1859-1952)
Type of plot: Social chronicle
Time of plot: Late nineteenth century
Locale: Norway
First published: 1917

Hamsun won the 1921 Nobel Prize for literature largely on the basis of this novel about simple, hardworking Norwegian peasants. Developments of mining interests and flirtations with town life come and go as does the prosperity of the individual characters, but the land remains and the protagonist Isak returns to sow it for his substance. This modern parable is written with Biblical simplicity and power.

Growth of the Soil is, in many ways, a brilliant novel. At the same time that it portrays the development of farming in an isolated Norwegian locale, it also portrays the psychological and sexual relationships between the settlers in much depth. Finally, Hamsun makes an argument about the significance of the soil in the life of man.

Farming is developed primarily through two types of men: Isak and Geissler. Isak, the central, even towering figure in the novel, is a selfless man wholly committed to the cultivation of the soil. This cultivation is, in Hamsun's narrative, equated with the primitive need for survival. It is Isak's dedication, honesty, and simplicity which, as they enable him to survive and then prosper, reflect those values of life promoted by work on the land. These values lend solidity and stability to his life and to the life of Inger.

Differing in character from Isak, but also necessary for the "growth of the soil" is the character of Geissler. Geissler is typical of a certain sort of man Hamsun was fond of portraying in many of his novels: the mysterious, restless, and interesting individual who wanders from place to place and thereby connects the lives of various people. Geissler, whose motives are never especially clear, but who seems clever and humane, connects Isak to the great world outside his land. Geissler, a man with connections, also protects the family when they are threatened by the law; and, on account of his worldly wisdom, he is able to involve Isak in a mining speculation which provides the money necessary to buy new agricultural machinery.

Another important aspect of the novel is the frank portrayal of the emotional and sexual relationships between people. The social and personal pressures exerted on relationships lead Hamsun to a discussion of infanticide, and he protests against the unfair treatment of mothers. These relationships, and the development of the new generation of farmers, are all communicated through a simple and sometimes profound style. Through his style, Hamsun conveys that sense of elementary decency and simplicity which he values so highly in Isak.

The sources of these values is the land itself. And it is here that a certain mysticism becomes evident. As Hamsun attempts to uncover the philosophical connection between men and the land, he sometimes tends to emphasize the metaphysical character of the tie between man and earth. Although he is realistic enough in showing the continuous work which makes the land productive, there is often an implicit claim that a mysterious transcendent meaning is hidden in the work.

DER GRÜNE HEINRICH

Type of work: Novel
Author: Gottfried Keller (1819-1890)
Type of plot: Autobiographical romance
Time of plot: Mid-nineteenth century
Locale: Switzerland and Bavaria
First published: 1854-1855; revised 1879

Der Grüne Heinrich *is one of the great German* Bildüngsromane *(educational novels). Its autobiographical content is unmistakable: it is an authentic description of Keller's life in Switzerland, his struggles in Munich, and his disillusioned return home. Keller reflected the Romantic Movement in his enthusiastic descriptions of nature; however, he added a strong note of realism and dry humor to his stories, which was somewhat shocking to his romantically inclined audience.*

Keller's *Green Henry* combines autobiography and irony, minutely observed realistic detail and poetic symbolism, to form a rich texture of inexhaustible fascination. It was for Keller himself something of a lifework and an education, beginning with its conception in 1842 through the appearance of the second, much revised, version of 1879. It is this later version that is always cited. In it, Keller turned from the original emphasis on the failure of the Romantic artist figure who ends in despair, to a less subjective representation, in which the mature Heinrich tells the story of his youth from a point of view that combines wisdom and resignation with a gentle sense of humor, as he looks on his own follies.

The novel shares with the revised version of Goethe's *Wilhelm Meister* this rejection of a youthful desire for irresponsible self-fulfillment typical of the Romantic personality, in favor of a commitment to finding one's place in society. The young Heinrich, an orphan with an indulgent martyr mother and no father to guide him in the direction of responsibility, lives a life colored by fantasy, unable to perceive reality as it is and measure himself against it. He paints from imagination rather than knowledge, and his painting, like his life, has no ties to the fabric of the natural world. In this sense, his art, rather than a calling, is a symptom of his false relationship to the world, and his life is one long process of disillusionment.

It is only at the end that Heinrich sees his proper calling in the life of his town, in a career of service. This wisdom comes too late to spare him guilt and suffering, and his education in life has been gained at a terrible cost. Yet in the end, he has learned, and the patient, loving humanity with which he tells his own story convinces us that his life is not, ultimately, a tragedy.

GUARD OF HONOR

Type of work: Novel
Author: James Gould Cozzens (1903-)
Type of plot: Psychological realism
Time of plot: Three days during World War II
Locale: An Air Force base in Florida
First published: 1948

The diverse and complex world of a large air force base in wartime becomes a microcosm, embracing on a smaller scale the personalities and conflicts found in the larger world. Specifically, Cozzens deals with the problems inherent in power relationships, authority, and suppression. The book indicts self-willed agitators and the noncomformists.

Although *Guard of Honor* is one of the best military novels published shortly after the end of World War II, the war itself seems almost incidental to the action. The central problem of the book is how to manage a huge, complex, necessary institution in which a large number of men and women from all social, economic, and ethnic backgrounds (which reflect the full spectrum of cultural, political, and racial attitudes) must cooperate if the system is to work. The war only acerbates and intensifies preexistent social problems and underscores the severe dangers that can result if the system fails to function as it should.

Cozzens sees two likely problems in any institution: incompetent or mismatched individuals will inevitably be placed in positions of authority; the impersonal necessities of the organization will conflict with the justified personal needs of its functionaries. Reconciling these problems is the test to which Cozzens puts his characters. The "heroes" are those who recognize both the system's fallibility and its necessity and who try to compensate for the former by accepting more than their share of responsibilities. The villains are those who cannot or will not accept their responsibilities within the system and those who try to "solve" the problems outside it.

Cozzens introduces us to a number of authority figures who fail for a variety of reasons to do their jobs adequately: old Colonel Mowbray, who simply lacks the requisite intelligence to perform in the job that seniority has given him; his superior, Major General "Bus" Beal, who is a strong leader in times of active crisis, but cannot handle the kind of problem that demands a slow, patient untangling of complex attitudes and relationships under continuing pressure; and Beal's co-pilot, Lt. Colonel Benny Carricker, whose youthful, impulsive courage predisposes him to recklessness. But, Cozzens suggests, such human weakness can be overcome if wiser and more dispassionate men are willing to accept additional responsibilities without thought of recognition or recompense.

The major action of the novel revolves around the racial tensions that surface at Ocanara when black Lt. Stanley Willis is struck by Carricker in a dispute over Willis' violation of the right of way. Subsequently, a confrontation ensues when the blacks are banned from the white Officer's Club. Willis, the potential black leader, is hospitalized, absenting him from the situation, and Beal, the base commander, issues hasty and extreme orders and then escapes by going on solo airplane rides.

The brunt of the crisis falls on the shoulders of Colonel Norman Ross who is a typical Cozzens hero. Although old and in precarious health, Ross accepts the responsibility for Beal's job as well as his own, because he knows how such incidents can get quickly out of control. Ross acknowledges that the blacks have a basic right to equal treatment, but he is more afraid of disrupting the morale of the much larger group of white officers. In other words, the immediate practicality of the situation demands a "moderate" approach to the rights of the offended minority. "A parachutist," he thinks to himself, "cannot climb back. . . . Gravity is a condition, not a theory. In our trouble with the colored officers we also have a condition, not a theory."

Accepting this "condition" Ross slowly works it out, devoting more energy to it than is good for his health and aware that nobody understands or appreciates what he is doing. He knows that "these are tough times. . . . We have a job; and a man who's given part of it has to do it right—or else." But he also knows that, since some are not going to "do it right," those others who see the difficulties as they arise must correct them immediately before they snowball into major disasters. Near the end of the book a practice parachute jump ends in many deaths precisely because, in the early planning stages, small details were not worked out and small responsibilities were not assumed.

Ross is, of course, not the only man who does more than his share. His problems are paralleled in those of several junior officers who take responsibility for the shortcomings of their men. And the crisis is finally resolved when Lt. Willis returns to duty, takes over the leadership of the black officers, and moderates their demands.

But while Cozzens accepts well intentioned failure with equanimity, he is less tolerant of overt challenges to authority. Lt. James Edsell represents the most destructive element in any organization, the individual who, acting out of a distorted moral sense, tries to force his own kind of "solution" to the problem. Edsell's kind of "liberalism" refuses to see the complexities of the problem and he agitates for a solution in accordance with his personal moralistic judgments. Edsell interprets all events in terms of his own assumptions and makes no attempt to learn the real facts.

Instead of helping the blacks to secure their demands, he intensifies the problem and sharpens the racial antagonisms by importing a black newspaperman to publicize the problem and Willis' father to embarrass the Air Force. He not only attacks military policy, which he does not understand, but he competes with it. When the authorities attempt to move in the direction of his "liberal" views, he consciously evades their help.

It is evident that Edsell is dedicated not to the betterment of the blacks at Ocanara, but to the aggrandizement of his own self-righteous ego. In the character of Edsell, Cozzens makes clear his attitude toward "reformers" and "radicals" who would force easy solutions to complex problems in accordance with their own abstract moral prejudices.

Thus, Cozzens makes no blanket approval of the system, but he demonstrates that its problems can be solved only within its institutional framework. There is, in *Guard of Honor,* no sudden revelation in time of crisis, but only a painful awareness of the problems and of the methods necessary to solve them. And at the center of those "solutions," which are usually temporary, inefficient compromises—the only kind available to men in the real, everyday world—are men like Colonel Ross; rational, moderate, sensitive individuals who are willing to do whatever must be done, even at the sacrifice of self, when the situation demands it. The success or failure of modern man, Cozzens seems to suggest, depends on whether or not, in times of continuing crisis, such "men of reason" can rise to the occasion.

Keith Neilson

GULLIVER'S TRAVELS

Type of work: Simulated record of travel
Author: Jonathan Swift (1667-1745)
Type of plot: Social satire
Time of plot: 1699-1713
Locale: England and various fictional lands
First published: 1726-1727

One of the masterpieces of satire among the world's literature, Gulliver's Travels *is written in the form of a travel journal divided into four sections, each of which describes a different voyage of ship's physician Lemuel Gulliver. In each section he visits a different fantastical society–Lilliput, Brobdingnag, Laputa, and Houyhnhnmland–and records the facts and customs of the country. Through Gulliver's adventures and observations, Swift aims his at times savage satire against the English people generally and the Whigs particularly, against various political, academic, and social institutions, and against man's constant abuse of his greatest gift, reason.*

When Jonathan Swift created the character of Lemuel Gulliver as his narrator for *Gulliver's Travels,* he developed a personality with many qualities admired by an eighteenth century audience, and still admired by readers today. Gulliver is a decent sort of person, hopeful, simple, fairly direct, and full of good will. He is a scientist, a trained doctor; and, as any good scientist should, he loves detail. His literal-minded attitude makes him a keen observer of the world around him. Furthermore, he is, like another famous novel character of the eighteenth century—Robinson Crusoe—encouragingly resourceful in emergencies. Why is it, then, that such a seemingly admirable, even heroic character, should become, in the end, an embittered misanthrope, hating the world and turning against everyone, including people who show him kindness?

The answer lies in what Swift meant for his character to be, and Gulliver was certainly not intended to be heroic. Readers often confuse Gulliver the character and Swift the author, but to do so is to miss the point of *Gulliver's Travels.* The novel is a satire, and Gulliver is a mask for Swift the satirist. In fact, Swift does not share Gulliver's values: his rationalistic, scientific responses to the world and his belief in progress and the perfectibility of man. Swift, on the contrary, believed that such values were dangerous to mankind, and that to put such complete faith in the material world, as scientific Gulliver did, was folly. As Swift's creation, Gulliver is a product of his age, and he is designed as a character to demonstrate the great weakness underlying the values of the "Age of Enlightenment," the failure to recognize the power of that which is irrational in man.

Despite Gulliver's apparent congeniality in the opening chapters of the novel, Swift makes it quite clear that his character has serious shortcomings, including blindspots about human nature and his own nature. Book III, the least readable section of *Gulliver's Travels,* is in some ways the most revealing part of the book. In it Gulliver complains, for example, that the wives of the scientists he is observing run away with the servants. The fact is that Gulliver —himself a scientist—gives little thought to the well-being of his own wife. In the eleven years covered in Gulliver's "travel book," Swift's narrator spends a total of seven months and ten days with his wife.

Thus, Gulliver too is caught up in Swift's web of satire in *Gulliver's Travels.* Satire as a literary form tends to be ironic; the author says the opposite of what he means. Consequently, we can assume that much of what Gulliver observes as good, and much of what he thinks and does, is the opposite of what Swift thinks.

As a type of the eighteenth century, Gulliver exhibits its major values: belief in rationality, in the perfectibility of man, in the idea of progress, and in the Lockean philosophy of the human mind as a *tabula rasa,* or blank slate, at the time of birth, controlled and developed entirely by the differing strokes and impressions made on it by the environment. Swift, in contrast to Gulliver, hated the abstraction that accompanied rational thinking; he abhorred the rejection of the past that resulted from a rationalistic faith in the new and improved; and he cast strong doubts on man's ability to gain knowledge through reason and logic.

The world Gulliver discovers during his travels is significant in Swift's satire. The Lilliputians, averaging not quite six inches in height, display the pettiness and the smallness Swift detects in much that motivates human institutions, such as church and state. It is petty religious problems that lead to continual war in Lilliput. The Brobdingnagians continue the satire in Part Two by exaggerating man's grossness through their enlarged size. (Swift divided human measurements by a twelfth for the Lilliputians and multiplied the same for the Brobdingnagians.)

The tiny people of Part One and the giants of Part Two establish a pattern of contrasts which Swift follows in Part Four with the Houyhnhnms and the Yahoos. The Yahoos, "their heads and breasts covered with a thick hair, some frizzled and others lank," naked otherwise and scampering up trees like nimble squirrels, represent the animal aspect of man when it is viewed as separate from the rational. The Houyhnhnms, completing the other half of the split, know no lust, pain, or pleasure. Their rational temperaments totally rule their passions, if they have any at all. The land of the Houyhnhnms is a Utopia to Gulliver, and he tells the horse-people that his homeland is unfortunately governed by Yahoos.

But what is the land of the Houyhnhnms really like, how much a Utopia? Friendship, benevolence, and equality are the principal virtues there. Decency and civility guide every action. As a result, each pair of horses mates to have one colt of each sex; after that, they no longer stay together. The marriages are exacted to insure nice color combinations in the offspring. To the young, marriage is "one of the necessary actions of a reasonable being." After the function of the marriage has been fulfilled—after the race has been propagated—the two members of the couple are no closer to each other than to anybody else in the whole country. It is this kind of "equality" that Swift satirizes. As a product of the rational attitude, such a value strips life of its fullness, denies the power of emotion and instinct, subjugates all to logic, reason, the intellect, and makes all dull and uninteresting—as predictable as a scientific experiment.

By looking upon the Houyhnhnms as the perfect creatures, Gulliver makes his own life back in England intolerable:

> I . . . return to enjoy my own speculations in my little garden at Redriff; to apply those excellent lessons of virtue which I learned among the Houyhnhnms; to instruct the Yahoos of my own family as far as I shall find them docible animals; to behold my figure often in a glass, and thus if possible habituate myself by time to tolerate the sight of a human creature. . . .

When Gulliver holds up rational men as perfect man, and when he cannot find a rational man to meet his ideal, he concludes in disillusionment that mankind is totally animalistic, like the ugly Yahoos. In addition to being a satire and a parody of travel books, *Gulliver's Travels* is an initiation novel. As Gulliver develops, he changes; but he fails to learn an important lesson of life, or he learns it wrong. His naïve optimism about progress and rational man leads him to bitter disillusionment.

It is tragically ironic that Swift died at the age of seventy-eight after three years of living without his reason, a victim of Ménière's disease, dying "like a rat in a hole." For many years he had struggled against fits of deafness and giddiness, symptoms of the disease. As a master of the language of satire, Swift remains unequaled, despite his suffering and ill health. He gathered in *Gulliver's Travels,* written late in his life, all the experience he had culled from both courts and streets. For Swift knew people, and, as individuals, he loved them. But, when they changed into groups, he hated them, satirized them, stung them into realizing the dangers of the herd. Gulliver never understood this.

Jean G. Marlowe

GUY MANNERING

Type of work: Novel
Author: Sir Walter Scott (1771-1832)
Type of plot: Historical romance
Time of plot: Eighteenth century
Locale: Scotland
First published: 1815

Set during the reign of George III, Guy Mannering *is notable not so much for its plot, whose events are often contrived and overburdened with coincidences, but for its characterizations, such as those of Dandie Dinmont and Meg Merrilies. Scott's flair for making his people come alive is at its best in the novel, and members of groups such as peasants, tradesmen, and gipsies are portrayed with particular warmth and realism.*

Scott's gift for making the history and manners of people remote in time and place come alive has long been considered his most enduring contribution to fiction; his reputation as the father of the historical novel is common knowledge. But Scott was essentially a romancer, perhaps the greatest in English literature. He told marvelously exotic and heroic stories. They were rarely well plotted, indeed often contrived; and they were never afraid of sentimentality or exaggeration. Despite the originality and brilliance of the historical or social coloring, Scott's primary purpose in almost all of his works was to fascinate and entertain.

Guy Mannering, with its astrological beginnings, haunting descriptions of the desolate Cumberland landscape, and mysterious portrait of Meg Merrilies, is as exotic as anything Scott wrote. Meg recalls the witches in *Macbeth* when she curses Godfrey Bertram, Laird of Ellangowan, and yet despite her curses and prophesies she is also the archetypal mother, protecting Harry Bertram and literally confirming his identity and title before she dies. This strange gipsy woman is more real, finally, than the more conventional characters of the novel. Her power comes largely from her asocial vitality and her mythic and choric function in the story; but it also has something to do with her importance to the plot. Unlike the interesting peasants in most of Scott's novels, Meg is not just part of the engaging background. She is integrally connected to the story. The same thing can be said for Dominie Sampson, the memorable tutor.

On the whole, the depiction of Scottish manners is more realistic than in *Waverley,* probably because the time pictured is closer to Scott's own. Nevertheless, at the thematic core of *Guy Mannering* is Scott's yearning for the richer tones of feudal life. The common people were still vessels of the older spirit, and Scott is characteristically at his best depicting their speech and action.

GUY OF WARWICK

Type of work: Poem
Author: Unknown
Type of plot: Chivalric romance
Time of plot: Tenth century
Locale: England, Europe, the Middle East
First transcribed: Thirteenth century

Undoubtedly French in origin, this metrical romance is made up of episodes anthologized, as it were, from earlier romances, epics, and sagas. The story of the various adventures of the knight Guy was frequently rewritten throughout the Middle Ages, later translated into numerous languages, immortalized in a play in 1620, and even adapted into a widely popular children's book in the nineteenth century.

This romance about Guy of Warwick, the "Hercules of England," apparently was extremely popular in English and Norman courtly circles. Twenty-one manuscripts of *Guy of Warwick* exist, which is unusual for medieval romances. For example, there is only one for *Sir Gawain and the Green Knight* and seven for the tale of Richard Coeur de Lion.

It is easy to understand why this long narrative held the high esteem of Anglo-Norman readers. Its hero is a young Saxon knight in the time of King Athelstan—a knight who through a series of incredible adventures in foreign lands (first in Normandy and Brittany) becomes the most valiant in the known world. He is a crusader knight who successfully fights the Saracens and finally wins the hand of the lady who repeatedly sent him off on these exploits. For the English Guy was also a symbolic national hero in the war against the Danes.

Guy of Warwick operates within the chivalric code and according to precepts of courtly love. There are enough tournaments, battles, and slaughter to suit the most bloodthirsty reader.

However, the narrative is stylized and replete with clichés and endless adventures which lack verisimilitude. Guy himself is not individualized like Havelok or Sir Gawain; he acts out his role according to established norms; the modern reader sees few touches that make this hero human or particularly appealing.

Like his adventures, Guy seems a composite. He is simply typical, and the recitation of his exploits at times becomes a mere catalogue. The structure of the work suffers as a result. Its author makes little attempt to devise an intricate plot; there is no theme in the work. And originality is completely lacking. The poet merely recites a series of adventures in linear succession.

However, medieval readers loved *Guy of Warwick* because it satisfied their desire for escape literature with all the necessary ingredients: an indomitable chivalric knight, fair disdainful ladies, adventures in faraway lands, brave and numerous enemies, and, finally, successful winning in love. These elements are sufficient to account for the great popularity of the work. Even Chaucer in his parody of metrical romance, "Sir Thopas," shows his familiarity with the famous hero, "Sir Gy" whom he lists, among others, with King Horn and Sir Bevis of Hampton. And Guy's appearance in adaptations through the nineteenth century attest to his endurance with readers of many periods.

GUZMÁN DE ALFARACHE

Type of work: Novel
Author: Mateo Alemán (1547-1613?)
Type of plot: Picaresque romance
Time of plot: Sixteenth century
Locale: Spain and Italy
First published: 1599, 1604

More popular than Don Quixote *in its own day, this picaresque novel went through thirty editions within six years of its publication; its vogue then spread to France and England, where it was translated in 1662 by James Mabbe under the title* The Rogue. *Typically Spanish in flavor, the work is realistic, comic, and often earthy; in numerous philosophical and moral digressions, Alemán reveals his qualities of frankness, broad humor, pessimism, wit, humility, and common sense. The plot follows Guzmán's travels and adventures as he moves freely from the highest to the lowest levels of society, living by his wits and shrewd cynicism and commenting freely on the follies and vices of mankind.*

Spain oscillated between the two poles of saintly mysticism and the picaresque novel, or romance of roguery, in the sixteenth century. Germs of protopicaresque fiction had first appeared in medieval Europe, in the Dance of Death of France and the jest books of Germany. The world's first genuine picaresque novel was Spain's *The Life of Lazarillo de Tormes* in 1554. Almost half a century later came a second major picaresque work, Mateo Alemán's *Guzmán de Alfarache,* which was about ten times as long as the earlier work, and had the subtitle *Watchtower of Human Life.*

Mateo Alemán was born in the same year as Cervantes (1547), and his life matches and contrasts with that of *Don Quixote's* author in odd ways. The son of a Seville prison doctor, Alemán led a riotous student life, and then careened into a life of wanderlust, penury, and wild sprees, interspersed with terms in debtor's prison. He was once in a Seville dungeon at the same time as Cervantes. Calamity had opposite effects on the two novelists—the noble Cervantes wrote a spiritual novel of the struggle between good and evil, while Alemán wrote one of world literature's most pessimistic novels, laced with human corruption.

Guzmán de Alfarache views human nature dimly, and is much more bitter than *The Life of Lazarillo de Tormes*. Woman are cunning vixens who fleece dullard men, the latter being selfish louts. The poor are coarse, greedy, and unlovable. Humans have appetites but not ideals, while color and humor are scarce. Thieves, scamps, and false friends festoon the novel's pages, along with cynicism (the Spanish word *cínico* is more negative than the English "cynical," implying total unscrupulousness). Guzmán, the protagonist, cheats and betrays, and wanders the rural roads and urban alleys of Spain and Italy. He is finally condemned to the ultimate horror of rogues—service as a galley slave. The novel's episodes are morbidly interesting and ripple casually on for hundreds of pages. Life is seamy to the core, honor can be bought like garlic at a fair, and dreams are fake. The novel follows the same autobiographical form as *The Life of Lazarillo de Tormes,* but stitches short stories, fables, allegories, satirical polemics, and long moralizations into its fabric. Unity is supplied by Guzmán's narration of his miserable life, and the novel alternates geographically between city and country, a technique that was to be followed by subsequent Spanish novelists, including Cervantes. The novel also bobs up and down from one social level to another with a range and energy new to Spanish fiction.

Alemán was nonetheless such a child of his Catholic culture that his novel views affliction as God's purification of man. It is implied that man can fight original sin, while suffering is the royal road to conversion. (Some critics contrast this to Daniel Defoe's *Moll Flanders,* where conversion leads to prosperity.) Guzmán attended mass regularly, thus leaving battered readers with hope of a better eternity despite all gross imperfections of this world.

Guzmán de Alfarache went through some thirty editions and many translations in its first five years. Alemán's massive notes for the second part were stolen, resulting in an apocryphal version, but he rewrote a genuine second part. He went to Mexico late in life and died in the faith, but still believing, as did Guzmán, that dreams are false: "It is all castles in the air! Fantastic silhouettes of imagination!"

HAJJI BABA OF ISPAHAN

Type of work: Novel
Author: James Morier (1780-1849)
Type of plot: Picaresque romance
Time of plot: Early nineteenth century
Locale: Persia
First published: 1824

Comparable to Gil Blas *and other early picaresque romances,* The Adventures of Hajji Baba of Ispahan *combines the details and interest of a travel book and the excitement of a story of rogues and daredevils. The book is significant for its picture of Persia at the time of Napoleon Bonaparte and for its satire and shrewd comments on human nature.*

Morier's romance is both an Oriental tale and a picaresque narrative. For its treatment of exotic customs and manners, the novel resembles such eighteenth century romances as Samuel Johnson's *The History of Rasselas, Prince of Abyssinia* (1759) and William Beckford's less philosophical *Vathek, an Arabian Tale* (1786). As a picaresque narrative, *Hajji Baba of Ispahan* resembles the episodic novels of Defoe and Smollett. Like most novels concerning a rogue-hero, Morier's book satirizes the foibles not only of the characters in the story, but also those of humankind. Hajji Baba is an amiable opportunist and schemer, experienced in the worldly arts of guile and deception, but not the sole rascal in the book. On the contrary, Hajji learns his impudent tricks from others, and although he is an apt pupil, he is simply more successful—not more wicked—than most people. As one of his teachers, the Dervish Sefer explains: "We look upon mankind as fair game—we live upon their weakness and credulity"; from such counsel, Hajji discovers how to expropriate, for the sake of his own ease, riches from the weak and stupid. In a world of scoundrels and fools, he is seen as amoral rather than immoral; the reader sympathizes with his desire, in the contest of life, to be the world's knave instead of its victim.

During the course of his roguish adventures, Hajji ranges through almost all the social levels and professions of Persian (and, indeed, Middle-Eastern) life. At various times he is a barber, a merchant, a robber, a slave, a "seller of smoke," a *saka* (water carrier), a *lûti* (privileged buffoon), a dervish, a physician's apprentice, a sublieutenant for the Chief Executioner, a scribe to a man of law, an ambassador to foreign powers, and finally, the Shah's deputy. He travels throughout the Middle East, from Cairo to Aleppo and Damascus; from Mecca and Medina to Lahore and Cashmere. Mostly, however, he travels through the cities and villages of early nineteenth century Persia, learning to understand the passions and weaknesses of his fellow men. In none of the ranks of society does he encounter true comradeship, civility, or altruism. At one point, after he escapes from the Turcoman robbers and throws himself at the mercy of his countryman, a Persian prince, he is robbed and threatened with further punishment by his protector. A simple muleteer chides Hajji for lamenting his losses. After all, what could he expect from a prince? "When once he or any man in power gets possession of a thing," the muleteer reasons, "do you think that he will ever restore it?"

In spite of Morier's broad-ranging satire, which sometimes approaches cynicism, his prevailing tone is comic rather than censorious. Hajji is, above all, an affable rogue, high-spirited and inventive, most resilient when he appears to be defeated. Through his resourceful imagination, he overcomes most of the obstacles in his way. Yet he is never wholly successful and triumphant, as are some other picaresque heroes in fiction. Morier is too much the realist to allow his adventurer the fullest enjoyment of his romantic dreams. Hajji's true love, Zeenab, is kept from him, first by the crafty physician Mizra Ahmak, and later by the Shah himself. Worse, as one of the royal executioners, poor Hajji is forced to witness her terrible death.

He suffers other misfortunes. When he is under the tutelage of the Turcoman bandits, he is forced to rob his own father; and years later, he arrives at his ancestral home just in time to watch the old man expire. After his father dies, Hajji and his mother quarrel and part on unfriendly terms. His marriage to the rich widow Shekerleb is dissolved by her kinsmen, when they discover that Hajji is not so rich as he had pretended to be. And he is not only humiliated but beaten on several occasions, once by order of the *Mohtesib* (inspector), who has our hero thrashed on the soles of his feet until he loses consciousness from the pain. Thus Morier avoids the romantic stereotype of the swaggering outlaw—the corsair, the highwayman, the outcast—popularized by Scott, Byron, Shelley, and others. Instead, his rogue-hero is a fellow mortal, perhaps less scrupulous than most of us, but unquestionably human in his weaknesses. In *Hajji Baba of Ispahan in England* (1828) Morier continues the tale of Hajji's adventures, this time as an envoy from Persia to the barbarians of the West.

HAKLUYT'S VOYAGES

Type of work: Travel narratives
Author: Richard Hakluyt (c. 1553-1616)
Type of plot: Adventure and exploration
Time of plot: c. 517 to 1600
Locale: The known world
First published: 1589

Valuable for its accounts of many sixteenth century explorations, for its indication of the temper of Elizabethan England, and for its vigorous and authentic style, this anthology of explorations and travels of early British adventurers remains fascinating reading, both for students of history and of literature. The idealism, courage, and optimism of the age are apparent throughout the narratives.

Richard Hakluyt, regarded as the first professor of modern geography at Oxford, made a point of getting to know the "chiefest Captains at sea, the greatest merchants, and the best Mariners of our nation." The result was *Hakluyt's Voyages,* an invaluable source book to students of the Age of Discovery and the place of England in it. As a boy, he watched the ships come to port from distant journeys, and early lessons in geography fired him with an eagerness to know more; studies at Oxford and a five-year period in Paris further set his resolution to collect the scattered records of English maritime discovery. Perhaps he began the work as a piece of propaganda, but it soon became more than that. The second edition grew to three volumes issued over as many years. He also translated narratives by Spanish explorers, but *Hakluyt's Voyages* remains his memorial, a true "prose epic" of the English people and nation. The massive work is more than a documentary history of exploration, for in it, alongside tales of adventure, are mingled historical and economic papers intended to establish British sovereignty at sea. The purpose of the huge undertaking was to encourage overseas settlement and foreign trade. (It was asserted that the income of the East India Company was greatly increased through *Hakluyt's Voyages.*)

To the modern reader, *Hakluyt's Voyages* is alive with Elizabethan spirit of adventure, and reflects the suddenly expanding world of the Tudors. The book contains, indeed, the raw material from which an English *Odyssey* might have been made. Although the work is basically an anthology, the stamp of Hakluyt's personality is over the entire book; his idealism, his admiration for brave men and noble deeds, and his ambitions for his nation are everywhere evident.

As much as anything else, *Hakluyt's Voyages* should be read as economic history; some of the pieces included might be considered real estate promoters' descriptions of lands to be developed. Merchants found the book invaluable, and the queen and her ministers saw it as a worthy psychological push toward the readiness of the nation to embrace an empire. The accounts of the voyages are told with a simplicity and directness far more effective than self-conscious artistry or literary pretensions; the tales are the matter-of-fact reporting of men of action. Among the most interesting accounts are those of Sir Walter Raleigh's unsuccessful attempts to found a colony in Virginia and the seeking of the fabled Northwest Passage to the Orient, but perhaps the most fascinating is the legendary voyage of Sir Francis Drake up the Western coast of America.

THE HAMLET

Type of work: Novel
Author: William Faulkner (1897-1962)
Type of plot: Psychological realism
Time of plot: Late nineteenth century
Locale: Mississippi
First published: 1940

Again rejecting the conventional forms of fiction, Faulkner in this book brings together a collection of views of his section of the South, focusing on the personalities and moral qualities of its inhabitants. His genius raises these ironic and merciless portraits to universality, providing the reader with a moral vision comparable to those of the greatest artists. A positive life force does endure, Faulkner implies, despite the existence, and often triumph, of men who are ruthless and corrupt.

In *The Hamlet,* Faulkner explores the triumph of those amoral qualities which collectively have come to be called "Snopesism." Though never at its center, Flem Snopes, who epitomizes the worst qualities characteristic of the society arising to fill the power vacuum created by the decline of the great ante-bellum Southern families, dominates the book as an almost diabolically evil presence. V. K. Ratliff, the unifying narrative voice and moral center against whose intelligence and humanity Flem's greed, rapacity, and inhumanity are measured, represents the most stable moral force in the novel.

Through his sympathetic portrayal of such diverse characters as Ike Snopes, idiot lover of a cow, and the murderer Mink Snopes, Faulkner suggests that it is Flem alone who represents the evil associated with the Snopses. Flem, who breaks no law, is simply without human feeling of any sort, and hence guilty of the greatest sin. This fact is dramatized repeatedly as we see various characters become victims of their own or other's passions, while Flem, passionless himself, uses these human weaknesses to his own advantage. Flem's marriage of convenience to Eula Varner is perhaps the most overt example of this theme. To other men, Eula, an almost irresistible sexual force, symbolizes life and fecundity. Flem alone is untouched by her sexuality, and he marries her only for the advantage she brings him.

Ratliff's deep sense of humanity and his moral strength make him Flem's most worthy adversary, and he does indeed defeat Snopes in their first encounter. Within the scheme of the book, however, Flem must triumph over all. Thus, he is finally able to tempt Ratliff into speculating on the Old Frenchman's Place so he too can be cheated. At that point, evil is ascendant and Flem Snopes has at last conquered the world of Frenchman's Bend.

HAMLET, PRINCE OF DENMARK

Type of work: Drama
Author: William Shakespeare (1564-1616)
Type of plot: Romantic tragedy
Time of plot: c. 1200
Locale: Elsinore, Denmark
First presented: 1602

One of the most popular and highly respected plays ever written, Hamlet *owes its greatness to the character of the Prince, a man of thought rather than action, a philosophical, introspective hero who is swept along by events rather than exercising control of them. Through the medium of some of the most profound and superb poetry ever composed, Shakespeare transforms a conventional revenge tragedy into a gripping exploration of the universal problems of mankind. In Hamlet's struggle with duty, morality, and ethics are mirrored the hopes, fears, and despair of all mankind.*

Hamlet has remained the most perplexing, as well as the most popular, of Shakespeare's major tragedies. Performed frequently, the play has tantalized critics with what has become known as the Hamlet mystery. The mystery resides in Hamlet's complex behavior, most notably his indecision and his reluctance to act.

Freudian critics have located his motivation in the psychodynamic triad of the father-mother-son relationship. According to this view, Hamlet is disturbed and eventually deranged by his Oedipal jealousy of the uncle who has done what, we are to believe, all sons long to do themselves. Other critics have taken the more conventional tack of identifying Hamlet's tragic flaw as a lack of courage or moral resolution. In this view, Hamlet's indecision is a sign of moral ambivalence which he overcomes too late.

The trouble with both of these views is that they presuppose a precise discovery of Hamlet's motivation. However, Renaissance drama is not generally a drama of motivation either by psychological set or moral predetermination. Rather, the tendency is to present characters, with well delineated moral and ethical dispositions, who are faced with dilemmas. It is the outcome of these conflicts, the consequences, which normally hold center stage. What we watch in *Hamlet* is an agonizing confrontation between the will of a good and intelligent man and the uncongenial role which circumstance calls upon him to play.

The disagreeable role is a familiar one in Renaissance drama—the revenger. The early description of Hamlet, bereft by the death of his father and the hasty marriage of his mother, makes him a prime candidate to assume such a role. One need not conclude that his despondency is Oedipal in order to sympathize with the extremity of his grief. His father, whom he deeply loved and admired, is recently deceased and he himself seems to have been finessed out of his birthright. Shakespeare, in his unfortunate ignorance of Freud, emphasized Hamlet's shock at Gertrude's disrespect to the memory of his father rather than love of mother as the prime source of his distress. The very situation breeds suspicion, which is reinforced by the ghastly visitation by the elder Hamlet's ghost and the ghost's disquieting revelation. The ingredients are all there for bloody revenge.

However, if Hamlet were simply to proceed to act out the role that has been thrust upon him, the play would be just another sanguinary potboiler without the moral and theological complexity which provides its special fascination. Hamlet has, after all, been a student of theology at Wittenberg. Hamlet's knowledge complicates the situation. First of all, he is aware of the fundamental immorality of the liaison between Gertrude and Claudius. Hamlet's accusation of incest is not an adolescent excess but an accurate theological description of a marriage between a widow and her dead husband's brother.

Hamlet's theological accomplishments do more than exacerbate his feelings. For the ordinary revenger, the commission from the ghost of the murdered father would be more than enough to start the bloodletting. But Hamlet is aware of the unreliability of otherworldly apparitions, and consequently he is reluctant to heed its injunction to perform an action which is objectively evil. In addition, the fear that his father was murdered in a state of sin and is condemned to hell not only increases Hamlet's sense of injustice but also, paradoxically, casts further doubt on the reliability of the ghost's exhortation. Is the ghost, Hamlet wonders, merely an infernal spirit goading him to sin?

Thus, Hamlet's indecision is not an indication of weakness, but the result of his complex understanding of the moral dilemma with which he is faced. He is unwilling to act unjustly, yet he is afraid that he is failing to exact a deserved retribution. He debates the murky issue and becomes unsure himself whether his behavior is caused by moral scruple or cowardice. He is in sharp contrast with the cynicism of Claudius and the verbose moral platitudes of Polonius. The play is in sharp contrast with the moral simplicity of the ordinary revenge tragedy. Hamlet's intelligence has transformed a stock situation into a unique internal conflict.

He believes that he must have greater certitude of Claudius' guilt if he is to take action. The device of the play within a play provides greater assurance that Claudius is suffering from a guilty conscience, but it simultaneously sharpens Hamlet's anguish. Having seen a recreation of his father's death and Claudius' response, Hamlet is able to summon the determination to act. However, he once again hesitates when he sees Claudius in prayer because he believes that the king is repenting and, if murdered at that moment, will go directly to heaven. Here Hamlet's inaction is not the result of cowardice nor even of a perception of moral ambiguity. Rather, after all of his agonizing,

Hamlet once decided on revenge is so thoroughly committed that his passion cannot be satiated except by destroying his uncle body and soul. It is ironic that Claudius has been unable to repent and that Hamlet is thwarted this time by the combination of his theological insight with the extreme ferocity of his vengeful intention.

That Hamlet loses his mental stability is clear in his behavior towards Ophelia and in his subsequent meanderings. Circumstance has enforced a role whose enormity has overwhelmed the fine emotional and intellectual balance of a sensitive well-educated young man. Gradually he regains control of himself and is armed with a cold determination to do what he decides is the just thing. Yet, even then, it is only in the carnage of the concluding scenes that Hamlet finally carries out his intention. Having concluded that "the readiness is all," he strikes his uncle only after he has discovered Claudius' final scheme to kill him and Laertes, but by then he is mortally wounded.

The arrival of Fortinbras, who has been lurking in the background throughout the play, superficially seems to indicate that a new, more direct and courageous order will prevail in the place of the evil of Claudius and the weakness of Hamlet. But Fortinbras' superiority is only apparent. He brings stasis and stability back to a disordered kingdom, but he does not have the self-consciousness and moral sensitivity which destroy and redeem Hamlet.

Gerald Else has interpreted Aristotle's notion of *katharsis* to be not a purging of the emotions but a purging of a role of the moral horror, the pity and fear, ordinarily associated with it. If that is so, then Hamlet, by the conflict of his ethical will with his role, has purged the revenger of his horrific bloodthirstiness and turned the stock figure into a self-conscious hero in moral conflict.

Edward E. Foster

A HANDFUL OF DUST

Type of work: Novel
Author: Evelyn Waugh (1903-1966)
Type of plot: Social satire
Time of plot: Twentieth century
Locale: England
First published: 1934

One of the certain masterpieces of the modern English novel, A Handful of Dust *conveys, in prose as pure as any written in the twentieth century, the absurdity of the lives of the English landed aristocracy and the inevitability of their decline and fall.*

Drawn from T. S. Eliot's *The Waste Land,* the title of Waugh's novel suggests its theme and his attitude toward post-World War I civilization. In its last stages English society is "dust," spiritually dead. Without belief or purpose, its members wander from one relationship to another, seeking energy and vitality. The atmosphere is of hectic, but empty activity.

The only still point in this whirlwind is provided by Hetton Abbey. Associated with the Middle Ages, a time of Christian belief and social order, Tony Last's estate is a symbol of values which informs not only this novel but all of Waugh's satires. Indeed, if *A Handful of Dust* has a hero at all, it is the Gothic abbey. For despite the destructiveness of its owners and visitors, it alone survives—and, in fact, gives promise of growth at the end.

Tony Last, of course, is an unsuitable lord of this richly traditional home. If he is presented as sympathetic, he is also dramatized as morally effete, specifically in regard to his profligate wife, Brenda. Besides, he is an anachronism, unable to adapt to the new age. Just as he cannot bring himself to renovate Hetton, he cannot live in the twentieth century. The absurd end which Waugh designs for him—reading Dickens aloud to a madman for the rest of his life—is an apt, if cruel justice.

Tony's successors at Hetton, the Richard Lasts, are of different mettle. Energetic, resourceful, and more importantly, a growing family, the Lasts seek to restore the abbey to economic independence. So if in part Waugh derives his inspiration from Eliot's apocalyptic poem, the final chapter of the novel is one of hope, both in the revival of Hetton and also in the values it symbolizes: order, family, and continuity.

HANDLEY CROSS

Type of work: Novel
Author: Robert Smith Surtees (1803-1864)
Type of plot: Humorous satire
Time of plot: Nineteenth century
Locale: England
First published: 1843; enlarged 1854

A typical example of nineteenth century English sporting tales, Handley Cross *contains little plot or dramatic motivation, but remains of some interest because of its detailed pictures of fox hunting and of the hard-riding, hard-drinking sporting set. Jorrocks, who appears in several of Surtees' books, was at one time an extremely popular literary character.*

For some twenty years, Robert Smith Surtees regaled the huntsmen of Britain with his amusing tales of the grocer Jorrocks and his undying passion for all things having to do with the chase. Abused and ridiculed for his extreme love of the hunt, he is never totally absurd: there is too much intensity, sincerity, and humanity in the man's love of sport for him to be destroyed by his enemies and detractors. Although a cockney in manners and speech, a mere grocer by trade, he achieves a lovable nobility all his own.

In his encouraging address to Benjamin, one of his huntsmen or glorified stable boys, Jorrocks reveals the highminded values of character and true wordliness he associates with expertise in things of the hunt: There is no saying what "keenness combined with sagacity and cleanliness may accomplish." Benjamin is flattered into believing that he has all the "ingredients of a great man," and "hopportunity only is wantin' to dewelope them."

The hunt is everything to Jorrocks; it is the measure of all he holds dear. Everything else in life, including his grocery business and home, takes second place to the call of the hounds. Even when he is sorting his clothes, the primary consideration is what can be preserved for use in the hunt and what must be discarded because it no longer can be adapted to the hunt. He is so obsessed with his passion that he cannot, without some anxiety, entrust anything connected with hunting to others. When his celebrated horse is being auctioned, he constantly interrupts the auctioneer with praise of the animal's speed and leaping ability. Eventually, Jorrocks' passion becomes a form of madness, but Surtees insists, in a shower of good honor, on vindicating Jorrocks. As exaggerated as it is, his love of the hunt is too sincere *and* authentic to cause his downfall. He must be free to hunt again.

HANDY ANDY

Type of work: Novel
Author: Samuel Lover (1797-1868)
Type of plot: Comic romance
Time of plot: Nineteenth century
Locale: Ireland
First published: 1842

A series of anecdotes rather than a cohesive novel, Handy Andy *became popular—and remains of interest—because of its excellent character portrayal and atmosphere, and its droll wit and description of Irish folkways. The book endures as a vigorous and amusing period piece.*

Musician, painter, songwriter, novelist, playwright, and performer, Samuel Lover was above all an entertainer, and it is as entertainment that *Handy Andy* has endured for nearly a century and a half. Farcical, full of dialect humor and slapstick comedy, the book stops at nothing in its efforts to provoke good humor and laughter.

One of the chief sources of amusement is Andy's ever-present ignorance. A poor, uneducated lad, Andy means well but invariably gets into trouble. To the unsophisticated readers of Lover's day, Andy's antics touched a familiar chord, as well as being funny in a very basic way. More than anything else, Lover possessed a horror of dullness, and perhaps this accounts for the frenetic pace of *Handy Andy*. Certainly, the little tales are full of action and nonsense. The humor is vigorous and rough-and-ready, but never malicious or cruel. Some of the humor directly attacks prejudices of and toward the Irish; one of the most amusing sequences deals with the potato, the Irish fondness for it and reliance upon it for nourishment and the English scorn towards it. A great deal of humor is made of the local elections, the canvassing for votes, and the competition between the parties. But whatever the issue involved, the characters tend to be portrayed in an affectionate and kindly light, and any humor at their expense is gentle rather than scornful or harsh. There is nothing satirical about this book. Lover has no intention of reforming anything with his humorous sketches.

Lover seldom attempted subtlety in his humor; the accounts of Sackville Scatterbrain on election day or of Andy's being kidnaped while disguised as a young girl are as broad as they are lively. The plot, such as it is, dealing with Andy's marriage, is contrived, and the surprise ending, revealing Bridget's actual husband, is hardly plausible, yet none of this matters, for it all is told with such humor that the reader willingly suspends disbelief. Although the novel is weak, Handy Andy himself nearly ranks with Pickwick and Micawber as a comic hero.

HANGMAN'S HOUSE

Type of work: Novel
Author: Donn Byrne (Brian Oswald Donn-Byrne, 1889-1928)
Type of plot: Regional romance
Time of plot: Early twentieth century
Locale: Ireland
First published: 1925

Intended as an Irish novel for Irishmen, Hangman's House *reflects the troubled times in which it was written. Sensitively drawn characterizations and vivid landscapes, and an honest passion for the land, give this book a unique place in Anglo-Irish literature.*

Ireland and the strangely heroic Irish race are the subject of *Hangman's House,* perhaps Donn Byrne's most noted novel. Certain medieval prophets had accurately predicted that Ireland would be tyrannized by England for "a week of centuries" (seven centuries); and that week ended during the 1920's, the decade in which Donn Byrne's novel is set. The end of tyranny is the story's background theme. Despite the cluster of characters, ranging from the Citizen, to Lord Glenmalure, to Dermot McDermot, the dominant presence in the novel is Ireland's finally realized struggle for freedom. Thus the real protagonist of *Hangman's House* is Irish history, with its centuries of oppression.

Nevertheless, Donn Byrne is not hateful or propagandistic; the few British personalities in the novel are presented as decent men doing their duty, while Catholics are not painted as saints or Protestants as cohorts of the Anti-Christ. The one touch of overt Irish flag-waving occurs when a fairly amiable British officer seeks to bribe an Irish child into singing British rather than Irish ditties, but is calmly rejected. Otherwise, the novel's characters move through their lives as their ancestors have done for centuries, living under an oppressive pall that never vanquishes them. The Citizen is the strongest symbolic personality of the story, and Connaught a victim figure that is almost representative of Ireland itself. A curious void exists in the rather mild treatment of Lord Glenmalure, "The Hangman," who wreaks vengeance on many Fenians and who coerces Connaught into marriage with a spineless traitor for the most spurious of economic reasons. The selfishness and violence of Glenmalure—whose base actions are outwardly respectable and dignified—are treated more as a commentary on weak human beings than as a portrait of a willfully evil individual. The author's sensitivity for tints and color, as well as ability to use words musically, are evident in the story.

HARD TIMES

Type of work: Novel
Author: Charles Dickens (1812-1870)
Type of plot: Social criticism
Time of plot: Mid-nineteenth century
Locale: England
First published: 1854

Dedicated to Thomas Carlyle, this book, based upon personal observations of life in Manchester, was Dickens' first novel of outright social protest. The author's vivid style, unforgettable characterizations, and detailed panoramas equalize the bitterness which sometimes threatens to overpower the narrative. The book remains as important for historical and social reasons as for literary ones.

Dickens began as an entertainer (*Pickwick Papers*) but gradually evolved into a moralist and social critic of major significance. In his early works there are heroes and villains; in his later, victims and victimizers. The distinction is important because it measures his development from a writer of fiction to an artist with a tragic vision.

Hard Times is a milestone in Dickens' art: caricature and allegorical names are used here in a form of Swiftian satire so bitter in its contempt and social rage that we almost forget that the same devices are used to create lovable human beings in his other works. Mr. Gradgrind is offensive in a very serious way. His reduction of everything to "facts" constitutes a *gradual grinding* away of the humanity of his pupils and his own children. Louisa marries to obtain advantages for her brother—in itself a noble act; but her blind willingness to set aside personal feelings and needs only makes her more vulnerable to Harthouse's attempts at seduction. It is finally Louisa's responsibility, from the depths of her own denied feelings, to educate Gradgrind to his deficiencies as a father and teacher.

Although Dickens' satirical dismissal of rationalistic Utilitarianism (the doctrine that the greatest good for the greatest number must be the goal of a statistically rigorous and "fact" conscious social reform) is brilliantly effective in the classroom scenes, he does not entirely convince us that Utilitarian education is directly responsible for the dehumanization of England. Dickens wanted to shock the middle-class reformers with the coldness of their ideas, but he himself was curiously limited in his own humanism. Humanitarian that he was, he did not entirely respect the humanity of the very working classes he championed. The portrait of Slackbridge, the trade union organizer, reveals Dickens' contempt of labor as a political force.

Throughout his life Dickens distrusted the people's ability to govern themselves; he always looked to the manufacturers and the aristocracy, the governing classes, to correct or avoid the evils of the society they held in trust. *Hard Times* is a blow at the ideas Dickens felt were preventing the leading classes from meeting their social responsibilities.

HARP OF A THOUSAND STRINGS

Type of work: Novel
Author: H. L. Davis (1896-1960)
Type of plot: Historical-philosophical romance
Time of plot: Late eighteenth and early nineteenth centuries
Locale: The American prairie country, Tripoli, and Paris
First published: 1947

History itself is the thousand-stringed harp of the title of this brilliant, difficult novel, and it is revealed as an instrument capable of endless vibrations and echoes. An unusual book, linking personalities and events of the French Revolution to the development of the American West, the work's philosophical considerations are as fundamental to its interest and merit as is its narrative power.

Harp of a Thousand Strings is not an easy novel to read. Characters are introduced abruptly, there are random digressions that seem to have little to do with the main narrative, and the writing makes no concessions to casual readers. Davis is not afraid to use coincidence in his plot as freely as Dickens did, occasionally straining the reader's credulity. But the novel has many merits, including the prose which is of a schooled intelligence, contemplative and elegant, and, subtle delineation of character. The reader comes to enjoy the play of the author's mind over the intricate—almost labyrinthine—situations and the equally scrupulous assessment of human motivation.

The style changes with the narrative. When Davis describes the three founding fathers in their dotage, he uses the garrulous, inventive ramblings of a frontier tale. As the scene shifts to France, the language takes on an epigrammatic, paradoxical elegance. He does not dwell on the tangible, surface impressions of the past found in most historical novels, but rather creates a dreamlike past, filled with shadow and light. Goyaesque images pervade the book, grotesque, shadowy scenes of hideous people engaged in vile acts. Yet the book is often very funny. This juxtaposition of wit and anger gives the novel a unique resonance and power.

Davis casts a wry eye at men such as Robespierre and Fouché and the hero of the novel, Tallien. The implication is that all men are mortal, are played on by history as much as they play upon history. The story shows how personal motives—and not always of the highest order—can influence the actions which make history. Many of the characters look back over their lives with anger and regret. Jory and the Commodore both gaze back on frustrated hopes and years of humiliation and bitterness, but the Commodore tells his friend that after a certain point one no longer should compare one's life to one's early expectations and hopes. Survival should be sufficient.

Like his contemporaries A. B. Guthrie Jr. and Walter Van Tilburg Clark, H. L. Davis was a literary pioneer of the American West, rediscovering and reinterpreting the past with the eyes of an artist and poet. Davis' novels are loosely plotted, almost picaresque, his style is quiet although at times complicated. What sets his work above the usual is his mood, what some critics have called "the magic qualities of place and emotion." He is a man who writes with the knowledge of the energies that make history and can present this awareness in tales which are lyrical, tragic, and sometimes comic.

Although an exact contemporary of the so-called Lost Generation which included Hemingway, Fitzgerald, and Dos Passos, Davis had little in common with them. He began fiction writing late and was never prolific. Almost twelve years elapsed between his first prize-winning novel, *Honey in the Horn,* and his next, *Harp of a Thousand Strings.* He always was a man and writer who followed his own vision, belonging to no coterie or school. First and foremost, he was a craftsman.

This craftsmanship is particularly evident in the complicated structure of *Harp of a Thousand Strings.* The story is framed by the rugged grandeur and squalor of the American frontier. The tale moves the reader from the American West to Tripoli to the France of the Revolution, back to Tripoli in the time of Napoleon, and then back to the American frontier. The reader seems to view the story through a series of refracting lenses. By the time he has finished the book, it has taken on the character of a legend: larger than life, abstract, and ripe with moral significance.

The theme of money and the craving for it runs through the novel beside the theme of lust for power. With the additional motifs of vengeance and thwarted love, these themes give the novel a bitter view of mankind. Only when he writes about nature does Davis attempt to paint a pretty picture. Men and man-created objects, whether cities or smaller creations, are treated harshly.

The author frequently makes comments about women. None of the female characters in the novel are very likable or admirable. Of the two principal women, one is passionately destructive, the other is cold and calculating. Both are self-centered. But this last is a trait shared by the male characters, as well. With the possible exception of Father Jarnatt, the characters are all self-seeking, concerned primarily with their own survival. Few of them are presented as vivid, living beings.

Only Anne-Joseph Théroigne emerges as a physical, dynamic human force, lingering in the imagination long after the book is finished. The best realized scenes are those of Anne-Joseph haranguing Parisian mobs during the Terror. Her animal vitality and vulgarity give the novel a needed push, and the book suffers when she drops from the scene.

But Davis is obviously not interested in that physical, dynamic side of characterization. His gift is for the analytical consideration of motives and emotions. The reader may not be able to visualize a character, but the reasoning processes of that character are quite clearly presented. The reader understands why the characters in the novel double-cross one another, even if he does not always care.

Harp of a Thousand Strings is an impressive achievement, a highly cerebral novel, which, although it does not greatly move the reader emotionally, provides rewarding moments of contemplation, and fascinating views of contrasting worlds. An intellectual maze, a collection of Chinese boxes, one inside the other, the novel draws the reader ever in, farther and farther, gradually demonstrating that the cycles we call history are all tightly fitted together. It is a book worth the effort of reading.

Bruce D. Reeves

HAVELOK THE DANE

Type of work: Poem
Author: Unknown
Type of plot: Adventure romance
Time of plot: Tenth century
Locale: England and Denmark
First transcribed: c. 1350

True to the conventions of the medieval romance, Havelok the Dane *presents the noble hero and pure heroine in a tale in which virtue is rewarded and villainy punished. The plot maintains a sense of suspense and the story manages to be both concise and coherent.*

Unlike many medieval romances, whose locale is some legendary land completely unanchored to the real world, *Havelok the Dane* seems to take place in a geographical area, marked by association to Lincolnshire and the town of Grimsby. A town seal with the names "Grym," "Habloc," and "Goldeburgh," the story's three main protagonists, still exists. Although other attempts to tie down its historical validity have failed, *Havelok the Dane* may well be based upon popular local events.

Its author, although anonymous, seems to have been a conscientious middle-class writer concerned with down-to-earth matters such as justice, the value of hard work, and a man's being true to himself. The author's description of King Athelwold stresses, before prowess in battle, the ruler's integrity, fairness and concern for the weak. Athelwold, like Havelok, relates to the poor and underprivileged.

In contrast, the villains Godard and Godrich seem darker and totally consumed with evil. There is nothing to relieve their wickedness except Godard's relenting enough not to kill Havelok outright; instead, he commands the fisherman Grim to throw him into the sea after having tied an anchor around his neck.

The Latin subtitle of *Havelok the Dane* which states "Here begins the life of Havelok once king of England and Denmark" shows that the author, if not his audience, realized their half-Danish heritage. Though we have nothing to prove this, perhaps the tale arose out of some actual political situation.

Notwithstanding its geographical place-names and subtitle, however, the story is a typical wish fulfillment depicting the disguised, mistreated hero of royal birth who finds his true status, regains his kingdom, and gets the princess. *Havelok the Dane* has a double plot of this nature because Goldeboru, the maiden, also undergoes mistreatment and must regain her royal status before they marry and become King and Queen of Denmark and England.

The author has composed no knightly romance with trappings of rich armor and vestments; Havelok is a middle-class folk hero who fights with a door bar, takes part in a stone-heaving contest, spends most of his time as a steady cook's helper, and, when victorious, dispenses land and women as rewards.

Havelok the Dane is a very English medieval romance, tied to the land and common folk, and told with the rugged gusto of *Beowulf*.

A HAZARD OF NEW FORTUNES

Type of work: Novel
Author: William Dean Howells (1837-1920)
Type of plot: Novel of manners
Time of plot: The 1880's
Locale: New York City
First published: 1890

A complex novel containing some of Howells' most deft characterizations, A Hazard of New Fortunes *reflects both the author's own life and his dissatisfaction with America. It also reveals his interest in social improvement. The novel is considered one of the finest of Howells' fictional works.*

The plot of *A Hazard of New Fortunes* is strikingly autobiographical; the various events reflect Howells' hazarding of his own fortunes in leaving his literary domain in Boston for New York City and the editor's chair at *Harper's Magazine*. It was an astute move, for the literary center of America seemed to follow him.

The protagonists of this novel are also autobiographical. Featured in Howells' first novel, *Their Wedding Journey* (1872), which parallels the Howells' own honeymoon, Basil and Isabel March are also central to several of Howells' works of the 1890's. In *A Hazard of New Fortunes* they mature noticeably and develop a sense of the complicity of all men in one another's affairs. But learning this lesson took Howells himself beyond the comfortable surface of American life and exposed him to social and economic problems that aroused his concern but with which he was temperamentally unable to deal. Mr. Dryfoos' attempt to make amends after the death of his son reads like the end of *A Christmas Carol*. However, the labor unrest that indirectly caused Conrad's death calls for more than the redemption of a Scrooge. Naturalists such as Dreiser and Norris were to provide the fiction that would bring such social forces into focus.

Howells after *A Hazard of New Fortunes* is, therefore, a changed man. While he struggled with a new range of experience, the school of literary realism he had developed and propounded as editor and novelist proved inadequate for dealing with the more grim aspects of real life in America. Howells' succeeding novels reveal a new pensiveness, tentativeness, and diminished self-assurance. While no abrupt transition can be noted, experimentation with new literary forms in the utopian Altrurian romances, psychological symbolism in *The Shadow of a Dream,* manipulation of point of view in *The Landlord at Lion's Head,* all point to a diminishing confidence in the capacity of literary realism, and in Howells himself, to render into fiction the increasingly complex reality of American life.

HEADLONG HALL

Type of work: Novel
Author: Thomas Love Peacock (1785-1866)
Type of plot: Comedy of manners
Time of plot: Early nineteenth century
Locale: Wales
First published: 1816

A satire on pseudo-philosophers of the nineteenth century, Headlong Hall *contains virtually no plot and no character development, yet the prose style, the dialogue, and the author's awareness of the ridiculousness of human nature give the book an enduring fascination.*

Headlong Hall, Peacock's first novel, has been characterized as apprentice work because his later exercises in the genre are even more successful. However, there is no awkwardness or hesitancy in this pioneer work; the later novels differ from it only in offering a richer variety of conversation and slightly more complex plots.

Plot is the least requisite element in a Peacock novel, and the author is inclined to mock even the minimal necessities of storytelling that he acknowledges. Chapter XIV of *Headlong Hall,* in which four marriages are clapped up in as many pages, is a reduction to absurdity of the propensity of popular novelists in his day to pair off their *dramatis personae* in the concluding chapters.

Characterization is not much more important to Peacock. What he provides instead is a group of quirky mouthpieces for different points of view, combined with caricatures, seldom malicious, of his associates. Aspects of his friend Shelley are caricatured in at least three of the novels (Foster is the Shelleyan figure in this one), and Shelley was highly amused by each portrayal. Peacock's wit, though sharp, is seldom wounding, and it touches virtually everywhere with a fine impartiality. He was delighted to learn of his readers' difficulty in ascertaining which, if any, of the opinions so entertainingly advanced in his novels he shared.

Opinions, or more precisely, the absurdity and pretentiousness with which people advance them and the gap between their propositions and their behavior, are the real subject of all the novels. Literary historians, noting the customary setting for Peacock's gatherings of indefatigable talkers, have called him the father of the "country house novel." His progeny have been numerous and often brilliant, including such dazzling performances as Douglas' *South Wind* and Huxley's *Crome Yellow,* but none has surpassed its progenitor in wit and geniality.

THE HEART IS A LONELY HUNTER

Type of work: Novel
Author: Carson McCullers (1917-1967)
Type of plot: Psychological realism
Time of plot: The 1930's
Locale: A Georgia mill town
First published: 1940

This distinguished first novel introduced many of the themes which reappeared in the author's later works. With subtle and precise art, Carson McCullers explores the moral isolation of the individual in society and the loneliness and longing of men in the modern world.

All of Carson McCuller's writing turns on the plight of the loving and the lonely, and it is this view of moral and spiritual isolation as the inescapable condition of man that makes *The Heart Is a Lonely Hunter* so impressive as a first novel. Although the book shows certain limitations resulting from the author's youth and inexperience, it nevertheless remains a remarkable work for a twenty-two-year-old to write. To read it as a novel of social criticism is to misunderstand the author's subtle art. One character is a fiery white radical and another is a fanatic black Marxist, but their political views are subordinate to the dominant theme of the novel: the loneliness of the individual and the frustrated struggle to communicate with others. Singer, the ironically named mute, is the focal figure in the story. It is to him that the other main characters turn when they wish to unburden themselves, to pour out their views, their ideas, their emotions.

It is ironic that Singer should be the one toward whom the others turn to release the tension and some of the confusion within them, since Singer hears nothing and is really the loneliest person in the story after the removal of his insane mute friend Antonapoulos to the asylum. With the death of Antonapoulos, Singer has no one to turn to and he shoots himself, while the others, who have given him nothing, continue their own self-centered lives.

Love and hatred struggle for mastery in McCuller's characters. Jake Blount, itinerant carnival worker, seethes with anger at the injustices which the common man endures in a capitalistic society that permits the rich to prey upon the poor. Dr. Copeland rages also against the inequities of capitalism, but he concentrates his hatred upon the whites who have for so long oppressed his race. Dr. Copeland's intemperance of thought and feeling brings him into conflict both with his family and with Blount, whose own intemperance makes a successful dialogue between himself and Copeland impossible despite their common anger at the political and economic system in which they live.

Mick Kelly is experiencing the pains of adolescence, suffering from self-consciousness, beset by the confusions which accompany her developing sexuality, indulging in dreams of the future—a future that will be frustrated forever by the economic situation of her family, and finally embittered by the realization that her Woolworth's job means doom to her hopes.

Biff Brannon, who keeps his café open at night as a haven for lonely people, seeks an understanding of those who come in not only to eat and drink but to talk. They are objects for his study, but they also help him to forget the loneliness he feels when they have gone. He is the last person one sees in the novel—alone, frightened, and awaiting the sun of a new day that will bring customers through the café door.

HEART OF DARKNESS

Type of work: Short story
Author: Joseph Conrad (Józef Teodor Konrad Korzeniowski, 1857-1924)
Type of plot: Symbolic romance
Time of plot: Late nineteenth century
Locale: The Belgian Congo
First published: 1902

Both an adventure story and the account of a philosophical and moral quest, this tale takes the reader on a symbolic journey into the blackness central to the heart and soul of man. A vagueness at its core has detracted little from the story's power and continued popularity.

Christened Teodor Jósef Konrad Nalecz Korzeniowski by his Polish parents, Joseph Conrad was able to write from firsthand knowledge of the sea and sailing. Early in his life he left the cold climate of Poland to travel to the warmer regions of the Mediterranean where he became a sailor. He began reading extensively and chose the sea as a vehicle for the ideas that were forming in his psyche. He traveled a great deal: to the West Indies, Latin America, Africa. Eventually he settled in England and perfected (through the elaborate process of translating from Polish into French into English) a remarkably subtle yet powerful literary style.

Criticism of Conrad's work in general and *Heart of Darkness* in particular has been both extensive and varied. Many critics concern themselves with Conrad's style; others focus on the biographical aspects of his fiction; some see the works as social commentaries; some are students of Conrad's explorations into human psychology; many are interested in the brooding, shadowy symbolism and philosophy that hovers over all the works. It is easy to see, therefore, that Conrad is a distinctively complex literary genius. E. M. Forster censured him as a vague and elusive writer who never quite clearly discloses the philosophy that lies behind his tales. Such a censure ignores Conrad's notion about the way some fiction can be handled. Partly as Conrad's mouthpiece, the narrator of *Heart of Darkness* states in the first few pages of the novel:

> The yarns of seamen have a direct simplicity, the whole meaning of which lies within the shell of a cracked nut. But Marlow was not typical (if his propensity to spin yarns be excepted), and to him the meaning of an episode was not inside like a kernel but outside, enveloping the tale which brought it out only as a glow brings out a haze, in the likeness of one of those misty halos that sometimes are made visible by the spectral illumination of moonshine.

The mention of the narrator brings up one of the most complex and intriguing features of *Heart of Darkness*: its carefully executed and elaborately conceived point of view. For one can detect (if careful in his reading) that the novel is in truth two narratives, inexorably woven together by Conrad's masterful craftsmanship. The outer frame of the story—the immediate setting—involves the unnamed narrator who is apparently the only one on the *Nellie* who is profoundly affected by Marlow's tale, the inner story which is the bulk of the entire novella. Marlow narrates, and the others listen passively. The narrator's closing words show his feeling at the conclusion of Marlow's recounting of the events in the Congo:

> Marlow ceased, and sat apart, indistinct and silent, in the pose of a meditating Buddha. Nobody moved for a time. "We have lost the first of the ebb," said the Director suddenly. I raised my head. The offing was barred by a black bank of clouds, and the tranquil waterway leading to the uttermost ends of the earth flowed sombre under an overcast sky—seemed to lead into the heart of an immense darkness.

Since Marlow's narrative is a tale devoted primarily to a journey to the mysterious dark continent (the literal heart of darkness, Africa), a superficial view of the tale is simply that it is essentially an elaborate story involving confrontation with exotic natives, treacherous dangers of the jungle, brutal savagery, and even cannibalism. But such a view ignores larger meanings with which the work is implicitly concerned: namely, social and cultural implications; psychological workings of the cultivated European left to the uncivilized wilderness; and the richly colored fabric of symbolism that emerges slowly but inevitably from beneath the surface.

Heart of Darkness can also be examined for its social and cultural commentaries. It is fairly obvious that a perverted version of the "White Man's Burden" was the philosophy adopted by the ivory hunters at the Inner Station. Kurtz's "Exterminate the brutes!" shows the way a white man can exploit the helpless savage. The futile shelling from the gunboat into the jungle is also vividly portrayed as a useless, brutal, and absurd act perpetrated against a weaker, more uncivilized culture than the one that nurtured Kurtz.

Here the psychological phenomena of Marlow's tale emerge. Kurtz, a man relieved of all social and civilized restraints, goes mad after committing himself to the total pursuit of evil and depravity. And his observation "The horror! the horror!" suggests his final realization of the consequences of his life. Marlow realizes this too and is allowed (because he forces restraint upon himself) to draw back his foot from the precipice of madness. The experience leaves Marlow sober, disturbed, meditative, and obsessed with relating his story in much the same way Coleridge's Ancient Mariner must also relate his story.

On a symbolic level the story is rich; a book could easily be written on this facet of the novel. An arbitrary mention of some of the major symbols must suffice here: the Congo River that reminded Marlow early in his youth of a snake as it uncoiled its length into the darknes of Africa and furnished him with an uncontrollable "fascination of the abomination"; the symbolic journey into man's own heart of darkness revealing blindingly the evil of man's own nature and his capacity for evil; the irony of the quest when the truth is revealed not in terms of light but in terms of darkness (the truth brings not light but rather total darkness). The entire symbolic character of the work is capsuled at the end of Marlow's tale when he is forced to lie to Kurtz's intended spouse in order to preserve her illusion; the truth appears to Marlow as an inescapable darkness and the novel ends with the narrator's own observation of darkness.

Heart of Darkness is one of literature's most sombre fictions. It explores the fundamental questions about man's nature: his capacity for evil; the necessity for restraint; the effect of physical darkness and isolation on a civilized soul; and the necessity of relinquishing pride for one's own spiritual salvation. E. M. Forster's censure of Conrad may be correct in many ways, but it refuses to admit that through such philosophical ruminations Conrad has allowed generations of readers to ponder humanity's own heart of darkness.

Wayne E. Haskin

THE HEART OF MIDLOTHIAN

Type of work: Novel
Author: Sir Walter Scott (1771-1832)
Type of plot: Historical romance
Time of plot: Early eighteenth century
Locale: Scotland
First published: 1818

Reputedly based on fact, The Heart of Midlothian *tells the story of a dairyman's daughter and her efforts to save her sister from being hanged on a charge of child murder. The narrative is exciting in the typical Scott style, and is filled with suspense, mystery, and romance. Many readers consider this Scott's greatest novel.*

Many critics have considered this novel Scott's best; but, although *The Heart of Midlothian* has received much praise, the reasons for its success are different from those of most of the Waverley series. The novel does not have the usual Gothic props of ruined abbeys, spectres, prophesizing old hags, or lonely windswept castles. Only one scene, where Jeanie Deans meets George Staunton at moonrise in Nicol Muschat's Cairn, is typical of wild, picturesque settings so frequent in Scott's fiction.

The plot is based upon authentic historical events; the Porteous Riot of 1736 in Edinburgh's famous Old Tolbooth prison, or as it was commonly called "the heart of Midlothian," sets the action on its course. But the story is not actually one of social history involving questions of justice. Nor is it a study of Scottish Presbyterianism. Long debates on both these issues take up major portions of the work, but Scott comes to no clear conclusions. These issues do not provide the unifying force that holds the story together.

A strong moral theme is the binding element, for most of the main protagonists are caught in dilemmas of conscience. Jeanie Deans must decide between telling a lie to save her sister Effie's life or speaking the truth and thereby condemning her to execution. Effie herself has the choice of attempting to live virtuously as she was taught or being faithful to her dissipated, criminal lover. Their father, stern David Deans, must decide whether to adhere to his Presbyterian principles or come to terms with the human condition and forgive Effie. George Staunton, alias Robertson, is forced either to follow his wild inclinations and stay with his desperate associates or to reform and assume responsibilities of position and inheritance. He must also confront his obligation to marry Effie, whom he has wronged. These varied dilemmas of conscience constitute the texture of the novel.

The heroine is the one strong character in the novel, but she differs strikingly from the usual Waverley heroine, who is tall, beautiful, exceedingly well bred, romantic and, of course, wealthy. Jeanie Deans is the unusual: a peasant heroine, plain in appearance, not trained in social deportment, and lacking a romantic, Gothic background to aid her. Perhaps the moral seriousness of *The Heart of Midlothian* plus the fact that Scott drew his heroine from the lower classes not only make the novel popular but also give it a coherence and unity unusual in his fiction.

In most of Scott's novels minor characters, who are largely drawn from Scottish rural life and humble occupations, are more real than upper-class figures. When dealing with them Scott has a more energetic and colorful style. Critics often remark that the strength of his work lies in such characters as Caleb Balderstone of *The Bride of Lammermoor,* Edie Ochiltree and Maggie Mucklebackit of *The Antiquary,* Callum Beg and Widow Flockhart of *Waverly.* Scott reproduces their speech faithfully and with obvious relish.

But in *The Heart of Midlothian,* although he still opposes the upper-class culture—with that of the lower and exploits resulting tensions, he elevates a dairyman's daughter to the status of heroine. And, in spite of the unyielding virtue of her character and the contrived situation in which she becomes involved, he not only makes her believable, but also enlists the somewhat skeptical, hesitant reader on her side. She has common sense, and the rough, matter-of-fact elements in her daily life leave no doubt that she will conquer all adverse forces to triumph in Effie's cause. The law of retribution is at work here as in Scott's other novels, but Providence has a fresh, indefatigable agent in Jeanie. It is interesting that she was Scott's own favorite heroine.

Believable, too, are several scenes in *The Heart of Midlothian,* particularly the Porteous Riot which opens the novel. Scott handles realistically the mob's capture of Tolbooth prison and the lynching of Captain Porteous. Another well constructed scene, and one which is moving, if sentimental, is that of Effie's trial. In such sections Scott tightens his control of character interaction and effects economy of language.

However, the entire account of Jeanie's journey to London to obtain from Queen Caroline Effie's pardon slows down the novel and fails to hold the reader's interest. And the last section of the work—almost an epilogue—though required by Scott's publisher, does not seem to be required by the story itself. Jeanie and Reuben with their children and old David Deans live out a mellowed existence in picturesque Roseneath; their rural domesticity is only enlivened by the reunion of Jeanie and her sister (now Lady Staunton) and George's murder by his and Effie's unrecognized son.

If some portions of the novel seem protracted and rather unexciting, still the whole is well-knit and more logical than much of Scott's fiction. Because Scott considered the function of the novel to furnish "solace from the toils of ordinary life by an excursion into the regions of imagination," he ordinarily was indifferent to technique; instead, he concentrated on subject matter. He stressed factual accuracy but felt that too much care in composition might destroy what he termed "abundant spontaneity." Following his own dicta, he wrote rapidly with disregard for planning and revision. He improvised with careless haste and his novels often suffer from poor style and construction. Critics have repeatedly faulted his work for improper motivation and lack of organic unity.

However, one does not get the impression from reading *The Heart of Midlothian* that the author wrote at his usual breakneck speed, casually assembling scenes and characters together without forethought. Motivation is more properly furnished, characterization consistent, and, as mentioned, the dilemmas of conscience are carried through logically. Scott has dispensed in this novel with excess supernatural escapades and the often flamboyant trappings of decadent nobility. He concentrates on the sincerity and integrity of his lower-class protagonists to effect a democratic realism new in the historical English novel, a genre he himself had invented.

Muriel B. Ingham

THE HEART OF THE MATTER

Type of work: Novel
Author: Graham Greene (1904-)
Type of plot: Psychological realism
Time of plot: World War II
Locale: British West Africa
First published: 1948

A fable of the conflict between good and evil, this novel portrays the fears and hopes, loves and hates of a small group of Europeans confined in a colony on the African coast during World War II. Greene's brilliant analysis of the moral state of a man's soul gives this book its lasting value.

The Heart of the Matter is an intelligent, perceptive, and humane *tour de force* on the spiritual capacities and moral dilemmas of Henry Scobie, husband, chief of police, and Catholic. Each of these roles contributes something to the complications of Scobie's situation. It must be admitted, however, that the novel, for all of its sensitivity and insight, is not a work of fiction of the first rank—perhaps just because it is a *tour de force*. Greene, while accepting a stern Roman Catholic framework, challenges us to find fault with a man who goes beyond dishonesty and infidelity to sacrilege and suicide. As Scobie degenerates, Greene dares us, despite the evidence, to cast the first stone by involving our sympathies and appealing to a higher law of mercy which is beyond man's capacity to understand or forgive.

The hothouse setting, in a British colony on the West African coast in the early 1940's, is interesting in its own right. It affords opportunity for commentary on the uncertainties of the period and the limitations of the colonial mentality. Yet, the setting is not the heart of the matter. Scobie's problems as a human being are always the central focus of the novel and they spring from the confluence of his circumstances, his roles, and his character. To the web of colonial life Scobie is a perpetual outsider. Too self-contained, too reflective, too honest with himself and others, he is not able to assume the roles and act out the rituals which will bring him local success. Circumstances contribute to the evolution of the central conflict, but the maritime warfare and diamond smuggling are, for Scobie, rather occasions for sin than sin itself. They provide a context in which Scobie's character agonizes and falters as he takes on his major roles. In each of these roles, his character shines through and it may be his ultimate transcendence that his strength of character maintains a stable core as its periphery comes into conflict with corrupting circumstances.

Scobie's first role is as husband to a wife who, to Scobie's credit, is far more irritating to us than to him. It is through Scobie's patience and understanding that we achieve any degree of sympathy for the human burden his wife bears. In the related role of father of a deceased daughter we see more of Scobie's, and his wife's, suffering. However, he understands her while she lacks the sensitivity, despite her love for poetry, to reciprocate. Paradoxically, Scobie's honesty about his own limitations and compassion for the plight of others leads to a kind of hubris, which manifests itself first in his attempts to make his wife happy. It is this same desire to fix up the world, to provide totally for another's security and happiness, that embroils him in his later relationship with the vulnerable Mrs. Rolt and occasions his infidelity.

In his role as chief of police, Scobie has the sort of reputation for impeccable honesty and fairness which, combined with a lack of ambition, is likely to stimulate the suspicion, gossip, and animosity of his small-minded peers. It is one of the novel's many fine ironies that Scobie's honesty is compromised by the compassion he feels for his wife's plight, for it is his, perhaps excessive and blameworthy, even selfish, desire to free her that leads him to borrow money and put himself in the hands of Yusef. Indeed, it may ultimately be a desire to free himself, but it also lays him open to the less publicly dangerous but morally serious dishonesty with Mrs. Rolt. His desire, whether it is to please his wife or free himself, leads to a compromise of his office. His desire to provide insulation against suffering, whether it is compassionate or selfish, leads to a compromise of his marriage.

Scobie does not wish anything but to be at peace, and he hopes that if he can fix everything for his wife, and thereby free himself of her, he can find peace. Subsequently, Scobie's compassion for Mrs. Rolt turns into a love that brings his desire to repair other lives to an impasse when he wins Mrs. Rolt and his wife decides to return. In the chain of consequences and of flawed moral decisions, his attempt to comfort Mrs. Rolt by a reckless declaration of love further leads to complicity in murder. Scobie's actions are, thus far, morally imperfect but entangled in mixed emotions and motives. It is in his role as Catholic that he commits the ultimate transgressions against God and the divine power of forgiveness.

Violation of public trust and infidelity can be pardoned or extenuated, but Scobie, as Catholic, proceeds to the institutionally "unforgiveable" sins. His love for Mrs. Rolt makes valid confession impossible because his selfishness and compassion make it impossible for him to promise to give her up. His concern for his wife forces him to receive Communion, without absolution, so that he will not betray himself to her and thus wound her. In so doing, he does violence to Christ in the Eucharist. Although well aware that Christ, for love of man, makes himself vulnerable to abuse by his availability in the sacrament, Scobie allows his human motives to lead him to desecrate that trust by receiving Christ while in a state of sin. Having sacrificed Christ to selfishness and human compassion, Scobie is left totally desolate, and, unable to live with these conflicts, he commits the sin which theoretically puts him beyond God's mercy—suicide.

Nevertheless, we do not condemn Scobie. It is not that he is an automaton, a victim of circumstance. To excuse him on those grounds would trivialize the theology of the novel: "to understand all is to forgive all." Rather, we clearly recognize his progressive sins, but are led by Greene to participate in the mystery of divine mercy by extending compassion without selfishness. The compassion that contributed to Scobie's corruption may also be, raised to the divine level, his only hope of salvation.

Edward E. Foster

THE HEAT OF THE DAY

Type of work: Novel
Author: Elizabeth Bowen (1899-1973)
Type of plot: Psychological realism
Time of plot: 1942-1944
Locale: London
First published: 1949

Treating of contrasting faiths and loyalties, this novel, set during World War II, analyzes complex personal relationships with a skill worthy of Henry James. The author's sensitive and involved style perfectly captures the truths inherent in her story of the collision of finely grained personalities.

Elizabeth Bowen often expressed her concern for the disintegration of tradition and value in the twentieth century by depicting the discrepancy between modern woman's changing aspirations and her felt desire for the traditional roles. In *The House in Paris* (1936) and *The Death of the Heart* (1938), heroines are restless or dissatisfied in the roles of wife or mother, and in *The Heat of the Day* Stella tests "free womanhood." *The Heat of the Day* combines the portrayal of modern woman's dilemma with two other representations of Bowen's concern—the neglected family estate and the events of World War II.

Stella Rodney is Bowen's "free woman." She is a professional working in military intelligence, a longtime divorcée, and the mother of a grown son. She has a lover whom she has known for two years, but she dates and knows other men. Still, the relationship with Robert is the most important. Stella is sensitive, strong, and articulate, not only about others, but also about her own problems. She has let her son and others believe for years that she left her husband, that she was the *femme fatale,* the self-sufficient one. In fact, she was divorced by her husband, who left her for his nurse. Stella's son Roderick discovers this fact and confronts his mother, saying it puts "everything in a different light." She admits that it was a matter of saving face; when most people believed that she was the guilty party, she let the story go on. She says to Harrison that it is better to sound like "a monster than look a fool." That remark suggests the paradox in Stella's psyche: she craves to be identified as a free woman, *"capable de tout,"* but her inner self is not quite in concert with that image. Thus, there is the divorce story, her relationship to Roderick (she takes pains to show that he is not tied to her, but worries a great deal about him), and her attitude to Robert (their relationship is a stable one, but Stella refuses Robert's marriage proposal).

Stella is not alone in her ambivalence about how to react to changes in society. Cousin Nettie Morris is driven to insanity by the difficulties of woman's "place" at the family estate, Mount Morris. It seems she takes refuge in madness. One of the novel's most memorable scenes is the nonconversation between Roderick and Nettie at Wisteria Lodge, the asylum. Nettie is not so mad as others would like to think. Stella, visiting Mount Morris in Ireland, understands how the lack of real choices for the "traditional" woman can drive her insane.

Stella's dividedness is expressed in her attitude toward Mount Morris. She had sold her own house, stored her furniture, and rented a luxury furnished flat in London, thus making herself more independent. Nothing in the flat reflected her personality. But Stella finds herself again saddled with place, family, and tradition when Cousin Francis wills Mount Morris to her son—whom he never met but who was conceived at Mount Morris where Stella and his father Victor honeymooned. Stella's ambivalence begins when she attends Cousin Francis' funeral; it grows as she revisits, after 21 years, Mount Morris, now knowing that Roderick will carry on the tradition she had rejected. (Elizabeth Bowen herself believed that the modern attitude against family estate was erroneous, that indeed it had contributed to the general disintegration of society. She became the first female Bowen to inherit Bowen's Court near Dublin since its construction in 1776. But in 1960 she was forced by financial exigency to sell the house and in 1963 it was torn down.)

Stella is repeatedly characterized as being typical of her generation, and the generation is often described as having "muffed" the century. She became an adult just after World War I, and now there is World War II. The specific details of the war years in London give concrete reality to Stella's own trauma, and are skillfully interwoven in her involvement with Robert. "The heat of the day" is Stella's middleage, her "noon," and the agony of the decision to question Robert's loyalty. It is also, of course, the height of the war, a turning point in the century.

As Bowen's structure and symbols both clearly suggest, the generation which follows Stella's, that of Roderick and Louie Lewis, represents both a new integration and a rebirth. Stella's story—her "defeat" as a free woman—is framed and intersected by the story of the working-class Louie Lewis, whose vague desires for motherhood culminate in a triumphant pregnancy while her husband is fighting abroad. She is unaware of the identity of the child's father. The novel ends with the birth of her son just after D-Day and her return to the south coast of England where her parents had been killed by a bomb in the early days of the war. Roderick intends to reside at Mount Morris: he has great plans about rejuvenating it with modern farming methods. Both members of the next generation, therefore, are able to resolve the dichotomies that so plagued their parents' generation—dichotomies about family, place, tradition, and role. The three white swans, a recurrent positive symbol in Bowen (they figure in *The Death of the Heart* as well) appear only at Mount Morris and at the end of the book as Louie wheels her new baby. The swans symbolize a positive rebirth, flying straight, and suggest also the resolution of the war in the "direction of the west." Bowen's symbols are more suggestive than absolute, though. Louie's and Roderick's clear choices are more than enough direction for interpreting the novel. Stella's generation has "botched" it; the only hope is in the next.

Margaret McFadden-Gerber

HEAVEN'S MY DESTINATION

Type of work: Novel
Author: Thornton Wilder (1897- 1975)
Type of plot: Social satire
Time of plot: 1930-1931
Locale: Middle West
First published: 1935

In this novel, Wilder portrays the tragic inconsistencies which he feels are locked into the American character. With deceptive simplicity and irony, he cuts open the hypocrisy of the hero, George Brush, and the many other colorful and unprincipled characters who wander through this episodic story.

Heaven's My Destination is structured around its main character, George Brush, and it is in many ways an involved and complicated study of an all-too-familiar comic hero. Brush is motivated by one outstanding desire, and that is to have a "fine American home." His exploits put him into contact with people and situations which thwart his search; but through these encounters, Wilder develops a George Brush whom we look at humorously and sympathetically. The reader would probably find Brush's evangelism obnoxious if he thought Brush to be consciously hostile and aggravating. But it is clear from the beginning that George Brush is motivated by a sincere desire to do good. For this reason he is pathetic. The causes of Brush's misery lie in his own method of reasoning and coming to conclusions. He bases his principles on Christian morality, but tries to interpret them strictly and apply them to all people—there is no flexibilty in the substance of Brush's ethics. He aspires by his example to change everyone with whom he comes in contact and he is repeatedly shattered when people laughingly reject him. Yet the impact of their rejection never truly scars George Brush, for he bounces back for more, oblivious to the reasons why people think him such a fool.

This novel is quite different from any other Thornton Wilder literary work. In many ways it is Wilder's way of immortalizing his own belief that eternity is all-important to the activities of man, and that Heaven is truly man's destination. Wilder uses plain descriptive prose in this novel, and remains fairly objective, allowing the reader to make his own inferences and observations. Wilder is not the philosopher he appears to be in other works. Rather, he attempts to reveal the influences upon him in his own youth and the results of his own religious upbringing. In *Heaven's My Destination* he tries to put these ideas into perspective in terms of a believable character. There are times in the novel when the thoughts and actions of George Brush are very funny, contemporary, and exceedingly familiar. His experiences cannot help but reinforce one's faith in goodness, no matter what the penalties are for trying to achieve it.

Brush is seen in the final pages of the novel as unchanged. Throughout he has been at odds with what is considered "normal" behavior, and there is no reason to expect that anything will be different in his future life style. He will continue his travels as a textbook salesman, probably never settling in that "fine American home." His failure is pathetic, and the routineness of his life and search are apparent. But it is difficult to put George Brush into a category and unequivocally say we like or dislike him. Wilder asserts that he has portrayed Brush with realism, not satire. It is not impossible, however, to see Brush in a highly satiric light today in terms of religious enthusiasts and their programs for salvation. Brush, like many with missionary intent, demands a great deal of acceptance and understanding and offers very little in return.

HEDDA GABLER

Type of work: Drama
Author: Henrik Ibsen (1828-1906)
Type of plot: Social criticism
Time of plot: Late nineteenth century
Locale: Norway
First presented: 1890

Perhaps the most perfectly structured play of the modern theater, Hedda Gabler *was the summing up of Ibsen's dramatic theories and skills. Within this flawless structure he created an unforgettable character, a woman filled with contradictions; she is both ruthless and afraid, desperate and tormented. The economy of writing and the compression of style in the play contribute greatly to its emotional impact.*

In *Hedda Gabler,* Henrik Ibsen constructed a complex play which caused considerable bewilderment among his contemporary critics. Some found fault; some simply confessed puzzlement. *Hedda Gabler,* as one of Ibsen's later plays, was, for example, often judged in the context of his earlier work instead of evaluated on its own merits. Hence, when the broad social issues treated in earlier plays were found lacking or deficient in *Hedda Gabler,* the latter play was pronounced inferior. The most common misperception of *Hedda Gabler,* however, stemmed from a tendency to see the play through its title and hence its protagonist. "How," it was asked, "could Ibsen present a 'heroine' so totally devoid of any redeeming virtues?" Again, critics who raised the question misconstrued the play—and drama criticism, as well—for a protagonist need not be a heroine or a hero.

Modern critical opinion has focused more carefully on the structure of the play. Hence, one critic has called attention to a typical Ibsen device which the critic characterizes as "retrospective action"—a theatrical method noted by many other critics but without the apt label. As a thearical device, Ibsen's dramatic innovation operates thus: the problem of exposition—revealing the crucial events which preceded the present action in the play (motion pictures solve the problem through flashbacks)—is handled in the first few scenes by having the major characters, reunited with other characters after a long absence, recapitulate past activities to bring the other characters up to date. Hence, the Tessmans, returning from their extended honeymoon, reveal much of themselves in conversation with Juliana and others. Yet, despite this sophisticated surmounting of theatrical obstacles, the play is not without structural weaknesses. Lovberg's apocalyptic attitude is unconvincing; Ibsen's view of scholarly enterprise as a batch of notes in someone's briefcase is ludicrous; and Hedda's potential disaffiliation with the play poses a threat to dramatic unity. These disabilities notwithstanding, the play holds up under critical review because dialogue, characterization, and theme carry it through.

For the verbal polish and linguistic sensitivity of the dialogue, Ibsen's method of playwrighting is largely responsible. After completing a play, Ibsen would rest, letting his mind lie fallow. Then he would begin incubating ideas for his next play. When he was ready to write, he wrote quickly, completing his first draft in about two months. Next, the draft was set aside for another two months or so to "age" properly, whereupon Ibsen would then attack the final job of refining each nuance to perfection, completing the job in two to three weeks and having the copy ready for the printer within a month's time; the following month, the play was off the press and ready for distribution. It was in the refining process, however, that Ibsen sharpened his dialogue to crystal-clear perfection. Thus it was that he added to the play George Tessman's fussy expostulations—the characteristic, questioning "Hmm's?" and "Eh's"; Brack's inquisitorial manner; the fillips of imagery such as "vine leaves in his hair"; and so on. Out of such stuff truly poetic dialogue is made, and Ibsen certainly made it. Few playwrights can match the exquisitely fine-tuned dialogue of *Hedda Gabler*.

As for characterization, one is hard put to resist the temptation to concentrate exclusively on Hedda without touching upon at least George, Lovberg, and Judge Brack. Yet the character of Hedda stands out in bold relief only by contrast with these other characters in the play. Thus the others must be given serious consideration at least as the medium for Hedda's development. Hedda's three major counterfoils are George Tessman, Eilert Lovberg, and Brack, but all of the men are rather static characters in the play. Although their personalities are revealed to us gradually as the play progresses, none of them undergoes any fundamental change. Thus, George Tessman begins and ends as a somewhat distracted "Mr. Chips" personality; Lovberg is revealed as an incurable incompetent; and Brack is exposed for the coldly calculating, manipulative Svengali he wants to be, on the face of it a perfect match for Hedda's own apparently predatory instincts. But against this background, Hedda dominates the scene: a creature of impulse and indulgence, her father's spoiled darling. Let us remember that the play is titled *Hedda Gabler,* not Hedda Tessman! Let us also remember Hedda's growing contempt for Tessman and her opportunism as it grows in inverse ratio to his declining prospects. And let us not forget that in the matrix of Lovberg's inelegant death, Tessman's ineffectuality, Brack's obscene proposition, and Hedda's unwanted pregnancy with Tessman's child, Hedda prefers an efficient suicide to a messy life. Hedda's life does not meet her exacting standards, but her suicide fulfills her sense of style in a way that living cannot. Ibsen's vivid insight into Hedda's personality thus constitutes the real meat of the play, for it is Hedda as an individual—not Hedda as a "case study" or Hedda as a "social issue" or Hedda as anything else—that constitutes the play *Hedda Gabler*.

If Hedda's character dominates the play, what does this have to do with the theme of the play itself? If the answer were as simple as the question suggests, long explanations would be unnecessary. But the theme of *Hedda Gabler,* like Hedda herself, is complex. It is complex because Hedda's personality is the theme of the play; because Hedda's personality is complex; and because complex personalities—instead of easily distilled social issues—are difficult to convey sympathetically to an audience of diverse and equally complex personalities. How can we understand Hedda? Certainly she is more substantial than a mad housewife or an ex-prom queen. Inchoately, she desires, but she has not the sophistication to focus her desires. She is thus directionless. Her *angst* is as much an identity crisis as a lack of goals. She does not know what she wants, much less how to get it. Her apparent hardheadedness, which so attracts Brack, is no more than a mask for her own insecurity. Hers is not a problem of social justice but of private insight. She knows nothing of personal or political power; hence, she appears to use people, to exploit them—but, in reality, more out of naïveté than cold calculation, for she does not recognize or appreciate her influence. The metaphorical evolution of Hedda's personality—from self-indulgent child, to falsely confident adolescent, to desperate and despairing (and pregnant) woman who puts a bullet through her head—starkly depicts the life of an individual, not a symbol of a social issue. As such, *Hedda Gabler* is a problem play, not a social problem play.

Joanne G. Kashdan

THE HEIMSKRINGLA

Type of work: Sagas
Author: Snorri Sturluson (1179-1241)
Type of plots: Historical chronicles
Time of plots: Legendary times to twelfth century
Locale: Norway
First transcribed: Thirteenth century

A collection of sixteen traditional sagas of the Norwegian kings, The Heimskringla *begins with the Yngling Saga, which traces the descent of the Northmen from the god Odin. The rest of the sagas cover the Viking Age, when Norwegians came into historical significance. This period, dating from 839, spans more than three centuries and includes the years of Norwegian occupation of foreign lands, the Christianization of their own country, and the consolidation of Norway itself.*

Though his name is hardly well known today, Snorri Sturluson was one of the foremost authors and politicians of the thirteenth century. He came from a rich and politically influential family in Iceland and was very active in the political intrigues of the Norwegian court which ruled Iceland. So much was he involved in politics, that he was assassinated in 1241 by an agent of his enemy, King Hakon of Norway. His political life notwithstanding, it was his role as historian and mythographer for which he is most remembered among scholars today. He wrote and compiled several works on Norse history/mythology, the most famous being *The Heimskringla.* In this work he combined his earlier *Olaf Saga* with stories of the ancient Norwegian kings which were part of Norse tradition to create *The Orb of the World,* which is the English translation of *The Heimskringla.* (Another title by which *The Heimskringla* is known in English is *The Lives of the Kings of Norway;* this is a translation of the work's title as it appears in other Old Icelandic versions of the saga.)

From evidence obtained from careful study of Snorri's works, we know that he was familiar with other historical works, and he made an attempt to be "scientific" in his writings. He was, however, what would be called a "vernacular" historian, that is, he took much of his writings from oral tradition rather than previous written sources. He cannot be called a complete mythographer, however, since, unlike other mythographers, he did not add any myths to his work which had never previously been written down.

In the twelfth and thirteenth centuries Iceland was alive with literary activity. There was great interest among Icelandic people in the myths and history of their own country and also in its ties with their rulers, the Norwegians. Many of the known sagas of Icelandic tradition were written down during this period. The early kings of Norway, the legendary heroes and gods, were dramatized in these writings so that the real people and the actual facts were difficult to separate from legend. One of the most important examples of this is the tradition created around the Norse God Odin. His story was told time and again throughout Norse history in various oral and written forms. There are numerous variations on Odin's story as one can see by comparing several of the written sources in existence today. Snorri explained Odin as one of the earliest kings of Norway who was glorified to such an extent that after his death he was deified by the Norwegian people. This is the "euhemeristic" interpretation of Norse history. Euhemeres was a fourth century B.C. Greek writer who was the first person to propose the theory that all mythological characters are actually based on real people who were deified and glorified after their deaths. Snorri was a follower of this theory. He said that he wrote "biographies" rather than mythological stories. In *The Heimskringla* he wrote sixteen such biographies to give a historical basis for Norse mythology. There are many other interpretations of these stories, however, and it should be noted that the problem of historicity versus mythology is something which cannot be definitely solved in this case.

Snorri did not simply treat the ancient, unreliable accounts of history. He intended to make his work an interpretation of more recent history as well. His work traces Norwegian history down to Snorri's own time, something which again adds to the dispute about how *The Heimskringla* should be categorized. He pays much attention to the part that Christianity played in Norwegian history, although he spends very little time moralizing or even discussing the effects of the Christian religion upon the Scandinavian peoples.

Because of the combination of myth and history in Snorri's work, it reads almost like a novel. He treats the ancient kings the way classical authors such as Plutarch did, glorifying their lives and interpolating anecdotes which are often missing from "textbook" treatments of history. He has been called the Scandinavian Herodotus because of his keen ability to combine myth with history and create an entertaining chronicle, but it is a rather high compliment to pay to Snorri.

A careful reading of *The Heimskringla* indicates that Snorri thought of himself certainly more as a historian than a mythographer. Compared to other treatments of Odin, for example, *The Heimskringla* is quite believable. Odin here is neither an amorphous being nor a sun-god. There are no religious connotations at all attached to his life. One can read this work as a piece of plausible history if one does not have previous knowledge of the flimsy historicity of the "facts" presented therein.

Perhaps it is best simply to define *The Heimskringla* as a "saga" in the traditional meaning of the word: a medieval treatment of sweeping magnitude which describes the history of various aspects of Scandinavian society. The saga usually included numerous battles and conquests, as does *The Heimskringla,* and was written for no other purpose than to illustrate history and increase national pride. It is perhaps difficult for readers more familiar with traditional histories to see the significance of the saga, but to medieval Norsemen it was an important cultural as well as educational device. This is important for modern readers to keep in mind, for *The Heimskringla,* like all sagas and most histories, was written more as an edification of past events than an explanation. It represented the themes which the author wanted to have illuminated and those are often different from the interpretations of other authors.

Patricia Ann King

HELEN

Type of work: Drama
Author: Euripides (c. 485-c. 406 B.C.)
Type of plot: Romantic adventure
Time of plot: Seven years after the sack of Troy
Locale: Egypt
First presented: 412 B.C.

Unusual in that the line of action seems to build toward a tragedy which then is averted at the last moment by a deus ex machina, *this play is adapted from an ancient tradition which suggests that Paris carried off to Troy only a phantom Helen fashioned by Hera, while the real Helen was taken to Egypt by Hermes.* Helen *is highly regarded for its consistent characterization and skillful rhetoric.*

A "happy ending" drama such as the *Helen* is as much a "Greek tragedy" as the most typically horrifying and saddening plays. Tragedy meant to the Greeks a dramatic performance drawn from a heroic, that is, mythologically significant, theme; the *Helen* fits that description in that its characters and situation are eminently well known (cf. Euripides *Iphigenia in Tauris* and *Alcestis*). Critics note the resemblance of the *Helen* to the much later love-adventure novels called Greek romances, in which (young) lovers are cruelly separated but are eventually reunited after a tangled succession of trials and misadventures. But in the *Helen,* as in any Greek tragedy, the action is not protracted, nor is the poet's only intention to entertain with spectacle and suspense; on the other hand, we must not try to fit Helen (or any other character) into the mold of the Aristotelian tragic hero.

Broadly this play deals with Helen's rescue-escape from a fate worse than death (widowhood and forced marriage to a *barbaros*). Her gloomy despair is genuine, or at any rate eloquently conveyed. She is a sympathetic character, intelligent as well as beautiful, and she is most exciting when she ruthlessly uses her wit and charm to demonstrate her faithfulness to Menelaus. Nevertheless, Theonoe, not Helen, is the key to this drama. Prophetic powers make her literally the center of attraction, and it is her personal decision of silence which allows Helen and Menelaus to escape. Theonoe enjoys the role of intermediary between men and gods, but as a mortal she is subject to human sympathy, which nearly proves her undoing. Like Helen, Theonoe is rescued from Theoclymenus in the end. All the once-threatening dangers have been removed with much the same ease as had the Helen phantom, which had caused so much death and suffering.

HENRY ESMOND

Type of work: Novel
Author: William Makepeace Thackeray (1811-1863)
Type of plot: Historical romance
Time of plot: Late seventeenth, early eighteenth centuries
Locale: England and the Low Countries
First published: 1852

One of the great English historical novels, Henry Esmond *is notable both for its accurate reproduction of the speech, manners, traditions, and historical events of late 1600's and early 1700's, and for its fascinating characterizations, especially that of the bewitching coquette, Beatrix. Thackeray was inspired by his low regard for the average historian of his day to write this novel, which he intended as a model of how history ought to be presented. He continued the story of Henry's descendants in America in another novel,* The Virginians.

Critical reaction to *Henry Esmond* is as varied as reader reaction to the characters themselves. What Thackeray attempted to do was to offset contemporary charges of his "diffusiveness" by providing a well-integrated novel, sacrificing profitable serial publication to do so. He concluded that *Henry Esmond* was "the very best" he could do. Many critics have agreed with him. Others, however, remain loyal to the panoramic social vision and ironic authorial commentary of the earlier *Vanity Fair*. What makes evaluation of *Henry Esmond* so variable?

Short of a full history of cycles and fashions in fiction, certain features may illustrate the problems. First is the narrative point of view. Thackeray cast *Henry Esmond* in the form of a reminiscential memoir—an old man recounts his earlier life, describing it from the vantage point of a later time and distancing it further with third-person narration. The occasional use of "I" suggests the involved narrator, either at emotional highpoints or moments of personal reflection. The distancing in time is increased by Esmond's daughter's Preface, wherein Rachel Esmond Warrington not only "completes" certain details of the plot but also suggests the ambiguities in characterization of her own mother, Rachel, and of her stepsister, Beatrix. Readers of Henry James may react favorably to this early use of a central intelligence whose point of view, limited not omniscient, can suggest the disparities between appearance and reality. They may also welcome the shifting interpretations readers themselves can form of the "reliability" of the narrator. Is Esmond providing a framework within which to reveal only the exemplary, vindicating himself consciously, or is he recollecting as honestly as the self can permit, with the reader knowing more than he at many points?

Another point of contention involves the historical setting of the novel, which purports to be a historical romance. Thackeray casts the novel in the early eighteenth century and attempts to catch the flavor of the Augustan Age, its military conflicts, its waverings between Church of England and Catholicism, and the problems of its monarchs, William, Queen Anne, George II, and the Stuart Pretender. Most readers laud Thackeray's adept handling of the technical problem of suggesting the language and manners of that earlier time without lapsing into linguistic archness or sending readers to glossaries. It is, then, praised by many as a polished example of the historical romance and relished as many relish Scott or Stevenson—for its adventure and its depiction of society, at least those levels that Thackeray chooses to treat. For as with *Vanity Fair,* he is less concerned with portrayal of the lackeys than of the masters, primarily the newly arrived and still aspiring scions of society. Their foibles were his special target.

Yet for others the novel's fascination lies in its domestic realism. Commentators find much to explore in the rendering of the marriage conventions. Lord and Lady Castlewood, new heirs to Castlewood, befriend the supposedly illegitimate Henry Esmond and gradually reveal the strained bonds which hold their marriage together. Esmond, as narrator, takes sides with Rachel, seeing the husband as carousing, unfaithful, not too intelligent. Readers, however, can also realize, despite the analysis of "domestic tyranny," that Rachel's purity and coldness might lead the husband not only to drink but to other fleshly delights. Devoted Henry Esmond may lament the waste of such a fine woman, but the reader perceives in the dramatic scenes that Rachel, who began by worshiping her husband, is also quite capable of both restrictive possessiveness and emotional repression.

Historical romance, novel of domestic manners—*Henry Esmond* also illustrates a favorite nineteenth century form, the *bildüngsroman,* or novel of development and education, which is also represented in such popular contemporary examples as *David Copperfield* and *Great Expectations.* Henry Esmond remembers his childhood vaguely, a time spent with poor weavers, a foreign language. Brought to Castlewood, he is treated with favor by Lord Castlewood but kept in place as a page. It is only with the death of Lord Castlewood that Henry receives any emotional response, this from the new heirs—and most especially from Rachel, Lady Castlewood. Thackeray carefully distances Esmond to be eight years younger than Rachel and eight years older than her daughter Beatrix. Esmond's growth is the principal subject but readers are also aware of the young son Frank and of Beatrix, both children who are alternately spoiled and then emotionally isolated from Rachel. The much sought after but "loveless" Beatrix reveals how isolated she was made to feel by the possessive nets her mother cast over the father and then over the seemingly favored brother. Momentarily consoling Esmond, Beatrix shows the motivation for her romantic conquests so that readers understand her complexity and ambivalence though Esmond may choose not to do so.

As Esmond progresses through Cambridge, through imprisonment following a duel fatal to Lord Castlewood, through military campaigns, through the loss of one idol after another and on to a slow knowledge of the way of the world, the reader watches for his "present" age to come closer to his recollected past. The reader watches for his insight to develop, for memory and maturity to coincide. Whether or not Esmond achieves that wholeness is yet another point for critics and readers to ponder.

Esmond has virtuously denied himself his birthright as legitimate heir to Castlewood so that young Frank may assume the title and Rachel and Beatrix can stay ensconced in society, but some might think Henry revels in the self-sacrifice. He has also chosen to believe that Beatrix will admire him for military daring and political plotting. Thus when the Stuart Pretender misses a chance for the throne in order to secure an amorous chance with Beatrix, Esmond loses two idols at once. "Good" Henry Esmond is settled at the end of the novel on a Virginia plantation in the New World, his marriage to the widowed Rachel compressed into two pages. All ends happily, except for those strange overtones and even stranger suggestions in the Preface by the daughter of this autumnal marriage. She reminds us that Esmond was writing for a family audience, that his role had been carefully established, and that she, Rachel Esmond Warrington, like Beatrix, had also suffered from her mother's possessiveness and jealousy.

Ultimately, then, what the modern reader may enjoy most is the psychological penetration into love bonds which Thackeray provides through the "unreliable" narrator. Dramatic irony permits the reader more knowledge than Esmond permits himself. And as readers circle back in their own memories to the daughter's Preface, the whole range of interrelationships and the ambivalences of human affairs unfold. The characters, in short, remain fascinating puzzles long after the historical details fade. Emotional life, the subtleties of rejection and acceptance, time rendered both precisely and in psychological duration—these are the elements which will continue to tantalize readers of *Henry Esmond.*

Eileen Lothamer

HENRY THE EIGHTH

Type of work: Drama
Author: William Shakespeare (1564-1616)
Type of plot: Historical chronicle
Time of plot: 1520-1533
Locale: England
First presented: c. 1612

Possibly written in collaboration with John Fletcher, this play vividly pictures British court life with its pomp and its behind-the-throne humanity. Filled with political maneuvering and ambition, the drama progresses to an eloquent prophecy regarding a newborn princess, to become Queen Elizabeth. This compliment paid to their monarch was received with enthusiasm by Shakespeare's audience.

Henry the Eighth is a relatively weak play: the relationships between the principal characters tend to be superficial, and the characters themselves are more or less transparent, lacking cogency and complexity. Buckingham, for example, although perfectly consistent, is one-dimensional; he is something of a stock character and finally emerges as little more than a display of Wolsey's corruption. Wolsey himself, whose arrogant cruelty together with a seeming nobility adds to his interest, is more or less a cliché of the steward who abuses his power.

Despite these weaknesess, the play remains historically interesting and significant because of its glorification of Elizabeth's reign, the majesty of which is foretold by Cranmer at the end of the drama. Written during the first decade of James the First's tenure, it reflects England's dissatisfaction with the Scottish monarch and a nostalgia for his predecessor. Throughout his history plays, written for the most part early in his career, Shakespeare had sought to legitimatize and honor the Tudors who had saved England from "Crookback Dick," Richard III, and had brought an end to the War of the Roses. Elizabeth, the Virgin Queen and the last Tudor, is glimpsed in *Henry the Eighth* as the crowning glory of that dynasty.

Henry himself is not presented here as the perfidious tyrant that some later historians recognize. Still the Tudor apologist, Shakespeare suggests Wolsey as the principal villain in the deposition of Katharine Aragon. A Machiavellian, the cardinal seeks to center the power in himself at the expense of the king and the Royal family. His motto, *Ego et Rexmeus,* which puts him above the monarch, insures his ignominious defeat. Despite his hatred of tyrants, Shakespeare, in one of his later plays, remains a Royalist to the end, paying his allegiance to the idea of the Divine Right.

HENRY THE FIFTH

Type of work: Drama
Author: William Shakespeare (1564-1616)
Type of plot: Historical romance
Time of plot: Early part of the fifteenth century
Locale: England and France
First presented: 1600

In The Life of Henry the Fifth, *Shakespeare skillfully combined poetry, pageantry, and history in his effort to glorify England and Englishmen. Although the characters are larger than life, they also are shown to be flawed like other men; even Henry at last achieves a necessary element of humility.*

Henry the Fifth is the last play in the cycle including *Richard the Second, Henry the Fourth, Part One* and *Part Two,* and *Henry the Fifth.* The three plays dealing with the reign of King Henry VI, mentioned in the epilogue of *Henry the Fifth,* were written much earlier and are not ordinarily grouped with this cycle. *Henry the Fifth* is itself almost a break with this cycle. However, there are important, if in some ways superficial, elements of continuity.

These elements of continuity are the great historical transition represented by the movement from the reign of Richard II to that of Henry V. Richard and, progressively, the two Henrys, are associated by Shakespeare with the medieval, then the Renaissance, even modern, world views. The second dominant element is the formation of Prince Hal, who becomes Henry V, as a Renaissance king.

In *Richard the Second,* the king, Richard, is deposed by Bolingbroke, who becomes Henry IV. What is important is the act of rupturing, symbolized by this usurpation, of an entire conception of humanity governed by ritual and tradition. This conception is sometimes referred to as "the great chain of being." It asserts an utterly planned cosmos which is considered the manifestation of God. To challenge and finally replace this world is a force not clearly understood by its protagonists, but nevertheless defines their own practical and political ambitions as individuals.

The two *Henry the Fourth* plays are continuations of Shakespeare's exploration of the shift in political perspective. The rebellions which follow Henry IV's usurpation had been predicted by Richard II, and seem, indeed, a kind of natural consequence to the break in the structure of authority.

But while his father is engaged morally by that break even to a death troubled by remorse for his "crime," the education of Prince Hal is pursued in a subplot mainly situated in taverns and places of public amusement. Hal's progress, in a few words, is between two extremes of individualism (characteristic of the Renaissance): the obsessive and bloody quest for glory in the person of Hotspur, and the pleasure-seeking, nearly total, incontinence of

Falstaff. What he learns from each of them could be said to be the sense of valor and honor of the one, and the wittiness and humanity of the other. But this is so, in a way, only "theoretically." For the nature of the prince in *Henry the Fifth,* as king, is quite removed from either the thesis or the antithesis which precedes him.

An explanation for this can be found symbolically in the two scenes at the end of *Henry the Fourth, Part Two,* where Hal, after his father's death but before his own coronation, takes as his own his father's Lord High Justice, and banishes Falstaff. The Chief Justice had expected—among all who feared Hal would become an irresponsible king—the worst personal damage, as he had punished Hal's revels in the name of Henry IV. Shakespeare seems to imply, in a very modern sense, that Hal was assuming fully his father's Law. In the historical perspective it is secular law, in contrast to the divine mandate of Richard II.

The opening scenes of *Henry the Fifth* show how secular, indeed, how free-and-easy, the new law has become. Individualism, in the form of self-interest, rules, but in an orderly, legalistic way. The bishops make the ancient laws fit the needs of their own financial interests and the ambition (concerning the French throne) of King Henry V.

These scenes already suggest a sense of *fait accompli* to the broad transitional process which is, at base, the rise of the bourgeoisie. Thus the play is a kind of break with the others. As a whole it is a kind of apotheosis of the powerful though incipient undercurrent of the times, the collective mentality we have come to ascribe to the bourgeoisie. This play has a lack of moral depth, which derives, perhaps, from a contradiction in bourgeois society. There is the economic base of cut-throat competition and an ideological superstructure of supposedly harmonious relations between men and nations. The loss of the sacred system of exploitation made the contradiction more apparent. The dynamic individualism of the new culture takes on the authority of the old order but sublimates the sense of responsibility into platitudes of doubtful logic.

The bishops are one example of this. The ease with which Henry allows his conscience to be soothed in those scenes is another. Later, he rather cavalierly blames the citizens of Harfleur for the impending destruction of their city, with all the barbaric effects he will not even try to control, by his invading army. Likewise, he shuns, by pure sophistry, any responsibility for the deaths, or souls, of his soldiers. He skirts the question of the justice of the king's cause with the assertion that, in any case, each man's soul is his own worry before God.

Shakespeare presents, then, a society in triumph, but one of atrophied moral sensitivity, escaping always in bad faith. The need to compensate for inner insecurity is shown, for example, in the absurd mortality statistic (twenty-nine to ten thousand). Again, it is shown in the aggressive, even hostile and puerile, clumsiness of Henry's wooing of Katharine. He tells her, on the one hand, that he will not be very hurt if she rejects him, and on the other hand, that she and her father are, in effect, his conquered subjects and have no real choice in the matter. This does not constitute, however, a definite condemnation by Shakespeare, of this society. But he does not wholly praise, either. More than the other plays of this cycle, the conventionality and moral opacity leave judgment to the reader's, or spectator's, understanding of history.

James Marc Hovde

HENRY THE FOURTH, PART ONE

Type of work: Drama
Author: William Shakespeare (1564-1616)
Type of plot: Historical chronicle
Time of plot: 1400-1405
Locale: England
First presented: 1596

Through the antics of Falstaff and his mates, comedy and history join in this play. Woven into and between scenes of court and military matters, the humorous sequences are used to reveal Prince Hal's character and to bring into sharp relief the serious affairs of honor and history.

Although there is no evidence that the cycle of plays including *Richard the Second, Henry the Fourth, Part One* and *Part Two,* and *Henry the Fifth* were intended by Shakespeare to form a unit, there is much continuity, of theme as well as of personages. There is a movement from one grand epoch to another, from the Middle Ages to the Renaissance. The main aspects of his transition implied at the end of each play are projected into the next, where they are developed and explored.

The reader of *Henry the Fourth, Part One,* should be familiar with some aspects of *Richard the Second,* for in that play the broad lines of the entire cycle are drawn and the immediate base of *Henry the Fourth, Part One,* is formed. In *Richard the Second,* the legitimate king, Richard II, is deposed by Bolingbroke, who becomes Henry IV. This event, to include both historical perspectives, must be viewed as at once a usurpation and a necessary political expediency. It is a usurpation because unjustifiable, indeed unthinkable, from the strictly medieval view of what has been called "the great chain of being." This notion postulates that the universe is ordered, hierarchical, that everything is given a place by God, from angels to ants, and that station is immutable. In this world, formed by ritual, an annointed king is representative of God's Order. To depose him is to call in question all order in the world. Tradition, especially ritual, presupposed and supported fixed order. Ritual in this larger sense is broken in *Richard the Second* first by the excesses of Richard himself and then, in a more definitive sense, by the usurping Bolingbroke. The irony of Bolingbroke's act, and the subject of *Henry the Fourth, Part One,* is the consequences of what was to have been a momentary departure from ordained ritual. As with Eve, the gesture of self-initiative was irrevocable, the knowledge and correlative responsibility gained at that moment inescapable.

At the opening of *Henry the Fourth, Part One,* then, we see the results of rebellion already installed; the security of the old system of feudal trust is forever lost. Those who helped the king to power are men instead of God, the guarantors of the "sacredness" (the term already anachronistic) of the crown. This means political indebtedness and, at this point in history, with the anxiety of lost certainty still sharp, terrible doubt as to whence truth, power, and justice rightfully emanate. The king is no longer sovereign as he must negotiate, in the payment of his political debts, the very essence of his station. At the historical moment of the play, distrust predictably triumphs. Men are guided by the most available counsel, a *personal* sense of justice, or merely, perhaps, their own interests and passions.

In the void left by the fallen hierarchical order Shakespeare dramatizes the birth of modern individualism and, as a model for this, the formation of a Renaissance king (Prince Hal), an entity now of uncertain, largely self-created identity.

Prince Hal's position in the play is central. He represents a future unstigmatized by the actual usurpation. However, he inherits, to be sure, the new political and moral climate created by it. Yet while Henry's planned crusade to the Holy Land will be forever postponed in order to defend his rule from his former collaborators, Hal's life looks to the future.

It is characteristic of Henry's uncertain world that he knows his son only through hearsay, rumor, and slander. Even the Prince of Wales is suspect. He is widely thought a wastrel, and the king even suspects his son would like him dead. But where is the pattern of virtue for Hal? The king, the usurper, is tainted, of ambiguous virtue at best. He has betrayed, perhaps out of political necessity, even those who helped him to the throne.

In this play Hal is clearly attracted to two figures, Hotspur and Falstaff. Both of these are removed from the medieval ritualistic structures that had once tended to integrate disparate aspects of life: courtesy, valor, honest exchange, loyalty, and the like. A new synthesis of this sort is symbolically enacted in Hal's procession through the experience of, and choices between, the worlds of Hotspur and Falstaff.

For Hotspur life is a constant striving for glory in battle. As has been remarked, time for him presses implacably, considered wasted if not intensely devoted to the achievement of fame. But his is an assertion of the individual enacted outside a traditional frame such as the medieval "quest." Hotspur's character is seen to be extremely limited, however breathtaking his *élan* may be. For it is finally morbid, loveless, incourteous, and even sexually impotent. He has not the patience to humor the tediousness of Glendower (which costs him, perhaps, his support); his speech is full of death and death's images; he mocks the love of Mortimer and has banished his wife from his bed, too absorbed by his planned rebellion.

Falstaff, on the other hand, is as quick to lie, to steal, to waste time with a whore or drinking wine, as Hotspur is to risk his life for a point of honor. Hal spends most of his time with him, and he seems at times a sort of apprentice to the older man in the "art" of tavern living. This means, for Hal, living intimately with common people, who naïvely call him "boy," and whose unpretensiousness strips him of the artificial defenses he would have among people who understand protocol.

The adventure with the robbery is the image of cowardice as the reputation of Hotspur is the image of valor. Yet both stories are in their ways celebrative. Falstaff's flexible ways are more human, certainly kinder than Hotspur's, kinder even than Hal's. Hal is awkward at joking sometimes, not being sensitive enough to know what is serious, what light. Hotspur has renounced sensitivity to human love; Falstaff has abandoned honor. In schematic terms, it is a synthesis of these two perspectives that Hal must, and in a way does, achieve.

James Marc Hovde

HENRY THE FOURTH, PART TWO

Type of work: Drama
Author: William Shakespeare (1564-1616)
Type of plot: Historical chronicle
Time of plot: 1405-1413
Locale: England
First presented: 1597

As in Henry the Fourth, Part One, *comedy is an outstanding feature of this play, Falstaff continuing to promise great things for his friends until the touching moment of his death. The pomp and drama common to Shakespeare's historical chronicles permeate the serious parts of the play, and the deathbed scene between Henry IV and Prince Henry is considered among the best in dramatic literature.*

Henry the Fourth, Part Two is, of course, the second part of the Henry IV narrative. But it is also the third part of the unofficial cycle composed of *Richard the Second, Henry the Fourth, Part One, Henry the Fourth, Part Two,* and *Henry the Fifth.* The continuity should be noted, especially from preceding plays. As a whole the cycle traces the historical transition from the reign of Richard II, a distinctly medieval king, to the reign of Henry V, a distinctly Renaissance king. And while it is an "unofficial" cycle, salient aspects of this transition are implied at the end of each play, projected into the next, and developed and explored. *Henry the Fourth, Part Two,* is, of course, a sequel (although an independent play), to *Henry the Fourth, Part One,* but to place it in its larger frame we must briefly look back to *Richard the Second.*

In *Richard the Second* the legitimate king, Richard II, is deposed by Bolingbroke, who becomes Henry IV. This act must be viewed as a usurpation and also as a necessary political expediency. It is a usurpation because unjustifiable, indeed unthinkable, from the strictly medieval view of what has been called "the great chain of being." This idea holds that the universe is ordered, hierarchical, that everything is given a place by God, and that one's station must not be changed. In this world governed by ritual, an annointed king is representative of God's Order. To depose him is to call in question all order in the world.

And indeed, the effects of Bolingbroke's (Henry IV) revolution initiated in England a new, and less innocent world. *Henry the Fourth, Part One,* presents the immediate political effects, the distrust and further rebellion of Henry's nobility (the men who helped him steal the crown), and the wider effects of the new-found sense of individualism relating to all facets of life. *Henry the Fourth, Part One,* is concerned, in large measure, with the struggle of various individualistic viewpoints trying to absorb the whole, to fill the vacuum left by the fallen absolute denoted by "the great chain of being."

The focus in this play, *Henry the Fourth, Part One,* is on Prince Hal, later

Henry V, and his attempt to reconcile, or at least compromise, the conflicting claims upon his person, as a Renaissance man and future king, of attitudes represented on the one hand by the glory-obsessed rebel, Hotspur, and, on the other hand, by the humorous wastrel, Falstaff. The world of the tavern, with its riotous submission to basic appetites, still has wit and irony. The battlefield represents reckless courage and the pursuit of personal honor and glory at any cost, shaming Hal. But he senses the need for an alternative to this sure path to early death. Hal learns to compromise, at least, the needs for rigidity and flexibility. The practical politician that the king, entering modernity, must be, is an eclectic solution rather than a great synthesis.

If in *Henry the Fourth, Part One,* Shakespeare showed the new world mainly as a burst of new energies, in *Henry the Fourth, Part Two,* he explores, we might say, some aspects of its darker side. The new freedom to express individual potential is not without costs at the very heart of things, any more than it had been at the political level. It is a "fallen" world and diminished too, having realized in some way that the power of the individual had, in fact, been exaggerated, misunderstood. This is not to say, however, that there is the radical loss of moral certainty in the problem comedies. But the characters, or what they represent, become almost travesties of their former selves.

Northumberland, the father of Hotspur, upon learning of his son's death, rages rhetorically, even beyond his son:

> But let one spirit of the first-born Cain
> Reign in all bosoms, that each heart being set
> On bloody courses, the rude scene may end,
> And darkness be the burier of the dead.

The morbidity of Hotspur's obsession for battle-glory is translated now into a manifest call for general slaughter.

King Henry, if he has seemed authoritative before, is now much less sure of himself. He cannot sleep, his worry looks fearfully back to the prediction of King Richard that corruption, "foretelling this same time's condition," would thrive as a result of his usurpation. He faces the rebellion with a fatalistic tone: "Are these things necessities / Then let us meet them like necessities," rather than, as he had said at Shrewsbury in *Henry the Fourth, Part One,* "rebuke and dread correction wait on us, / And they shall do their office," or, "And God befriend us as our cause is just."

The world of the tavern is altered as well. The Boar's Head is now clearly a brothel. The humor now reflects the real corruption of the place. The butt of jokes, more often than not, is now someone unable to defend himself, such as Doll, Shallow, or Mistress Quickly. The Braggart Soldier element in Falstaff is now the frenzied mind and speech of Pistol. Falstaff himself is seen to be the victim of ailments of all sorts, results of his long life of excesses. His lust for Doll, and his callous exploitation of Shallow and (he would hope) of his relation to Hal, are now particularly unseemly.

Perhaps as much as in any other, it is in the person of the Lord Chief Justice that we get an idea of the meaning of the coming society. There is a motto on some court houses that suggests the new orientation: "This is a court of Law, not of Justice." That is, institutions are plainly secular, no longer having pretensions beyond human capabilities to control, through human efforts, a moral order. And it is to him, and his administration of efficient Law, that the new king, Henry V, adheres.

It is in deference to such a conception of order, a legalistic social hierarchy, that Henry V banishes Falstaff at the end of the play. For, as Eric Auerbach has shown (in commenting upon Hal's knowledge of Poins's laundry), the absolute distinction between high and low has been lost (through a process of leveling ultimately engendered in Christian doctrine). Hal, Henry V, represents a firm step on the path that will lead, as a character in Stendhal's *The Red and the Black* laments, to a time when there will be no more kings in Europe, but only prime ministers and presidents.

James Marc Hovde

HENRY THE SIXTH, PART ONE

Type of work: Drama
Author: William Shakespeare (1564-1616)
Type of plot: Historical chronicle
Time of plot: 1422-1444
Locale: England and France
First presented: c. 1592

Filled with political intrigue, battles, courtly pomp, and witchcraft, Henry the Sixth, Part One *is typically Shakespearean historical drama; however, the play is more flagrant than most of the other histories in its distortions and inaccuracies of historical detail, and it uses more boldly melodramatic devices to further character development.*

Some modern critics see an overall design in the three *Henry the Sixth* plays plus *Richard the Third,* and treat them as an epic of the suffering England must undergo in retribution for the deposition and slaying of a rightful monarch, Richard II. Only with the reign of a legitimate successor—Henry VII, the first Tudor king—can England regain peace and greatness.

Henry the Sixth, Part One, while it may seem fragmented, is actually a well-structured episodic play based on the theme of the loss of France and the ruin of England. A concomitant theme, the breakdown of order, is set in motion early in Act One when the Duke of Gloster and the Bishop of Winchester quarrel, disrupting the solemn order at Henry V's funeral. In contrast to the English disintegration into chaos, the French, under Joan of Arc's forceful leadership, unite; England's weakness, however, results more from her own division than from French strength.

As a contrast to the bickering and deceit which is directly responsible for England's decline, Talbot's role in the play is to provide a picture of what England's successes could be if the English emulated his loyalty, steadfastness, and courage. With no English unity to back him, Talbot falls, and with his fall, the prospects of English strength collapses.

The final scene illustrates the play's unified construction. Margaret, of whom we have seen little, would seem not to belong in the play at all. She does belong, however, primarily so that Suffolk can establish her on the English throne purely to further his own power. At the end of the play, Suffolk's deceitful and self-aggrandizing action mirrors the actions of other nobles, and the final scene reinforces the important theme of English loss through selfishness.

HENRY THE SIXTH, PART TWO

Type of work: Drama
Author: William Shakespeare (1564-1616)
Type of plot: Historical chronicle
Time of plot: 1444-1455
Locale: England
First presented: c. 1592

This second one of the Henry the Sixth *plays contains scenes which reflect the social implications of the drama, making clear the social strata of the commoners and nobles and giving the chronicle a fuller historical perspective. As is true of the first part of* Henry the Sixth, *this drama is a revision of an earlier play.*

Henry the Sixth, Part Two, generally considered the best of the three *Henry the Sixth* plays, is, like all of Shakespeare's history plays, a rich mixture of fact and fancy. Shakespeare was not a historian; his main concern was to dramatize a political era and comment upon political processes that seriously weakened England a century and a half before he wrote.

Shakespeare's themes are fully realized in the play. Although the play ends at an inconclusive historical point, with the king in retreat but not entirely defeated, a full dramatic action has been concluded and important themes have been fully explored. The most significant themes are the need for loyalty to the monarch, the danger of a weak sovereign, the dangers of perfidy and rebellion, and the success an evil schemer can achieve if not effectively opposed. Shakespeare, as always in his early career, was in the mainstream of Elizabethan political thought: somewhat conservative, patriotic, and optimistic about man's ultimate potential.

The play's many episodes and characters may best be understood in their relationship to the king: Henry stands at the center of the play. He occupies the office that should lead the nation into harmonious order, but he is pitifully ineffectual. Among the characters there are two chief attitudes toward the throne: selfless devotion to its protection, as embodied in Gloster, and selfish desire to possess it, as embodied in York.

Gloster is a key figure early in the play, as York is later. Many of the play's early episodes are intended to establish Gloster's identity as protector of the throne; while most later episodes, including the Jack Cade affair, identify York as the chief threat. Through these two men Shakespeare successfully presents the problem of how a man of power may use his power either for the enhancement of the national welfare or for his own enrichment. In this world the position represented by York often wins, but clearly Shakespeare had a vision of a political order in which man's higher qualities would prevail.

HENRY THE SIXTH, PART THREE

Type of work: Drama
Author: William Shakespeare (1564-1616)
Type of plot: Historical chronicle
Time of plot: 1455-1471
Locale: England and France
First presented: c. 1592

Although not a tragedy in the classical sense, this play is more poignant than many tragic dramas; infinite and unswerving ambition in the characters and closely developed plotting unite to make the play a masterpiece of gripping drama.

In *Henry the Sixth, Part Three,* which belongs to Shakespeare's tetralogy of history plays dealing with the political upheaval that followed Henry Bolingbroke's overthrow and murder of Richard II, England continues to suffer the evils of civil strife and social disorder arising from the war between the houses of York and Lancaster. Shakespeare's general purpose in this series of plays is to reassert the power of Providence, and to glorify England and suggest the nature of her salvation; but only with the restitution of the rightful heir at the end of *Richard III* will England be able to bind her wounds and enjoy peace once again.

Henry the Sixth, Part Three is a powerful study of disorder and chaos; the play interweaves a cohesive body of imagery and symbolism with the action of its plot to create a strong unity of impression centering on the theme of anarchy and disunity. Chaos prevails on all levels of society, from the state, to the family, to the individual. At the highest level of authority and social organization—the throne—anarchy has replaced traditional rule. The king, who must be the center of political strength and embody the sanctity of social duty, oath, and custom, is instead the essence of weakness; Henry not only yields the right of succession to York, but eventually abdicates in favor of Warwick and Clarence. Whenever he attempts to intervene in events, his weak voice is quickly silenced; finally he is silenced permanently, and his murder represents the ultimate overturning of political order and rejection of the divine right upon which his rule was founded. Contrasted to Henry, the representative of rightful power, is Richard, who in this play becomes the epitome of total anarchy. Richard murders the prince, the king, and his brother Clarence, boasting later, "Why, I can smile, and murder whiles I smile"; he scornfully disregards any form of moral obligation; and eventually falls victim to unreasoning fears and nightmares.

The primary social bond—that of the family—is likewise in a state of dissolution. Again, the malady begins at the level of the king; Henry disinherits his own son, the rightful heir, thus causing his wife Margaret to cut herself off from him, sundering their marital bond. York's three sons become hopelessly divided by their conflicting ambitions. And in Act II, scene 5, Shakespeare shows, by means of the morality tableau, that the same family breakdown prevails among the common people as well. Simultaneously with its presentation of political and social chaos, the play dramatizes the disruption that is occurring in individuals' morality. Hatred, ambition, lust, and greed are the keynotes, while duty, trust, tradition, and self-restraint are increasingly lost.

Henry the Sixth, Part Three thus depicts a society in the throes of anarchy and war, a society where kings surrender their duties, fathers and sons murder each other, and brothers vie for power at any cost. Yet the play contains an ocasional feeble ray of light, such as in Henry's weak protests against the cruelty of the usurpers, his pleas for pity for the war's victims, and his ineffectual calls for an end to the conflict and a restoration of peace and order. These scattered flickers, dim as they are, along with several prophecies planted throughout the play, foreshadow the coming hope, resolution of conflict, and return of peace and rightful authority which will follow in *Richard III.*

HERAKLES MAD

Type of work: Drama
Author: Euripides (c. 485-c. 406 B.C.)
Type of plot: Classical tragedy
Time of plot: Remote antiquity
Locale: Thebes
First presented: c. 420 B.C.

One of the most puzzling of Euripides' plays, Herakles Mad *begins with a stereotyped situation, builds to a powerful climax in the mad scene of Herakles, and is followed by a moving tragic reconciliation. The hero reaches tragic stature when, finally, he refuses to commit suicide and decides to face whatever life has in store for him.*

Euripides has deliberately reversed the tradition that Herakles was forced to perform his labors to atone for the murder of his family, thereby achieving ultimate greatness. There is no evidence to assume that in this play Herakles had not actually performed the labors, as has been suggested; nevertheless Euripides has demeaned them as mere feats of strength and cunning by demonstrating the greater strength of soul which Herakles must summon from the depths of his misery. True nobility requires that the hero persevere against the uncontrollable whims of immortals, in this case Hera, who is virtually abstracted into Tyche, or Fortune. Herakles' nobility of soul is contrasted with the wealth and might of his antagonist Lycus ("Wolf"), and his killing of this inhuman creature may be seen, then, as merely a "thirteenth" labor.

The first half of the drama is, therefore, appropriate to the variety of Herakles' glories. Note the ironic dependence of Herakles' family on the hero who will save them by killing Lycus to bring about a "happy ending" to the melodrama; but this glorious figure will promptly be transformed into the pathetic wreck that must be restored in the "tragic" half of the drama (compare lines 631 and 1424).

The fact that Madness seizes the innocent hero without cause shows that man must be prepared for any event in this life ruled by unconcerned or unfriendly external forces. Man's only hope or resolution is to turn to his own kind, not to the gods; this is exemplified by Amphitryon's complaint against Zeus and by Theseus' role in giving aid to his former savior. This friendship, *philia,* is Euripides' answer to the cruel and brutal blows of Fortune, epitomized by the rapid succession of horrors unequaled in any Euripidean play. When man's world is violently turned about, humanity must triumph over inhumanity. This realistic rather than nihilistic philosophy prevents life from becoming absurd.

HERCULES AND HIS TWELVE LABORS

Type of work: Classical myth
Source: Folk tradition
Type of plot: Heroic adventure
Time: of plot: Remote antiquity
Locale: Mediterranean region
First transcribed: Unknown

Not born a god, Hercules achieved godhood at the time of his death because he devoted his life to the service of his fellow men. Some authorities link Hercules with the sun, as each labor took him further from his home and one of his tasks carried him around the world and back. Whatever their origin, the adventures remain fascinating stories which can support varied interpretations.

Hercules (Latin form of Greek "Herakles," meaning "Hera's (Juno's) fame") rightfully deserved to rule Mycenae and Tiryns, but because of the machinations of Juno, his cousin Eurystheus had become his lord. Driven mad by Juno, Hercules killed his own wife and children, and was required by the Delphic oracle to atone for his crime by becoming King Eurystheus' vassal. Eurystheus originally assigned ten *athloi* (ordeals for a prize), but he refused to count both the killing of the Hydra, since Hercules had been assisted by his nephew Iolaus, and the cleansing of the Augean stables, since Hercules had demanded payment. These *athloi* required twelve years and are described above essentially according to Apollodorus, the first- or second-century A.D. mythographer (the third and fourth labors are reversed as are the fifth and sixth). Sometimes the last two labors are reversed, which subtracts from the supreme accomplishment of conquering death, as it were, by returning from Hades. The same twelve exploits were sculpted nearly life-size on the metopes of the Temple of Zeus at Olympia in the mid-fifth century B.C.; four scenes have been reconstructed from the fragments. Euripides perhaps reflects an earlier tradition, which begins with Homer, when he lists encounters with the Centaurs, with Cycnus the robber, and with pirates in place of the boar, the stables, and the bull *(Herakles Mad).*

Nevertheless, the twelve labors are not the extent of Hercules' fame. Apollodorus (*Library* 2.4.8-2.7.7), as well as Pausanias and Diodorus Siculus detail the "life" of this folk-hero; Ovid briefly recounts the labors and death of the hero in Book 9 of the *Metamorphoses*. From their accounts, and from numerous other sources, we have a wealth of exploits accomplished before, during, and after the labors. Among those before is Hercules' fathering a child by each of the fifty daughters of King Thespius. During the labors, Hercules performed a number of well-known *parerga,* or "side deeds," such as joining Jason's Argonauts in quest of the Golden Fleece. He never completed the journey, however, since he was left at Mysia looking for his lost squire and boy-love Hylas. Among other *parerga* are his rescue of Alcestis from Death after she had volunteered to die in place of her husband King Admetus of Pherae (see Euripides *Alcestis*). He also rescued Hesione, daughter of King Laomedon of Troy, who was to have been sacrificed to Poseidon's sea-monster. In Italy he killed the fire-breathing Cacus who had stolen the cattle of Geryon(es) which Hercules was driving back to Eurystheus (see Vergil *Aeneid* 8.193-270). In Libya he lifted the giant Antaeus from his mother Earth, from whom he derived his strength, and crushed him. He rescued Prometheus from the rock in the Caucasus and Theseus from the Underworld.

After the labors, Hercules sought to marry Iole, daughter of Eurytus, King of Oechalia and the man who had taught him archery. Eurytus refused, and Hercules killed the king's son, for which he was sold into slavery to Omphale, queen of Lydia. There he performed numerous feats, including killing a great snake, fathering a child on Omphale, and burying the body of the fallen Icarus, who had flown too near the sun. Freed, Hercules went on to seek revenge on Laomedon and Augeas for their refusal to honor their debts for services rendered. He later married Deianira, whom he soon had to rescue from the lustful Nessus, who instructed Deianira to dip Hercules' tunic into the dying centaur's blood. The wearing of the tunic, she was told, would prevent Hercules (notorious for his *amours*) from loving another. Soon Hercules returned to Oechalia where he murdered Eurytus and abducted Iole. In desperation and ignorance, Deianira sent the tunic, and as soon as Hercules put it on, it began to sear his flesh (since Nessus' blood had been poisoned by an arrow which long ago had been dipped in the Hydra's blood). Hercules' horrible death is vividly described in Euripides' *Trachiniae*.

By the twelve labors Hercules earned the immortality promised by the Delphic oracle, and so when Hercules died (having mounted his own funeral pyre), Jupiter persuaded all the gods, including Juno, to accept him into the pantheon. He took Hebe ("Youth") to wife and was thereafter universally honored. If Hercules' mythic origins are indeed solar, it is appropriate that he enjoyed *apotheosis,* or deification, and allegorical union with Youth, since the sun, having passed through the twelve zodiacal constellations, returns each year, renewed in strength. On the other hand, Hercules may well have been the original male consort to a pre-Greek mother goddess (Hera) as his name would imply. But whatever his origins, throughout the ancient world in religion and literature, he was welcomed as the ultimate folk-hero, simple but not obtuse, powerful but humane, whose myths symbolized the pains and indignities that even great men, beloved of 'Jupiter, must undergo to attain undying glory. On him, the Athenians modeled their local hero, Theseus. Numerous other localities variously worshiped Hercules as a hero, if not a god. The Cynics and Stoics admired his hardy self-reliance and attention to duty.

In art, Hercules is a favorite subject—his broad, muscled shoulders draped with the skin of a Nemean lion. Although he gained fame for his archery and physical strength, he is usually represented wielding a knotted club. In Roman art representations of his brutality seem to tend toward brutishness, so that he becomes more the gladiator than the noble demigod who courageously submitted to the will and whims of the lesser. More than any other figure, Hercules drew together the mythic experiences of Olympians and Titans, monsters and men, death and immortality.

E. N. Genovese

HEREWARD THE WAKE

Type of work: Novel
Author: Charles Kingsley (1819-1875)
Type of plot: Historical romance
Time of plot: Eleventh century
Locale: England, Scotland, Flanders
First published: 1866

Both an interesting fictional story and a valuable historical study, Hereward the Wake *is one of the few extended fictions which deals realistically and credibly with the Anglo-Saxon period of English history. Kingsley re-created the age and its people in a believable and interesting manner.*

In his last novel, *Hereward the Wake,* Kingsley treats a heroic figure whose character and adventures form the core of the *Gesta Hereward.* Based on the past, it is, however, more than an adaptation of existing legends. Kingsley makes the most of the rich material provided by this colorful period in history. He chooses to assign a new past to Hereward, making him the son of Lady Godiva, and he also gives much attention to the courtship and winning of Torfrida, a woman of exceptional virtue and talents, who is reputed to be a witch.

Yet what undoubtedly attracted Kingsley to the legend were the various elements that he himself felt were missing in his own time. An advocate of "muscular Christianity" as well as social benevolence to the poor and underprivileged, the Reverend Kingsley found in Hereward's life an opportunity to champion militant heroism blessed by the Church. After Hereward returns from exile, one spent in reparation for his youthful rebellion, he goes to his uncle, Abbot Brand, and is knighted, literally annointed, as a soldier of the Church to battle the Normans. He displays all the virtues, even in his death, of the medieval soldier whose embassy is charity as well as bloodshed.

Hereward stands for the last "pure" English knight, moreover, because the foreigners, the Normans, are successfully installed as England's rulers after his death. It was also this racial purity which the Saxon represents that led Kingsley to the legend. Unspoiled by any alien influence or blood the knight, although finally defeated by the Normans, is apotheosized and even in death his body is saved from his Norman wife by the mysterious Torfrida. It is these chauvinistic qualities which accounted for the success of the novel in England, a society which felt threatened by the Continental political revolutions of the nineteenth century.

A HERO OF OUR TIME

Type of work: Novel
Author: Mikhail Yurievich Lermontov (1814-1841)
Type of plot: Psychological romance
Time of plot: 1830-1838
Locale: The Russian Caucasus
First published: 1839

In this realistic novel of social and military life in nineteenth century Russia, Lermontov pointed to the development of the Russian psychological novel. The protagonist, Pechorin, was intended to be a collective personification of all the evil and vice then found in Russian life. Structurally, the novel is made up of five related stories, narrated in a compact and vivid style.

Russian literature came of age during the nineteenth century. Mikhail Lermontov, one of the most seminal writers of that century, produced in *A Hero of Our Time* an insightful social document rarely duplicated during the golden century of Russian literature. It was the author's misfortune—and that of all those interested in the development of Russian literary and social thought—that he died at the age of twenty-seven. While Lermontov's literary followers prostrated themselves before the genius of Gogol, claiming "we all crawled out of Gogol's *Overcoat,*" it is just as likely that they were in fact epigones of Lermontov and very well ought to have said—"it is time we acknowledged Lermontov as our hero."

The Russian literary debt owed to Lermontov was and is great. His steadfast desire to depict accurately Russian social types and social conditions led him to create and develop several Russian literary myths which remain an integral part of the Russian literary imagination today. He created the cultivated yet weak and passive "superfluous man." While Pechorin was a soldier, he was not a man of strength or warrior skills; he was a *bon vivant* on horseback, a gay seducer who genuflected to his own pleasure, not to the needs of society. As the passive exploiter, he became the harbinger for a century of similar literary types. The superfluous hero enjoyed a long life, and perhaps a permanent residency, in Russian literature. The novels of Gogol, Turgenev, and Goncharov, to name but a few of the premier writers of the nineteenth century, perpetuated and therefore reaffirmed the accuracy of Lermontov's creation.

Lermontov also clearly defined the relationship of the Russian writer to his society. Desiring to free the writer from a "superfluous" position *vis à vis* Russian society, Lermontov aimed to criticize conditions in Russia, most notably the serf-landlord relationship which was the basis for Russian social and economic life. Lermontov felt that a society changed only through criticism of existing social conditions and values. Lermontov's *A Hero of Our Time* is the first significant attempt in Russian *belles lettres* to define a social role for the writer. His literary followers have perpetrated, with dogged if unacknowledged faithfulness, the correctness of Lermontov's mission.

HERSELF SURPRISED

Type of work: Novel
Author: Joyce Cary (1888-1957)
Type of plot: Social comedy
Time of plot: First quarter of the twentieth century
Locale: London and the English southern counties
First published: 1941

With compassion and irony, through his rich and colorful language, Joyce Cary portrays the story of Sara Monday in this episodic, virtually plotless novel. The characters in this book possess a common creative energy and joy in creating. The world of art is a symbol for the creative process that Cary felt was the basis of life.

Herself Surprised is the first novel in a trilogy published in the early 1940's (the other titles are *To Be a Pilgrim* and *The Horse's Mouth*). Each novel may be read by itself with satisfaction, but for greatest enjoyment and understanding the trilogy should be experienced as a unit. In the trilogy each novel is given over to a single character who tells his or her story with wonderful personal style and inflection. These novels establish Cary as one of the great mimics of literature. The basic scheme of the trilogy involves the conflict between the conservative attitude represented by the lawyer and landholder Tom Wilcher (*To Be a Pilgrim*), and the liberal attitude represented by the painter Gulley Jimson (*The Horse's Mouth*). Sara Monday, the heroine of *Herself Surprised,* has loved both these men. She stands between them in a mediating position.

Sara is a warm, comfortable woman. She likes to make her men feel at ease. Her narrative is full of the imagery of the home and the kitchen. She has been Jimson's mistress and endured his rages as well as his ecstasies. He has painted some of his finest nude studies using her as a model. Basically, however, he rejects her because she threatens to domesticate him and dampen his creative fires. Her next companion is Tom Wilcher, a fussy old bachelor who is largely concerned with maintaining the traditions represented in the family estate of Tolbrook. Sara soothes and smooths Wilcher's thorny nature. He is a perfect object for her feminine arts.

In Cary's world Sara Monday stands for the womanly virtues of love, acceptance, gratification, and nurturing. She may make her way in the world by employing these skills with some calculation, but it is a kind passage.

A HIGH WIND RISING

Type of work: Novel
Author: Elsie Singmaster (Mrs. E. S. Lewars, 1879-1958)
Type of plot: Historical chronicle
Time of plot: 1728-1755
Locale: Pennsylvania
First published: 1942

The story of the Pennsylvania settlements beyond the Schuylkill during the French and English struggle, this novel brings to life the frontier world of that time. The virtues needed to rise above the hardships and dangers of the era are illustrated in the lives of the characters; many great figures, as well, are viewed briefly in this crowded canvas of people and events.

Elsie Singmaster is an author who has attracted little literary criticism. The bulk of her writing is in the genre of the historical novel, and is either written for juveniles or dealing with youthful heroes. Born in a small town in the German region of Pennsylvania in 1879 and educated at Radcliffe, Singmaster's fiction is largely regional, concerned with the span between colonial times and the mid-twentieth century in America. *A High Wind Rising* is one of her later works, and is set in the years of the French and Indian Wars; it details the efforts of local German settlers to secure the Ohio River Valley for the British during the conflict. The writer's straightforward narrative and careful characterizations downplay the historical importance of these people. Instead, she dramatizes the struggle of their everyday lives as pioneers who must cope with both natural and political forces in order to survive.

The author has clearly been influenced by historical romanticists like James Fenimore Cooper. In contrast to Cooper, however, who creates larger-than-life characters such as Natty Bumppo for the purpose of dramatizing significant historical themes, Singmaster wishes to depict the lives of the early settlers without exaggerating for thematic effect. If Cooper is interested in the ethical, historical, and metaphysical aspects of the frontier, Singmaster is interested in the details of everyday lives; whereas romance is central to Cooper, it is incidental to her.

It is, finally, her attention to the orderly lives of her characters that remains her most modern feature. There is, furthermore, a pervasive tone of good feeling toward humanity in her work. That healthy tone, in *A High Wind Rising* and in her other work as well, undoubtedly accounts for her popularity with the young.

THE HILL OF DREAMS

Type of work: Novel
Author: Arthur Machen (1863-1947)
Type of plot: Impressionistic romance
Time of plot: Late nineteenth century
Locale: England
First published: 1907

In part an autobiography, this unusual novel is the study of a man who, while searching for a way to express life, lost both himself and the power to understand humanity. The author maintained that many of the trials and weird experiences put into the life of the fictional hero were, in reality, his own experiences as he wrote the novel.

The Hill of Dreams is the depressing but haunting tale of an apparent failure. Lucian Taylor dreamed impractical dreams, failed to earn a "respectable" living, failed in his writings (which were plagiarized by unscrupulous publishers), and died unnecessarily, having ruined his own health. He was not liked by "respectable" people, even by his landlady to whom he left money, and he had been the cause of strain to his father. Yet, through the story of Lucian, Machen tells us that many *apparent* failures at the time of their deaths, such as Jesus Christ or Lucian, are the *eternal* victors. Lucian's neighbors in his home town and in West London could well be the eternal failures, for they fail to see the proverbial beam in their own eyes, and ignore the Biblical injunction to "judge not, that ye be not judged."

Although Lucian is the target of criticism and condemnation throughout the novel, and although this condemnation seems justified and crushingly final when he is found dead in his dismal rented room amidst his illegible scribblings, *The Hill of Dreams* is not, ultimately, a novel of failure. It breathes of another life beyond the grave, a life that Lucian might have won, for he was loyal to his tortured dreams until the end. Lucian seemingly succumbed to satanic visions only under the unnatural influence of opium, when he had lost his reason. The real Lucian, however, is the youth of the early parts of the novel, who hates cruelty and mediocrity, who has not yet known opium, and who one afternoon walks up an old, neglected country lane when the air is still and breathless. He walks up his "hill of dreams" where wild, bare hills meet a still, gray sky. It is on such occasions, when his sensitive spirit vanquishes harsh reality and the ugly purgatory that enshrouds him in the "real" world, that the reader sees the victorious Lucian Taylor.

HILLINGDON HALL

Type of work: Novel
Author: Robert Smith Surtees (1803-1864)
Type of plot: Comic romance
Time of plot: Nineteenth century
Locale: England
First published: 1845

The final novel of the Jorrocks series, this book emphasizes the charms and oddities of country life. Good satire predominates in the electioneering scenes and in Emma Flather's attempts to get a husband; also, some current farming fads come in for goodnatured ridicule. As in all of Surtees' work, the cockney speech is accurately represented.

The third of Surtees' novels treating the comic misadventures of "Cockney sportsman" John Jorrocks, *Hillingdon Hall* is somewhat less episodic and more conventionally plotted than the picaresque *Jorrocks' Jaunts and Jollities* (1838) or *Handley Cross* (1843). The author continues the career of Jorrocks, now in his late middle age and fairly prosperous from the success of his London grocery business, who determines to settle down with his wife and hounds at a country estate in order to enjoy the vigorous life of a sporting squire. By placing his parvenu hero among the landed gentry, Surtees is able to develop the amusing possibilities of an idea that he had proposed in his first novel: that if Jorrocks' lot had been "cast in the country instead of behind a counter, his keenness would have rendered him as conspicuous—if not as scientific—as the best of them."

The test of this proposition occurs at Hillingdon Hall, where Jorrocks, in spite of his urban background in vulgar commerce, is entirely at ease among both the aristocrats and simple country folk of the vicinity. Jorrocks is, after all, "frank, hearty, open, generous, and hospitable"—possessing virtues certain to prevail no matter where fortune leads him. There is no question that the onetime grocer is shrewder than his lordly neighbors, the effete Duke of Donkeyton and his blue-blooded but insipid son, the Marquis of Bray. And Jorrocks is honest enough to recognize his own limitations in dealing with farm matters that he cannot comprehend. So he allows the pragmatic James Pigg—another of Surtees' memorable creations—to manage the business part of the estate.

Thanks to his common sense (along with a measure of luck and the political acumen of Pigg), Jorrocks even wins a contested Parliamentary seat from his highborn rival Bray. Although the issue at stake in the election—the question of repealing the Corn Laws—is treated farcically, Surtees was in earnest about the matter in his personal life. A staunch conservative, he feared that a rising middle class would destroy the privileges of wealth and the stability of country life as he had known it. Jorrocks' Hillingon Hall, to be sure, is a very modest estate compared to Surtees' own inherited properties: Milkwellburn, Byerside Hall, Espershields, and Hamsterley Hall in Durham.

Because of his experience in public life as well as his high social station, Surtees could view Jorrocks from two vantages: that of an aristocrat laughing at the common man's foibles, but also that of an adopted Londoner who appreciates the rugged strengths of the ambitious middle class. Consequently, he treats his hero both as bumpkin and solid citizen—or "cit." In the third novel of the Jorrocks series, the grocer is not so much a sportsman as he is a landholding squire. Much of the impetuous hilarity of the hunting scenes from the other two novels is missing. But in its place is a fuller portrait of the "cit" as a man of warmth and dignity. By the time Surtees takes his leave of Jorrocks, the master of Hillingdon Hall, he seems to resemble less Dickens' Sam Weller, the Cockney who similarly confuses his *v*'s and *w*'s, and more the great-hearted gentleman Pickwick.

HIPPOLYTUS

Type of work: Drama
Author: Euripides (480-406 B.C.)
Type of plot: Classical tragedy
Time of plot: Remote antiquity
Locale: Troezen in Argolis
First presented: 428 B.C.

In this tragedy Euripides relates the story of Hippolytus, who scorns women and pays homage to Artemis rather than the goddess of love, Aphrodite; in her anger, Aphrodite avenges herself by causing the young man's stepmother to fall in love with him. Theseus, Hippolytus' father, and Phaedra, who hangs herself after only a brief appearance in the play, command the audience's sympathy and pity much more than the title character, since they are seen as tragic victims of a relentless fate.

Hippolytus is an intriguing play from both a religious and a psychological standpoint. Euripides dramatizes the traditional rivalry in Greek religion between Aphrodite, the goddess of love, and Artemis, the goddess of chastity. The three major characters—Phaedra, Hippolytus, and Theseus—are caught in that antagonism and must suffer for it. Just as a statue of each goddess frames the stage, so the dramatic action is set between the appearance of Aphrodite in the prologue and the appearance of Artemis at the end. The contrast between these two, as Euripides shows it, however, is not between carnal love and spiritual love, but between uncontrolled passion and artificial restraint.

Aphrodite is an intense, volatile goddess who does not hesitate to destroy her own devotee, Phaedra, in order to wreak vengeance upon Hippolytus, who, she believes, has deeply offended her by his conduct and attitudes. Artemis appears, however, as the revealer of truth, the calm reconciler of father and son. After passion wreaks its damage only a clear-eyed view of things is left, sobering and immeasurably sad.

The goddess of passion works her will through two violently emotional people, Phaedra and Theseus. Although perhaps not technically incestuous, Phaedra's love for the young man is clearly immoral and wrong. However, the intensity of her feelings—they are obviously beyond her control—and the sincerity of her guilt and anguish, make her the most sympathetic and moving figure in the play. Hippolytus, on the other hand, is innocent of any actual wrongdoing, but his self-righteous moralism and abnormally rigid sexual behavior not only render him personally unsympathetic, but, more important, are major stimulants to the sequence of actions that lead to the final catastrophe. Theseus' impulsive vengeance adds the third element to the drama. Thus, uncontrollable passion, arrogant self-righteousness, and mindless revenge combine to provoke multiple tragedy.

From a dramatic standpoint, the main problem in the play is that the most important character, Phaedra, dies when the action is little more than half over. Her tragedy finished, the intensity of the play flags. The debate between Theseus and Hippolytus over the causes of her death and Theseus' subsequent condemnation of Hippolytus lack the feelings present in Phaedra's scenes, although they do resolve the action and grant to the males, especially Hippolytus, a measure of sympathy and tragic stature absent earlier. But it is the vividness, intensity, and tragic ambiguity of Phaedra's character that makes *Hippolytus* one of Euripides' greatest and most provocative plays.

THE HISTORY OF COLONEL JACQUE

Type of work: Novel
Author: Daniel Defoe (1660-1731)
Type of plot: Picaresque adventure
Time of plot: Late seventeenth century
Locale: England, France, Virginia
First published: 1722

Defoe intended, in Colonel Jacque, *to show the ruination of youth through lack of proper training and to prove that a misspent life may be redeemed by repentance; along the way, he carefully included many sensational and scandalous scenes which would insure the popularity of his book. The vitality of the writing and the attention to detail make the story as interesting today as it was 250 years ago.*

At its very commencement the English novel indicated the direction of its subsequent development. In *The History of Colonel Jacque* as well as in his other novels, Defoe detailed the adventures of the rogue, society's outcast, in his attempt to find station, security, and identity in culture. So even at the beginning of the eighteenth century, the novel was a middle-class, democratic genre, growing out of the political and social rise of that class. It is middle-class in its concern for wealth and station; it is democratic in its insistence that power, which lay in aristocratic hands, be dispersed and allowed to filter down to the parvenus.

Typically, Colonel Jack is an unwanted child who is excluded by his birth from the goods of society. Simply but accurately put, his aim during his adventures is to accumulate wealth, which, he soon discovers—and this is of course the edge of Defoe's moral satire—will give him power and place. But it is also a part of Defoe's wisdom, which is as well that of the middle class, that the pleasure goods afford gives man a fundamental nobility. It is a dignity achieved when he frees himself from poverty and gains substance in the eyes of society. Those goods, Defoe also tells us, make possible the pursuit of virtue; for if material security does not necessarily lead to virtue, the moral life is impossible without it.

Colonel Jack's conversion, then, like the more famous one of Moll Flanders, should not be seen as mere hypocrisy. It is a knowledge won at the expense of suffering and deprivation. If one condemn Jack's means to his end, one should be prepared to honor his middle-class sagacity that if man cannot live by bread alone, neither can he live without it.

THE HISTORY OF MR. POLLY

Type of work: Novel
Author: H. G. Wells (1866-1946)
Type of plot: Comic romance
Time of plot: Early twentieth century
Locale: England
First published: 1909

The story of a gentle man who rebels at last against the insults heaped upon him by the world, The History of Mr. Polly *is a timeless comedy, highly original and moving, and full of Wells's special genius for a quiet humor that startles even as it amuses.*

Alfred Polly, the English Walter Mitty, closely resembles some of Wells' other protagonists. He is a more middle-class version of Artie Kipps and a less aggressive counterpart of the heroes of *Tono-Bungay* and *Love and Mr. Lewisham.*In *Mr. Polly,* the objects of Wells's attack are the same as in those earlier works: England's stultifying class system; the mind numbing quality of lower-class education; the boredom of "a nation of shopkeepers"; the repression of sexual joy. The novel's humor and pathos derive from Polly's wonderfully confused ways of letting his romantic spirit find expression in such an unfavorable environment.

Like a Don Quixote on a bicycle, Polly seldom discovers a correspondence between his real and imaginary worlds. "The Three P's"—Polly and two fellow apprentices—do enjoy a robust picaresque fellowship. Polly summons up all his malapropistic poetry in wooing his mysterious "lady" in the woods (while her hidden school chums stifle hysterical giggles). But the world of commerce and convention always interrupts such halcyon episodes. So, bewildered Mr. Polly is dragged into matrimony by the heavy tides of custom. His courtship is hilariously painful. Terrified by the proposal he almost offered Minnie, he impulsively proposes to Miriam, only to discover that he would rather have had Minnie. During the wedding, Polly imagines far off "a sweet face in sunshine"; he then awakens to the drab little person next to him: "It was astounding. She was his wife!"

Never quite able to identify the source of his dissatisfaction, Polly nevertheless knows that a change must come. His suicide attempt is successful—in killing the resigned, conformist, "practical" Polly. But what is the connection between the liberated romantic of the final chapters and the earlier spineless protagonist? The world of the Potwell Inn is almost purely feudal; Mr. Polly, now transformed into a latter-day Robin Hood, defends his damsel from the wicked Uncle Jim. The novel remains wonderfully comic, but Wells rather toys with our sense of psychological reality.

H. M. S. PINAFORE

Type of work: Comic opera
Author: W. S. Gilbert (1836-1911)
Type of plot: Humorous satire
Time of plot: Latter half of the nineteenth century
Locale: Portsmouth harbor, England
First presented: 1878

Written in collaboration with his composer-partner, Arthur Sullivan, Gilbert produced in H.M.S. Pinafore *a delightful satire on jingoism and a spoof on the extravagances of grand opera. The plot disregards the element of time and is crowded with incident, while every song and scene abounds with adroit and ingenious dialogue and mischievous and clever rhymes.*

In December 1878, one year after the moderately successful production of *The Sorcerer,* William Schwenck Gilbert offered his musical collaborator, Arthur Seymour Sullivan, a libretto for a new comic opera, with a note appended: "I have very little doubt whatever but that you will be pleased with it." Sullivan was indeed pleased, and although he was suffering intense pain from a kidney disorder, he composed the music rapidly. On the evening of May 25, 1878, three nights after *The Sorcerer* completed its run, the Comedy Opera Company presented *H. M. S. Pinafore, or The Lass That Loved a Sailor,* which was to become one of the great triumphs of the musical theater.

Curious to say, the opening performance of *H. M. S. Pinafore* was nearly a failure. Even though some scandal attached to the caricature of Sir Joseph, who was clearly a satirical portrait of Sir William H. Smith, a publisher appointed by Queen Victoria as First Lord of the Admiralty, the first season of the production languished during the June heat. Most affluent Londoners simply vacationed outside the city, and the cast and chorus, threatened with cancellation of the whole production, agreed to accept a cut of one-third of their salaries. Eventually, however, *H. M. S. Pinafore* began to attract a following. The Savoy Company, under D'Oyly Carte, performing at such theaters as the (English) Opéra Comique, the Imperial, and the Olympic, enjoyed a London run of two years, and was a remarkable success.

Almost concurrently, *H. M. S. Pinafore* was performed in pirated and often poorly staged versions in America. To secure American royalty rights and correct misconceptions about the quality of the work, Gilbert, Sullivan, Alfred Cellier (another composer for the Carte company), and selected members of the original cast, mounted an impressive production of the comic opera at the Fifth Avenue Theater in New York City, starting December 1, 1879. The authorized version of *H. M. S. Pinafore* was widely hailed, and touring companies performed it throughout the United States as well as England.

Reasons for the popularity of Gilbert's comedy are not difficult to identify.

Apart from Sullivan's tuneful score, the book itself is delightfully arch, bubbling over with high spirits and clever invention. Gilbert satirizes with wit, but little malice, pretensions of social superiority in class-conscious Victorian England. In the pecking order of rank, Sir Joseph Porter is superior to Captain Corcoran, and the Captain in turn lords it over his crew. Yet even the lowly British tar is snobbish about his rank. After all, every sailor "is an Englishman," and his national pride, for which he feels superior to seamen of other nations, makes him better than "a Roosian, a French or Turk or Proosian." Even the revelation by Buttercup that the Captain is of lowly birth and Ralph Rackstraw of high, scarcely disturbs the Victorian audience's sense of social justice. Now Sir Joseph, who likes to think of himself as democratic but who is really a snob, will have to marry his cousin Hebe instead of Josephine, who has fallen in class as the daughter of a humble sailor. At the same time the former Ralph, elevated in rank to the Captain of the *H. M. S. Pinafore,* can claim Josephine. As for the one-time Captain (now plain Ralph), he is free to marry at his own social level, and wisely chooses the buxom Little Buttercup.

Buttercup, like the gypsy Azucena in Verdi's *Il Trovatore* or like Miss Prism in Wilde's *The Importance of Being Earnest,* had been slightly addled when she was "young and charming." She had mixed up the infant Ralph and the infant Captain, a worrisome mistake perhaps, but obviously no serious harm was done. No matter what his social caste, each Englishman (and Englishwoman too, including sisters, cousins, and aunts) knows what is the proper duty and decorum for that prescribed caste. And since the crew of the *H. M. S. Pinafore* is happy with Buttercup's mistake, so must the audience be.

THE HOLY TERRORS

Type of work: Novel
Author: Jean Cocteau (1889-1963)
Type of plot: Psychological fantasy
Time of plot: The present
Locale: Paris
First published: 1929

A tender and compassionate account of the creativity and destructiveness of adolescence, this novel exists in a stifling and narrow world of its own. A psychological fantasy, it is, like the author's films, the product of a romantic imagination which has been much influenced by Freudian imagery.

The Holy Terrors possesses many of the qualities of a fairy tale, but it is an erotic and frightening fairy tale. It is a novel which works on the basis of contradictions; little is as it seems in this unusual masterpiece. Layer by layer, reality is stripped away, exposing the fascinating and bizarre personalities of the principal characters. The plot seems almost haphazard, incidents piling up as they are needed (as in the convenient Isadora Duncan-like death of Elisabeth's new husband, Michael). The perverse and yet charming brother and sister never think of the consequences of their actions (for example, Elisabeth's marriage and Paul's letter and, always, the taking of drugs). The characters in the novel seem to plummet forward, toward their ultimately tragic fates.

Cocteau frequently uses the word "devouring" to describe the relationship between the brother and sister. The book begins when they are fourteen and sixteen respectively, and carries them into their early twenties, yet the author always considers them "children." If their actual ages are considered, their actions do not seem so innocent or amusing; their heedlessness becomes selfishness and their games lose the charm of their rather forced spontaneity. Paul and Elisabeth never worry about money, accepting as their due after their mother dies the charity of the Doctor and Gérard's uncle. Michael's convenient death, which results in their inheriting his fortune, seems to them merely an act of the gods, and they refuse to change their morbid existence. Paul and Elisabeth do not care about other people; they never consider the effect they will have on others. They are unnaturallly tied up in themselves, and this obsessive relationship leads to their mutual destruction, carrying along the innocent Gérard and Agatha. They are not likeable, but thanks to the artistry of Cocteau, they are fascinating.

THE HONEST WHORE, PART ONE

Type of work: Drama
Author: Thomas Dekker (c.1572-1632?) with Thomas Middleton (1580-1627)
Type of plot: Tragi-comedy
Time of plot: Sixteenth century
Locale: Milan, Italy
First presented: 1604

Assisted by Thomas Middleton, Dekker created in this play an amazingly complicated and brilliantly worked out plot, one which manages to border the improbable while remaining affecting and fascinating. The humor which runs through the drama, particularly in the subplot, helps to lift it from the essential sordidness of much of the subject matter and to infuse it with vitality and interest.

Although *The Honest Whore, Part One,* taken as a whole, is not a typical comedy of humors, some of its characters display the peculiarities common to the type. Indeed, the advertisement from the title page of the play—"With the Humors of the Patient Man and the Longing Wife"—identifies two characters who suffer from a form of psychological unbalance. Unlike Ben Jonson's comedy of humors, in which the afflicted persons' unbalance often approaches madness, the humors characters in this play appear to suffer milder derangements.

The chief example from the subplot is Candido, the linen draper, whose patience—a Christian virtue usually considered admirable—is exaggerated to the point of stubborn eccentricity. Although Candido has "no more gall in him than a dove, no more sting than an ant," he is rewarded for his meek forbearance with abuse instead of kindness. Candido's problem is that his patient apathy torments his shrewish wife Viola, who is driven nearly lunatic in her futile attempts to rouse him. As the "longing wife," Viola's humor is rage. Nettled, she is ready to bite off her own tongue "because it wants that virtue which all women's tongues have, to anger their husbands." Count Hippolito, the protagonist from the main plot, also suffers early in the play from a humor, that of the "tyrant melancholy." As a dour moralist, he lectures the whore Bellafront on her vice until he reforms her character. Sourly he listens to and rejects her protestations of love. In spite of his otherwise attractive quality as the faithful lover of Infelice, the count is—to modern readers—far too sober a hero to deserve the fullest sympathy.

The strength of the play is, however, in its plot rather than its characters. Complexly structured, *The Honest Whore, Part One* has three distinct actions which are ingeniously entangled and finally unified. In the main plot, Count Hippolito seeks to wed Infelice. Opposed by her father, the Duke of Milan, Hippolito succeeds in his endeavor by overcoming obstacles that, in *Romeo and Juliet*, had proved tragic to the lovers. Though in the first act Infelice appears to be dead, she has merely been drugged. In the high subplot Bellafront, a harlot, first confounds her many lovers and later is driven desperate herself for love of Hippolito. She eventually marries her first seducer, Matheo. In the low subplot Candido, the model of patience, vexes his wife and is in turn persecuted by her. All the plots converge in the triumphant concluding scene at Bethlem Monastery (the madhouse). All the characters are revealed for what they are—virtuous and wise, or vicious and foolish. The ending, undeniably sentimental and pat, is difficult to accept as realistic. But the play, despite a few realistic scenes in the draper's shop, is essentially a romantic entertainment and is meant to be amusingly heartwarming, not perfectly logical.

THE HONEST WHORE, PART TWO

Type of work: Drama
Author: Thomas Dekker (c. 1572-1632?)
Type of plot: Tragi-comedy
Time of plot: Sixteenth century
Locale: Milan, Italy
First presented: c. 1605

This sequel, written entirely by Dekker, capitalized on the features of the first play; it also continued the high moral tone of the earlier drama, this time, however, making gambling as well as prostitution the object of its strictures.

The Honest Whore, Part Two, continues in a more realistic, indeed often cynical fashion the story of *The Honest Whore, Part One.* As is true of many literary sequels, in the second play Dekker changes his concept of the characters in order to satisfy the demands of his different plot. In *Part One,* Count Hippolito was the melancholy but faithful lover of Infelice; Gasparo Trebazzi was the inflexible father-tyrant who crossed the young lovers until the concluding scene; and Bellafront was the whore reformed through her unrequited but pure love for Hippolito. In *Part Two* Hippolito, now married to Infelice, is no longer the melancholy saint of love: "turned ranger," his passions are roused by Bellafront's beauty; Gasparo is judicious instead of rancorous; and Bellafront is a model of wifely virtue, deaf to Hippolito's seductive entreaties. Only Candido, the patient linen draper, remains quite the same in both plays. His "humor"—an exaggerated meekness and forbearance—is tested by his young skittish bride (his former wife Viola, the shrew, having fortunately expired), by pranksters, a bawd, a pander, and by assorted whores and knaves at Bridewell prison. The single important new character, Orlando Friscobaldo, who is Bellafront's father, is intended to arouse in the audience sentimental affection, but his meretricious disguise and mean intrigues serve only to make his motivation appear inconsistent, and he is ultimately unsympathetic.

To be sure, the major difference between the plays is the change from romantic tragicomedy approaching comedy of humors in *Part One* to tragicomic realism in *Part Two.* So far as we can judge from what remains of Dekker's many plays, the author's talents would not appear to run toward authentic tragedy. He is at his best with comic scenes of London lower class or lower-middle class life. In *Part Two,* he is most convincing when he treats Candido in the linen shop, fretted by apprentices; or when he brings all his characters, in the final scene, to Bridewell Prison. Like the conclusion of *Part One* in Bethlem Monastery (a madhouse), the Bridewell scene is vivid with caricatures of the denizens of London's sordid underworld. Unlike such dramatists as Marston, Chapman, or Jonson, who often flail these wretched creatures with indignant satire, Dekker sees them as amusing although pitiful.

His humanity rather than moral power is most clearly displayed in the play.

In the character of Matheo, Dekker's failure in moral vision seriously weakens the otherwise happy ending. In *Part One,* Matheo was a minor figure, a friend of the count. In *Part Two,* as Bellafront's husband, he is an evil, scheming, luxurious brute. Contrasted to Hippolito's amateur philandering, Matheo's studied lust and depravity are the greater vices. Yet Matheo is pardoned at the end, thanks to the intercession of Bellafront, who dutifully forgives her husband. Thus the patient generosity of the wife nearly matches the patience of Candido. Nevertheless, for modern audiences, Bellafront sacrifices too much of her self-respect for her worthless spouse; his reformation, it would seem, is only temporary, and he is likely to abuse her afterward—a destiny that any woman, even an "honest whore," should not have to endure.

HONEY IN THE HORN

Type of work: Novel
Author: H. L. Davis (1896-1960)
Type of plot: Regional romance
Time of plot: 1906-1908
Locale: Oregon
First published: 1935

The well-told, fast-moving story of this pioneer novel is actually less important than the character studies of the individuals whose lives are portrayed. The reader is given an accurate picture of the migrants who were continually seeking new homes in better lands, and finally came to Oregon in the early part of this century.

Oregon in the homesteading days was colorful, raw, rollicking, and often brutal. West of the Great Plains meant west of civilization, but the frontier nevertheless profoundly influenced American culture. *Honey in the Horn* is Harold Lenoir Davis' Pulitzer Prize-winning attempt to render the unique and captivating quality of that experience.

The title, from a boisterous square dance lyric, introduces a tall-tale dimension popularized by local colorists such as Bret Harte and Artemus Ward. The story derives much of its power and inspiration from the poker-faced comic sketches of the rustic characters the young protagonist encounters. When Clay Calvert flees the ramshackle toll bridge station (under shady circumstances which eventually unfold and help relieve the rambling plot of its dependence on coincidence), his adventures encompass a spectrum of incidents infused with local color, including vivid scenic description, and scenes involving random brutality, frontier lore, backwoods politics, human dignity and degradation, squalor and sensibility.

Davis' story combines authentic frontier language with huge infusions of first-hand knowledge and backwoods lore which are occasionally fabulous, but which nevertheless ring true of human situations. Davis refuses to mythologize his material, but rather allows the tension between the myth and the revealed reality, between the ideal of the Old West and fact, to impel its own conclusions. While his characters tend to be one-dimensional, subtleties of frontier character and nuances of commonplace personal interaction are rendered perceptively and deftly, though without deep probing.

Although his vivid and lovingly rendered descriptions of homesteading life and landscape ranging from Oregon's rain forest to its alkali desert occasionally threaten to overwhelm his story and characters, Davis may be considered a frontier realist of sorts. His honest and authentic portrayal of the scene as it actually was helps to break the grip of the romantic myth on the American imagination.

THE HOOSIER SCHOOLMASTER

Type of work: Novel
Author: Edward Eggleston (1837-1902)
Type of plot: Regional romance
Time of plot: About 1850
Locale: Indiana
First published: 1871

A regional study, this book captures the twists of phrasing, the rough frontier conduct, and the morality of its country characters. With great charm and detail, the author faithfully reconstructs a picture of Indiana in mid-nineteenth century.

As one of America's early literary realists, Edward Eggleston was part of a movement to counter the excesses of bucolic romanticism with "truth-telling" about the bleakness of agrarian life, the bitter—and often petty—rivalries of small-town life, and the very real hatreds and resentments of class conflicts. Influenced by the French critic Hippolyte Adolphe Taine, Eggleston—like such contemporaries as Hamlin Garland and William Dean Howells—followed the dictum, "he writes best who writes about what he knows best." Thus, in *The Hoosier Schoolmaster,* Eggleston based his novel upon the experiences—with which he was intimately familiar—of his brother George, a teacher in his early years and later a noted journalist, biographer, historian, and novelist in his own right. Edward Eggleston also made a special effort, in all of his work, to capture accurately and reflect the peculiar speech and behavior patterns of the people he depicted.

A direct offshoot of this particular version of realism was Eggleston's regionalism, for in writing of what he knew best, he wrote of his native Indiana whose residents were called Hoosiers. The Hoosiers who people the novel are dour, small-town folk preoccupied with the façade of respectability. Accordingly, since pauperism is construed as a major social transgression, Pete Jones's attempt to have the Pearsons declared indigent so that Shocky Thompson could be indentured is a deliberate expression of the region's value system, as is Matilda White's refusal of shelter to Shocky's "pauperized" mother who is subsequently aided by Nancy Sawyer and other members of Miss Sawyer's church.

But Eggleston softened the rigid mores of the region with his own uncompromising morality. Tempered by his ministerial experience and his Christian commitment, Eggleston gave high priority to the didactic value of his work. Swift and sure justice was thus meted out to malefactors according to the severity of their offenses. The repentant Walter Johnson was therefore spared punishment; the guilty Jones brothers were sentenced to prison, and the nonparticipating mastermind of the robbery scheme, Dr. Small, was hanged. The implacable vengeance of a wrathful Christian God was accomplished.

One need not accept or reject the demanding moral code of Eggleston or of the characters he so vividly portrayed. It is sufficient to recognize the existential mode of life which Eggleston filtered through his own sensibility in *The Hoosier Schoolmaster,* for that lifestyle was a distinct reality as the author related it. As such, the novel contributes both to our knowledge and to the author's goal of contributing to the history of civilization in America.

HORACE

Type of work: Drama
Author: Pierre Corneille (1606-1684)
Type of plot: Neo-classical tragedy
Time of plot: Remote antiquity
Locale: Rome
First presented: 1640

Corneille turned to Livy for his plot in this tightly constructed play, in which the classical unities of time, place, and action are rigorously followed. The story tells of the arranged combat in which Horace and his two brothers, representing Rome, oppose Curiace and his two brothers, who represent Alba. The theme of patriotism or love for one's country as opposed to private love for an individual is explored through the complication of Horace's sister Camille's love for her betrothed, Curiace.

Horace is typical of Corneille's tragedies in that the tragic hero is caught in a dilemma. He must make a choice, in this case between the exigencies of patriotism and those of familial affection. In this respect, the play belongs to a long classical tradition, exemplified by Sophocles' *Antigone*.

In its construction *Horace* adheres to the dramatic principles generally followed by Corneille and his great younger contemporary, Racine. The plot develops rapidly, with considerable emphasis on suspense. After a brief expository opening, setting the stage for the war between Rome and Alba, there is an initial surprise, or *coup de théâtre*: the war will be averted (in reality, the outcome will be decided by three warriors on each side). Then comes the crisis: the three Horace and the three Curiace brothers have been chosen to represent their respective states. The first news of the struggle indicates that the Curiace brothers have triumphed. Then the truth, the second *coup de théâtre,* is revealed: Horace ran momentarily, merely as a ruse to enable him to eliminate the Curiace brothers one at a time. The struggle is resolved, in favor of Rome. A second crisis now arises, for which Corneille was much criticized by his contemporaries because he appeared to violate the law of the unity of action. Horace's sister Camille bitterly condemns the harsh Roman ethic that has caused her the loss of Curiace. The third surprise is, of course, Horace's unexpected murder of Camille.

Horace is a singularly unattractive hero. One can hardly sympathize with his single-minded approach to glory, ignoring all human sentiment. A hero who murders his own sister inevitably strikes the spectator, or reader, as an impossible extremist. It is difficult to see, at least at first glance, how Horace can qualify as an acceptable tragic hero who inspires any feelings other than disgust.

The circumstances of his struggle with the Curiaces hardly make him hesitate a moment. He never expresses any sense of revulsion at the task facing him, as does Curiace. We can assume that Horace is probably capable of normal human feelings, though he quickly suppresses them in favor of his patriotic proclivities. Lacy Lockert agrees that the conflict in the soul of Horace is not expressed in words; he suggests that it can be revealed by the actor who plays the rôle. This is undoubtedly the locus of difficulty in accepting *Horace* as tragedy: the tragic hero evinces a distressingly low degree of capacity for suffering. Most critics who have written on the nature of tragedy would agree with Cleanth Brooks' assertion that tragedy deals "with the meaning of suffering," and that in no tragedy "does the hero merely passively endure."

About all that can be said in defense of Horace is that after his orgy of blood-letting he seems to be momentarily pervaded by a feeling of despair. To the accusations of Valère, a disappointed suitor of Camille, he responds by agreeing that he deserves death. But it soon turns out that the real reason behind Horace's desire for death is that he feels that anything he does henceforth is bound to be anti-climactic. He has attained the apogee of glory, from which the only path open to him leads downhill, to mediocrity.

Out of frustration with Horace, one is almost tempted to seek the real tragic hero elsewhere. Curiace, for instance, suffers deeply because of the dilemma in which he is caught. Out of the wide range of attitudes toward duty explored in the play, his is the most human. But he is not the active character that Horace is. He does nothing to shape his destiny.

Besides Horace, the only character whose rôle is active is Camille. She resembles the heroines of Racine in that her inability to control her passion results in her destruction. As far as her rôle goes, she is tragic, though she cannot be considered the central character. In reality, the situation in *Horace* is such that everyone's rôle is essentially tragic, since everyone is inextricably caught in a wave of conflicting emotions.

There is, however, no escaping the conclusion that Horace is the central character and that, if this play is tragic, Horace must be considered a tragic hero, in spite of his apparent insensibility. Lockert's view that Horace must force himself to be inhuman can be most helpful here. He says that Horace has had to do violence to his gentler feelings, and as a result he cannot permit any doubt that he is right. Hence the appearance of insensibility. The very fact that he must rationalize his position to himself makes him highly vulnerable to any allegation that his ideal is unworthy. When Camille attacks his patriotism, he reacts violently as a man who will stop at nothing in order to prevent his painfully acquired position from being destroyed.

Horace can be compared to Lady Macbeth, who calls upon the spirits of night to dry up her human feelings, thus revealing that the heartlessness she later displays is not natural to her. This is made manifest in her sleepwalking scene, in which we see the terrible guilt that weighs on her conscience. Of course, it was not Corneille's intention to show such a development in his tragic hero, nor could he have done so in the limits prescribed by the unities, especially of time. Nevertheless, the last scene does present a rather apathetic Horace, disillusioned and doomed to an existence devoted primarily to justifying, at least to himself, what he did.

Robert Eisner

THE HORSE'S MOUTH

Type of work: Novel
Author: Joyce Cary (1888-1957)
Type of plot: Picaresque romance
Time of plot: The 1930's
Locale: London
First published: 1944

One of several novels depicting the life and times of Gulley Jimson, artist and social rebel, The Horse's Mouth *is a delightful combination of humor, pathos, and down-to-earth philosophy. It is a familiar picaresque romance brought up to date and enlivened by the supple, witty qualities of Cary's style.*

The Horse's Mouth is the third novel in a trilogy published in the early 1940's (the other titles are *Herself Surprised* and *To Be a Pilgrim*). Each novel may be read by itself with satisfaction, but for greatest enjoyment and understanding the trilogy should be experienced as a unit. In the trilogy each novel is given over to a single character who tells his or her story. These novels establish Cary as a keen observer and a mimic. Gulley Jimson, the hero of *The Horse's Mouth,* stands in conflict with Tom Wilcher, the conservative lawyer and landholder in *To Be a Pilgrim,* with Sara Monday (*Herself Surprised*) mediating between them.

When Cary was a young man, newly graduated from the university, he went to Paris to study art and to perfect his skills as a painter. He continued to draw and paint all his life. His treatment of Gulley Jimson as a painter was thus written from "inside." Many consider *The Horse's Mouth* to be the finest novel about painting and the painter's way of seeing.

In contrast to the traditionalist Wilcher, Jimson is constantly looking for new ways of expression. As an experimentalist he is committed to rejecting the old forms. His early work may hang in the best museums and be worth a great amount of money to collectors such as Hickson, but it is meaningless to Jimson. He confronts the present like an innocent; no past solutions are of any use. His big work on the Creation, which seems so intractable and frustrating (partially because he is too poor to buy proper working materials), is an image of his own creative situation; it is full of the potential risks and problems incurred by any free, creative effort. Gulley Jimson is like the experimental, original writer and artist William Blake, whose poem "The Mental Traveller" is used as a kind of running commentary throughout the novel. In all of Cary's fiction, Jimson is the hero who most meets the demands of Cary's free, creative world.

HORSESHOE ROBINSON

Type of work: Novel
Author: John P. Kennedy (1795-1870)
Type of plot: Historical romance
Time of plot: 1780
Locale: The Carolinas
First published: 1835

Both a love story and a war story, Horseshoe Robinson *offers a good narrative description of the effect of the American Revolution on the people of the Carolinas without stooping to flag-waving sentimentality. The confusion of divided loyalties between England and the Colonies is well portrayed.*

John Pendleton Kennedy is principally remembered as a patron of Edgar Allan Poe and for two of his own books—*Swallow Barn* (1832), a loosely linked series of sketches of plantation life in Virginia written in the manner of Washington Irving's *Bracebridge Hall*; and *Horseshoe Robinson: A Tale of the Tory Ascendency,* with a plot reminiscent of James Fenimore Cooper's *The Spy* and a hero who resembles Cooper's Leatherstocking.

Just as Cooper had built *The Spy* upon the theme of divided loyalties of the Tories and the American rebels in New York during the Revolution, so Kennedy pictures a division of loyalties in the Carolinas at a time when any stranger one met might be either a friend or an enemy. Kennedy is unoriginal in his plot development, using both characters and incidents that seem to have been borrowed from Cooper. Major Butler and Mildred Lindsay are conventional romantic lovers such as may be found in many earlier English and American novels. Also as in Cooper's frontier romances, the lower-class characters are more appealing than the genteel upper-class ones.

Horseshoe Robinson has survived mainly because of Horseshoe himself—Kennedy said he modeled him upon a real Galbraith Robinson—and though the modern reader may object to the slow pace and the contrived plot of the novel, he can still enjoy, as did Kennedy's contemporaries, the character of the stalwart soldier whose good heart and stout body were dedicated to the service of the Revolution and the safety of his friends. In addition, the novel offers, to some readers at least, the pleasure of relishing Kennedy's polished narrative and descriptive style marked by touches of genial humor, directed sometimes at Horseshoe himself. William Gilmore Simms, a South Carolina author of later historical romances, complained in 1852 about faults in Kennedy's dialect, history, and geography; but Kennedy has otherwise been praised for the accuracy of his period detail in this, the first novel which dealt with the Revolution in the South.

THE HOUSE BY THE CHURCHYARD

Type of work: Novel
Author: Joseph Sheridan Le Fanu (1814-1873)
Type of plot: Mystery romance
Time of plot: Late eighteenth century
Locale: Chapelizod, a suburb of Dublin
First published: 1863

Often regarded as the author's masterpiece, this tale is rich in atmosphere and suspense, although it possesses more humor than many of his other stories. Death, mystery, and the supernatural pervade the book.

Although Joseph Sheridan Le Fanu is best remembered as a master of the psychological horror story, his first literary efforts were in the field of the Irish historical romance. However, since these early works were ignored by critics and readers, Le Fanu abandoned the novel in favor of editing and short fiction. It was not until after the death of his wife in 1858 and the long seclusion which followed that he returned to long fiction and produced the major novels of his last years, the first of which was *The House by the Churchyard.* The major topics of the work, violent murder and retribution, are characteristic of his late novels, but the novel also reflects Le Fanu's earlier interest in historical and social subjects and thus serves as a transition book between the two phases of his career.

The setting of the novel, the Dublin suburb of Chapelizod, was an area Le Fanu knew personally and affectionately from his own youth. He clearly demonstrates this intimacy in the way he captures the atmosphere and character of small town Irish life in the late eighteenth century with considerable warmth and humor. Some critics have faulted the novel as too diffuse and fragmentary, but, in fact, Le Fanu carefully balances the activities of the various social and economic groups as he gradually brings the different plot lines together. The "serious" courtship of Mr. Mervyn and Gertrude Chattesworth and the "doomed" love between Captain "Gipsy" Devereux and the Rector's daughter, Lilias Walsingham, are carefully juxtaposed against the farcical romantic entanglements of the clownish members of the Royal Irish Artillery and their equally comic lady friends. Even the primary villainy, Paul Dangerfield's murder of Dr. Sturk, is set opposite Mary Matchwell's absurd attempt to defraud Charles Nutter's widow of her inheritance. It is this balance between the comic and the horrific, coupled with Le Fanu's acute social observations, that gives *The House by the Churchyard* its unique place in the Le Fanu canon.

All of this is not to minimize the "sensation" element in the novel, only to put it into proportion. Murder and violence do dominate the second half of the book, although the comic is never completely subdued. But after Sturk's beating there is a definite acceleration in the pace and intensification of the suspense. While the focus of the novel is constantly shifting in the early sections of the book, the action in the latter half concentrates on a few characters and their activities, notably Mervyn's efforts to vindicate his father's name, Zekiel Irons' sinister partial confession and bizarre actions, Paul Dangerfield's ambiguous machinations, and, most vivid of all, the mute, zombie-like victim, Barnabas Sturk.

Since Sturk alone can unravel the mystery, the question of his recovery, or at least his speaking, comes to dominate the novel. The climax of the book is the "trepanning" scene which gives Sturk the strength and stimulus to expose Dangerfield ("trepanning" is the archaic medical practice of drilling a small hole in the skull to "relieve pressure"). As mystery writer and historian Dorothy Sayers has rightly stated: "For sheer grimness and power, there is little in the literature of horror to compare with the trepanning scene in Le Fanu's *House by the Churchyard*. . . . That chapter itself would entitle Le Fanu to be called a master of murder and horror."

And once the aristocratic Paul Dangerfield is revealed to be the nefarious Charles Archer, he assumes a kind of evil grandeur that makes him almost the equal of Le Fanu's arch Gothic villain, Silas Ruthyn. Trapped and condemned, Dangerfield-Archer confesses and rationalizes his crime with a cool, stylish audacity that places him in the best tradition of the Gothic hero-villain. "I assure you," he tells Mervyn, "I never yet bore any man the least ill-will. I've had to remove two or three—not because I hated them—I did not care a button for any—but because their existence was incompatible with my safety which, Sir, is the first thing to me, as yours is to you." And then he casually commits suicide.

All things considered, although *The House by the Churchyard* may not possess the sustained, mounting terror and the continuing dramatic intensity of Le Fanu's Gothic masterpiece *Uncle Silas,* it has a breadth, scope, humor, and social realism that the later novel lacks. For this reason, in spite of the greater popularity of *Uncle Silas,* many critics and readers consider *The House by the Churchyard* to be the crowning achievement of Le Fanu's career.

THE HOUSE BY THE MEDLAR TREE

Type of work: Novel
Author: Giovanni Verga (1840-1922)
Type of plot: Impressionistic realism
Time of plot: Mid-nineteenth century
Locale: Sicily
First published: 1881

This novel, also translated under the title The Malavoglia, *is an example of modern Italian realism, dealing with poor, simple people who never rest from their struggle to stay alive. The novel bridges the gap between realism and naturalism.*

The House by the Medlar Tree was designed by Giovanni Verga to be the first of five novels dealing, each in its turn, with the economic, social, and ethical aspirations of the five principal social classes in nineteenth century Italy. It is generally agreed that Verga drew the inspiration for this literary structure from the cyclical works of Balzac and Zola. Only two of Verga's five novels were finished: *The House by the Medlar Tree* and *Maestro-don Gesualdo*. The former is striking for its choral presentation of human relationships, its success in achieving a poetic, eternalizing tone to realistic investigation, and its astounding objectivity. The latter makes near-perfect use of classical novel structure by depicting in a linear manner the inner life of one man through his outward existence. It is common to assume that Italian Realism dealt almost exclusively with the so-called "primitive" classes, wherein, theoretically, the essential nature of man, neither hidden nor distorted by refinement, most clearly manifested itself. The five-volume *I Vinti* ("The Conquered") was, however, to address itself as a realistic study to all of society; and *The House by the Medlar Tree,* while complete in itself, must also be considered as but one level of interest in Verga's vast design.

Notwithstanding the author's objectivity, the central theme common to this design is that a man, no matter what his discomforts and tragedies, is ultimately better off in the position in which he is born. Portrayal of a static world is hardly the result. Verga's characters fight desperately and in infinitely different ways against the cruelty of this state. Nor does Verga pronounce judgment upon their reactions—the heroic, the pathetic, and the cruel are alike portrayed realistically.

The mainstream of criticism on *The House by the Medlar Tree* views the disintegration of the Malavoglia family somewhat in the terms of Greek tragedy. The family, headed by paterfamilias Padron 'Ntoni, who unquestioningly guides their moral, social, and economic life with ancient Sicilian proverbs, begins the novel in a state of relative prosperity on all three levels. A familiar theme of Padron 'Ntoni's proverbs is that prosperity is possible only when the family works together, completely together, at all times, and does not try for more than its due share. Strangely enough, it is he who arranges to buy the black beans on credit. Although La Longa is afraid, almost the entire family is enthusiastic about the possibility of sudden profit; thus the family commits what may be considered an act of collective hubris by trying to gain what is beyond their proper realm. The ensuing shipwreck, in which Bastianazzo dies and the family is literally torn asunder, may be seen as the resultant nemesis. It is only in their working together, unquestioningly, that the family is able to survive economically and retain a portion of their former prestige and dignity in the eyes of their fellow villagers.

The struggle is long, however—too long for some of the family to bear. Young 'Ntoni is the first family member to question the struggle, and the only one to question it on a rational level. Having been conscripted, he has seen other social environments and other values while in service and soon refutes his grandfather's principle that only total loyalty will bring the meager success so long accepted in Trezza as the maximum hope. He abandons the family when they need him most in order to find his fortune in the world outside, thus proving himself unchristian in the eyes of the village and committing hubris on a personal level. When he returns home in failure, he is greeted with ridicule from Trezza and openly displays antisocial behavior.

Lia likewise commits individual hubris when she acknowledges Don Michele's attentions. Because he is of a superior class, the relationship is doomed and can only end in destroying her reputation and that of her family. Yet her desperation and her attraction to his material gifts are overwhelming. While she is rebelling on an emotional rather than a rational level, the result is the same as it was for young 'Ntoni—her own reputation is ruined, her family is dragged further down in the eyes of Trezza, and the beginning of her moral decline occurs. Thus, by a family member again acting as an individual bent on individual survival, the total family unit sinks deeper into extreme poverty.

In the end, the united efforts of the least questioning—La Longa, Mena, Luca, Alessio, and Padron 'Ntoni—reverse the trend. Yet lines of good and evil, reward and punishment, cannot be clearly drawn. La Longa has died from suffering and exhaustion as wife and mother. Gentle and virtuous Mena cannot marry because of her sister's reputation. Luca has been drafted and killed in a war no one in the village really knows about. Padron 'Ntoni has had to be sent to the poorhouse in his last illness. Alessio has inherited the family's somewhat reversed fortunes. And young 'Ntoni, after serving a prison term, has set out for the world again, partly because of village ostracism and partly because he is determined again not to be strangled by life. There is no comment by Verga on his rightness or wrongness, or his chances of failure or success.

In 1881 the author wrote:

> This account [*The House by the Medlar Tree*] is the sincere and impartial study of how most probably the first inquietudes for well-being must be

> born and develop in the humblest of conditions; and what confusion and disturbance the ill-defined desire for the unknown and the realization that one is not well-off, or could at least be better off, must bring into a family which has lived until now in a relatively happy state.

Interpretation and conclusion are the right of the reader; but, in *The House by the Medlar Tree,* Giovanni Verga's contrary purpose of almost scientific objectivity as an author must be kept continuously in mind.

Roberta Payne

THE HOUSE IN PARIS

Type of work: Novel
Author: Elizabeth Bowen (1899-1973)
Type of plot: Psychological realism
Time of plot: After World War I
Locale: France and England
First published: 1936

Perhaps Elizabeth Bowen's greatest achievement, The House in Paris *unfolds with subtlety and precision the complex relationships of a group of individuals hemmed in by circumstances and their own fears. With brilliant style and penetration, the author peels aside the layers of half-truths and lies that confine the innocent and not-so-innocent.*

Unwed mother and illegitimate child—Elizabeth Bowen uses these traditional social pariahs to express her perennial concern for the value of the child's perspective concerning adult society, the changing role of woman, and the importance of accepting the past.

Even though Henrietta and Leopold seem so at first, the children are not the most important characters in *The House in Paris.* Bowen is capable not only of detailing the consciousnesses of children but of using the child's perspective in her portrayal of adults. Bowen's real concern is with adults, but she is very much aware of the connection of adult reality to the child's world. The structure of *The House in Paris* clearly suggests both the connection between the two realities as well as the absolute gulf separating them. The first and last sections of the book, both headed "The Present," frame the longer middle section, "The Past." The consciousnesses of Henrietta and Leopold dominate "the Present," while those of their parents' generation dominate "The Past." A character like Naomi Fisher, who appears in both parts, is very different when viewed by a nine-year-old child as "Miss Fisher" and when viewed by a contemporary as "Naomi."

A child's loneliness is often Bowen's metaphor for that human loneliness brought about by fate or misfortune. Thus Leopold—abandoned as an infant by his mother, his father dead—sees himself as utterly alone and bereft of identity. He is, therefore, a stranger to the values of his biological family and the community of the "house in Paris." At nine years he expects to be "initiated" into those mysteries, accepted by his mother, and made a part of the community. But instead he must cope with his mother's rejection; he weeps because this is the end of his hopes and plans. Much of the material devoted to Leopold is narrated through the consciousness of the second child, Henrietta. Henrietta's perception of her contemporary helps to balance Leopold's solipsistic self-analysis.

Bowen often uses the discrepancy between women's changing aspirations and the traditional roles assigned by society as metaphor for the disintegration of society as a whole. Karen is ambivalent about the roles of wife and mother. Maturing in an upper-class environment free of anxieties about family or money, she still feels unfulfilled. Even after she becomes engaged to the man she is expected to marry, she keeps asking, "What next? What next?" She wants to escape from the too-secure future which is held out to her, and she complains bitterly to her Aunt Violet that she will be too "safe" with Ray as a husband. Karen thus rebels, taking her best friend's fiancé as lover and cancelling her own engagement. Ironically, Karen had regretted that no one would ever know of her action. She believes that her "revolution" has changed nothing. But consequences do occur: Max and Karen fall in love and want to marry; Karen is pregnant; Max commits suicide when he learns that Madame Fisher had planned for him to break with Naomi, so his rebellion was useless.

Karen gives up Leopold for adoption, but cannot rid herself of ambivalent feelings toward her son and her past. She makes an attempt to see him again—thus the day at the house in Paris. But although she desperately desires this union of her past with Leopold's present to make a new future, she lacks the courage to take the final step.

The House in Paris uses structure, symbol, and plot to achieve a clear statement about the value and organic character of the past. In the book's structure, "the Past" is bounded by "the Present," showing the essential interpenetration of the two. Leopold personifies the past's ongoing character; in him are embodied Madame Fisher and Naomi, Karen, Ray, Max. The house itself is a symbol of the past's inserting itself into the present: the events of the present were begun on their inexorable course by the meeting of the characters in the house when Karen was a schoolgirl.

In her use of enclosed spaces to give meaning to her characters, Bowen reminds one of Jane Austen and George Eliot. Not only in "the house in Paris," but at 2 Windsor Terrace in *The Death of the Heart* (1938), in Stella's apartment and at Mount Morris in *The Heat of the Day* (1949), and in her early works *The Hotel* (1927) and *The Last September* (1929), Bowen places her female and adolescent characters within architectural structures. Rooms, houses, apartments, mansions—these are the spaces where the drama of female lives takes place. Employing little natural description, Bowen fills her works with depictions of interiors.

Here, of course, the house is Madame Fisher's. She is the strongest personality in the book, and both Karen and Max come to realize that if they fail to assert their wills, she will dominate them. Ray also senses this, and takes the courageous step Karen could not: he decides to accept Leopold (and Karen's past). Ray's gesture is not totally romantic; he understands the difficulties involved. But that Karen can reintegrate past and present and break through to the future may now be hoped for. Unwed mother and illegitimate son have been accepted and taken into society; but will that society really change now that the "revolution" has taken place? Or will Karen still be wondering, "What next? What next?" Bowen is not too hopeful here; all that can be said is that a beginning, an attempt at reintegration, has been made.

Margaret McFadden-Gerber

THE HOUSE OF ATREUS

Type of work: Drama
Author: Aeschylus (525-456 B.C.)
Type of plot: Classical tragedy
Time of plot: After the fall of Troy
Locale: Argos
First presented: 458 B.C.

Aeschylus won first prize with this trilogy about the doomed descendants of the cruel and bloody Atreus. The atmosphere of the play is one of doom and revenge, as the playwright delves into the philosophical issue of the problem of evil and human suffering.

The House of Atreus (also known as the *Oresteia*) won first prize in the Athenian drama competition when it was initially presented in 458 B.C. This was the thirteenth time Aeschylus had been awarded the highest honors in a career of forty-one years as a tragedian. No one had done as much to establish the drama as a soaring art form capable of exploring the most compelling problems of human existence. And this dramatic trilogy—the only one in Greek drama to survive intact—was a fitting climax to his life. *The House of Atreus* is not merely a magnificent work, it is one of the supreme achievements of classical culture.

In it Aeschylus took up the theme of the ancestral curse, as he had done in *Seven Against Thebes*. But here he uses that theme to probe the metaphysical problem of evil. The question amounts to this: in a divinely ordered universe why are atrocities committed, and what is the reason for human suffering? Aeschylus brought all of his dramatic skill, all of his lofty genius for poetry, and all of his intelligence and feeling to bear on the issue. And he came as close as any writer ever has to expressing the profoundest truths of human life.

The legend of the dynasty of Atreus is a series of crimes, each committed in retaliation against a close relative. The murder of kin was the most hideous sin a person could perform, according to Greek morality. The blood curse was brought on the house of Atreus when Atreus murdered his nephews, and from there on the history of the family is one of slaughter. *Agamemnon,* the first play in the trilogy, reveals the homecoming and murder of Agamemnon by his wife Clytemnestra and his cousin Aegisthus, who is also her lover. The second play, *The Libation-Bearers,* shows Orestes' arrival in Argos and his revenge upon his mother and Aegisthus for killing Agamemnon. Then he is pursued by the Furies. And in the final play, *The Eumenides* (or "The Kindly Ones"), the curse is put to rest when Orestes is absolved from guilt in the Athenian law court of Athena.

The action of this trilogy is simple enough, but it is in the way Aeschylus develops the action, with layer upon layer of meaning, that these dramas engross us. The curse theme operates on several planes at once, and it is given concrete expression in the recurring images of the web, the net, the coiling snake full of venom.

On the simplest level *The House of Atreus* is a revenge trilogy. Agamemnon kills his daughter Iphigenia, which enables him to make war on Troy. When he returns Clytemnestra kills him in retaliation, aided by Aegisthus, who wants to avenge his father, Thyestes. Then Orestes slays the two of them to avenge Agamemnon, for which the Furies persecute him. Conceivably this chain of butchery could continue forever, if it were not for the intervention of the gods.

Yet on the personal plane crime begets crime not because of any abstract law, but because human motives require it. Aeschylus' characters have freedom of choice, and must take full responsibility for what they do. However, their personalities are such that their deeds seem inevitable. On this level character is fate and impels acts of violence. So Agamemnon brings Troy to rubble because family honor and his own pride demand it. But in the process he kills his daughter and nearly wipes out all the youth of Greece. The tragedy of the Trojan War is repeatedly emphasized, and Agamemnon is in large measure responsible for that waste of life. He is rather a monster, grown fat and arrogant in his power.

Clytemnestra is equally prideful. Her vanity is injured when Agamemnon brings his mistress, Cassandra, home. And out of personal honor she avenges Iphigenia. Also, she is tied by sex to Aegisthus, a demagogue who turns tyrant.

Here another level of meaning becomes visible—that of political intrigue and the lust for power. Agamemnon is king. With him out of the way Clytemnestra and Aegisthus become co-rulers of Argos. And we must not forget that Agamemnon went to Troy fully aware of the wealth and fame in store for him. But Orestes knows, as well, that Argos will fall to him when he kills his mother and her lover. Every act of vengeance in these plays carries some motive of gain.

We see the inevitable sequence of events. Power or the drive for power breeds insolence and crime, which brings retribution. But Orestes breaks this chain. Why? Because he was encouraged to the crime by Apollo; because he feels pain and remorse afterward; because he does not take over Argos once the crime is committed; and because the gods feel compassion for such a man, even if the Furies do not.

Now the final level of meaning emerges—the divine revelation. That this occurs in the Areopagus is Aeschylus' patriotic salute to the notion that Athenian law had supernatural sanction. God, or Fate, tempers retribution with mercy in the end. And the vengeful Furies are placated with an honorary position as tutelary goddesses. If Orestes is absolved by a sophism about paternal lineage, this merely underscores the fact that Athena and Apollo, as the agents of Zeus, have compassion for him and would use any legal pretext to get him off the hook. Man must learn by suffering, Aeschylus says, and

Orestes has shown himself to be the only character in the trilogy who is able to learn by agony. Success makes men proud and amoral, but pain teaches men the true way to live. As a vindication of divine justice *The House of Atreus* is splendid, and as a depiction of the cumulative power of evil it is unsurpassed.

James Weigel, Jr.

A HOUSE OF GENTLEFOLK

Type of work: Novel
Author: Ivan Turgenev (1818-1883)
Type of plot: Psychological realism
Time of plot: Nineteenth century
Locale: Russia
First published: 1858

One of Turgenev's simple, powerful romances, A House of Gentlefolk *exhibits a greater degree of Slavophilism than is usually found in his novels. Lavretzky and Liza stand as symbols of Russia in the heroic mold.*

The publication of *A House of Gentlefolk* established Ivan Turgenev as a great novelist, and although modern critical opinion has generally awarded *Fathers and Sons* the honor of being Turgenev's masterpiece, this earlier novel was for over half a century his most universally acclaimed work. *A House of Gentlefolk* is to be appreciated on two separate, yet interlocking and organically unified levels: the social-historical and the artistic. Although in the novel as a work of art these two aspects are inextricably fused, they may nevertheless be studied individually in order to illuminate more clearly some of the work's underlying themes and to gain deeper insight into its characters.

Any discussion of Turgenev is enriched by a basic understanding of social movements which were under way in Russia in the mid-nineteenth century. A cultural controversy had arisen during the author's lifetime centering around the question of the relative worth of foreign (that is, Western European) versus exclusively Russian ideals. The so-called "Westerners" were a group of Russians who believed in the efficacy of democracy in curing the ills of society; they repudiated Russia's autocratic government as well as her Greek Orthodox religion as outmoded and repressive institutions. They viewed their homeland as morally, intellectually, and politically primitive by comparison with countries such as England, France, and Germany, which had, either through philosophical soul-searching or actual practical experimentation, advanced toward increasingly democratic institutions.

In bitter opposition to the Westerners there grew up a group known as the Slavophiles, composed of many of Russia's finest poets and novelists and the most gifted philosophers and scholars. These men viewed Western European culture as decadent, corrupt, morally rotten; they looked to a new and pure Slavonic race, headed by Russia, to rejuvenate Western philosophy. In their enthusiasm over Slavonic culture, the early Slavophiles often lived among the Russian peasant population studying their way of life, their art and music, their social customs and legal arrangements. Yet ironically, rather than leading to the seemingly obvious conclusion of condemning the tyranny under which the bulk of the Russian population suffered, their near-worship of all things Slavonic led them instead to deny the obvious and condone autocracy and Orthodoxy simply because the masses accepted them unquestioningly.

Although Turgenev is classified as a Westerner in terms of this debate, such narrow categorizing is misleading in that it does not account for his uniquely clear thinking on the issue. With his usual brilliant insight and objectivity, he saw the pitfalls of either camp and avoided the excesses of both; a lover of the people, he was a passionate believer in democracy like the Westerners, but he understood from his heart the deep and powerful force beneath the Slavophile argument. Nowhere is Turgenev's lucidity and freedom of spirit more evident than in *A House of Gentlefolk,* where, in the character of Lavretzky, he has embodied all the emotional and psychological richness of Slavophilism with none of its rigidness or excess. In a lengthy digression about Lavretzky's lineage before he makes his appearance in the novel, the author is careful to stress his hero's dual background: his mother was a peasant, while his father belonged to the landed aristocracy and had become totally cut off from his people because of his extended residence in Europe. Lavretzky himself enters the story just returned from a stay in Paris with his shallow and unfaithful wife, Varvara, which has ended in their separation; he is coming home to his neglected ancestral estate in order to reestablish closeness to the land. In the sole political scene in the novel, it is Lavretsky who eloquently summarizes Slavophile doctrine, insisting that the essential life and spirit of Russia resides in the common folk; he completely annihilates the feeble platitudes of the unhealthy, superficial, and egotistical bureaucrat, Panshin. It is crucially important, however, that Lavretzky, unlike his real-life counterparts, is a democratic revolutionary spirit in the truest sense of the word, as witnessed in his freedom and individuality, in his abiding love for the land and its people.

The woman who grows to love and be loved by Lavretzky is Liza, the heroine of *A House of Gentlefolk*. Turgenev has endowed her character with all the attributes shared by generations of Russian women and thus given her a timeless and universal quality. Liza's personality, since it represents the spirit which is at the heart of the novel, is of central importance. She is a religious girl, beautiful in her moral strength and purity rather than physical attractiveness, impressive in her calm passivity, her endurance, and her single-minded devotion. She is never revealed directly to the reader by the author, but rather develops as a character through her reflection in the people around her; we learn the most about Liza through the eyes and heart of Lavretzky, but in the last analysis she remains an elusive, if entrancing, figure.

Artistically, *A House of Gentlefolk* is more like an extended short story than a novel. Its plot is slight: in a time span of only two months (not counting the brief epilogue), Lavretzky returns home and falls in love with Liza; his wife returns after she was believed dead; Liza enters a convent and

Lavretzky goes to his estate brokenhearted. The central theme is embodied in the love story, around which all the elements in the novel center; setting, atmosphere, and minor characterizations all combine to produce the single effect of the love sequence. This powerful singleness of effect gives the novel an incredible cohesiveness and perfection of structure.

This cohesiveness is perhaps best seen in Turgenev's evocation of a summer atmosphere which coincides throughout the story with the emotions of the hero and heroine; the spirit of summer pervades the scene of Liza meeting Lavretzky in the garden, for example, imbuing the passage with a lyrical beauty unsurpassed in fiction. Likewise, the minor personages in the story, while they are among Turgenev's most brilliant sketches of character, nevertheless owe their foremost importance to their relationship to either the hero or the heroine. The odious Panshin; the passionate old German, Lemm; Liza's mother and her crusty, wise old aunt, Marfa Timofyevna; Lavretzky's worthless and malicious wife, Varvara; all these unforgettable figures serve to reveal something about the two central characters. Along with the summer atmosphere and country landscape, of which they almost seem a part, they set the stage for the love story long before its participants make their entrance. Thus we are given detailed portraits of a collection of minor characters before we receive any more description of Liza than that she is "a slender, tall, dark-haired girl of nineteen"; and Lavretzky's belated appearance is preceded by a nine-chapter (Chapters 8-16) digression on his genealogy.

In his usual fashion, Turgenev in *A House of Gentlefolk* uses his characters' love affairs to test their strength and worth. When in the epilogue Lavretzky returns after eight years to visit the house where Liza used to live, we find that despite his shattering loss of happiness, he has not only survived but emerged from the ordeal a better and kinder man. On one level Turgenev has produced in his hero a symbol of the indomitable strength of the Russian soul; on another he has shown us the capacity inherent in all people for transcendence of pain and growth through suffering. *A House of Gentlefolk* is an elevating tale of melancholy, but not defeat; of sadness mingled with hope.

Nancy G. Ballard

THE HOUSE OF MIRTH

Type of work: Novel
Author: Edith Wharton (1862-1937)
Type of plot: Social criticism
Time of plot: Early twentieth century
Locale: New York
First published: 1905

One of Wharton's finest novels, this is the story of a girl alone trying to survive in a hypocritical and shallow society, in which a young woman's only assets are her beauty and her ability to amuse the rich who might be her protectors. The book is a devastating criticism of the emptiness and cruelty of people who calculate individual worth only in terms of dollars.

"Life is the saddest thing," Edith Wharton once wrote, "next to death." *The House of Mirth* perhaps comes as close to tragedy as any novel written in America. Neglected by a generation bored with stories of high society, *The House of Mirth* is now recognized as one of Wharton's outstanding works. One reason for this recognition is that the novel deals with more than high society. It contains the very arresting sequence in which Lily Bart works in the millinery factory. Here Wharton examines the oppression of laborers, a recurring theme in her work, although she is not so sentimental as to overlook the cruelty of those same laborers toward one another. She also explores the character of Mr. Selden, who is not a member of the upper class. But Selden and the millinery factory do not alone explain the novel's newfound appeal.

The House of Mirth is primarily about the degradation of the members of the upper class, and it is one of the most powerful novels of its kind. It illustrates, in bold and clear detail, what the members of the upper class—the "right people"—undergo to keep their places in that class: the meaningless rituals, their loveless marriages, their face-saving loans to friends. Also illustrated is the pervasive influence of the "right people" on those who do not belong, and who should be, but are not, able to see the emptiness of class values. Rosedale, an outsider because of his birth and religion, is overpowered by a need to belong. To satisfy this need, he has worked hard to acquire a fortune; to satisfy this need, he is willing to marry Lily Bart, even if he has to assume her debts.

Lily Bart is a victim of her birth into the upper class. Her artistic sensitivity might have developed into a superior talent, but has been allowed to atrophy because of her acceptance of the teaching that ladies of her class have only one destiny—to make a "good marriage." Thus educated, Lily pursues this "good marriage" in the way a businessman would pursue a good investment, passing up Rosedale in the hope that Percy Gryce might be available. Yet her good qualities get the better of her just as she has almost won Percy Gryce. To maintain her contacts and her place in society, she is obliged to play bridge and to gamble away money she does not have. She misses a second chance to marry Rosedale when the Dorsets invite her on a trip to Europe, thinking that they are thus helping out a fellow member of high society by taking her away from her troubles. The trip, however, ends in disaster, causing Lily to feud with Mrs. Dorset and ruin herself as a respectable members of the upper class. No longer eligible for protection by her social peers, or for marriage to the social-climbing Rosedale, Lily must seek a job. She goes to work in the millinery factory, and there discovers that birth and breeding do not provide one with usable skills.

Lily's ruin is partly treated as a naturalistic drama in which the victim of environment and chance is inexorably crushed. A sense of fatality hangs over the book. But throughout, most especially toward the end, the possibility of escape presents itself, in the person of Selden. At the beginning, he is willing to rescue Lily from the emptiness of being one of the "right people." At the end, he tenders an offer, subject to entirely reasonable conditions, to rescue her from poverty and uselessness. But she is essentially unable to communicate with him, despite her concern that he not be victimized by her corrupt entanglements. Such lack of communication is as much a theme of *The House of Mirth* as is criticism of high society.

Like many communicative failures in real life, that of *The House of Mirth* takes many forms. At first, it is Lily who cannot express her love for Selden because he is not one of the "right people." She offends him by offering to be his friend while continuing her mercenary search for a "good marriage." Later, it is Selden who becomes harsh toward Lily because of unfounded suspicion, although he cannot set aside his genuine feeling for her. In the end, and most pathetically, it is Lily who cannot reach out, because she feels unworthy of Selden.

Most of the action is told from Lily's viewpoint. But, at the beginning, the middle, and the end, it is the story of Selden. A sympathetic character because of the genuineness of his love and because of his freedom from the false values of high society, Selden nevertheless suffers from an inability to see things in context, and, no less than Lily, from a failure to make his true feelings known. For this, he assumes a disproportionate share of the blame for Lily's death.

The House of Mirth can be seen as either the story of Lily or the story of Selden. Lily's story is an indictment of a class, and is somewhat limited in its appeal by the subsequent changes which have occurred in our society. The American upper class is no longer as powerful or prestigious as it was in Edith Wharton's time, and its values have changed. Its members betray a certain amount of guilt because of their privileges and the interests of the quest for proper marriages has been mitigated. Even so, Lily's story is relevant so long as meaningless social rituals, class envy, and the belief that women can have only limited destinies continue.

The plight of Selden is universal. Stories of lovers who cannot express themselves are as old as literary history. But the irony and power of Selden's story lie in what the reader knows that Selden does not. Such is the technical brilliance of Wharton's use of point-of-view. The shift to Lily's consciousness for the bulk of the story enables us to know that she is not having an affair with Gus Trenor, and that her love for Selden is what restrains her from trying to ruin Mrs. Dorset. Ironically, the reader understands more than do either Lily or Selden. Edith Wharton's mastery of point of view—with the authorial voice always in command in the background—helps make the novel as powerful as it is.

Charles Johnson Taggart

THE HOUSE OF THE SEVEN GABLES

Type of work: Novel
Author: Nathaniel Hawthorne (1804-1864)
Type of plot: Psychological romance
Time of plot: 1850
Locale: Salem, Massachusetts
First published: 1851

Woven into the ingenious plot of this novel is the theme that the sins of the fathers are passed on to the children in succeeding generations. The book reflects the author's interest in New England history and his doubts about a moribund New England that looked backward to past times.

In reputation *The House of the Seven Gables* usually stands in the shadow of its predecessor, *The Scarlet Letter*. It is, however, a rich and solid achievement, a Gothic romance whose characters are among Nathaniel Hawthorne's most complex. The author himself thought it, in comparison with the earlier work, "more characteristic of my mind, and more proper and natural for me to write."

In his preface, Hawthorne explicitly states his moral: "the truth, namely that the wrong-doing of one generation lives into the successive ones, and, divesting itself of every temporary advantage, becomes a pure and uncontrollable mischief." This of course echoes the Biblical adage that "The fathers have eaten sour grapes, and the children's teeth are set on edge." Hawthorne's interest in the heritage of sin was probably whetted by the history of his own family. His first American ancestor, William Hathorne (Nathaniel himself added the *w* to the family name), was a soldier and magistrate who once had a Quaker woman publicly whipped through the streets. William's son John, having, as Nathaniel said, "inherited the persecuting spirit," was a judge at the infamous Salem witch trials, during which a defendant cursed another of the three judges with the cry, "God will give you blood to drink!" Thenceforth, as Hawthorne noted, although the family remained decent, respectable folk, their fortunes began to decline.

The fate of the Pyncheon family of the novel is considerably more dramatic. Matthew Maule's curse on Colonel Pyncheon, who has persecuted him for witchcraft and wrested from him the land on which the seven-gabled house is to be built, is precisely that which Judge John Hathorne had heard in a similar trial. It is apparently fulfilled on the day of the housewarming, when Colonel Pyncheon dies of apoplexy, the hemorrhage rising through his throat to stain his white shirt. But, Hawthorne would have us believe, such sins as Pyncheon's are not so easily paid for. The family occupies the mansion, but misfortune is their constant lot. There are repeated apoplectic deaths, sometimes heralded by an ominous gurgling in the throat; greed leads Judge Jaffrey Pyncheon, like his ancestor, to participate in a trumped-up trial, this time against his own cousin; and years of pride and isolation have thinned the family blood so that, like the scrawny chickens that peck in the Pyncheon garden, they are an unattractive, ineffectual lot. Judge Pyncheon is a monster who hides his avarice and callousness behind a façade of philanthropy and civic service. Clifford, like Hawthorne's Young Goodman Brown, is a sensitive soul who is unmanned by his confrontation with evil; after years of imprisonment he is poised on the brink of madness. Hepzibah, a spinster who has spent most of her life waiting for her brother's release, is virtually helpless either to resolve her precarious financial situation or to deal with her malevolent cousin.

Only young Phoebe possesses both goodness and energy. It is significant that she is the "country cousin" whose father married beneath his rank, and that Hepzibah observes that the girl's self-reliance must have come from her mother's blood. Thus Hawthorne casts his vote for the energizing effects of a democratic, as opposed to an aristocratic, social system; he has Holgrave, the daguerreotypist, support this view with the comment that families should continually merge into the great mass of humanity, without regard to ancestry.

The other fully vital character in the novel is Holgrave, the young daguerreotypist. He is one of Hawthorne's most charming creations: a perceptive, adventurous man who has been, it seems, almost everywhere, and done almost everything. His conversations with Phoebe reveal him as a radical who believes that the Past "lies upon the Present like a giant's dead body," preventing any generation's true fulfillment—a thesis frequently expressed by Hawthorne's contemporary, Ralph Waldo Emerson. Holgrave goes so far as to suggest that institutional buildings should "crumble to ruin once in twenty years, or thereabouts, as a hint to the people to examine into and reform the institutions which they symbolize." He is also a psychologist; his daguerreotypes, which inevitably go beyond mere pictorial likeness to expose personality, symbolize his own insight into human nature.

At the end of the novel we are led to believe that the curse is broken as Phoebe, the last of the Pyncheons, plans to marry Holgrave, who turns out to be a descendant of old Matthew Maule. The curse's effects can all be explained naturally: Holgrave observes that perhaps old Maule's prophecy was founded on knowledge that apoplectic death had been a Pyncheon trait for generations. Avarice and cruelty can certainly be passed on by example; and pride, isolation, and inbreeding can account for the "thin-bloodedness" of the once aristocratic family. Now, as Phoebe, whose blood has already been enriched by plebian stock, and Holgrave, who has escaped the stifling influence of his own declining family by traveling widely, replace a tradition of hatred with that of love, it seems plausible that the curse may indeed have run its course. Perhaps the chain of ugly events—what Chillingworth of *The Scarlet Letter* termed "dark necessity"—can be terminated by positive acts of good will.

The novel is replete with Gothic characteristics: mystery, violence, a curse, gloomy atmosphere, archaic diction, and visits from the spirit world. Yet though it is not realistic, it demonstrates what Henry James called Hawthorne's "high sense of reality," in that it reveals profound truths about how the effects of the sins of the fathers are felt by children for generations to come. The ending, however, discloses that although he recognized the deterministic effects of heredity, environment, and man's predisposition to evil, Hawthorne was essentially a hopeful man who believed that the individual does possess a residuum of will that can cope with and perhaps change "dark necessity."

Sally Buckner

THE HOUSE WITH THE GREEN SHUTTERS

Type of work: Novel
Author: George Douglas (George Douglas Brown, 1869-1902)
Type of plot: Regional realism
Time of plot: Late nineteenth century
Locale: Rural Scotland
First published: 1901

Rebelling against quaint and sentimental representations of Scotland, the author presented here a realistic picture of Scottish life in the late nineteenth century. In this fatalistic story, the scenes and atmosphere and the rough characters are presented with authority and power.

George Douglas Brown's reputation rests on this single novel, *The House with the Green Shutters.* Born at Ochiltree in Scotland, to a poor family, he managed to attend Glasgow University and Oxford, and in 1895 went to London as a freelance writer. Not until 1901 with *The House with the Green Shutters* did he win recognition. The novel was praised by Andrew Lang and was well received in England and the United States. His royalties in the summer of 1902 brought him the only financial ease he ever knew, but in August of that year he suddenly died.

This one great novel is modeled on classical Greek tragedy. It is a vivid picture of cottage life in a Scottish village, with finely drawn characters and realistic atmosphere; the peasant humor running through the book has been compared to that of Hardy. The citizens of Barbie are preoccupied with scandal when they are not grubbing for an existence. Beyond work, their concerns are narrow and petty; they are malicious, often from mere boredom. The villagers act as a Greek Chorus, standing around the square commenting on the principal characters and the life in the village. They also fill in background for the reader.

The author places a heavy emphasis upon "character." If a person is weak, he is doomed. As hubris might cause the fate of a Greek tragic hero, so stupidity or moral weakness causes the fate of these Scottish villagers. John Gourlay is proud and ambitious, eager to make a big showing; his house is a symbol for him of his place and dignity. But he is a stupid man and is easily provoked. Understanding nothing, he is able to sneer at everything. His son cannot build upon his first success at college. Young Gourlay is morally weak and lazy, and must inevitably come into conflict with his father.

The relentless realism of the narrative, detailing every grimy inch of the town and the house and mercilessly describing the characters as if they are under a microscope might be too much for some readers. (Some critics of 1901 thought the grimness of the tale overdone, while others compared its effect with that of Balzac's *Father Goriot.*) The dialect is not easy for modern readers, but it lends a richness and verisimilitude to the tale, if the reader is patient enough to stick with it. The story moves forward to its tragic conclusion sweeping the reader along. If the narrative does not quite evoke the "pity and terror" of a Greek tragedy, it does provide the reader with a rich and rewarding emotional and intellectual experience. Although the novel seems to be a "slice of life," it is a highly sophisticated and artfully structured book, ingeniously creating a calculated effect, and thus is a work of art of a very high order.

HOW GREEN WAS MY VALLEY

Type of work: Novel
Author: Richard Llewellyn (Richard D. V. Llewellyn Lloyd, 1907-)
Type of plot: Domestic realism
Time of plot Nineteenth century
Locale: Wales
First published: 1940

How Green Was My Valley *is the story of the life of a Welsh boy seen through the eyes of an old man who has only memory to sustain him. The novel was extremely popular in the years immediately following its publication, probably because its gentleness and kindly optimism provided a welcome contrast to the bitterness of the war years.*

How Green Was My Valley is part of a large body of literature which has developed in England since the end of the eighteenth century. It is a literature of nostalgia; a longing for the past where all *was* (and this is the significant word in the title of Llewellyn's novel) peaceful, ordered, and tranquil. It is associated with the literature of arcadia, possessing a pastoral quality that is inevitably contrasted to the blight of the new industrial city. Goldsmith's "The Deserted Village," bemoaning the rural life that has been destroyed, is one of the earliest and best known poems in the same tradition as *How Green Was My Valley.*

In particular, Llewellyn's novel, narrated by Huw Morgan, is a lament for a Welsh valley with all its connotations of Eden. Moreover, it is a dirge for his own childhood, secure in a large family headed by his temperate and wise father, Gwilym. The principal foe is the mine, or rather the miners who insist upon breaking down the traditional relationship of employer-employee, that of patronage, by forming a modern union. Huw's brothers, enraged by the owners' treatment of the men and their own father's abandonment of the union, leave the family, making the first crack in Huw's happiness and the first step toward the fragmentation of the family. It is, metaphorically, the beginning of the end of the valley life. From that point the modern world with its new ideas of family, work, and society continues to impinge on Huw.

When the Morgan family disintegrates either through death or immigration, Huw is left absolutely alone. What begins as a powerful celebration of a family whose members are deeply in touch with one another and the community, ends in a lament of a single voice: a pattern repeated so often in modern literature that it has become an identifying characteristic.

HOWARDS END

Type of work: Novel
Author: E. M. Forster (1879-1970)
Type of plot: Domestic realism
Time of plot: Early twentieth century
Locale: England
First published: 1910

A carefully plotted, subtle novel, Howards End *illustrates E. M. Forster's deft use of irony and genius for characterization as well as his belief in the eternal contrast between illusion and reality.*

The country house has long been an important image and symbol in English literature. From its appearance in such an early seventeenth century poem as Jonson's "To Penshurst," to its celebration by Pope in the eighteenth century, to its centrality in the nineteenth century fiction of Jane Austen, Anthony Trollope, and Henry James, to its prominence in the modern works of E. M. Forster and Evelyn Waugh, the manor house has provided not only a dramatic setting, but also an embodiment of certain social, moral, and spiritual values. Despite its various literary manifestations, the apotheosis of the country estate is in essence a reaction against the introduction of the mercantile ethic, its manifestation in the phenomenon of industrialism, and the consequent growth of large cities. It is, in brief, a nostalgic image for a way of life, based on the land, that possessed a definite social hierarchy and took its rhythms from nature. While it pays special homage to individuality, intellect, and imagination, its chief virtues are the classical ones of restraint and moderation. The country house, then, is a correlative for a human ideal which found its first flowering in the Renaissance.

Besides these attributes, the house in Forster's novel, Howards End, represents an image of cultural unity. The book's epigraph, "only connect . . . ," suggests the major theme and describes the prescription required to bring about moral health to Edwardian England. To Forster this society, on the verge of becoming completely urbanized and industrialized, is fractured, lacking order and direction. For a solution to this dilemma he looks toward the traditional values embodied in Howards End.

Three principal forces are at work in *Howards End.* The first is embodied in the Schlegel family, which stands for the past, art, imagination, and culture; second, there are the Wilcoxes, representing the present, practical intelligence, and business acumen. The third force points to the future and is found in the parvenu, Leonard Bast. The drama of the novel resides primarily in the conflict between the Schlegels and the Wilcoxes, both solid middle-class families, for the right to direct England's future—or at least to determine its dominant values. Leonard Bast, a member of the working class and always on the periphery, is seemingly lost in the shuffle. He is without manners, culture, or any business sense. Yet he aspires to the center of power, held jointly by the Schlegels and the Wilcoxes. And, after his ignominious death "resolves" the conflict between the two families, it is, ironically, his illegitimate child, conceived by Helen Schlegel in an act of moral protest against the establishment, who will inherit Howards End and—we may infer—the spoils of the battlefield, the future of England.

From the beginning it appears that these three forces have nothing in common. Margaret, Helen, and their brother celebrate the "poetic" inner self, the passion of existence, while despising the world of telegrams, profit and loss, and machines. That world, peopled and directed by their rivals, Henry Wilcox and his son, Charles, dedicates itself to practicality, to the "prose" of life, as Forster phrases it.. Although he is not fully a part of either, Leonard does have one foot in each; he is a small business clerk, yet, he ravenously and superficially fills his life with cultural items, books, concerts, and intelligent conversations.

But as the novel unfolds, the deep connections between these three forces begin to appear: in a private will Ruth Wilcox leaves Howards End to Margaret in recognition of their mutual identities and Jacky, Leonard's wife, is revealed to have been Henry's mistress. These connections are further strengthened by the real attractions that grow up among them. Initially Paul Wilcox and Helen fall in love; the engagement, however, is broken off as unseemly. Later Henry and Margaret discover in each other a passionate need—a fact apparently recognized by the late and mysterious Mrs. Wilcox—and eventually marry. And last, there is the fruitful if misdirected union of Helen and Leonard. Thus, *Howards End* describes a society which on the surface seems fractured and disjointed, but as it is gradually revealed, one which is fundamentally joined by needs and desires of love and fellowship. All that is required to cement the connection is human will and a place to validate the union.

Under the influence of Ruth Wilcox, Margaret provides the will which is constantly directed to the acquisition of Howards End, her rightful legacy. But it finally takes the tragic-comic death of Leonard at the hands of Charles Wilcox to force the principal characters into making *all* of the "connections." With Charles imprisoned and the Wilcox clan disgraced, Henry Wilcox, the practical man-of-action, is thoroughly deflated and it remains for the "poetic" Margaret to assume the leadership and direction of the family.

In the denouement Forster gathers all his principal characters at Howards End for one last conversation. The atmosphere is of peace and joy, not unlike the aftermath of a wedding in which all tensions are abated and passion, fruitfulness, and unity are celebrated. The house itself, cut off from the demands of culture and the workaday, allows its inhabitants to feel the rhythms of nature and the ties which bind them. It is autumn and around them a bountiful harvest proceeds; it is a time of expectations, further attested by the health of Helen and Leonard's child. Yet Forster is too much of a realist to conclude on a note of simple optimism. For he sees, like Helen and Margaret, that the smog of London is encroaching on the house. It is a complete moment, to be sure, but one stolen from the past. At last Forster knew that it was also the autumn of the country house as well as of the Renaissance and that it was the spring of the modern world.

David L. Kubal

HUASIPUNGO

Type of work: Novel
Author: Jorge Icaza (1906-)
Type of plot: Social criticism
Time of plot: Twentieth century
Locale: Ecuador
First published: 1934

Stark, brutal realism overlies the artistry of this novel of protest against the enslavement of the Indian in rural Ecuador. It is made up of a series of episodes whose power lies in a graphic account of the lives and trials of the Indian.

This brutal novel flows swiftly. Technically, it is one of the better Spanish-American novels. Its virtues are legion, as are its defects, and among the former are interesting dialogue, bitter irony, sardonic humor, interesting plot, effective use of detail, exposure of social injustice, and crispness of style with short sentences that get to the point. *Huasipungo* presents the Ecuadorian Andes so clearly that we see them in stark detail. Even the sounds of the sierra are heard, while the odors, temperature changes, and direction of the night wind are experienced. Nevertheless, *Huasipungo*'s crowning virtue is its defense of Ecuador's oppressed Indians. For this reason it has been considered Jorge Icaza's most significant novel, and has attained Continental prestige. It helped launch the cycle of so-called *Indianista* novels, devoted to telling the story of the long-abandoned Indians. The novel's protagonist, thus, is the Indian, who is characterized collectively but clearly, even to the peculiar flavor of his Spanish.

Decay is a prominent and depressing note in *Huasipungo;* images of garbage, filth, mold, slime, and rotten meat are frequent. Trash, dirt, and profanity are always present; everything is sloppy and unkempt, reflecting life's hopelessness. Depression is thus a constant note, accentuated by dismal mountain fogs, clammy cold, foul speech, and superstition. *Soroche* (altitude sickness) occasionally strikes, as do other afflictions. Alcoholism is the Indian's bane, for the *huasipunguero* abandons everything—chickens, corn, potatoes, children—for alcohol.

The characters of *Huasipungo* generally fail to change or develop. At the novel's end they are almost the same personalities and characters that they were at its start. The principal exception is the Indian community itself, for "from all corners of the soul, from every pore, grow the secret rebellions of a slave." Icaza also implied that the mestizo or mulatto suffers from a psychological inferiority complex in Ecuador, as is exemplified by Juana la Chola's (Juana the Half-breed) inert submission to rape by a landowner and a cleric. The latter villains, unfortunately, are crudely drawn. Don Alfonso Pereira is a second-rate Simon Legree, a consistent rascal, self-server, hypocrite, and uncomplicated brute from start to finish of the novel. He snarls, curses, and brutalizes Indians, but cringes from those above him. The priest is worse; he is so utterly depraved as to be comical. He extorts money from hungry Indians; sells passages out of purgatory or burial plots "close to Heaven" at alarming prices; builds a lucrative trucking business on ill-gotten money; and commits ridiculous rascalities too numerous to mention, including the drunken rape of Juana the Half-breed. Referred to as "the Cassocked One," the priest is a symbol of Icaza's disenchantment with religion, and it is puzzling that this "larger-than-life" caricature has not aroused disdain or even criticism from many generations of college students and professors.

Other ogres in *Huasipungo* are wealthy people, businessmen, whites, property owners, and Gringo capitalists. The Gringoes careen about in Cadillacs oblivious to Indians; they relish money and lack human feelings. It is possible that they were grotesquely overdrawn by Icaza to appeal only to readers blinded by prejudice, but it should also be recalled that the novel was intended as a tirade against the social injustice that then blighted Ecuador. Icaza possibly had the illusion that his novel would bring a better life to the Indians, but initially his work was better received and lauded abroad than it was in his own country. In any event, Icaza exposed the plight of Ecuador's peons and also the decay of the rural aristocrats, who had left the work of their fathers to live luxuriously in the city. The novel also promotes the conflict of red race against white. White aristocrats are portrayed as hard, unfeeling, and cruel. They are contemptuous of Indians and exploit the poor. Some critics feel that Icaza's work had political motivations, others compare him to John Steinbeck (*The Grapes of Wrath*) and consider him a social reformer.

No one in *Huasipungo* apparently wishes to live in the country, since life in Quito is much richer. The countryside is backward, isolated, and uncomfortable; the city is cultured and far superior. Nature is unattractive; its beauties are unmentioned and unextolled. Nature's dangers are stressed, however, such as the scene where a man dies horribly by drowning in mud. Little interest is shown in animals, birds, or plants. The novel is almost devoid of color. Tints of sunrises, sunsets, mountains, skies, fields, or towns are generally lacking, and even the grayness of the constant mountain mist is assumed rather than described. The author's treatment of color is a deliberate stylistic device to increase the feeling of dismal hopelessness.

Although of Spanish blood and comfortable background, Icaza decided as a youth to champion Ecuador's poor of all races. Having attracted international attenion, his novel *Huasipungo* eventually won acceptance in Ecuador and undoubtedly helped the Indian. It has therefore helped to implement some social reform and to attract attention to the cause of the Indian. Some of the political attention has been lip-service, but the life of Ecuador's highland Indians is today improved over that described in *Huasipungo*. Thus, like *Uncle Tom's Cabin,* Icaza's novel has, in spite of its propagandistic qualities and superficial characterization, attracted much attention through its literary readability, and has made considerable impact on Ecuador and Spanish America in general.

William Freitas

HUCKLEBERRY FINN

Type of work: Novel
Author: Mark Twain (Samuel L. Clemens, 1835-1910)
Type of plot: Humorous satire
Time of plot: Nineteenth century
Locale: Along the Mississippi River
First published: 1884

The title character of this famous novel tells his own story with straightforwardness laced with shrewd, sharp comment on human nature. The boy's adventures along the Mississippi form the framework of a series of moral lessons, revelations of a corrupt society, and contrasts of innocence and hypocrisy.

Little could Mark Twain have visualized in 1876 when he began a sequel to capitalize on the success of *Tom Sawyer* that *Huckleberry Finn* would evolve into his masterpiece and one of the most significant works in the American novel tradition. Twain's greatest contribution to the tradition occurred when, with an unerring instinct for American regional dialects, he elected to tell the story in Huck's own words. The skill with which Twain elevates the dialect of an illiterate village boy to the highest levels of poetry established the spoken American idiom as a literary language, and earned for Twain his reputation—proclaimed by Ernest Hemingway, William Faulkner and others—as the father of the modern American novel. Twain also maintains an almost perfect fidelity to Huck's point of view in order to dramatize the conflict between Huck's own innate innocence and natural goodness and the dictates of a corrupt society.

As Huck's own story, the novel centers around several major themes, including death and rebirth, freedom and bondage, the search for a father, the individual versus society, and the all-pervasive theme of brotherhood. Huck's character reflects a point in Mark Twain's development when he still believed man to be innately good, but saw social forces as corrupting influences which replaced with the dictates of a socially determined "conscience" man's intuitive sense of right and wrong. This theme is explicity dramatized through Huck's conflict with his conscience over whether or not to turn Jim in as a runaway slave. Huck, on the one hand, accepts without question what he has been taught by church and society about slavery. In his own mind, as surely as in that of his southern contemporaries, aiding an escaped slave was clearly wrong both legally and morally. Thus, Huck's battle with his conscience is a real trauma for him, and his decision to "go to Hell" rather than give Jim up is made with a certainty that such a fate awaits him for breaking one of society's laws. It is ironic, of course, that Huck's "sin" against the social establishment affirms the best that is possible to the individual.

Among the many forms of bondage, ranging from the widow's attempt to "civilize" Huck to the code of "honor" which causes Sherburn to murder Boggs and the law of the vendetta which absolutely governs the lives of the Grangerfords and Shepherdsons, that permeate the novel, slavery provides Twain his largest metaphor for both social bondage and institutionalized injustice and inhumanity. Written well after the termination of the Civil War, *Huckleberry Finn* is not an anti-slavery novel in the limited sense that *Uncle Tom's Cabin* is. Rather than simply attacking an institution already legally dead, Twain uses the idea of slavery as a metaphor for all social bondage and injustice. Thus, Jim's search for freedom, like Huck's own need to escape both the Widow and Pap Finn, is as much a metaphorical search for an ideal state of freedom as mere flight from slavery into free-state sanctuary. Thus it is largely irrelevant that Twain has Huck and Jim running deeper into the South rather than north toward free soil. Freedom exists neither in the North nor the South, but in the ideal and idyllic world of the raft and river.

The special world of raft and river is at the very heart of the novel. In contrast to the restrictive and oppressive social world of the shore, the raft is a veritable Eden where the evils of civilization are escaped. It is here that Jim and Huck can allow their natural bond of love to develop without regard for the question of race. It is here on the raft that Jim can become a surrogate father to Huck, and Huck can develop the depth of feeling for Jim which eventually leads to his decision to "go to Hell." But, while the developing relationship between Huck and Jim determines the basic shape of the novel, the river works in other structural ways as well. The picaresque form of the novel and its structural rhythm are based upon a series of episodes on shore, after each of which Huck and Jim return to the peaceful sanctuary of the raft. It is on shore that Huck encounters the worst excesses of which "the damned human race" is capable, but with each return to the raft comes a renewal of spiritual hope and idealism.

The two major thrusts of Twain's attack on the "civilized" world in *Huckleberry Finn* are against institutionalized religion and the romanticism which he believed characterized the South. The former is easily illustrated by the irony of the Widow's attempt to teach Huck religious principles while she persists in holding slaves. As with her snuff taking—which was all right because she did it herself—there seems to be no relationship between a fundamental sense of humanity and justice and her religion. Huck's practical morality makes him more "Christian" than the Widow, though he takes no interest in her lifeless principles. Southern romanticism, which Twain blamed for the fall of the South, is particularly allegorized by the sinking of the Walter Scott, but it is also inherent in such episodes as the feud where Twain shows the real horror of the sort of vendetta traditionally glamorized by romantic authors. In both cases, Twain is attacking the mindless acceptance of values which he believed kept the South in its dark ages.

Many critics have argued that the ending hopelessly flaws *Huckleberry Finn* by reducing its final quarter to literary burlesque. Others have argued that the ending is in perfect accord with Twain's themes. But all agree that, flawed or not, the substance of Twain's masterpiece transcends the limits of literary formalism to explore those eternal verities upon which great literature rests. Through the adventures of an escaped slave and a runaway boy, both representatives of the ignorant and lowly of the earth, Twain affirms for us that true humanity is of men rather than institutions, and that we can all be aristocrats in the kingdom of the heart.

William E. Grant

HUDIBRAS

Type of work: Poem
Author: Samuel Butler (1612-1680)
Type of plot: Satirical burlesque
Time of plot: 1640-1660
Locale: England
First published: 1663-1678

Butler's poem Hudibras *was intended to ridicule the Presbyterians, Dissenters, and others who had fought against the Crown in the conflict between Charles I and Oliver Cromwell. It has been called a mock epic; certainly the use of burlesque unmasks the hypocrisy and absurdity of Dissenting reformers in seventeenth century England.*

Hudibras opens with terse, end-stopped couplets that immediately impede the building of an epic narrative's flow; the impatient reader may be lost in this awkward beginning that sounds to the modern ear like a succession of commercial jingles. Butler, however, redeems himself after this perfunctory start by proving the necessity of that form in establishing a tonal solidity of ridicule toward Sir Hudibras, magically sustained throughout the long poem. About line 300, the couplets open up, assuming a near-speech rhythm in spite of the archaic diction and syntactical inversions; Butler executes this loosening and subsequent flow through frequent use of enjambment.

The paradoxical ridicule of a hero in his own epic poem is accomplished by the successful juxtapositioning of crude, occasionally vulgar language with overblown rhetoric and empty terms. Use of the latter group of words allows Butler to satirize the overly ambitious pedantry of his time; his use of the former group constitutes a strong argument for the stupidity and commonness of man. Butler's contention that moderation is the proper course unfolds as the only alternative to the ludicrous extremes. Other purposeful travesties against a "natural-ness" of language include obscure references to tax even the most resourceful historian of trivia, and heavy use of Latin words and idioms. Both allude to the many quackeries that were springing up in the guise of scientific fields, and the arbitrariness that gave these fields their minute substance. In addition, the characters' epigrammatic speech parodies the religious dogma responsible for the bitter conflict that Butler found so deplorable.

One should note the interesting and unorthodox invocation of the Muse that suggests the unheroic doings through which Fate will drag the knight and his squire. In the same passage (little escaping the satirical sweep), Butler even takes a swipe at the art of writing itself.

HUGH WYNNE, FREE QUAKER

Type of work: Novel
Author: Silas Weir Mitchell (1829-1914)
Type of plot: Historical romance
Time of plot: 1753-1783
Locale: Colonial America
First published: 1897

One of the best novels of the American Revolution, this book is also a touching revelation of a child-parent relationship and of the consequences of too much doctrinal discipline.

Written more than a hundred years after the Revolution, Mitchell's historical romance recaptures the tone as well as the letter of the Philadelphia scene before and during the struggle with Great Britain. Tolstoy recreated the time of the Napoleonic invasion of Russia and its effects on the aristocracy with brilliantly conceived characterizations and dramatized historical events. Mitchell's method is modest by comparison, and if not as effective as Tolstoy's, is curiously satisfying in its own right.

What Mitchell does is play memoirist. His main character, Hugh Wynne, begins by apologizing for "having no gift in the way of composition" and a distaste for fiction. By chance, his friend Jack Warder, a major character in the novel, bequeathes Hugh his diary which is as fulsome and sensitive as Hugh is forgetful and unliterary. This "convenient" bequest does not seem contrived because it is a reflection in point of view of one of the novel's central themes: Warder's protection, through thought and deed, of his less perceptive friend.

The memoir style is very well done: cooly observant, precise in detail and limpidly clear throughout. The eighteenth century elegance of the tone forms a poignant counterpoint to the emotional turmoil of the irrational relationship between father and son, Hugh and John Wynne. The portrait of Washington is meticulously historical, but the vindictiveness with which Mitchell attacks the zeal of conservative Quakerism mars his pretension of complete historical objectivity. The characters are largely wooden, and motivation is mechanical rather than psychological; Darthea's love is a thing difficult to believe in. Perhaps spirited Gainor Wynne, with her Whig independence and brashly lovable integrity, is the novel's best creation: "The good old lady was lamenting her scanty toilet, and the dirt in which the Hessians had left her house. 'I have drunk no tea since Lexington,' she said, 'and I have bought no gowns. My gowns, sir, are on the backs of our poor soldiers.' "

THE HUMAN COMEDY

Type of work: Novel
Author: William Saroyan (1908-)
Type of plot: Sentimental romance
Time of plot: Twentieth century
Locale: Ithaca, California
First published: 1943

The story of a family which loses a son in the war, this frankly sentimental novel has for its theme the idea that no human can ever die as long as he lives in the hearts of those who loved him.

In *The Human Comedy* William Saroyan details the life of a small town during World War II. The book is full of vignettes which recall such homey matters as Homer buying the day-old pies; Ulysses waving to the train; and Ma Macauley comforting her working son with late night conversations. There is, then, a noticeable mixture of childlike innocence and adult homily in Saroyan's book. The world is seen through the eyes of children, and yet we are always aware of the author whose presence adds complexity to the experience just as we are always aware of the fact of war. While the ordinary problems of human existence, such as school rivalries, adolescent love, and the first experience of evil, are being dealt with by the Widow Macauley and her children, the larger world drives toward cataclysm and challenges the pieties and conventions of innocent, rural America. To be sure Ithaca, an ancient symbol of home itself, comes no closer to actual hostilities than its Greek namesake came to the battlements of Troy. But the arrival and departure of the daily train and the ominous click of the telegraph bring the outside world very close to Ithaca's consciousness.

Saroyan's conclusion is positive if it is melodramatic and sentimental. While Homer is conveying the message of Marcus' death in battle to his family, pensation, Katey Macauley finds comfort, sustenance, and belief in the continuity of human experience. By the title of the novel itself, Saroyan seems to suggest that all tragedy, finally viewed from a wide enough perspective, dissolves into a comedy of joy and affirmation. If we are uncomfortable with this philosophy, it may be we have lost the innocence of faith which Saroyan finds so sustaining in Ithaca.

HUMPHRY CLINKER

Type of work: Novel
Author: Tobias Smollett (1721-1771)
Type of plot: Social satire
Time of plot: Mid-eighteenth century
Locale: England, Scotland, Wales
First published: 1771

An epistolary novel, full of life and continually amusing, Humphry Clinker *offers a picture of a somewhat eccentric eighteenth century family and of the society in which it moved. It is considered a masterpiece of English humor.*

Humphry Clinker is considered by many critics to be the best of Tobias Smollett's works. First published in the very year of the author's death, the lively novel was written while Smollett was, like his character Matthew Bramble, in retirement seeking recovery from his failing health. Despite the novel's artful treatment of the effect of health on the individual's mentality, *Humphry Clinker* caters delightfully to the tastes of its eighteenth century audience. It focuses primarily on travel, distant societies, and manners since eighteenth century readers thrived on novels of the exotic. Smollett, however, lent that same exotic excitement to the travels of Bramble and his party as they made their excursion through England, Scotland, and Wales. Smollett combined, then, his audience's thirst for the remote with their increasing desire to learn more of history and social structure, particularly their own.

The structure of *Humphry Clinker* is at first glance deceptively simple. It is an epistolary novel, a genre very popular during its time, and as such, it lends itself readily to a straightforward, chronological structure. Dates and locations are given with every letter; even directions are given about where the author will be to receive an answer by return mail. Yet it is not the passing of time that is important for, during any particular period of time, nothing really changes; no one's opinions metamorphose from one point to another. Lydia continues to love "Wilson"; Jerry continues to despise him; Tabitha continues to struggle for masculine attention; Clinker continues to devote himself to a humble way of life; and Matthew Bramble continues to reaffirm above all else a distinct social division. Instead, action is of prime importance. Although there appears to be a tremendous change of orientation toward life at the conclusion of the novel, there is not. The social structure, having been tampered with by chance, has been rectified, and all continue to love and despise as before, now that the labels of the objects have been returned to normal.

Another characteristic of the structure is its semblance of the picaresque. Although it is quite clear that the novel fulfills many of the requirements of the picaresque novel—it is episodic and treats various levels of society—one is asked to question, who is the picaro? He is not the titular hero, who actually appears long after the novel is under way. The "picaro," then, is Bramble. Bramble is a particular type of picaro who appeared often in the eighteenth century. He is not a criminal, loose in his morals, nor is he an anti-hero; he is a reflection of the author, Smollett himself. Most important of all, Smollett-Bramble is a moralizer.

Bramble's moralizing is Smollett's avenue for displaying one of the novel's unifying features—humor. Above all, Smollett-Bramble is a special kind of moralizer—an idealist. According to Bramble's view of humanity, society is to be separated into strict social classes. The classes give society order, and through order men are essentially safe from the many bothersome problems which could prevent them from pursuing the style of life to which they feel entitled. Such is the latent subject of the majority of Bramble's letters to his dear Dr. Lewis. But the ironic and humorous vehicle for these moralistic treatises is his encounters with the oddest assortment of "originals." Although, for the most part, they concur with Bramble's views of society, socially they are not what they seem. Sons of refined blood appear to be lowly; people of adequate means conduct themselves only with the richest of tastes; worthy gentlemen are treated ill by life and reduced to poor, nearly inescapable circumstances. Most of Bramble's acquaintances are eccentrics and as such they are "humorous" in the true sense of the word. Each has a master passion that he fervently pursues, often to ludicrousness. And Bramble, in his effort to comprehend them in a magnanimous manner, is equally humorous—the conflict between his head and his heart is never resolved, and his endearing desire to help everybody is obviously his own master passion.

Humor, in *Humphry Clinker,* eventually lends itself to satire, and at this task Smollett is at least partially successful. Unfortunately Smollett's satire is often against personal enemies, and one of his faults is that his allusions are too obscure to be appreciated. But one means through which his more appreciable satire is executed is that of opposites. Town *versus* country, commoner *versus* gentleman are both opposite extremes which at first appear to have one side clearly preferable to the other. But one soon sees that Smollett does not present his reader with logical alternatives when opposites are in conflict. We know, for example, that the characters have common views of propriety because of their actions and, especially, their verbalized reactions. But the result when the reader tries to reconstruct what these guidelines are, is elusive. What are they based on? And what really are the consequencs if they are ignored? Although we know that the commodities used in pursuit of propriety are good favor, a good name, and money, it is difficult to see what it is these commodities secure when put to use.

Above all, what makes *Humphry Clinker* the successful novel it is, is Smollett's reaffirmation of the genuine emotional response. Bramble is a man of sensitivity to his physical and social surroundings and experiences. He is tempted, for example, to believe that his trip through Scotland is a glimpse into the ideal way of life he has been both proselytizing and searching for. However, Bramble senses that modernization threatens Scotland with the laziness and complacency that consume England. In addition, Smollett emphasizes how a man's character is shaped by his experiences and emotional responses, by anticipating the very responses a reader might have to such a travel novel. But most important, Bramble's solitary reflections imply that the most intense and meaningful emotions a person might have are those he does not feel obligated to verbalize. In this way Smollett's characters are safe from both our pity and our ridicule.

Bonnie Fraser

THE HUNCHBACK OF NOTRE DAME

Type of work: Novel
Author: Victor Hugo (1802-1885)
Type of plot: Historical romance
Time of plot: Fifteenth century
Locale: France
First published: 1831

In this masterpiece of romantic writing, Hugo tells of the love of a grotesquely ugly, hunchbacked deaf-mute for a mysteriously beautiful gipsy dancer. The compelling theme of the novel is that God has created in man an imperfect image of Himself, an image fettered with numerous handicaps, but one which has the potential to transcend its limitations and achieve spiritual greatness.

Victor Hugo was inspired to write *The Hunchback of Notre Dame (Notre Dame de Paris* in the original) when he accidentally discovered the Greek word for "fate" carved into an obscure wall of one of Notre Dame Cathedral's towers. Each personality is built around a "fixed idea": Claude Frollo embodies the consuming, destructive passion of lust; Esmeralda, virgin beauty and purity; Quasimodo, unshakeable devotion and loyalty. Hugo's characters do not develop but simply play out their given natures to their inevitable conclusions.

In analyzing the character of archdeacon Claude Frollo, it is helpful to understand Hugo's theory that the advent of Christianity in Western Europe marked a new era in literature and art. Because Christianity viewed man as a creature half animal and half spirit—the link between beast and angel—writers could present the ugly and lowly as well as the beautiful and sublime. They could attain a new synthesis, more meaningful because realistic, not achieved by writers of antiquity, who only depicted idealized, larger-than-life subjects on the grounds that "Art should *correct* nature." Claude Frollo excludes all human contact from his life and locks himself up with his books; when he has mastered all the legitimate branches of knowledge, he has nowhere to turn in his obsession but to the realm of alchemy and the occult. He is ultimately destroyed, along with those around him, because in denying his animal nature and shutting off all avenues for the release of his natural drives and affections, he falls into the depths of a lustful passion that amounts to madness.

As the novel develops, Quasimodo, the hunchback of the novel's title, is increasingly trapped between his love for the gipsy girl, Esmeralda, and his love for the archdeacon, his master and protector. These two loyalties finally create an irreconcilable conflict; a choice must be made. When the priest destroys the gipsy, the bell ringer hurls his master from the heights of Notre Dame: a fitting death for Frollo, symbolic of his descent in life from the sublime to the bestial. In Quasimodo, Hugo dramatized his belief that the grotesque and the sublime must coexist in art and literature, as they do in life; the modern writer, he says, "will realize that everything in creation is not humanly beautiful, that the ugly exists beside the beautiful, the unshapely beside the graceful . . . and [he] will ask . . . if a mutilated nature will be the more beautiful for the mutilation." Esmeralda is the embodiment of innocence and beauty. She is held in reverence even by the criminal population of Paris, who vaguely equate her in their minds with the Virgin Mary. But her beauty is too innocent and pure to exist amid the brutality and sinfulness of her world. Of all the men in the book, only one is worthy of Esmeralda: the hunchbacked Quasimodo, who loves her so totally and unselfishly that he would rather die than go on living after she is executed. Appropriately, it is Esmeralda and Quasimodo who are finally "married" in the charnel-house at Montfaucon; theirs is the perfect union of physical and spiritual beauty.

Almost more than by any of the human characters, the novel is dominated by the presence of the cathedral itself. The hero, Quasimodo, understands Notre Dame: he is in tune with her "life." Like her deformed bell ringer, Notre Dame is both ugly and beautiful, both strong and vulnerable, both destructive and life-giving. Quasimodo's monstrous face hides a loving, faithful spirit, while his twisted body conceals a superhuman strength; Notre Dame's beautiful sanctuary is enclosed by a rough exterior encrusted with gargoyles, while her vulnerable treasures are guarded by doors that six thousand maddened vagrants cannot batter down. The cathedral and the ringer work together, almost as one entity, to protect Esmeralda in her room hundreds of feet above the city; to repulse invaders with hurled stones and molten lead; to dash the blasphemous student, Jehan, to death against the massive walls; and to cast off the priest whose lustfulness defiles the purity of the place.

Setting was all-important to Hugo. As the foremost French Romanticist of the nineteenth century, he was fascinated by the medieval period, and strove to reconstruct it in such a way that it would live again in his novel. Hugo believed that a description built on exact, localized details would recapture the mood of a historical period; that setting was as crucial as characterization in engraving a "faithful representation of the facts" on the minds of his readers. Early in the novel, therefore, he devotes an entire section (Book Three) to a description of the cathedral and the city of Paris; and throughout the book, he offers brief passages of historical background which add verisimilitude to his narrative.

In the Preface to his play *Cromwell,* Hugo wrote, "The place where this or that catastrophe took place becomes a terrible and inseparable witness thereof; and the absence of silent characters of this sort would make the greatest scenes in history incomplete in the drama." Thus, in *The Hunchback of Notre Dame,* not only does the cathedral live almost as a personality; so also does the Place de la Grève spread its influence over the lives of all the characters. The cathedral and the square are the two focal points not only of the setting, but of the plot and the theme of the novel; the former embodies the spiritual and beautiful, the latter the lowly and cruel. It is the cathedral that enfolds the humble and loyal Quasimodo and the Virgin-like Esmeralda, while the square, the scene of poverty, suffering, and grisly death, with its Rat-Hole and its gibbet, claims Esmeralda, her lunatic mother, and Claude Frollo as its victims.

Nancy G. Ballard

HUNGER

Type of work: Novel
Author: Knut Hamsun (Knut Pedersen Hamsund, 1859-1952)
Type of plot: Impressionistic realism
Time of plot: Late nineteenth century
Locale: Norway
First published: 1890

In Hunger *we find a striking study of a man's mind under stress; realistic in subject, the novel's form and treatment are highly impressionistic. This is the novel that established Hamsun's reputation.*

Knut Hamsun's works have been neither well-known nor popular for almost a generation. When the Germans invaded Norway during World War II, Hamsun lent his support and prestige to the Quisling government. The reaction against him both during and after the war helps to explain in part why Hamsun's works are no longer popular. But more to the point is the fact that his style of novel writing, impressionistic realism, fell out of favor after World War II. Hamsun's *Hunger* is part of the literary tradition leading to Steinbeck and other writers of the first part of the twentieth century. This so-called "modernistic" school deals in part with subjective reality and it is particularly in this regard that Hamsun's position in the movement is most secure.

Hunger grew out of the same general environment that produced at the end of the nineteenth century Sigmund Freud and his works. Hamsun delves into the subconscious of his protagonist and comes up with an excellent depiction of madness as seen from inside the mind of the madman. The fact that this madness derives from hunger is significant because this story of a young journalist literally starving to death is autobiographical to some extent. When Hamsun first presented the manuscript of his work for publication, the editor was so struck by his emaciation that he paid Hamsun an advance on the work, without even bothering to read the title. The story told by the editor is closely paralleled in the novel.

On one level, this is a madman's story of a madman, but on another it is an account of life in a large city of the industrial age. The city where the action takes place, Christiania, is like any city where people try to sell their art, their literature, or their journalism and discover that there is no market for the best they have to offer. Like modern day Los Angeles and New York, Christiania is presented as a city full of people who seek fame and fortune but who find instead they are not capable of reaching their goals. Characteristically, this sort of person often becomes discouraged and is obliged to seek employment in a field far removed from his original ambition. The protagonist of *Hunger* finds himself in just this situation. He is unable to make a career for himself in the environment of a large city of the industrial age.

What lifts this novel from a mere story about a poor boy doing poorly in the big city is Hamsun's depiction of the internal workings of the human mind. He demonstrates the foolish pride and motiveless behavior that come from a tenuous existence such as the protagonist of the novel leads. The starving man in this novel is one who lies, as the saying goes, even when it is not necessary. He has no regular habits and is at the mercy of his own strange whims. The incident of his persistence in telling a strange woman on the street that she has lost her nonexistent book is a case in point. He lies to save his pride time and again, even in the face of starvation. Hamsun explains that at the stage when the body is starving, the mind falters and mistakes the inconsequentials of life for life's necessities and cannot distinguish between the two. Hamsun terrifyingly depicts in this book the odd sort of seemingly lucid logic that is to an impartial observer nothing but the worst sort of nonsense.

While Hamsun is able to depict the workings of such a mind broken by the stress of hunger, he does not present a full picture of the book's protagonist. Yet, because of this omission his study of psychological pressure is all the more vivid and effective. We do not know much about the young man in the novel, only that he is starving and periodically reduced to chewing on wood shavings or bits of cloth. Hamsun focuses the reader's full attention upon the issue of the mind, and he does so in a masterful fashion.

On yet a third level this book is also a portrait of a failure. Indeed the book is a collection of episodes that are united only by the underlying themes. The book is divided into four sections, each one describing the thoughts and actions of the protagonist as he suffers the effects of starvation at different times. There is, strictly speaking, no beginning or end to the novel. At the end of each section there is a stroke of good luck. The protagonist sells a story, or gets a loan. Then the novel immediately jumps to the next episode in his life when he is starving, and the cycle begins again.

At the end of the book the young writer joins the crew of a steamship bound for England. The effect of this ending, though, is one not of escape but of pessimism. There is a flaw in this man's character, one that Hamsun only hints at, that damns him to a continuing cycle of luck and hunger. It is a cycle that the reader at the end of the novel feels can lead eventually only to death.

Glenn M. Edwards

HUON DE BORDEAUX

Type of work: Chanson de geste
Author: Unknown
Type of plot: Chivalric romance
Time of plot: Ninth century
Locale: Paris, Jerusalem, Rome, the fairy kingdom of Mommur
First transcribed: First half of the thirteenth century

In this lengthy medieval French verse romance, we see a chanson de geste*—a "tale of a deed"—in a developed and perhaps impure form. The events are supposed to take place late in the reign of Charlemagne, after the betrayal and defeat of Roland at Roncesvalles.*

The French romance, of which the *chanson de geste* forms the first example, is part of the earliest major classification of romantic literature. The three categories of romantic literature are traditionally the Matter of Roma, which is based upon classical myth and legend, occasionally utilizing Roman history; the Matter of Britain, which is based upon the Arthurian legends and the courtly love device which was so essentially a part of the Arthurian romances; and the Matter of France. The basis for the Matter of France is the *chanson de geste,* of which about twelve hundred are in existence. These fall into three main groups. The *geste du roi* is centered around the legends and history of Charlemagne. He is usually presented as the champion of Christendom against the heathens. The best known of these is the *Song of Roland.* The second group, the *geste de Donnde Mayence,* is the history of his vassals; the third, the *geste de Garin de Monhane,* is the history of William of Orange.

Huon de Bordeaux was first translated into English in 1530 by John Bourchier, Lord Berners. It remains today as a great translation, one of the earliest in English. Berners had previously translated the works of Jean Froissart, which were to have an immense influence on the late English Renaissance. *Huon de Bordeaux* was no less influential for the course of English literature. In it the English caught their first glimpse of Oberon, king of the fairies, and the entire work proved to be a gold mine of information for English dramatists. The subject matter of *Huon de Bordeaux* is most closely related to the Charlemagne cycles, hence it is considered part of the *geste du roi.* Although the plot bears little, if any, relation to history in its latter part, it is nonetheless an interesting picture of the French general attitude toward, and knowledge of the Near East. From it the modern reader may assume that the information given here is indicative of the level of knowledge of the educated classes in the Middle Ages. That *Huon de Bordeaux* was accepted is proof that this mythical interpretation of what was in the not so distant past was the accepted method of transmitting information.

HYDE PARK

Type of work: Drama
Author: James Shirley (1596-1666)
Type of plot: Comedy of manners
Time of plot: Early seventeenth century
Locale: London
First presented: 1632

Hyde Park, *the second of Shirley's comedies, paved the way for later Restoration drama. The play looks forward to a more sophisticated theater, but it is still based on the works of Shakespeare and other Elizabethan and Jacobean playwrights.*

The most prolific of the later Elizabethan dramatists and the only major surviving dramatist until the Restoration was James Shirley. Although he was equally adept at all forms of drama—tragedy, tragi-comedy, and comedy—comedy was his forte. This can be attested to since of the more than thirty of his plays that remain extant, the largest and most distinctive group is his comedies. His best plays in this grouping deal with London's fashionable life and can be categorized as comedies of manners. *Hyde Park* is a distinguished example of this comedic type.

Hyde Park might be considered at first glance to be a drama written for the stage advertisement of a new popular diversion or as an "occasional piece" because it was written to commemorate the opening to the public, in 1632, of the previously private park by its owner, Lord Holland. The play, however, demands closer scrutiny. It provides an example of the apparent trends within the dramatic writing of the later Elizabethan period as well as a view of the foibles of London society.

Great attention to the use of ceremony and pageantry had been paid within early Elizabethan dramatic writing; however, *Hyde Park* seems representative of the trend away from this practice, having only a half-dozen entrances that ask for formal presentation. This is quite a reduction compared with, for example, Thomas Middleton's *Women Beware Women* (c. 1620) which has twelve formal entrances and as many formal exits, a masque, and a staged banquet which includes a procession to it and formal toasts.

Accompanying these reductions came an attempt to cater to the audience's growing taste for a greater realism on stage through the use of ingenious effects and elaborate settings. The undertaking, therefore, in *Hyde Park* was to make the audience feel as though it was *in* the park; and to this end, contemporary reports say the play was staged with bird song.

The content of *Hyde Park,* in the comedy of manners style, exposes the life style of London during the period. Shirley chose the comedic technique to expose man's foibles and vices, believing, as he expressed later in the prologue of the *Duke's Mistress* (1636):

> For satire, they do know best what it means
> That dare apply; and if a poet's pen,
> Aiming at general errors, note the men,
> 'Tis not his fault. The safest cure is, they
> That purge their bosoms may see any play.

In Act I, through the description of the Cavalier Lord Bonvile, Shirley also remarks on the aristocracy's belief that one's station in life brings with it certain privileges.

The aristocratic life with its promenading, horse-racing, and lovemaking is not the only life portrayed, however. There is a wide representation of the Elizabethan class structure: a milkmaid, a jockey, bagpipers, park-keepers, a merchant, officers, lords and ladies, and so on. The feeling for the country life evidenced by the list of the *dramatis personae* and the treatment of those representative characters was uncommon for Shirley's time, and was one of the few characteristics of his writing not generally adopted by the Restoration dramatists that followed him.

Indeed, James Shirley in *Hyde Park* set the pace for the dramatic writing of the Restoration in his comedy of manners. With his later play, *The Lady of Pleasure* (1635)—which gave the stage the characters of Sir Thomas Bornwell and his lady Aretina, who foreshadow so well Sir Peter and Lady Teazle of Richard Sheridan's *The School for Scandal* (1777)—and *Hyde Park,* perhaps one might remark: James Shirley was to Elizabethan drama the spark that William Wycherley was to Restoration drama. He at least was the bridge over the "void" of the Commonwealth period.

HYPATIA

Type of work: Novel
Author: Charles Kingsley (1819-1875)
Type of plot: Historical romance
Time of plot: Fifth century
Locale: Egypt and Italy
First published: 1853

Hypatia *is the story of the conflicts between pagan, Christian, and Jewish forces all struggling for the souls of men in the fifth century after Christ's death. The larger background of the novel is the dissolving Roman Empire.*

Charles Kingsley was the son of a clergyman and received his education at King's College and at Cambridge. He chose to follow a religious profession, and he became rector of a Hampshire parish, a position which he held for the remainder of his life. His activities were not limited to the religious, for he acted as an instructor in modern history at Cambridge for nine years. His fields of interest were equally broad. He contributed to political pamphlets under a pseudonym and was active in the area of social reform. He was influenced by Carlyle's writings, and continually opposed the Chartist movement.

In addition to his other obligations, Kingsley somehow found time to work in the literary fields which interested him. He wrote songs and ballads, at least one play, numerous children's books, and several novels. His work *Alton Locke,* which appeared in 1850, is an early treatment of the changing view of the worker in society and reflects his essentially left-wing sentiment which prompted so much of his political activity. His other principal novels include *Hypatia, Westward Ho* (1855), and *Hereward the Wake* (1866), an attempt at the historical novel which is admirably accurate in its portrayal of history, but which suffers greatly from the complexities of plot and custom imposed upon it by the author's attention to detail and meticulous accuracy. Kingsley also published reviews of theological works and several volumes of sermons. It was one of his reviews which prompted Newman to write the *Apologia.*

Like *Hereward the Wake, Hypatia* suffers from the sort of overattention to detail which formed a feature of Kingsley's work. The plot is well worked out and of itself interesting, but the author loads a great deal of philosophical and theological discussion into an already overcomplicated plot structure and the predictable happens: the reader is tempted to gloss over the sometimes three to four page dissertations on Platonic logic as it related to the fundamentals of early Christian thought, and to resume reading where the action begins. This flaw is unfortunate, for Kingsley's sermons—and this is what they are—hold a wealth of information in a reasonably readable style. His classical education made him ideally suited for the sort of essays which he published with success elsewhere, but he was unable to resist the temptation to insert them into his novels.

THE HYPOCHONDRIAC

Type of work: Drama
Author: Molière (Jean Baptiste Poquelin, 1622-1673)
Type of plot: Romantic comedy
Time of plot: Seventeenth century
Locale: Paris, France
First presented: 1673

With this, his last comedy, Molière turned his satirical pen on the medical profession. His usual wit and humor are well-displayed in this attack on doctors and pharmacists but are secondary to the bitter irony which dominates the play.

On February 17, 1673, the fourth performance of *The Hypochondriac* was staged with Molière playing the role of the hypochondriac Argan. Toward the end of the final scene, Molière was seized with a fit of choking brought on by a hemorrhage of the lungs. However, such was his dedication and strength of will, that he managed to finish the scene and take his bows without his fellow actors even realizing his condition. He collapsed immediately after the final curtain call, was carried home, and died within a few hours. It was one of the most dramatic deaths in literary history, and much has been written about it. But aside from its poignancy, the incident reflected the most crucial aspect of Molière's genius: his ability to convert painful realities into joyous farce, to defy the limitations of human life through comedy of the most superb and transcendent quality.

The Hypochondriac, the last of Molière's plays, is the culmination of an art which had its roots both in the traditions of old French farce and in the Italian *commedia dell'arte* form. We can see features of the former in the play's irrepressible high spirits, in its uproarious slapstick, and in its hilarious and rollicking episodes. The influence of the latter shows in Molière's use of masks, a device with which he never ceased to experiment throughout his entire career. Beginning in his first plays with masks adopted from the Italian theater by French neoclassicists, he soon modified and expanded their function until they became a device perfectly suited to the expression of his comic genius; in *The Hypochondriac* they are employed with particular effectiveness in the characterization of the various doctors.

But Molière would not have become the great writer that he was if he had not transcended his artistic origins, transforming his raw materials with the spark of genius. As it was, that spark kindled comedies whose characters are unforgettable and whose themes are universal; it produced plays of unsurpassed comedy inspired by passion, fraught with meaning, and rich with implication.

The Hypochondriac contains some of Molière's most memorable characters; Argan is one of his finest creations. Like all of Molière's comic heroes, Argan has fallen prey to an obsession which dominates his every thought and action. He is a domestic tyrant whose entire household revolves around treatment of his imagined illness, and whose selfishness extends to such a point that he attempts to force his daughter into marriage with a witless doctor, so that he can profit from free medical attention. He is opposed every step of the way and eventually duped by the bold, clever, and inventive maid-servant, Toinette. Surrounding these two central figures are a cluster of minor characters including Argan's lovely and generous daughter Angélique; his scheming and greedy second wife Béline; his practical, sensible brother Béralde; his daughter's suitor, the automaton Thomas Diafoirus; and a motley assortment of doctors and apothecaries such as Monsieur Purgon, Monsieur Fleurant, and Monsieur Diafoirus the elder. In all of these characterizations, Molière presents universal types rather than unique individuals; he concentrates only on the character's dominant traits while he passes over his other qualities, simplifying in order to create a single powerful dramatic effect. As in all his comedies, Molière subordinates plot to characterization in *The Hypochondriac;* he created the roles to fit the actors who were to perform them, supplying them with a plot just sufficient to allow them room to develop those roles. Above all, the plays were written to be performed rather than read; and the plots are marked by their blissful disregard of probability and their constant intrusion of musical interludes, song, and dance.

The Hypochondriac is a play of considerable thematic complexity. On the surface, of course, this comedy is an attack on incompetent doctors and unscrupulous quacks; but many critics have discussed the deeper parallels between the open satire on medicine and a disguised attack on religion which they perceive in the play. Whether or not the author consciously intended any parallels, one can certainly see many analogies between the doctors in *The Hypochondriac,* and priests and theologians. Like Argan's doctors, churchmen preach with unbending dogmatism, summarily condemn anyone who questions their authority, and propagate more of their kind through obscure and inaccessible initiation rites. Just as Monsieur Purgon and Monsieur Fleurant dispense their drugs, priests dispense blessings, and Argan is as dependent on his apothecary as a religious fanatic on his confessor.

Beneath this parallel between medicine and religion lies the crucial theme in the play: blind obedience to fallible authority is dangerous. This theme is conveyed in a number of ways; the primary one is through the characterization of Argan, who is the extreme example of a man who has totally surrendered his free will to others and thereby lost his ability to reason clearly. He is so at the mercy of the doctors that he accepts without question the curse which Monsieur Purgon delivers as punishment when his patient delays taking his enema for several minutes past the prescribed hour: "I will that before four days are up you get into an incurable state." This central power-submission theme is also reflected in several minor relationships as well: Monsieur Fleurant, the apothecary, takes orders blindly from his superior within the medical hierarchy, Monsieur Purgon; Thomas Diafoirus worships the ancients and follows his father's commands as a puppet obeys a puppeteer.

The theme is also conveyed, and the parallel between medical and theological dogmatism stressed, through the dialogue. The Biblical echo is unmistakable, for example, when Toinette, disguised as a doctor, advises Argan to cut off one arm and gouge out one eye; one hears behind the line the admonition to sinners in Mark, 9:43-47, "And if thy hand offend thee, cut it off . . . And if thine eye offend thee, pluck it out. . . ." The implications are provocative. At least one viable interpretation is that Molière is objecting to the abuse of the body and denial of its natural needs, and consequent warping of the spirit, occasioned both by absurd medical practice and the excesses of Christianity. Also fascinating is Molière's constant use of numbers, suggestive both of meaningless medical jargon and religious superstition. Argan in the opening scene equates the quantity of medicines consumed and enemas administred in a month to the quality of his health, much as a scrupulous devotée might worry that he had recited too few rosaries or lit too few votive candles during the week. Likewise, Monsieur Purgon's absurd formula for the proper number of grains of salt to put on an egg ("Six, eight, ten, using even numbers; just as in drugs, you use uneven numbers.") may be Molière's way of satirizing not only contemporary medical gimmicks but also similar Church practices such as indulgences sold to cut down the length of one's stay in purgatory.

It is Molière's unsurpassed comedy, however, which the viewer remembers, and which insures that future productions of *The Hypochondriac* will always be well attended. Scenes of sheer fun, such as Argan's tabulation of his monthly medical expenses, or Thomas Diafoirus' bungled attempt to recite his memorized avowal of love, are unforgettable; when the invalid flies out of his chair brandishing a stick, to chase a maidservant around the table before he suddenly realizes he cannot walk, the audience today roars with laughter as it did in 1673.

Nancy G. Ballard

I, CLAUDIUS

Type of work: Novel
Author: Robert Graves (1895-)
Type of plot: Historical chronicle
Time of plot: 10 B. C.-A. D. 41
Locale: Rome
First published: 1934

A semi-fictional reconstruction of a period in the history of the Roman Empire, the novel contains snatches of history, records of conquest, and notorious historical figures. Sophisticated and ironic, the story is infused with humor even in the midst of descriptions of decadence and pageantry.

From one of the most violent centuries in Western civilization Robert Graves drew his material for *I, Claudius.* After the rule of Augustus and Tiberius, the Roman empire reached a peak of violence and vulgarity under Caligula and after his death—rather incongruously—fell into the hands of Tiberius Claudius. The protagonist is the son of Germanicus, the noble and virtuous son of Augustus Caesar. As Graves presents him, he is the least blessed of all the imperial family: lame, weak in body, cursed with a stutter and a tendency to drool. Yet he is also a scholar and a historian who is able, because he is an outcast, to record with objectivity the events of his turbulent century. He sees his father poisoned, his various aunts, uncles, and cousins murdered; watches his mother starve to death; and manages to survive Caligula's madness. Indeed, bcause of his knowledge of history, and his position as an outcast, he is able to outlast the insanity of all the Roman power seekers. Ironically, when he is finally made emperor, all he thinks about, like most authors, is that now his books will be read.

Throughout the narration Claudius is fascinated and bemused by the delight his family takes in the pursuit of power. Told in an informal manner, a method which undercuts the apparent horrendous nature of their crimes, the various and complicated plots and counterplots become exercises in the banality of evil. Seen from the long, historical perspective such actions seem monumental, but viewed from the inside as Claudius sees them, they appear all too often petty, all too often the greedy sins of ordinary if perverse human beings. The corruption of the empire does not so much arise out of any grand evil plan of supermen but out of the lust of mere mortals.

I SPEAK FOR THADDEUS STEVENS

Type of work: Biography
Author: Elsie Singmaster (Mrs. E. S. Lewars, 1879-1958)
Type of plot: Historical chronicle
Time of plot: 1792-1868
Locale: Vermont, Pennsylvania, Washington, D. C.
First published: 1947

A biography in the form of a novel, this work strives to make understandable the complex and often contradictory character of the famous partisan statesman of the Civil War period, Thaddeus Stevens. The author tells the story of his life as a series of dramatic episodes, each of which presents some crisis, triumph, or defeat.

Elsie Singmaster's *I Speak for Thaddeus Stevens* is less a work of fiction than a work in which fiction and history compete as standard-bearers for the story of humanity's triumphs and failures. It is the historical novel of the Age of Emancipation and the fictional biography of Thaddeus Stevens, uncompromising champion of the underprivileged and disadvantaged.

In overcoming his own personal weakness, the deformity with which he was born, Thaddeus Stevens found symbolic strength in defending the weak and poor. He championed the rights of Pennsylvanians to have free education, risking his own career in the process; he stood for the rights of black people, and attacked the Fugitive Slave Law when it was politically damaging to do so. Singmaster's portrait of the man, whose uncompromising opinions were "imbibed with his mother's milk," creates a convincing psychological *gestalt* of Thaddeus Stevens, who became a superior man by overcoming his innate feelings of inferiority.

As a historical novel, *I Speak for Thaddeus Stevens* recreates an earlier age by infusing it with life. The Free-Soil Whigs, Masons, and Jackson Democrats come to life as men in a political drama unfolding before Thaddeus Stevens. Singmaster's scrupulous use of historical data sheds new light on the Civil War Congress and the struggle for the Thirteenth Amendment. The novel's climax, the attempted impeachment of Andrew Johnson which failed in the Senate, underscores the tragic theme of Thaddeus Stevens, advocate for the sovereign rights of the people.

Singmaster's style is unobtrusive and sparse, devoid of rhetorical flourish and pretense. She writes in clear, unelaborate language whose intention is to present, close to reality, the struggle of Thaddeus Stevens against the forces of ignorance and oppression. *I Speak for Thaddeus Stevens* is the very personal statement of Elsie Singmaster about man's inhumanity to man, and humane forces which can rise to the challenge.

AN ICELAND FISHERMAN

Type of work: **Novel**
Author: **Pierre Loti (Julien Viaud, 1850-1923)**
Type of plot: **Impressionistic romance**
Time of plot: **Nineteenth century**
Locale: **Brittany and at sea**
First published: **1886**

This unadorned tale exemplifies the virtues of French literature: clarity, simplicity, power. A warm, touching story of the fishing fleet in Iceland waters, the book and its characters possess wide appeal.

The great popularity of Pierre Loti's exotic works at the close of the nineteenth century and in the early years of the twentieth was in part the result of a reaction to the literary naturalism of Émile Zola, the Goncourts, and other novelists in France and elsewhere. Loti had himself, in his wide-ranging voyages as a French naval officer, seen the people and places he described in his fiction. Various works by him are set in Turkey, Tahiti, Africa, Japan, and Persia.

In *An Iceland Fisherman,* Pierre Loti combines realism and impressionism in a simple tale of primitive people living in an elemental world filled with occasional beauty and many natural dangers. The story's theme of love and separation is one frequently repeated by Loti who in his years at sea had learned how often a sailor's farewell to his loved ones is final though he does not wish it so. The sea dominates most of the scenes in the novel, whether the action is on shipboard or on land. The sea is called "the foster mother and destroyer" of generations of Breton fishermen. It shows a "dark and sinister" look before a storm, and when some drunken sailors drown their cares in mirthful song, the sea, "their grave of tomorrow," sings a booming, dirge-like accompaniment. Such poetic language stems from the author's own nautical impressions, an aspect of the novel that heightens the reader's enjoyment of the story.

Loti's characters are realistic but somewhat sentimentalized. Because the author seems to care so much, though, for these doomed people (he mentions that he himself conducted the sad funeral in Singapore of the valiant young Sylvester), the reader does also. One is touched by the handsome young sailor's death far from home, by the deep grief of his grandmother, and by the desperate, vain longing of Gaud for her drowned husband, taken from her by her cruel rival the sea after Yann and Gaud had spent only one week of happiness together.

THE IDES OF MARCH

Type of work: Novel
Author: Thornton Wilder (1897-1975)
Type of plot: Historical chronicle
Time of plot: 45 B. C.
Locale: Ancient Rome
First published: 1948

This retelling of the last months of Caesar's life was written with sophistication and depth of feeling. From imaginary letters and documents, Wilder reconstructed the plots and intrigues leading to the stabbing of the great Roman.

Thornton Wilder twice received the Pulitzer Prize for his work as a playwright (*Our Town,* 1938; *The Skin of Our Teeth,* 1943). However, he is also respected as a novelist. His reputation was first made by *The Bridge of San Luis Rey,* a best-selling novel that won him his first Pulitzer Prize in 1928. After the success of this work came a succession of other novels, many of which employed Wilder's characteristic device of centering on a group of persons whose lives at some point in time are all in some way interconnected.

This is also the technique Wilder was to use in *The Ides of March,* a novel whose use of "documents" to tell its story fits it into at least two major novel categories: the historical and the epistolary. Wilder's use of these fictitious documents—only the parts from the Catullus and the last entry are authentic—allows him an omniscient point of view in telling his story. He is thus able at the same time to maintain a sense of unfolding progression, as the same facts are discussed again and again from a different viewpoint, and are filled in more completely by each character's successive letter.

This technique of multiple viewpoints also allows Wilder to present a more comprehensive picture of the novel's characters. Caesar is seen as rational, truly unvengeful, dedicated to the responsibilities he accepts as Dictator, and generally superior in every way to those around him. His virtues are not understood by the other characters because they are incapable of possessing such strengths themselves. Brutus, for example, is incapable of the strong convictions, about Rome or himself, which are needed by a man in Caesar's position. Caesar's private character is revealed through his own letters to Lucius Mamilius Turrinus, but we also see different and complementary sides of him in the letters of Clodia Pulcher, Julia Marcia, Pompeia, and others. These in turn are understood through their own and others' letters, so that the reader has a sense of completeness as well as objectivity in Wilder's characterizations.

Wilder's scrupulous accounting of his "documents' " origins, his knowledge of Roman history and customs, and his ability to simulate the Roman epistolary style and language lend further verisimilitude to the work. His unique talent for weaving several lives and points of view into one coherent, fascinating whole is the novel's strongest structural and stylistic asset.

THE IDIOT

Type of work: Novel
Author: Fyodor Mikhailovich Dostoevski (1821-1881)
Type of plot: Psychological realism
Time of plot: Mid-nineteenth century
Locale: St. Petersburg, Russia
First published: 1868-1869

One of the author's great masterpieces, this novel deals with the fundamental issues of good and evil, purity and corruption. In the center of this vast panorama of Russian life stands Prince Myshkin, a man so simple as to seem complex to those who do not possess his innocence. Although difficult to read, the novel rewards the effort with its undeniable power and breadth of vision.

The Idiot has been faulted for technical imperfections as a novel. Such imperfections do indeed exist. The novel begins well—in fact shows outstanding promise—but as it progresses, the author's control over his material seems to deteriorate. Consequently, the latter part of the novel, despite occasional flashes of brilliance, appears ill-conceived and sloppily written. In all fairness, however, consideration must be given to the circumstances under which Fyodor Dostoevski was working when he wrote *The Idiot*. He was living abroad with his second wife (the first had died in 1864), moving too frequently to put down roots in any one place. During this period, he suffered severe attacks of epilepsy. His first child was born and died hardly three months after birth. He gambled compulsively, was constantly in debt to his publisher for advances on the novel, and felt intermittent guilt about subjecting his wife and child to privation because of his gambling. Shortly after the death of the first child, whom Dostoevski mourned excessively, his wife became pregnant again, adding more worries and responsibilities to Dostoevski's already heavy burden. Under these conditions and demands Dostoevski wrote *The Idiot*. If the novel is technically imperfect, the author is nevertheless entitled to mercy.

The Idiot has also been accused of obscurity. Without a doubt, it has languished in the shadow of its two more renowned siblings, *Crime and Punishment* (1866) and *The Brothers Karamazov* (1879-1880). That kind of obscurity, however, is an equivocation of the term. The obscurity charge leveled at *The Idiot* is really one of impenetrability, the inability of the reader to grasp what is happening in the novel. Much of this confusion is simply a failure not of the novel, but of the Western mind to apprehend the essence of the Russian soul, for *The Idiot* is a quintessentially Russian novel. Its uniqueness—and hence its so-called obscurity—derives from the distinctive qualities of the Russian psyche unfamiliar to Western readers. At least seven such qualities can be identified.

First of all is the concept of Russian brotherhood. It is illustrated, among other places, in Myshkin's return from Switzerland when he is befriended en route by Rogozhin, a complete stranger, and on arrival by the Epanchins. But the concept is not thus limited. Myshkin's enduring reputation as "the idiot" with the Epanchins and others throughout the novel evidences an affectionate alliance or brotherhood often under-appreciated in the West.

Another trait is the unmethodical approach to life. Western people tend to place high value on social ritual and punctuality; however, Russians express themselves spontaneously and observe time schedules only when the schedules do not interfere with the more important business of living. Such a tendency leads to a rather irrational attitude toward handling the necessary trivialities as well as the serious aspects of everyday life. Hence, against all logic and reason, Myshkin proposes marriage to Natasya. Myshkin does not calculate advantages and disadvantages; he simply responds autonomically to what the situation calls for. His impulsive behavior, like the impulsive behavior of many others in the novel, is typically Russian.

The Russian is also compassionate and humble. The Epanchins, with affectionate compassion, refer to Myshkin as "the idiot." Myshkin's own compassion is demonstrated in his impulsive proposal of marriage to Natasya. In fact, Myshkin, throughout the novel, remains kindhearted and compassionate. Likewise, he is humble, just as are—ultimately—Natasya, Rogozhin, Ganya, and the Epanchins.

Religiosity is yet another Russian characteristic manifested in *The Idiot*. This quality is particularly demonstrated in Myshkin's peculiar diatribe at Mme. Epanchin's party when he launches upon a recollection of four conversations which he had concerning the matter of faith. It is evidence of the Russian's unquestioning devotion to Eastern Orthodox Christianity. In fact, Dostoevski even goes so far as to allege that Roman Catholicism and socialism are working conjointly toward imposing authoritarian goals and standards, whereas Eastern Orthodoxy encourages individuality—albeit within a set standard of ethics. This logic can be understood only within the framework of the faithful believer.

The belief in the messianic destiny of Russia adds still another dimension to Dostoevski's view of the Russian soul in *The Idiot*. This belief manifests itself as a sense of honor, which is best displayed when Myshkin goes to Rogozhin's apartment only to find the dead body of Natasya. Myshkin spends the night with Rogozhin, the murderer, and Natasya's corpse—performing his honorable duty. The next morning, Rogozhin confesses to the police that he murdered Natasya. These dutiful observances of honorable behavior are, in the context of the novel, attributed to proper Russian conduct. As such, they are individual contributions to Russia's manifest destiny in fulfillment of her obligation to save the world from perdition.

Closely allied to this Russian mission to save the world is the practice of public confession. This practice, too, is intimately connected with the difference between Roman Catholicism and Eastern Orthodoxy. The former requires whispered revelations to a closeted priest; the latter mandates publicly spoken admission of wrongdoing to the full congregation. Consonantly, Ganya and Rogozhin make "confessions" of misdeeds early in the novel. Other characters as well confess transgressions—as Rogozhin confesses murder to Myshkin—throughout the novel. Everyone, it seems, has some dirty little secret hidden away and, finally, can hide it no longer, "confessing" it to someone else. Such purgation is but another typical Russian trait.

The last essential Russian quality in *The Idiot* is the warping effect of the conflict between humility and pride. On the most literal level, this trait is demonstrated by Rogozhin's vow to kill "the idiot" because Rogozhin is sure that Natasya left him for Myshkin, while, as a consequence, Myshkin becomes an extortion victim for being deluded by the same misapprehensions. On a more sophisticated level, all of the characters in the novel are warped by the conflict between pride and humility. They are, in effect, the double or schizophrenic personalities so typical in Dostoevski's novels. Myshkin, for example, is Dostoevski's penultimate Christ figure as well as the idiot-savant of folklore. Natasya is a sado-masochist, reveling in her exploitation while she revenges it. Other characters follow suit.

These factors make the novel uniquely Russian. Since they differ from conventional Western standards, they make *The Idiot* a novel too dense and too complex for most Western readers; hence, misunderstanding is bound to occur. The novel is, finally, too Russian for the non-Russian reader. It can be appreciated only from the Russian point of view—native or trained.

Joanne G. Kashdan

THE IDYLLS OF THE KING

Type of work: Poem
Author: Alfred, Lord Tennyson (1809-1892)
Type of plot: Chivalric romance
Time of plot: Fifth century
Locale: England
First published: Separately, 1859-1885

Divided into twelve sections, each symbolic of one month of the year, these poems present to the reader the span of a man's life, extending from the coming of Arthur to his death. Filled with mystic and spiritual meanings, Tennyson's stories of the Knights of the Round Table are rich in allegorical significance and beauty of narrative.

As England's poet laureate from 1850 until his death in 1892, Alfred Lord Tennyson spoke to a complex and paradoxical age. His widely varied poetry made the author of *Idylls of the King* the most representative poet of the Victorian age. Writing sometimes with the optimism of his contemporary Robert Browning, sometimes with the brooding melancholy of Matthew Arnold, Tennyson wrote of the demands of love and duty, of the conflict between the public and private selves.

Tennyson's own life, particularly the early days, was one of tension and conflict. Born in 1809, he began writing poetry at an early age, stimulated perhaps by his wide reading and by a desire to escape the morbid atmosphere of his home. His father, the rector of Somersby, was a man of erratic behavior, sometimes kind, but more often melancholy and harsh toward his family. Even after Tennyson left home his life was not easy; he suffered from poverty, the lack of public recognition of his poetry, and the death of his friend, Arthur Hallam—events which must be at least partially responsible for the introspective quality of much of the early poetry. The last section of *Idylls of the King,* "Morte d'Arthur," was written during this period of his life.

But most of the poem was written after 1850. This is the great year of Tennyson's life, when *In Memoriam* was published and he was made poet laureate. With public recognition came financial security, and the opportunity to marry Emily Sellwood, his fiancée of fourteen years. But if the main part of *Idylls of the King* took shape after the bitter conflicts (at least the external ones) were past, many of the themes of the early poetry recur in the mature work. Contrasting motifs that surface in the early lyrics (the passive acceptance of the sensual life in "The Lotus-Eaters," the ultimate rejection of that subjective world in "Palace of Art") come together in many of the later poems, including *Idylls of the King*. In "The Coming of Arthur," for example, the young king sees Guinevere, falls in love with her, but rides on to duty and to battle.

The decision and the conflict seem typically Victorian. The years 1837 to 1901 (Victoria's reign ends neatly just as the new century begins) saw change and reform in England. The Chartist Movement of the 1840's and the various Reform Bills (in 1867, 1884, 1885) were real if not entirely effectual attempts to right the wrongs of a world irreparably altered by the Industrial Revolution. For many Victorians, and certainly for Tennyson, a sense of duty was as real and immediate a part of life as love and pleasure.

But there was often a paradoxically introspective quality about the literature of this age of social action. New developments in science and their religious and philosophical implications turned writers away from the outer world and inward to the self as they tried to discover through meditation and reflection the values and the God that, in J. Hillis Miller's sense of the word, seemed to be "disappearing." Tennyson read widely in the sciences, in astronomy and geology, while he was a student at Cambridge. He knew Lyell's *Principles of Geology,* an unsettling precursor of Darwin and the Theory of Evolution. Undoubtedly this reading reinforced his early predilection for subjectivity—an attitude that would always be at war with the demands of the public role of poet laureate.

A problem that arises when analyzing these tensions in *Idylls of the King* is that Tennyson's epic (like the earlier *In Memoriam*) was written over a long period of time. The question must be asked: are the twelve idylls separate, fragmentary, or is there a unifying theme—or set of themes? Taken from a chronological point of view the problem is even more difficult here than in *In Memoriam,* which was written over a period of about sixteen years. Although "The Coming of Arthur" was conceived in 1833, the first idylls (four in number) were not completed and published until 1859; expanded versions followed in 1869, 1871, and 1872. The complete work did not appear until 1885, seven years before the poet's death. Thus the reader is dealing with a poem that was written over a period of fifty years, begun when the poet was twenty-four and finished when he was seventy-four.

There is, of course, one obvious unifying theme—the Arthurian legend which Tennyson derived mainly from Malory's *Morte d'Arthur.* But just as *In Memoriam* transcends its original theme (Tennyson's sense of personal loss at the death of Hallam), *Idylls of the King* becomes more than a retelling of an ancient romance. Written in the Victorian spirit, the poem speaks not only of the mystique of the Round Table, but of man in and out of society, of what was and what might have been.

The plot centers not on one man, but on a vision of the better world that Arthur and his good knights would create. Tennyson's tale is not of a man who would be king, but of a man who must be king—of a society that is destined to be born, come to fruition, and finally to die because of perfidy from within.

A number of the idylls are concerned with the sharp contrast between the high ideal and the actuality. In "Vivien" Merlin is enticed by the vixenish Vivien into giving up a magic formula known to the magician alone. Merlin sometimes sees Vivien without illusion, but at other times allows himself to be ensnared by her false but charming façade. Even the wise Merlin must be reminded that the world is not always as it seems, that in life exists the potentiality of death, in love the possibility of deceit, and in all idealistic endeavors the opportunity for treachery.

This knowledge of the good in evil, the evil in good, appears throughout the poem. The search for the grail, for instance, is a highly idealistic mission. Through the quest for the cup from which Christ drank and the various tests of character to determine whether he would succeed, the quester is strengthened and purified; he returns a better knight. But the vision can only come to a few; despite the noble motives that initiate the adventure, the end result is the weakening of Cameliard because of the absence of her leaders.

Ultimately, it is not the search for the grail, but Guinevere's guilty love for Lancelot that becomes the catalyst for Cameliard's destruction. But it is only one of a flood of incidents. Many events in the poem lead to the defeat of the Round Table; many perfidies—Tristan's, Gawain's, Modred's—destroy the ideal society. Like the period in which it was written, *Idylls of the King* cannot be interpreted simplistically. The problem it examines is perhaps the basic modern and Victorian dilemma: what is to become of society, and more importantly, what is to become of man, destined to exist simultaneously within himself and among others.

Alice Guise

IF WINTER COMES

Type of work: Novel
Author: A. S. M. Hutchinson (1879-1971)
Type of plot: Social criticism
Time of plot: 1912-1919
Locale: Southern England
First published: 1920

If Winter Comes *is the heartwarming story of a man who loved all humanity but was persecuted and betrayed by those who did not understand him. The book makes no pretensions to great literature, but has remained a favorite among all classes of readers.*

A. S. M. Hutchinson's *If Winter Comes* is a prime example of a novel which cannot be called universal in its appeal, yet which has remained a minor classic among twentieth century British and American readers. The simplicity of its theme, man's discovery of universal love and forgiveness, coupled with the overly complex plot puts it more on the level of a daytime television serial than a great work of literature. However, as one critic has put it, Hutchinson's works are second rate, but good second rate, which is a distinction in itself.

One of the principal reasons why *If Winter Comes* is not considered first rate is that it plays entirely too much on the audience's emotions. The tragedies which befall the principal characters border on the maudlin. The reader may become very engrossed in the plot, but he does so on an emotional rather than an intellectual level. It is difficult to relate the bizarre turns of plot to real life.

The best aspect of the novel is the characterization of Mark Sabre, a simple man who appears too complex to his acquaintances because he takes a different view of life from their own. He, like many people, desperately tries to find an uncomplicated existence but is prevented from doing so by the complexities of life. In many respects the characterization of Mark is drawn from Hutchinson's own personality. Although he had a great deal of success from his literary career during his own lifetime, he was somewhat of a recluse and desired to live a very simple, peaceful life, devoid of notoriety.

Aside from the picture of Mark Sabre, the descriptions of life and manners during the era of World War I in the English town are valuable to students of social history. By analyzing situations and the moralistic reactions of the townspeople, an interesting picture of English country life emerges; although chronologically removed from the Victorian era, the people in the novel are basically as staid and unrelenting as their nineteenth century counterparts.

THE ILIAD

Type of work: Poem
Author: Homer (c. Ninth century B.C.)
Type of plot: Heroic epic
Time of plot: Trojan War
Locale: Troy
First transcribed: Sixth century B. C.

Set during a three-day period in the Trojan War, The Iliad *tells the story of the wrath of Achilles against King Agamemnon. The battle episodes reveal the true characters of the warriors, their strengths and their weaknesses. These figures emerge as human beings not of one era, but of all eras and for all time.*

The earliest extant work of European literature, Homer's epic poem, the *Iliad,* is also one of the most enduring creations of Western culture. Of the author, or possibly authors, we know nothing for certain. Tradition says that Homer was a Greek of Asia Minor. Herodotus surmised that Homer lived in the ninth century B.C., which seems reasonable in the light of modern scholarship and archaeology. The poet drew on a large body of legend about the seige of Troy, material with which his audience was familiar, and which had been part of a bardic tradition. Homer himself may not have transcribed the two epics attributed to him, but it is probable that he gave the poems their present shape.

The *Iliad* was originally intended to be recited or chanted, rather than read. Its poetic style is vivid, taut, simple, direct, full of repeated epithets and elaborate visual similes. The treatment is serious and dignified throughout, and the total effect is one of grandeur. With Homer we are clearly in the presence of a great poet.

His greatness also reveals itself in the action of the *Iliad,* where, within the scope of a few weeks in the tenth year of the seige of Troy, Homer gives the impression of covering the whole scope of the war by a few deft incidents. The appearance of Helen on the walls of Troy forcibly reminds the reader that she was the cause of the war. The catalogue of ships and warriors calls to mind the first arrival of the Greek army at Troy. The duel between Paris and Menelaus would properly have come in the first years of the war, but its placement in the poem suggests the breakdown of diplomacy which leads to the bloodbath of fighting. And Hector's forebodings of his own death and of the fall of Troy as he talks to his wife, not to mention his dying forecast of Achilles' death, all point to the future of the war and its conclusion. Homer thus gives the rather narrow scope of the poem's immediate action much greater breadth.

However, the *Iliad* is not a mere chronicle of events in the Trojan War. It deals with one specific, and crucial, set of sequences of the war: the quarrel of Achilles with his commander, Agamemnon; Achilles' withdrawal from the war; the fighting in his absence; Agamemnon's futile attempt to conciliate Achilles; the Trojan victories; Patroclus' intervention and death at Hector's hands; Achilles' re-entry to the war to avenge his friend's murder; the death of Hector; and Priam's ransom of Hector's body from Achilles. The poem has a classical structure, with a beginning, middle, and end.

This sequence is important in its effect on the war as a whole for two reasons. Without Achilles, the ablest fighter, the Greeks are demoralized even though they have many powerful warriors. It is plain that Achilles will die before Troy is taken, so the Greeks will have to capture Troy by other means than force in his absence. The second reason is that the climax of the poem, the killing of Hector, prefigures the fall of Troy, for as long as Hector remained alive the Greeks were unable to make much headway against the Trojans.

Achilles is the precursor of the tragic hero according to Aristotle's definition. Young, handsome, noble, courageous, eloquent, generous, and of unsurpassed prowess, his tragic flaw lies in the savage intensity of his emotions. He knows he will die young. In fact, he has chosen to die at Troy, and thereby win a lasting reputation, rather than to grow old peacefully. It is precisely his pride, his supreme skill in warfare, and his lust for future glory that makes him so ferocious when he is crossed. He has a hard time restraining himself from killing Agamemnon, and a harder time bearing Agamemnon's insult. He puts pride before loyalty when his Greek comrades are being overrun. And only when the war touches him personally, after he has allowed his friend Patroclus to enter the combat and be slain, does he come to terms with Agamemnon. Then his rage against the Trojans and Hector consumes him, and he is merciless in his vengeance, slaughtering Trojans by scores, gloating over Hector's corpse and abusing it, and sacrificing twelve Trojan nobles on Patroclus' funeral pyre. His humanity is restored in the end when, at Zeus' command, he allows old King Priam to ransom Hector's body. Trembling with emotion, he feels pity for the old man and reaches out his hand to him. It is the most moving moment in the epic.

If Achilles lives by a rigid code of personal honor and fights to win a lasting reputation, he has nothing to lose by dying. Life is worthless to him except insofar as it allows him to prove his own value. Yet, paradoxically, this very ethic makes his life more intense and tragic than it might have been. Hector, by contrast, is fighting on the defensive for a city he knows is doomed, and his responsibilities as a leader tend to burden him. He has others to think about, even though he foresees their fate, and all of this hinders his becoming a truly effective warrior like Achilles. Whereas Achilles' life seems tragic, Hector's life is one of pathos, but the pathos of a man fighting heroically against overwhelming odds.

The gods play a prominent part in the *Iliad,* and they are thoroughly humanized, having human shapes, sexes, and passions. Although they have superhuman powers, they behave in an all-too-human fashion—feasting, battling, fornicating, cheating, protecting their favorites from harm. Just as the Greek army is a loose confederation under Agamemnon, so the gods are subject to Zeus. What is interesting is the way superhuman and human forces interact. Divinity penetrates human action through oracles, dreams, visions, inspiration; it shows itself in inspired warfare where a hero seems invincible, and in miraculous interventions where a wounded hero is spirited away and healed. However, the gods are not omnipotent. Zeus can merely delay the death of a man, but in the end must bow to Fate. Further, men have free will; they are not mere puppets. Achilles has deliberately chosen his destiny. Men, finally, have more dignity than the gods because they choose their actions in the face of death, while the gods have no such necessity, being immortal. It is death that gives human decisions their meaning, for death is final and irrevocable. The *Iliad* is a powerful statement of what it means to be human in the middle of vast and senseless bloodshed.

James Weigel, Jr.

THE IMPORTANCE OF BEING EARNEST

Type of work: Drama
Author: Oscar Wilde (1856-1900)
Type of plot: Comedy of manners
Time of plot: Late nineteenth century
Locale: London and Hertfordshire
First presented: 1895

A play built on a pun and plotted around a misunderstanding over the name Ernest, this comic masterpiece is an attack on earnestness; that is, the Victorian solemnity of a false seriousness which results in priggishness, hypocrisy, and so-called piety.

Oscar Wilde, the leading spokesman for the so-called Yellow Nineties, stood at the end of the nineteenth century and jeered at his Victorian forefathers. All their sacred values—name, position, and money—are ridiculed in his most popular work, *The Importance of Being Earnest.* Turning on a play of words, the drama also satirizes the idea of earnestness. If there were any virtue to which the Victorians attached the greatest significance, it was that of earnestness. To work hard, to be sincere, frank, and open with a high degree of seriousness was a social ideal which underpinned their whole notion of society and religion. Wilde not only satirized hypocrisy and sham virtue, but also mocked its authentic representation.

If the play has any heroes at all, they are Algernon Moncrieff and Jack Worthing, the two dandies; neither are what they seem. The polar opposites of earnestness, placing no value on sincerity or work, they create "night identities" to live out their instinctual life which is forbidden in society. Algy invents a sick friend and goes "Bunburying," while Jack assumes the identity of his nonexistent brother, "Ernest," for his London escapades. It is while they are engaged in such masquerades that they feel themselves to be real and authentic. It is only when they take on their social identities, Jack as the warden of Cecily Cardew, and Algy as the nephew of the fearsome Lady Augusta Bracknell, that they are unreal and hypocritical. The play, however, does not pursue the serious implications of these circumstances and dissolves into a comic farce where Jack and Algy struggle to convince everyone, even Miss Letitia Prism, that they are their social identities, in order to win Cecily and Gwendolen, two empty-headed Victorian maidens. They fall victim, in fact, to the attractions of earnestness and are appropriately rewarded.

IN DUBIOUS BATTLE

Type of work: Novel
Author: John Steinbeck (1902-1968)
Type of plot: Social criticism
Time of plot: The 1930's
Locale: California
First published: 1936

One of the most successful proletarian novels written in the United States, In Dubious Battle *is a forceful book, with vivid characterizations and a sharp, angry focus. A story of the clash of social and economic forces during the early part of the Depression of the 1930's, this intensely vital narrative stands among the best of Steinbeck's novels.*

In Dubious Battle, Steinbeck's fifth book—the first after *Tortilla Flat* (1935), which had brought him immediate fame—solidified his literary reputation. As an embodiment of the author's reforming vision, derived from the explosive social and economic problems of California in the 1930's, this novel is his most obviously "proletarian" comment on class struggle. It has been looked upon by critics as the source for his Pulitzer Prize-winning masterpiece, *The Grapes of Wrath* (1939). Although its dialogue captures the rough idiom of the migrant workers and strike organizers, the novel is too "pat" in the inevitability of plot and abrupt character development to be considered among Steinbeck's best work.

Yet it is notable for Doc Burton's expression of the concept of "group-man," an organic, animal-like entity which Jim, the hero, learns to recognize as something quite apart from the individual men who compose it. Jim realizes that "the Holy Land, Democracy, Communism," are only words invented by group-man to "reassure the brains of individual men" and that the group has a will of its own that no individual can discern accurately. The novel's major theme is the organizers' recognition that anger must be sublimated into wrath; only then can it be dispassionate and indifferent enough to become mechanistically effective. Steinbeck presents his story with the stark realism of the muckrakers. The idyllic pastoral vision of Frost's "After Apple Picking" is trampled by the actual brutality of the applepickers' lives; only at the end does Mac even taste an apple—and that is a withered one. Jim, a person of feeling and dreams contrasted to Mac who is "too busy to feel" because he is always planning, moves from frustrated bystander to charismatic leader to symbolic martyr. And Mac, the pragmatist, finally realizes that Jim is more useful dead than alive.

IN THE WILDERNESS

Type of work: Novel
Author: Sigrid Undset (1882-1949)
Type of plot: Historical chronicle
Time of plot: Early fourteenth century
Locale: Norway
First published: 1927

This novel by the 1928 winner of the Nobel Prize for Literature deals with the invasion of Norway by Duke Eirik of Sweden in 1308. This tale of medieval life is full-bodied and vivid in detail, as well as enriched by scenes of vast happenings and portraits of great historical figures.

More than the others, this third novel of *The Master of Hestviken* tetralogy depends for its action on the large historical movements of the time. It is vastly interesting, especially since Olav's viewpoint on these events is one not likely to be represented in the actual chronicles of the period, for it is the viewpoint of the rank and file. But the colorful details of war and trade are in fact merely the background for a concentrated examination of Olay's character and spiritual condition.

With Ingunn's death in *The Snake Pit,* Olav had expected to be able to abandon the lie in which he had lived so long; instead, he finds himself more closely bound to it than before, for he must continue in it for Eirik's and Cecilia's sake. When the struggles of his conscience come to a head at the pilgrimage church near London, he decides to resolve the problem by going on pilgrimage to Jerusalem without returning to Hestviken first; but he changes his mind when he realizes that his resolution is prompted as much by his desire to avoid the vexed situation at home as by a wish to humble himself before God and be cleansed of his old sin.

In taking up his old life as a cross to be born for his children's sake, he acts out the Christian precept that sin is its own punishment; his decision not to take Torhild into his house again carries out the penitential theme. But in consciously giving up his soul that his children might thrive, he regresses, in effect, into a pre-Christian state of being. The last part of the book shows him immersing himself in thoughtless paganism: attempting to call Ingunn from her grave, applauding Cecilia's fierceness, and glorying in the panoply and comradeship of war. In a way, he comes full circle, experiencing again the emotions of his youth and young manhood. But with the passing of his physical beauty, the link with his early life with Ingunn dissolves, making way for the renewed Christian conflict of *The Son Avenger.*

INAZUMA-BYÔSHI

Type of work: Novel
Author: Santô Kyôden (1761-1816)
Type of plot: Feudal romance
Time of plot: Fifteenth century
Locale: Japan
First published: 1806

Using the central theme of rivalry for succession to a great feudal house and the triumph of good over evil, Santô Kyôden took his materials from traditional Kabuki *plays. The scenes change rapidly and the plot is complicated by the appearance of a large number of secondary characters, but the author's ability carries the reader through the succession of intrigues and subplots.*

Kyôden, better known in the West by his artist's name of Kitao Masanobu, followed his early successes in both print-designing and fiction, by concentrating his attention on the latter. He was the most versatile and gifted of the popular Edo (modern Tokyo) writers. Besides the picture books and fanciful didactic *yomihon* reading books to which he turned under the pressure of Tokugawa censorship, he wrote many excellent *sharehon* ("books of wit"), sophisticated sketches of manners in the Yoshiwara and other pleasure quarters. Though these were limited in subject matter, their realistic dialogue technique greatly influenced the two leading kinds of realistic Edo fiction of the nineteenth century. This tendency toward realism is evident in *Inazuma-byôshi*.

Like many of Santô Kyôden's works, this novel is written in a vigorous, popular style, simple and direct, and often melodramatic in plot. Because of the skillful handling of action and the true-to-life emotions of the characters, the novel was very widely read in Japan. A somber history of vengeance, the novel abounds in violence, suicides, torture, combat, and rapid shifts of plot. It reads often like an early nineteenth century European romantic novel, filled with Gothic horrors and boiling emotions, but, at the same time, a lusty quality and a certain vigorous humor raises the book to a greater level of realism. Kyôden was considered one of the leaders in Japan in the development of the realistic, romantic school of fiction.

Although the plot at times is confusing, owing partly to the large number of characters, a vigor of style and narrative drive carries the action steadily forward. The minor characters tend to be stylized, boldly sketched figures, but the principal characters are much more realistically portrayed. *Inazuma-byôshi* possesses an almost cinematic sweep and power of movement, and the Western reader should not become sidetracked by attempting to follow every minute plot thread; the novel's romantic vision of feudal life in Japan is rendered in an exciting, enjoyable style.

INDEPENDENT PEOPLE

Type of work: Novel
Author: Halldór Laxness (1902-)
Type of plot: Social chronicle
Time of plot: Twentieth century
Locale: Iceland
First published: 1934-1935

Independent People *provides a faithful picture of the bleak, difficult life in Iceland; written in a style and with a scope approaching the epic, the book gives some of the feeling of the traditions of the Vikings and shows how the old ways yield to the new.*

Laxness' *Independent People* is an excellent example of the naturalistic novel, for it demonstrates the thesis that man has no connection with a religious or spiritual world and is subject to the natural forces of heredity and environment. According to naturalism, one must confront the social and economic forces of his background which are usually presented by an author of this school with elaborate and minute documentation. The characters usually show strong animal drives, but they are helpless in their fight against sociological pressures. All of these characteristics fit *Independent People.* In it Laxness starkly presents all the grim details of the life of Bjartur, the "independent man," who fights to rise above his environment, becomes successful for a period, and then sinks back into the miserable life he had worked so hard to escape.

Except for occasional references to automobiles and electricity, one would not know that the novel is set in the twentieth century, for the life style of the crofters is no better than that of peasants in medieval times. The poverty of the crofters is almost unbelievable. They live in small, one room hovels above the stables and are plagued by the smoke of peat stoked fires, the dampness of spring, and the bitter cold of winter when snow may cover the entire house. In an environment where humans live little better than beasts, it is almost unavoidable that they become animalistic and lose all compassion and emotion. In *Independent People,* there is no communication nor understanding among the characters, and any attempt at communication is viewed with suspicion.

The role of women in such circumstances is particularly hard. This is shown in the grotesque death of Rosa who, left alone to die in childbirth, is found dead on the croft floor in a pool of blood. Her infant is kept alive by the warmth of the dog that lies upon it until Bjartur returns. The harshness of a woman's life is also seen in the yearly pregnancies of Finna and in the miserable life Asta is forced to live after Bjartur drives her from the house.

But even more interesting is the perverted response man is conditioned to making to the hard life he is locked into. For instance, Bjartur mourns for neither of his wives. When looking for a housekeeper to care for the infant Asta, he admits that he talks more about animals than about human beings. He dismisses Rosa's death by telling the minister that she just died from loss of blood. No effort to care for her seems to have entered his mind.

There are several prominent themes running through the novel; politics, economics, social reform, and the clash between religion and ancient superstitions are all dealt with in some detail. For years Laxness had searched for a sustaining religious and political ideology, and in *Independent People* the restless energy generated by that search found its first powerful outlet in his bitter attack on materialism. He held the greed and oppression inherent in the materialistic philosophy responsible for the sordidness and suffering which filled the lives of his countrymen in rural Iceland. In exposing the cruelties of rural conditions with all the merciless determination of the naturalist, the author at once enraged many Icelanders—who resented having such a brutal picture of their emerging nation published abroad—and delighted liberals all over Europe and America. Yet for all Laxness' revolutionary vigor, his hatred of power and authority, his scorn for bourgeois morality, and his anger and grim satire, he still was able to express his artist's love of beauty. Alongside scenes of coarseness and themes marked by their bitterness, Laxness displays throughout *Independent People* a great compassion and sensitivity, a capacity for tenderness and concern, and a burning devotion to the spirit of individualism and idealism.

But the center of interest is always the character Bjartur. At times, his seeming indifference is nothing more than an attempt to cope with life's harshness. In the spring following Helgi's disappearance, for instance, Bjartur, looking for a lost ewe, finds the decayed body of a young boy which did not look like a human being. Bjartur touches it once or twice with his stick, takes a good pinch of snuff, and leaves.

Yet Bjartur reveals, at times, that affection is possible in this life. Although he knows Asta is not his child, she is his favorite. He calls her his "little flower" and is horrified when he finds his fingers undoing the fastenings of her undergarment in the townhouse bed they share. He also has a poetic side, for he continually composes complicated verses and teaches the ancient poems of Iceland to Asta. But poetry is the only fancy he allows himself; all else is harsh reality. To Bjartur the sheep and the land are the most important things in the world, for after years of debt his only desire is to be considered an "independent man." When he brings his bride, Rosa, to Summerhouses, he says that independence is the most important thing in life. He intends to maintain his independence. This is the great irony of the book, for his independence is false; he is completely at the mercy of his environment. His stubbornness and false pride lead him to disaster when he refuses to take the advice of wiser men and falls into bankruptcy when he borrows money to build a "real" house which he hopes will rival the Bailiff's mansion.

Bjartur defies everything and everyone. He refuses to believe in either the Christian religion or in the ancient superstitions of the country. In a show of bravado he defies the spirit of Gunnvor, the witch buried upon his land, who was supposed to have killed most of her children and to have drunk the blood of those who survived. Everyone else in the district adds a rock to her grave when they pass, but this Bjartur refuses to do. Instead he purchases a headstone for her grave marked "To Gunnvor from Bjartur." It is after this act of defiance that his financial troubles begin.

Laxness was reared in the country and is able to give an intimate picture of the starkness of Icelandic life on the frontier. This great attention to detail makes the book approach epic proportions. However, there are some flaws in the author's style. He uses the omniscient point of view, but he often violates this with authorial intrusions commenting upon politics, economics, or human nature. The style is also uneven. At times it is smooth and poetic, but at others it is extremely awkward. On the whole, however, the book is valuable both as a social document and as the story of Bjartur, the independent man, who, struggling against impossible odds, is never defeated psychologically even when he loses all he has worked so hard for. Without remorse, he plans to begin again at the wrteched, abandoned croft of his mother-in-law.

Vina Nickels Oldach

INDIAN SUMMER

Type of work: **Novel**
Author: **William Dean Howells (1837-1920)**
Type of plot: **Domestic realism**
Time of plot: **Shortly after the American Civil War**
Locale: **Florence, Italy**
First published: **1886**

A masterpiece of the realism of the commonplace, this book details life in the American colony in Florence shortly after the American Civil War. Howells wrote with sympathy and affection of his aging, cultured characters. Some critics consider this work his best novel.

Indian Summer represents Howells at his best; psychological acuteness, facile development, and deft delineation of character all typify Howells at the top of his form. A European love story in the American mode, the delicate handling of manners, marriage, and travel made *Indian Summer* an immensely popular work.

Howells was well equipped for this particular task. Set in Italy, the novel capitalizes on Howells' experience as consul to Venice during the Civil War. He revisited Italy a few years before writing *Indian Summer,* and worked on that novel concurrently with *Tuscan Cities,* thus keeping the intricacies of the place of Americans in Italian society fresh in his mind. Howells was, in 1886, in the ripe Indian summer of his own career, and the Old World setting and subtle, intricate relationships of the characters provided a most appropriate vehicle for the delicate touch he had perfected in *A Modern Instance* and *The Rise of Silas Lapham.*

Furthermore, while Howells' later fictions were to strain his social consciousness and force him to question the ability of literary realism to deal with real life, *Indian Summer* is a precise embodiment of his own critical theory. It is the commonplace, rather than the fantastic, elaborate, or unusual that provides the material for the novel. The focus of the story is not on plot but rather on the development of character. The story is deliberately antiromantic; real life is shown to be more good than evil, and democracy comes off better than decaying European aristocracy.

Recent criticism, moreover, has uncovered symbolic and even allegorical levels of meaning beneath the quaint and quiet surface of *Indian Summer.* The novel is to be appreciated as vintage Howells, most of all because he was perhaps never to write as well again.

INDIANA

Type of work: Novel
Author: George Sand (Mme. Aurore Dudevant, 1804-1876)
Type of plot: Sentimental romance
Time of plot: Early nineteenth century
Locale: France
First published: 1832

Written at the height of French Romanticism, Indiana *exhibits all of the conventions of the movement. The chief value of the book derives from the fact that it typifies a popular literary form and a philosophy which still survive, to a lesser degree, in contemporary literature.*

Resurgent interest in female and feminist writers ensures that the question of George Sand's literary contribution will again receive attention. Yet it seems likely that her life will remain the central object of controversy and fascination. Calling her a female Lord Byron would not be incorrect, for she scandalized France and England as he had done, and the reading public doted on the autobiographical aspects of her novels. But it is important to recognize the specifically feminist—as opposed to the romantic—dimension of her activities. Her bisexuality, her romantic liaisons, and her opposition to the institution of marriage frequently obscure the fact that she was one of the earliest female writers to make her living by her pen. Her use of a male pseudonym and her masculine dress were occasioned by constraints against women: novels written by women were not often given a fair reading by male editors and critics; likewise, many of the clubs and theaters were closed to women, so her male disguise enabled her to participate more fully in literary Paris. Her first published work under the renowned pseudonym, *Indiana* enjoyed success and convinced Sand that she could support herself and her children by means of her writing.

Indiana, as a heroine of a new order, comes to believe, as did her creator, in the primacy of love over society's moral strictures. The romantic movement, with its emphasis on the individual, championed passionate love as the basis for a relationship—as opposed to the old contractual arrangements based on family, estate, or power. Indiana, says George Sand, "is will battling against necessity . . . love beating its head against the barriers raised by civilization." The novel suggests this new ethic even in the extremes of its romanticism—the suicides and near-suicides, the fainting spells, the exaggerated speech and pleas of everlasting faithfulness. Indiana rebels against the bonds imposed by society, first by refusing to submit her will to her husband, then by offering herself to Raymon, and finally by living in harmony with Sir Ralph, unmarried and away from society's laws ("to resist mentally every species of moral restraint had become with her second nature"). *Indiana* is a good introduction to the concerns and style of George Sand, even though commentary throughout the novel emphasizes differences between males and females, especially of temperament, that a modern reader might find outmoded.

INÊS DE CASTRO

Type of work: Drama
Author: António Ferreira (1528?-1569)
Type of plot: Romantic tragedy
Time of plot: 1354-1360
Locale: Portugal
First presented: c. 1558

In construction, this drama follows Greek models, with a chorus which serves as spectator and the voice of Fate. Moments of dramatic brilliance and scenes of suspense and moving poetry have caused the work to endure for four hundred years, despite flaws of exposition and dull passages.

This is one of history's most famous love stories, describing "the love that endured beyond the grave." It is set in fourteenth century Portugal, about a century after the Islamic Moors had been expelled, when Portuguese nobles were still fanatical Christians, wearing chain mail, red crosses on their breasts, and wielding two-handed broadswords.

The counselors of old warrior King Alfonso IV became worried when his son, Crown Prince Pedro, developed an unusually absorbing interest in Inês de Castro, a beautiful lady-in-waiting to the Queen. Many people feared that this union would endanger Portugal, since Inês' brothers were notoriously ambitious. This situation led to a bizarre tragedy, dramatized later by António Ferreira, as well as by Portugal's national poet, Luis de Camoëns, in his masterpiece *The Lusiads*.

Everyone was surprised when Pedro refused to leave Inês, even after pressure had been put upon him. More pressure was exercised, but still Pedro would not abandon Inês. Her enemies finally induced the King to order her assassination, but she made so moving an appeal to Dom Alfonso that he relented—"before the frowning King fair Inês stands, her tears of artless innocence, her air so mild, so lovely, and her face so fair, mov'd the stern monarch. . . . "

The influence of the nobles persisted, however, and she was murdered. As the assassins' swords plunged into the "swan neck" of green-eyed Inês, some small white flowers at her feet, watered with her tears, turned red. Inês is still remembered by the maidens of the university town of Coimbra, where the murder occurred, tradition having it that their tears formed a fountain of love around Pedro's statue there.

Maddened by sorrow, Pedro took the throne in 1357. He exercised ferocious revenge on Inês' killers, staking them out on stone slabs and cutting out their hearts. He then declared that he had been legally married to Inês. Tradition has it that he exhumed her body from the grave, brought it to the palace in Alcobaça, and had her crowned with sumptuous ceremony, obliging the highest nobles of the kingdom to kiss the icy hand of "the Queen after death." Pedro and Inês are buried today in marble tombs in Alcobaça, foot to foot, so that, upon arising on Judgment Day, they will see each other immediately. This tragedy has long been a favorite theme, not only of Portuguese playwrights, but of the playwrights of other literatures.

THE INFORMER

Type of work: Novel
Author: Liam O'Flaherty (1896-   )
Type of plot: Psychological melodrama
Time of plot: The 1920's
Locale: Dublin
First published: 1925

An outstanding example of modern Irish realism and a masterpiece of suspense, this novel was a popular as well as a critical success. Adhering to the classical unities of time, place, and action, the story covers a single night in Dublin.

This novel is set in Ireland during the 1920's, in a period when the Irish Republican Army was dormant after its civil conflict with the Free State. There were several isolated bands of rebels still waging a quasi-war. Some of these were units of the IRA and some were communist. Gypo Nolan had belonged to one of these communist groups, but this is not a story about Irish politics or about the way rebels deal with informers. The politics of Gypo Nolan are kept vague by O'Flaherty, partly because Gypo himself understands them so vaguely, and partly because the author wishes to focus his attention, and the reader's, upon the fact of Gypo's abandonment. Gypo's torment, its nature and progress, is the central focus of the novel.

In spite of the fact that relatively little critical work has been done on O'Flaherty, he has long been recognized as one of the central figures of the literary movement called the Irish Renaissance. Seán O'Faoláin felt that O'Flaherty shared center stage in this period with James Joyce only. One of his claims to this honor is *The Informer*. Some feel that of all O'Flaherty's novels this one is the most universal and the least provincial. It, more than any other of his works, is a novel about humanity and the human condition.

O'Flaherty's focus on the human condition in this novel is existential. It is the condition of anxiety. The fact that Gypo Nolan is cut off from human society for being an informer is not as important as the fact that he is cut off. O'Flaherty feels that this is the state of all people. We are all cut off from others to a greater or lesser degree. The purpose of this novel is to explain what the pain of this condition is like, and to describe it as it seems to an observer, to one outside the soul. This same existential loneliness is described internally, as it seems from inside the soul, in one of O'Flaherty's earlier novels, *The Black Soul,* which is the most autobiographical of all his works. He put a great deal of his own loneliness and suffering into the characterizations of *The Black Soul,* and *The Informer* can best be understood as a companion piece. The two novels explore the same problem in different ways.

O'Flaherty makes excellent use of his skill in describing things in order to create atmosphere. He adds to the reader's understanding of loneliness by making him see the misery of Gypo's surroundings. O'Flaherty is able to paint with deft strokes the environment in which Gypo Nolan, Gallagher, and all the other characters operate. He is able to make settings, rooms, household objects, trolley tracks, and paper packages all speak volumes. His use of words is so seemingly magical that he not only can conjure up a scene in the mind's eye of the reader, but also can use this same scene to illuminate the lives, thoughts, and the very essences of the characters in them. It has been said that O'Flaherty writes more for the eye than for the ear. This criticism is all the more appropriate in view of the stunning artistic success of the movie version of this novel. In the motion picture, as in the book, inanimate objects and scenes of action serve only to intensify and illuminate the spiritual lives of the main characters. It is in this visual regard that the movie is most faithful to the form of the novel. Gypo is a miserable man, a fact that we understand more clearly when we see him moving in a miserable world. It is a world that O'Flaherty makes the reader see.

One of the themes runing through the book on several levels is that of New Testament parallels. This is not dissimilar to the existential anxiety which forms the central core of *The Informer,* but rather it is one of the vehicles for its expression. Gypo Nolan can be understood in these terms as a figure of Judas, if one takes Judas also to indicate the nature of Everyman. The parallel with the New Testament is most explicit in the final scene when Gypo, while dying, asks the mother of Francis McPhillip to forgive him. She does so because he did not know what he was doing. This book does not admit of simple substitution of names in order to say that Gypo equals Judas, Gallagher equals Pontius Pilate, and Francis' mother equals the Virgin Mary. O'Flaherty's novel is much too varied and complex for that. Yet Gypo does have much in common with Judas and can be said to be a Judas figure. Gypo turns in his friend to the authorities for a sum of money, and like Judas he finds out that this betrayal cuts him off from his fellow men and women. Neither does the betrayal bring him any sort of happiness. Gypo and Judas both throw the money away and die.

No one, O'Flaherty seems to be saying, can find any sort of happiness if one is cut off from humanity. This is the tragedy of Gypo Nolan, Judas Iscariot, and everyone. Gypo does manage to do some good with the money. He gives a woman in a brothel enough money to enable her to go home, but in the end nothing is left. He has dissipated all the money and is left with only the loneliness that is his birthright, with the existential agony that is the central concern of *The Informer*.

Gypo is not bright. He really was unaware of the consequences of his betrayal. He knew only that he had no money for a bed for the night and that there was a reward of twenty pounds for his friend. By going to the police, he could afford a bed. That was as far as his reasoning went. This lack of intelligence was the immediate cause of his downfall, even though on a deeper level, his humanity made him an outcast from human society.

It is important to remember that Gypo is really a very immature person. O'Flaherty is able to build sympathy in the course of this novel, sympathy even for an informer, by gradually pointing out that Gypo is only a child. This is an amazing example of literary skill, for the Irish hate no one so much as an informer. They and their families have for generations suffered too much from traitors for there to be much sympathy left for informers, but O'Flaherty is able to make one see that this informer is still a boy-man torn by the loneliness that all boy-men must live with. And we are all, after all, children in one way or another. Sympathy also arises from the fact that in O'Flaherty's eyes, and ultimately in the eyes of the reader, Gypo Nolan is only incidentally a traitor. He is primarily Everyman, and the author is able to bring about a growing sympathy for him by careful exposition of Gypo's humanity. This special ability was one of the great strengths of O'Flaherty's art.

Glenn M. Edwards

THE INNOCENT VOYAGE

Type of work: Novel
Author: Richard Hughes (1900-)
Type of plot: Psychological realism
Time of plot: Early nineteenth century
Locale: Jamaica, the high seas, England
First published: 1929

This classic novel, with its insights into the childhood psyche, displays a varied humor that runs from macabre playfulness to biting satire. It combines with unusual effectiveness the events of an adventure story—a hurricane, capture by pirates, murder—and psychological analysis of the most subtle kind.

In *The Innocent Voyage* or *A High Wind in Jamaica,* as the novel is now universally known, melodramatic and fantastic events are united with innocence and humor, all blended with craftsmanship and style. A powerful and blunt realism combined with the delicacy of the poetic descriptions gives the narrative a strange, disturbing quality. Yet the author is careful never to overwrite when describing the bizarre incidents of the story. The plot is based upon an actual event related to Hughes by an old lady who had been one of the children. Joseph Conrad previously utilized the same actual happening in *Romance* (1901).

Emily's maturing during the novel is rendered as a symbol, yet Hughes never lets any outside meanings interfere with the tale he has to tell. The sudden awakening of Emily's consciousness is detailed with charming and touching truth. The account of the girl's development is *right,* portrayed with sensitivity and with humor. Her sudden questioning at the age of ten of the universe and its maker and her amazement at her own being are the finest pages in an extraordinary and perceptive novel.

Hughes's attitude toward the children is unique in fiction, never condescending and unusually objective, as if he were writing of a different species being observed under experimental conditions. Because the characters are handled with unassuming honesty, the strange events of the story become almost matter-of-fact. Hughes seems to be implying that, yes, life is bizarre and frightening, but also beautiful and amazing—especially for those with the awareness and fearlessness of children. But with knowledge and maturity must come fear and deception and unhappiness—and the gradual clouding of vision. And this loss of innocence is the real tragedy of human life. (Perhaps the worst aspect of the loss is that adults do not even remember what they have lost, or even seem to realize that they have lost anything.) Yet Hughes does not romanticize either the children or their condition. His power comes from the cleanness of his objectivity and the purity of his prose.

THE INSPECTOR GENERAL

Type of work: Drama
Author: Nikolai V. Gogol (1809-1852)
Type of plot: Political satire
Time of plot: Early nineteenth century
Locale: Russia
First presented: 1836

This comedy was written as a protest against the fumbling, venal bureaucracy of Russia's small towns. Gogol satirized here the practice of giving and accepting bribes and favors, creating as he did so a large number of lively, hilarious characters.

Although most of Nikolai Gogol's highly praised work consists of prose fiction, *The Inspector General* established his reputation in the theater as well. In the history of Russian literature, Gogol was a pioneer of realistic prose. When he turned his hand to playwrighting, Gogol set equally important precedents for later Russian drama, for he applied his skills at realistic fiction to the stage. He wrote two other plays and left a dramatic fragment unfinished at the time of his death. But Gogol's theatrical laurels rest on his masterpiece, *The Inspector General.* The play has been translated under several titles: *The Inspector, The Government Inspector,* and *Revizor* (transliterated from the Cyrillic, this is the Russian word for "Inspector" or "Auditor"). But by whatever name it is called, it has deservedly been given unstinting critical acclaim.

This satiric comedy on corrupt bueaucrats in the Russian provinces blazed the trail for the realistic social drama of the later nineteenth and the twentieth centuries. However, Gogol was by no means a doctrinaire realist, nor was he even a devoted social or political reformer in the ideological-polemic sense. In fact, Gogol saw himself not as a social satirist but as a moral satirist, unmasking human frailties and related social imperfections. Yet regardless of his intent, *The Inspector General* is broad social satire, and it set the pace for the realistic comedies of social and political satire which followed.

In addition, lively characterization and spirited language contribute to the play's realistic flavor. The town's minor functionaries, for example, are properly resentful about Anton Antonovich's so-called unwarranted criticism of them and in retaliation endeavor to undermine his reputation with "The Inspector"; and later they are equally indignant about having been bilked of several hundred rubles by "The Inspector"—all of these part of the perdurable behavioral repertoire of civil servants. And the dialogue among these petty bureaucrats and merchants, from Anton Antonovich on down, is likewise authentic: a broad and salty jargon reflected in some of the better translations by such English equivalents as "ain't," the double negative, lack of subject-verb agreement, malapropisms, mangled French expressions, vulgar allusions, pretentiousness, and the like. Here, as nowhere else, Gogol's dialogue is flawless, with never a wrong word or false tone, always with an eye toward intensifying the comic effect. Gogol, in a brilliantly puckish stroke, even named his characters to reflect their qualities. Skvoznik-Dmukhanovsky translates rougly to Rascal-Puffed-up, for instance, and Hlestakov means "Whipper-snapper." Zemlyanika is strawberry; Lyapkin-Tyapkin literally signifies "Bungle-Steal"; and Hlopov designates a "bedbug." Gogol's astute satiric eye, it seems, overlooked no opportunity.

One of Gogol's innovations is the omission of the conventional "love interest," for Ivan's passes at Maria and Anna have nothing to do with love for any of them. And in another departure from convention, Gogol includes not a single sympathetic character in this many-peopled play, a device that his enemies were quick to fault. But serious critics agree about the genius of the ploy, for its satiric quality is enhanced immensely by it. In fact, the play is unerringly constructed from start to finish, and, aside from its topicality, has remained popular because it is plainly and simply good entertainment.

INTRUDER IN THE DUST

Type of work: Novel
Author: William Faulkner (1897-1962)
Type of plot: Social realism
Time of plot: Early 1930's
Locale: Jefferson, Mississippi
First published: 1948

In this novel, Faulkner juxtaposed his views regarding the problem of the black in the South against a bizarre tale involving murder, grave robbing, and lynching. The book succeeds because Faulkner's skill makes the reader believe in its central characters, and understand and sympathize with them.

Intruder in the Dust is an excellent introduction to William Faulkner's numerous and complex novels of the Deep South. Set in Faulkner's mythical Yoknapatawpha County, his standard fictional location, *Intruder in the Dust* also includes such familiar inhabitants as attorney Gavin Stevens and farmer Carothers Edmonds. But this novel includes only a few examples of such famous Faulknerian stylistic devices as elongated, periodic sentences, disconnected narratives, multiple narrative perspectives, psychological time, and stream of consciousness. While the very substance of *The Sound and the Fury, Absalom, Absalom!, Light in August,* and *As I Lay Dying* consists of these variations in style of form, *Intruder in the Dust* (except for Chick Mallison's meditations and flashbacks) is a relatively straightforward narration. Faulkner novels typically use parable and folklore as a basis for forming a vision of life as a neurotic and involved psychological process. But *Intruder in the Dust* blends folklore and parable with a formula mystery story and strikes a much simpler note than most of Faulkner's work.

Aspects of folklore permeate *Intruder in the Dust.* Faulkner's panorama of rural local color includes a generous sampling of cracker-barrel philosophers, bigoted rednecks, mischievous, shoeless youngsters, and fading ladies of breeding long past their prime. The plot crackles with anecdotes, bits of country wisdom, humor, and superstition. It is thematically enriched by Gavin Stevens' philosophical speeches. After Chick, Aleck, and Miss Habersham discover that Vinson Gowrie's grave contains the body of Jake Montgomery, *Intruder in the Dust* becomes a highly suspenseful mystery story with Sheriff Hampton and Lawyer Stevens solving the crime in barely enough time to prevent Lucas Beauchamp from being lynched by a mob far more interested in violence than justice.

The novel also contains several parables, one of which is a Southern version of the Biblical Cain and Able story. The brothers Vinson and Crawford Gowrie have joined forces in several business ventures including timber dealing. Crawford, increasingly greedy for his own profits, steals timber from his brother and sells it to the shady Jake Montgomery. When Lucas Beauchamp sees Crawford stealing the timber and threatens to expose him, Crawford kills his brother in a way to make Lucas appear as the murderer. Crawford relies on the townspeople's readiness to blame a black man for the murder of a white man. But, like Mink Snopes in Faulkner's *The Hamlet,* Crawford learns too late that violence, instead of eradicating problems, creates more violence, and eventually one's downfall. Truth simply will not stay buried, Faulkner seems to be saying. In a hair-raising midnight scene combining the best of Edgar Allan Poe and Raymond Chandler, plus his own inimitable sense of place and wry humor, the author has three very frightened individuals uncover the truth that frees Lucas.

Beyond the Cain and Abel story, Gavin Stevens' speeches expand *Intruder in the Dust* into a parable about the people's right to govern themselves. Critics have frequently condemned Stevens' rhetoric as the propaganda of an unfeeling and aristocratic bigot. While this interpretation holds some validity, Stevens is not a mouthpiece for Faulkner's views; nor should Stevens' pleadings, however prolix, be discounted. In the filibuster tradition of Southern oratory, he articulates a code of noninterference, following Candide's final words of "till your own garden." The intruder of the title may refer not only to those who open Vinson Gowrie's grave, but also "outlanders" who would dictate moral action to these people. With their own sense of justice, the Southerners close this incident in their own way. They come to realize that Beauchamp could have little to do with what is fundamentally a family feud. Because of his cruel victimization, Lucas in the future will be shown innumerable courtesies by white people. He has suffered and he is wise. Lucas will endure. The true villains here are the poor whites, those who have perverted the opportunities of their position.

The elderly spinster Eunice Habersham supports Beauchamp enough to rob a grave to prove his innocence. Had Miss Habersham been less sentimental and more skeptical, Crawford Gowrie, guilty and white, would have escaped. On the other hand, Hope Hampton, Sheriff of Yoknapatawpha County, is highly skeptical and totally unsentimental. Hampton seeks justice, not conviction; evidence, not the will of the voters, persuades him to action. He is a diametric opposite to the familiar stereotype of the rural Southern sheriff, a big-bellied bounty hunter who catches victims and tells them "you in a heap of trouble, boy!" The villains of *Intruder in the Dust* behave in predictably stereotyped and evil ways, while the figures in power—Hampton, the prosecutor; Stevens, the defender; and Miss Habersham, the moral sentiment—are humane, rounded characters.

As a story of initiation, the novel is an unqualified success. Young Chick Mallison must unlearn old values as well as learn new ones. In attempting to pay Lucas for his act of kindness, Chick denies the old black man his humanity. What others often interpret as arrogance is really Lucas' unyielding demand that he be treated as a human being, worthy of respect. Gradually

Chick comes to realize the moral rightness in the demand Lucas makes. After the death of Mrs. Beauchamp, Chick sees Lucas and understands that grief can come to a black man as well as to a white. By the time Lucas has been accused of committing murder, Chick knows that he must act with the same humanity Lucas showed him. Through Lucas, Chick also learns to accept Aleck as an equal. Thus, through the initiation of Chick Mallison, Faulkner makes a powerful, positive statement about race relations as fundamentally an encounter between one human being and another.

Because *Intruder in the Dust* includes Gavin Stevens' philosophical discourses on the South's ability to handle its own problems *after* the action has essentially been resolved, this novel is too often dismissed as a distasteful polemic, a lapse in Faulkner's series of brilliant novels. Yet, *Intruder in the Dust* is not so much inferior to such works as *The Sound and the Fury* or *Absalom, Absalom!* as it is different in its approach to the genre. Always an experimenter and innovator, here Faulkner turned with considerable success to establishing his vision in formula fiction, as he did earlier with *Sanctuary* (1931), an even more Gothic murder mystery, and *Pylon* (1935), an adventure story about flying. While *Intruder in the Dust* will probably never rank with his greatest fiction, this work, along with *The Reivers* (1962), does present the famous Faulkner world in a form understandable to many readers.

Patrick Morrow

THE INVISIBLE MAN

Type of work: Novel
Author: H. G. Wells (1866-1946)
Type of plot: Mystery romance
Time of plot: Late nineteenth century
Locale: England
First published: 1897

One of the pseudoscientific romances which Wells wrote early in his career, The Invisible Man *achieves an air of probability by means of the realistic details with which it is built up. The psychological implications of the central situation have continued to fascinate readers.*

Three factors account for the immense effectiveness and enduring popularity of *The Invisible Man*: its believability, its structure, and the profundity of its main theme.

Wells, a keen observer of English village life, evokes a completely convincing picture of Iping and the people of Sussex. The scenes of Griffin in London—especially the department store incident—are almost photographically vivid. Wells's account of Griffin's transformation abounds in carefully thought out details. Providing enough optical and physiological explanation to gain the reader's confidence, Wells meticulously recounts the difficulties which Griffin must surmount. The iridescent material in the eyes of the experimental cat refuses to become invisible, but since Griffin is an albino, the conversion process is somewhat easier. Yet food shows until it is digested, and sleep is a problem when eyelids are transparent. Rain, fog, and sweat reveal the "glistening surface of a man."

Wells employs a masterful three-part structure. The first part, constituting over half of the novel, presents Griffin through his encounters with the villagers and tells of his unsuccessful attempt to keep his invisibility secret. In the second part, Griffin himself recounts the history of his experiments, describes his motives, and narrates the events which led him to Iping. The final section could be called "The Betrayal of Griffin"; its protagonist is Dr. Kemp. Each of these parts has a dramatic unity with a characteristic tone. The reader is drawn from an almost Dickensian atmosphere into the Kafkaesque nightmare world of Griffin's London; then he is plunged into the frenzied, sunlit action at Burdock. The tension in the novel, broken and reestablished, mounts to higher levels as each section unfolds.

The novel's main ethical concern is revealed in the relationship of Griffin and Kemp. In betraying his guest to the police, Kemp destroys all hope of using Griffin's genius for the benefit of society. Nor does Kemp display sufficient empathy for Griffin's psychological suffering; he therefore ranges himself with the narrow-minded Iping villagers who do nothing to make Griffin feel secure. At the same time, Griffin is clearly a moral monstrosity. He is an archetype of the gifted scientist who craves knowledge for the power it will bring. He disregards "the common conventions of humanity," and Wells introduces the frightening thesis that the process of scientific investigation itself makes men like Griffin possible.

IOLANTHE

Type of work: Comic opera
Author: W. S. Gilbert (1836-1911)
Type of plot: Humorous satire
Time of plot: Nineteenth century
Locale: England
First presented: 1882

The story of a shepherd lad, the upper portion of whose body is a fairy but whose feet are molded in human form, this comic operetta satirizes many human foibles and makes gentle fun of the British House of Lords.

While *Patience* was still enjoying a long run at The Savoy Theatre, William Schwenck Gilbert prepared for his musical callaborator, Arthur Seymour Sullivan, the libretto for a new comic opera. Sullivan, as usual, was not wholly satisfied with the preliminary draft of the book, and at his urging Gilbert rewrote the first act. Gilbert himself had trouble with the title. Because his last three successful D'Oyly Carte productions had begun with the letter *P*—*Pinafore* (1878), *The Pirates of Penzance* (1880), and *Patience* (1881)—Gilbert thrashed about for another title beginning with the "lucky" initial. He considered and then rejected "Perola," "Phyllis," and "Princess Pearl" before he chose *Iolanthe,* with the acceptable subtitle *The Peer and the Peri.* This last matter settled, Gilbert and Sullivan's "entirely new and original fairy opera" opened at The Savoy on the evening of November 25, 1882, and continued to hold the stage for a year and two months.

No doubt Gilbert wished to emphasize the "fairy" elements of *Iolanthe* in order to soften any possible criticism of his spoof upon the House of Lords. In the course of Parliamentary debates running throughout Victorian England, the House of Lords, a privileged and largely hereditary body lacking any democratic representation, was under constant fire as antiquated, unresponsive to the people, and ultra-conservative. Almost every reform bill intended to widen the franchise, limited at the same time the powers of the Lords, who eventually lost most of their real authority to the House of Commons. Gilbert, clearly on the side of the liberals, wished to satirize the absurdity of the Peers, but not so directly as to excite political controversy. For the framework of his plot, he reworked an old idea from one of his *Bab Ballads* concerning a hero who is the child of a fairy and is, therefore, half fay and half human. Not even a crusty Tory could complain that the adventures of Strephon could possibly insult the dignities of a modern Lord; and when, at the conclusion of *Iolanthe,* all the Peers marry the fairies, the doughtiest Lord in Parliament would have to acquiesce in pleasure to Gilbert's romantic jest.

But behind the jest, Gilbert's satire applies not only to the House of Lords but also to the notion of a privileged class. The Peers announce their arrival ("Loudly Let the Trumpets Bray") with the contemptuous salutation: "Bow,

bow, ye lower middle classes . . . ye tradesmen, bow ye masses!" And the powerful Lord Chancellor, who argues that the law is the "true embodiment of everything that's excellent," cynically changes the law to suit himself and insure that every fairy shall die who does *not* marry a mortal. In "Spurn Not the Nobly Born," Lord Tolloller insists that high rank "involves no shame," so women should never withhold affection from "Blue Bloods." Finally, Lord Mountararat, in "When Britain Really Ruled the Waves," looks backward to the good old days of Queen Bess, when the House of Peers "made no pretence to intellectual eminence or scholarship sublime. . . . " By their own merry words, the Peers indict themselves as a class of drones, bores, and fools. And Gilbert, not disposed to press the point, permits the Lords to grow wings to fly off to a fairyland blessedly distant from the responsibilities of office.

ION

Type of work: Drama
Author: Euripides (c. 485-c. 406 B.C.)
Type of plot: Tragi-comedy
Time of plot: Remote antiquity
Locale: The temple of Apollo at Delphi
First presented: Fifth century B.C.

In this curious and compelling drama, Euripides treads such a middle road between tragedy and comedy that it is sometimes difficult to predict which way the story will go. One intriguing thematic question in Ion *concerns the ambiguity of Euripides' attitude toward the gods. On the one hand, the action demands that we accept Apollo's power and godhood; on the other, he is described so anthropomorphically that he appears as a knave trying to wriggle out of a tight spot after having been caught cheating.*

The *Ion* falls into the category of Euripides' *Helen* and *Iphigenia in Tauris,* since the three dramas bring their principal characters to the brink of destruction before sudden and marvelous rescues resulting in lives lived happily ever after. Into no other play of Euripides are the techniques of reversal and recognition more tightly woven; so too, irony abounds in the actions and intentions of not one but all parties. The sympathetic wishes of Ion and Creusa for each other in the first half of the play are sharply and ironically reversed in the second half to mutual intentions of murder. In the first half Xuthus connives with Ion to hide from Creusa what they believe to be the lad's true identity, but in the second half it is Xuthus who is deceived by Creusa.

This play has been the occasion of much debate since it does not fall neatly into a tragic or comic mold. On the one hand scholars insist that it is a propagandistic piece, aimed at flattering the Athenians by deifying their origins. The traditions of Hesiod and Herodotus had Ion the son of Xuthus and grandson of Hellen, who himself was the grandson of Prometheus. Evidently Euripides borrowed a less-known tradition in order to trace the lineage of the Ionian Athenians directly to the Olympian god Apollo, patron of the arts. The *Ion* seems to be the last of Euripides' so-called patriotic plays, which include the *Herakleidae, The Suppliants,* and *Herakles Mad.* On the other hand, some critics prefer not to attach any real profundity to the play, citing the complexity of the plot and the melodramatic climax as designed solely for the absorbing entertainment of the Athenian audience, unused to plays on the less familiar myths and always expecting a different twist to the Euripidean version of a well-known myth.

IPHIGENIA IN AULIS

Type of work: Drama
Author: Euripides (480-406 B.C.)
Type of plot: Classical tragedy
Time of plot: Beginning of Trojan War
Locale: Aulis, on the west coast of Euboea
First presented: 405 B.C.

Despite its heroic background, this play is in many respects a domestic tragedy. It lacks the terrible and compulsive passions which motivate the story of Clytemnestra and Agamemnon in the dramas of Aeschylus.

This play has been characterized by the best of classical scholars as one of Euripides' finest creations but also a play full of weaknesses. It is formally a tragedy, but it lacks the traditional tragic concentration and heroic figures. Unlike other tragedies which succeed as adaptations of myths, the *Iphigenia in Aulis* seems controlled by the myth, unable to rise above the complexities of the original story. Thus it has been called a "nontragedy" or a "tragedy *manqué*." Nevertheless, an attempt has been made to resolve its appeal with its flaws by finding its structure in the "ironic lack of cohesion" in the various attempts to save Iphigenia; thus the drama reflects the tragic disorder of the world.

The characters themselves are not genuinely "tragic"; that is, both their situations and their reactions seem too incredibly removed from reality. On the other hand, if we look beneath the spectacle of deceptions and discoveries, we may see that the basic notion of the sacrifice is credible and absorbing. Thus the play seems to succeed by a tension between two levels: the intrigues of the relatively dimensionless mythic characters versus the real prospect of a horrifying death, lurking, tugging at the entertainment.

As in so many of Euripides' plays, the vanity of war is thematic to the *Iphigenia in Aulis*. The less than noble characterizations of Agamemnon and Menelaus, revealed particularly in their "contest of words" beginning at line 317, help us to see the baseness of this whole affair. Because of Agamemnon's personal ambition and Menelaus' exaggerated outrage, a protracted, destructive war must be waged. The irony becomes unbearable when Iphigenia selflessly yields herself to sacrifice, apparently influenced by Agamemnon's rationalization that she will be dying for all Greece. At this point, no longer able to identify with the girl, we are dragged into the pathetic plight of Clytemnestra and distracted by the heroic overtures of Achilles, and here the play all but collapses. Evidently the bathos tests even Artemis, who demanded the sacrifice in the first place, since in the final report to Clytemnestra we discover that at the sacrificial blow Iphigenia vanished from view, and in her place lay a bloody deer gasping out its life.

IPHIGENIA IN TAURIS

Type of work: Drama
Author: Euripides (480-406 B.C.)
Type of plot: Romantic tragedy
Time of plot: Several year- after the Trojan War
Locale: Tauris, in the present-day Crimea
First presented: c. 420 B.C.

More of a romantic melodrama than a classic tragedy, Iphigenia in Tauris *abounds in breathtaking situations of danger and in sentimental passages of reminiscence. The feelings of Iphigenia after many years in a barbaric land are described touchingly by Euripides.*

Like Shakespeare, Euripides turned to the romance in his later years to convey a more optimistic view of the world. In fact, he invented this new dramatic form. *Iphigenia in Tauris,* along with *Helen* and *Ion,* are the few surviving examples. As a play *Iphigenia in Tauris* is masterly. It is carefully plotted, full of suspense, and genuinely moving. The setting is distant, dangerous, romantic. And a wistful love for all of Greece illuminates the action, especially in the beautiful choral odes. The characters are realistically drawn, and their reactions at tense moments are both unexpected and credible. The mixture of accurate psychology and miraculous occurrences is typical of Euripides. Further, the long recognition scene between Iphigenia and Orestes is thrilling in its execution. It would be hard to find a better piece of pure theater in the repertoire of classical drama. But this play has the penetrating depth of Euripides' finest works, in addition to being high entertainment.

Euripides seems to have been fascinated by the legend of the House of Atreus. From the final years of his life five plays on the subject have come down to us. *Iphigenia in Tauris, Electra, Helen, Orestes,* and *Iphigenia in Aulis* treat this story in different ways mostly, and sometimes the depiction of a character is inconsistent from play to play, particularly with Orestes and Helen. Of these works *Iphigenia in Tauris* comes closest to *Helen* in mood and plot. Both are romances in which a woman has been supernaturally transported to a remote, barbaric land and there held in chaste captivity. Iphigenia and Helen long for one deliverer whom they believe to be dead. Promptly they meet the man and a recognition scene follows. Then they plot a means of escape, trick the king, and return home by divine intervention. The similarities are remarkable and suggest that one of these plays attempts to repeat the success of the other, although Euripides may have written more plays along these lines.

The plot of *Iphigenia in Tauris* has two major climaxes and can be divided into two parts. The first part begins with Iphigenia believing her brother, Orestes, to be dead and ends with her accepting the captive Orestes. The second part begins with the two of them planning the escape and ends as they overcome all obstacles with Athena's aid.

Euripides uses an interesting technique. Often a character will state a principle by which he intends to act and then immediately betray the principle. Thus, Iphigenia states her intention of being harsh to the Greek captives because of her own misery (lines 350-353), and melts on hearing news of her homeland, offering to spare Orestes. In this case the technique points up her intense homesickness for Greece and Argos, a passion that animates not only her, but the chorus of Greek maidens, Orestes, and Pylades as well.

With Orestes, Euripides varies the technique in relation to a major theme. When Orestes appears before Iphigenia as a prisoner he says he disdains self-pity; and a few lines after, when Iphigenia asks his name, he replies sullenly, "Call me unfortunate." The method indicates his misery. But it also underscores his nobility of character later when he insists on being sacrificed to free his friend, Pylades. Disinterested love is always a sign of redemption in Euripides.

The barbarian king, Thoas, claims no barbarian would murder his mother, as the Greek, Orestes, had done. Yet he has no compunction about ordering a massacre of all Greeks, including the temple virgins. Euripides uses Thoas as a gullible, vengeful foil to the clever Greeks.

However, the most important theme of the play has to do with divine injustice and human suffering. Iphigenia is in thrall to the goddess Artemis, a victim who has been offered up herself for sacrifice, transported far away from home, and then set to aid in the sacrifices of all strangers and Greeks, a task she loathes. Artemis has been the perpetrator of this whole sequence.

But Artemis' twin, Apollo, has visited similar suffering on Orestes, causing him to kill his mother, be pursued and driven mad by Furies, and sent to Colchis (not Tauris), where he is captured for sacrifice. At first glance the gods Apollo and Artemis appear to be arch-villains ruthlessly dealing out anguish.

There is another perspective, however, that mitigates this view. Orestes is working out his redemption and must enter the gates of death almost literally before he can free himself of the guilt of matricide. He is offered a chance to live, but he chooses to save Pylades. Presumably Apollo sent him to Colchis for that very purpose, to act as a free man rather than an embittered victim. Once this choice occurs things begin falling into harmony. Iphigenia accepts him as her brother and contrives an escape. Orestes repays the favor by saving her life as they board the ship. Then in the moment of greatest danger the goddess Athena arrives to rescue the Greeks, showing that the gods give help to those who help others.

Euripides is showing us that as long as a person regards himself as a victim he can only suffer. Only when someone acts freely and unselfishly does their suffering cease and gods come to their assistance. By disinterested love divine injustice is transmuted to true justice.

James Weigel, Jr.

ISRAEL POTTER

Type of work: Novel
Author: Herman Melville (1819-1891)
Type of plot: Social satire
Time of plot: 1774-1826
Locale: Vermont, Massachusetts, England, France, the Atlantic Ocean
First published: 1855

A mock picaresque novel, Israel Potter *satirizes a great many ideas and institutions, from the pious morality of Benjamin Franklin to the brutality of wars and the idiocy of jingoistic patriotism. The hero, Israel Potter, wanders about America and Europe for more than fifty years, forever innocent and often stumbling into difficult situations.*

"Is civilization a thing distinct, or is it an advanced state of barbarism?" Melville asks the question after describing in vivid detail, but with cynical detachment, the canine ferocity of the fight to the death between John Paul Jones's *Bon Homme Richard* and the British man of war *Serapis.* Joined by their smashed and burning rigging, the two vessels are a fitting symbol of the fratricidal struggle between Britain and the young United States. What bemuses Melville is the insanity of a fight in which both parties literally destroy themselves in pursuit of victory over the other; when the *Serapis* finally strikes her colors, it is almost impossible to determine the true victor because both ships were disemboweled wrecks with half their crews killed or wounded. Ironically, Jones and his men board the *Serapis* the morning after battle because they are unable to put out the flames on the *Richard.*

In *Moby Dick* and *Pierre,* written a few years before *Israel Potter,* Melville had traced the consequences of erratic and self-destructive behavior in titanic and tormented individuals: satanic Ahab and maddeningly idealistic Pierre. In *Israel Potter* Melville broadens his focus to include the world at large; instead of cosmic tragedy, we have cosmic laughter, a kind of grim snicker at the absurdity and contemptuous pettiness of the real world. There is no doubt that this minor work is an important bridge between *Moby Dick* and *The Confidence Man,* that dark social satire which Lewis Leary has called "the inevitable sequel" to *Israel Potter.*

The famous portraits in the novel of actual historical figures (Franklin, John Paul Jones, and Ethan Allen) are artful exercises in debunking and anticipate by more than sixty years the biographical intentions of Lytton Strachey. Great men are mirrors to the corruption and vanities of their time. Israel Potter, the common man, despite the adventurous promise of his youth fails to realize the American imperative of independence and self-realization. Although brave and gifted with the shrewdness necessary for survival, he lives out his days in mediocrity and helpless exile. When he finally does return to America, he is unrecognized and denied his pension—a hero of Bunker Hill.

IT IS BETTER THAN IT WAS

Type of work: Drama
Author: Pedro Calderón de la Barca (1600-1681)
Type of plot: Cape-and-sword comedy
Time of plot: Seventeenth century
Locale: Vienna
First presented: 1631

A comedy of lovemaking among the nobility in which the outcome is not definitely known until the final lines, this play was written as an optimistic contrast to the earlier It Is Worse than It Was.

Calderón's *It Is Better than It Was* falls into that subdivision of his cloak-and-sword plays known as the Palace Plays. Although the techniques applied to this type are essentially the same as in the cloak-and-sword plays, the distinguishing feature is that the Palace Plays revolve around incidents in the lives of the upper nobility.

The primary purpose of *It Is Better than It Was* is simple amusement, and consequently there is little of the philosophy of Calderón's later plays. Yet there are on display many of the traits for which the playwright is noted. The stylization of balance and contrast for which Calderón had so strong a penchant is found not only in the linguistic style and imagery, but also in the arrangement of the plot. The main plot deals with Don Carlos' love for Flora, who is aiding his escape from his pursuers. The secondary plot centers around the love of Arnaldo and Laura. This situation turns on the appearance versus reality theme brought by misunderstanding, deceptions, veiled ladies, and forbidden suitors. Comic situations arise because of the discrepancy between illusion and reality and are accentuated by the compromising circumstances in which the characters find themselves.

The linguistic style and imagery are full of the gyrations of conceptual and formal language, particularly characteristic of the seventeenth century Spanish court. The rigid formality of this style and imagery, although seeming artificial today, served to create the courtly atmosphere of the society in which the action took place and its vogue for expressing matters of the heart in veiled language.

It Is Better than It Was, while not being one of Calderón's most notable plays, was characteristic of his early efforts and was a great favorite of audiences who enjoyed the tricks and deceptions of Calderón's comedies.

IT IS WORSE THAN IT WAS

Type of work: Drama
Author: Pedro Calderón de la Barca (1600-1681)
Type of plot: Cape-and-sword comedy
Time of plot: Seventeenth century
Locale: Gaeta, Italy
First presented: 1630

To compete with the plays of Lope de Vega, Calderón added to his own plays an interest in philosophy and logic, with the result that, as one critic has remarked, his characters make love like debaters. But the plot and style of the drama are well-executed and exciting to follow.

It Is Worse than It Was is a fairly representative example of a cloak-and-sword play, so-called because of the cloak and sword worn by the gentlemen of the era depicted in the play. This type of play, the purpose of which is to amuse, reached its zenith with Calderón de la Barca. *It Is Worse than It Was,* while not being as important as some of Calderón's other cloak-and-sword plays, notably *The House with Two Doors,* excellently showcases the traits of the genre. It contains the zestful ingredients of a romantic love, universal in its appeal: Boy (César) meets girl (Lisarda), all kinds of obstacles arise, especially a vigilant father, and the audience is kept on edge by the rapidity of the action, the excitement of the chase, and the various intrigues, deceits, and misunderstandings.

The character portrayals are the weakest part of the play's fabric, as they usually are in cloak-and-sword plays. César is somewhat insipid in professing to love Lisarda, whose face he has not seen. Lisarda is a little better portrayed. She is forward, clever, bold, and deceitful. She is of major importance in determining the flow of the action.

The play makes use of a number of stock devices inherited from classical Roman comedy as found in the works of Plautus and Terence and continued in the Italian comedies of intrigue. Some of these devices are seen in the manipulation of the intrigue where mistakes, identity, trickery, misunderstanding, and surprise disclosures combine to produce an effect of suspense, bewilderment, and comic irony. The purpose of the intrigue is to create a farcical situation which reveals character and satirizes manners of the day. The audience enjoys sorting out the deceptions, and interest is sustained by the onlookers' natural desire to determine the workings and outcome of the intrigues.

THE ITALIAN

Type of work: Novel
Author: Mrs. Ann Radcliffe (1764-1823)
Type of plot: Gothic romance
Time of plot: 1758
Locale: Italy
First published: 1797

As in Mrs. Radcliffe's other novels, in The Italian *she mingles the wild, idyllic beauty of nature with scenes of nightmare and terror. This is wholly a work of the romantic imagination, lacking both the fantastic supernaturalism and turgid sensationalism of her rivals in the specialized genre of the gothic novel.*

The Italian is one of the most skillful and successful examples of the Gothic novel, a literary sub-genre whose aim is to astound, terrify, and thrill its readers. More controlled and convincing than her earlier *The Mysteries of Udolpho,* Mrs. Radcliffe's novel is filled with the conventional Gothic qualities: a highly melodramatic (and unlikely) plot set in the remote past, a minimal degree of character development, and a painstakingly developed setting and atmosphere.

The plot is a familiar one to readers of the Gothic: a mysterious and black-hearted villain, Schedoni, plots against a beautiful damsel, Ellena, who spends most of the novel either imprisoned or in imminent danger of death, while her chivalrous and faithful lover, Vivaldi, struggles against incredible odds to rescue her. Character delineation is crude, limited primarily to blacks and whites. Predictably, the villainous monk Schedoni is much more fascinating than the somewhat vapid hero and heroine. The air of mystery and terror in the monk is strikingly described: "An habitual gloom and severity prevailed over the deep lines of his countenance; and his eyes were so piercing that they seemed to penetrate, at a single glance, into the hearts of men, and to read their most secret thoughts."

Setting is crucial to *The Italian.* Here are the gloomy monasteries, the dank dungeons of the Inquisition, the dizzying precipices and crags of Abruzzo, as well as scenes of quiet but spine-tingling terror, such as the one between Ellena and Schedoni on the deserted beach. Just as the evil characters are made even more menacing by their contrast to the good characters, the wild landscapes and brooding interiors are made even more threatening by their contrast to the beauty of Naples at the beginning and end of the novel.

The excesses and improbabilities of the lurid plot are tempered by a number of qualities. First, despite the manifold mysteries and hints of ghostly or demonic forces pervading the work, nothing magical or supernatural actually does occur; unlike the events in *The Castle of Otranto,* for instance, there is ultimately a rational explanation provided for everything. Also, Radcliffe's handling of suspense, mystery, dramatic pacing, and realistic detail and description is expert and gripping throughout. Finally, the author displays a serious concern for the main Gothic theme of man's inhumanity to man, as seen, for instance, in Vivaldi's outburst against the brutalities of the Inquisition: "Can this be in human nature!—Can such horrible perversion of right be permitted! Can man, who calls himself endowed with reason, and immeasurably superior to every other created being, argue himself into the commision of such horrible folly, such inveterate cruelty, as exceeds all the acts of the most irrational and ferocious brute . . . !"

Such novels as *The Italian* were adroitly satirized by Jane Austen in her *Northanger Abbey*. But Radcliffe's novel is significant not only in its own right, but for the influence it had on later writers, such as Scott, Charlotte Brontë, Coleridge, Keats, and Poe, all of whom made use of the mysterious and threatening Gothic settings and atmospheres in many of their own works.

THE ITCHING PARROT

Type of work: Novel
Author: José Joaquín Fernández de Lizardi (1776-1827)
Type of plot: Picaresque satire
Time of plot: The 1770's to 1820's
Locale: Mexico
First published: 1816

Considered the first Spanish-American novel and reputed to have sold over one hundred million copies, The Itching Parrot *included many of the polemical tracts which the author had written previously and which had earned him nationwide fame. The work is an often-savage satire and an indictment of corruption and inefficiency in Mexican society.*

The Itching Parrot is of special interest to literature students. Besides being the first true novel of Latin American literature, and the only important Spanish American representative of the picaresque novel, it is of definite sociological interest. It compares reasonably well in entertainment value with good modern novels. It paints Mexican society in the last phase of the colonial period and the first years of national independence. *The Itching Parrot* is still a widely-read Mexican novel, and has been published in approximately twenty editions.

The novel's primary aim was to satirize socio-economic conditions in Mexico. Lizardi's criticism of the abuses of his time was sound, and he became an apostle of reform. Realism dominates *The Itching Parrot,* making it primarily a call for social reform, but the book has other virtues as well. It not only exposes charlatans and fakes at all levels, but draws them well, whether they be lower social types or aristocrats. The book is not pessimistic, even though its many episodes, mutually independent, are usually depressing. Life is not meaningless to Lizardi, for God is not dead, and good will eventually conquer evil. The novel has a cheerful ending, proving that man is capable of reform, and indeed Lizardi always seems honest and attracted by good. Class hatreds are lacking even while social inequalities and evils are scorched. Religious bias is also lacking even though individual Catholic priests are lampooned. Lizardi's patriotism glows throughout the book, in glaring contrast to the selfishly corrupt politicians who mislead Mexico during the initial years of independence, and whose stupidity leads directly to the loss of half of Mexico's national territory to the Americans.

The book is written in the good, basic Spanish that has almost always characterized Mexican literature. Its one thousand pages and three hundred thousand words expose many evils, not only social but political, for the last Spanish viceroys and the first rulers of independent Mexico were absolute monarchs who failed to use their powers wisely. Lizardi flayed the vicious town bosses, who wallowed in extortion, "bites," and corruption. He also exposed court clerks, tax collectors, police, jailers, the swarms of beggars, and the merchants who used false weights. Even though a Catholic himself, who defended worthy clerics, Lizardi blasted individual priests, such as the one who drank at a party and squabbled over a woman, or another who refused to interrupt his card game to give the last rites to a dying person, and the incredible cad who collected money to pray for the soul of Christ.

Lizardi's arrows did not spare the unsanitary Indian wet nurses who tied the hands and feet of babies to prevent them from striking themselves, nor the ignorant and lecherous teachers, lawyers, and doctors who infested the unhappy Mexico of his days. Hospitals were often horrible; pharmacists gouged for drugs, doctors peddled fake nostrums. Nor was the antiquated university system spared—students argued logic all day, as was done in the Middle Ages, and learned little of practical value. Lizardi especially resented the fact that the aristocracy and even the middle class scorned manual work, causing their young to waste their time as con men, card sharps, embezzlers, pimps, and the laziest of thugs.

The style of *The Itching Parrot* is direct. Action is never lacking, and a sense of anticipation tinges most of the book, along with several episodes of adventure and travel.

IVANHOE

Type of work: Novel
Author: Sir Walter Scott (1771-1832)
Type of plot: Historical romance
Time of plot: 1194
Locale: England
First published: 1820

For a hundred and fifty years, Ivanhoe *has held its charm in the popular mind as the epitome of chivalric novels. Among its characters are two of the most popular of English heroes, Richard the Lion-Hearted and Robin Hood. It may not be Scott's greatest novel, but it is without doubt his most popular.*

Scott himself wrote that he left the Scottish scenes of his previous novels and turned to the Middle Ages in *Ivanhoe* because he feared the reading public was growing weary of the repetition of Scottish themes in his books. Since he was fascinated with history all of his life, it was logical that Scott should turn to the past for subject matter. Many faults have been found with the historical facts of the book; Robin Hood, if he lived at all, belonged to a later century than that represented in the novel, and by the time of Richard I the distinction between Saxons and Normons had faded. But the thrilling story, the drama and action, still grip the reader, whatever liberties Scott took with history.

Scott's four great chivalric novels all possess similar structures in that they all focus on a moment of crisis between two great individuals, a moment which determines the survival of one of the opposed pair. In *Ivanhoe,* the symbolic contrast is between Richard the Lion-Hearted and his brother John. The struggle between these two helps to raise one of the principal questions of the novel: the decadence of chivalry. For generations of juvenile readers, *Ivanhoe* represented the glory of chivalric adventure, but actually Scott entertained serious doubts about the chivalric tradition. At several strategic points in *Ivanhoe,* passages occur which unequivocally damn the reckless inhumanity of romantic chivalry.

The novel is symmetrically designed in three parts, each reaching its climax in a great military spectacle. The first part ends with the Ashby tournament, the second with the liberation from the castle of Front de Boeuf, and the third with the trial by combat of Rebecca. The beginning chapters draw together all of the character groups for the tournament, Ivanhoe being present only as the mysterious palmer. The problem of seating at the tournament provides a sketch of the cultural animosities that divide the world of the novel.

Richard is the moral and political center of the book, and, therefore, the proper object of Ivanhoe's fidelity. The captive king does not appear until he fights the mysterious Black Knight during the second day of the tournament. He saves Ivanhoe and then disappears until the scene of his midnight feast with Friar Tuck. The reader's impression of him is of a fun-loving, heroic fighter. The friar thinks of him as a man of "prudence and of counsel." Richard possesses a native humanity and a love of life, as well as the heroic chivalric qualities. He is always ready to act as a protector of others.

John, by contrast, is an ineffectual ruler whose own followers despise him. His forces quickly disintegrate, his followers abandoning him for their own selfish ends. He is a petulant, stupid man, incapable of inspiring loyalty. It is inevitable that the historical climax of the novel should be the confrontation between Richard and John. The chivalric code has become completely corrupt in the England left to John's care. Both the narrator and the characters make clear that chivalry is no more than a mixture of "heroic folly and dangerous imprudence."

Rebecca speaks against chivalry, asking during the bloody siege of the castle if possession by a "demon of vainglory" brings "sufficient rewards for the sacrifice of every kindly affection, for a life spent miserably that yet may make others miserable?" (Rebecca is antichivalric, yet she is the most romantic character in the book, suggesting the traditional chivalric attitudes towards women.) The narrator speaks most sharply of the chivalric code at the end of the tournament: "This ended the memorable field of Ashby-de-la-Zouche, one of the most gallantly contested tournaments of that age; for although only four knights, including one who was smothered by the heat of his armour, had died upon the field, yet upwards of thirty were desperately wounded, four or five of whom never recovered. Several more were disabled for life; and those who escaped best carried the marks of the conflict to the grave with them. Hence it is always mentioned in the old records as the 'gentle and joyous passage of arms at Ashby.' "

An argument has been made that Scott's historical novels, such as *Ivanhoe,* are inferior to his earlier novels based on his direct, personal knowledge of the Scottish customs and characters and land. But even in the historical novels, Scott's characters are colorful, full of vitality, and realized with amazing verisimilitude. Scott's knowledge of the past about which he was writing was so deep that he could draw upon it at will to clothe out his fictions. He did not find it necessary to research a novel such as *Ivanhoe* in order to write it; the historical lore was already part of him. Years before, at the time when he was beginning the Waverley series, he had written a study about chivalry. His prolific writing did not seem to exhaust his resources.

Sir Walter Scott was one of the most prolific writers in the history of British fiction; only Trollope could stand up against his record. Scott's novels were published anonymously, although their authorship came to be an open secret. His friends found it difficult to believe that he was the author of the novels, for he lived the life of a county magistrate and landowner, spending hours daily on these occupations, as well as entertaining lavishly and writing poetry and nonfiction works. His secret was that he would rise early and finish novel-writing before breakfast. In time, his compulsive working injured his health, and while he was writing *Ivanhoe*, he was tortured by a cramp of the stomach and suffered such pain that he could not physically hold the pen, but was forced to dictate much of the story.

Like many great novels, *Ivanhoe* betrays a complexity of attitude on the part of the author. Although much of the book makes clear Scott's severe view of the code of chivalry, beyond the antichivalric attitude the reader can see a definite attraction on Scott's part for the romantic traditions of the period. It is in Richard that Scott seems to instill the chivalric virtues, although his personality is not romantic. Through the characters of Rebecca and Rowena, Ivanhoe and Richard, Scott dramatized his ambivalent feelings about the chivalric period. The tension created through these mixed feelings, coupled with the dramatic (if historically inaccurate) story and the vast accumulation of detail as to costume and social customs and historical anecdotes, all worked together to create a novel which has remained popular for more than a hundred and fifty years. *Ivanhoe* is no longer considered as seriously as Scott's Scottish novels, but its achievement remains impressive.

Bruce D. Reeves

JACK OF NEWBERRY

Type of work: Novel
Author: Thomas Deloney (1543?-1607?)
Type of plot: Picaresque adventure
Time of plot: Reign of Henry VIII
Locale: England
First published: 1597

Not truly a novel, this fictional work marks the first successful attempt by any writer to use the material found in the lives of ordinary people as material for prose fiction. For this reason, the book marks a great step toward the novel as we know it today. The pictures Deloney drew of bourgeois England were exaggerated, but highly entertaining.

Very little is known about the pamphleteer and balladeer who was Thomas Deloney, the English writer whose works were precursors of the English novel. By trade a silk weaver, probably of Norwich, Deloney wrote topical ballads and, through his pamphlets, took part in the religious controversies of the day. Even the date of his birth is not certain, some sources suggesting 1543, others the more likely date of 1560. But it seems certain that Deloney died early in 1600, after producing at least three "novels" (that is, episodic narratives) in a short but crowded life. He seems to have had more education than most weavers of the time would have had, and he translated from Latin into his uniquely vigorous English. The ballads of the day were the newspapers of the period, and Deloney's apprenticeship, like that of so many novelists, might be said to have been in journalism. Probably, that was how he learned how to write concisely and how to choose popular subjects. He wrote broadside ballads on such subjects as the defeat of the Spanish Armada, great fires, the execution of traitors, and domestic tragedies, but current events were not Deloney's only ballad subjects. Using Holinshed and other sources, he drew on English history for subject matter. A collection of Deloney's ballads titled *The Garland of Good Will* appeared in 1631, and earlier editions, like those of his prose fictions, were probably read out of existence. More than once, Deloney's pamphlets and more than fifty ballads put him in trouble with the authorities, even sending him to spend time in Newgate. One ballad in particular, showing disrespect for the queen, caused him serious difficulties.

Though widely read, Thomas Deloney's novels were scorned by the university educated writers of the day as mere plebian romances from the pen of a ballad-maker, and it was not until the twentieth century that his merits as a writer were recognized. The three novels, all approximately the same length, appeared between 1597 and 1600. Probably, *Jack of Newberry* was the first one written and published. Each novel was in praise of a trade: *Jack of Newberry* of weaving, *The Gentle Craft* of shoemaking, and *Thomas of Reading* of the clothiers' trade.

Deloney's stories contain excellent pictures of contemporary middle-class London life, introducing a variety of quaint characters. But the realism of the novels is only in matter of setting and dialogue; probability is disregarded and wish-fulfillment fantasy prevails as members of the hardworking trade class are rewarded for their diligence by large fortunes. The tales are rich with humor and told in a straightforward way, except for "ornamental" language used in some romantic passages.

Deloney may have been commissioned by the cloth-merchants to compose a life of one of their order, the result being *Jack of Newberry*. Jack was a real person who lived in Newberry under Henry VII, but his history is merely traditional. Deloney, however, knew the town and had a gift for elaborating a tale with circumstantial facts and humorous episodes.

Despite its popularity in its own day, Deloney's fiction probably had little real effect on the subsequent development of English prose fiction, which had to wait a hundred years and more for the geniuses of Defoe and Richardson to get it off the ground. On the other hand, *Jack of Newberry* may be considered the first really dramatic novel in English. The fictions of Nash and Greene are witty and satirical, but they do not have the dramatic plots of Deloney's work. Sidney's *Arcadia* and John Lyly's *Euphues* were only minor influences, if any, on Deloney, who seems to have been more impressed by the Elizabethan stage than anything else (the widow and the other characters display a sense of rhetoric in their dialogue reminiscent of the stage). Deloney's view of life was essentially dramatic, and the people he wrote about in *Jack of Newberry* and his other novels are people of action, people who set out to accomplish material things.

Deloney's focus is on the details of everyday life. Love and marriage and money and food are the main topics of conversation. Materialist to his heart, he is fascinated by business and household matters. Like Dickens, Deloney plunges into scenes that summarize dramatically an entire situation, painting a picture of an entire culture along the way. There are few irrelevant incidents in *Jack of Newberry*. The story of the middle-aged widow who falls in love with her young apprentice, and of his subsequent adventures (including that concerning the king) is told with great enthuiasm. The widow is portrayed as a lusty, self-sufficient female, a woman who knows what she wants and goes after it—in this case, Jack. Jack is apparently as virtuous and industrious an apprentice as Ben Franklin, but he is not as innocent as he pretends and soon moves up in the world.

The tradesmen heroes such as Jack are rather idealized characters. Jack rises less from his own efforts than from those of the people around him. It almost seems that he is above certain efforts, as the king, himself, is. The women in *Jack of Newberry* are the book's finest characterizations. In creating the gallery of female portraits, Deloney leaves behind him all of his rivals in the prose fiction of the time and approaches the best of Elizabethan stage comedy. Queen Catherine, the first Mistress Winchcomb, and other women in the story are colorful figures, alive with natural vitality. As the plots develop, the women are in the midst of the action. Perhaps it is a man's world, but the wife seems to be responsible for her husband's success. Deloney knew and understood middle-class women, and recorded their foibles and unique characteristics with a sharp eye and a precise pen. For the author, the good wife was one who was never idle, but knew her place and did not "gad about." Jack and his first wife made no headway at all until she decided to stay at home and manage the household.

The minor characters are well drawn, especially Randoll Pert. Recently out of debtor's prison, Pert becomes a porter to support his family. His description is delightful, and his antics add both comic and pathetic touches to the novel. The meeting of Jack and Pert at the Spread Eagle in London is superbly handled. The whole episode, including the part where Jack agrees not to collect five hundred pounds until Pert is sheriff of London, is excellent comedy.

Although the novel is episodic, it forms a coherent and often dramatic whole, and is filled with humorous scenes and witty dialogue. *Jack of Newberry* stands as a good "novel" in its own right, as well as the first example of its kind in English literature.

Bruce D. Reeves

JACK SHEPPARD

Type of work: Novel
Author: William Harrison Ainsworth (1805-1882)
Type of plot: Picaresque romance
Time of plot: 1702-1724
Locale: London and its environs
First published: 1839

Jack Sheppard *differs from most of Ainsworth's work in that it has a rogue instead of a historical figure for its title character. The plot is based on the life of a famous English criminal. Abounding in characters, circumstantial incident, and action, the novel illustrates the typically Victorian treatment of the rogue in fiction.*

William Harrison Ainsworth held the editorship of *Bentley's Miscellaney* for two years beginning in 1840, and then edited his own publication, *Ainsworth's Magazine,* for eleven years following. It was during these years that some of his best-known novels were written, giving us astounding evidence of this enormous capacity for work. As is to be expected in view of such productivity, not all his works are of even quality.

Jack Sheppard is Ainsworth's attempt at the form already explored in English literature by Smollett, Defoe, and Fielding. He differs from the picaresque form as it existed in English in several ways. The pure picaresque novel is episodic and concerns itself essentially with the rogue figure, but also is a vehicle for satirizing the institutions of the society which exclude the rogue. The rogue generally ends his career in a secure social position which he assumes not as the logical consequence of his own actions, but through the machinations of an irregular and sometimes perverse Fate. The picaresque novel is written from a point of view which expresses sympathy for the rogue, who should be the central point of interest. Ainsworth's narrative point of view is that of the good society; his rogue is neither ironic nor the vehicle for satire, and he does not end in a better position than before, all violations of the picaresque form.

The true hero of the novel, though Ainsworth thought to create the second plot line in him, is Thames Darrell, who in the end rises to inherit untold fortune and marry his true love. This is the picaresque ending, but Thames is a romantic hero, not a picaro. Ainsworth, while using elements of the picaresque, is much more at home with the romantic hero. The characterization of Jack Sheppard is more thorough than that of Thames, but it is generally true of Ainsworth, as with many of his generation, that character development for villains proves much more interesting than for that of romantic heroes.

JALNA

Type of work: Novel
Author: Mazo de la Roche (1885-1961)
Type of plot: Domestic realism
Time of plot: The 1920's
Locale: Canada
First published: 1927

One of a series of novels dealing with the Whiteoak family, Jalna *is dominated by the towering and somewhat frightening figure of Grandma Whiteoak, whose character lifts the book above the level of popular fiction.*

Jalna and all the books of the Jalna series are unusual in that each stands alone on its own merits; the mass of exposition needed to set the stage for the events of the plot is deftly incorporated into the musings of the characters or their dinner-table conversation. Yet we feel from the first that the characters have had a life prior to the novel, just as we feel that their lives continue beyond the end of it. The characters, painted with a critical detachment, are extremely amusing. The author has achieved an impressive balancing of the dozen portraits of hardy egoists going about their nagging, fighting, and loving. But there is too much material in the book—too many characters and a confusion of incident. Some descriptions and scenes are brisk and fresh, but other passages are weak and amateurish in execution. The characters never develop; they are born in full bloom, as it were. It is the sense of *family,* the cumulative effect of the group, that provides the real charm of the novel, despite its shortcomings. The elderly matriarch holds together both the family and the book.

The very quarrelsomeness of the family prohibits us from taking any of the members solely at his own self-estimate. Finch is both a stupid, sulky young whelp and a person of almost clairvoyant sensitivity to the moods and motives of those about him, just as Eden is talented, sinned against, and at times a cad. Neither is readily likable, and the somewhat perverse claims they make upon the reader seem the very essence of their being Whiteoaks. The many-sidedness of these quarrelsome people and the sparks they strike from one another find their synthesis in the character of Grandma Adeline Whiteoak. The living symbol of the family's covenant with the land, she draws warmth from the friction of their communial life, and strength from their vivid physicality. *Jalna* is a well-crafted popular novel that comes close to being literature.

JANE EYRE

Type of work: Novel
Author: Charlotte Brontë (1816-1855)
Type of plot: Psychological romance
Time of plot: 1800
Locale: Northern England
First published: 1847

The poetry and tension of Jane Eyre *marked a new development in adult romanticism in fiction, just as Jane herself was a new kind of heroine, a woman of intelligence and passion, but one lacking in the charm, beauty, and grace usually associated with romantic heroines. Likewise, the strange and unconventional hero, Rochester, is a new type, who sets the often eerie, moody, or even violently passionate atmosphere of the novel.*

Charlotte Brontë was always concerned that her work be judged on the basis of its art and not because of her sex. Thus the choice of the pseudonym which she continued to use even after her authorship was revealed, often referring in her letters to Currer Bell when speaking of herself as writer. *Jane Eyre,* her first published novel, has been called "feminine" because of the romanticism and deeply felt emotions of the heroine-narrator. It would be more correct, however, to point to the feminist qualities of the novel: a heroine who refuses to be placed in the traditional female position of subservience, who disagrees with her superiors, who stands up for her rights, who ventures creative thoughts; more importantly, a narrator who comments on the role of women in the society and the greater constraint experienced by them. Those "feminine" emotions often pointed to in Jane Eyre herself are surely found as well in Rochester, and the continued popularity of this work must suggest the enduring human quality of these emotions.

Brontë often discussed the lack of passion in her contemporaries' work and especially in that of Jane Austen, about whom she said, "Her business is not half so much with the human heart as with the human eyes, mouth, hands and feet." Coldness, detachment, excessive analysis, and critical distance were not valued by Brontë. The artist must be involved in her subject, she believed, and must have a degree of inspiration not to be rationally explained. Such a theory of art is similar to that of the romantic poets, an attitude not altogether popular by mid-nineteenth century.

In *Jane Eyre*, therefore, Brontë chose the exact point of view to suit both her subject matter and her artistic theory, the first-person narrator. The story is told entirely through the eyes of the heroine Jane Eyre. This technique enabled Brontë to bring the events to the reader with an intensity that involved him in the passions, feelings, and thoughts of the heroine. A passionate directness characterizes Jane's narration: conversations are rendered in direct, not indirect dialogue; actions are given just as they occurred, with little analysis of either event or character. In a half-dozen key scenes, Brontë shifts to present tense instead of the immediate past, so that Jane Eyre narrates the event as if it were happening just at the present moment. After Jane flees Thornfield and Rochester, when the coachman puts her out at Whitcross having used up her fare, she narrates to the moment: "I am alone. . . . I am absolutely destitute." After a long description of the scene around her and her analysis of her situation, also narrated in the present tense, she reverts to the more usual past tense in the next paragraph: "I struck straight into the heath." Such a technique adds greatly to the immediacy of the novel and further draws the reader into the situation.

Jane Eyre, like all Brontë's heroines, has no parents and no family that accepts or is aware of her. She, like Lucy Snowe (*Villette*) and Caroline Helstone (*Shirley*), leads her life, then, cut off from society, since family was the means for a woman to participate in society and community. Lacking such support, Jane must face her problems alone. Whenever she forms a close friendship (Bessie at Gateshead, Helen Burns and Miss Temple at Lowood, Mrs. Fairfax at Thornfield), she discovers that these ties can be broken easily —by higher authority, by death, by marriage—since she is not "kin." Cutting her heroines off so radically from family and community gave Charlotte Brontë the opportunity to make her women independent and to explore the romantic ideal of individualism.

Jane Eyre is a moral tale, akin to a folk or fairy tale, with nearly all ambiguities—in society, character, and situation—omitted. Almost all the choices that Jane must make are easy ones, and her character, although she grows and matures, does not change significantly. Her one difficult choice is refusing to become Rochester's mistress, leaving Thornfield alone and penniless instead. That choice was difficult precisely because she had no family or friends to influence her with their disapproval. No one would be hurt if she consented; that is, no one but Jane herself, and it is her own self-love that helps her to refuse.

Again like a fairy tale, *Jane Eyre* is full of myth and superstition. Rochester often calls Jane his "elf," "changeling," or "witch"; there are mysterious happenings at Thornfield; Jane is inclined to believe the gipsy fortune-teller (until Rochester reveals himself) and often thinks of the superstitions she has heard; the weather often presages mysterious or disastrous events. And, most importantly, at the climax of the story when Jane is about to consent to be the unloved wife of St. John Rivers, she hears Rochester calling to her —at precisely the time, we learn later, that he had in fact called to her. This event is never explained rationally, and we must accept Jane's judgment that it was a supernatural intervention.

Numerous symbolic elements pervade the novel; most often something in nature symbolizes an event or person in Jane's life. The most obvious example is the chestnut tree, which is split in two by lightning on the night that Jane accepts Rochester's marriage proposal, signifying the rupture of their relationship. The two parts of the tree, though, remain bound, as do Jane and Rochester despite their physical separation.

Likewise, the novel is full of character foils and parallel situations. Aunt Reed at Gateshead is contrasted with Miss Temple at Lowood; the Reed sisters at the beginning are contrasted with the Rivers sisters—cousins all—at the end; Rochester's impassioned proposal and love is followed by St. John's pragmatic proposition. Foreshadowing is everywhere in the book, so that seemingly chance happenings gain added significance as the novel unfolds and each previous event is echoed in the next.

Thus, the novel's artful structure and carefully chosen point of view, added to the strong and fascinating character of Jane herself, make *Jane Eyre,* if not a typical Victorian novel, surely a classic among English novels.

Margaret McFadden-Gerber

JASON AND THE GOLDEN FLEECE

Type of work: Classical legend
Source: Folk tradition
Type of plot: Heroic adventure
Time of plot: Remote antiquity
Locale: Ancient Greece
First transcribed: Unknown

The story of Jason and the pursuit of the Golden Fleece has been repeated in story and song for more than thirty centuries; its form has often changed, but its substance remains unchanged. The peculiar poignancy of the myth lies in the contrast between the image of the youthful Jason, strong and arrogant, and the aged Jason, a homeless outcast who wanders until he is killed by the falling prow of his old ship, the Argo.

The journey of the Argonauts ("Sailors of the *Argo*") and/or Minyae may well be one of the oldest of Greek adventure myths. Homer alludes to it, and it is placed in the generation preceding the Trojan War (the roster of heroes includes Telamon, the father of Ajax, and Peleus, the father of Achilles). No doubt its folktale theme of a sea journey to inhospitable lands in quest of a valuable prize was the model for the adventures of Odysseus, Herakles, Theseus, and others. Compare, for example, the dragon-guarded golden fleece with the dragon-guarded golden apples of the Hesperides (the eleventh labor of Herakles); the beautiful young princess who aids her father's enemy and is eventually cast aside (as was Ariadne by Theseus); the journey to Aeaea, the island of Circe (Odysseus); a kingdom usurped (Herakles) and regained with a vengeance (Odysseus). Typical of such tales is the accomplishment of an impossible task, a confrontation with death and the fantastically inhuman, all to prove one's nobility of birth and right to reign. The retrieval of the fleece, then, is not the subject of this myth, but the occasion; it is a device by which the hero becomes involved with the heroic. Futhermore, the entire expedition would not have come about were it not for Hera, whom Pelias had refused to honor. Her tortuous plan was to have Jason sent off to Colchis so that he would bring back with him the sorceress Medea who would kill Pelias (which she did, by convincing the old king's daughters to kill him so that she might rejuvenate him).

Despite the age of this myth, the earliest extensive literary account is found in Pindar's Fourth Pythian Ode (462 B.C.), and it was not until the third century B.C. that the myth received formal expanded treatment by Apollonius of Rhodes, who revived the epic genre. His romantic effort, the *Argonautica,* would henceforward not only be the model for other versions of the quest, but would greatly influence Roman epic poets, notably Vergil.

Apollonius' work, despite its obvious stylistic and structural inferiority to Homer's poems, nevertheless contains some very charming, if not masterful, descriptions and characterizations. The first two books are devoted to the voyage from Thessaly to Colchis. Among the more prominent episodes are the Argonauts' landfall at Lemnos, where they are entertained for a year by the women who, having once been plagued with a malodor, killed their men because they had taken Thracian brides. Reaching the Asian mainland, they soon were forced to fight six-armed giants and were involved in two other battles before rescuing the prophet-king Phineus. Book III contains the arrival at Colchis and Medea's falling in love with Jason. Unlike the *Iliad,* in which Hera and Athena are at odds with Aphrodite, the *Argonautica* portrays them as allies who instigate the mischievous Eros (Cupid) to fire a shaft into the princess Medea. Torn between filial loyalty and her uncontrollable passion, she soon yields to love. Her escape with Jason and their eventual arrival at Iolchus (Book IV) include the murder of Medea's brother Absyrtus and the necessary expiation on Circe's island, Aeaea. Apollonius has Jason kill Absyrtus through Medea's treachery; in the earlier version Medea herself murders her brother and scatters the butchered remains over the sea in order to delay the pursuing Colchians, who have to gather the pieces for burial.

The exact return route supposedly taken by the Argonauts was disputed in ancient times. Doubtless the various versions were based on the trade routes begun in the Mycenaean age. Apollonius takes the Argonauts from the mouth of the river Phasis on the Black Sea to the Ister (Danube), overland to the Adriatic, where they are confronted by Absyrtus; thence to the Eridanus (Po?) overland to the Rhone to the Tyrrhenian Sea and Circe's island. Other accounts include (1) a return by the same route as they came; (2) sailing east up the Phasis to the world-encircling river Ocean, then southwest to Africa and overland to the Mediterranean (Pindar's version); and (3) up the Phasis, through Russia and over northern sea routes past Britain and through the Pillars of Herakles. Apollonius includes in the journey the perils of the Sirens, Scylla and Charybdis, and the Wandering Rocks; Medea and Jason are, like Odysseus, given refuge in hospitable Phaeacia on the west coast of Greece, but only after the young lovers marry to void Æetes' claim to his daughter.

The myth receives brief attention in Ovid's *Metamorphoses* (Book VII), and would have been retold at length in the Latin hexameters of Valerius Flaccus (A.D., first century), but his *Argonautica* is incomplete. Jason's adventure is, nevertheless, included in Apollodorus' *Library,* the invaluable (Greek) collection of myths (A.D., first or second century). Like most myths, the search for the fleece was subject to the rationalizing minds of classical writers: Strabo the geographer theorized that the Argonauts were an expedition in search of alluvial gold; but whatever the origins of the myth, it stands out as a magnificent prototype of the perilous search for the marvelous prize. In a sense this is also the theme of the Trojan cycle, in which the greatest figures of a distant glorious age attempt to retrieve the most beautiful mortal woman. But the voyage of the *Argo,* like the wanderings of Odysseus, belongs to that entertaining genre, *Märchen,* which attends to the unnatural, the exotic, the romantic. Jason-like heroes are not only seen in the many local legends of ancient Greece, but in history (Alexander's oriental conquests were romanticized). Comparisons may be drawn between Jason and Celtic heroes, and between the Fleece and the Grail. In 1867, William Morris revived the original myth with a 7,000-line Victorian epic entitled *The Death of Jason.* Robert Graves has authored a novel about the search for the fleece—*Hercules, My Shipmate* (1944).

Classical authors seemed to be more concerned with Medea than with Jason. Euripides' masterpiece tragedy, *Medea,* deals with Jason's cruel rejection of the woman who sacrificed all—even murdered—for him (cf. Ovid *Metamorphoses VII*). Her vengeance, to deprive Jason of the things he loves most, requires that she kill not only the girl he intends to marry, but Jason's (and Medea's) own sons as well. Her refuge in Athens as wife of aging King Aegeus is brief; she escapes to Colchis after an unsuccessful attempt to poison Theseus. Nothing is known of her death—if she died at all. Jason, however, overcome with grief, loneliness, and shame, returned to the rotting hulk of the *Argo* which he had beached at Corinth, and there he was struck by a falling beam and died.

E. N. Genovese

JAVA HEAD

Type of work: Novel
Author: Joseph Hergesheimer (1880-1954)
Type of plot: Period romance
Time of plot: 1840's
Locale: Salem, Massachusetts
First published: 1919

A novel of colorful detail and romantic incident, Java Head *is set in a historic port town during the period when the clipper ship was making America mistress of the seas. Each chapter is written from the point of view of a different character.*

Java Head is essentially a novel about the struggles of outsiders with the powerful and closed society in which they find themselves. Although Joseph Hergesheimer did not give full effect to the dramatic possibilities inherent in the story, his feeling for surface impressions and the honesty of his statement produced a vivid spectacle and a thought-provoking book. Technically, the different parts—each from the viewpoint of a different character—remain "set" pieces, never quite fusing into a whole, but the book is worth reading for the skill of the sketching of atmosphere and characterization. Hergesheimer writes of a sailing ship, for example, as if she were a living creature, and conveys great insight into sea psychology. One of the highlights of the narrative is the dramatic and detailed description of the ship *Nautilus* docking in Salem port.

Gerrit Ammidon tends to reduce the other characters to the background. Almost bigger than life, he stands for romance, eternally protesting against the conventional and bigoted, rebelling against the restrictions laid down by others. Only his old father, Jeremy Ammidon, is equal to him. Reliving his past glories and old voyages, and reworking bygone grievances, Jeremy is frustrated by his beached existence. The characters symbolize the conflict of old and new, the struggle between the "clerk-sailors," as Jeremy calls them, and those who would cling to the romance and danger of old ways. The tide of trade is turning from Salem to the railway and docking facilities of larger cities; although Gerrit and Jeremy are noble figures, they cannot win out against the pettiness of the majority and the lure of "progress."

Taou Yuen is presented with subtlety and restraint. Hergesheimer resists the temptation to use her as a mere exotic counterpoint to the other characters. Viewed merely as a study of the ancient opium habit, the section of the book dealing with her is impressive and interesting. She is an outsider by birth, but her husband is an outsider by nature of his character, as his father has become one by virtue of his age. The destiny of the outsiders is martyrdom. Although their story is told in a strangely passive style, it is effective and significant.

JEAN-CHRISTOPHE

Type of work: Novel
Author: Romain Rolland (1866-1944)
Type of plot: Social chronicle
Time of plot: Late nineteenth and early twentieth centuries
Locale: Germany, France, Switzerland
First published: 1904-1912

Jean-Christophe, *a two thousand-page novel originally published in ten volumes, is the painstaking record of the artistic development of a musical genius. Rolland endeavored to portray the adventures of the soul of his hero; Jean-Christophe's experiences are those of every genius who turns from the past to serve the future.*

The subject matter in *Jean-Christophe* is more important than the technique. The style of composition and manner of construction are straightforward and plain; with few exceptions, the narrative moves smoothly forward, like a river, carrying Christophe through his life. The first sentence establishes the continuous symbolism of the river. Days, weeks, and months are seen as a tide, ebbing and flowing, always beginning anew. First the Rhine and then the Seine dominate the setting. Christophe's first experience of love-making, with Ada, is on the river, and his father drowns in the river. When Christophe dies, the image of the river recurs.

The importance of honesty and integrity forms a continuing theme in the novel. Only one thing is asked of a baby, Christophe's grandfather says at his birth: that he grow into an honest man. Old Jean Michel, one of the finest characters in the novel, has a fondness for spouting aphorisms; he suggests many of the thematic beliefs—honesty, duty, industry—that will later be developed in the book.

Rolland effectively attempts to reveal the world from the point of view of the baby and tiny child. From infancy, music has a special, magical effect on Christophe, whether it is the ringing of church bells or the playing of the church organ. He does not understand the feeling, but it foreshadows the dominant influence in his life. An old piano becomes a source of magic and joy to the child and soon is the most important power in his life. Christophe dreams and muses through childhood. The first crisis of his life occurs when he realizes that some men command and others are commanded. Injustice torments him all of his life. The name Jean-Christophe suggests Jesus Christ, and he later thinks that to create music is to be God on earth.

The maturing process is shown in great detail; the reader is spared none of the pains and joys of Christophe's development. Christophe's grandfather set him on the path of composing, and his Uncle Gottfried taught him to respect music. He saw the faults of the composers around him, and labored to avoid those faults in his own work. He struggled always to make his work *true*. He was torn between the instincts of his family and those of his genius; this struggle is at the heart of the novel. Christophe's "progress" seems to move inevitably from the horror of his grandfather's death, to the importance of his first friendship at fifteen with Otto, to the civilizing influence of Frau von Kerich and the beauty and pain of his first love for Minna.

Occasionally, the reader wonders if it is really necessary to learn about each and every quarrel in which Christophe is involved or to see every suffering moment and witness every betrayal and agonized failure. The catalogue of pain is somewhat excessive. The moral growth of the protagonist is shown with special sensitivity, beginning with the religious crisis that he experiences in his late teens. Before then, he does not have time or education enough to consider philosophical or religious questions. Sabine's sudden death teaches him another painful lesson about the injustices of life, but, perhaps it is Ada who teaches him the most of the inconsistencies of the human heart and the treacherousness of life. Ada, ignorant and vain, petty and jealous, with nothing appealing about her but her physical appearance, is particularly well-drawn. She hates Christophe's music because she hates anything that she cannot understand, but Christophe is captivated by her until he catches her in an affair with his brother. The least sympathetic characters, such as Ada, are often the best drawn in the book.

The narrator holds up Christophe as an example of a man who refuses to give up in the face of defeat, a man who is made stronger by setbacks. The theme of endurance, survival at all costs, is important in the book. If Christophe can be said to possess any one outstanding characteristic, it is tenacity. Perhaps it begins when his uncle Gottfried tells him that what men *will* and what they *do* are seldom the same, but the important thing is never to give up either. Christophe becomes disillusioned with both German and French music, because he feels it is filled with cheating and superficialities. He realizes that honesty must be everything to him. The novel, in large part, is the story of this honesty confronting the sham and lying of the world. Life is always a struggle for Christophe; without his music and friendships, he would not be able to endure the hardships that he faces. The theme of the importance of friendship runs through the many volumes of *Jean-Christophe*; Olivier recalls Otto of so many years before. But Christophe realizes that he is a man alone; it is the man who counts only on his own efforts in life and does not lean on others who wins the author's respect. Rolland does not moralize, but he makes his opinions clear. *Jean-Christophe* is more than the romantic story of a struggling young musician; intellectual and moral beliefs play an important part in the narrative.

The account of the world of the arts, and particularly music, as no more than a great marketplace is superbly detailed. A better indictment of Philistinism has never been written. Christophe's vain efforts to find an unmercenary musician or writer are poignantly described. The section of Christophe's confrontation with the artistic establishment of Paris is well-written, although at times it turns into a diatribe. The book is filled with many intellectual conversations about the arts, politics, science, and philosophy, as well as about psychology and human nature. Christophe is amazed and horrified, in particular, by French politics. The descriptions of Christophe's first impressions of Paris and later efforts to succeed in the French capital are fascinating, filled with both humorous and pathetic details. Vast numbers of characters pass through the book, many only slightly touching Christophe's life; this device stresses Christophe's immersion in the world. He moves in a complex and real society, and he cannot retreat into isolation.

The frustrations and ultimate successes of the protagonist are detailed fully, but Christophe is one of those true artists who creates without hope of glory. Despite loneliness, illness, and poverty, Christophe is patient; he feels that suffering purifies the soul, a romantic notion that runs throughout the book. *Jean-Christophe* is an immense achievement, perhaps somewhat dated in its romantic attitudes, but nonetheless impressive.

Bruce D. Reeves

JENNIE GERHARDT

Type of work: Novel
Author: Theodore Dreiser (1871-1945)
Type of plot: Naturalism
Time of plot: The last two decades of the nineteenth century
Locale: Chicago and various other Midwestern cities
First published: 1911

This naturalistic novel tells the story of a beautiful and vital young girl who is beaten by the forces of life. These forces are accidental and inevitable, and stronger than any man's will or purpose. The social and economic details in the book provide an interesting picture of urban life in the American Middle West at the end of the nineteenth century.

In his second novel, *Jennie Gerhardt,* Theodore Dreiser continues his exploration of themes first introduced in *Sister Carrie.* Central to the novel's vision is Dreiser's belief that the misery in people's lives arises from the conflict between natural human instincts and artificial social and moral standards. Man denies his basic animal appetites, condemning them because they violate the codes of society; yet, ironically, he himself has not only created, but come to believe in, those very social mores which thwart his true desires and bring him great unhappiness. Thus, Jennie is condemned by society for acting on motives of selfless love and generosity. She violates moral codes in becoming Lester Kane's mistress, although she does so in order to save her family from poverty; and when that relationship proves to be a loving and happy one, it is nevertheless considered sinful because it lacks the legal sanction of a marriage license. Likewise, Lester's natural desires are blocked on both sides: if he marries Jennie he will be disinherited and ostracized for marrying beneath his social class, while if he does not, he will be condemned for "living in sin."

In terms of the novel, the people most guilty of perpetuating a social framework so destructive of human happiness are the fathers, who represent the rigid old morality. Mr. Gerhardt, who stands for the blindness and bigotry of religious conviction, turns his own daughter out of her home for trying to help him in a time of financial distress. For similar reasons, Mr. Kane condemns his son's alliance with Jennie, although for his moral arbiter he has replaced the Christian God with the gods of money and respectability.

Within the naturalistic vision embodied in *Jennie Gerhardt,* man is seen as a powerless victim, a creature without free will who therefore lacks the means to control his own destiny. It would be a mistake, however, to assume that, in the absence of free will, chance rules men's lives. It is true that the story of Jennie's career is filled with chance incidents which seemingly bring about important changes in her life; but actually, these chance occurrences are mere catalysts. What really dictates the course which each character's life takes is his or her temperament and personality. Dreiser creates in each character a particular set of limitations which predetermine how he or she will respond to any new circumstances. Thus, when it appears that Jennie or Lester have a free choice to make between two alternatives, what is actually the case is that their respective temperaments cause them to choose as they do. Given Jennie's generous and caring nature, she has no choice but to become Lester's mistress; given Lester's lack of ambition, and his love of an easy life, it is inevitable that he leave Jennie in order to secure his inheritance. By the same token, such seemingly crucial chance events as Senator Brander's untimely death or Letty Pace Gerald's sudden appearance do not materially affect the characters' lives in the long run; if it were not for these *particular* two incidents, some other incidents would eventually occur through which Jennie and Lester would play out the inevitable roles determined for them by the essential qualities of their personalities.

JERUSALEM DELIVERED

Type of work: Poem
Author: Torquato Tasso (1544-1595)
Type of plot: Historical romance
Time of plot: Middle Ages
Locale: The Holy Land
First published: 1580-1581

One of the great poems to come out of the Italian Renaissance and a landmark of heroic literature, Jerusalem Delivered *treats the Crusades in a highly romantic way, with rapid action and vivid, kaleidoscopic scenes.*

As the son of a poet, Torquato Tasso grew up knowing the hardships and insecurities of the poet's life, but he could not be dissuaded from his own pursuit of poetry and a career as a court poet. After thorough grounding in the classics, Tasso wrote in Italian. Early success with *Rinaldo,* a narrative poem, was followed by his two best works: *Aminta,* a pastoral play, and *Jerusalem Delivered (Gerusalemme Liberata),* a romantic epic completed when he was hardly thirty years old. His later works included a tragic drama, a biblical poem, and *Jerusalem Conquered (Gerusalemme Conquistata),* an ill-advised and best-forgotten revision of his masterpiece. In his lifetime, Tasso also produced a prodigious quantity of lyric poems. But in his thirty-third year, he was affiicted with severe mental illness which required his confinement off and on until his death, only days before he was to be awarded the laurel wreath for poetic achievement.

Jerusalem Delivered is a literary epic divided into twenty cantos of *ottava rima* (an eight-line stanza rhyming abababcc). The historical matter of the poem deals with the First Crusade (1097-1099). In substance, however, it reflects the renewed power of Catholicism in Tasso's time, in the wake of the establishment of the Holy Office. Yet, in structure, it clearly shows the influence of Tasso's classical education as well as the contemporary vogue for classical rules of poetics. The central issues developed in the plot are the effectiveness, or ineffectiveness, of Godfrey's military leadership; the banishment and infatuation of Rinaldo; and the three-sided love relationship among Tancred, Clorinda, and Erminia. All of these issues bear on the final victory of Christendom over the pagans. Other aspects of the poem become important as elements in its romantic attitude. Magic, in particular, plays a heavy part in the romantic quality of the poem: the enchantress Armida, the angel who heals Godfrey's wounds, and Godfrey's visions of Hugh and of Archangel Michael. Other super-human (Clorinda's warrior-like skills) and supernatural (Satan's intervention in the early success of the Christian campaign) occurrences contribute to the romantic atmosphere. Likewise, the ultimate triumph of Good over Evil indicates the romantic orientation of the poem.

The artful integration of all of these many features places *Jerusalem Delivered* in the front ranks of the Italian epic tradition in the Renaissance.

THE JEW OF MALTA

Type of work: Drama
Author: Christopher Marlowe (1564-1593)
Type of plot: Romantic tragedy
Time of plot: Fifteenth century
Locale: Malta
First presented: c. 1589

The Machiavellian character of Barabas dominates The Jew of Malta; *he is both a tragic figure and an unrepenting villain. The drama observes unity of place and covers a lapse of time of little over a month. The stage techniques are superbly handled.*

Although Marlowe may have found his initial inspiration for the story and its hero in the person of Juan Michesius, recorded in Philip Lonicerus' *Chronicorum Turcicorum* and in Belleforest's *Cosmographie Universelle,* it is clear from a comparison that the character of Barabas in this play owes at least as much to the tradition of Italian revenge tragedy, to the English morality plays, and to his own preferences in characterization as demonstrated in *Faustus* and in *Tamburlaine*. Considered the most important English dramatist before Shakespeare, Marlowe's social background was similar to that of his illustrious successor, although Marlowe's formal schooling was more extensive just as his theatrical career was, unfortunately, much briefer. Perhaps it was because he himself was gripped by a master passion that Marlowe constructed his greatest plays around characters obsessed with one thing or another; for them, the obsession itself is all-imporant, not particularly its object. Marlowe has been given credit for raising the formerly stilted and academic English theater to the level of a both serious and entertaining art.

Though *The Jew of Malta* is written in Marlowe's most masterful and fully-developed style, it nonetheless remains an enigmatic and difficult play because of the unevenness of its structural impact and emotional effect. Perhaps this is inevitable in the very combination of the morality drama with the drama of personality; it is hard to maintain Barabas as both a typical figure of evil and as a sympathetic, understandable person in his own right. Although the play is usually considered a "romantic tragedy" or a "tragedy of blood," T. S. Eliot considered it a farce, characterized by "terribly serious even savage comic humor." What is certain is its thematic resemblance to Marlowe's other great plays. With *The Tragedy of Doctor Faustus* and *Tamburlaine, The Jew of Malta* shares a concern with exploring the limits of human power; a self-made hero who rises to power from lowly origins, compelled to his own end by an over-arching passion; and the play itself is unified by this hero's personality alone. Moreover *The Jew of Malta* is Marlowe's first Machiavellian play, the first in which the word "policy" appears. As he speaks at the play's opening, Machiavelli embodies in general and final fashion the vices that

Barabas' history will reenact: unbounded greed, accompanied by a complete absence of conscience or moral scruples. In many senses, a major theme of the play is amorality rather than immorality—the amorality displayed by Ferneze as a representative of the political realm, or by the friars as representative Catholics, as well as by Barabas himself as a type of the commercial sphere.

The Jew of Malta is critically difficult because of its apparent structural disjunction, as it moves from an emphasis on Barabas' mind and motivations in the first part to a concentration solely upon his evil actions in the second. In the first part, the familiar Marlovian themes are presented. Barabas' Machiavellian egocentrism is apparently well-founded on the hypocrisy of his "Christian" enemies; the splendor of his wealth is delineated, not in the grandiose general terms of *Tamburlaine,* but in appropriate mercantile detail. The scene between Barabas and Ferneze develops the satirical tone, as it seems to contrast the hypocrisy of the Maltese Christians with the Jew's overt wickedness, their greed with his—an extension of the quarrel between Christians and infidels in *Tamburlaine Part Two*. Barabas nearly captures the sympathies of the audience by making us believe that he will suffer from Ferneze's decree; and that decree *is* manifestly unjust.

In the second part, as the play moves from what M. C. Bradbrook calls the "technique of verse" to the "technique of action," we see that Barabas has fooled the audience; his subterfuge thereby exposes him now as the completely villainous Machiavellian. Marlowe therefore no longer presents introspective revelations of Barabas' mental and emotional processes but turns instead to concentrate on verbal and narrative reversals in the last three acts. The primary interest now is in clever stage situations and adroit manipulation of the narrative, as, for example, when Barabas constantly reverses his overt meaning by his tagged-on asides. The entrapment of Lodowick and Mathias, of the two friars, of Ithamore and Bellamira, and the final series of double-crosses between Ferneze, Calymath, and Barabas, are obviously influenced by the revenge tragedy tradition as brought to England by Kyd's *The Spanish Tragedy*. The plot of *The Jew of Malta*, then, is largely episodic, constructed through the "symmetrical pairing" of a series of figures around that of Barabas: the three Jews at the beginning, the abbess and the nun, Mathias and Lodowick, Friar Bernardine and Friar Jacomo, Bellamira and Pilia-Borsa, the Calymath and Del Bosco.

The focus of the play is Barabas' own character. He is at one and the same time, according to David M. Bevington, the "lifelike Jewish merchant caught in a political feud," an "embodiment of moral vice," and the "unrepenting protagonist in [a] homiletic 'tragedy.' " Once our initial sympathies for Barabas have vanished, we see him only as the heinous culprit who unintentionally fashions his own downfall by the very complications of his evil schemes and his ultimate inability to control those around him who, in their own lesser ways, are also evil schemers. It would be, clearly, a mistake to consider Barabas as an epitome of a race persecuted by prejudice; he shows, at the very beginning, that he himself has no more respect for Jews than he does for Christians or Turks. Abigail, before entering the convent for the second time, now in earnest, makes this point when she says, "But I perceive there is no love on earth,/Pity in Jews, nor piety in Turks." Barabas, instead, proclaims himself "a sound Machiavell," as the Prologue predicts, when he instructs Ithamore in the ways of evil: "First, be thou void of these affections,/ Compassion, love, vain hope, and heartless fear." It is supremely ironic that he calls Ithamore his "second self," since in the end Barabas murders the slave, figuratively revealing the self-destructive bent of his own narcissistic selfishness. On a larger scale, the same irony pervading the entire play is proclaimed in the absurdly righteous closing words of Ferneze: "So, march away; and let due praise be given/Neither to Fate nor Fortune, but to Heaven." Heaven has had little hand in this story; instead, the hand of the pessimistic atheist Marlowe leaves its prints everywhere.

Kenneth John Atchity

THE JEWESS OF TOLEDO

Type of work: Drama
Author: Franz Grillparzer (1791-1872)
Type of plot: Historical tragedy
Time of plot: About 1195
Locale: Toledo and vicinity
First presented: 1872

Grillparzer uses the dramatic form with a poetic clarity and tragic force reminiscent of Shakespeare; he balances form and content and adds new psychological insights and moral perspectives. This drama tells of a monarch's lapse from duty because of his sudden passionate affection for a beautiful but vain young Jewess.

Although *The Jewess of Toledo* was first performed in 1872, the five-act tragedy had been completed in the 1850's, and the idea dated back to 1824, when Grillparzer read Lope de Vega's *La Judea de Toledo,* upon which *The Jewess of Toledo* is closely based. Into it he wove not only his own experience of an overpowering sensual love, but also his observation of a major political scandal of the day, the passion of King Ludwig I of Bavaria for the Spanish dancer, Lola Montez, which ended in her banishment and his abdication. The play is thus doubly motivated, and has been criticized as falling into two pieces: a love tragedy and a political tragedy.

In fact, the two are inseparably intertwined. The fortunes of the state are inextricably bound up with the personal fate of the naïve king, just awakening to the power of the senses. His English wife, Eleanor, is coldly virtuous, though not above jealousy, but it is Rachel to whose charms he succumbs so utterly as to neglect his duty as king. Rachel is a creature of impulse, not of deep emotion, and embodies the absence of moral obligation. Queen Eleanor places duty above all, but lacks warmth and sensuality. It is the king's tragedy and the tragedy of the state, that this division of attributes places his desire and his duty in conflict. His tragedy is, therefore, personal and political. The throne is as good as vacant as the king forgets his divinely ordained role, and the nobles and the queen have no choice but to act to restore the order of the state. In this play, all incur guilt, not so much legal as moral. Rachel pays with her life, and in a sense, so do the king and nobles, as the king embarks upon a crusade against the Moors to atone his guilt by committing his life to the judgment of God in defense of his state.

JOANNA GODDEN

Type of work: Novel
Author: Sheila Kaye-Smith (1888-1956)
Type of plot: Domestic realism
Time of plot: Early twentieth century
Locale: Rural England
First published: 1921

Joanna Godden *is the powerful story of a strong and vibrant woman who ruled her sister and her farm with an iron hand, although she was often bewildered by emotions she could not understand. The novel is notable for reconstructing the atmosphere of the English countryside in all weathers and seasons.*

Joanna Godden is a novel about a remarkable woman who not only survives, but thrives through her efforts to carve out a niche for herself within a man's world. Her strength and independence are such that she wastes no time after her father's death in building her inherited property, Little Ansdore, into a prosperous farm. This she manages to do at a time when many men are sinking under financially in similar enterprises. Her gift for management and insight into business matters finally earns her the grudging admiration of her neighbors who had been at first so disapproving of what they considered her indecorous and unfeminine behavior.

Sheila Kaye-Smith creates the character of Joanna with skill and sensitivity; her heroine is a vibrantly real figure who blends both strength and vulnerability, sharp judgment and naïveté, staunch independence and the need for human relationships within her personality. Through an unfolding of her interpersonal relationships with her younger sister Ellen, her devoted admirer Arthur, her fiancé Martin, and the father of her child Albert Hill, the author reveals Joanna as a very complex and deep woman. Her almost paternal relationship with Ellen, for example, brings out both the loving and the controlling, dominating sides of her character. In her tender affection and instinctive desire to protect her weaker sister, she exerts such control that the latter feels stifled and longs to escape into some kind of independence.

Likewise in her relationships with men, Joanna is an odd mixture of strong and weak, sensible and foolish. She feels nothing for Arthur, the man who truly loves her. She is actually able to pressure him into marrying Ellen, yet when he finally leaves Little Ansdore, she begins to see him as more desirable; and after he is dead, it is his memory and the imagined approval of her actions that give her strength in selling the farm and refusing to marry Albert. When Joanna finally does meet a suitable man in Martin Trevor, her tough-minded devotion to the farm causes her to delay the marriage; she decides too late that Martin's love is more important than the farm: he becomes ill and dies. When an undesirable man comes into her life in the form of Albert Hill, the woman who can unerringly choose the best sheep or barter for the highest price is unable to judge a potential lover wisely. And yet it is this very blend of qualities that make Joanna Godden such a human and sympathetic heroine.

Sheila Kaye-Smith, dubbed the "Sussex novelist" by some critics to suggest a comparison to her contemporary, the "Wessex novelist" Thomas Hardy, sets her story against the rural setting of the Sussex countryside. The novel is rich in local-color detail; it abounds with loving descriptions of both the people, their habits and dialect, and the beauty of the land. In *Joanna Godden,* Kaye-Smith realizes her early ambition, recounted in her autobiography, to become an excellent novelist of rural life; in so doing, she brings that life back for her readers.

JOHN BROWN'S BODY

Type of work: Poem
Author: Stephen Vincent Benét, (1898-1943)
Type of plot: Historical romance
Time of plot: 1859-1865
Locale: The United States
First published: 1928

John Brown's Body, *which won the Pulitzer Prize for 1929, tells, in free and formal verse, the tragic story of the Civil War and its effects upon the nation. Benét weaves several small plots concerned with fictional characters into the main plot of the history of the time.*

Stephen Vincent Benét's poem *John Brown's Body* is the only American poetic work which reaches epic proportions; its nearly fifteen-thousand-line length qualifies it as an epic in the classical sense, and ranks it, in form and purpose at least, with the great epics of Western literature. But although the poem as a whole is traditional in its classic structure, it is distinctly and uniquely American in its atmosphere, imagery, style, and symbolism. In his Invocation, Benét calls upon the American Muse to aid him, providing inspiration for what he humbly acknowledges to be an almost impossible task because of the magnitude of its scope. The poet's Muse becomes a symbol of America, his elusive subject: she is beautiful and strong, colorful and diverse, a unique, mysterious offspring of European and native parentage. Within the poem (line 311), Benét describes his work as a "cyclorama": a series of large pictures of America spread around the reader, who views them from the center.

The major unifying element in this cyclorama is the spirit of John Brown. Based on the historical figure of the man who raided the arsenal at Harper's Ferry, Benét's hero becomes the focal symbol of the epic; although he is condemned and hanged early in the work, his memory grows into the legend that gives hope and inspiration during the dark days of the Civil War. The second unifying thread throughout the loosely woven eight books is provided in the characters of Northerner Jack Ellyat and Southerner Clay Wingate. Other minor characters help round out the scheme whereby all the regions and social groups of a huge nation are represented: Melora Vilas and her father typify the Border States and the expanding West; Lucy Weatherby is the Southern coquette; Luke Breckinridge, the independent mountaineer; Jake Diefer, the settled farmer; Spade, the runaway slave, and Cudjo, the loyal slave; and Shippy, the Northern spy. By tracing the fortunes of such diverse people, Benét dramatizes not only how the war affects their lives, but how their lives shape the nation.

One of the greatest achievements of *John Brown's Body* is Benét's accurate and balanced picture of Southern life. With realism and insight he probes the character of John Brown and of his legend; judging the raid as foolish, he sees Brown as a murderer and a fanatic, a man so caught in his zealous dream that he remains coldly unmoved by his son's horrible death. Brown the man was a failure; but dead, he became a crucial legend and symbol. Likewise, the Southern slaves are portrayed in all the complexity, ambiguity, and irony of their situation; and the Wingates embody the dilemma of the genteel Southern aristocrat. Unfortunately, Benét fails to capture the culture and way of life in the North; his portraits of the Ellyat household, in contrast to those of the Wingate plantation, are rather flat and one-dimensional.

JOHN HALIFAX, GENTLEMAN

Type of work: Novel
Author: Dinah Maria Mulock (Mrs. George Craik, 1826-1887)
Type of plot: Domestic realism
Time of plot: Turn of the nineteenth century
Locale: Rural England
First published: 1857

The story of John Halifax depicts the simple pleasures of lower middle-class life in rural England. Mulock makes the plea that a man be judged by his merits rather than by his social class or his birth.

Few readers today probably know this once widely read novel, a domestic idyll extolling Christian virtues and plain values of family life. Its simplicity and seeming artlessness have little appeal for readers who have accustomed themselves to ambiguity, violent realism, and sophisticated innovations of style. But *John Halifax, Gentleman* enjoyed decided popularity in its Victorian milieu. The author, Dinah Maria Murlock, or Mrs. Craik, wrote fifty-two works of fiction, poetry, and children's stories. Whatever judgment modern critics might place upon her output, she was honored by some of the most famous writers of her period. Indeed, after her death, a committee which included Lord Tennyson, Matthew Arnold, Robert Browning, Professor Huxley, James Russell Lowell, and Mrs. Oliphant, erected a marble medallion in Tewkesbury Abbey in her memory.

As background for her story of John Halifax and Ursula March, Mrs. Craik chose one of the most picturesque sections of Gloucestershire; she faithfully described the small English homesteads clustered in the pleasant valleys, the softly rolling hills, and the town of Tewkesbury itself, which she terms Norton Bury. Like Hardy and others, Mrs. Craik chose an area with which she was familiar; one who knows the locale easily recognizes Nunnely Hill as Selsley Hill and Enderley Flats as the real Amberley Common.

As a novelist, Mrs. Craik shows herself cognizant of some of the most important principles of the craft, as seen, for instance, in her method of allowing dialogue to carry the plot, instead of relying on authorial reportage. And her characters develop; John Halifax, Ursula, Lord Ravenel, and especially the elder son, Guy Halifax, go through experiences which effect changes in their outlooks or adjustments to society or to themselves. Though the novel emphasizes ideals, the characters are not ideal. They act and react like human beings and are therefore believable. John Halifax must come to terms with his own pride, Ursula with her tendency to direct situations. Lord Ravenel must choose between a decadent luxury which is empty, and effort in a new world which exacts of him his latent strength and belief. A simple story simply told, *John Halifax, Gentleman,* in spite of its quaint Victorian tone and exaltation of old-fashioned ideals, is based upon clear principles of good writing and can still for this reason involve today's reader.

JOHN INGLESANT

Type of work: **Novel**
Author: **Joseph Henry Shorthouse (1834-1903)**
Type of plot: **Historical-philosophical romance**
Time of plot: **Seventeenth century**
Locale: **England and Italy**
First published: **1881**

This historical romance follows the complicated political and ecclesiastical affairs in England during the stormy years of the reign of Charles I and the ensuing Civil War. The author emphasizes philosophical content in the novel, but the modern reader is likely to find the historical aspects more interesting.

Judged as a philosophical novel, *John Inglesant* is a product of Tractarianism, deriving from the Oxford Movement of mid-nineteenth century England. For his Victorian audience, Shorthouse attempts to mediate between the conflicting claims of Anglicanism and Roman Catholicism. He provides a historical perspective for the conflict by setting the novel in the seventeenth century, a period of great religious upheaval, to show that it is possible to bridge the gap between the two religions and their underlying cultures. In a letter to his friend Dr. Abott, Shorthouse writes that perhaps the chief object of his novel is to "promote culture at the expense of fanaticism."

His spokesman for tolerance, John Inglesant, is trained as a Jesuit by Father St. Clare, but is permitted freedom to exercise his own religious conscience. During the course of his adventures, Inglesant meets representatives of different Christian viewpoints, from those of the High Anglican monastic colony under John Ferrar at Little Gidding to the "Quietist" followers of Michael de Molinos; from Puritans hostile to King Charles I to followers of the Benedictine Order directed by Hugh Paulin Cressy. He comes to understand the intricate politics of electing a Pope and discovers secrets of the Jesuits. Wherever he goes, he meets Christians of principle, conviction, and dignity. Devoted to the "ideal of Christ," he remains to the last a member of the Church of England. Yet he is neither exceedingly zealous in his own faith nor bigoted toward any other. Except for the Puritans, whom he considers narrow-minded fanatics, he finds among all other Christians the same high-minded dedication to Christ's ideal that he professes.

Searching for spiritual perfection, Inglesant moves freely through the different levels of seventeenth century society, both in England and on the Continent. His quest is also a romantic one. Mary Collet and Lauretta Capace, his two loves, help to perfect his character as a gentleman, just as his religious teachers perfect his moral nature. Always his enemy is Malvolti, slayer of his brother Eustace, master of disguises, resourceful and cunning betrayer. The romantic climax of the novel is Chapter 32, the scene in which Inglesant delivers Malvolti, now in rags and begging for pity, over to the priest of the Capella for justice, leaving his sword on the altar. In his letters, Shorthouse reveals that he wrote the entire novel expressly to describe this scene (based upon a historical anecdote concerning one Giovanni Gualberto of Florence). Just as Inglesant foregoes religious fanaticism through love of Christ, so he spares his enemy, making possible Malvolti's later reformation. Thus Inglesant's romantic quest is fulfilled; he becomes a true gentleman in Christ.

Inspired by William Smith's *Thorndale, John Ingelsant* in turn influenced many late-Victorian philosophical novelists, including Mrs. Humphry Ward (*Robert Elsmere*, 1888). Most important, it created an interest in philosophical romance that helped to develop an audience for Walter Pater's *Marius the Epicurean* (1885), probably the most important English work of this genre.

JONATHAN WILD

Type of work: Novel
Author: Henry Fielding (1707-1754)
Type of plot: Social criticism
Time of plot: Late seventeenth century
Locale: England
First published: 1743

The characters of this satirical novel are vivid, the plot sure and swift, and Fielding's barbs at society both delightful and accurate. The book presents the story of a "great" man, but not a good one, for, says Fielding, a great man must necessarily be a villain.

Jonathan Wild is an exceptionally brilliant novel. It reflects and comments upon the life of London and, at the same time, offers a profound moral analysis of human behavior.

The London in which Henry Fielding lived was characterized by wildness, extravagances and corruption. London was a "wide-open" city, a sort of American frontier town on a huge scale. During the years when Fielding was beginning his career, Sir Robert Walpole dominated the Parliament, the King, and the Courts. He stifled opposition and succeeded in amassing enormous power and wealth; he also attracted the brilliant and biting satire of some of England's most talented writers, including Swift, Gay, Pope, and Fielding. Jonathan Wild, a "great man," is intended as a satire of Walpole as well as of the moral position he occupied. Viewing this "great man" as a gangster and an opportunist, Fielding combined him with another personage, an actual small time criminal named Jonathan Wild, who was hanged at Tyburn before a large, interested crowd.

Henry Fielding offers an alternative to the blind respect that those in authority often demand. By stressing throughout the novel the distinction between "greatness" and "goodness," Fielding makes moral judgments independent of social standing. He implies not only that we must distinguish between greatness and goodness, but that the two are mutually exclusive.

But there is a further point that Fielding makes about "greatness": it amounts to nothing but the untrammeled selfish instincts of men. For Jonathan Wild, it means stealing from friend and foe alike, taking advantage of women whenever possible, and, above all, thinking and acting in behalf of no one but himself. This unrestricted and uncivilized behavior accounts for his name: he is wild indeed. But although he is as wild as an animal, he is basically not free. At every step, he is entirely possessed by his own desires and driven by his own selfish instincts. The more he looks after "number one," and the more he lets himself go, the fewer choices he has left open to him. Thus it is philosophically appropriate, as well as morally necessary, for Jonathan Wild to be jailed and hanged at the conclusion of the novel.

Fielding intends Wild to be contrasted with his enemy, Heartfree, who, because he thinks of others and lacks ambition, is basically free as well as morally acceptable. Freedom for Henry Fielding, then, lies not in the possession of power or wealth or license, but in the practice of a simple morality and a consideration for others. Thus, in *Jonathan Wild*, freedom arises from social responsibility and not from individual prerogative.

JORROCKS' JAUNTS AND JOLLITIES

Type of work: Tales
Author: Robert Smith Surtees (1803-1864)
Type of plot: Comic romance
Time of plot: The 1830's
Locale: England and France
First published: 1838

This volume of Jorrocks' sporting adventures differs from the others in that there is no connecting plot; the work is a series of tales given unity by the irrepressible personality of Jorrocks. A wealth of detail provides a good contemporary account of town and country life in early Victorian England.

Appearing in serialized form in *The New Sporting Magazine*, the episodic sporting adventures of Mr. Jorrocks, the rich Cockney grocer, captured the English imagination. His exploits were discussed in stable and dining room alike; among sportsmen he enjoyed as great a popularity as Dickens' Mr. Pickwick did in the society at large.

Although Surtees subjects Jorrocks to one social or physical humiliation after another, it would be a mistake to assume that the mudfalls and dunkings, the ridicule in court and the gulling by the French, are calculated primarily to reduce Jorrocks to the level of an exploited clown, or a lower-class tradesman satirized for his social pretensions. He *is* funny, and he is ridiculed for his sports mania, but Surtees' humor is not informed by social snobbery.

Jorrocks suffers from enthusiasm,from an over-involvement with all forms of sport. He is punished comically for the exaggerated role the hunt and chase play in his life, but at the same time he is humanized by the very weakness that makes him ridiculous. What Surtees seems to be suggesting is that the true sportsman, no matter how disastrous the weather or how foul his luck, is always ready for the morrow, for the next hunt when everything will be perfect. In short, the sheer joy of the sportsman's expectations make him impervious to disappointment. There is greatness in that.

Surtees is the original apologist for the "sporting life." The secret of Jorrocks' appeal lies very much in the way Surtees managed to graft eighteenth century sentimentalism to what is essentially a robust social satire. It is as if Sterne and Smollett had joined forces in the same work. Dickens was to carry that kind of blend to far greater heights than Robert Smith Surtees, a yarn-spinning journalist who stumbled into comic fiction.

JOSEPH ANDREWS

Type of work: Novel
Author: Henry Fielding (1707-1754)
Type of plot: Comic epic
Time of plot: Early eighteenth century
Locale: England
First published: 1742

Originally begun as a satiric rebuttal of what Fielding felt was the distasteful, maudlin sentimentality of Richardson's Pamela. Joseph Andrews *takes its title from the hero, who is Pamela Andrews' brother. However, the work soon grew into something much more serious than a mere takeoff. Often called the first realistic novel of English literature, the work brilliantly satirizes affectation and the vanities of human nature. The structure of the novel is loose, but its realistic settings and vivid portrayal of eighteenth century English life more than compensate for this weakness.*

Joseph Andrews is many things: a parody of Richardson's *Pamela,* a sentimental tale of virtue rewarded; a realistic portrayal of the English road in the eighteenth century; a resetting of the values of comic epic poetry in prose, resulting in what Fielding calls a "comic epic romance" and by which he has in mind the model of Cervantes' *Don Quixote*; an experiment in social satire which brands affectation as ridiculous. All these characteristics blend in a master function. It is an oversimplification merely to conceive of this function in generic terms, to formulate an all-encompassing descriptive label like "comic epic in prose" or "comic novel" and consider the book defined.

Fielding, along with Richardson, is sometimes called the father of the English novel because he ventilated the concept of narrative itself; his brilliant plotting in *Tom Jones* and the desultory Odyssean travels of *Joseph Andrews* are contrasting patterns for realizing a broadly imagined action rich in human nature. *Joseph Andrews,* then, is one of the earliest examples of modern literature's successful extension of mimetic possibilities beyond the models of classical antiquity and the folk tradition. The novel is a mixed genre; it is composed of tale, parable, ballad, and, of course, epic. But the mixture becomes a whole greater than its parts with true innovators such as Fielding.

What holds Fielding's book together is its cosmic exposure of appearance. Wherever Joseph and Parson Adams go, their naïveté and innocence make them inadvertent exposers of affectation. Affectation is the most ridiculous form of "appearance" among men. It invites derision and must be exposed: the effect is morally healthy, but even more to the point, mimetically revealing. Behind appearance lies the "true springs of human action." The essence of a man is often better than his appearance, even though his vanity may commit him to affectation. Parson Adams is a loveable character mainly because under his pedantries and vanities beats a heart of gold. His naïve trust in human goodness, and his unshakeable belief in practiced Christianity define the true man: the "real" Adam is better than his affectations. Similarly, when Joseph is robbed, beaten, and stripped of his clothes, Fielding takes the opportunity to demonstrate the fact that true human charity may emanate from a person whose appearance and life history would seem to mark him incapable of any kindness: "the postillion (a lad who has since been transported for robbing a hen-roost) . . . voluntarily stripped off a great-coat, his only garment; at the same time swearing a great oath, for which he was rebuked by the passengers, that he would rather ride in his shirt all his life, than suffer a fellow passenger to lie in so miserable a condition."

Fielding trusts in his satiric method—the exposure of affectation and the questioning of appearance—because he senses that it will not ground his comic vision in despair or cynicism. He avoids the satiric fate of Swift, whose contempt for human imperfections of character and principle drove him to contempt for men in general. Fielding maintains a love of life itself, an essential state of mind for an artist who presumes to epic achievements in the imaginative grasp of social reality. Swift could never have written *Tom Jones* (1749), Fielding's great comic novel with its tolerant but firmly objective picture of human nature. *Joseph Andrews* is a preface, in theme and style, to the more carefully plotted masterpiece.

As tolerant as Fielding is of human nature, he is also capable of biting judgment. Not a misanthrope like Swift, as Walter Allen reminds us in *The English Novel* (1954), Fielding is nevertheless a tough-minded moralist who delights in passing harsh comic judgment when it is called for. He was, after all, a court judge in real life. Parson Trulliber is a case in point. Fielding has Parson Adams fall into the mud with Trulliber's pigs, but this embarrassment is typical of the many other physical beatings and discomforts that the good Parson suffers throughout the novel. They are emblematic of Fielding's mild judgment of Adams' clerical vanity. Once the mud is washed off, the naïve but true Christian in Parson Adams is all the more shiningly revealed. Things are exactly the opposite with Trulliber. His Christianity is completely superficial; Parson Adams' innocent request for fourteen shillings of charity is met by cries of thief. Once Trulliber's fake Christianity is exposed, he is all hog's mud underneath. This is established from the beginning of his encounter with Parson Adams, whom he mistakes for a hog merchant. Trulliber sees and feels with the eyes and temperament of a hog. He is stingy with food as well as money and like his angry pigs is quick to belligerence. The only way he can defend himself against Parson Adams' accusation that he is not a good Christian is by clenching his fist. The most telling irony is Trulliber's contempt for Parson Adams' appearance. How can this horseless man with a torn "cassock" call himself a man of the cloth? Because Trulliber's Christianity is all surface, it is he who is dripping in hog's mud from first to last, not Parson Adams.

Fielding's pursuit of essential humanity in his characters, through the stripping away of affectation and appearance, is so successful that by the end of the novel he can indulge in burlesque without dehumanizing. Two chapters from the end, Parson Adams, thinking he is about to rescue Fanny from rape, finds himself wrestling with Slipslop, whom he mistakes for the rapist. Aroused to his mistake by Slipslop's huge bosom and Lady Booby's entrance, he staggers back to what he mistakenly thinks is his own room and lies down beside Fanny. In the morning Joseph discovers them lying together. Everything is explained and everyone is appeased. Even Slipslop seems to have enjoyed the "attention" of both the rapist (Beau Didapper) and her attacker, the Parson. All this is pure farce, a broad joke to usher in the warmly comic conclusion of the novel. It is a measure of Fielding's fictive power that he can people a story with characters rich enough to shift from burlesque to comedy without compromising their credibility. In fact, both plot and character seem to benefit mutually from the author's comic exuberance.

Peter A. Brier

JOSEPH VANCE

Type of work: Novel
Author: William De Morgan (1839-1917)
Type of plot: Simulated autobiography
Time of plot: Mid-nineteenth century
Locale: England
First published: 1906

This autobiographical novel relates the life of the protagonist from earliest recollections until the last years of his life. Humor and pathos are mixed in the sometimes precious, but always lively narrative. Much of the humor derives from the character of Vance's father, who firmly believes that to be a success, a person must know nothing about the job he is hired to do.

The influences of Sterne and Dickens are very clear in *Joseph Vance.* Sterne especially is evident in the tone of the narration, the descriptions of the characters, and in the philosophizing and digressions, for instance, on Joe's Father's Hat and Human Nature. The author's style is not as smooth and graceful as Sterne's, however, resulting at times in a rather strained and arch humor. The protagonist's father, for example, is too obviously intended to be a grand old "character." The narrative vitality and sense of place, and the minor characters, suggest Dickens. The lower-class dialect is often skilfully utilized, but it is carried to the point of preciousness; mispronunciations and absurd grammar alone do not make a character comic. But the story is crowded with telling and often amusing details, despite the occasionally excessive use of letters to move the story forward, and the minor characters are sketched with precise and vivid portraits.

The development of the protagonist is interesting, for the most part, although the narrative is sometimes confusing. Joseph's bouts with education (especially geometry) and the results when he tries to demonstrate his new learning to his old friends are amusing. De Morgan's power to create character and convey atmosphere provide the principal merits of the novel. Some of the scenes in the house of the Thorpe family, Joseph's adopted relations and protectors, possess a quaint and touching charm.

William De Morgan did not begin his career as a writer until after retiring from his first career as a ceramic artist and inventor. A member of the Pre-Raphaelite circle, he was famous for the quality and beauty of his glazes; much of his work with pottery and tiles is preserved in museums. His second career as a novelist brought him a wide literary reputation and considerable financial success. His last two works were published posthumously. *Joseph Vance,* De Morgan's first novel, is still considered his best fictional effort. The richness of the prose, the humor, and the delightful characterizations should ensure the book a secure, if minor, place in English literature.

JOURNEY TO THE END OF THE NIGHT

Type of work: Novel
Author: Louis-Ferdinand Céline (Louis Ferdinand Destouches, 1894-1961)
Type of plot: Naturalism
Time of plot: World War I and following years
Locale: France
First published: 1932

Pessimistic and experimental, this unusual novel reveals in a very personal way the mental condition of the author. The action is seen through the eyes of a neurotic narrator who reduces all experience to a disillusioned, cynical level. Above all, images symbolic of the fear of death dominate Journey to the End of the Night.

In Louis-Ferdinand Céline's *Journey to the End of the Night,* night is a symbolic descent through fear into approaching death. Ferdinand Bardamu, Céline's anti-hero, is obsessed with fear. His fear of bodily death expands into a fear more encompassing than death—the dark night of a life without a reason for death. Ferdinand's travels are a series of escapes from everything, always searching for something. He sees in the ruthless, cynical light of his intellect, the demi-gods—heroism, patriotism, fatalism, sex—to which people are devoted, and he runs from them.

Most of Ferdinand's acquaintances are duped by delusions, fearlessly unaware of their own deaths. Captain Ortolan, the patriot, obediently and enthusiastically gives himself and others to death. Ferdinand's psychiatrist, Dr. Bestombes, and the doctor at the Ford Motor Company in Detroit, share the opinion that for one to be intelligent is a hindrance. Ferdinand's mother resigns herself to a fatalistic view that the small are meant to suffer; and the little American, Lola, dedicates herself to the romantic ideal of French suffering by heroically tasting and distributing apple fritters daily. All of these characters are blind.

But Ferdinand cannot give himself to illusion; he cannot escape his awareness of death. Those without imagination seldom fear death, but Ferdinand does have imagination, and he suffers because of it. He is one of the unhappy ones, thoughtful, searching, alone, contemplating his eventual death and abhorring it.

Ferdinand is nonheroic and nonpatriotic, anti-war, anti-psychiatry, anticlerical. His longing goes far beyond satisfaction with negativisim. He is lost in a void, yearning to discover his own "great idea" that will be stronger than the idea of his death. His fear is that he will reach the end of the night without having made that discovery.

JOURNEY'S END

Type of work: Drama
Author: Robert C. Sherriff (1896-)
Type of plot: Impressionistic realism
Time of plot: March, 1918
Locale: A battlefield in France
First presented: 1929

Produced with the help of George Bernard Shaw, this study of men under pressure began Sherriff's writing career. An antiwar play based on personal experience, it probes skillfully the psychological anguish of soldiers and the nature of conflict.

It was not until 1929, eleven years after the end of World War I, that England had its first memorable "anti-war" play (Sean O'Casey's *The Silver Tassie* being Irish), and that one was largely accidental. Robert C. Sherriff, a junior insurance clerk, was called upon by his boat club to write an all-male play and he complied with *Journey's End*. But, as soon as Sherriff tasted play-writing, he became enthused, abandoned insurance for artistic creativity, and persisted in marketing *Journey's End* until it was commercially produced. Once on the boards, it was a tremendous success, both popularly and critically, and Sherriff seemed destined to become one of England's most important post-war dramatists. Unfortunately, however, he was never able to match his first theatrical achievement.

By contemporary standards the "anti-war" message of *Journey's End* is quite muted. Sherriff certainly creates a believable milieu, demonstrates that combat is an unpleasant experience, and points out the insensitivity of those who plan and carry out the war from a distance, using combat troops as mere pawns in a grand design. But the absolute necessity of the war and the correctness of the long-range vision of those who oversee it are never questioned. However meaningless the men's activities may seem to the contemporary reader, Sherriff leaves no doubt that there is purpose in their sacrifice. War, he suggests, is a necessary evil, and the important thing is to face up to it with intelligence and courage. Thus, the lasting importance of *Journey's End* lies not in its rhetoric, but in its dramatic potency and psychological insights.

In spite of its context of combat violence, *Journey's End* is, for the most part, a leisurely play. Most of the action occurs offstage, and except for the final moments, the pacing is deliberately slow. The atmosphere in the trenches is one of anxious boredom as the men wait for the big German assault. To escape the tedium and forget the sudden destruction and death hovering about, they indulge in aimless banter, stale jokes, and a kind of grotesque parody of domesticity. But the more casual the men try to be, the more tense the atmosphere becomes.

The play focuses on the contrasting reactions of the five officers. Each of them has his own special "defense" against the pressures of combat. Lieutenant Osborne, the second in command, is the most stable of the five. A middle-aged schoolteacher in peacetime, he has managed to keep himself under control by scrupulously separating his civilian and military roles and by viewing the entire process with an ironical distance and detachment. Throughout most of the action, Second Lieutenant Trotter seems to be an unimaginative clod, until he reveals, in a heated exchange with Stanhope, that he has suppressed his imagination as a way of keeping his emotions in hand. Second Lieutenant Hibbert has no effective defense at all and so, when denied the chance to malinger out of combat, he cracks. Only Stanhope's threat to kill him on the spot forces Hibbert to a precarious self-control. Second Lieutenant Raleigh, fresh from training, is still buoyed up by the clichés of military honor and personal glory; given the almost suicidal mission to kidnap a German soldier in the face of the enemy's fire, he says "it's most frightfully exciting." But, once exposed to active fighting and the death of Osborne, he quickly sheds these clichés, comes to understand the anguish and fears of his companions, and dies with stoic courage at the final curtain.

But the most interesting and important study of a man under pressure is that of the Commanding Officer, Captain Dennis Stanhope. Lacking Osborne's detachment, Trotter's unimaginativeness, or Raleigh's naïveté, he cannot adopt any of their survival strategies and so teeters near the edge of breakdown during most of the play. An impressive man in college and sports, Stanhope has brought considerable ability to the military. He is an excellent leader, a good strategist, a perceptive judge of his men, and an extremely capable officer in an emergency. At the same time he is intense, emotional, and depressed. His "decline" is given special emphasis by the arrival of Raleigh, who has known and idolized him before the war and now sees him in a haggard and dissipated condition. The Captain's decline is most obvious in the way he abuses himself physically, drinks to excess, and doubts his own sanity out loud.

Late in the play he almost goes into an hysterical rage over Raleigh's slighting of the other officers following Osborne's death. But he gets control over himself and later, in the final, crucial moments he holds himself together. When he returns to combat after Raleigh's death, it is clear that he has faced the worst in himself and comes out of it with purpose and confidence.

Thus, *Journey's End* may be pessimistic about the nature of war, but it is optimistic about the men who must fight them. In the end it is a powerful tribute, not to battlefield glory, but to the practical heroics of survival with dignity.

A JOVIAL CREW

Type of work: Drama
Author: Richard Brome (?-1652 or 1653)
Type of plot: Farce
Time of plot: Seventeenth century
Locale: England
First presented: 1641

A Jovial Crew; or, The Merry Beggars *is a goodnatured, unpretentious comedy presenting a world filled with pleasantly unreal problems that permit equally unreal solutions. The play succeeds as a light and gay entertainment, although less frivolous realities lurk beneath the surface.*

"You are a jovial crew," says Springlove to the beggars, "the only people whose happiness I admire." Springlove was not alone. When this play was produced, England was on the threshold of one of the darkest periods in its history, and the gathering storm (that was to lead to civil war, regicide, and finally military dictatorship under Cromwell) was already shaking the nation to its foundations. Little wonder that the carefree and rancorless life of the beggars was a pleasant and soothing spectacle to contemporary audiences, or that the escapist romances that Brome laments in his prologue (and to which this play is a mirthful alternative) were the vogue in "these sad and tragic days."

The motif of the jolly beggars is an enduring one in English literature. Taking dramatic hints from plays such as Fletcher's *The Beggar's Bush* and Middleton and Rowley's *The Spanish Gypsy,* Brome worked a rich comic mine that was to be rediscovered by writers like Gay, in *The Beggar's Opera,* and Burns, in his dramatic poem, "The Jolly Beggars." *A Jovial Crew* was Brome's most popular play, being frequently revived in the Restoration period (Pepys saw it three times in one year) and in the eighteenth century. The underlying thesis of this and other such works, of course, is that the freedom, mirth, fellowship, and nobility of the beggar makes for a far happier life than the commercial accounts, debts, responsibilities, of the respectable gentleman. A corollary of this romantic idea is that there is, after all, a striking similarity between the "statute beggar" and the "courtier beggar"; indeed, the fact that the former is motivated by need and hunger, rather than pride or ambition, makes him a figure of greater sympathy and dignity.

Unlike some of Brome's earlier plays, *A Jovial Crew* is not overloaded with plot values, but owes its success, rather, to an appealing group of characters, especially the two sets of lovers, who develop, through lively dialogue, a warm rapport with one another. Their essential humanity is not obscured by battles of wit, but comically revealed as they earnestly try to assume new social roles to which they are not at all suited. In addition, the aura of benevolence that surrounds the faithful steward, part-time beggar-king, and long-lost son, Springlove, and the generous openhearted landlord Oldrents—along with the utmost utopian community he governs—augment the nostalgic sense of good feeling and social stability that had vanished from the outside world.

The play for years has been received as gay and lighthearted; but recent critics have noted that the grim realities beneath the pleasant fun are constantly showing through the surface. The commonwealth of beggars is, after all, an escape from the world of cares and anxieties that is faced even by the utopian Oldrents, and outside his sheltered domains is a virtually unchecked reign among thieves, cheats, usurers, corrupt justices, and bloodsucking landlords. It is also plain to see that beneath the lighthearted comic treatment of Justice Clack is a picture of a petty and egocentric tyrant whose self-confessed philosophy is "punish 'em first and be compassionate afterwards." Nor is the traditionally romanticized portrait of the jolly beggars unshaded by darker hues. The lovers soon discover to their discomfort that the beggar's lot is not as carefree as they had imagined, and added to the natural hazards of the profession are constant dangers of arrest and persecution by the authorities.

The mirthful and pleasant nature of the outward action and the happy ending gave audiences some of the last fragments of good feeling of the era. The following year, the theaters were closed by the Puritans, not to reopen for another eighteen years. Meanwhile, the nation underwent a course of events remarkably paralleled by the prediction of the poet-beggar in *A Jovial Crew*: "I would have the country, the city, and the court, be at great variance for superiority. Then I would have Divinity and Law stretch their wide throats to appease and reconcile them; then would I have the soldier cudgel them all together and overtop them all."

JUDE THE OBSCURE

Type of work: Novel
Author: Thomas Hardy (1840-1928)
Type of plot: Philosophical realism
Time of plot: Nineteenth century
Locale: Wessex
First published: 1894

Hardy's sexual frankness and unconventional treatment of the theme of marriage in this novel outraged readers when the book was first published; now Jude the Obscure *is seen as one of the author's most powerful achievements. A somber, at times grim novel, it is rich in its portrayal of suffering, powerful in its evocation of nature, and tragic in its vision of a universe where men are powerless to avert the fates inflicted by impersonal external forces.*

A unique transitional figure between the literary worlds of the Victorian and the modern, Thomas Hardy was an undistinguished architect whose novels and poems were to become his chief profession. Although his rustic characters and some of his poems exhibit a humorous hand at work, invading most of his creations are a brooding irony reflecting life's disappointments and a pessimistic belief that man is a victim of a neutral force which darkly rules the universe. Hardy himself divided his novels into three groups: Novels of Ingenuity (such as *Desperate Remedies*); Romances and Fantasies (for example, *A Pair of Blue Eyes*); and Novels of Character and Environment. This last class includes his best and most famous works, *Tess of the D'Urbervilles, The Return of the Native, Far from the Madding Crowd, The Mayor of Casterbridge,* and *Jude the Obscure.*

First published in a modified form as an 1894 serial in *Harper's, Jude the Obscure* is considered by many to be Hardy's top-ranking novel. Yet today it is read less often than many of his works, and it was the outraged reception of *Jude the Obscure* which turned Hardy from the novel to a concentration on his poetry. His disgust at the reactions, which ranged from moral outrage to an incident where an American gentleman furiously flung the book across the room when he found it was not as harmful as touted, was bitter and enduring.

The best explanation of the book's basic framework was stated by Hardy himself in his preface: the novel, meant for adults, was intended "to tell, without a mincing of words, of a deadly war waged between flesh and spirit; and to point the tragedy of unfulfilled aims." To these, we may add two other important themes: an attack on convention and society, and an examination of man's essential loneliness.

Exhibiting the flesh-spirit division is, of course, Jude's conflicting nature. His relationship with Arabella represents his strong sexual propensities, while his attraction to intellectual pursuits and his high principles reveal his spiritual side. His obsession with Sue is a reflection of both sides of his personality, for while he is compelled by her mind and emotion, he is also drawn to her physically. At the crucial moments of his life, Jude's fleshly desires are strong enough to temporarily devour his other hopes. His two major goals are checked by this flaw, for his initial attempt at a university career is halted when he succumbs to Arabella, and his plans for the ministry end when he kisses Sue and decides that as long as he loves another man's wife he cannot be a soldier and servant of a religion which is so suspicious of sexual love.

"The tragedy of unfilled aims" is forcefully present in both Jude and Sue. For years Jude, in a truly dedicated and scholarly fashion, devotes himself to preparing to enter Christminster (Hardy's name for Oxford). Even when he frees himself from the sexual entanglement with Arabella, his hopes for an education are dashed, for the master of the college who bothers to reply advises him to "remain in your own sphere." Through no fault of his own, despite his seeming ability, he is again denied what he so desperately seeks. The fact of his birth as a poor person is unchangeable, and Jude must accept its results. His second great desire, a spiritual (as well as sexual) union with Sue, is also doomed. When Jude first sees Sue's picture, he thinks of her as a saint, and he eventually derives many of his maturing intellectual concepts from her. His passion for Sue is true and full, yet as the deeply flawed character she is, she must destroy Jude as well as herself. She drains Jude while simultaneously serving as a source of his growth, for she is irresponsible, cold, and cruel. She is an imperfect being, afraid not only of her physical side but of her very ideas. She tells Jude that she does not have the courage of her convictions, and when he adopts her iconoclastic stance, she abandons it and demonstrates how conventional she really is. Her pagan shouts, her free thought, her brave spirit prove as much a sham as Christminster's promises. Her tragedy, the gap between what she is and what she might have been, is not hers alone, but is shared by Jude and becomes his.

As an attack on convention and society, *Jude the Obscure* focuses on three major areas: the British university system, marriage, and religion. Jude's exclusion from Christminster is an indictment of the structure of an institution which allegedly symbolizes the noble part of man's mind yet actually stands only for a closed, tightly-knit social club. In its criticism of marriage, a union which Hardy said should be dissolvable by either side if it became a burden, the novel reveals how false is the view of marriage as a sacred contract. Marriage, as in Jude's merger with Arabella, is often the fruit of a temporary urge, but its harvest can be lifelong and ruinous. Sue's fear of marriage also suggests that the bond can be one of suffocation. Perhaps most important are the novel's charges against Christianity. The fundamental hollowness and hypocrisy of Christianity, Hardy asserts, damn it dreadfully. A farmer thrashes Jude for lovingly letting the birds feed, and the sounds of the beating echo from the church tower which the same farmer had helped finance. Hardy's scorn for such inconsistencies rebounds throughout the book, and he proposes that the only valuable part of Christianity is its idea that love makes life more bearable.

Mirroring the development of these themes is the final impression that the book is also a cry of loneliness. Jude's hopelessness is in the final analysis a result of his alienation not only from Arabella and Sue but from his environment. Used in connection with Jude, the word "obscure," in addition to conveying his association with darkness, his lack of distinction in the eyes of the world, and his humble station, suggests also that he is not understood, that he is hidden from others and is only faintly perceptible. In Hardy's world, the happiest people are those who are most in touch with their environment, a condition which usually occurs, of course, in the least reflective characters. But Jude, ever grasping for the ideal, ignores the unpleasantness about him as much as he possibly can and inevitably places himself on the path to isolation. Such, Hardy hints, is the price man must pay for the refusal to accept unquestionably his status.

All the ills which Hardy ascribes to this world are, he feels, merely a reflection of the ills of the universe. Man ruins society because he is imperfect and caught in the grip of a fatal and deterministic movement of the stars. Defending his dark outlook, Hardy tells us: "If a way to the better there be, it demands a full look at the worst." In a philosophy which he terms evolutionary meliorism, Hardy further amplifies this concept in both a brighter and a more disastrous vein. That philosophy proposes that not only may he improve, but that man *must* find the way to that better condition if he is to survive.

Judith Bolch

JUDITH PARIS

Type of work: Novel
Author: Hugh Walpole (1884-1941)
Type of plot: Historical chronicle
Time of plot: Nineteenth century
Locale: England
First published: 1931

Judith Paris *is the second of four novels dealing with the history of the Herries family. Like the others, it contains many characters and covers about half a century. The book was popular in its day, but today Walpole's style seems lifeless and dated.*

Judith Paris picks up the story of the Herries family where it left off in *Rogue Herries,* the preceding volume of the Herries chronicle. Hence, as a chronicle, the action of this second novel moves forward as one would expect; Walpole's style, however, while remaining the same in many ways, differs significantly from the preceding novel. It is an interesting discovery that the stylistic changes in *Judith Paris,* when compared with *Rogue Herries,* appear as weaknesses; yet, ironically, they emerge as strengths in the context of this second novel.

Judith Paris, like *Rogue Herries,* is the story of one character. Judith enters the world at the moment of her parents' death; however, she serves to combine and to perpetuate their strong characteristics. Judith, therefore, inherits aggressiveness and the need to dominate others from her father; fidelity and inexorable honesty from her mother. These prime forces in Judith's personality make her a dynamic character, though she lacks the vitality and appeal of her father, the protagonist in *Rogue Herries.* The major weakness in Walpole's characterization of Judith is not only the lack of a "double" to clarify the protagonist's character, but the fact that there is none of the psychological introspection which figures so strongly in the "rogue's" personality. In the preceding novel, Francis Herries' idiosyncracies were, at once, the subject and the results of his search for self-realization and self-fulfillment. Judith's personality, however, is resolved from the beginning. She inherits a combination of strong characteristics from both her parents, with an added touch of practicality developed from her exposure to David Herries. Her personality remains consistent throughout the novel. She does not question her motives; she merely recognizes the qualities of her character and acts according to them.

An inner struggle, though not as intense as in *Rogue Herries,* does take place in *Judith Paris.* For Judith's actions are characterized by firm self-control, and she allows herself few indulgences, though recognizing temptations as they arise. This is not to say that she does not relish life in all its facets; like her father, the "rogue," she exhibits the distinctive Walpole zest for life. Nevertheless, all her actions occur only after careful consideration, in accordance with the primary drives of her personality. Her father, in the preceding novel, does not display any appreciable self-control until the final portion when his destiny is fulfilled in Mirabell Starr, and he becomes an ennobled figure. Hence, prudence assumes an exalted position in the value systems of the novels, and Judith's character is enhanced by this quality. Her residence at Uldale, following George's death, is a decision based on her loyalty to her nephew, Francis, and her need to dominate others, in this case to rescue the management of Fell House from the inept Jennifer. Even though Judith suffers from Jennifer's feeling of contempt towards her, she sacrifices her own comfort to obey the more powerful forces of her nature. Later, after Francis' suicide, she remains at Fell House to manage the Uldale estate and provide the necessary obstacles to Will and Walter Herries' insanely exaggerated need for revenge after the "broken fan" incident. She chooses to do this while yearning for the peace and good cheer she could find in her adored Watendlath. While Judith's character is certainly forceful, the characterization is weakened by its predictability and its clearly resolved nature.

In spite of weak characterization, including the figures involved in the various subplots of the novel, *Judith Paris* gathers its strength from features that were not so strongly developed in *Rogue Herries*. In the second novel, historical setting plays a much more influential role, and Walpole's use of the "sensational" is of a different nature from that in the preceding work. Where before the historic setting provided only a backdrop, a context, upon which the drama of the "rogue's" life played itself out, in the present work historic events prove to be prime factors in the evolving action. For example, the fall of the Bastille causes the outburst between David Herries and his son, Francis, leading eventually to the father's death and the resultant chaos at Fell House. The social upheaval felt throughout Europe and England consequent to the French Revolution becomes an underlying motive for the growing dissension among various members of the Herries family. In a similar fashion, while Walpole's use of the "sensational"—in the preceding novel it was the influence of supernatural forces—served before as an incidental force, in the second novel the "sensational," in the form of extreme violence and murder, plays a more substantial role. The French Revolution, Stane's murder by Georges, Georges' death at the hands of Stane's father, the attack upon Fell House, and the violent death of Reuben Sunwood are all events that significantly affect the action of the novel. They are far from incidental occurrences.

In *Judith Paris,* therefore, shallowness of characterization, lack of psychological investigation, and the failure to make characters better in condition or nature at the end of the novel, are all weaknesses compared to the first volume of the Herries chronicle. However, the ill effects of these weaknesses subside somewhat in view of the more integral functions of historical setting and the use of the "sensational." These positive features, along with the distinctive Walpole zest for life and his perceptive view of the conflict between good and evil forces, emerge as strengths to make *Judith Paris* a work with a good story and memorable characters, the traditional requirements of a good novel.

JULIUS CAESAR

Type of work: **Drama**
Author: **William Shakespeare (1564-1616)**
Type of plot: **Romantic tragedy**
Time of plot: **44 B.C.**
Locale: **Rome**
First presented: **1601**

The story of Brutus rather than of Caesar, this drama transforms history into a tragedy of character. Brutus emerges as a forerunner of Hamlet, while Caesar appears as a rather shallow individual and the so-called villain Cassius develops into a sympathetic figure.

The first of Shakespeare's so-called "Roman plays"—which include *Coriolanus* and *Antony and Cleopatra*—*Julius Caesar* also heralds the great period of his tragedies. The sharply dramatic and delicately portrayed character of Brutus is a clear predecessor of Hamlet and Othello. With *Titus Andronicus* and *Romeo and Juliet, Julius Caesar* is one of the three tragedies written before the beginning of the sixteenth century. It is, however, more historical than the four great tragedies—*Hamlet, Othello, Macbeth,* and *King Lear*—being drawn in large part from Sir Thomas North's wonderfully idiomatic translation of Plutarch's *Lives of the Noble Grecians and Romans* (1579). A comparison of the Shakespearean text with the passages from North's chapters on Caesar, Brutus, and Antony reveals the remarkable truth of T. S. Eliot's statement: "Immature poets borrow; mature poets steal." For in instance after instance, Shakespeare has done little more than rephrase the words of North's exuberant prose to fit the rhythm of his own blank verse. The thievery is nonetheless a brilliant one, and not without originality on Shakespeare's part.

Shakespeare's originality, found in all his "historical" plays, is analogous to that of the great classical Greek playwrights. Aeschylus, Sophocles, and Euripides faced a dramatic challenge very unlike that offered to modern writers who are judged by their ability of sheer invention. Just as the Greek audience came to the play with full knowledge of the particular myth involved in the tragedy to be presented, the Elizabethan audience knew the story of the assassination of Julius Caesar. Shakespeare, like his classical predecessors, had to work his dramatic art within the restrictions of known history. He accomplished this by writing "between the lines" of Plutarch, offering insights into the mind of the characters that Plutarch does not mention—insights which become, on the stage, dramatic motivations. An example is Caesar's revealing hesitation about going to the Senate because of Calpurnia's dream, and the way he is swayed by Decius into going after all. This scene shows the weakness of Caesar's character in a way not found in a literal reading of Plutarch. A second major "adaptation" by Shakespeare is a daring, dramatically effective telescoping of historical time. The historical events associated with the death of Caesar and the defeat of the conspirators actually took three years; Shakespeare condenses them into three tense days, following the Castolvetrian unity of time (though not of place).

Although prose is used in the play by comic and less important characters or in purely informative speeches or documents, the general mode of expression is Shakespeare's characteristic blank verse consisting of five stressed syllables, generally unrhymed. The iambic pentameter, a rhythm natural to to English speech, has the effect of making more memorable lines such as Flavius' comment about the commoners ("They vanish tongue-tied in their guiltiness") or Brutus' observation, "Men at some time are masters of their fates." As in most of the tragedies, Shakespeare here follows a five-part dramatic structure, consisting of the "exposition" (to Act 1, Scene 2), "complication" (1.2 to 2.4), "climax" (3.1), "consequence" (3.1-5.2), and "denouement" (5.3-5.5).

The primary theme of *Julius Caesar* is a combination of political and personal concerns, the first dealing with the question of justifiable revolutions—revealing with the effectiveness of concentrated action the transition from a republic of equals to an empire dominated by great individuals (like Antony, influenced by the example of Caesar himself, and Octavius, who comes to his own at the end of the play). The personal complication is the tragedy of a noble spirit involved in matters it does not comprehend; that is, the tragedy of Brutus. For, despite the title, Brutus, not Caesar, is the hero of this play. It is true that Caesar's influence motivates the straightforward and ultimately victorious actions of Antony throughout the play, accounting for Antony's transformation from an apparently secondary figure into one of solid stature. But it is the presence of Brutus before the eyes of the audience as he gradually learns to distinguish ideals from reality that dominates the sympathy of the audience. Around his gentle character, praised at last even by Antony, Shakespeare weaves the recurrent motifs of honor and honesty, freedom and fortune, ambition and pride. Honor is the theme of Brutus' speech to the crowd in the Forum, honor as it interacts with ambition: "As Caesar loved me, I weep for him; as he was fortunate, I rejoice at it; as he was valiant, I honour him, but, as he was ambitious, I slew him." After the deed Brutus comments, "Ambition's debt is paid." One of the great, dramatically successful ironies of the play is that Antony's Forum speech juxtaposes the same two themes: "Yet Brutus says he was ambitious / And Brutus is an honourable man." By the time Antony is finished, the term "honour" has been twisted by his accelerating sarcasm until it becomes a curse, moving the fickle crowd to change their opinion entirely and call for death to the conspirators.

The conjunction of Brutus and Antony in this particular scene (Act 3, Scene 2) reveals the telling difference between their dramatic characterizations. Though Caesar may have had too much ambition, Brutus' problem is that he has too little; Brutus is a man of ideals and words, and therefore cannot succeed in the corridors of power. Cassius and Antony, in contrast, have no such concern with idealistic concepts or words like honor and ambition; yet there is a distinction even between them. Cassius is a pure *doer,* a man of action, almost entirely devoid of sentiment or principle; Antony, however, is both a doer of deeds and a speaker of words—and therefore prevails over all in the end, following in the footsteps of his model, Caesar. To underline the relationships among these similar yet different characters and the themes that dominate their actions Shakespeare weaves a complicated net of striking images: monetary (creating a tension between Brutus and Cassius); the tide image ("Thou are the ruins of the noblest man / That ever lived in the tide of times") connected with the theme of fortune; the stars (Caesar compares himself, like Marlowe's Tamburlaine, to a fixed star while Cassius says, "The fault, dear Brutus, is not in our stars, / But in ourselves, that we are underlings"): and the wood and stones used to describe the common people by those who would move them to their own will.

Julius Caesar, in yet another way, marks the advance of Shakespeare's artistry in its use of dramatic irony. In this play the Shakespearean audience becomes almost a character in the drama, as it is made privy to knowledge and sympathies not yet shared by all the characters on the stage. This pattern occurs most notably in Decius' speech interpreting Calpurnia's dream, showing the ability of an actor to move men to action by duplicity that is well-managed. The pattern is also evident when Cinna mistakes Cassius for Metellus Cimber, foreshadowing the mistaken identity scene that ends in his own death; when Cassius, on two occasions, gives in to Brutus' refusal to do away with Mark Antony; and, most effectively of all, in the two Forum speeches when Antony addresses two audiences, the one in the theater (that knows his true intentions), and the other the Roman crowd whose ironic whimsicality is marked by the startling shift of sentiment following Brutus' speech ("Let him be Caesar!"), from admiration to the immediate and very opposite feeling after Antony's ("Die, honourable men!"). The effect of the irony is to suggest the close connection between functional politics and the art of acting. Antony, in the end, wins out over Brutus—as Bolingbroke does over Richard II—because he can put on a more compelling act.

Kenneth John Atchity

THE JUNGLE

Type of work: Novel
Author: Upton Sinclair (1878-1968)
Type of plot: Social criticism
Time of plot: Early twentieth century
Locale: Chicago
First published: 1906

The power of this novel derives from the anger the author felt at the social injustices of the meat-packing industry. An honestly told and gripping story, The Jungle *at the time of its publication aroused public sentiment and eventually led to reforms in the practices of the meat industry.*

"Here it is at last! The *Uncle Tom's Cabin* of wage slavery! And what *Uncle Tom's Cabin* did for black slaves, *The Jungle* has a large chance to do for the white slaves of today." So wrote Jack London in 1905. His hopes were exaggerated, for labor's Magna Carta, the Wagner Act, was not enacted until 1935. Nevertheless, Sinclair's muckraking classic was a singularly important factor leading to the Pure Food and Drug Act.

In *The Jungle*, superb investigative journalism and the art of a master melodramatist combine. Sinclair spent two months gathering his material; he ate in settlement houses, visited workers at home, interviewed strike leaders, and spoke to professional and political leaders who knew "the Yards." On a Sunday stroll he happened into a Lithuanian wedding and so obtained his characters. At first, publishers balked, so horrifying were Sinclair's revelations. Finally, after verifying key facts, Doubleday sent the book to press. Sinclair was invited to the White House to advise an outraged Roosevelt on the conduct of a secret Presidential investigation. Only the charge that men who had fallen into lard vats went out to the world as "Armour's pure leaf lard" could not be substantiated.

The effectiveness of Sinclair's story lies in the gradual and relentless way in which the picture of a terrifyingly oppressive system is revealed. He allows us to believe, with Jurgis, that some hope exists in "the American way." Then, even the few positive factors are shown to be related to corruption. The democratic institutions which might have provided a means of change have all been bought off by the "Machine." The opportunity to "rise" causes men to betray their fellow workers and countrymen.

The Jungle is a naturalistic work: Jurgis' environment forces him into violence and crime; fault lies with "the system," not with him. But Sinclair's pessimism is not like that of Zola. The Socialism he preached implied a human ability (collectively expressed) to master that system.

THE JUNGLE BOOKS

Type of work: Short stories
Author: Rudyard Kipling (1865-1936)
Type of plot: Beast fables
Time of plot: Nineteenth century
Locale: India
First published: 1894, 1895

Nobel Prize winner Kipling brought his sophisticated, flawless style to these children's stories, constructing them with an apparent simplicity that only partially obscures their true polish and depth of purpose. The tales in these two volumes attempt to teach the lessons of justice, loyalty, and tribal laws, yet are always entertaining and often exciting.

Rudyard Kipling's *The Jungle Books* — both of them — are a throwback to medieval beast fables. Fables, as such, are not exclusively restricted to animals, since even humans or inanimate objects may be protagonists in these tales. But beast fables *per se* rely entirely upon animal characters. Subject matter is often drawn from supernatural or unusual incidents, commonly originating in folklore. Aesop's fables are perhaps the best known of the genre; however, the beast fable has been popular through the ages as a satire of mankind's follies. La Fontaine (France), Gay (England), Lessing (Germany), and Krylov (Russia) used the device, as well as—more recently—Joel Chandler Harris (United States) and George Orwell (England). The moral thrust of these works has invariably been didactic, and thus it is with Kipling's *The Jungle Books*. In fact, Kipling's tales so closely follow classic models that an analogy between Romulus and Remus (nurtured by a wolf) and Mowgli (also nurtured by wolves) is inevitable.

Kipling's tales, however, are set in India, also the locale for many of his poems, short stories, and novels. Through this setting, and through his depiction of characters and events, Kipling reveals—consciously and unconsciously—a strong Anglo bias. Hence, Mowgli may be viewed as the white man under seige in an alien culture. He tries to bring civilization to the natives, but knows that ultimately he will have to depart for the sake of his own survival. Kipling thus demonstrates his Victorian conviction that "civilized" concepts of justice, loyalty, and law and order cannot be inculcated in "primitive" peoples.

Such a view causes one to question whether *The Jungle Books* are to be construed as children's stories or as adult literature. There is no ready answer as to what Kipling's purpose really was, but what exists is a collection of traditional stories which have—not surprisingly—both entertainment value and moral value for young and old alike.

JUNO AND THE PAYCOCK

Type of work: Drama
Author: Sean O'Casey (1884-1964)
Type of plot: Satiric realism
Time of plot: 1922
Locale: Dublin
First presented: 1924

In Juno and the Paycock *the Irish dramatic renaissance reached a new peak of realism; O'Casey dispensed with elaborate plotting and formal dramatic technique to show characters with the vigor and vitality of real life. Drenched in local color and apparently formless, the play nevertheless had a powerful impact on audiences and, indeed, caused riots when it was first produced in Dublin.*

"The whole worl's in a state of chassis!" (chaos) says "Captain" Jack Boyle, the "paycock" (peacock) of Sean O'Casey's *Juno and the Paycock,* and it was against this background of "chassis"—in particular the turbulence of the civil wars that wracked Ireland during the first quarter of the twentieth century—that O'Casey wrote his great trilogy of realistic plays about violence and strife in Dublin. *The Shadow of a Gunman* (1923), *Juno and the Paycock* (1924), and *The Plough and the Stars* (1926).

However, although civic disorder provides the atmosphere of general bitterness and tension, as well as determining the fate of the son, Johnny, *Juno and the Paycock* is the most domestic of the plays. That is, what happens to the Boyle family is largely the product of their own actions. But, because they embody personal qualities that are common to the Irish, the Boyles become a symbolic family and their actions illuminate the follies, evils—and *strengths*—of the national character in a time of turmoil.

Twice, in the early moments of the play, Mary tells her mother that "a principle's a principle," once in reference to her own support of a fellow striker and once in regard to her crippled brother's nationalistic activities. A short time later Johnny repeats the same slogan to Juno, but this time she answers it emphatically:

> JUNO: Ah, you lost your best principle, me boy, when you lost your arm; them's the only sort o' principles that's any good to a workin' man.

And that exchange sets up the thematic dichotomy of the play—abstract moral principles, based on generalized causes such as nationalism, Marxism, or religion, versus a practical morality based on human loyalties, needs, and sympathies. The abstractions are used either as justifications for violence or as rationalizations for no action at all.

Captain Boyle is a veritable catalog of Irish weaknesses. His capacity for strong drink is exceeded only by his capacity for self-deception and pompous moralizing. Most of his time is spent in idle chatter and drinking with his equally irresponsible crony, "Joxer" Daly. If offered honest work, Boyle has a sudden attack of leg pains. He continually complains about the moral state of the world ("is there any morality left anywhere?" he asks Joxer), but he refuses any involvement with the problems of others ("We've nothing to do with these things, one way or t'other"). But, for all of that, Boyle is charming; he sings, he recites poetry, and, when not in a drunken stupor, he speaks with style and vigor. He has opinions on every current political, social, and religious subject and, although they are trite, they are not stupid. If he is never exactly lovable, he is at least likable at the beginning of the play; these defects do not seem too harmful and, most important, he is very funny. His early scenes with Joxer are masterpieces of comic repartee.

But our attitude toward Boyle changes during the course of the play. As the action progresses it becomes clear that his buffoonery has serious implications. When his daughter's unsanctified pregnancy is revealed, he rises to heights of moral indignation as though she did it as a personal insult to him ("when I'm done with her she'll be a sorry girl!"). He continues to squander money on credit even after he learns that it has been lost, in spite of the serious damage that it will do to the household. So when, at the end of the play, he and Joxer come in very drunk and do a repeat of their earlier routine, what was previously funny becomes grotesque. The consequences of his braggadocio are too real and serious to laugh at a second time. Dramatically this mixture of tragedy and farce is most powerful. Thematically O'Casey is suggesting that many of those "lovable" Irish failings, so celebrated in popular myth and song, may, on closer inspection, prove to be dangerous and destructive.

Although Boyle's faults may be the most blatant, the kind of self-righteousness he exhibits infects others in the play. Jerry Devine's abstract pieties prevent him from marrying Mary because she is a "fallen woman." It is strongly hinted that the death of Tancred was the inevitable result of his "Diehard" politics. The men who take Johnny make sure that he "has his beads" so that the proper religious proprieties will not be missing from his murder. All of the men in the play cling to their narrow patterns of thought and rigid moral postures and they fail in every situation that requires practical, humane responses. Thus, instead of "freedom," their ideas produce confusion, violence, and pain.

But, if the men are a damning influence, the women in *Juno and the Paycock* are the redeeming one—although, even for them, there are important lessons to be learned. The difference is that they are capable of learning and growing because they react to personal needs and sorrows, not abstract ones. At the play's beginning, Mary chides her mother about the need for "principles," but by the end of it, having been impregnated and deserted by Charlie Bentham and rejected by Jerry Devine, she has come to understand

and accept human weakness without bitterness. As she says to Jerry: "I don't blame you . . . your humanity is as narrow as the humanity of the others."

It is Juno Boyle, however, who is the supreme embodiment of compassionate action. Throughout the play it is evident that it has been her strength which has kept the Boyle household intact. But even Juno has been tainted by the atmosphere of the times and the prospect of easy money. She is casual about the Captain's defects, intolerant of her children's feelings and opinions, and somewhat callous toward those outside the family. She feels no special sympathy for her bereaved neighbor, Mrs. Tancred, and even plays her new phonograph while the rituals of mourning are going on nearby. But, after Juno faces the loss of the money, her husband's betrayal, Mary's pregnancy, and Johnny's execution, she gains a new insight into her fellow man and a deeper, more sympathetic humanity. She overcomes her grief for Johnny, casts aside her political and moral prejudices ("why didn't I remember that when he wasn't a Diehard or a Stater, but only a poor dead son!"), leaves Boyle, accepts the burden of Mary and her unborn child, and hopefully assumes the "biggest part o' the trouble."

Whether or not the strength evidenced by Juno is enough to overcome the weaknesses, follies, and evils the men exhibit is not answered in the play. In the end it depends upon whether or not it is possible to give a positive response to Juno's final, plaintive prayer:

> JUNO: Sacred Heart o' Jesus, take away our hearts o' stone, and give us hearts o' flesh! Take away this murdherin' hate, and give us Thine own eternal love!"

Keith Neilson

JURGEN

Type of work: Novel
Author: James Branch Cabell (1879-1958)
Type of plot: Fantasy
Time of plot: Middle Ages
Locale: Poictesme, a land of myth
First published: 1919

Jurgen, A Comedy of Justice, *is one of a series dealing with the mythical country of Poictesme. The novel can be read on different levels—as a narrative of fantastic love and adventure, as a satire, and as a philosophic view of life.*

Jurgen possesses the artificiality and mannered style of much of Cabell's writing. Somewhat reminiscent of the satires of Anatole France, this novel does contain scenes of humor worthy of the French master, but other sections are heavy-handed and obscure. A fairy tale for adults, *Jurgen* assumes a certain sophistication in its reader; even its humor tends to be artificial and mannered. The novel illustrates Cabell's persistent avoidance of "realism" in his work, as well as his essentially antiromantic point of view. *Jurgen* presents the full range of Cabell's skeptical vision of human nature and his biting opinion of mortal existence on earth. Nevertheless, much of Cabell's supposedly sophisticated approach to sex is little more than suggestive snickering or is borrowed from *Tristram Shandy*.

A picaresque fantasy, inspired by medieval chivalric romances, *Jurgen* follows its hero in his search for his lost shrewish wife. The plot, such as it is, reminds one of Maeterlinck's *The Bluebird,* for Jurgen finds his wife at home, the one place where he had not thought to look for her. Many of the hero's adventures are humorous, and most of them are improbable, including, as they do, figures from ancient history and mythology. Cabell does not develop his characters as much as he lets them represent certain viewpoints or symbolize particular conditions of being.

In a sense, Jurgen's search is into his own past, as well as the past history of the world, for he encounters people from his own life as well as from antiquity. His hopes are all frustrated as he wanders, and he comes to realize that time is merciless; the past cannot be recaptured. Youth, when regained, he discovers, proves to be less desirable than one would think. A dreamlike quality pervades much of the narrative, and a charm and gaiety often surfaces, despite the artificiality of the tale. A reaction against the prevailing trend of realism in American fiction at the time, *Jurgen* stands isolated with its author, a brilliant oddity in the history of American literature.

JUSTICE

Type of work: Drama
Author: John Galsworthy (1867-1933)
Type of plot: Social criticism
Time of plot: 1910
Locale: London
First presented: 1910

This drama is a protest against dehumanized institutionalism, with particular attention directed toward evils of solitary confinement and the strict parole system. Although prison reforms have progressed considerably since 1910 when the play was written, Justice *remains a powerful work.*

John Galsworthy considered himself to be a "naturalistic" playwright, by which he meant "to create such an illusion of actual life passing on the stage as to compel the spectator for the moment to lose all sense of artifice, to think, talk and move with the people he sees thinking, talking and moving in front of him." But most of his dramas are the antithesis of what writers like Zola, Strindberg, or Norris meant by "naturalism." Galsworthy's characters have too much free choice in determining their lives and, although pressured by society, too much responsibility for their own fates to fit into the bleak, deterministic naturalist category. An important exception, however, can be seen in *Justice.* It follows the pattern typical of such plays and novels; one extremely fallible human being, acting impulsively and irrationally, makes a small, unavoidable mistake and is thus caught up in the implacable, impersonal social system and destroyed by it.

In the powerful second act courtroom scene, Hector Frome, the defense attorney for the victim, sums up the case for mercy—and charts the course of the play:

> *Frome*: If the prisoner be found guilty, and treated as though he were a criminal type, he will, as all experience shows, in all probability become one. . . . Justice is a machine that, when some one has once given it the starting push, rolls on of itself. Is this young man to be ground to pieces under this machine for an act which at the worst was one of weakness?

And that is, of course, exactly what happens to him. Given the rigidity of the law plus the Victorian attitudes toward private property, marriage, and sex, William Falder is convicted and sent to prison. The qualities which make him most sympathetic to the reader, his love and devotion toward Ruth Honeywell and her children and his willingness to risk prison for them, become primary charges against him; in the eyes of proper English society he is a home wrecker and suspected adulterer. After his release, broken by solitary confinement, hounded by the "ticket-of-leave" system which controls his every movement, and rearrested on a technicality, Falder commits suicide.

The most frightening thing about his fate is that, once the process is set in motion, Falder has no chance to escape regardless of what he, or anyone else, does. And this is not because the system is consciously malevolent; it is simply impersonal, unyielding, and automatic. All of those involved in Falder's fate desire the best for him and for society. Old James How, who first accuses him, states "one must think of society"; the Judge denies him mercy on the grounds that *"the Law is what it is*—a majestic edifice, sheltering all of us, each stone of which rests on another"; the prison Doctor declines to release him from solitary confinement because, should he do so, he would have to do the same for others; in short, the authorities are as much trapped by the system as the victim. As Cokeson tells Falder: "You must give them credit for the best intentions. Really you must. Nobody wishes you harm, I'm sure."

The relentless progression of Falder's destruction gives the play considerable cumulative power, and several of the separate scenes are extremely potent, especially the trial scene and the short, wordless, almost hallucinatory scene in which Falder nearly goes insane in his solitary whitewashed cell. On the other hand, the absence of human decision and the emphasis on social process in this play keeps the characterization on a superficial level and deprives the play of that thematic complexity and ambiguity which is characteristic of Galsworthy's best work. In *Justice* the "certain detachment" that Galsworthy thought essential to good playwrighting is missing; it is a didactic play which to some extent succeeded in its immediate aim—as a result of it the solitary confinement and "ticket-of-leave" policies were mitigated—but, as happens in all works narrowly directed at particular social abuses, the play has become one of Galsworthy's most dated dramatic efforts.

THE KALEVALA

Type of work: Poem
Author: Elias Lönnrot (1802-1884)
Type of plot: Folk epic
Time of plot: Mythological antiquity
Locale: Finland and Lapland
First published: 1835

The national epic of Finland, The Kalevala *was fashioned from folk legends and oral traditions by Elias Lönnrot. Kaleva, from whom the title derives, was, in legend, the ancestor of all of the heroes in the poem; as such, he is a unifying force in the tales.*

Dr. Elias Lönnrot was less the author of *The Kalevala* than its scribe. For fifteen years Lönnrot collected, edited, ordered, and revised the songs which comprise this epic cycle. The first version, *The Old Kalevala,* which appeared in 1835, was significantly altered and augmented in the 1849 edition (*The Kalevala* we know today) largely through the use Lönnrot made of songs collected by David Europaeus. Lönnrot linked the oral and written traditions in Finnish, and regarded himself as a singer as authentic as the peasant singers from whom he gathered the songs.

The tradition of ceremonial singing, passed from generation to generation among the Finnish peasants of Savo and Karelia, centers on the two singers, a leader and his supporting singer, surrounded by a circle of listeners. The singers sat facing each other, hands joined and knees touching, *à deux*: the lead singer chanted the first verse, accompanied by his second on the final syllable; the second singer then repeated the verse, allowing the leader to prepare a second verse, accompanying the leader on the final syllable. Usually a flagon of beer was present to provide the singers inspiration before and in between songs, which often lasted far into the night. When a harp player was present, he accompanied the singers with music.

The Kalevala, a collection of these songs, with two others by Lönnrot himself, is not a closely-knit narrative, but an interrelated group of story cycles. The story cycles concern the love and loss of love of the three heroes, Väinämöinen, Ilmarinen, and Lemminkäinen. Francis Peabody Magoun, Jr., in the introduction to his translation of *The Kalevala*, suggests that each of the story cycles might be read independently and that the magic charms and incantations interspersed throughout the epic cycle may be read out of context. This is particularly true of "A Fisherman's Charm" or the several Milk and Cattle Charms. The Wedding Lays of Väinämöinen constitute a story by themselves, and as such may be read as a record of the Finnish folk attitudes toward husband and wife. In whatever way *The Kalevala* is read, whether sequentially as a narrative, as story cycles, or as independent lyrics, it remains both epic song and folklore, a true story and cultural artifact.

KATE FENNIGATE

Type of work: Novel
Author: Booth Tarkington (1869-1946)
Type of plot: Domestic realism
Time of plot: Twentieth century
Locale: The Middle West
First published: 1943

Published twenty years after Alice Adams, *this novel also explores the condition of a woman in American middle-class society. Tarkington raises many questions, but his probing is always hesitant and gentle; nevertheless, his portrayal of character and milieu is honest and authentic.*

Booth Tarkington wrote like a gentle Balzac: in other words, like a writer totally aware of the venality and hypocrisy of the "human comedy," but somehow disinclined to form harshly realistic or cynical judgments. This may be simply another way of saying that he was a commercial novelist, a writer trained to provide the kind of fiction suitable for serialization in women's magazines; as a matter of fact, a portion of *Kate Fennigate* was printed in *The Ladies Home Journal* under the title, "The Hardest Wife to Be."

Nevertheless, Tarkington was more than merely a commercial hack. His fiction ranges from such a memorable children's book as *Penrod* to the realism of the novel in question. He had the talent and intelligence to see American manners and the American mind very objectively. (*The Magnificent Ambersons* provided the basis for one of Orson Welles' greatest films), but he lacked the anger of a Sinclair Lewis or the tragic vision of a William Faulkner. He was, finally, an entertainer, and anyone reading his fiction seriously is always slightly amazed and disappointed by Tarkington's reluctance to deal with the social and philosophical problems which his realism raises. For example, in *Kate Fennigate* the closing pages present Kate and Ames in a sobering moment of confrontation. They are about to express the "truth" concerning their feelings, to probe the actuality of their relationship. The scene has all the dramatic promise of an illuminating final confrontation in a novel by Henry James. Instead it settles for a vague pathos. Yes, Kate will tolerate more truth, but later. We sense that Kate has been brought to the point where she must finally face the deep-seated psychological reasons for her managerial personality, but Tarkington only hints darkly at the consequences. He is content to draw the portrait of a good but manipulative woman, as if that paradox would serve. Tarkington's talent seems strangely stillborn.

KENILWORTH

Type of work: Novel
Author: Sir Walter Scott (1771-1832)
Type of plot: Historical romance
Time of plot: 1575
Locale: England
First published: 1821

Scott spends much time in this historical novel establishing the setting and background for the slight action, and his immense knowledge and skill give these passages literary merit. As always in Scott's novels, the characters are well-portrayed and the story handled in a professional manner.

To a historical novelist like Sir Walter Scott, vivid and accurate settings were invaluable tools for summoning a past age before readers' eyes; but nowhere in his novels was the masterful use of place more central to theme and meaning than in *Kenilworth.* In this novel of love and intrigue in Elizabethan England, the moral statements dramatized through the story are buttressed by their association with either of the two places where all the major action occurs—Cumnor Place or Kenilworth; both places are described in highly-charged images and richly symbolic language. Cumnor Place is like a gilded prison. Decorated lavishly, its rooms sumptuously comfortable and filled with expensive finery, it is nevertheless designed as a place of detainment and hiding. In one vivid and eerie passage, Scott describes its specially designed oaken shutters and thick drapes, which allow the rooms to be ablaze with light without the slightest flicker showing to an observer on the outside. Leicester uses this strictly private place as the hiding place for his wife Amy Robsart, whose existence he wishes to keep secret from Queen Elizabeth; he also uses it as a place of escape and relief from court life for himself. He travels to Cumnor in disguise, and while there sheds the finery which identifies and validates him at court.

As opposed to Cumnor Place, Kenilworth is a thoroughly public manor house. With the entire court and nobility preparing for the royal entertainments, it exhibits all the pomp and splendor of a regal palace in its most concentrated form; it is literally exploding with feverish activity. The atmosphere at Kenilworth is one of unreality; in his initial picture of the place, Scott describes a row of guards, along the battlements, who are intended to represent King Arthur's knights—but uncannily, some are real men, some mere pasteboard figures, and it is impossible to distinguish from a distance which are which. A more sinister and frightening instance of the confusion between illusion and reality occurs when Elizabeth encounters Amy in the garden; unable to understand her muddled replies, the queen quickly assumes that Amy is one of the wandering actresses, planted throughout the grounds to pay her homage, who has forgotten her lines in embarrassment or fright.

Between these two places, the two major characters—Leicester and Amy—are torn, and close beside each of them throughout their trials are their personal servants, whose relationships with their master or mistress point up a major theme in the novel. This is the theme of the moral connection or interdependency between masters and their servants; a master, being responsible for his choice of servants, may be judged to a large extent by their attitudes and behavior. Thus, when Varney interviews Michael Lambourne as a prospective employee for himself—and, therefore, ultimately for Leicester—he is very pleased with Lambourne's list of desirable qualities in a courtier's servant, which includes "a close mouth" and "a blunt conscience." These are Varney's specifications exactly, to which are added cunning, greed, and consuming ambition. The proper scheme of things is turned topsy-turvy early in the story, in the symbolically prefigurative scene in which Varney persuades his master to disguise himself as a servant, while he impersonates the master. Leicester's moral guilt is clear when he recognizes his servant's true nature, yet keeps him in service; he calls Varney a devil, but he is a devil indispensable to the Earl's ambitious plans. In contrast to Leicester's and Varney's standards of a good servant are those of the admirable Tressilian, who warns Wayland Smith against knavery, pointing out that transgression committed "by one attending on me diminishes my honour." In addition to Wayland, Amy's maidservant offers another example of a loyal servant who reflects her mistress' worth; Janet Foster is totally devoted, even to the dangerous extreme of aiding her lady's escape from Cumnor Place in defiance of her father, Amy's jailer.

KIDNAPPED

Type of work: Novel
Author: Robert Louis Stevenson (1850-1894)
Type of plot: Adventure romance
Time of plot: 1751
Locale: Scotland
First published: 1886

This tale of high adventure, told simply but colorfully, is woven around a true incident; Stevenson's characters, from all classes, noble and ignoble, are skillfully drawn, and develop convincingly as they pass through kidnapings, battles at sea, murders, and other adventures.

Robert Louis Stevenson directed many of his works to young readers in deference to nineteenth century Romanticism's idealization of the presumed innocence of childhood, and the fecundity of children's imaginations. It was his strong personal conviction that youngsters were an important segment of the reading public. *Kidnapped* was originally published as a serial in a boys' magazine, and Stevenson first won fame as a novelist with a children's adventure story, *Treasure Island* (1883). *A Child's Garden of Verses* (1885) also falls in this category, as does *Kidnapped.*

A large part of the popular appeal of *Kidnapped* lies with the historical-romantic nature of the plot. Typical of such plots, the novel revolves around a genuine historical incident, the murder of Colin Campbell, the Red Fox of Glenure; and other historical figures appear—King George among them. However, nonhistorical incidents and characters—David Balfour's trials and Alan Stewart's escapades, for example—constitute the largest part of the novel, even though the pivotal action in the plot is tied to actual history. This intertwining of history and fantasy has the effect of both personalizing history and making fantasy credible to the reader.

Another factor which enhances the verisimilitude of *Kidnapped* is the narrative technique. David Balfour tells his own story in the first-person narrative voice. As a consequence, the reader develops a close rapport with the narrator and sympathizes with his plight. Most important, the first person narrative makes the story highly plausible.

Stevenson emphasized plot over characterization, for his goal was to entertain—to transport the reader from mundane, daily existence to a believable world of excitement and adventure which the reader might otherwise never experience. To create this effect in *Kidnapped,* Stevenson combined the extraordinary with the commonplace. On the one hand, such extraordinary events as David's kidnapping. Alan's rescue, and the shipwreck take place. On the other hand, such commonplaces as family hostilities (David versus Ebenezer), drunken sailors and sober sailors, and Scottish feuds (Alan versus the monarchist Colin) lend a measure of reality to the unusual or extraordinary. This combination produces an exceptionally convincing tale.

Still, Stevenson does not ignore the impact of character development. His juxtaposition of David—the canny Lowlander—and Alan—the proud Highlander—brings the story to its highest pitch of excitement by synthesizing two opposing value systems into a compatible working unit. David and Alan have contradictory points of view and antithetical socio-political commitments; yet they work together and form a lasting bond on the basis of friendship and loyalty which transcend their differences. Here is Stevenson the novelist at his best—forsaking dogma and eschewing ideology in favor of humanistic values. Such are the qualities which make *Kidnapped* a novel of enduring appeal.

KIM

Type of work: Novel
Author: Rudyard Kipling (1865-1936)
Type of plot: Adventure romance
Time of plot: Late nineteenth century
Locale: British India
First published: 1901

Kim *gives a vivid picture of the complexities of India under British rule. Kipling's vast canvas, crowded with action and movement, is painted in full detail, showing the life of the bazaar mystics, of the natives, and of the British military.*

Rudyard Kipling wrote many poems, short stories, and novels about India. Whether by design or accident, most of these works assumed a tone that implied acceptance of the caste system and a class-conscious society. This position is diametrically opposed to that of E. M. Forster, who in his classic novel, *A Passage to India,* castigated British colonial depredations. *Kim* is a remarkable exception to Kipling's Tory allegiance, for this novel paints an almost affectionate—not condescending—portrait of the Indian masses. It affords sympathetic insight into some of the most important aspects of Indian life, including among them, popular beliefs, life in the streets, bazaars, and life on the road.

Popular beliefs are often labeled superstitions when such beliefs are strange or foreign to the one who applies the label, as though the labeler were hardly aware of the pejorative connotations of "superstition." The Tibetan lama thus believes that his search will ultimately lead him to the holy River of Arrow which will wash away all sin. An Anglo-American reader might scoff at such naïveté, whether it is called popular belief or superstition, but Kipling lends both credibility and dignity to the lama's faith by allowing him to find the river at the end of the novel. In this way, as in others dealing with uniquely Indian beliefs, Kipling pays respect to a culture other than his own.

The teeming life on India's streets and in its bazaars is relatively common knowledge today. At the turn of the century, however, it was unfamiliar territory and hence quite exotic. Although Kipling did nothing to diminish the exotic ambience of street life, neither did he varnish or gloss over its harsh realities. Particularly vivid is the depiction of Kim's early experiences in the streets of Lahore—opium, extortion, fighting, and the like.

With equal verisimilitude, Kipling described the rigors of travel—life on the road. There were dangers, such as the two men who plotted to kill Mahbub Ali; there were discomforts and inconveniences, such as having occasionally to sleep in the open. But a spirit of friendship and hospitality could also be found, as, for example, when the old woman gives the exhausted and emaciated Kim a resting place. All in all, this nostalgic tale captured a flavor of tolerance and humane feeling for the most part lacking in Kipling's other Indian literature.

A KING AND NO KING

Type of work: Drama
Authors: Francis Beaumont (1585?-1616) and John Fletcher (1579-1625)
Type of plot: Tragi-comedy
Time of plot: Indefinite
Locale: Armenia and Iberia
First presented: 1611

Extremely popular in its time, this tragicomedy employs a dazzling array of technical devices to maintain emotional intensity. A good example of baroque sensibility, the play does not tackle moral issues but provides sophisticated entertainment through the use of contrasts and parallels of character, sudden reversals and surprises, and abrupt speeding up or retarding of the action.

A King and No King is the first play in which the Beaumont and Fletcher formula for tragi-comedy is firmly established. Several of the charges leveled against *A King and No King,* and often against the tragi-comedy in general, are that the play makes little comment on the state of mankind and fails to deal with the characters from a standpoint of rational psychology, thus making it hard to find a way in which one can identify with the characters.

The error against decorum in *A King and No King* was the introduction of the seemingly incestuous affair between Arbaces and Panthea—with somewhat the Braggadoccio and somewhat the Doll Common within them respectively. That Fletcher felt a break from conventional morality was acceptable as long as it was not excessive is apparent in lines from his prologue to *Rule a Wife and Have a Wife* (1624): "Nor blame the poet if he steps aside/Sometimes lasciviously, if not too wide." Besides, it is the "incestuous" affair that provides the play with the characteristic of mystification —a part of the tragi-comic formula developed by Beaumont and Fletcher and an element demanded by their contemporary audiences.

Aside from the element of mystification, the characterizations of Arbaces and Panthea provide some of the other elements necessary to maintain the middle ground of tragi-comic form. Arbaces' character is designated from the first scene of the first act with Mardonius' description: "he is vain-glorious, and humble, and angry, and patient, and merry and dull, and joyful, and sorrowful in extremity in an hour." His excesses provide the vehicle for some highly emotional and impassioned speeches. The moments when he seems to be consumed by his passions may fill the audience with a sense of terror and impending evil at his loss of control. This sense of impending evil became a characteristic of the tragi-comedy. When dealing with his love for Panthea, the poetic form chosen by Beaumont and Fletcher for the language of the play meets the compromise necessary in tragi-comedy and serves Arbaces' emotional purposes well. There is nothing stiff or elaborate about the formal, declamatory verse; and though it is not representative of conversational dialogue, the vocabulary is familiar and the sentence structure is simple. An actor well-trained in a declamatory style could easily sway an audience emotionally with the values provided in rhythm and length. Another characteristic of the form the tragi-comedy took after *A King and No King,* one that grew from the love relationship and the language, was the "lively touches of passion" admired by John Dryden in his preface to *Troilus and Cressida.*

The ending of *A King and No King* may be slightly "theatrical" for some. The almost perfect alternation of scenes between the plots of Arbaces and Panthea and Tigranes and Spaconia may be too much like watching a tennis match to others. The fact remains, however, that *A King and No King* is a milestone in the development of drama. It provided the dramatists of the Restoration a "new," fully-developed form—the tragicomedy.

KING JOHN

Type of work: Drama
Author: John Bale (1495-1563)
Type of plot: Historical allegory
Time of plot: Early thirteenth century
Locale: England
First presented: c. 1548

Although too long and tedious for dramatic effectiveness, Bale's King John *is interesting as a scathing and uncompromising attack on the Church of Rome and as a version of history different from that usually accepted. The play shows the transition from old techniques to the new, an allegorical play using the devices of the medieval morality, but using them to dramatize historical events.*

This work well illustrates John Bale's position as a follower of the so-called "New Learning" as it was espoused by Cambridge reformers during the reign of Henry VIII. Two of these reformers particularly link Bale to that group. William Tyndale's book on Christian obedience (1528) sets out the theme that Bale followed. To both Tyndale and Bale, King John was a king who was prevented from the exercise of his royal duty by the usurping power of an anti-Christian Papacy. Thomas Cranmer, another member of the Cambridge Protestant circle, gave this play its first performance in his house on January 2, 1539. Henry was still king then, and even though the play was amended later, it is still interesting in its historical context.

This is because Henry's reformation consisted of dissolving many monasteries and religious houses of England, and removal of the pope as the Church's recognized head. In matters of doctrine Henry was conservative. He retained the Mass and sacraments, and although he permitted the Bible to be translated into English and the vernacular liturgy, he tended to reject many of the Lutheran doctrines and those of the more radical reformers in Switzerland. Yet of all the Protestant sects, Bale attacks only the quasi-anarchical Anabaptists. He attacks monks very strongly, as would be expected in Henry's England, but goes on to rail against the Mass, sacraments, relics, bells, vestments, and other "Papist" accouterments retained by Henry. All this fits in very well with the more radical reformation that reached England after Henry's death. Led by Cranmer and others, the Protestants of the old Cambridge school were riding high during the reign of Edward VI. The beliefs of Edward's time were presaged by Bale's play, but it is surprising to see such sentiments expressed so strongly when Henry was alive and vigorous. This play, then, gives the reader a full picture of one part of religious belief during the reign of Henry VIII, and a belief moreover that was later to come powerfully into its own.

Bale also expresses in *King John* a significant idea that usually is called

"Erastianism" after Thomas Erastus, but is more correctly ascribed to Marsiglio of Padua. Marsiglio held, in his book *Defensor Pacis,* that the church was not an equal of the state, but instead was subject to civil authority as an arm of the state, like the army or any bureaucracy. Tied up in this concept is the idea of Empire. England is an Empire rather than a kingdom, and that England is an autonomous political body is at the heart of both Bale's *King John* and the Henrician reformation. It was Henry who first declared that England owed no allegiance to any other organization, and the reign of his daughter Elizabeth can partly be understood as an attempt to make Henry's dream of Imperial Majesty into a reality.

KING JOHN

Type of work: Drama
Author: William Shakespeare (1564-1616)
Type of plot: Historical chronicle
Time of plot: Early thirteenth century
Locale: England and France
First presented: c. 1594

One of Shakespeare's earliest histories, King John *is uneven, although it contains passages of brilliance. Its strongest feature is the depiction of character; John, Constance, and the Bastard Faulconbridge all are memorable personalities, and Constance and the Bastard particularly have opportunities to reveal in remarkable speeches unexpected and affecting sides of their natures.*

An uneven product of Shakespeare's early period and one of his first history plays, *King John* is neither as good as it might have been nor as bad as it has been considered. Written entirely in verse, the play sometimes fails to distinguish among the various characters in its portrayal of their speech—almost homogeneously filled with conceits and wordplays that, only in the case of the Bastard, fit the personality who speaks them. Its themes include the relationship between fortune and the individual's nature, the powerful finality of a king's words, the corrupt and conniving influence of the Roman Church, and the degree of individual responsibility in the face of a leader's folly. This last is studied in Act IV, when John upbraids Hubert for taking him at his word in killing young Arthur; he tells Hubert that a king, too, has moods and his followers must protect him from his rash emotions. In general, as the brief abdication scene in the first part of Act V demonstrates, *King John* is generically a part of the *de casibus virorum illustrium* ("the fall of illustrious men") motif popular in medieval and Renaissance literature.

The play suffers from structural deficiencies that suggest Shakespeare had not yet mastered that peculiarly difficult combination of historical verisimilitude and artistic inspiration, that is, giving psychologically convincing motivation to actions that are "givens" of historical record. When Blanch and Lewis fall in love to order when Pandulph enters as a *deus ex machina* to alter the course of events dramatically and unpredictably, when the Bastard carries Austria's head across the stage, when young Arthur whimsically decides to escape and kill himself, and when Lewis' rebuff to Pandulph goes unanswered, we suspect that Shakespeare nods. But Arthur's speech on his sadness, Hubert's mercy, the Bastard's touching pardon of his mother's folly, and his saucy exchange with Austria, plus Constance's speech about the fears of a queen, a woman, and a mother contain the fertile seeds that will blossom into the full flower of Shakespeare's imagination.

KING LEAR

Type of work: Drama
Author: William Shakespeare (1564-1616)
Type of plot: Romantic tragedy
Time of plot: First century B.C.
Locale: Britain
First presented: c. 1605

The theme of filial ingratitude is portrayed in two parallel stories with overwhelming pathos in this majestic achievement, considered by many the greatest of Shakespeare's tragedies. The heights of terror and pity achieved through the poet's treatment of his story equal those of the great tragedies of antiquity. Although generally considered one of the noblest utterances of the human spirit, the play often proves to be difficult to stage. Its world is more legendary than concrete and its figures larger than life, although the vehicles for universal feelings.

King Lear's first entrance in Act I is replete with ritual and ceremony. He is full of antiquity, authority, and assurance as he makes his regal way through the ordered court. When he reveals his intention to divide his kingdom into three parts for his daughters, he exudes the confidence generated by his long reign. The crispness and directness of his language suggest a power, if not imperiousness, which, far from senility, demonstrate the stability and certainty of long, unchallenged sway. The rest of the play acts out the destruction of that fixed order and the emergence of a new, tentative balance.

In the opening scene Lear speaks as king and father. The absolute ruler has decided to apportion his kingdom as gift rather than bequest to his three heirs. In performing this act, which superficially seems both reasonable and generous, Lear sets in motion a chain of events which lay bare his primary vulnerabilities not only as a king and a father but also as a man. In retrospect it is foolish to expect to divest oneself of power and responsibility and yet retain the trappings of authority. However, this is exactly what Lear anticipates because of his excessive confidence in the love of his daughters. He asks too much, he acts too precipitously, but he is punished, by an inexorable universe, out of all proportion to his errors in judgment.

When he asks his daughters for a declaration of love, as a prerequisite for a share of the kingdom, he is as self-assured and overbearing a parent as he is a monarch. It is thus partly his own fault that the facile protestations of love by Goneril and Regan are credited: they are what he wants to hear because they conform to the ceremonial necessities of the occasion. Cordelia's honest response, born of a greater, ingenuous love, are out of keeping with the formalities. Lear has not looked beneath the surface. He has let the ritual appearances replace the internal reality or he has at least refused to distinguish between the two.

The asseverations of Goneril and Regan soon emerge as the cynical conceits that they are, but by then Lear has banished Cordelia and the loyal Kent, who saw through the sham. Lear is successively and ruthlessly divested of all the accoutrements of kingship by the villainous daughters, who finally reduce him to the condition of a ragged, homeless madman. Paradoxically, it is in this extremity on the heath with Edgar and the Fool, that Lear comes to a knowledge of himself and of his community with all mankind that he had never achieved amid the glories of power. Buffeted by the natural fury of the storm, which is symbolic of the chaos and danger that come with the passing of the old order, Lear sees through his madness the common bond of humanity.

The experience of Lear is mirrored in the Gloucester sub-plot on a more manageable, human level. Gloucester too suffers filial ingratitude but it is not raised to a cosmic level. He too mistakes appearance for reality in trusting the duplicitous Edmund and disinheriting the honest Edgar, but his behavior is more clearly the outgrowth of an existing moral confusion reflected in his ambivalent and unrepentant affection for his bastard. His moral blindness leads to physical blindness when his faulty judgment makes him vulnerable to the villains. In his blindness he finally sees the truth of his situation, but his experience is merely as a father and a man.

Lear's experience parallels Gloucester's in that his figurative madness leads to a real madness in which he finally recognizes what he has lacked. He sees in the naked Edgar, himself a victim of Gloucester's moral blindness, the natural state of man, stripped of all external decoration, and he realizes that he has ignored the basic realities of the human condition. His experience finally transcends Gloucester's because he is a king, preëminent among men. He not only represents the occupational hazards of kingship but also the broadly human disposition to prefer pleasant appearances to troubling realities. However, because of his position, Lear's failure brings down the whole political and social order with him.

Lear has violated nature by a culpable ignorance of it. The result is familial rupture, physical suffering, and existential confusion. Brought low, Lear begins to fashion a new salutary view of himself, of human love, and of human nature. In his insanity, Lear assembles the bizarre court of mad king, beggar, and fool which reasserts the common bonds of all men. Once these realizations have come, the evil characters, so carefully balanced against the good in this precarious world, begin to kill each other off and succumb to the vengeance of regenerated justice.

However, it is a mark of Shakespeare's uncompromising view of reality that there is no simple application of poetic justice to reward the good and punish the wicked, for the good die too. It is true that Edgar finishes off his brother in trial by combat and that the machinations of Goneril and Regan result in the destruction of both, but the redeemed Lear and Cordelia, the perfection of selfless love, also die. That Lear should die is perhaps no surprise. The suffering that he has endured in his confrontation with the primal elements does not allow an optimistic return to normal life and prosperity. He has, on our behalf, looked into the eye of nature and there is nothing left but to die.

The death of Cordelia is more troublesome, at least tonally, because she is the perfectly innocent victim of the evil and madness that surround her. But Shakespeare refuses to save her. She dies gratuitously, not because of any internal necessity of the plot, but because the message to save her is too late. The dramatist has created his own inevitability in order to represent the ruthless consequences of the evil and chaos that have been loosed. When Lear enters with the dead Cordelia, he accomplishes the final expiation of his unknowing.

Out of these sufferings and recognitions comes a new moral stasis. Yet the purged world does not leave us with great confidence in future stability. Kent is old and refuses kingship. Edgar assumes authority but, despite his rectitude, there is an unsettling doubt that he has the force or stature to maintain the new order in this volatile world where evil and chaos are always rumbling beneath the surface.

Edward E. Foster

THE KING OF THE GOLDEN RIVER

Type of work: Fairy tale
Author: John Ruskin (1819-1900)
Type of plot: Heroic adventure
Time of plot: The legendary past
Locale: Stiria
First published: 1851

The plot of this fairy tale is not new: the good youngest brother triumphs after the evil older brothers fail and are punished. But the story retains a charm and emotional effectiveness derived probably from the sincerity of Ruskin's intention when he composed it.

John Ruskin, aesthetician, art historian, reformer, and economist, would seem an unlikely author of a world-famous fairy tale. In fact he himself wrote slightingly of it in his autobiography *Praeterita*: "*The King of the Golden River* was written to amuse a little girl . . . it is totally valueless . . . I can no more write a story than compose a picture." Yet Ruskin unjustly demeaned his story which, more than a century after it was first published, still has its charm for children as well as for adults.

As Ruskin admitted, his principal literary influences were Grimm and Dickens. From Grimm came the grotesque elements and the German setting; the geniality, the colloquial tone and, more important, the character of the child, Gluck, and the social theme were derived from Dickens.

Like many of Dickens' fictive children—Oliver Twist, Little Nell, Tiny Tim and Paul Dombey—Gluck is the image of the tyrannized child, dear to Victorian hearts, who is victimized by the adult mercantile world. Preternaturally innocent, unspoiled by his environment, Gluck works generously under his brothers' sadistic direction. He never responds to them or anyone else but in the spirit of Christian charity. Also like Dickens' children he is close to a magical world which takes particular care of him.

Opposed to magic and spirit is a recognizable adult world of profit and loss. Schwartz and Hans can be taken as Ruskin's version of Scrooge. The visits of the South West Wind and the King of the Golden River would then parallel the various ghosts which visit the terrible miser on Christmas Eve. Yet unlike Scrooge they fail to learn the lesson of charity, preached so eloquently by their brother's example, and are turned to stone. Appropriately Gluck triumphs, and becomes a benevolent farmer who ministers to the poor, not unlike the reformed Scrooge.

THE KING OF THE MOUNTAINS

Type of work: Novel
Author: Edmond François About (1828-1885)
Type of plot: Adventure romance
Time of plot: Mid-nineteenth century
Locale: Greece
First published: 1856

A response to his own travels abroad, this satirical novel was the perfect instrument to display About's ingenious and clever wit. Many of the characters are hilarious representations of national types, and the view of Greece in the mid-nineteenth century is both trenchant and devastating.

Edmond About visited Greece in 1851, approaching his first experience with that country armed with superficial, almost schoolboy, ideas. His preconceived notions were, of course, disappointed, and he spent the next two years reëvaluating his impressions.

After his return to Paris in 1853, he wrote a number of books dealing with his Grecian experiences. His first work was the sparkling and satiric volume *La Grèce contemporaine* (1854), whose portrait of Greek society gave great offense in Athens but was widely read in other parts of Europe. *The King of the Mountains,* which followed, is even more satirical, drawing on the juxtaposition of the ancient and modern in Greece for its wit. A satirist like About could not have a finer theme, and the book gained a wide popularity in its time. The author made cosmopolitan fun of his subjects. The German botanist, so brave, simple, and honest, deeply in love without knowing it, is the literary ideal of the Germans before the war of 1870. The British banker's wife, with her appetite and her ungracious gratitude is a fair caricature of that terrible being—the rich, middle-aged, middle-class British female. The grave irony of the king himself is worthy of Swift. His item of expenditure, "Repairs of the road to Thebes, which has become impracticable, and where unfortunately, we found no travelers to rob" is inimitable.

The King of the Mountains is, in short, a caricature of the same devastating sort as Dickens' *American Notes* (1842), showing that while human nature does not really differ much anywhere, we become much more sensitive to our own faults and limitations when they are exhibited in the context of other worlds and cultures.

KING PARADOX

Type of work: Novel
Author: Pío Baroja (1872-1956)
Type of plot: Social satire
Time of plot: Early twentieth century
Locale: Spain, Tangier, and the imaginary Bu-Tata, in Uganga, Africa
First published: 1906

A novel of protest and social satire, King Paradox *utilizes different styles and forms to attack the injustices and cruelties of the world in general and of Spanish society at the turn of the century in particular. Somewhat rambling and confusing, the novel nevertheless maintains a certain power throughout its length, chiefly because of the author's anger and intellectual force.*

Spain's literary "Generation of 1898" was unhappy with society. It was goaded by Spain's ignominious defeat at American hands in 1898 and, pessimistically introspective, it sought the reasons for the puzzling decadence of Spain. Pío Baroja was the most important novelist of the "Generation of 1898." He scorned injustice, cruelty, and hypocrisy. He also opposed mediocrity, considered himself a spiritual vagabond, and felt that men were forlorn creatures in an enormous universe. Having witnessed many scenes of poverty in Spain, he studied medicine in order to be of social help. He eventually became a philosopher, visionary, and satirist, while from his medical studies arose an interest in pathology and abnormality that was to influence his writing. Since he considered life devoid of logic and reason, full of chaos and confusion, his novels lack strong organization.

Baroja viewed *King Paradox* as a symbolic creation, representing an attempt to achieve a better world. The fictional Utopia created by a motley throng of adventurers is symbolically destroyed by a cruel government which represents the false aspects of civilization, especially its destructive bureaucracy. The novel mingles fantasy and satire to condemn Spain's stagnant aristocracy and bureaucracy. The author creates an imaginary Double Spain, one a progressive New Spain, symbolized by light and movement, the other a petrified Old Spain, contentedly ignorant. Baroja also wove three prose poems into his novel, including "A Metaphysical Ode to Destruction," wherein he paraded many of his most positive and philosophical ideas.

Originally influenced by Darwin, Pasteur, and Nietzsche, Baroja was sometimes viewed as Maxim Gorky's Spanish counterpart. As time went on he became ever more convinced that spirit was superior to matter. He also became the most prolific novelist of the Generation of 1898 and, in the opinion of some, its most genuine representative. It is often felt that, although Baroja fell short of greatness, he is the novelist of 1898 most likely to receive a niche in literary history.

KING SOLOMON'S MINES

Type of work: Novel
Author: H. Rider Haggard (1856-1925)
Type of plot: Adventure romance
Time of plot: Nineteenth century
Locale: Africa
First published: 1886

The story of the search for King Solomon's legendary lost treasure, hidden in the land of the Kukuanas, has remained popular for generations. Rooted in precise details and vivid descriptions, the fantastic narrative is both convincing and engrossing.

King Solomon's Mines was the first great African adventure novel and set the pattern for a host of jungle stories to follow, from Edgar Rice Burroughs' *Tarzan* epics to serious novels such as Joseph Conrad's *Heart of Darkness* (1902) and Saul Bellow's *Henderson the Rain King* (1959).

Haggard chooses his heroes for maximum dramatic effect. Allan Quatermain, the narrator, is the thorough professional. He is a moderate, practical, cost-conscious man, courageous when he has to be, but quite willing to avoid danger if given the option; he is a firm believer in brain over brawn.

Sir Henry Curtis is the more typical hero. Where Quatermain is rational and careful, Curtis is emotional and extravagant. Quatermain is the mechanical expert, especially with guns, but Curtis is most at home with primitive weapons and becomes awesome in hand-to-hand combat. In short, Curtis is the natural warrior; it is he who kills the one-eyed villain, King Twala.

Captain John Good, the ex-naval officer, is the one hero who seems out of place in the depths of Africa. He is fastidious and fussy. His personal quirks and unusual accessories, such as his monocle, his false teeth which "snap" into place, his formal attire, and his delicate white legs, provide the necessary comic relief. Late in the novel, however, these humorous details become crucial plot elements when Good's half-shaved face and bare legs are taken as signs of divinity by the hostile natives. Thus, if the characterizations are neither deep nor complex, they are vivid and thoroughly convincing.

Haggard also keeps the plot simple and the language plain, as Quatermain states in offering his "apologies for my blunt way of writing . . . simple things are always the most impressive, and books are easier to understand when they are written in plain language." The plot is organized around the most basic adventure formula—the treasure hunt—and has all the necessary ingredients: a mysterious map; an exotic, even mythic destination; an unknown, dangerous terrain; and a pair of grotesque, diabolical villains. Haggard carefully develops his story by subjecting his heroes to a series of crises that become progressively more dangerous, more extreme, and more fantastic.

But, however exotic these adventures become, the author keeps them believable with his matter-of-fact language and his careful, realistic use of detail. Calling upon his own youthful experiences in Africa, Haggard supports every incident with relevant particulars. Quatermain is a thoroughly seasoned professional. He uses the best equipment, detailed accurately, and demonstrates his expertise in dozens of small ways: handling animals, negotiating with natives, organizing and directing their hunts, and supervising the day to day safari routine. As the men encounter more unusual environments, Haggard continues to reinforce his narrative with concrete details. The natives' equipment, social and military organizations, tribal customs, and religious rituals are described with precision. Even the most fantastic sequences in the novel—the exploration of Solomon's mines, the discovery of the giant figures and the Place of Death, the search through the treasure room, and the escape through the underground tunnel—are "explained" minutely and logically by historical speculation, Biblical references, and native folklore. Since the novel takes place in an area which was, at the time, as yet unexplored, the book seems "authentic" and many of its first readers even thought that the story was true.

Thus, as one of the first and best of the popular modern adventure novelists, Rider Haggard understood the basic rule of "escapist" fiction: if the imaginative adventure is to succeed, the world the reader "escapes" to must be as real as the one he lives in, however improbable the particular events may be.

THE KING, THE GREATEST ALCALDE

Type of work: Drama
Author: Lope de Vega (Lope Félix de Vega Carpio, 1562-1635)
Type of plot: Tragi-comedy
Time of plot: Sixteenth century
Locale: Spain
First presented: c. 1623

A social drama, this play portrays vividly the struggle of the peasantry against the nobility; power is on the side of the aristocracy, but honor on the side of the poor. Comedy, pathos, and an overriding sense of justice all combine to make this a stirring work, one of the finest dramas to come from the author's prolific pen.

The King, the Greatest Alcalde is one of the best works (along with *La fuente ovejuna*) of one of the most remarkable literary men of all time. Like Dr. Johnson, Byron, and the composer Liszt, Lope is as much of a "personality" as he is an artist. Born of humble parents, he became a soldier, a sailor in the Spanish Armada (taking part in the ill-fated expedition of 1588), a duelist, an exile, a lover of innumerable ladies and a husband of two, a priest of passionate if temporary convictions, an arbiter of the theater, and reputedly the writer of about eighteen hundred plays and other dramatic works, less than a third of which have survived. A contemporary of Shakespeare, he has often been compared to the English bard for his breadth of vision, his vitality, his role in the creation of a national theater, and the similar innyard-type theater (the *corral*) for which he wrote. Inevitably for such a prolific dramatist, however, his artistry falls far short of Shakespeare's. We cannot say of his role in Spanish dramaturgy, as Johnson said of Dryden's in refining English poetry, that he found it brick and left it marble; perhaps, without undue aspersion, we can say that he found it sand and left it brick.

Lope wrote with a disdain for classical precedent and an open appeal for popular approval. "When I set out to write a play," he observed, "I lock up all the rules under ten keys, and banish Plautus and Terence from my study. . . . For I write in the style of those who seek the applause of the public, whom it is but just to humor in their folly, since it is they who pay for it." The Spaniards called him "Monstruo de la Naturaleza" or "the freak of nature," for his plays have the vices of their virtues: bubbling with inventiveness, energy, and variety, they are also too often careless in their construction, shallow in their characterization, and uneven in their poetic power.

The King, the Greatest Alcalde exhibits both the virtues and the vices and also exemplifies Lope's dramatic outlook. The play, a tragi-comedy, is a mixture of romance and realism. Sancho and Elvira are closely related to the Corydons and the Phyllises of pastoral romance in their rustic idealized love for each other, and in the miseries they must endure before they are finally reunited. But they are observed with a realism, as well as a pessimism, that takes due note of the branding power of evil in the world. "There is no interest beneath the sun by which an honest woman may be won," Feliciana assures Don Tello, underestimating the savage determination of her brother. In the standard pastoral or romance, the honest woman would remain chaste to the end, despite all temptations and menaces. But Lope realizes that life is not like that, and Elvira is raped before the king can restore her to Sancho.

The primary interest of the play for us, however, is Lope's treatment of social forces, especially as they interact among three poles: the peasants, the feudal lord Don Tello, and the king. We can examine each of these poles in turn.

The dramatist has an unalloyed admiration for the peasant class that we find in no other drama of the time, including Shakespeare's. In our own time, Marxist critics have seized on such plays as this one and *La fuente ovejuna* as examples of Lope's "proletariat" theater, which portrays an oppressed and hearty peasantry struggling against a corrupt and depraved aristocracy. Without necessarily subscribing to such an overall interpretation of the action, we can certainly discern a tendency toward idealization of the peasants in the play. Sancho's opening paean to nature, and his elevated sentiments throughout (a little *too* elevated for a peasant) mark him as a noble character indeed, far more noble, certainly, than the outwardly refined Don Tello. Sancho himself feels that "in the passion of the heart" he is a lord, and the king is highly impressed with Sancho's eloquence and lofty sentiments. But just as important, the king is equally taken with the honest and open nature of the peasants when he questions them about Don Tello's villainy: "The guilelessness of these folk is the most convincing proof," he remarks.

Lords like Don Tello were intermediate in the social structure between the peasants and the king (Lope gives virtually no hints of a middle class). But Spain, in this period, was still in transition between a feudal and a national governmental structure, and Don Tello makes a fatal miscalculation as to just how much power he retains in the new structure. Traditionally, the peasants living within the province of a lord are subject to his absolute authority in all matters of daily life (such as marriage). "You serve Don Tello in his flocks, who rears his powers over these lands, and is supreme through all Galicia," Nuño tells Sancho. Apparently, Don Tello's permission to marry is no longer strictly required, though Nuño strongly advises his future son-in-law to ask for permission anyway in the hope of receiving a generous gift. And Don Tello can indeed be generous when he is in the mood, but he is also arrogantly proud of his undisputed authority. Living quite distant from the king, he accepts no remote challenges to this authority. Even when presented with a direct order in writing from the king he asserts his independence: "I reign here and here I do my will as the King does his in Castile. My forebears never owed land to him—they won it from the Moors." Only when the king personally appears before Don Tello does the once haughty lord crumble and acknowledge his higher authority.

The king himself is presented as the only recourse, this side of God, for the injustices heaped on the peasants. First, he is their special friend. As one of Don Tello's courtiers warns him, "Alfonso was reared in Galicia . . . and for that reason they say he will never close his door to any Gallegan, though never so humble his birth." And indeed, our first view of the king reveals him asking his own courtiers whether there are any suppliants waiting with appeals to him; as he confesses, he is unable to resist the poor. As an indication of his lack of pretentiousness, Alfonso (unlike Don Tello) is unostentatiously dressed; when Sancho is first admitted he must ask a lord which person is the king. But this unpretentiousness does not in the least diminish the king's real importance and power, for he is nothing less than God's regent on earth. His face, Sancho declares to him, is the "Image of God," and "you reflect his glory!" Later, a humbled Don Tello admits that he has "offended God—God and the King!"

The motif of the king in disguise is a fairly common theatrical and literary device, having high dramatic potential (Scott uses a disguised Richard the Lion-Hearted, for instance, in *Ivanhoe*). Lope uses it, though, not only for its suspense value, but also as an emblem of his attitude toward the king. When Alfonso tells Sancho that he intends to intervene personally in the matter, disguised as an alcalde, or justice of the peace, the youth fears that the king is humbling himself by concerning himself so much with a peasant's honor, and he urges instead that the king simply dispatch an alcalde to the scene. But Alfonso, conscious of his judicial, as well as his executive role, replies, "The King the greatest Alcalde!"

It must be noted that this play is not free from the flaws that mar the playwright's other, less important work. The poetry often sags, and the lyrical passages, apart from the fact that they sound faintly incongruous in the mouths of Sancho and Elvira, often become artificial and declamatory. There are inconsistencies of characterization. For instance, Don Tello's passionate desire for Elvira is condemned by her as mere lust. Yet at the opening of the play Sancho tells us repeatedly that his own love for Elvira is based entirely on her physical beauty, and is, in fact, in direct proportion to it: "may your beauty grow, so that in me may grow the love I bear!" And Lope's hasty writing betrays itself in careless construction. For example, Elvira, in the final scene of the play tells us that she has been taken out to a wood and raped; but we have seen her, only a page or so earlier, still untouched, fleeing from Don Tello. The lord could barely have had time to perform the deed, let alone have her taken to a wood, "a fourth league removed."

For such reasons, perhaps, the plays of Lope de Vega are seldom performed outside his own country. Still, he is an important and influential playwright. The dramatic vitality and skillful inventiveness of his plays, despite their frequent lapses, make for exciting reading, if not playing. He was to influence other, more highly regarded dramatists, such as Racine and Molière—note, for instance, how kingly intervention in *Tartuffe* saves the day. And his concern with the social importance and dignity of the peasant, who had been conventionally represented in drama as a fool or a clown (such as Pelayo), marks his plays, thematically, as far ahead of their time.

Laurence Behrens

THE KINGDOM OF GOD

Type of work: Drama
Author: Gregorio Martínez Sierra (1881-1947)
Type of plot: Social criticism
Time of plot: Early twentieth century
Locale: Spain
First presented: 1915

This drama of Christian charity relentlessly pursues its theme through three carefully presented scenes; on a large canvas, the author dramatizes three stages in Sister Gracia's devotion to what she considers her duty. Her moving story is no less effective for being told in a quiet manner.

The warm color, delicate shading, beautiful form, and deep philosophy of Martínez Sierra's dramatic craft is evident in *The Kingdom of God.* This play presents Martínez Sierra's philosophy of practical Christian charity, wherein religion is expressed through treating even the least of men as Christian brothers. Such treatment is needed even more by evil men than by good men, the play's theme indicates, for such men are innately weak and naturally capable of only minor amounts of grace. Social significance is given to charity in an apostolic and almost revolutionary sense, for Sister Gracia gives her life to unfortunate waifs and old men, even though some of them are incorrigible.

The play also presents the Biblical theme that God's kingdom will come at the end of the New Testament age, the end of which mankind could now be approaching, and that humans should work toward its early implementation. Sister Gracia therefore consoles her children in the final scene, admonishing them to work—ignoring all discouragement and suffering—so that the kingdom of the Lord's Prayer will come more speedily to anguished mankind. Sister Gracia's charity also links the three separate acts of the play. Her service to the charitable order of Saint Vincent de Paul reflects her faith in human beings, and Martínez Sierra's conviction that women represent life's nobler instincts. Although some critics allege that *The Kingdom of God* is coated with sugary sentimentality, the play obviously does not merit such reproof when judged by Spanish rather than by Anglo-American standards.

KINGS IN EXILE

Type of work: Novel
Author: Alphonse Daudet (1840-1897)
Type of plot: Political romance
Time of plot: Nineteenth century
Locale: Paris
First published: 1879

A forerunner of the highly imaginative and popular Graustarkian romance, this novel combines the simple and the grand, the archaic and the new in its presentation of a tale of political intrigue and adventure. The satirical elements in the story guaranteed its success when it was published and remain of interest to the reader.

Kings in Exile, or *Les Rois en exil* as it is known in France, was completed by Daudet in the summer of 1879. It appeared first as a serial in *Le Temps,* and was subsequently published in book form, going through twenty editions in only a few weeks. The immediate success of the book was in no small part due to the fact that certain of the characters were reminiscent of well-known personages. For example, Elysée Méraut, hero of the novel, is based on Constant Theroin, a royalist orator who held sway in the Latin Quarter, a man of exceptional erudition who harangued whatever audience he could command in the cafés and reading rooms of Paris. While the fictional King of Illyria, around whom the novel revolves, is a wastrel without honor or dignity, and the rest of the exiled royalists are a sorry sight, it is the humble tutor Elysée Méraut who passionately pleads the monarchic cause, and who preserves unsullied the high ideal of the divine right of kings.

Daudet's irony in *Kings in Exile,* however, almost landed him in trouble. Since the models for the characters were alive and in Paris at the time of the novel's publication, many readers found the author's irony too scathing, and the exposure too complete. There was a feeling that Alphonse Daudet was becoming too scandalous—an impression heightened when the novel was dramatized four years later, and the royal personages in its pages appeared as beings of flesh and blood upon the stage. In general, though, most found the book to be brilliant. Flaubert devoured it in one day and hailed it as a triumph. Modern readers, too, find the novel interesting, for it combines both simple and complex techniques in the formation of a timeless political romance.

KING'S ROW

Type of work: Novel
Author: Henry Bellamann (1882-1945)
Type of plot: Social criticism
Time of plot: Late nineteenth century
Locale: The Middle West
First published: 1940

The story of Parris Mitchell and his town of King's Row, this long novel combines sentimentality and sensationalism with realistic portrayals of character and setting to produce an effective if uneven story. The characters develop in unexpected yet convincing ways, and are so vividly drawn as to seem to possess lives beyond the pages of the novel; this quality no doubt accounted for the book's enormous popularity.

King's Row is long and uneven, but it provides the reader with an engrossing, somewhat more romantic and less satiric view of "Main Street" in the late nineteenth century and the early years of the twentieth century. Some characters, such as Jamie Wakefield, the would-be poet, are unoriginal and insufficiently individualized to stand up, while others, notably Madame von Eln, are skillfully drawn and unique portraits. The characters and story possessed possibilities that Bellamann did not always realize. He drew back at the point where Sherwood Anderson or William Faulkner would have penetrated more ruthlessly to the heart of small-town tragedy.

But Bellamann did attempt to show different levels of society, with the rise of some individuals and the fall of others, representing the interacting fears and hopes and frustrations of these people. None of these individuals stands alone; the inherent dependence of human beings upon one another is a vital thread that weaves through the book from the beginning to the end.

King's Row is presented as no idyllic country town. The scandal of the sadistic Dr. Gordon, the suppressed tragedy of Cassie Tower and her father, and the pathetic tale of Vera Lichinska, the brilliant young violinist who stops playing and comes home to King's Row to stare at the asylum which terrified her as a child, are all skillfully woven into the dominant stories of Parris Mitchell and Drake McHugh. Some scenes, such as the peaceful death of fat, crazy old Lucy Carr, while young Parris plays the out-of-tune piano in her shanty, are perfectly handled and very moving, while other scenes do not quite succeed, but Bellamann is successful more often than not. Some human beings grow as they live, Bellamann seems to suggest, others are incapable of growth. But, despite the tragedy inherent in the human condition, the town and its people endure.

KIPPS

Type of work: Novel
Author: H. G. Wells (1866-1946)
Type of plot: Domestic romance
Time of plot: Early twentieth century
Locale: England
First published: 1905

Kipps, The Story of a Simple Soul, *is a gentle satire on social pretensions and an admonition that one should never try to be what one is not. The hero of this comic novel, the delightful Kipps, never takes himself too seriously and thus endures the quirks of fortune.*

Of his first comic novel, Wells wrote, "*Kipps* is designed to present a typical member of the English lower middle-class in all its pitiful limitation and feebleness, and beneath a treatment deliberately kind and general provides a fairly sustained criticism of the ideals and ways of the great mass of middle-class English people." Wells was in an excellent position to comment on both these social types.His father had kept a shop much like that of Kipps's uncle. Wells too was forced to study at a commercial academy and apprentice himself in a drapery shop. Marriage brought him squarely into the middle-class milieu, and the agony which Ann and Arthur experience in building their house is reminiscent of Wells's ordeal in getting Spade House erected near Folkestone.

It is precisely that quality of feebleness which makes Arthur Kipps such a superb comic figure. Impressionable, undereducated, always a bit bewildered, this unself-conscious "simple soul" is incapable of mastering the "social graces," and his attempts only highlight the silliness of polite society. Led by the omniscient and sympathetic narrator, we see Kipps struggling with "The Art of Conversation," French sauces, the "social call," the Anagram Tea, and tipping in London's Royal Grand Hotel.

Wells treats the Walsinghams very harshly. Not wealthy, their sense of class is nevertheless boundless. *Noblesse oblige* draws them into charitable activities, through which they express their utter contempt for working people. Barely deigning to speak to Kipps in the drapery shop, when they learn of his inheritance they organize a cynical conspiracy to capture his wealth. To Helen, Kipps means "money and opportunity, freedom and London." She introduces him to grammar, idleness, gardening, and afternoon tea. Not really hopeful that he can be reformed, she takes comfort in the anticipation that he will at least change the spelling of his name to *Cuyps* and "cut dead" his old friends.

THE KNIGHT OF THE BURNING PESTLE

Type of work: Drama
Author: Francis Beaumont (1585?-1616)
Type of plot: Mock-heroic comedy
Time of plot: Early seventeenth century
Locale: England and Moldavia
First presented: c. 1607

Most likely inspired by Don Quixote, *this innovative comedy revealed, through its hilarious burlesque of a dramatic plot, the author's warm sympathy for and large understanding of the London lower middle classes. With its parody of heroics and romances and its clever use of audience participation, the play was a startling departure from the usual dramatic techniques of its time.*

The prologue to the 1635 Beaumont and Fletcher Folio reprint of *The Knight of the Burning Pestle* makes clear that Beaumont's comedy was innovational when it was first presented about 1607. At that time the theatergoers' rage was all for satires full of "invective . . . touching some particular persons." So the mock-heroic play, with its parody of romantic bombast and its war treatment of the London lower-middle class enjoyed little success until it was revived about 1635; then the aristocratic court audience delighted in its word-play, wit, and ingenious construction. *The Knight of the Burning Pestle* has really three plots cleverly unified in one: a frame-story concerning George the grocer, his outspoken wife Nell, and his cloddish apprentice Ralph; a mock-romantic play, *The London Merchant,* which parodies stock conventions and concerns Jasper Merrythought, the witty apprentice who loves Luce, Venturewell's comely daughter; and finally a parody of chivalric romances, featuring the apprentice Ralph, now cast as "the right courteous and valiant knight," whose actions travesty the heroic traditions.

As Knight of the Burning Pestle, Ralph utters archaic, confused, hyperbolic language as he goes about his business of knight-errantry. Instead of performing brave, wonderful deeds, he confronts a monster who is in reality a barber; instead of being a noble warrior, he is in reality a grocer's boy who is faithful to his profession; instead of marrying a beautiful princess, he remains faithful to his cobbler's maid, Susan. Finally, instead of succeeding in the end, he dies; indeed, he does not even die on stage, but walks off with a forked arrow through his head.

Thus the play successfully parodies the whole gamut of romantic and heroic conventions. In addition to Ralph's misadventures, other stock elements of the theater are employed in satirical jest. Jasper and Humphrey are the traditional "rival wooers"; Jasper and Michael are the "double sons." George and Nell consistently support the wrong lover, as they display their lack of artistic sense. Venturewell, the rich London merchant, portrays the typical protective father-figure, just as Luce is the typical independent-minded daughter. Yet

Beaumont's parody of stock theatrical situations and personalities never descends to the level of insult. His intent is to "move inward delight, not outward lightness . . . soft smiling, not loud laughing." Despite this modest disclaimer, *The Knight of the Burning Pestle* is Beaumont's most amusing, inventive comedy.

THE KNIGHTS

Type of work: Drama
Author: Aristophanes (c. 448-385 B.C.)
Type of plot: Political satire
Time of plot: Fifth century B.C.
Locale: Athens
First presented: 424 B.C.

This political satire was written by Aristophanes in answer to the accusation of Cleon, tyrant of Athens, that the playwright used the privileges of citizenship fraudulently. Both witty and wise, the comedy teaches that as long as men will not look beyond their noses they will continue to sell each other short and to give themselves the shortest weight.

This political allegory is one of Aristophanes' most obvious attacks. But to understand its impact on the Athenian audience who voted its author first prize at its Lenaean performance, we must be aware of certain historical and political events.

Cleon was a jingoistic demagogue of the worst sort who had harangued, bullied, and stumbled his way into a position of leadership in the Athenian assembly. Some six years into the Peloponnesian War and four years after the death of his arch rival Pericles, Cleon had accused the Athenian generals Demosthenes and Nicias of cowardice for their slowness in dealing with a Spartan contingent on the island of Sphacteria. Nicias resigned, and the people sent Cleon, who, as promised, returned victorious in twenty days—though the victory resulted from the strategy designed and executed by Demosthenes. Cleon (not a "tyrant" in the technical sense) had thus worked his way through flattery and fear into the management of the affairs of the people (Greek *demos*), having supplanted two honest servants who might well have lived up to their names, "People's Strength" and "Victory" (Demosthenes and Nicias).

Aristophanes produced the *Knights* one year after the Sphacterian affair, when Cleon was at the height of his power, and he himself is said to have played the Paphlagonian. The chorus, representing the thousand young nobles who made up the well-equipped Athenian cavalry, was an obvious counterbalance to the singularly influential and singularly despicable figure of Cleon, who in fact *was* a tanner. The portrayal of Cleon as a Paphlagonian from Asia Minor emphasizes his un-Athenian manners and his undemocratic politics. In his portrayal of old Demus, the playwright is careful not to offend; after all, Demus is his audience, whom he must prod from its political senility by revealing Demus miraculously rejuvenated as the idealized Athenian of Marathon and Salamis. Amid this concluding optimistic fantasy we begin to suspect that the Sausage-Seller who bested Cleon in the *agons* (debates), who is now suddenly revealed as Demos' wise and inspirational guide, and who answers to the name Agoracritus ("Forum-Judgment"), is none other than Aristophanes himself.

THE KREUTZER SONATA

Type of work: Novel
Author: Count Leo Tolstoy (1828-1910)
Type of plot: Social criticism
Time of plot: Late nineteenth century
Locale: Russia
First published: 1889

A sardonic attack upon the problem of sex, The Kreutzer Sonata *has been much misunderstood as representing Tolstoy's views on marriage and the relationships of the sexes in Russian society. Actually, the story is the confession of an insane man and should be viewed as a work of art in which Tolstoy again expresses with poignancy the passions of the human heart.*

One of the strangest of Tolstoy's works, *The Kreutzer Sonata* is almost entirely a raving monologue concerning sex and marriage. Indeed, it is hardly a work of fiction at all, for it takes few pains to explore a verisimilar situation for its own sake. Instead it engulfs us at once in a deluge of fanatic ideas. This short novel can be viewed as a study in suffering and deracination, but it was intended as a piece of propaganda and its sources spring directly from Tolstoy's life. After Tolstoy had experienced his conversion and attempted to turn away from the world and material concerns, he came increasingly into harsh conflict with his wife. Their quarrels largely concerned the family fortune, which Tolstoy wished to give to the poor, but it also concerned sex, for despite their arguments Tolstoy strongly desired his wife, though he found such desires loathsome. To compound the matter, he found himself in a state of violent jealousy over his wife's harmless flirtations with her violin teacher.

Pozdnishef, the central character of the story, has murdered his wife in a fit of sexual jealousy and madness. His monologue is a feverish attempt to explain this act to himself. He locates the causes in woman's corrupt desires to enslave men through sensuality; all love is false because it is based on sensuality. Men must practice sexual continence in order to encourage reason and avoid passionate excitements which are essentially destructive. Sexual intercourse should be practiced only for the purpose of producing children. Only those arts which calm the passions should be condoned. Music should be banished as the most dangerous art. Pozdnishef murders his wife when he finds her with her music teacher, a violinist. It is a harmless relationship but Pozdnishef is determined to see it as a corrupt one. Indeed, he has encouraged the relationship to prove his theories. He is hopelessly trapped in his own obsessions, incapable of balanced perceptions.

The Kreutzer Sonata was written out of Tolstoy's desperate need to objectify and thus to understand his own obsessions and the fearful consequences which could follow from them. It is, in the deepest sense, a piece of utilitarian fiction because it practices that most useful and crucial act, the encounter with the self.

KRISTIN LAVRANSDATTER

Type of work: Novel
Author: Sigrid Undset (1882-1949)
Type of Plot: Historical chronicle
Time of plot: Fourteenth century
Locale: Norway
First published: 1920-1922

A trilogy, Kristin Lavransdatter *is characterized by consummate artistry in delineation of character, in selection of detail, and in sweep of storyline. These three novels, laid in medieval Norway, illustrate Undset's psychological depth and ability to visualize the mind and temper of bygone ages.*

Alexander Woollcott, a popular radio critic of the 1930's, once commented that there were some books that made one want to distribute them by the wheelbarrow loads, handing one to everyone he met and saying, "Take this and read it!" *Kristin Lavransdatter* is such a book. It begins like a family chronicle and, indeed, it maintains the deceptively simple narrative form of a straightforward historical account, yet it carries the reader along and gradually draws him into a vortex of events and problems as only a moving story which is deeply true to our sense of genuine human experience can do.

Kristin Lavransdatter, written in Sigrid Undset's middle years (*Kransen* or *The Bridal Wreath* was published in 1920; *Husfrue* or *The Mistress of Husaby* in 1921; and *Korset* or *The Cross* in 1922, when she was forty) is her finest work. It is the study of a woman first in her early prime, then as mother and manager of household and estate, and finally in her declining years—the story of a woman who is forced either to bow to unfavorable circumstances or grow to a remarkable stature. This aspect of the work has considerable psychological depth of insight. The trilogy is also a historical novel of significant penetration and validity. As one reads he finds himself feeling that he knows what it was like to live in that medieval environment.

Both aspects of the work, and with them its technical excellence, are the products of years of preparation. Genius may be a gift with which one is born, but it must also be cultivated, and Sigrid Undset worked steadily at developing her knowledge, her understanding, and her skill. The daughter of a well-known professor and archaeologist, she had a lifelong interest in history, especially of the Scandinavian past. Her own home was to be one of the sturdy old Norse houses—nearly a thousand years old—and she would fill it with antiques of the medieval northland. She not only read history; she was thrilled with the practical and ornamental products of her homeland's history.

In the period before *Kristin Lavransdatter,* her life was not easy; she was engaged in a constant struggle between the unrestrained acceptance of life and asceticism. Not that she wanted to live an immoral life. Her conflict went much deeper. Miguel de Unamuno, in his *The Tragic Sense of Life,* says there is an inevitable conflict between faith and reason, between an attachment to or yearning for the unknown, and a clinging to the known. Sigrid Undset felt the call of faith, which to her meant stern control of her existence, a life like that of the cloister; she was also strongly attached to everything of this earth. Both aspects wanted to be first; both pulls were so strong no compromise could be found. Eventually, the call of the Church was to prove the stronger, but before *Kristin Lavransdatter* there was no resolution—and her trilogy was a natural battleground where this personal conflict could be waged with full force. The fourteenth century furnished an ideal setting, for the Viking Age was then still fresh in memory and a powerful cultural influence, while Christianity was struggling to reach the hearts and minds of the populace.

At the age of twenty-five Undset published her first novel, *Fru Marta Oulie* (1907) and followed this in 1909 with *Viga-Ljot og Vigdis,* a study of pre-Christian Norse paganism. In 1911 came her first great success, *Jenny.* Already, with two novels about women and one historical study, she had made great strides in preparation for her masterpiece. Her technical literary skills were honed with a volume of poetry, *Youth* (1910). In the next few years came an autobiographical fragment which centered on women's problems (she was an ardent feminist, working for recognition of women as equals of men, but not one who wanted the roles of men and women to be interchangeable) and a study of the three Brontë sisters, centering on Emily. She also wrote on pagan witchcraft and on the development of Christianity as a decisive force in life. She had become a cultural historian, a psychologist, a careful thinker, and a craftsman skilled in the arts of leading her readers to deeper understanding while carrying them along with narratives of compelling force and action. She was ready to gather these qualities together in her Nobel Prize novel, *Kristin Lavransdatter.*

A historical novel should give the reader not so much a set of historical facts (though it should not distort these) as a strong and valid sense of what it was like to live in the age represented. The historian may deal in bones; the novelist's trade is the living flesh, the pulsating heart, the yearning spirit, the questioning mind. These, although seen in relationship to a time and culture remote from our own, are valid for and relevant to us because human nature remains essentially the same and because we have the capacity to adapt ourselves, at least in imagination, to a wide range of circumstances. The fourteenth century was an age of transition from a life centered on hunting, fishing, and adventure to a settled agricultural existence, from deeply rooted Nordic faith and superstitions to Christianity.

The physically strong—those with the capacity for adventure, hardship, excitement—mostly clung to the old ways which not merely allowed but required these. The old, the crippled, the weak, who were unfitted for a stern struggle for survival, turned readily to the sheltering faith, to the priesthood, sometimes to the cloister. But if the Church was to gain dominance, the strong had to turn to it, to hold to it, not only for support but from conviction. These aspects of the age are brought to vivid life for us in *Kristin Lavransdatter*. Our own age (like every other, an era of transition) has its parallels, its divided populace, with those who cling to established values and those who seek to seek out and establish new ones. The impact of *Kristin Lavransdatter* is not, then, simply a matter of information about the past of a faintly remembered minor culture; in that setting it is the story of every significant generation and of the men and women who will not, cannot, yield their convictions for the sake of an easier accommodation to life: Sigrid Undset's trilogy is not timeless; it is timely at all times.

Kenneth Oliver

THE LADY FROM THE SEA

Type of work: Drama
Author: Henrik Ibsen (1828-1906)
Type of plot: Psychological realism
Time of plot: Nineteenth century
Locale: A small town in northern Norway
First presented: 1889

This play was the first of the psychological dramas written by Ibsen, who had formerly devoted himself almost entirely to social criticism. The story of Ellida Wangel's struggle with the threat of insanity is very moving; her character and those of the other people in the play are all strongly drawn, without condescension or social pigeonholing. The drama revolves around the problems of communication, individual freedom, and responsibility for one's fate.

In the last phase of his career, Henrik Ibsen turned from the realistic social plays of his middle period in the direction of a more psychological and, eventually, symbolic drama. He also shifted his emphasis from characters who were "normal," if extreme, to those who were obviously "abnormal." He became fascinated by what he called the "trolls" or "demons" present in the back of the mind; that is, the irrational, subconscious side of the human personality that could erupt and dominate the actions of the most apparently stable individuals. Although there are important aspects of this transition in such earlier plays as *The Wild Duck* (1884) and *Rosmersholm* (1886), it was in *The Lady from the Sea* that he first overtly dramatized this new preoccupation with the "demonic." Thus, while *The Lady from the Sea* may lack the stature of Ibsen's major plays, either in the quality of its craftsmanship or in the depth of its perceptions, it still remains a pivotal play in his development—as well as offering one of Ibsen's most fascinating female characters, Ellida Wangel, "the lady from the sea."

Ellida immediately impresses us as an intelligent, sensitive, vivacious, sensuous woman. She is also, clearly, on the edge of an emotional breakdown. She feels oppressed by her domestic routine and alienated from her immediate surroundings. Her husband, Dr. Wangel, loves her, but is unable to either understand her or communicate with her. Ellida respects and feels gratitude toward him, but, because she feels her marriage to have been a "business arrangement," she can neither confide in him nor respond to him emotionally. She is even more isolated from Wangel's daughters, Boletta and Hilda, who treat Ellida as an intruder. They make this evident to her by celebrating their dead mother's birthday behind her back.

Such a stifling environment is, of course, common to many of Ibsen's great heroines—Nora Helmer, Mrs. Alving, Gina Ekdal, Hedda Gabler—but only in *The Lady from the Sea* does it actually threaten to drive the woman to madness. Ellida's grasp on reality is precarious. She cannot forget that her own mother died in an asylum; she is irrationally drawn to the sea; she is obsessed by the memory of her dead son, whose eyes, she believes "changed with the seas." Her mood shifts are abrupt and erratic; she cannot even remember what people look like when they are out of her sight.

The focus of her obsession is, of course, the mysterious sailor she married prior to meeting Wangel. Although the vow she made to him was unsanctioned by law, Ellida cannot disregard it. She has felt his presence ever since her marriage to Wangel, and especially since the death of her son. The final crisis is provoked by his return to claim her as his "bride."

But when he does appear, Ellida's reaction is a curious one—she does not recognize him until she looks him directly in the eyes. Thus, it is not the Stranger that Ellida longs for, but what he has come to represent to her. The sea, not the sailor, is the primary symbol, and it suggests the life of the imagination, of daring (he once killed a man), of extreme experience, and of total personal and spiritual fulfillment—but at the risk of self-destruction. The real contest, all three participants realize, lies not in any contention over the physical possession of Ellida, but within the mind and heart of the woman herself. "The root of that fascination lies in my own mind," she tells Wangel, "what can you do against that?"

Wangel finally realizes that, even if he forces her to remain with him, he will lose her—to insanity. But as a trained and sensitive doctor, he also sees that she will be destroyed if she goes with the Stranger. Caught on the horns of this dilemma, he makes a desperate and, for him, soul-wrenching decision: he gives her the absolute "freedom" to make her own choice and be "responsible" for the consequences of it.

Those two words, "freedom" and "responsibility," give Ellida power over herself and resolve the play. Three factors free her from the Stranger's power: Hilda's emotional reaction to the news that she will be going away suggests to Ellida the real possibility of a relationship with the girls; Wangel's obvious agonizing over his decision demonstrates the depths of his devotion; and her own "responsibility" has given her the strength to look directly at the man who has come to "claim" her. Once she sees things clearly, the choice is not that hard. Because Ellida has been allowed—*forced*—to take control of her own life, she does so, and not only resolves her marital difficulties, but, more importantly, solidifies her mental and emotional stability.

LADY INTO FOX

Type of work: Novelette
Author: David Garnett (1892-)
Type of plot: Fantasy
Time of plot: 1880
Locale: England
First published: 1923

A fantasy written with scrupulous attention to detail, Lady into Fox *presents the story of a bridegroom who finds himself married to a fox. Many interpretations of the book's underlying meaning are possible, but it remains an entertaining story.*

A comparison of *Lady into Fox* with Franz Kafka's *Metamorphosis* seems possible on the basis of their sharing a theme hardly encountered elsewhere in modern literature—the sudden and inexplicable transformation of a human being into a totally different form. It is hard to find any further likeness: Kafka's grim and sardonic tale cries for symbolic interpretation, but Garnett's delightful literary prank is pure fun of no discernible allegoric significance.

The English reading public in the 1920's, perhaps in reaction to the horrors of World War I, was particularly receptive to witty fantasy, and *Lady into Fox* shared the best seller lists with works of Ronald Firbank, A. A. Milne, and "Saki." Its continuing popularity, however, attests to Garnett's comic skill.

The idea for the story came from the author's wife during a playful conversation, but what particularly engaged him was the problem of how to induce credulity toward an intrinsically incredible situation. He chose Daniel Defoe as his guide, and the novella employs the same devices Defoe used to convince his readers of the factuality of his fictions. The unremittingly sober narrator constantly reiterates his skeptical insistence on total accuracy, solemnly decrying all gossip, rumor, and imaginative invention. Subtly archaic in diction and syntax, the style is eighteenth century, firm, balanced, and full of moral sententiousness. The narrator applauds Mrs. Tebrick's early efforts to remain a lady even in fox form and deplores her descent into beastliness, he debates at length the moral and religious implications of Mr. Tebrick's godfathering her cubs, and he approaches eloquence in the final catastrophe.

The total effect is both funny and oddly touching, one of the most successful exercises in English of the deadpan tall tale.

THE LADY OF THE LAKE

Type of work: **Poem**
Author: **Sir Walter Scott (1771-1832)**
Type of plot: **Semihistorical romance**
Time of plot: **Sixteenth century**
Locale: **Scottish Highlands**
First published: **1810**

One of Scott's best-known poems, The Lady of the Lake *delves into Gaelic history, retelling a legend that had been popular for generations; Scott's poetry is in a sense painting, for his descriptions are both intense and colorful. It is obvious that he loved the locale he described and understood the people who inhabited the wild Highlands of Scotland.*

The Lady of the Lake followed *Marmion* by merely two years and achieved instant success. Its popularity was attributable to a twofold appeal. It is a romance drawn straight from folk tradition, complete with a disguised king and an innocent maiden. Ellen Douglas, first described as a "Nymph, a Naiad or a Grace," eventually is realized in a manner less classical or pastoral than essentially Romantic. As many commentators have remarked, Ellen is one of Wordsworth's children of nature. Even more than its story or heroine, the poem's setting and scenery captured the imagination of Europe. This one poem literally opened up the Highlands to tourism. Within six months of its publication, *The Lady of the Lake* had made the Loch Katrine section of the Trossachs a literary mecca. The poem served as a dramatic guidebook and started a craze for travel in "Romantic" Scotland that included artists as well as tourists. Keats took a memorable journey to the Highlands, and Mendelssohn's Scotch Symphony is an eloquent testimonial to the hold of Scott's landscape on the European mind.

The verse is less spirited than in *Marmion,* but the story is more carefully plotted and the occasional lyrics, songs, and dirges highlighting the action are among Scott's finest. The Coronach, or dirge, in Canto III is particularly famous.

Finally, the scene painting, that is merely decorative in *Marmion,* is so expertly done here that it becomes an end in itself, a form of program music providing an intensely lush background for the action. The opening of the poem, the episode describing Fitz-James's pursuing of the stag and his accidental discovery of the lovely Ellen, guides both characters and reader through a landscape emblematic of the Romantic promise of the poem's action, a landscape where

> Each purple peak, each flinty spire,
> Was bathed in floods of living fire.

LADY WINDERMERE'S FAN

Type of work: Drama
Author: Oscar Wilde (1856-1900)
Type of plot: Comedy of manners
Time of plot: Nineteenth century
Locale: London
First presented: 1892

Known as one of the wittiest and best-constructed first acts in dramatic history, this play still conveys, despite a dated plot, the flamboyance of its attitudes and the brilliance of its satire. The polish and economy of Wilde's style make the play as enjoyable today as when it was written.

Lady Windermere's Fan is but one example of Oscar Wilde's skill at letting the truth peek gaily from beneath flippant skirts. The play, which was the first of four almost simultaneous successes which once made Wilde an astounding hit in London's West End, is in the Restoration comedy tradition, but Wilde is also able to present emotional scenes without sentiment because of careful timing. In addition to some of the wittiest lines ever heard on stage, the play also has aspects of both the problem play with its comments on social issues and of the well-made play with its neat, compact, and often contrived plot.

A comedy of reversed attitudes, the play offers as its central idea the saucy proposal that a "good" woman may cost more than she is worth and thereby castigates the snobbish, holy attitude of many Victorians. It also presents several other motifs: the woman with a past (who in this instance emerges victorious); children's fated repetition of their parents' errors (again a pitfall which is avoided); and the enlightenment of a narrow conscience (Lady Windermere advances from being a creature who expresses horror at a joint mention of herself and "that" woman, to becoming a person who can say, "I don't think now that people can be divided into the good or the bad, as though they were two separate races or creations.")

As usual in Wilde's plays, the characters are subordinate to the biting wit, and even Mrs. Erlynne, the most fully developed figure, is less sympathetic than amusing, less moving than flamboyant. Lady Windermere, her husband, and her friends are merely attractive and/or absurd mouthpieces for the play's pertinent points. The fan, the major symbol of the play, is also an appropriately casual social trifle, lightly conveying its multiple meanings.

THE LADY'S NOT FOR BURNING

Type of work: Drama
Author: Christopher Fry (1907-   )
Type of plot: Poetic comedy
Time of plot: About 1400
Locale: The small market town of Cool Clary
First presented: 1948

A mixture of poetry and comedy, Fry's verse drama presents a group of characters and a plot which might have been conceived by Shaw; the particular style of verbal humor, however, and the lusty wit and symbolism are unique to Fry's own works.

The Lady's Not for Burning poses intelligence against stupidity and prejudice, the quest for knowledge against self-centered complacency, and honesty against corruption, but it does these things with a lightness of touch and sense of style rare in the modern theater. Although the intent of the work is serious, the play is very funny. The play is also about the power of love, which sometimes can achieve what wit and intelligence cannot; it is love that saves Thomas and Jennet from the stupidity and cruelty of the townsmen.

Thomas Mendip and Jennet Jourdemayne are two of a kind; one of them wants to die and the other wants to live, but both are intelligent and rational beings and both are outsiders in the community. Jennet announces that she believes in the human mind, despite all evidence that her belief is futile. When this "witch" takes refuge in the mayor's house, she cries "Oh, this is the reasonable world, again!" Yet, she soon sees that power and authority do not necessarily go along with reason. Above all, states the mayor, the status quo, the *average,* must be protected. And if that means that she must be sacrificed, so be it. Each of the characters in the play is totally self-centered, until touched by genuine love; only then do some of them begin to think of others, and thereby save themselves. But all of them find that nothing is quite as it seems, and life can hold surprises even for the most complacent individual. And, perhaps most important, these sudden changes may very well shock a person into a better existence.

The language of the play is rich and graceful, and always civilized and delightful, whether coming from the mouths of the pompous town officials, of the philosophical hero, or of the rather befuddled monk. Christopher Fry's dialogue is filled with precise and beautiful metaphors, and has a suggestive power almost unheard of in contemporary drama.

L'AIGLON

Type of work: Drama
Author: Edmond Rostand (1868-1918)
Type of plot: Historical romance
Time of plot: 1830-1832
Locale: Austria
First presented: 1900

Rostand's portrayal of Napoleon's idealistic but weak son is sympathetic, but the character is not strong enough to carry the play for a modern audience's satisfaction. Despite many effective scenes, this verse drama never reaches the heights of Rostand's Cyrano de Bergerac. *However, the play remains of interest for historical reasons, as an example of stagecraft in the year 1900.*

L'Aiglon belongs to a period of dramatic history in which plays were considered chiefly as performing vehicles for star actors or actresses. It is rich in dramatic speeches, filled with elaborate rhetoric and poetry, yet it is essentially static. Perhaps the reason for this fault lies with the protagonist more than with the author, for the Duke of Reichstadt is a weak and vacillating individual. He devotes, in this long and rambling play, much time and energy to proclaiming the need to act, but never acts. Indecisive and full of self-pity, he bemoans his fate to everyone who will listen. If the quality of his speeches were not on such a high level, he would be one of the greatest bores in dramatic literature. The play does not at any time reach the heights of *Cyrano de Bergerac,* and its alexandrines carry to excess the dislocation already visible in that finer play.

Rostand wished to be thought of as the poet of bravery in quest of an unattainable ideal, and made more noble by its heroic paradox, but he worked much better with a more dynamic hero. It is difficult for an audience to sympathize with impossible goals unless the protagonist is willing to fight for them. Style, or panache, Rostand's self-proclaimed ideal, is not enough for a six-act drama.

Rostand's plays were hailed as a welcome reaction against the naturalistic drama of the period, but they actually were Romanticism brought up to date, with new symbols woven into old fabrics. Rostand was the master of language and rhyme and was able to construct speeches that were as moving as they were beautiful. *L'Aiglon* will survive chiefly becaues of its sentiment and poetry, although it fails as a piece of dramatic craftsmanship. The characterizations are highly stylized, as if each individual in the drama is consciously playing a part; the result is that the audience seems to see masks upon masks and poses upon poses. The only characters who possess a substantial reality are Metternich, the Emperor Franz, and—occasionally—Marie-Louise, the young duke's mother. But even they seem often to be partaking in a glorious pageant rather than trying to survive a real-life crisis.

Much attention is paid, in both dialogue and stage instructions, to settings and costumes. The exquisite gowns and elaborate uniforms seem almost to assume symbolic status; certainly, the white uniform with the scarlet-lined cape and eagle buttons that the duke orders for himself is intended as a symbol of his lost glory and power. At the end of the play, the audience or reader pities the duke, but cannot feel that his end was in any way tragic. The Duke of Reichstadt simply did not possess the stature to be a tragic hero.

THE LAIS OF MARIE DE FRANCE

Type of work: Poetry
Author: Marie de France (fl. late twelfth century)
First transcribed: c. 1175

Marie de France may have composed some of these verse romances at the court of Henry II of England and his wife, Eleanor of Aquitaine. These are tales of magic and courtly love, in which the characters experience quick and deep emotions and move toward inexorable fates. Violence, love's partner, is the dark shadow in most of the stories.

Marie de France started a "literary fiction"—if not a genre—in the Breton *lai*. This form, a short poem with romance elements dealing mainly with love and the supernatural, in Marie's hands, became immediately and widely popular. Its success in England and on the Continent may have been due to her position in court but more likely it was due to the charm and magic of her plots drawn from long-forgotten Celtic and Breton material. Her lays, more simple and dramatic than the usual romances, could easily be sung by minstrels. They were escape literature without the intricacies or subtleties of the extended medieval romance.

Marie says in the prologue of her *Lais* that she first started the vogue. She intended to translate some works from Latin but found too many others engaged in this practice so she turned to retelling lays she claims to have heard as a child from Breton bards. Her statement may not be quite true, since some of the lays have German, English, and Scotch analogues and one has its source in the Orient, but her work had considerable impact.

Marie's delineation of aristocratic life affords today's readers much historical information on the customs, dress, and household arrangements of the twelfth century. Despite typical exaggeration of medieval romance where ladies and their knight-lovers move in a world of unreal beauty and wealth, Marie's *lais* furnish details of social behavior, court furnishings, battle gear, household service, and even games like chess and draughts, in which noblemen indulged. These touches in her well-told, charming stories make them informative as well as delightful almost eight hundred years later.

More important is the fact that in a period when men dominated the literary field, Marie de France stands out as one of the few women artists to make a substantial contribution to English and Continental literature. When most women were satisfied to be the inspiration of literary works by men, Marie in her well-frought, sensitive poems, proved herself a capable, self-conscious artist, who in style and plot influenced many subsequent works such as Thomas Chestre's *Sir Launfal* and perhaps "The Franklin's Tale" and "Sir Thopas" of Geoffrey Chaucer.

LALLA ROOKH

Type of work: Poem
Author: Thomas Moore (1779-1852)
Type of plot: Oriental romance
Time of plot: c. 1700
Locale: India
First published: 1817

A romantic tale told in prose and poetry, Lalla Rookh *is filled with rich descriptions of persons and places; its style is graceful and the narrative fluent and not without humor. The ornate structure and style of the poem and its laborious scholarship and occasional preciousness, however, have contributed to its loss of popularity.*

Though nearly forgotten today, Thomas Moore's *Lalla Rookh* was one of the most popular poems of the Romantic period. The public fascination for the exotic and the Orient was in such vogue that publishers bid thousands of guineas for Moore's Oriental romance before seeing a single line. Moore was able to capitalize on a popular theme and on popular enthusiasm for "light o' love" fictions written in verse form, and thereby secure his reputation, though it proved ephemeral.

Through conventional use of dramatic irony, Moore interwove two conflicting themes of love between Feramorz and Lalla Rookh: the romantic, or love of the heart, and the troth, or promised love. The dramatic conclusion of *Lalla Rookh* unites the two: the minstrel Feramorz is revealed to be Aliris, the young king whom Lalla Rookh will marry.

Fadladeen, the Harem's eunuch portrayed by Moore as a hypocrite and detractor, serves as the butt of Moore's satiric jests. He is the unsympathetic and ignorant critic of Feramorz's lyrical ballads until the minstrel reveals himself as Aliris. Moore set up Fadladeen as a straw man mouthing insipid commonplaces in order to lend authority to the themes which underlie the songs of Feramorz. Particularly in "The Veiled Prophet of Khorassan" and "The Fire Worshippers" we see, thinly veiled, the theme of religious and political revolt against tyranny, which bears obvious resemblance to the Irish-English conflicts of the period.

The language of *Lalla Rookh* is flowery, saccharine sweet, and rhetorical to the point that today it is a labor to read. Yet Moore was defensive toward his critics, who thought of him as a light versifier, and he included extensive footnotes as proof of his scholarly devotion, thereby compounding his faults. Moore's Orient is an abstraction of the exotic which gives off the scent of cloying incense and mildewy volumes. It is the relic of a popular style now extinct; and, whatever interest it may have today as a historical relic, Moore's *Lalla Rookh* no longer attracts the attention it once did.

L'AMOROSA FIAMMETTA

Type of work: Novel
Author: Giovanni Boccaccio (1313-1375)
Type of plot: Psychological romance
Time of plot: Fourteenth century
Locale: Naples
First transcribed: 1340-1345

Reputedly autobiographical in origin, this story of jilted love is distinguished by its psychological revelation of fourteenth century life and manners. Despite Boccaccio's imitative style and his labored references to mythological figures, L'Amorosa Fiammetta *presents a realistic picture of two lovers in fourteenth century Naples.*

For some time there has been doubt about the authorship of *L'Amorosa Fiammetta.* There is no known copy of the work earlier than the middle of the fifteenth century. The style does not much resemble that of the young Boccaccio, nor that of his greatest work, the *Decameron.* These difficulties are not major obstacles to ascribing the work to Boccaccio's pen, but one must consider that Boccaccio could not have published this work if it were true, for then the husband of Mario d'Aquino would have killed him for revenge. If the story were false, the author would have been killed for insulting the lady. None of these doubts are really grave, however, and can be accounted for in some measure. But they do lead to a consideration of Boccaccio's image of love in fourteenth century Naples.

The emergence of a modern literature from its European past first becomes apparent in Italy with the works of Dante, Petrarch, and Boccaccio. Yet all these men, Boccaccio included, were by no means modern, and the thoughts of Boccaccio on romantic love must not be assumed to be the same as our own. All these men were far more medieval than they were modern, and there is a rich and varied love literature in the Middle Ages that can shed some light on Renaissance Italian attitudes towards love and sex.

Medieval works like Andreas Capellanus' satire on love, the various parodies of Ovid's *Ars amatoria,* and allegories such as the *Romance of the Rose* all have at least one thing in common. The emotion we think of as love, the kind of passionate desire and longing for another shown by Fiammetta's weeping for Panfilo, was basically foolish behavior to be expected of adolescents, but not of anyone with any sense. Such was the medieval attitude that Boccaccio would be expected to share.

It is possible, then, that Boccaccio did not write this work, but it seems far more likely that he did and intended it to express his anger toward the woman who had jilted him. For his revenge, he wrote out this fable, making Maria d'Aquino appear foolish by making her counterpart suffer such ridiculous torments. If this were the case, the work would certainly not be intended for publication because of the predictable reaction of Maria's husband, and this fact could explain the lack of manuscript copies of this work in the first century after it was written.

THE LAST ATHENIAN

Type of work: Novel
Author: Viktor Rydberg (1829-1895)
Type of plot: Historical romance
Time of plot: Fourth century
Locale: Athens
First published: 1859

This novel presents a strong plea for freedom of religious conscience and worship. While it is a glorification of the Greek ideals of reason, wisdom, truth, and harmony, it is not an anti-Christian novel, but rather a thesis against bigotry and cruelty. As a historical novel it is crowded with knowledgeable detail of the period and of the attitudes and fears of the people.

The Last Athenian presents an awesome analysis of a crumbling civilization heading precipitously into the Dark Ages; detailed descriptions of fourth century dress, customs, political conflicts, and beliefs fill out the narrative. There is much discussion of the changing philosophical attitudes and of the demise of the ancient gods and the problem of the seeker after truth in an age of absolute belief is one of the central concerns of the novel.

Just as the great architecture of the Golden Age was dismantled to construct new Christian churches, so the great philosophies of the past were sacrificed to current prejudices. Many old customs were discontinued simply because they were associated with the old "heathen" ways; even the ancient custom of bathing fell into disrepute. Only a man of the sternest integrity could dare to stand against the blind will of the majority.

Deeply rooted in scholarship, *The Last Athenian* is a well-written and often moving novel of people who search for truth according to their own hearts and minds, even when it is dangerous for them to do so. The moral choices of the individual form the real conflict in the book, aside from melodramatic turnings of the plot. As the narrator explains, all of life in the fourth century was colored by theology, from the Emperor's down to the slaves'. The full social spectrum is included in the novel, with lives and beliefs carefully presented.

Hermione is an unusual and exceptional heroine, intelligent as well as beautiful, a young woman brought up by her philosopher father to be true to her convictions. She comes to learn that there are more subtle evils than hypocrisy and deliberate cruelty; great crimes can be committed with complete sincerity when people believe they are doing God's will. From the self-torture of a religious fanatic such as Simon of the Pillar it is but a little distance to the torture of others. Hermione's suicide is the final, futile act of an individual battling against social forces larger than she can comprehend.

THE LAST CHRONICLE OF BARSET

Type of work: Novel
Author: Anthony Trollope (1815-1882)
Type of plot: Domestic realism
Time of plot: Mid-nineteenth century
Locale: "Barsetshire," England
First published: 1867

As in the other novels set in the shire of Barset, this last book in the series displays Anthony Trollope's genius for understanding both human wisdom and human ignorance. The gentler satire of the earlier Barsetshire stories is replaced by a criticism of materialism more cutting than usual for Trollope.

In this novel Trollope brings to a close the great Barsetshire series: *The Warden* (1855), *Barchester Towers* (1857), *Dr. Thorne* (1858), *Framley Parsonage* (1861), and *The Small House at Allington* (1864). The ecclesiastical and social controversies of the earlier novels are extended in *The Last Chronicle of Barset* to a satire of a society which is becoming increasingly materialistic. The Reverend Josiah Crawley represents the extreme rejection of worldly ambition; he is so absorbed in ministering to his poor parishioners that he literally cannot remember what became of a check for twenty pounds that passed through his hands. To be accused of stealing is the utmost irony for a man of Crawley's uncompromising integrity. His old friend Archdeacon Grantly is equally honest, but he lives "in the world," enjoying prosperity and good living. He is dismayed at his son Henry's desire to marry Crawley's penniless daughter instead of looking about for a more suitable match. Henry's sister Griselda had previously set an excellent example by marrying Lord Dumbello and thus bringing both wealth and title into the family. Trollope implies an ironic contrast between this loveless marriage of social ambition and the genuine attachment of Henry and Grace Crawley; and like Lady Lufton in *Framley Parsonage,* Archdeacon Grantly learns that he must at last give way or lose his son's affection.

The scenes in London in this novel emphasize the ugliness of materialistic society. In the dark world of the Dobbs Broughtons and Van Sievers, only the acquisition of money has any reality. The world of Barsetshire, for all its petty jealousies and minor skirmishing, seems sunlit compared with this urban world devoid of all moral values.

The Last Chronicle of Barset closes the Barsetshire series with the deaths of two memorable characters, Mrs. Proudie and the Reverend Harding. Bishop Proudie, the classically henpecked husband, at last asserts himself on the issue of Crawley's innocence, and the shock symbolically—and perhaps literally—brings on Mrs. Proudie's death. The Reverend Harding, the Warden of the first novel, represents the balanced character that Trollope sees as the ideal: he is as honest as Crawley, but gentle and affectionate where Crawley is stiff-necked and proud. With Harding's passing, the world of Barset also passes into irrevocable change.

THE LAST DAYS OF POMPEII

Type of work: Novel
Author: Edward George Earle Bulwer-Lytton (1803-1873)
Type of plot: Historical romance
Time of plot: A.D. 79
Locale: Pompeii
First published: 1834

The Last Days of Pompeii *offers one of the longest and most sustained fictional views of the classical world of antiquity. A work of scholarship as well as a romantic novel, the book has fascinated many generations of readers. Today, the style seems somewhat verbose and leisurely, but the author's craftsmanship and vividly portrayed characters have assured the novel of a place in literary history.*

Edward George Bulwer-Lytton, first Lord Lytton, was one of the most prolific authors of the nineteenth century, an age abounding in prolific authors. The young Lytton was born to a well-to-do family, educated first privately and then at Cambridge in the classics. After leaving the university, he married against the wishes of his family and consequently was forced to rely upon writing to provide his income. His early works were detrimentally influenced by Byron, but after publishing a few excessively sentimental novels he began to write criminal novels, an interest which was to continue and reappear in many of his works. He next became interested in the historical novel, of which *The Last Days of Pompeii* is probably the best example. In addition to this and many varied later works, Lytton is known for his translations from Schiller and also for a translation of Horace's *Odes*. Towards the end of his life he became active in politics, publishing pamphlets on various current issues.

Lytton visited the continent as a young man, arriving in Pompeii in 1833, with the intention of viewing the site. He remained almost a year, studying the excavations and writing his novel. The end result was a novel which recreated for his readers the life of the city and its inhabitants at the period preceding Pompeii's cataclysmic end. The author takes particular care to describe clearly and accurately the clothing of the population, their utensils, the furnishings and decoration of their houses, the construction of various shops, temples, and public buildings. Vivid descriptions of the customs and various forms of religion also color his work. Modern archaeological scholarship has proven certain small details of this novel inaccurate, but on the whole Lytton manages to portray with clarity an impressively detailed picture of a complex and fascinating society, made all the more interesting by his cast of characters.

The hero, though not the central character, is Glaucus, an Athenian. He is associated with all of the virtues ascribed to the culture of Greece in the Golden Age, and he is seen as the inheritor and representative of beauty and nobility. He falls in love with Ione, a fellow Greek, and saves her from the evil Arbaces, a necromancer who represents the dark forces of Egypt. The story is a continual struggle between Glaucus and Arbaces, representing the widely-scattered conflict between the Greek ideal (light) and Arbaces, the Egyptian mythos (darkness). In the complexities of the book, one finds only a single connecting thread, portrayed with delicacy in the character of the blind slave girl, Nydia. She is a composite of light and darkness, being herself Greek, but from that portion of Greece where magic and witchery abound, Thessalonia. In her, the conflicting forces personified by Glaucus and Arbaces are combined, and her personal struggle is in reality the central theme and unifying element of the novel. The triumph of good on both her personal level and on the main level of action is initiated by her love of Glaucus. The resolution of the novel is the victory of Glaucus/light over Arbaces/darkness, and the concluding pages place Glaucus again in Athens, now a convert to Christianity (the true light). The novel is therefore on one level a portrait of a dead civilization, and on a second level an examination of a universal conflict. Read on any of several levels, it remains an excellent, exciting work.

THE LAST OF SUMMER

Type of work: Novel
Author: Kate O'Brien (1897-1974)
Type of plot: Naturalism
Time of plot: 1939
Locale: Eire
First published: 1943

Set against a background of imminent war, the story of this novel is tense and stark, one of conflict between strong individuals. With great restraint and simplicity, Irish novelist Kate O'Brien portrays the struggle between individuals who want to be free and those who refuse to relinquish their selfish grasp.

Kate O'Brien was born and reared in Ireland. She worked for years in Spain and France, however, and was thus exposed to European culture to an extent rare for a graduate of Dublin's University College at the time. Her novels reveal her blended French-Irish cultural background, and she became one of the few cosmopolitan novelists able to treat the delicate question of Irish isolationism fairly and perceptively. Her works reflect deep understanding of Ireland's human qualities and the beauty of its culture.

The Last of Summer is more than the story of an intense love triangle on an isolated estate in Ireland. It is also the story of a much-criticized man, Tom, who refuses to be a fool, and of his mother, Hannah, who believes in Ireland's right to isolationism and in her own right to live among her loved ones on Kernahans Estate as she sees fit. The novel's action occurs during the three brooding weeks just before World War II explodes late in the summer of 1939. The wild love of Tom and Martin for Angèle is poignantly told. Angèle is beautiful "in a queer sort of way," and her oddly angelic, yet adult, innocence mesmerizes the Kernahans clan. The story's cross-cultural theme fades in importance before the brusque rupturing of the Kernahans' pleasant isolation on the black eve of war.

Character delineation is subtle. Allegedly spineless, Tom had suffered childhood losses when he was too young to grasp them; as a child, for example, he had seen his father taken into the living room to die from hunting wounds. Tom bore the scars ensuing from such incidents without complaint, and lived happily on Kernahans' Estate, the place that he loved best on earth. His apparent submission to the legendarily steel-willed Hannah was partially a deliberate coalescence of his will with hers. Tom loved Angèle, but saw that his duty was on the estate and that, unlike Martin, he was not free. He also knew that Angèle could not be permanently happy with him on the estate, for her heart was in threatened France. Tom thus resisted war's false glamor and mummery, along with anti-German hate propaganda, choosing to rebuild Ireland instead of meddling in Continental wars.

Kate O'Brien's novel raises the question of a human's right to live as he sees fit, fulfilling home and family obligations, rather than bowing to allegedly inevitable changes. But the true tragedy of the Kernahanses is that they have dwelt on an idyllic estate, untested by affliction, and thus have not developed their personal potential. Aunt Hannah, for example, while loving her family and blindly defending its right to be itself, is smugly callous because a geographic accident immunizes her from war's horrors. Some critics thus consider *The Last of Summer* a study of mediocrity. Others praise Kate O'Brien for not answering the issue of isolationism and self-determination that her novel raises. For the river's sound courses through the entire novel, broodingly noncommittal, just as it had in all the Irish stories that Angèle's father had told her as a child in France.

THE LAST OF THE BARONS

Type of work: Novel
Author: Edward George Earle Bulwer-Lytton (1803-1873)
Type of plot: Historical romance
Time of plot: 1467-1471
Locale: England
First published: 1843

The Last of the Barons *is a complex, involved, and fascinating novel of a troubled period in English history. Bulwer-Lytton presents the struggles which followed the Wars of the Roses and captures, with attention to detail for which he was known, the vast panorama of that society and its people.*

Edward Bulwer-Lytton's astounding success was due in part to an accurate understanding of the tastes of the middle-class reading public, which had been created by Sir Walter Scott's vast historical panoramas. But more than his ability to cater to an already formed taste for historical romance was involved in his immense popularity. Bulwer-Lytton was a member of the House of Commons which brought political reform to England that in its eventual success spelled the end of aristocratic rule and shifted the governing power to that same middle class.

In *The Last of the Barons* he tells the story of the downfall of the Earl of Warwick, a powerful baron of the House of Lancaster, who had managed to secure the throne for Edward IV at the expense of the rightful monarch, Henry VI, the saintly if unworldly head of the House of York. Importantly, Henry was also backed by the London middle class, the tradesmen and mercantilists who were themselves about to assume a measure of political power in the fifteenth century.

By relating with his evident approval the eventual restoration of Henry, Bulwer-Lytton was advocating the rights of the commons to determine its own political destiny. In Bulwer-Lytton's version of Warwick's failure and Henry's success we witness an express denial of the concept of the divine right and a delineation of the idea of representative government, a political philosophy which, if it was not accepted until the seventeenth century, in England found its initial impetus during the time of his novel.

Finally, in the wisdom, brave deeds, and demand for equality on the part of the London goldsmith, Nicholas Alwyn, whose heroics are accomplished at the expense of the power-hungry aristocrats, we see the author's democratic values celebrated, all designed to appeal to the political prejudices of the growing middle class of Victorian England.

THE LAST OF THE MOHICANS

Type of work: Novel
Author: James Fenimore Cooper (1789-1851)
Type of plot: Historical romance
Time of plot: 1757
Locale: Northern New York State
First published: 1826

This novel remains the most popular of Cooper's Leatherstocking tales, a classic story of the French and Indian War. The battles and exciting pursuits which constitute the book's plot are rounded out by interesting Indian lore and descriptions of the wilderness.

The Last of the Mohicans is the second title published in what was to become a series of five entitled collectively The Leatherstocking Tales. When Cooper published the first of these "romances," as he called them to distinguish them from the somewhat more realistic contemporary novels, he had no plan for a series with a hero whose life would be shown from youth to old age and death. In *The Pioneers* (1823) Natty Bumppo or Leatherstocking is in his early seventies. Responding to a suggestion from his wife, Cooper went back, in *The Last of the Mohicans,* to Natty's early thirties when he was called Hawkeye. The great popularity of *The Last of the Mohicans* led Cooper then to move chronologically beyond *The Pioneers* and to picture in *The Prairie* (1827) the last of Natty's life when he was in his eighties, living as a trapper and finally dying on the Great Plains far from his early home. At the time, Cooper did not intend to revive Natty in further romances. One minor romance of the forest, *The Wept of Wish-ton-Wish* (1829), was followed by a stream of nautical novels, socio-political novels, and nonfictional works of social and political criticism extending until 1840, when Cooper finally answered the pleas of many literary critics and readers, and revived the hero whose death he had so touchingly portrayed at the end of *The Prairie.* In *The Pathfinder* (1840), Natty is called Pathfinder and the action shifts from land to the waters of Lake Ontario and back again. Pleased by the resounding praise he gained for having brought back his famed hero, Cooper now decided to write one final romance about him in which Natty would be younger than in any of the earlier books. In *The Deerslayer* (1841), Natty is in his early twenties and goes by the nickname Deerslayer. In 1850, Cooper brought out a new edition of all five Leatherstocking Tales arranged according to the order of events in Natty Bumppo's life: *The Deerslayer, The Last of the Mohicans, The Pathfinder, The Pioneers, The Prairie.* For this edition he wrote a Preface in which he remarked (prophetically, as it turned out): "If anything from the pen of the writer of these romances is at all to outlive himself, it is, unquestionably, the series of *The Leather-Stocking Tales.*" Despite the many complaints, particularly from Mark Twain and later critics, about

Cooper's style, plots, structure, characterization, and dialogue, the Leatherstocking Tales continue to be read, both in the United States and in many foreign countries, and they seem assured of a long life to come.

In Cooper's day, *The Last of the Mohicans* was the most popular of the five tales and it has continued to be so. It has been filmed by American and British companies, and the British version was serialized on American television. Structurally, the novel is superior to the other tales, with three major plot actions and a transitional though bloody interlude (the massacre after the surrender of Fort William Henry). Cooper's chase-type plot, with bad characters chasing good ones or good characters chasing bad ones, has since become standard in many action novels as well as motion pictures and television dramas.

Romantic love was conventional in the plots of novels in Cooper's day. His portrayal of Duncan Heyward and the Munro sisters, Cora and Alice—who carry most of the love interest in *The Last of the Mohicans*—shows no originality. They are all genteel characters and they speak in a stiff, formalized manner that seems unreal to present-day readers. Duncan is gentlemanly and the two "females" (as Cooper repeatedly calls them) are ladylike. Cooper contrasts Cora and Alice as he does the pairs of women who keep turning up in his books. Cora, the dark one, is passionate, independent, and unafraid, even defiant; blond Alice is timid and easily frightened into faints—she resembles the sentimentalized helpless girls of popular early nineteenth century fiction.

Cooper does much better with his forest characters. Hawkeye is talkative, boastful, superstitious, scornful of the book learning he does not possess, and inclined to be sententious at times. Yet he is brave, resourceful, and loyal to his two Indian friends. His French nickname, La Longue Carabine, attests to his shooting skill. He is religious but sometimes seems more pantheistic than Christian in any formal sense. Hawkeye's arguments with David Gamut oppose his generalized beliefs and Gamut's narrow Calvinism. With his dual background of white birth and early education by Moravian missionaries on the one side and his long experience of living with the Indians on the other, he is, as Balzac called him, "a moral hermaphrodite, a child of savagery and civilization."

Chingachgook and Uncas are idealized representatives of their race. As "good" Indians, they are dignified, taciturn, even noble despite their savage ways, which Hawkeye excuses as being simply their native "gifts." Uncas is lithe, strong, handsome, and he reminds the Munro sisters of a Greek statue. Magua is the "bad" Indian, sullen, fierce, cunning, and treacherous. His desire for Cora as his squaw is motivated by his wish to avenge a former whipping ordered by Colonel Munro.

In addition to the love theme, which provides for the marriage of Heyward and Alice, Cooper includes others. Related to the love theme is miscegenation, which Cooper has been accused of evading by killing off both Cora, who is part Negro, and Uncas, who had wanted to marry her. Another theme is suggested by the title of the romance. Chingachgook is left mourning for his son, the last of the Mohican sagamores. He grieves also because he foresees the eventual vanishing of his race. Both he and Hawkeye despair as they envision the end of their way of life in the great American wilderness, which will gradually disappear. Implicit in much of the novel is the opposition of savagism and civilization, with Hawkeye realizing that civilization will triumph.

It is easy to complain of Cooper's faulty style, his verbosity, his heavy-handed humor (with David Gamut), his improbable actions, the insufficient motivation of his characters, the inconsistency and inaccuracy of his dialogue, yet many readers willingly suspend their disbelief or modify their critical objections in order to enjoy the rush of action which makes up so much of *The Last of the Mohicans*. They sorrow over the deaths of Cora and Uncas, and their sympathies go out to Chingachgook and Hawkeye in the loss of what had meant so much in their lives. Also, especially in a time when ecologists are fighting to preserve some of the natural beauty of our country, they enjoy Cooper's relishing of that beauty in his descriptions of the northeastern wilderness as it was in the eighteenth century.

Henderson Kincheloe

THE LAST OF THE VIKINGS

Type of work: Novel
Author: Johan Bojer (1872-1959)
Type of plot: Regional realism
Time of plot: Early nineteenth century
Locale: Norway
First published: 1921

The Last of the Vikings *tells the story of a Lofoten fisherman in a style as simple as it is compelling. The pictures of fishermen in the book are local in time and place, but they are universal in their representation of the qualities of courage and endurance exhibited by these intrepid men of the sea.*

The Last of the Vikings is an epic of the lives of Norwegian fishermen who spend the greater part of their days on the sea, and of their wives who are condemned to bitter anxiety during the months of their husbands' absence. In open boats scarcely different in construction from those used by their Viking ancestors, these fishermen, in constant battle with the elements, sail the long distance north in search of cod. Bojer vividly depicts the struggle against wind and weather, with danger lurking in every wave.

It is a simple story that Bojer has to tell, and yet it is most effective. It is one of those books that unrolls a canvas on which the artist has employed no bright colors to attract the eye, and yet the characters become living personalities and grip the onlooker. With a few strokes of the pen, Bojer can produce a striking contrast between the peace of the land and the danger of the sea. The peace on shore is a peace made almost insufferable because of the difficulty of the humble peasants of the Norwegian coast country to make a bare living on the land.

Kristàver Myran, the protagonist of *The Last of the Vikings,* is one of the great characters of modern Norwegian fiction. He is the embodiment of a starkly realistic spirituality characteristic of a race with special depths of darkness to set off the beauty of its northern sunlight. Kristàver had become sole owner of a boat with a reputation for capsizing so often that when it was put up for auction he was the only bidder. He had been a headman for many years, but only part owner in the boat; an occasionally successful fishing season did him little good because the profits had to be divided among six men. He owed for the boat, it is true, and would have had to go deeper in debt if he alone had to equip six men for a winter's fishing. It was foolhardy, but he had made his choice. This attitude is characteristic of Bojer's pessimistic realism or perhaps of a vague optimism in which things can get no worse so one strikes out hoping to improve his lot a little. It is not the sort of vision to lift the author into the charmed circle of the purveyors of gladness or of that benign optimism which is soothing to, and eagerly consumed by, some readers.

Kristàver's wife presents a touching picture of a woman who had passed the seventeen years of her married life on the coast but who had lived her earlier life in a valley among the forests and mountains and was now as little reconciled to her life by the sea as she had been on the first day of it. Kristàver was out on the sea the greater part of the year, chaining Marza to a life on the barren shore and filling her with such fear and unrest during the long winter nights that it was all she could do to restrain her impulse to flee from it all. She was as homesick now as she had been through the first year of her married life; she might do the work of two or three, but she never succeeded in working herself into a feeling of belonging.

It is in the person of Lars, Kristàver's son, at sea for the first time, that Johan Bojer tells of his own experiences as a Norwegian fisherman. He writes of a life of which he has been a part, and his vivid descriptions are the result of his experiences with the fishing fleet. He is quoted as saying: "I have written the novel as a monument to my comrades of the Lofoten fishing life." Bojer was a poor boy, born March 6, 1872, at Orkdalsøra near Trondheim. The greater part of his childhood was passed at Risen, on the other side of the fjord. He fished in the fjord, tended cattle in the fields in summer, and went once a week to school, to stay two days. On Sundays he went to church with his parents and in the evenings he sat around the fire and listened to stories. All was preparatory to the time when Bojer turned to writing.

Bojer's novel is a worthy monument to the life of the Norwegian fisherman and it is proving to be an enduring one. Bojer has done for the Lofoten fisherman what Bjornson, in his early peasant tales, did for the simple Norwegian peasants. Bojer's unique talent lies in his psychological study of the fishing society in which the fishermen and their families participate, an analysis as profound as any that has been made of one of the more complicated existences. Bojer is deceptively simple in his depiction of character and yet in this simplicity there is a ruthless objectivity and a dispassionate view. He declines to destroy his objective stance by interjecting himself in the novel or by interfering on behalf of his central figures. He steps back and allows the worst to happen if it must for his is an uncompromising realism stemming from his own experience.

No other Norwegian writer of his generation has succeeded in gaining the ear of the American public more quickly than did Bojer. Before 1919 his name was virtually unknown on this side of the Atlantic Ocean. *The Great Hunger* was the first of his books to appear in English. *The Face of the World* was also published in English in 1919. Three other works followed in 1920, which was the heyday of his literary activity. *The Last of the Vikings* is a work from the latter part of this productive period and while lacking some of the fire of his earlier works, stands unexcelled as a sea story in the Jack

London tradition of intense realism.

Stephen Hanson

THE LAST PURITAN

Type of work: Novel
Author: George Santayana (1863-1952)
Type of plot: Social criticism
Time of plot: Early twentieth century
Locale: Connecticut, Massachusetts, England
First published: 1936

This fictionalized biography of Oliver Alden, the solemn New England prig who was ruined both by heredity and education, is told with wit, kindness, and wisdom. The world of the protagonist is sketched in with tender satire, and the individuals he comes up against in his varied career are portrayed with both humor and shrewdness. An unusual book of intelligence and charm, The Last Puritan *has attained the status of a minor classic since its first publication.*

Novels and their authors are the products of time and place, of personal knowledge and observation. Santayana—a student of Josiah Royce and William James and known to many as a philosopher exclusively—and his only novel, *The Last Puritan,* are no exception. As with changes in historical interpretation, analysis of this book reveals to the informed reader of the 1970's many inaccurate assumptions and details, yet the intellectual and emotional challenge of the work remains strong.

The parallels between Oliver Alden's early life and the author's are not merely coincidental. Before the appearance of this volume in 1935, Santayana dabbled in poetry and literary criticism. The author, like his principal character, reaped both the advantages and the frustrations of a proper education in the blue-blood tradition by attending the Boston Latin School, and later Harvard. Born in Spain, and reared on both sides of the Atlantic, Santayana's rootless wanderings were transposed into the restlessness and uncertainty that Oliver personified. The author disliked teaching, but this activity provided a financial base for his habit of writing learned tracts; Oliver became a teacher because he could do nothing else. Both Oliver and his creator faced the dilemma of possessing demanding personalities in an imperfect world full of imperfect people.

For Santayana, Oliver embodied all of those traits that were popularized as Puritan: stoic acceptance of life's shortcomings, an exacting mind, and the inability to love another human being or to express emotion. Unlike the iconoclast H. L. Mencken, who defined Puritans as those people who feared that someone, somewhere might be having fun, Santayana was more sympathetic about human frailty.

The Last Puritan is an account of the decline of American gentility, and the sense of finality and fatalism that accompanied the demise of that tradition. The Puritan of early New England did not survive industrialization, but the essence of his life style and his ideals remain. The challenges of life to the original Puritans were no less real to Oliver Alden, nor are they today.

THE LAST TYCOON

Type of work: Novel
Author: F. Scott Fitzgerald (1896-1940)
Type of plot: Social criticism
Time of plot: The 1930's
Locale: Hollywood
First published: 1941

This unfinished novel is perhaps the most highly regarded fragment in American literature, for in it, Fitzgerald's prose is said to have achieved its greatest power, flexibility, and economy. The heart of the novel is the love affair of Hollywood producer Monroe Stahr with the girl Kathleen, who resembles his dead wife.

After the overwhelming success of his autobiographical novel, *This Side of Paradise* (1920), and *Tender Is the Night* (1934), describing the precipitation of what he later termed "emotional bankruptcy," F. Scott Fitzgerald settled in Hollywod. There, he died in 1941 while pursuing a fruitless career as a screenwriter. *The Last Tycoon,* Fitzgerald's last and unfinished novel, is a sobering picture of society written by a man who had experienced both ends of prosperity's spectrum.

Although Fitzgerald intended this novel to be ". . . an escape into a lavish, romantic past that perhaps will not come again in our time," the fragmentary novel has at least two qualities that transcend its nostalgia: the manner in which the narrative is handled and the characters' views of society. Cecilia Brady functions as both narrator and character and is able to piece the story together by collecting fragments from people involved in various incidents. However, by means of a retrospective device revealed in the novel's projected outline, she is shown to be as limited in her view of American society as anyone else in the novel connected with the motion picture industry. It is this limited viewpoint that gives unity between plot and theme to the novel as well as credibility to the characters.

Fitzgerald's decision to use Cecilia Brady instead of a detached narrator allows him to reveal only those elements of reality that he deems thematically essential. Reality is filtered through life in Hollywood; Hollywood, in turn, is revealed only in relation to Stahr; and Cecilia reveals only the aspects of Stahr's life that she finds interesting. The narrator functions as a personification of the illnesses of Hollywood life; the illnesses physically manifest themselves in the form of her tuberculosis.

The major significance of this unfinished novel is the evidence in its stylistic daring and social criticism that Fitzgerald was far from through as a novelist. The moral subtleties of Stahr's characterization recall Fitzgerald's greatest achievement: *The Great Gatsby*. Like the hero of that novel, Stahr is involved with the underworld in order to preserve a dream. The difference between Gatsby's illusion of Daisy and Stahr's professional integrity is the measure of Fitzgerald's own hardwon maturity as a writer and man.

THE LATE GEORGE APLEY

Type of work: Novel
Author: John P. Marquand (1893-1960)
Type of plot: Simulated biography
Time of plot: Late nineteenth and early twentieth centuries
Locale: Boston
First published: 1937

In this brilliantly constructed novel, the satire is double-edged, aimed not only at the society portrayed but at the style of the book itself, for Mr. Willing, the supposed biographer of these memoirs of George Apley, is as much a source of satire as Apley himself. The humor is subtle and often gentle, but always accurate and knowing.

The Late George Apley, considered by many to be the best of John P. Marquand's novels, was a turning point in its author's career. For fifteen years prior to its publication Marquand had, as a "slick" popular writer, enjoyed considerable commercial success, but no critical recognition. *The Late George Apley,* however, was immediately recognized as an important book and its author was promoted by the critics from "popular" to "serious" writer. This elevation was certified when the novel earned Marquand the Pulitzer Prize in 1938. Throughout the remaining years of his writing career he confirmed and further consolidated this reputation, although never completely abandoning the commercial marketplace.

The Late George Apley is the first of a trilogy of novels in which Marquand minutely describes and analyzes the social patterns, behaviors, mores, and conflicts in upper class Boston society during the rapidly changing 1880-1920 period. This novel pictures that part of old Boston society with Puritanical antecedents and commercial traditions, the second of the books, *Wickford Point* (1939), shows the decline of Bostonians with Transcendentalist ancestors and artistic pretensions, while the last, *H. M. Pulham, Esquire* (1941), examines the present day (1920-1940) Boston businessman as he tries to accommodate his geographical and class inheritances to the pressures of the contemporary world.

In each of these books Marquand explores the ways in which social forms and cultural assumptions left over from the past bind those in the present; how, in short, those environments which evolved to assure familial and social protection, identity, and continuity, become prisons for the individuals who inherit them.

This is most obvious in *The Late George Apley*. Actually, the book chronicles three Apley generations. George's father, Thomas, represents the old nineteenth century individualistic businessman. He is highly intelligent, austere, rigid, hard working, and uncompromising. His relationship with his son is reserved and formal, almost institutionalized, although he shows concern and, on occasion, affection for the boy. The doubts that are to plague his son are foreign to Thomas. He knows who he is and what his roles are as father, as businessman, as member of the community, and as "Apley." When he and George have their only real public disagreement, the older man emphatically quashes George's fuzzy democratic ideas: "You and I do not stand for the common good. We stand for a small class; but you don't see it. . . . Nobody sees it but me and my contemporaries." But Thomas is saved from Robber Baron status by a sincere Puritan "stewardship" ethic; he truly believes that the Apley position and fortune are signs of Godly favor and that the money must be conserved and shared with the community—but only on terms dictated by that "small class" of superior people at the top of the social pyramid.

George Apley envies his father his certainty and strength, but cannot emulate him personally. Early in his life he accepts the verdict of his Uncle William, and subsequently Thomas, that he is "not a businessman," that he is "too easy going" and "erratic" and so accepts permanent placement as an investment counselor (of other people's money), lawyer, and civic leader. George assumes from the beginning that his environment is the only one he "could have survived in," but neither he nor the reader can ever be sure. He is never able to test his well-meaning mediocrity; he is given the opportunity neither to succeed nor to fail, but only to fit into a predetermined groove.

In his youth George makes a few feeble attempts at nonconformity; he chooses some dubious friends, questions a few Apley dogmas, and, most importantly, has a brief, intense love affair with a middle-class Irish Catholic girl. It is squelched, of course; George is sent on a Grand Tour and Mary Monahan becomes a sad memory (until the end of the book). But throughout his life George is plagued by the sense that he is trapped and is living a life filled with activity, but devoid of action or meaning. The most important events of his life are family disputes: what to name the baby, how to prevent cousin John from divorcing his wife, where to bury cousin Hattie, whether or not to move the rose bushes.

George's few attempts to find even momentary respite from his milieu fail before they begin. He travels abroad, but carries Boston with him. "I am a raisin," he says, "in a slice of pie which has been conveyed from one plate to another." He buys an island as a masculine retreat from Bostonian formality and its guardians, the womenfolk, and before he knows it, the ladies arrive and "Boston has come to Pequod Island." Throughout his life he suspects that he cannot escape the "net" (young John's phrase) of an environment that stifles more than it supports, and shortly before his death he acknowledges it. Worst of all he realizes that it has cost him the one important thing that he might have had from his life—happiness.

As his father before him, George tries to pass the Apley ethic down to his own son. John rebels more directly and emphatically than his father did. His social and political views baffle and alarm George. John pushes the rebellion further by refusing to join his father's firm, by going to New York City, and by marrying a divorcée. He is much more attuned to the modern world than his father is, and his World War I experiences at the front have matured and sophisticated him. But, in the end, John proves to be his father's son; he returns to Boston and sets up housekeeping at Hillcrest, the family estate. George dies secure in the knowledge that the Apley niche in Boston remains filled; the cycle continues.

But *The Late George Apley* is more than a sad story of the environment's tyranny over individuals. For all of the bleakness of its conclusions, the novel is most entertaining and amusing. The comedic and satiric center of the novel lies in its narrator, Mr. Willing. Marquand decided to tell the story as "a novel in the form of a memoir" for two reasons: first, to parody the then common sub-literary genre of the "collected papers" and, more importantly, to filter the information about the Apleys through the mind and language of a character even more dogmatically committed to the proper Bostonian vision of life.

Willing understands none of George Apley's incipient rebellions and his son's more blatant social improprieties. Much of the novel's rich humor and gentle satire comes from his fussy, polite, pseudo-literary apologies and rationalizations for the errant Apley behavior. In the end, in spite of Willing's stuffy shortsightedness, the reader gets to know and understand the subject very well, is amused and saddened by his weaknesses and narrowness, but is finally tolerant of, and sympathetic toward, the late George Apley.

Keith Neilson

THE LATE MATTIA PASCAL

Type of work: Novel
Author: Luigi Pirandello (1867-1936)
Type of plot: Psychological realism
Time of plot: Early twentieth century
Locale: Italy
First published: 1904

Pirandello's most famous novel and the first of his works to win international acclaim, The Late Mattia Pascal *uses fully realized characters to probe metaphysical problems, particularly the relationship between semblance and reality. The events of the protagonist's life, strange as they are, are wholly credible, and are not without humor or universal significance.*

Themes and images present in other works by Luigi Pirandello are fully integrated in this tale of Mattia Pascal who attempts to become someone else by creating his own life, only to be confronted with the realization that the form one's life takes is created for one by time, circumstance, and chance. A related theme in this novel depicts the dilemma of contemporary man, and is presented through two images: the "hole in the sky" and the "lantern."

Anselmo, a character Mattia meets in his "new life" as Adriano Meis, tells Mattia of a puppet show depicting the tragedy of Orestes. Anselmo muses on the possibility that during the performance, at the moment when Orestes is to kill his mother, he would suddenly look up at the paper sky and see a hole in it. At that moment, according to Anselmo, Orestes would become Hamlet. Orestes lived in an age of certainty; existence was accepted as finite and knowable. Hamlet, as well as contemporary man, lived in an age in which the only certainty is that nothing is certain. Both the seventeenth and twentieth centuries are ages in which everything has become problematic. A hole has appeared in the sky causing us to question everything while seeking certainty and yearning for meaning in life.

Pirandello presents another aspect of the contemporary dilemma through the image of the "lantern." Anselmo tells Mattia (Adriano) that each one of us carries a lantern that projects a limited amount of light. This lantern is equated with the individual form in which we live, a form imposed upon us by internal as well as external necessities. In addition, we are subject to the social lantern, by such constructs of our particular society as virtue and truth, that impose limitations upon the freedom of life. These lanterns cause us to believe that everything outside the limited vision of our projection is darkness. Were we to extinguish the lanterns, we would see that there is no darkness, only light (or life) that we had not seen because we were confined within our narrow constructs.

Mattia Pascal attempts to escape these narrow constructs by clinging to his old form, but soon realizes the situation he desires is impossible. In order to exist he finds that he must take on some form. And while he attempts to create a new existence for himself (that of Adriano Meis), this new existence gradually assumes the shape of his former existence. In desperation, Adriano is "killed" to enable Mattia to live once more.

On his return to his home town, however, Mattia is confronted with a new situation, the marriage of his former wife and a friend. Whereas Mattia (as Adriano) had attempted to remove himself from life, time, and change, the characters of his former existence had continued to live in time and thus had changed. He finds that he cannot return as Mattia Pascal, but must accommodate himself to the new situation by becoming "the late Mattia Pascal."

LAVENGRO

Type of work: Novel
Author: George Henry Borrow (1803-1881)
Type of plot: Simulated autobiography
Time of plot: Nineteenth century
Locale: England, Scotland, Ireland
First published: 1851

Lavengro *is a long novel, in part fiction and in part autobiography, which gives an interesting and unusual picture of England during the early nineteenth century. The book tells of nomadic gipsy life and offers character studies of tinkers, beggars, and thieves who roamed the English highways more than a hundred years ago.*

Lavengro may or may not be an autobiographical novel. George Borrow was trained in law and traveled widely; yet, his primary interest was literature. How much of himself he put into that literature—and how much he fantasized—is really irrelevant, for the writing itself must stand on its own merits. And Borrow's writing has considerable merit. Although he contributed to the *Newgate Calendar*—a compilation of infamous crimes—Borrow is best known for the novels about gipsy life: *The Zincali* (1841), *Lavengro,* and *The Romany Rye* (1857). That Borrow was well traveled and proficient in languages may account for some of his knowledge of and easy entrée into non-Anglo cultures, hence his familiarity with esoteric customs.

As Borrow depicts it, Romany life certainly differs from Western European life. *Lavengro,* in the Romany tongue, means "philologist"—a student of languages. In Borrow's novel, the lust for language amounts to a lust for life—a theme carried more or less explicitly through his other novels. Knowledge of languages is the key to a gipsy's survival, since the gipsy is by definition a nomad and must adapt to differing linguistic circumstances upon a moment's notice. Linguistic facility is thus at a premium; hence, Borrow's novel is aptly titled to suggest the central ingredient in a gipsy's life.

One consequence of the peripatetic Romany life, however, is a selective skepticism toward political and religious institutions. Here, *Lavengro* delivers the message clearly: Popery, radicalism, and anything inimical to the Church of England were abhorrent, Romany customs nothwithstanding. Gipsies can adapt to and live within a system while still maintaining their own customs and integrity. But because their way of life is dissident, they cannot tolerate dissidents from their own ranks, as these individuals endanger the gipsy community's safety. Borrow has really not been given proper credit for this astute political insight, for he demonstrates it rather than preaches it.

To nineteenth century readers, Borrow's *Lavengro* was at least a curiosity and at most a perplexity. It depicted a totally foreign way of life—something exotic and appealing, yet simultaneously repugnant for its unconventional ways. The Western reader, even today, may be caught in such a dilemma. For all the compelling fascination of *Lavengro,* the novel nonetheless depicts an experience largely alien to the Western reader because gipsies are essentially private people with their own customs and values. Assimilation with the dominant culture is incompatible with Romany life. From this novel, the Western reader can understand the features which human beings hold in common as well as appreciate differences which may seem anomalous.

THE LAY OF THE LAST MINSTREL

Type of work: Poem
Author: Sir Walter Scott (1771-1832)
Type of plot: Semihistorical romance
Time of plot: Mid-sixteenth century
Locale: The Scottish Border
First published: 1805

This semihistorical long poem describes the manners and scenery of the Scottish Border country during the middle of the sixteenth century. As in Scott's other metrical romances, he tells a picturesque story vividly and paints scenes with the skill of a great artist.

In *The Minstrelsy of the Scottish Border* (1802-1803) Scott had collected authentic ballads and revised some that were imperfect. *The Lay of the Last Minstrel* (1805) was the first of his series of original "metrical histories." Although *Marmion* (1808) is of greater literary merit, *The Lay of the Last Minstrel* is the poem that changed Scott's life. The enormous popularity of the poem (it sold an astounding 30,000 copies) induced Scott to abandon his work as a lawyer and part-time antiquarian in favor of a literary career. Whatever the poem's defects of plot and structure, it was full of the mystery and the Romantic manner the public longed for and it was all the more attractive because the bizarre matter was native British lore.

The poem is a medieval romance gone wild, compounded of supernatural events, folk motifs, and loosely connected episodes, but without a central, controlling theme. Its most effective element is the narrator, who allows Scott to imitate the oral character of balladry. The origins of the poem, as described by Scott, were in a commission from the Countess of Dalkeith to render the weird story of Boblin Gilpin Horner. The poem developed randomly so that the Gilpin (or dwarf) episodes now ironically seem unassimilated excrescences.

Scott recognized the limitations of the extreme regularity of the traditional ballad meter. He was influenced by Coleridge's *Christabel* to allow himself greater freedom in the construction of rhythms and stanzas, although he does not always escape a kind of formulaic doggerel. Scott also attempted to assume the linguistic simplicity of the Lake poets and he is generally successful despite an appropriately archaic diction. The greatest virtue of *The Lay of the Last Minstrel,* removed from the context of contemporary taste, is as a finger exercise in narrative techniques for Scott's subsequent novels.

LAZARILLO DE TORMES

Type of work: Novel
Author: Unknown
Type of plot: Picaresque romance
Time of plot: Sixteenth century
Locale: Spain
First published: 1553

This early picaresque novel is actually a series of brief sketches which give a vivid picture of the stratagems used by the poor to stay alive. Without a trace of self-pity the author shows the humorous side of continual penury and want. The book greatly influenced later picaresque tales such as Gil Blas.

In the fifteenth and sixteenth centuries, the Spanish novel began to develop into the modern form in which we now know it. This early novel form—particularly during the sixteenth century, the Spanish Golden Age of literature—evolved into four types. The earliest was the novel of chivalry. *Amadís de Gaul,* written in about the mid-fourteenth century but not published until 1508, is one of the best known of this type. Next in chronological order was the dramatic novel—a novel in dialogue—of which *La Celestina* is the prime exemplar. The other two types appeared at approximately the same time, mid-sixteenth century. One was the pastoral novel, the first and greatest being Jorge de Montemayor's *La Diana.* The other was the picaresque novel, exemplified by *Lazarillo de Tormes (La vida de Lazarillo de Tormes y de sus fortunas y adversidades).*

The anonymous *Lazarillo* is generally conceded to be the earliest and the best of the picaresque novels. Episodic in form, the picaresque novel's narrative is usually told in the first person, the story dealing with the life of a *pícaro* or rogue, who is both narrator and protagonist. In spite of much scholarly investigation, the origin of the terms *picaresque* and *pícaro* is still doubtful, and etymological research has so far proved fruitless. However, *pícaro* is understood to designate a wandering knave, a poor adventurer, who lives by his wits on the fringes of a class-conscious society and who must subordinate the luxury of ethics to the necessities of survival—in other words, the very essence of Lazarillo. Since the *pícaro* typically serves several masters sequentially and in the course of his service observes their weaknesses and those of others, the picaresque novel becomes an ideal vehicle for depicting a wide cross-section of society and, with its satirical tone, manages to attack broad segments of that society in the process. Of course, these picaresque elements of satire, parody, caricature, and the like were not unique to picaresque novels; they also existed in earlier literature—such as Juan Ruiz, the Archpriest of Hita's *El libro de buen amor* and Fernando de Rojas' *La Celestina* —which influenced the development of the picaresque novel. Still, it was in the picaresque novel that society was held up to most careful scrutiny and given the most scathing denunciation.

In addition, *Lazarillo de Tormes* is often thought, by virtue of its form, to be autobiographical. The likelihood of such an eventuality, however, is slim. The anonymous author refers to Latin authors—improbable for a real-life Lazarillo—and reveals a distinct influence of the philosopher Erasmus—equally improbable for Lazarillo whose formal education might charitably be described as lacking. But the intrinsically fascinating adventures of Lazarillo need no autobiographical buttress. The instant and enduring popularity of the novel—three editions from 1554 alone are extant—is testimony to its compelling qualities as literature. So, too, is the number of translations: French, English, Dutch, German, and Italian versions appeared within less than seventy years of *Lazarillo's* first publication; others followed. Imitation is another gauge of the novel's popularity and influence: in addition to Le Sage's *Gil Blas,* among many others, there were even two sequels to *Lazarillo* written. Perhaps the ultimate accolade, however, was that the novel was placed on the *Index librorum prohibitorum* for its anti-clericalism. (This anti-clericalism is routinely attributed to the influence of Erasmus.) The work's popularity and influence evidently posed a threat to the Roman Catholic Church.

As a character, Lazarillo is not original, cut from the whole cloth of the author's imagination. Before becoming the novel's protagonist, he was a character in folklore, with his name appearing in early proverbs and anecdotes. In fact, a quarter century before *Lazarillo de Tormes* was published, Lazarillo had a cameo role in Francisco Delicado's novel *La lozana andaluza,* which features a *pícara,* a female rogue after the *La Celestina* model. Following *Lazarillo de Tormes,* however, Lazarillo himself became such a staple that the very name itself became a generic term. Most particularly, the name was associated with the first episode in the novel: Lazarillo's service to the blind man. Hence, *un lazarillo* is, even now, a term used to designate a guide for blind persons.

Nevertheless, the most important aspect of *Lazarillo de Tormes* is satiric, and the targets of this satire are precise. All in all, Lazarillo serves seven masters before becoming his own master, so to speak. The story is thus divided into seven *tratados* (treatises or chapters), each dealing with a particular employer. The first is the blind beggar; the next, a priest; the third, a nobleman; the fourth, a friar; the fifth, a seller of indulgences; the sixth, a chaplain; the last, a constable. After narrating his unconventional background, Lazarillo launches his attack on social stratification, beginning with the blind man and continuing through the penniless nobleman and the constable. But his harshest commentary is reserved for the clergy—priest, friar, seller of indulgences, and chaplain—whose duplicity and venality are a constant source of amazement and embarrassment to him. Lazarillo's implicit and explicit criticism of the clergy constitutes the preponderant thrust of the novel. Yet

Lazarillo's observations are astute and the account accurately reflects contemporary conditions. Nonetheless, in such perceptivity lies a challenge to the *status quo,* a challenge which those in power must suppress, as they did by banning the novel.

Above all, *Lazarillo de Tormes* conveys a mood, a temper, a tenor: a cynical antidote to idealistic world views, secular or religious, which characterized the medieval age of faith. In this sense, the novel is refreshingly Renaissance, breathing clear air into a musty, closed era and musty, closed minds. It wafts a clarity which should, but does not, make the blind man see, the exploiter turn philanthropist, the self-seeking cleric become true shepherd, and so on. The unalloyed power of this novel in fact stems from its lack of malice: it deplores corruption, but it does not hate. Although it focuses on the lower levels of society, it is not Balzacian social criticism designed to reform. Although it attacks clerical depredations, it is not sacrilegious. Still, *Lazarillo de Tormes* is, in the last analysis, more than a bitter tale of personal privation. It is a realistic commentary—counterfoil to the competing idealism of somewhat earlier chivalric romances—on life as it is actually lived by common people who have neither privilege nor power but try to exercise those prerogatives in order to maintain or improve their positions in a hostile environment. Beyond cynicism and despair, it offers hope for better things to come, for Lazarillo ultimately gets his foot on the bottom rung of the ladder to respectable success. As town crier, he has a steady, assured income, even if his wife is a hand-me-down mistress of the archpriest of Salvador. Lazarillo is willing thus to compromise. The reader must finally respect Lazarillo's judgment.

Joanne G. Kashdan

THE LEGEND OF SLEEPY HOLLOW

Type of work: Tale
Author: Washington Irving (1783-1859)
Type of plot: Regional romance
Time of plot: Eighteenth century
Locale: New York State
First published: 1819-1820

American literature's first great writer, Irving was responsible for two trends in American letters: one toward local color and the legendary tale, the other toward the historical novel. This tale belongs to the first trend, and has fascinated and delighted readers for almost two hundred years.

The two best-known of Washington Irving's stories are "Rip Van Winkle" and "The Legend of Sleepy Hollow," both of which appeared originally in *The Sketch Book of Geoffrey Crayon, Gent.*, a collection of tales and familiar essays. Both stories are based on German folklore which Irving adapted to a lower New York State setting and peopled with Dutch farmers.

In "The Legend of Sleepy Hollow" the Dutch farmers make up most of the folkloric elements, for Ichabod Crane is an outsider, a Yankee schoolmaster among the canny Dutch settlers. As an outsider, and a peculiar-looking one at that, Ichabod Crane becomes the butt of local humor and the natural victim for Brom Bones' practical jokes. Most of the humorous sallies of the Sleepy Hollow Boys are in the vein of good-natured ribbing. But Brom Bones' practical jokes were somewhat more serious because of the rather unequal rivalry between Brom and Ichabod for the hand of Katrina Van Tassel. It is in the relationship between Brom and Ichabod that the common folk theme of the scapegoat is most clearly seen.

Other folk themes appear in the story as well. Among them is the belief that one can ward off evil spirits with religious symbols; thus, Ichabod sings psalms on his fear-filled homeward treks after evenings of storytelling. The distinction of having a special ghost—one with a definite identity—to haunt a specific locality is a matter of honor and prestige, highly respected as a folkloric theme. Here, the putative Hessian, the Headless Horseman of Sleepy Hollow, fills the role with grace, wit, and style. The character of the comely wench, over whose favors men wrangle, dispute, and plot is as common a catalyst in folklore as in life; hence, Katrina Van Tassel functions as fulcrum and folk theme in "The Legend of Sleepy Hollow."

These and other themes from folklore and legend appear in "The Legend of Sleepy Hollow" as well as other tales by Washington Irving, for folk and legendary material was one of Irving's two major interests, the other being history, a closely related field. As far as Irving's work is concerned, the two interests seem to feed upon each other to the mutual benefit of both. Irving's historical writings are thus enlivened by his cultural perceptions, and his stories are made more vivid by his knowledge of history. This symbolic relationship between Irving's interests has generally been neglected, and as a result, his other writings have generally been underrated. Although he was a prolific author, most people know him only for "Rip Van Winkle" and "The Legend of Sleepy Hollow." Perhaps it is now time to reexamine the entire body of Irving's work in order to make a more valid assessment of his place as the First American Man of Letters, the Ambassador of the New World to the Old, and the Father of American Literature, all of which titles have deservedly been accorded him by both popular and critical acclaim.

LEGEND OF THE MOOR'S LEGACY

Type of work: Tale
Author: Washington Irving (1783-1859)
Type of plot: Folklore
Time of plot: Seventeenth century
Locale: Granada, Spain
First published: 1832

One of the tales from The Alhambra, *this story shows Irving's love of the picturesque and his interest in fantastic and legendary narratives from many lands. It combines the qualities of reverie, gentle humor, and romantic imagination which made Irving a perfect writer of traveler's tales.*

When Washington Irving wrote "Legend of the Moor's Legacy," he did not have to rely, as one might expect, upon his imagination to produce the exotic and colorful setting—he had been there. When he lived in the Alhambra, a fifteenth century Spanish fortress, in 1829, it had undergone no restoration whatsoever; it was literally a ruins, inhabited by gipsies and beggars, invalid soldiers and ragged peasants. In the central court was a Moorish well which attracted a constant congregation of gossipers, storytellers, and water carriers who were the models for Pedro Gil, his wife, and neighbors. For the plot of "Legend of the Moor's Legacy," as for those of most of the tales in his collection *The Alhambra,* Irving fused together scraps of legends which he heard, and peopled them with standard folktale characters. For this reason, the story is familiar to anyone who has read fairy tales or folktales, stories of a traveler's strange adventures or Scherherazade's stories for the Sultan.

Irving's tale has all the stock figures: Peregil, the humble and kindly water carrier who is naïve about the greedy and scheming ways of the world; his lazy, nagging wife, forever dreaming of wealth and finery; the spying, talebearing mischief maker Pedrillo Pedrugo; and the corrupt and tyrannical authority figure, the Alcalde. The story itself is the well-known one about an honest, hard-working poor man who is rewarded for an act of charity with a great treasure and then almost cheated out of it, and who lives happily ever after in the end. What sets "Legend of the Moor's Legacy" apart from countless other tales like it is the author's skillful use of local color. All of Irving's writing reflects his love of faraway places and distant times, of the picturesque and the exotic, and is inspired by his desire to escape imaginatively from the humdrum actuality to these romantic realms. Thus it is that he so masterfully describes a sunset over Granada or a mule trail winding through barren mountains, a poor man's hovel or a cave brimming with ancient treasure, that each is brought vividly before the reader's eyes.

The original 1832 edition of *The Alhambra* was revised by the author in 1850. This later version, written nine years before his death, is superior to the first in that its several tales are unified by a common mood; they share a feeling of melancholy and longing, a sense of loss and disillusionment, mingled with Irving's distinctive strains of romance and magical possibility.

THE LEGEND OF TYL ULENSPIEGEL

Type of work: Novel
Author: Charles Théodore Henri de Coster (1827-1879)
Type of plot: Historical romance
Time of plot: Sixteenth century
Locale: The Low Countries
First published: 1867

A heroic epic based on folk legend and history, a story complete with visions, high adventures, traitors, and heroes, The Legend of Tyl Ulenspiegel *is well known to readers of most countries of the world. This account of the Flemish hero who represents the spirit of his native land remains popular to this day.*

Preoccupied with his Flemish heritage, Charles de Coster in 1858 published his first work entitled *Flemish Legends,* which was immediately successful. His new reputation brought him a job which freed him from material problems and allowed him to write. In 1867 he produced his masterwork *The Legend of Tyl Ulenspiegel,* an epic reworking of the German legends collected about 1519 by Father Thomas Murner and published at Strasbourg. Coster's version of the legends, however, bears little resemblance to the original.

The figure of Tyl was originally that of a lowly peasant turned merry prankster. His tricks and practical jokes, although often cruel, generally sprang from the impulse of an essentially good heart; they were most often perpetrated on greedy merchants, foolish noblemen, or hypocritical priests. The earliest written versions of the legends, which appeared in two different texts in Germany in 1483 and 1515, were satirical in spirit, and emphasized Ulenspiegel's triumph over his social superiors; his roguish adventures embodied peasant wit victorious over the snobbish pretentiousness of the townspeople.

In Coster's work, written in French, the character of Tyl has been infused with symbolism. Coster's hero is born during the years of Flanders' domination by foreign powers; Tyl and King Philip are born on the same day. Tyl Ulenspiegel is more than a mere peasant—he is the Flemish spirit incarnate. His destiny is to struggle to avenge not only his father's death, but the blood of all the people of Flanders who have died cruelly at the hands of foreign oppressors. Tyl is presented in symbolic terms from the very beginning, when his birth is accompanied by supernatural signs, portents, and prophesies. That his mission is successful is symbolized in the resurrection scene in which Tyl throws off the dirt covering him and rises from the grave, following his prophetic dream in which he envisions that he and his wife will never die, because they are Flanders. Thus, Coster's book is much more serious and fraught with meaning than the original legends, and as a result is less a chronicle of pranks than an epic of a nation. It is a work steeped in the richness of Flemish folklore, complete with scenes of brutal and violent death, redemptive virtue and humanity, noble high adventure, and mystical and supernatural happenings.

LETTERS FROM THE UNDERWORLD

Type of work: Novel
Author: Fyodor Mikhailovich Dostoevski (1821-1881)
Type of plot: Impressionistic realism
Time of plot: Mid-nineteenth century
Locale: St. Petersburg, Russia
First published: 1864

An unorthodox novel, this book is as much a philosophical statement as a work of fiction. Written after Dostoevski's return from exile in Siberia, it serves to point the direction of his later novels.

In *Letters from the Underworld* Fyodor Dostoevski creates a character—the "Underground Man"—who is crucial not only to his own best fiction, but also to the whole of nineteenth and twentieth century literature. Indeed, some critics even date the beginning of "modern" literature from the publication of this short novel and identify the Underground Man as the archetypal modern anti-hero. At the very least, *Letters from the Underworld* can be seen as the "prologue" to the five great novels that climaxed Dostoevski's career: *Crime and Punishment* (1866), *The Idiot* (1868), *The Possessed* (1871-1872), *A Raw Youth* (1875), and *The Brothers Karamazov* (1879-1880).

On the other hand, however, it is sometimes denied that *Letters from the Underworld* is actually a "novel" at all: the first part is too fragmentary and incoherent, the second too short and arbitrary, and the relationship between them too unclear to allow it that formal designation. But, in fact, the form and style of *Letters from the Underworld* are as radical as its content and fuse perfectly into an organic, if unorthodox (by nineteenth century standards), work of art.

The first part (subtitled "Underground") presents the Undergroundling's philosophy; the second part ("Apropos of Wet Snow") recounts a series of early experiences that explain the origins of that world view, while suggesting a possible alternative to it. Without part two, part one is little more than the bitter rantings of a semi-hysterical social misfit; without part one, the second part is only the pathetic narrative of a petty, self-destructive neurotic; but, together, they combine into a powerful statement about the nature and situation of man in the nineteenth century and beyond.

In the first sentence of the book the Undergroundling states that he is "sick," but later defines that sickness as "acute consciousness"—a malady characteristic of the sensitive modern man. This consciousness has made the narrator aware of the contradictions in his own behavior and the consequent impossibility of acting forcefully and meaningfully in his society. He feels superior to his fellow men, yet knows he is incapable of dealing with them. He despises them, yet obsessively wants their acceptance and approval. He acts spitefully toward them, yet feels personally insulted when they ignore or berate him. He asserts his need for dignity and then forces himself into situations that can only end in humiliation. The Narrator is not the first Dostoevskian character to have such contradictory, self-defeating qualities, but he is the first to be aware of them and their sources and so he represents a significant development in the novelist's career.

Even the Underground Man's attitude toward his own pain and humiliation is ambivalent. He does not actually enjoy his sufferings, and yet he takes satisfaction in them because they make him conscious of himself and give him a feeling of power over his own actions. The Narrator claims to admire the "man of action" who does things and has experiences unfettered by the doubts, hesitations, and defeats that plague the Narrator. But he sees a profound contradiction in the very notion of a "man of action"; although such a person acts, he does so not of his own volition, but as the end result of a long cause and effect sequence. This, then, is the basic reason for the Underground Man's rebellion; it is a reaction against the deterministic "scientific" view of man that was prevalent in the nineteenth century. If all human activity is regulated by environmental and hereditary factors, of which the individual is not even conscious, then man is reduced to the status of an "organ stop." The Underground Man denies that conception of himself, even while conceding that it is probably true.

This posture explains Dostoevski's apparently ambiguous attitude toward his fictional creation. While the author obviously despises the Undergroundling's pettiness, nastiness, cruelty, vanity, and spite, he clearly admires the man, because the Narrator possesses the one basic virtue: he asserts his *freedom* in the face of logic, self-interest, and nature itself; he insists on his "fatal fantastic element."

Dostoevski's real targets in writing *Letters from the Underworld* are the social theorists and human engineers who would "rationally" create the perfect society—symbolized by the "Crystal Palace"—in which man's happiness and fulfillment would be "scientifically" designed and implemented. The Underground Man rejects this view of human nature; he insists on using his free choice to assert his individuality. But the actions he takes to demonstrate this freedom are, he admits, meaningless. Thus, the dilemma of the sensitive insightful modern man: if he accepts a logical, well-ordered, "scientific" society, he gains happiness, but he gives up free will; but, if he rejects such a rational society and insists on expressing his individuality, he can do so only with impulsive, arbitrary gestures that have neither real meaning nor lasting effect. Is there any way out of this apparent impasse?

Dostoevski suggests an answer—or at least an approach to one—in part two, although the fact that the Undergroundling is incapable of seizing upon it underscores the difficulty of the solution. We also come to understand how he became the way he is. The action takes place sixteen years earlier and shows his contradictory attitudes in practice. He alienates those he would cultivate, plots revenge against "enemies" who are unaware of his existence, and creates situations that guarantee the humiliations and frustrations he fears.

After a number of minor skirmishes, he gives his theories a final test in two important human activities—friendship and love. Having forced himself on some old school acquaintances, he gets drunk and nearly provokes them to violence. Then, his attempt at friendship a failure, the Underground Man pursues the role of lover. He follows the others to a brothel where he purchases the favors of a prostitute named Liza. Upon awakening the next morning, he berates her for her profession, describes her inevitable and appalling future, and urges her to change her life. She responds with contrition and deep emotion.

But when she comes to him the next day, the Underground Man is in the midst of a vicious, demeaning argument with his manservant. Humiliated, he feels the need for "revenge" on her for witnessing his degradation. He realizes that it was a desire for power over another human being, not sincerity or compassion, that accounted for his moral strictures of the previous night. That power gone and his true pettiness revealed, he reacts brutally; she offers him love and he turns on her, rebukes her, mocks his earlier statements, and finally drives her off by "paying" for her "services." Sensing his pain and desperation, however, she demonstrates her moral superiority in her response to his tirade. Thus, the Undergroundling is denied even the satisfaction of bringing another human being down to his own level—a fact he realizes immediately after she leaves.

The Underground Man is, therefore, given a chance to escape from his self-imposed exile and he rejects it, dooming himself to pschological fragmentation and social isolation. But had he been able to accept and respond to Liza's love, he might have transcended the narrow confines of his narcissistic world and become a whole, purposeful human being.

This last positive possibility is a very muted one, however. *Letters from the Underworld* leaves the reader with feelings of depression and frustration. Although he espouses the saving capacities of spontaneous love, Dostoevski does not explicitly tie that love to the Christian vision which was to become central in his last great works. Thus, *Letters from the Underworld* remains Dostoevski's great transitional work, not just for his own writing, but for Western literature in general.

Keith Neilson

LIEH KUO CHIH

Type of work: Novel
Author: Feng Meng-lung (1574?-1645?)
Type of plot: Historical romance
Time of plot: 770-220 B.C.
Locale: China
First published: Probably early seventeenth century

A popularized history based on Chinese classics, this chronicle of the feudal states under the Eastern Chou Dynasty contains no fictitious figures. The numerous cast engages in political assassinations, incest, massacres, heroic actions, and noble deeds; the reader thus sees graphically the feudal world of China at that period—both the elements that tore it apart and those which brought it together.

Feng Meng-lung was more of a collector and editor of stories than an original fiction writer. His works were issued under various pseudonyms, and it is only through the careful investigation of modern scholars that he has been identified as the author or editor of the works now attributed to him. His prolific career was cut short by the overthrow of the Ming dynasty, which cost him his life. He was closely associated with the book trade in Soochow, where his great story collection, *Stories Old and New,* was published. Besides giving new titles to earlier tales and incorporating stylistic changes, Feng Meng-lung sometimes made drastic revisions in the works he collected, rearranging the sequence of events, adding new material and episodes, and remolding the plot of the story.

Three factors influenced the popularity of Feng Meng-lung's literary efforts: the influence of the storytelling tradition, the use of realistic narrative technique, and the prevalence in his stories of an urban middle-class attitude toward life. The championship of popular literature, short story as well as novel, by Feng Meng-lung was a significant literary event. Before his time, fiction was highly stylized and intended to be appreciated only by the court and scholars. His novels and stories, such as the *Lieh Kuo Chih,* were intended to be understood by the common people; they were written in the language of everyday speech. This "novel" covers nearly every phase of Chinese life: tales of kings and generals, of faithful friends and filial sons, romantic yarns and supernatural stories, as well as realistic stories of scandals and of daring exploits of brigands and thieves and domestic tragedies, even social comedies. The accent is always on a realistic presentation of life. Even the historico-romantic tales are described as happening in the present. The supremacy of realism in technique and style can be attributed to the fact that Feng Meng-lung always kept in mind the tastes and demands of the rapidly growing urban population, for whose reading pleasure this "novel" was compiled.

The richness of the details, the clever handling of plot with its surprises and crises, and a new articulation and mellowness of language marked a great and important advance in the development of fiction writing. True to the concepts of bourgeois morality, the characters can be divided into two clear-cut types, the good and bad. Tragedy results when the virtuous and innocent fall victim to the intriguing evil forces. But, in spite of near-tragic situations, usually everything ends well, in accordance with folk justice. The characters are not stereotypes, but are men and women of flesh and blood, whose individual traits are clearly depicted and thrown into sharp relief by the extreme situations of the plots. They develop and change as their conditions in life alter. They are so lifelike that they can be easily recognized as real and familiar types in traditional Chinese society. There is little doubt that Feng Meng-lung's sympathies were mostly with the weak and oppressed in society, particularly with women, who were victimized on every level of society.

LIFE IN LONDON

Type of work: Novel
Author: Pierce Egan (1772-1849)
Type of plot: Picaresque romance
Time of plot: Early nineteenth century
Locale: London
First published: 1821

This period piece about life in Regency London provides a detailed account of the amusements of the day, from cock fighting and boxing to masquerades and tavern-going. The heroes, known as Tom and Jerry, wander with good humor through their picaresque adventures. Egan's comic spirit made him a forerunner of Surtees and Dickens.

Pierce Egan's popularity in his own day was based on two works: *Boxiana, or, Sketches of Modern Pugilism* (1818-1824) and *Life in London,* originally published in monthly serial form and illustrated by George and Robert Cruikshank. The book was immensely popular for a time, and was the rage in London; at one point in *The Roundabout Papers,* Thackeray pictures himself as a boy getting boxed on the ears by his schoolmaster because he is caught reading a copy of *Life in London* which he has hidden behind a pile of Greek and Latin books. Years later, the adult Thackeray, in an article for the *Westminster Review,* relates how he was unable to find a single copy of the book in the British Museum and five major circulating libraries. Copies of Egan's tale are still scarce today, owing to the fact that the work lacks great literary merit; but this is unfortunate, since *Life in London* is not only highly entertaining, but offers one of the most complete pictures available of life in the big city during the reign of George IV.

Life in London is most often classified as a picaresque novel. Although it does utilize some of the more obvious features of the picaresque, however, Egan did not intend to write in that genre. The two central characters, Corinthian Tom and Jerry Hawthorn, are not rogues in the usual sense, but fun-loving rakes out on the town looking for a good time; Egan does not use their adventures as a tool for social satire, but merely for entertainment. Above all, *Life in London* is humorous. The plot is fast-paced, filled with madcap action from the first page to the last. In a breathtaking whirl, we follow Tom, Jerry, and Bob Logic from saloon to saloon, from Temple Bar to theater, from nightclub to dancing hall, as they sing, dance, drink, flirt, and generally make merry. It is said that Egan had intended to bring all three young men to ruin at the end, the proper punishment for their lives of carefree dissipation; but the young rakes are so lovable and captivating in their way that we are grateful to Tom and Jerry's original audience for persuading the author to settle them into happy marriages instead.

LIFE IS A DREAM

Type of work: Drama
Author: Pedro Calderón de la Barca (1600-1681)
Type of plot: Romantic melodrama
Time of plot: Sixteenth century
Locale: Poland
First presented: 1635

A play filled with vigor and brilliance, Life Is a Dream *uses its Polish setting as freely as Shakespeare used the seacoast of Bohemia or the forest of Arden. A gothic quality in the mountain scenes suggests the popular atmosphere of eighteenth century fiction. There is considerable psychological insight in this metaphysical melodrama.*

A dramatic genius and eminent mind of Spain's "Golden Century," Calderón resembled the gaunt, ascetic figures from El Greco's canvases. He was calm, withdrawn, reserved and courtly, and, as time went on, ever more religious and theological. Calderonian theater mirrored Christian principles but was best known for its "Cape and Sword" dramas featuring the delicate Spanish "point of honor." At one time, Calderón rivaled Shakespeare in European esteem.

Orphaned as an adolescent, Calderón wrote his first book while still a lad. He was sixteen years old when Cervantes and Shakespeare died. Between 1615 and 1619 he attended the famous Golden Century universities of Alcalá de Henares and Salamanca "the Golden." Even though declining at this time, Spain was still great, its red and gold flag floating over an immense world empire and its citizens excelling in many aspects of human activity. During his first literary phase following graduation, Calderón wrote poetry and one-act, sacred allegorical plays called *autos sacramentales*. He wrote his first major play in 1623, entitling it *Love, Honor, and Power*. As Calderón's star truly began to rise in drama—at which Spaniards were then considered Europe's masters—the "giants" of the Spanish Golden Age drama, such as Lope de Vega, Tirso de Molina, and Alarcón were closing their careers. El Greco had died in 1614, but Spain's most famous painting masters, including Ribera, Zurbarán, and Velásquez, produced some of their richest canvases during Calderón's ascendancy.

Calderón became a skilled swordsman, soldier, playwright, courtier, and eventually priest and theologian. He produced his masterpiece, *Life Is a Dream,* when he was thirty-five years old, whereas Shakespeare's *Hamlet* and Goethe's *Faust* were products of their respective author's ripest maturity. *Life Is a Dream* premiered at the Royal Court of Spain, and in the same year of 1635 Calderón was appointed Court dramatist upon the death of Lope de Vega. He was made a Knight of Santiago in 1637 (Spain had three great exclusive military-monastic orders dating from its earliest, medieval crusades against the Moors: Santiago, Calatrava, and Alcántara) and spent much of his life at the Royal Court, where intrigues and points of honor were rife. He eventually became the last giant literary figure of the vanishing Golden Age, far outliving all other greats. Information on the last three decades of his life is scant, but he is known to have lived calmly and in almost mystic seclusion.

Life Is a Dream has mysterious appeal, a will-o'-the-wisp lure. It is a metaphysical drama difficult to interpret, but moves its audiences deeply. It merits its fame as one of Spain's greatest plays, but puzzles commentators who strain to summarize it or probe its mysteries. Its verses are lyric and beautiful and it is prismatic, since new meanings can be derived from rereading it. Its basic theme is that life is a dream, filled with chaos, beauty, and torment. Thus it is partially based on the awakened sleeper theme (which Calderón did not originate, since it dates from antiquity as well as the time of Marco Polo, who brought back to Europe the tale of The Old Man of the Mountain, who drugged youths). Segismundo, Prince of Poland, represents man, but the play also stresses the evanescent nature of human life and the vanity of human affairs. It also emphasizes that salvation can be gained through good works and that, despite a strain of divine predestination, free will defeats astrological fatalism. Human bestiality is conquered by reason, while threads of freedom, grace, sin, and unreality are also a part of the play. The dramatic scenes in the tower and palace have often been praised. *Life Is a Dream* has basked in international fame for more than three centuries and still rates as one of Spain's most representative plays.

Oddly, few critics have detected that Calderón seems to have set his masterpiece in Poland because the latter nation was akin to Spain in its devout Catholicism, rich seventeenth century culture, and, above all, its heroic historic role as a defender of Christendom's "marches" against nonbelievers. (In Poland's case against pagan invaders from the endless East; in Spain's against Moors, Turks, and all anti-Catholics). George Tyler Northrup was evidently the first scholar to notice that Calderón borrowed much for *Life Is a Dream* from *Yerros de la Naturaleza y Acierto de la Fortuna,* a work that he and Antonio Coello wrote in 1634, and also set in Poland. Most characters in *Life Is a Dream,* excepting Astolfo and Estrella, had their prototypes in *Yerros de la Naturaleza y Aciertos de la Fortuna.*

Calderón was Spain's most poetic dramatist. He was thus influenced by the stylistic obscurities of the Cordoban bard, Góngora, "the Prince of Darkness." "Gongorism" was richly obscure and featured classical-mythological references, metaphors, contrived words, strained references, and the flaunting of erudition. Other features of the Spanish Golden Century have to be studied to understand Calderón. To appreciate his "Cape and Sword" theater, for example, the modern reader must comprehend the "point of honor" with which Spain was obsessed. A Spaniard's honor was a cherished possession, while personal dignity and family honor were also sacred. Male members of a family were vehement defenders of their family, and Spanish husbands were overly suspicious of wifely fidelity; indeed, they were prone to avenge even supposed breaches of it by dispatching their spouses.

The erudite Menéndez y Pelayo labeled Calderón a less spontaneous dramatist than Lope de Vega. He also felt that Calderón was Tirso de Molina's inferior in characterization. But Menéndez y Pelayo also rated Calderón above everyone in conceptual grandeur, poetry, symbolism, and Christian depth. In short, alleged Mendéndez, Calderón was history's greatest playwright after Sophocles and Shakespeare.

Calderón died on Pentecost Sunday in 1681, while writing an *auto*. He had ordered that his coffin be left ajar so as to stress the corruptible nature of the human body. His death left a void in Spanish literature, which declined into a long sterility; Calderón's theater, however, especially *Life Is a Dream*, has remained popular with Spanish and foreign audiences.

William Freitas

LIFE ON THE MISSISSIPPI

Type of work: Reminiscence
Author: Mark Twain (Samuel L. Clemens, 1835-1910)
Type of plot: Regional romance
Time of plot: Mid-nineteenth century
Locale: Mississippi River region
First published: 1883

Despite a certain carelessness of construction, Life on the Mississippi *is a vivid, dramatic, and extremely interesting collection of reminiscences. Like the mighty river with which it is concerned, the book has become part of the American tradition.*

Twain's book is not really a novel or regional romance. Generically, it is beyond classification—unless the reader is willing to be objective (and humorously enough inclined) to see it for what it is: an open-ended reminiscence, as rambling and broad as its subject, the Mississippi River itself. Readers of *Huckleberry Finn* (1884) will remember the dramatic role of the river in that work. Many critics feel the river is the structural foundation of *Huckleberry Finn.* Both T. S. Eliot and Lionel Trilling called the river a "God." It watches over Huck and Jim but also demands wrecked houses and drowned bodies as propitiating sacrifices. In *Life on the Mississippi* the river is seen with the eyes of a comic reporter, not the creative vision of a dramatic and philosophical novelist posing as a juvenile romancer. Nevertheless, the same characteristics that determine the river's symbolic function in *Huckleberry Finn* are singled out and examined here: the dangerous and changing channels, the mud infested villages, the floods. One way of reading *Life on the Mississippi* is to see it as the objective research from which Twain ultimately fashioned the art of his greatest story. Indeed, *Life on the Mississippi* and *Huckleberry Finn* stand in relation to each other much in the same way as the chapters describing whaling relate to the story of Ahab and his mad hunt in Melville's *Moby Dick* (1851).

The primary quality of the Mississippi River basin is its enormous size. How can such a geographic miracle be contained in a memoir? Twain begins by recalling his youth as an apprentice pilot. Even here the foreshadowing of Huckleberry Finn is astonishing: Twain learns to pilot down the same river on which Huck effortlessly floats his raft. Twain must master every curve, point, and bar. The feats of memory necessary to perform the skills of the river pilot are almost superhuman. "Nothing short of perfection will do." Just as Twain recalls first the map of the river as his mind mastered it, in *Huckleberry Finn* Twain had to strain his creative memory to bring back the Mississippi of his boyhood.

There is something humbling about the later chapters in *Life on the Mississippi*. True, they are fragmented and often look like padding. But there is an undeniable charm in their rambling quality: they seem to attest to Twain's continual deference to the giant and changing river. Although he learned its every curve as a youth, its natural evolution and the effect of social and technological "progress" astonishes him so much that he is reduced to gathering tall tales and newspaper clippings.

LIFE WITH FATHER

Type of work: Short stories
Author: Clarence Day, Jr., (1874-1935)
Type of plot: Humorous satire
Time of plot: Late nineteenth century
Locale: New York City
First published: 1935

This narrative of personal recollections is a humorous commentary on American manners in the Victorian age. Mr. Day's petty tyranny is seen as the last resort of masculine aggressiveness in a woman-dominated world.

Much of the charm and humor of the recollections in *Life with Father* are derived from the precise and careful detail with which they are narrated, which brings to life a past era. The stories suggest that the Victorian world was a golden, tranquil age, far happier than aggressive modern society. Clarence Day skips over those aspects of life in America that were not so pleasant for the majority who were not as well off as the Day family.

The book represents an interesting documentation of the relative positions of men and women in Victorian society. Mrs. Day can only obtain what she wishes from her husband by subtly maneuvering him, playing tricks, or resorting to tears and other "feminine" devices. The patriarch rules the household; his rule is absolute, for if it were not, such wiles on the part of his wife would not be necessary. The boys in the family also feel the strong rule of their father, but they grow up secure in their place in the household, and sure of the values which rule it. It is this security, above all else, which gives the Day household and the Victorian era such an appealing quality to the modern reader.

The powerful personality of Mr. Day provides the axis upon which the reminiscences turn; he is one of the striking figures in American literature. He is both a type and an individual, and has come to represent the Victorian father, the stern parent, and the dominating husband. There is no plot to connect the episodes, but the personality of Mr. Day holds the book together. The style of the book is simple and unpretentious. More than anything else, *Life with Father* remains a delightful social document, a glimpse into attitudes of America's recent past.

LIGEIA

Type of work: Short story
Author: Edgar Allan Poe (1809-1849)
Type of plot: Gothic romance
Time of plot: Early nineteenth century
Locale: Germany and England
First published: 1838

Poe considered this tale of terror combined with fantasy his best story. Ligeia *embodies perfectly the author's belief that in a perfect piece of writing, all elements—plot, setting, and characterization—must be fused and subordinated to a single effect.*

First published in the *Baltimore American Museum* in September, 1838, "Ligeia" was included in Poe's *Tales of the Grotesque and Arabesque* (1839-1840). The final text appeared in the *Broadway Journal* in 1845. "Ligeia" is one of Poe's most famous tales, and it is also among his most brilliantly written—he himself once declared it his best. He apparently considered it an "arabesque," a term Poe seems to have used to refer to tales which, though incredible or scarcely credible on the realistic level of meaning, are told "seriously" or without the tone of mockery or satire that Poe used in his "grotesques," such as "King Pest," with its fantastic group of characters, "every one of whom seemed to possess a monopoly of some particular portion of physiognomy," or "A Predicament," in which a lady writer tells in shuddery detail how she felt when the minute hand of a giant clock cut off her head. Critics since Poe have called "Ligeia" a tale of terror, since the narrator is frightened and horrified by what he sees, or thinks he sees, at the story's end. Similar terror is experienced by Roderick Usher in "The Fall of the House of Usher" and by Fortunato before he is buried alive in "The Cask of Amontillado." We see it also in a number of Poe's narrators during the harrowing experiences they undergo in other tales.

The narrator of "Ligeia" should not be directly identified in any way with Poe. He is simply the husband of Ligeia (and later of Rowena) who never tells us his name. Poe often employs a first-person narrator whose name is not given to the reader. He uses such narrators in "The Pit and the Pendulum," "The Tell-Tale Heart," "The Black Cat," and many other tales. Telling the story from a first-person point of view increases the final dramatic "effect," a predetermined element which, as Poe said in his famous review of Hawthorne's *Twice-Told Tales,* should always be the aim of a serious artist in short fiction.

Two themes in "Ligeia" appear elsewhere in Poe's tales. Psychic survival through reincarnation is the theme in an early tale, "Morella," in which a bereaved husband learns that his dead wife has taken over the body and the character of the daughter who was born just before the mother died. In the climactic closing scene of "Ligeia," the supposedly dead first wife, Ligeia, has (or seems to have) appropriated the body of the second wife, Rowena. A second theme, that of premature burial, appears in the early tale, "Berenice," and in such later tales as "The Fall of the House of Usher" and "The Premature Burial."

In fictional technique, "Ligeia" well illustrates Poe's skill in achieving the unity of impression which, like his "predetermined effect," he regarded critically as of primary importance in telling a tale. Throughout, the tone of the narrator is intensely serious as he tells of his two marriages. He dwells on his love for and passionate adoration of the beautiful, mysterious, intellectual Ligeia. There is foreshadowing when he speaks of his suffering and of the loss "of her who is no more." The final scene is prepared for in several ways. The description of Ligeia at the beginning emphasizes "the raven-black, the glossy, the luxuriant, and naturally-curling tresses," and her eyes are repeatedly mentioned: "Those eyes! those large, those shining, those divine orbs!" The brief, hectic excitement of the second marriage, to the "fair-haired and blue-eyed Lady Rowena Trevanion, of Tremaine," is quickly followed by the husband's obsessed memories of "the beloved, the august, the beautiful, the entombed" Ligeia. In the second paragraph of the tale, Ligeia's beauty of face is described as "the radiance of an opium-dream." This anticipates the actual opium-dreams which result from the husband's addiction following his loss of Ligeia and which accompany his loathing and hatred of Rowena. These dreams are filled with Ligeia, and the intensity of the husband's longing for his lost love is climaxed by her return as the story ends. When she opens her eyes he is sure of her identity and he shrieks " . . . these are the full, and the black, and the wild eyes—of my lost love— . . . of the LADY LIGEIA."

The theme of psychic survival is suggested first in the epigraph from Joseph Glanvill, with its final sentence, "Man doth not yield himself to the angels, nor unto death utterly, save only through the weakness of his feeble will." This theme first appears in the story itself when the narrator recalls having read the passage from Glanvill, which he quotes. He connects Glanvill's words with Ligeia when he speaks of her *"intensity* in thought, action, or speech" as "a result, or at least an index" of her "gigantic volition." After she fell ill he was struck by "the fierceness of resistance with which she wrestled with the Shadow." He recalls that just before she died she asked him to repeat a poem she had written some days before, a symbolic poem portraying life as a tragic drama with "its hero, the conqueror Worm," which finally devours each actor. As he concluded the poem, Ligeia shrieked and pleaded, "O God! O Divine Father! . . . shall this conqueror be not once conquered?" Her last murmured words were Glanvill's: *"Man doth not yield him to the angels, nor unto death utterly, save only through the weakness of his feeble will."* Yet her own fierce will to live did not save her from death—or so her husband thought. He left Germany, moved to England, purchased a decaying abbey, extravagantly refurnished its interior, and led to its high turret bedroom his new bride, the fair-haired and blue-eyed Rowena. But, though entombed, Ligeia continued to "wrestle with the Shadow." She filled her husband's memories and in final triumph replaced her blond successor. Or did she?

"Ligeia" has achieved considerable twentieth century fame as the subject of many widely divergent interpretations. It has been argued that Ligeia is not a real woman but symbolically "the very incarnation of German idealism, German Transcendentalism provided with an allegorical form." One critic has suggested that Ligeia never existed at all but was merely imagined by a madman. Another has called her a witch and still another a "revenant—a spirit who has spent immemorial lifetimes on earth." As for the husband, he has been termed a liar and even a murderer, who killed Rowena, his second wife, by poisoning her with the "ruby drops" which fall into her wine glass.

Perhaps the most acceptable interpretation of the story is a literal one. The narrator marries the beautiful, brilliant Ligeia and they live happily in Germany until she dies of a mysterious disease. He then marries Rowena in England but soon turns against her. Rowena suffers spells of illness and her husband endlessly dreams of his lost Ligeia for whom he longs deeply. His increasing use of opium causes his dreams to become so confused with reality that in a final frightening hallucination he believes he sees standing before him the beloved dark-haired and large-eyed Ligeia who has taken over the body of her fair-haired successor. By the strength of her intense will, Ligeia *has* defeated Death, the Conquering Worm!

Dramatically, the scene achieves the effect for which the Glanvill quotation prepared us. But that the return of Ligeia is only imagined is also prepared for by the narrator's repeated references to his drug addiction:

> I had become a bounden slave in the trammels of opium. . . . I was habitually fettered in the shackles of the drug. . . . I was wild with the excitement of an immoderate dose of opium. . . . Wild visions, opium-engendered, flitted, shadow-like, before me . . . passionate waking visions of Ligeia . . . a crowd of unutterable fancies . . . had chilled me into stone.

In his numbed state he has regained his intensely desired Ligeia, but surely it is a drug-induced "fancy" that shocks him into shrieking the words which end the story.

Henderson Kincheloe

LIGHT IN AUGUST

Type of work: Novel
Author: William Faulkner (1897-1962)
Type of plot: Psychological realism
Time of plot: 1930
Locale: Mississippi
First published: 1932

Light in August *is a study of the race problem in the South and of the psychological obsession with the Civil War which lingers there. A fascinating narrative with little regard for strict time sequence, the novel is important for its vivid treatment of a theme of wide social significance and for the intensity of Faulkner's moral vision.*

Faulkner was thirty-five when he wrote *Light in August* as the final explosive creation of the richest part of his artistic career that saw the production of *Sartoris* (1929), *The Sound and the Fury* (1929), *As I Lay Dying* (1930), and *Sanctuary* (1931). Only *Absalom, Absalom!* (1936) would approach again the intensity and splendid richness of this, his tenth book published and the seventh in the series about Yoknapatawpha County. Armstid, who appears in the novel's first chapter, is the same farmer of *As I Lay Dying;* and Joanna Burden mentions Colonel Sartoris in her account of her own family's blood-spattered history. *Light in August* is Faulkner's longest work, his most varied "in mood and character" (as Richard H. Rovere points out), and perhaps equaled only by *The Sound and the Fury* as a penetrating and compelling analysis of Southern society.

The style of this novel has often been criticized for its inconsistency, often pointed to as an example of Faulkner's "undisciplined genius." Indeed, its stylistic characteristics are manifold and complex: sudden changes of narrative tense, from present to past and back again; abrupt shifts in point of view, ranging from the viewpoints of the major characters to viewpoints of characters who apparently have no part in the main action at all; occasional use of the stream-of-consciousness technique based on the Proustian obsession with key images, or on what Joyce termed "radiating imagery"; the frequent use, also Joycean, of run-together words like "womanpinksmelling," "August-tremulous," "stillwinged," "womanshenegro"; the appearance of Joycean epiphanies, as when Chapter 16 ends with Hightower's "extended and clenchfisted arms lying full in the pool of light from the shaded lamp" or Joe Christmas caught in the glare of headlamps after the murder; the suggestion of Eliot's emphasis on all the senses—"an odor, an attenuation, an aftertaste"; and the use of Frost's simplicity of imagery, mixed with the kind of flamboyant poetic diction characteristic of Wallace Stevens—with the repetition of implicit interrogatives, and phrases such as "grown heroic at the instant of vanishment" and the "two inescapable horizons of the implacable earth." There is, in fact, awkwardly repetitious use of manneristic expressions such as "by ordinary," "terrific," and the adverb "quite" (as in "quite calm, quite still") that seem to support the argument that the composition of this admitted masterpiece was at times hurried and even heedless.

But the last two chapters of the novel—Hightower's rambling retrogression into Civil War history, and the resumption of Lena's travels (this time with Byron) as told by the unnamed furniture dealer who has nothing to do with the plot—achieve a sense of open-ended comprehensiveness that indicates Faulkner's epic concept of his novel. And it is the universality of the epic genre that may account for the apparently arbitrary concatenation of stylistic elements. Every angle of insight, every avenue of perspective, every mode of entry is used by the author to compel the reader into the world of the novel—a world complete with its own dimensions, of time as well as of space, of emotions and events. As an epic, *Light in August* falls into the genre of "search epics" that began with Homer's *Odyssey*. Joe is searching for a light that will give meaning to his existence, exploring, in turn, the light of McEachern's "home," the light of his adolescent town, the lamp of Bobbie Allen's room, the inordinate street—and room-lights of nameless Negro ghettos, the light of Joanna's candle and, finally, the light of the flames of Joanna's burning house—the "light in August" around whose central, sinister radiance all the main characters' lives resolve. For that burning light brings their identities into momentary and terrible focus: disillusioning Lena of her dreams of trust and security, forcing Lucas Burch and Gail Hightower to confront their cowardice, coercing Byron Bunch to throw his lot irrevocably with his love, ending Joanna's ambiguously introverted life in perverted horror, and, with supreme irony, ultimately identifying Christmas through the reaction of the outraged town and, through the identification, ending his search in death.

The novel is also epic in its thematic scope, a scope embodied in the ambivalence of Christmas himself who, like Homer's Helen, is tragically made to straddle, through no fault of his own, two worlds—neither of which will accept him because of his relations to the other, neither of which he will accept because of his inherent inability to be singularly defined. The two worlds, as Faulkner steeps them through the very fiber of his novel, may be described as a kind of movable equation—an equation generally defined by the Jungian distinction betwen the *anima* and the *animus,* and also by the racial distinction between black and white. On one side Christmas confronts his (possible) Negro blood, death (as stasis), darkness or artificial light, evil, fire, the female, sleeping, insanity, sin, savageness, violence, secrecy, cunning and deceit, softness, the fugitive state, belief, and passivity. Opposed to these elements, but also mingling and combining with them in unpredictable and unmanageable (for Christmas) patterns, are his white skin, life (as kinesis and fluid movement), light, good, the sun, the male, being awake and aware, control, righteousness, calm, openness, durability and determination, domestic security, knowing, and activity. "He never acted like either a nigger or a white man," one of his murderers comments at the end. Because Christmas could not find himself on either side of the equation, because his entire life was a confusion between the two sides, his epic quest ends in his own individual death and in the symbolic death of the community of Jefferson.

It is because Faulkner envisioned Christmas as an epic hero that he identified him with Christ—not only in name, but also in his peculiar silences; his master-disciple relationship with Brown; his capture on a Friday; the nurse who offers him a silver dollar bribe; Joanna's resemblance to both Mary Magdalene and the Virgin Mary; his thirty years of private life (about which the narrator tells of nothing specific); his refusal to complain when beaten at the end; and the town's final comment that "it was as though he had set out and made his plans to passively commit suicide." But *Light in August* is Christological only in the sense that it draws upon the Christian myth to complicate and deepen the essentially secular, sociological myth Faulkner constructs consistently in all the saga of Yoknapatawpha County. *Light in August* professes only the religion of man, a religion that must function in a world "peopled principally by the dead," as Hightower, the rejected minister, remarks. This is a novel of "mighty compassion."

Kenneth John Atchity

LILIOM

Type of work: Drama
Author: Ferenc Molnár (1878-1952)
Type of plot: Fantasy
Time of plot: Early twentieth century
Locale: Budapest
First presented: 1909

A story of love and loyalty among the working classes, Liliom *presents believable, living human beings in realistic and affecting situations. Even when the plot turns to fantasy, the honesty of the emotional thrust of the play gives the action plausibility. This drama has touched the emotions of millions of theatergoers around the world since it was first produced in 1909.*

Ferenc Molnár called his play a legend in seven scenes. True, *Liliom* has mythic dimensions, echoing Hungarian folktales; some have called it a Budapest folk play. It also contains elements of the fable. However it is classified, the play—after a tepid premiere in Budapest—has enjoyed great popularity, from the time of its first production in Vienna to its warm reception in North America. In fact, it furnished the basis for the highly successful American musical show *Carousel* (1945), although the adaptation ultimately bore little resemblance to the original.

Liliom's popularity notwithstanding, critics still dispute whether the play is so-called serious drama or "merely" a facile bit of entertainment. Molnár himself would be the first to point out the false dichotomy of these two positions. They are not mutually exclusive because a play can be both serious and entertaining at the same time. In addition, Molnár explicitly said in many places that he wrote to entertain his readers and his audience. In his best work—*Liliom* included—the seriousness is there as an organic part of the whole when Molnár succeeds in his honest search for truth about individuals and the human condition. He is not especially concerned with burning social issues involving masses of people; rather, his interest lies in people as unique individuals. This narrow concern, however, does not in itself necessarily render Molnár's work frivolous.

Liliom is so effective a blend of fantasy and reality that to distinguish between the two is specious. We must accept the heavenly policemen just as we accept Mrs. Hollunder's knife, and accept Liliom's return visit to earth on the same terms as we accept the reality of the attempted robbery. All are cut from the same cloth of Molnár's design where the surreal supplements the real to bridge lacunae in empirical reason. Artificial as this blend of fantasy and reality may at first seem, it is not without purpose, for Molnár uses it skillfully to explore the dilemma of mortal man trying to cope with hopes of eternity. In this sense, Liliom represents all mortal men.

In Hungarian, "liliom" means "lily," a slang term for a strong-arm man.

It is certainly an apt characterization of the protagonist, who is a bully and a brute of the first rank though nonetheless lovable and capable of love, as the final scene reveals. Liliom, in fact, is not an evil man—lazy and venal, perhaps, sometimes cruel, but not evil. He simply adapts poorly to conventional society, and his misanthropy magnifies his flaws. Lilioms, of course, have always been with us: men with Lucullan desires but meager ambition and limited talent have rarely lived orderly or happy lives. Insofar as Liliom shares the qualities of this archetypal figure, he transcends national boundaries and the other specifics of Molnár's setting and time to become a universal character type in Western literature, not just a quaint folkloric phenomenon. Much of the strength of the play—as well as its powerful audience appeal—rests on Liliom's sometimes unsteady shoulders.

THE LINK

Type of work: Drama
Author: August Strindberg (1849-1912)
Type of plot: Social criticism
Time of plot: Late nineteenth century
Locale: Sweden
First presented: 1893

The Link, *a one-act play in sixteen scenes, is one of Strindberg's briefer attempts to deal dramatically with the problems of marriage and divorce—problems which concerned him personally throughout his adult life. The "link" which gives the play its title is the child of two people who wish to be separated.*

From the beginning of his career, the conflict between the sexes was one of August Strindberg's most constant, even obsessive, subjects, and he produced several of the most memorable dramas ever written on the topic, notably *The Father* (1887), *Miss Julie* (1888), and *The Dance of Death* (1901-04). Although, as a one-act play, *The Link* may lack the scope and depth of the above masterpieces, it is their equal in thematic directness and dramatic impact. Like other great Strindberg plays, it begins as a starkly naturalistic drama and then, by the sheer intensity of the presentation, assumes larger-than-life, even symbolic, stature.

In the early moments of the play, the inevitable inequity and arbitrariness of the law is demonstrated. The young Judge has no experience and little training for his job. The jury is made up of semi-educated local types who vote according to their provincial prejudices and personal likes and dislikes. The Attorneys have no regard for justice, only a facility in manipulating technicalities in order to collect their fees. But it is the law, itself, which is the major villain.

The injustice to the Baron and Baroness is clearly foreshadowed in the treatment accorded to the honest farmer Alexandersson. Because legal technicalities make it impossible for him to defend himself, and he is unwilling to lie to the court, the farmer is fined and ruined on a slander charge brought against him by an ex-employee—even though the employee was guilty of the accused crime and everyone knows it. All are helpless in the face of an impersonal, absurd judicial system. The legal process, in Strindberg's view, is not a quest for justice, but a contest between manipulators and liars.

Thus, as the Baron and Baroness contend for the custody of their child, it is a foregone conclusion that the court will act in the worst interests of both. But, as the play progresses, the legal contest becomes secondary to the elemental struggle between husband and wife. *The Link* becomes a profound exploration of the tensions, conflicts, and passions inherent in the love-hate relationship between men and women.

Both parties agree to part amicably and not let their private dispute erupt into public view. Most importantly, they promise not to argue about the custody of the boy lest he be taken away from both of them. But once they are face to face in the courtroom, their competitiveness and need for self-vindication provokes an intense clash. Each accuses the other of poisoning the child's mind and of trying to make the youngster over in their own image. Thus, the child is not only a "link" between them, but also an object of contention that separates them. As they argue they become oblivious to the court and concentrate only on exposing and probing the most vulnerable spots in each other.

But as they do so they also reveal their powerful attraction to each other. "Parting is hard," he laments to her, "living together is impossible." Each sex, in Strindberg's view, longs to emulate the other, hence the struggle for dominance. So once they are put into opposition, considerations of logic and strategy must give way to the primal struggle: "Do you know—do you know what we have been fighting against?" the Baron asks his wife. "You call it God—I call it Nature! And Nature drives us to hate each other, just as it impells us to love each other."

The struggle ends, of course, in a defeat for both of them. The child is lost to the Baron's ignorant, narrow enemies on the jury. The final impression the play leaves us with is that of people trapped—trapped in a maze of absurd legal rituals and procedures that will financially and emotionally ruin everyone involved; trapped even more thoroughly by their own powerful emotional needs, frustrations, and hates.

THE LION OF FLANDERS

Type of work: Novel
Author: Hendrik Conscience (1812-1883)
Type of plot: Historical romance
Time of plot: 1298-1305
Locale: Flanders
First published: 1838

The father of modern Flemish literature, Hendrik Conscience revived a dying literary language in this and other books. This novel presents a period in the history of Flanders and the Flemish-speaking people in a manner similar to that of Scott; in its ample historical detail and pageant-like descriptions, it is typical of Conscience's work.

When the Kingdom of Belgium earned its nationhood in 1830, it was only after centuries of foreign oppression; but throughout that time the inhabitants of the Low Countries had somehow managed, in spite of incredible outside pressures, to retain a sense of nationality. Nevertheless, the feeling of unity in the artistic sphere was precarious and in danger of extinction when Hendrik Conscience began his drive to bring the Flemish language to life through a national literature.

When he began, Conscience was working with a debased dialect, scorned by the French and Walloon and rejected by the French-speaking educated Fleming; it was the language of the peasant, incapable of expressing complex ideas or emotions or painting beautiful images, and barely sufficient for dealing with the basic needs of everyday life. By the time of his death in 1883, Conscience—through his one hundred books translated into all the major European languages—had transformed this uncouth dialect into a language beautiful and lyrical, strong and sensitive, flexible and adaptable to all the demands of sophisticated literature.

Hendrik Conscience's fiction falls into two main categories. The first, which includes his most popular novel, *The Lion of Flanders,* is made up of stories in the historical romance tradition reminiscent of Sir Walter Scott. These novels are generally set in Belgium's medieval period; they are filled with scenes of colorful pageantry and heroic, daring deeds, and were intended by the author not only to demonstrate the beauties of the Flemish language, but also to inspire pride in Flemish readers by dramatizing their illustrious heritage. Because Conscience's historical novels have enjoyed the most popularity abroad, his other works have suffered some neglect; these are the novels detailing contemporary Flemish life and culture. In these stories, which have all the color, vividness, and rich texture of a seventeenth century Dutch painting, Conscience demonstrates his abilities as a first-rate realistic writer. His sympathy and affection for his subject, as well as his intimate knowledge of the simple and homely scenes he describes, give the stories a charm and glow all their own.

THE LITTLE CLAY CART

Type of work: Drama
Author: Shudraka (fl. 100 B.C.)
Type of plot: Tragi-comedy
Time of plot: Fifth century B.C.
Locale: Ancient Hindu city of Ujjayinī
First presented: Unknown

Regarded by Western critics as one of the two best extant Sanskrit plays, The Little Clay Cart *is more like Western drama than any other Sanskrit play. It shows realistically a courtesan in love with a Brāhmana and presents characters from various strata of Hindu society.*

The Little Clay Cart should be studied according to the philosophical thought of the East, although it has found popularity in the Western world because the tragi-comedy is similar to that found in Western dramas such as those of Shakespeare.

Hindu philosophy considers life as a sphere or circle. There is neither complete happiness nor complete despair because Destiny, or Fate, steps in to see that what seems to be an inexorable force is stopped and life is returned to natural sources. Throughout the drama nearly all the characters speak of Destiny and Fate.

The title itself is a complete summation of this "wheel of fortune" concept even though the section of the drama dealing with the cart is extremely short. Chārudatta's young son had been playing with a gold cart belonging to a friend. The friend then wants it back. Chārudatta, an impoverished Brāhmana, can afford only to have his servant make a clay cart for the boy. When the courtesan Vasantasenā, of whom Chārudatta is enamored, sees the boy crying for the gold cart, she gives him jewels with which to buy one for himself. Thus the circle is complete.

Many other minor circles occur to make the sphere a whole. Āryaka, an exiled prince, is imprisoned but escapes. The mad king is killed and Āryaka becomes king. A gambler who has lost his money and owes much, is rescued and becomes a friar. As all turns out well in the end, he is asked what ambition he might have. He replies that having watched the instability of human fortune, he prefers to remain a friar.

The overall circle that encloses all the rest is the story of Chārudatta and his lover, Vasantasenā. The Brāhmana has become poor because he has given away his fortune to help others in need. But his nadir is not reached until he is accused of the murder of Vasantesenā and actually has his head on the chopping block with the axe raised above his head. Miraculously, Vasantasenā appears and points out the attempted murderer, Samsthanāka, who is arrested while Chārudatta is freed. Āryaka, the king, whom Chārudatta had protected when he escaped from prison, names him viceroy of the city of

Kusavati.

The opening and closing dialogues by Chārudatta bring the total drama to its complete circle. In the beginning dialogue he is scattering grain for the birds and notes that when he was wealthy his offerings were of better quality; swans and cranes fed upon his terrace. Now the poor seed is thrown into the tangled grass where even wrens despise it. In the ending dialogue he remarks that "Destiny, as it plays with us, teaches us that the world is a union of opposites, an alternate recurrence of fortune and misfortune. . . ."

The drama is acted out in mime with no setting, as such, as in the Oriental Noh plays. A minimum of properties is used and each may represent a number of things, from an altar to a tree or a carriage. The tempo is rapid, with one scene following the next so quickly that illusions created by the actions, gestures, and dialogues of the players are of prime importance. The actions are carried out like a ritualized dance. Emotional impacts are played down so that viewer or reader has a continuous feeling of repose and enjoyment at the finale. There is no catharsis as in Western drama.

We learn about the characters through what they say and what is said about them. No physical descriptions are given; one knows only that the courtesan is beautiful, which is an abstraction. In *The Little Clay Cart* the characters are from all walks of life and their dialogues are apropos of their station. Vasantasenā comes through as the strongest and most astute character; Samsthānaka is the most pompous and ridiculous.

The play has much wit, humor, buffoonery as well as wisdom, which appears in similes and metaphors, aphorisms and maxims. When presented properly, *The Little Clay Cart* can be a delight.

LITTLE DORRIT

Type of work: Novel
Author: Charles Dickens (1812-1870)
Type of plot: Sentimental romance
Time of plot: Early nineteenth century
Locale: England
First published: 1855-1857

Written during Dickens' middle period, this novel deals with life in the Marshalsea debtors' prison and with the complicated procedures and inefficiencies of the British government and bureaucracy. In the center of this we have the pathetic figure of Amy Dorrit, known as Little Dorrit, and her bankrupt father. As always in Dickens' work, the narrative is crowded with memorable characters and scenes of London life.

In *Little Dorrit* Dickens deals directly with the worst trauma of his difficult childhood: his father's imprisonment for debt. In autobiographical notes written some years after that event, he inveighed against a system which inflicted worse punishment on debtors then it did on felons, and he claimed pity for the unfortunates confined in Marshalsea prison.

Nursing and comforting her father in that prison, Little Dorrit gives voice to these sentiments. But Dickens also introduces another view of the debtors in the novel: Folly leads people to prison which often results in an unbecoming self-pity. For William Dorrit, the "Father of the Marshalsea," self-depracation becomes a relatively lucrative profession. Nor is his malady confined to the population he rules. Few characters in the novel are free of the taint of moral self-indulgence. At one end of the scale, those who have injured others most deeply, Blandois and Mrs. Clennam, display their own injuries most blatantly. At the other end, with the best of intentions, Arthur Clennam loses his company's funds in stock speculation; Pet Meagles marries Henry Gowan hoping to improve him, but instead furthers his corruption; Flora Finching indulges her romantic fancies to the detriment of the real feelings of Arthur Clennam; and poor Tattycoram estranges her best friends in the name of some vague idea of injustice done her by life.

In this sense the whole world is a prison and all the people prisoners, isolated from one another by self-deceit. Still, of course, Dickens reserves his sympathy for those caught in the mazes of London. If they do pursue their own self-interest, they do so to survive in an inhuman world. It is not so much that they have chosen to become prisoners, but rather, like Little Dorrit, they have been born into a prison.

THE LITTLE FOXES

Type of work: Drama
Author: Lillian Hellman (1905-)
Type of plot: Social realism
Time of plot: 1900
Locale: The Deep South
First presented: 1939

Perhaps Lillian Hellman's major achievement, The Little Foxes *is both a technically well-knit piece of stage writing and a realistic and shrewdly accurate picture of one aspect of the rise of industrialism in the post-Civil War South.*

Lillian Hellman's play *The Little Foxes* is a story of illusion and sterility set in a small town in the South around the turn of the century. The principle characters are all members of a family, either through association, marriage, or birth. Within the major family are smaller family units, formed by the marriage of one major family member to an "outsider." These marriages serve both to break down the authority of the major family and to enlarge the reduced family by the addition of the husband or wife and any resultant offspring.

The Hubbard family members are marked by their greed and by the absolute lack of scruples which enable them to fulfill it. Oscar is characterized as a man who hunts daily for sport, having forbidden the town poor to kill game even to supplement their diet. He himself throws away all that he shoots, while depriving the poverty-stricken blacks of food. He and his brother have made their fortunes through a store which overcharges the town's poor, black and white, for food. A major image in the play is starvation. Hellman makes constant references to hunger and lack of food. The image of hunger (for love) is a powerful counterpoint to the hate-filled reality of this family. Both Oscar and Benjamin are avaricious, as is their sister Regina. The three of them conspire against each other and against Horace to deprive him of control of his own fortune. Again the author plays on the theme of deprivation and hunger.

Just as the Hubbards conspire to attain power in order to satisfy their insatiable greed, Regina's daughter Alexandra suffers from the effects of lack of affection. Her father being absent, her only source of affection is Addie, the black house servant. Hellman indicates strongly that of all the play's characters, only Addie, Horace, and Alexandra are capable of feeling a need for love. They are also the only ones capable of giving it, though Horace is not capable of loving Regina. These three are played against the three Hubbards, Regina, Horace and Benjamin. The contrast builds until, by the climax of the play, when Regina has in effect killed Horace, the conflict has become an open battle between love and the death of love. That love wins (barely) is indicated by Alexandra's leaving the sterile household of her mother to go with Addie, who also loves, in search of a better life.

Hellman's characters are made memorable by her sharp, bitter portrayal of them; there is an acid bitterness about the play characteristic of her early work, as also seen in *The Children's Hour*. In her later work Hellman left behind the anger and bitterness which pervades her earlier plays; but it is her early plays which are considered her strongest work.

THE LITTLE MINISTER

Type of work: Novel
Author: James M. Barrie (1860-1937)
Type of plot: Sentimental romance
Time of plot: Mid-nineteenth century
Locale: The village of Thrums in Scotland
First published: 1891

This early novel by James Barrie set in a small Scottish village is known for the brilliant portrayal of the contradictory, fascinating heroine, Babbie. The book displays Barrie's gift for character delineation and a spontaneous, whimsical, ironic style.

A master of situation and dialogue, Barrie produced his first best-selling success with *The Little Minister,* but the mixture of clowning and sentimentality in the overrich prose is perhaps not as much to modern taste as it was to that of his contemporaries. The Scottish dialect also might be difficult for some readers. But the characterizations are vivid and original, transcending the other dated aspects of the book.

Babbie is a character of contradictions, fascinating, willful, headstrong, and beautiful, and the mystery lurking behind her presence makes her all the more interesting to both Gavin and the reader. Gavin's sincerity makes his priggishness bearable, and the intensity of his feelings eventually transform him into a genuine hero. The minor characters, from Gavin's mother to old Nanny Webster to Rob Dow and the doctor, are all sharply etched and convey an aura of authenticity. The reader feels that if nineteenth century life in a Scottish village was not as portrayed in this novel, it should have been. A rich vein of humor, arising at its best from the characterizations rather than the situations, gives the novel a lightness of tone which makes more palatable the sentimentality of the tale.

The device of having Gavin's unknown father tell the story is awkward and unconvincing. The little clues placed occasionally into the narration are distracting from the main story line and confuse the reader without preparing him sufficiently for later revelations.

It is the impulsive, generous, and loving character of Babbie which dominates this novel and lifts it above the ordinary. She is one of the great heroines of British fiction; whether she is dropping barefooted from a tree, thrusting a diamond ring at poor old Nanny, or teasing and later loving the rigid young minister, she breathes life and excitement onto every page on which she appears.

LITTLE WOMEN

Type of work: Novel
Author: Louisa May Alcott (1832-1888)
Type of plot: Sentimental romance
Time of plot: Nineteenth century
Locale: A New England village; New York City; Italy
First published: 1868

This largely autobiographical story of four sisters growing up during and after the Civil War has remained popular for generations because of its realism and humor, its tough-minded heroine, and its innate honesty and compassion. The book is far less sentimental than is supposed by people who have not read it. There are more than a few hints in the novel of Alcott's concerns with equal opportunities for women in society.

Little Women long has been unfairly characterized as a sentimental children's novel. Actually, it is a surprisingly tough-minded and realistic book dealing with strong and resilient people and their efforts to survive in an often bleak world. In large part it is concerned with ideals, but these ideals are integrated as part of the lives of the characters. It would have been impossible for the daughter of Bronson Alcott not to incorporate certain ideals of living in her fiction. But Louisa May Alcott possessed a much stronger character than her father, and this is evident in her powerful and at times angry picture of the place of women in mid-nineteenth century America. Any reader who approaches the book objectively will note this continuous theme. The restless Jo, not surprisingly, bears most of the weight of this important theme. In her later novels, notably in *Jo's Boys,* Alcott was to carry on and intensify her concern with women's rights. The mature Jo, in that later novel, would actively encourage young women to study medicine and other previously unacceptable occupations for women. These aspects of Jo's character and Alcott's radical preoccupations are visible in this early, excellent novel.

The importance of the family unit was vital to all of the Alcotts and this conviction gives *Little Women* much of its power. The family circle is shown as a force which can help individuals survive against all odds, against war, poverty, narrow-minded self-interest, and social change. Individuals suffer, struggle, and die, but the family endures. At the center of this family unit stands the mother. But Mrs. March is not the saccharine figure which she often is supposed. In the novel, she is a tough and courageous woman with a temper which she has had to struggle to control and a character strong enough to hold together her family even when it is divided by war and other trials.

Above all, *Little Women* is a novel rich with fine characterizations. The portraits of Aunt March, of Professor Bhaer, of old Mr. Lawrence, and so many other individuals, as well as the March clan, have endeared the book to millions of readers. These people are not sweet, idealized figures, but genuine human beings, with faults and foibles and tremendous vitality. Louisa May Alcott's artistry was so unself-conscious and natural as to seem almost nonexistent, but it was this skill which created such memorable and real characters. *Little Women* has survived the patronizing of many critics and will continue to be a popular and loved book, because it is an extraordinary and vigorous piece of writing and because it presents a picture of human endurance that is both touching and inspiring.

LIZA OF LAMBETH

Type of work: Novel
Author: W. Somerset Maugham (1874-1965)
Type of plot: Naturalism
Time of plot: Late nineteenth century
Locale: England
First published: 1897

W. Somerset Maugham's first novel, Liza of Lambeth *was based upon his own experiences and observations as a doctor serving his internship among the poor of the London slums. Inspired by the manner of Maupassant, the novel is as blunt and unsparing as a clinical report. Maugham's prose, as always, is straightforward and unadorned, the work of a professional.*

Although akin to the naturalistic style of fiction emerging at the end of the nineteenth century, *Liza of Lambeth* is not as relentlessly bleak as George Moore's *Esther Waters* or Dreiser's *Sister Carrie*. Rather, the novel possesses a lightness of touch closest to the fiction of Maupassant, and Maugham has acknowledged that the book was modeled after the straightforward, realistic manner of Maupassant and was influenced by the socially conscious plays of Ibsen. The novel presents an eloquent—if implied—picture of the need among the poor for birth control. The irony occasionally is heavy-handed, but the boisterous humor of the slum characters is usually amusing and always interesting. The scenes of the slum life of eighty years ago are vividly detailed.

Liza is a girl of spirit, with a strong, if untutored, native intelligence. She possesses a vague desire to better herself, and would like to marry (since she can think of no other fate than marriage for herself) someone better than any of the men she knows. But her inarticulate dissatisfactions have no outlet other than Jim, the married man down the block. She is cornered by her place in society and by convention. Without even understanding her own feelings, she plunges ahead, hoping for the best, but not expecting it.

The only joy the people in the novel have is in basic physical pleasures: dancing and singing, running and playing games, eating and drinking, and sex. Their pints of beer ease the aches and pains of everyday life and their moments of lovemaking provide a brief escape into another world. But their pleasures necessarily are fleeting, and are paid for with years of boredom and drudgery. It is their lusty humor which carries them along, helping them endure their gray lives. Maugham catches with precision and economy the essence of their humor and the taste of their brief gratifications. Their efforts to make life bearable are all the more poignant for the lack of moralizing on the part of the author.

The pressures of the group on the individual are dramatically presented. As much as Liza and Jim want to have their freedom and bit of happiness, they are hedged in by the opinion of the neighborhood. Vere Street is the center of the world to Liza, and she cannot escape it, whatever she does.

The black humor of the closing scene, with Liza's mother and the old midwife, Mrs. Hodges, guzzling brandy and whiskey and gossiping, as Liza lies dying a few feet away, is chilling in its effectiveness, and worthy of Dickens. Finally, nobody seems to be to blame for what happened. The incidents of life just piled together, and fate closed in on Liza. Unlike the naturalist novelists, Maugham makes no plea for social reforms; he has simply presented a piece of life as directly and vividly as possible.

THE LONG JOURNEY

Type of work: Novel
Author: Johannes V. Jensen (1873-1950)
Type of plot: Cultural epic
Time of plot: The Age of Man
Locale: The world
First published: 1923-1924

The Long Journey's *title refers to the journey of mankind, for this epic book ranges from before the Ice Age to the twentieth century. It is a great work of cultural mythology, as well as a novel, a new integration and sensitive reinterpretation of the progress man has made in the world since that remote age when he first began to walk upon the earth.*

Although a winner of the Nobel Prize for literature in 1944, the Danish writer Johannes V. Jensen is little known in the United States—a remarkable oversight in view of the fact that for almost 50 years after his first visit to this country in 1897, Jensen was a major interpreter of American life and letters for Scandinavian readers. This preoccupation with the United States was only part of a larger interest in and frank acceptance of the modern age in all its nervous variety. Jensen's probing curiosity and rich imagination ranged over the whole of the modern world and found expression in a large published body of novels, verse, essays, short stories, and travel impressions.

The author was born in that section of Northern Jutland which is known as Himmerland, a region characterized by large tracts of somber landscapes broken only by a few sparse settlements and an occasional farm. His descent from peasant stock and a boyhood spent in play among the burial mounds of Jutland left a distinct mark on Jensen's writings. It shows up not only in a dry and often mordant humor but also in the fact that throughout his career Jensen kept his origin and the distant past which lies behind his people as constant points of reference. He was a prolific writer. Besides the monumental *The Long Journey,* he published a number of books dealing with a variety of subjects, often with his own interpretations of Darwinism. Few writers have done so much to interpret in creative terms the past of their own race and to point to the interdependence of past, present, and future. And perhaps no writer has caught the intimate charm of Danish nature quite as has Jensen.

The Long Journey, the author's most ambitious work, is a long cyclic novel of three volumes. Although some critics would find a place in the saga for some of Jensen's earlier works beginning with *The Glacier* in 1908, the three volumes generally regarded as comprising *The Long Journey* are: *Fire and Ice* (1923), *The Cimbrians* (1923), and *Christopher Columbus* (1924). The epic traces the long journey of the man of the North from the Tertiary forest through the rigors of the Ice Age and out on his many journeys in search of the "lost land," which in the author's mind is represented symbolically by the warm tropical forest of the race's infancy. Its aim is to show the development of mankind from primeval chaos to modern civilization. The narrative is in story form showing how the actual stages of the ascent of man and of the climactic conditions of the earth's surface have left their traces in mythology and religion. On a symbolic level, the work shows how the forest became a ship and the ship became a church until men like Christopher Columbus changed the church back into a ship in their quest for the new world. With the discovery of the new world and its natives the ship reverts to the forest and the cycle is complete.

The Long Journey should not be taken seriously as anthropology, yet to refer to it simply as a novel falls short of an accurate appraisal of its merit. It is a work of mythology which in the boldness of its conception deserves a place among the finest works of fiction of the modern era. It is similar in its effect to *The Divine Comedy* or perhaps to *Gulliver's Travels*—creative works that embodied unique approaches to particular stages in the evolution of literature and its applications to the world in which we live.

To the reader who is of the firm conviction that the account of the world related in the first five books of the Bible is literally true, *The Long Journey* comes as a heretical shock. Jensen is convinced that the world, as it stands, is open to various explanations. Although he is silent about evolution as far as direct statements are concerned, Jensen regards this theory as another and obvious interpretation of the advance of mankind. Few readers will contend, however, that Jensen wrote this novel as a conscious and scientific attempt to refute Biblical interpretation, or that he has unconsciously refuted it. Indeed, evolution, according to Jensen, is a strong proof ascertaining the existence of a supernatural deity and is probably the one principle of life that makes homage to God obligatory. He implies that the world would be found lacking as a piece of divine handiwork if there had been no progress, no evolution within the most recent thousands of years.

In many respects, *The Long Journey* is similar to Knut Hamsun's *Growth of the Soil* in that both novels go back to a primitive state of the world, both deal with elemental traits in man, and both rise in some instances to great heights as truly epic portrayals of the workings of the human heart. But here the similarities stop. When Hamsun's novel concludes, the sons of Isak and Inger have grown up, and even Barbro, the once citified lady, has married and settled down. So in reality Hamsun covers the period from about 1916 to roughly 1950. In contrast, when Jensen's Gunung Api stands in airy solitude in the third paragraph of *The Long Journey* chewing the fire within him, there was no fire, no ice; there was nothing but unmeasured time, millions of years before the Christian era. And when Jensen is through, Christopher Columbus has discovered America. Jensen does not note time except by its passing, and it passes slowly.

Jensen's work necessitated a familiarity with some of the more significant sciences such as archaeology, geology, ethnology, and mythology, for *The Long Journey* deals with the unfolding of a particular idea and the delineation of that theory of origin, growth, and development through a long period of time. Parts of the novel are ostensibly irrelevant in that they apply neither to science nor literature. Yet on the whole the work is a unique and epic treatment of the genesis of man and the world.

Stephen Hanson

THE LONG NIGHT

Type of work: Novel
Author: Andrew Lytle (1902-)
Type of plot: Historical romance
Time of plot: 1857-1862
Locale: Alabama, Mississippi, Tennessee
First published: 1936

A remarkable first novel based in part on actual people and events, The Long Night *is a work of originality and true historical imagination. The writer presents a realistic regional picture of ante-bellum life on the southern frontier and deals convincingly with the moral struggles of the young protagonist in a violent world.*

Andrew Lytle was one of the earlier novelists and theorists of the Southern Literary Renaissance. In the mid-1920's he was drawn into the literary orbit of the influential Nashville poetry magazine *The Fugitive,* joining such notable southern writers as John Crowe Ransom, Robert Penn Warren, Caroline Gordon, and Jesse Stuart. His contribution to the Agrarian manifesto *I'll Take My Stand* (1930) marked him as deeply and articulately involved with the reinterpretation of Southern tradition in agrarian terms.

One of the main concerns of *The Long Night* is the reassessment of shaken values in a South marked by change. In Lytle's story the McIvor family is presented as a unified moral force. Their private moral duty, revenge of the murder of the father, coincides with public responsibility, ridding the community of thieves and killers. Pleasant McIvor takes up his grim task with a vengeance, and in the first half of the novel systematically, single-handedly kills nearly a dozen of his father's murderers. The scenes in which he carries out his mission are blood-tingling, mixing local color and back-woods lore against a background of almost Biblical intensity of purpose. Although the novel is structurally flawed, the reader is given an extraordinary insight into the politics and morality of Southern frontier life.

With the onset of the Civil War the revenge motif, Pleasant McIvor's long night of retribution, begins to yield to a theme of moral development. The war, which brings into focus an entire civilization with its traditions and moral code, shows up the inadequacy of the old morality. As a Confederate soldier, Pleasant finds his personal vendetta superseded by the greater purpose of the war; his story implies that the strength of the Southern tradition, re-examined and reassessed, will inspire a new generation in the South.

THE LONGEST JOURNEY

Type of work: Novel
Author: E. M. Forster (1879-1970)
Type of plot: Social criticism
Time of plot: Early twentieth century
Locale: England
First published: 1907

In this novel Forster is primarily concerned with the story of a sensitive young man and the problems he encounters on his introduction into the world. Structurally and stylistically, the novel had a great influence over the generation of writers immediately after Forster.

Best known for his haunting novel, *A Passage to India* (1924), E. M. Forster's *The Longest Journey* is less exotic in setting but nearly as powerful in delineation of character and exploration of humanist values. The Cambridge scenes constitute Forster's affectionate salute to his beloved university, and the caustic portrait of Herbert Pembroke and Sawston School his bitter recollections of humiliation and cruelty at Towbridge Public School.

The "Longest Journey" is Rickie Elliot's development from unloved child to responsible brother, a process crystallized in his growth from an amateur writer of pallid and shallow fantasies to an artist of humanist insight. The debate that opens the novel about the "existence" of "cows" is an ironic prologue to Rickie's spiritual education; he moves from reflection on the meaning of objects to a sentimental marriage devoid of honest feeling. Not until his half-brother's brutal but emotionally straightforward intrusion into Rickie's life is he ready to confront the demands of his own heart and mind. Stephen frees him from his melancholic attachment to their dead mother's spirit. After his marriage he reflects on his mother and concludes that it is the "dead . . . whose images alone have immortality." After leaving Agnes he travels with Stephen to Salisbury and while looking at the cathedral spire hears Stephen boldly announce, "When a man dies, it's as if he's never been."

Inspired with Stephen's vital sense of life and nature, Rickie defies his strong aunt's insistence on the authority of "conventions" in life. Although Stephen's drunkenness indirectly loses Rickie his life, the irresponsible brother has already contributed to Rickie's immortality in art by inspiring his last and best work. Rickie will live in his work more vitally than he ever did in his life. Stephen has the last word when he upbraids Rickie's pompous cleric of a brother-in-law for trying to cheat him of his due share in the profits resulting from a posthumous publication of Rickie's stories. "There's one world, Pembroke, and you can't tidy men out of it." Men triumph over conventions—and cows.

LOOK HOMEWARD, ANGEL

Type of work: Novel
Author: Thomas Wolfe (1900-1938)
Type of plot: Impressionistic realism
Time of plot: 1900-early 1920's
Locale: North Carolina
First published: 1929

An attempt to re-create the whole American experience in Wolfe's own terms, this sprawling novel combines a large cast of brilliant and vital characters and a chaotic, romantic representation of the United States in the early days of this century. In the center of this swirling mass stands the young hero Eugene Gant—Wolfe himself—trying to cope with the world and with his own emotions and genius.

Essentially plotless, *Look Homeward, Angel* covers roughly the first twenty years of the life of both Thomas Wolfe and his autobiographic hero, Eugene Gant. The three sections of the novel portray the first three stages in Eugene's life: his first twelve years, his four years at the Leonards' school, and his four years at the university. Wolfe's subtitle, "A Story of the Buried Life," partly suggests the way in which the story is developed. Though there is much external action, talk, and description, the reader is frequently taken into the consciousness of Eugene as well as into that of Ben, of Eliza, and of Gant. Eugene's double inheritance from his rhetoric-spouting, self-pitying, histrionic father and his more practical and dominating mother, brings him into a series of conflicts with family, school, society, and all that is outside himself. He is the young artist seeking isolation from a world that constantly impinges upon him. Like most highly imaginative and passionately intense young persons, he reacts through both mind and senses to this external world, and his responses are often phrased in a lyrical prose that sweeps the reader emotionally along with Eugene. Young Gant is inclined to take himself very seriously, as when he becomes a hero in his many fantasies. Yet he is capable of self-mockery, particularly as he is growing out of adolescence during his university years. Stylistically, the novel shows an amazing variety: sensuous, evocative description; symbolism with shifting meanings; realistic, pungent dialogue; bawdy humor; parody and burlesque; satire; fantasy; and dithyrambic passages in which the author becomes intoxicated with the flow of his own words. The shifts of style are often so abrupt that the reader needs a keen awareness to appreciate what Wolfe is doing. *Look Homeward, Angel* is a novel of youth slowly developing into maturity, and perhaps it is best appreciated by readers who can more or less identify with young Eugene. Yet older readers can also lose themselves in it, remembering the turmoil, the joys, and the sorrows of their own maturation.

LOOKING BACKWARD

Type of work: Novel
Author: Edward Bellamy (1850-1898)
Type of plot: Utopian romance
Time of plot: A.D. 2000
Locale: Boston, Massachusetts
First published: 1888

The main interest of Looking Backward: 2000–1887 *lies in its credible presentation of a socialist Utopia; the book has served to introduce many people to the theory of socialism. Its prophecies for the world by the year 2000 are sometimes strikingly shrewd, and the judgments made of modern society are pointed and witty.*

Not even Skinner's renowned *Walden Two* promises to replace *Looking Backward* as America's premier utopian novel. Commonly judged one of the most influential American publications of the period 1885-1935, *Looking Backward* inspired the formation of 150 "Nationalist" clubs and strengthened the Populist cause. Its success derived from its having presented socialism in a way which made the idea uniquely appealing to Americans.

Bellamy disarmed his skeptical readers by viewing socialism as the natural outcome of capitalism. The tendency towards monopoly has its logical conclusion in the dominance of a single corporation which essentially employs the whole nation. From this point, said Bellamy, the conversion of this "Great Trust" into a public interest firm would be easy and obvious. He thus joined with economic conservatives in praising the productivity and efficiency of Big Business, defending it against all forms of "trust busting." He further pleased his readers by denying Marx's predictions of catastrophic class warfare.

But the greatest appeal of the utopia is its promise of minimal government and liberty. Here Bellamy nourishes several illusions. He places all economic and political power in the government's hands, but expects nonconformity and dissent to flourish. He prohibits all private trade and assumes that a small, innocuous police authority can enforce this rule. He implies that the involuntary conscription of workers into the Industrial Army for twenty-four years poses no threat to liberty. (The revelation that lazy workers get "solitary imprisonment on bread and water" is very chilling.) He eliminates federalism, judicial review, and congressional co-equality without providing fresh safeguards against presidential tyranny. In truth, the freedoms Dr. Leete boasts of presuppose a marked improvement in human nature.

Yet *Looking Backward* remains relevant, both for its clear statement of a particular socialist ideal and for its superb satire on capitalism's absurdities. That education should be more closely related to industrial realities; that the retired worker needs more social power; that civic beauty and a vibrant common life should be the first fruits of abundance—these are Bellamy's ideas whose time has come.

LORD JIM

Type of work: Novel
Author: Joseph Conrad (Józef Teodor Konrad Korzeniowski, 1857-1924)
Type of plot: Psychological romance
Time of plot: Late nineteenth century
Locale: Ports and islands of the East
First published: 1900

A psychological novel in the setting of an adventure story, Lord Jim *has achieved renown for its breakthrough in narrative technique; the complicated manner in which the story is told has been copied and adapted by many writers. Through this device, Conrad avoids a direct judgment of his protagonist and leaves the reader to evaluate Jim's character.*

Joseph Conrad, born in the Polish Ukraine in 1857, was the son of a political exile who championed Poland's resistance to Russian rule and was, in turn, forced to leave his native land. Since Conrad lost both parents before he was ten, he was brought up by an uncle. In 1874 he went to sea, and by 1886 had earned his master mariner's certificate and had become a naturalized British citizen. Working in the merchant service, Conrad served mostly in eastern waters, with the exception of one trip to the Congo. His first novel, *Almayer's Folly,* was written in 1895; in 1896 he married Jessie George and settled down to his profession as a novelist. Suffering from rheumatic gout and worrying about his work and finances throughout his last years, Conrad died in 1924. His major works include *Nostromo, Heart of Darkness, The Nigger of the Narcissus,* and *Lord Jim.*

Critics have said that *Lord Jim,* which was first published as a magazine serial, began as a short story but became a novel because its author lost control of his material. Conrad, however, in a Note to *Lord Jim,* defended his work and claimed its credibility as a novel. Readers and critics alike seemed to feel that Jim's long, tragic story could not logically be told to a group of men sitting on a veranda; yet Conrad claims that men do sit up for hours at night exchanging stories. Besides, he claims that Jim's story is interesting enough to hold the listeners' attention. Conrad also states that his readers, too, should be interested in Jim and the meaning of his experiences; for, as suggested by the motif of the novel, "He is one of us." Because Jim, like all of us, is an enigmatic paradox of strength and weakness, Conrad allows the reader to judge Jim's actions but reminds him that often there is "not the thickness of a sheet of paper between the right and wrong" of something.

The novel often confuses its readers. Shifts in point of view and a seeming disregard for a logical time sequence give the novel a meditative but rambling style. Narrating the first four chapters himself, Conrad first shifts in Chapter Five to Marlow's oral narration and then in Chapter Thirty-Six to a letter written by Marlow. As Jim's story unfolds, however, Conrad also allows other reliable characters to comment on Jim and his actions: the French lieutenant, who saves the *Patna* after Jim deserts it; Stein, who gives Jim another chance to prove himself; and Jewel, the native girl who loves him. Thus Conrad gives his readers the pieces to a gigantic puzzle—the connection between human motivation and human character—but admits that, in spite of one's best efforts toward interpretation, much will remain inscrutable.

Conrad himself says that the central theme of *Lord Jim* is the "acute consciousness of lost honour." Although he admits that Jim may be uncommonly idealistic, he denies that Jim is a figment of cold imagination, for he says that he saw Jim's "form" in an Eastern port. To help the reader understand Jim's desperate preoccupation with his failure to live up to his dreams of himself, Conrad plants several clues to the development of those dreams. In his youth Jim spent his time, Conrad says, reading "light holiday literature," and he imagined himself "always an example of devotion to duty, and as unflinching as a hero in a book." In addition, Jim had been brought up by a minister-father who held absolute ideas of right and wrong and who wrote Jim, just before he joined the *Patna* as chief mate, that one who "gives way to temptation . . . hazards his total depravity and everlasting ruin." That Jim is a dreamer who becomes lost in his own imagination is revealed by the training ship incident in which Jim fails to respond to a cry for help from a wrecked schooner because he was reveling in his dreams of heroism. His inability to face the reality of his failure is seen in his blaming nature for catching him off guard and in his rationalizing that he is saving himself for bigger emergencies. Yet when the crucial emergency comes—that of the *Patna's* crisis—he again fails to act because he imagines the chaos and the screaming desperation of eight-hundred pilgrims fighting for seven lifeboats; instead, he stands as if entranced while the other members of the crew lower their lifeboat and prepare to jump. Jim wants to make it clear that he did not plan to jump, nor did he help to lower the boat. His jumping, then, is to him a subconscious but understandable urge for survival. He tells Marlow: "I had jumped. . . . It seems."

The French lieutenant does not condemn Jim's actions. He blames Jim's youth and natural fear. He believes that "Man is born a coward" but that he does brave deeds to make others believe he is heroic. Jim, he notes, faced a situation in which he thought no one would ever know that he acted cowardly: during the *Patna* crisis it was dark, and Jim thought all the passengers would die. Still, the lieutenant recognizes Jim's self-condemnation: "the honour . . . that is real. . . . And what life may be worth when . . . the honour is gone" is the real question of *Lord Jim*.

Stein diagnoses Jim's problem: "He is romantic. . . . And that is very bad. . . . Very good, too." He sees in Jim the potential found in the tragic hero who has high ideals but who fails as the result of a tragic flaw. Jim's flaw, then, is his excessive imagination and his inability to face the reality of his weakness and his guilt. Not until the end of the novel, when he knows his limitations and accepts his guilt for Dain Waris' death, does he redeem his lost honor by giving his own life unflinchingly in atonement for his error in misjudging Gentleman Brown. For it is Brown who finally makes Jim see man's depravity and the ugliness of reality. Yet in his death Jim remains true to his concept of the hero; he has transcended his guilt and declares that "Nothing can touch me now." Earlier, when Jewel expresses to Marlow her fear that Jim will leave her, Marlow assures her that Jim will not go back to his world because "he is not good enough." Still, in the end Marlow seems to believe in Jim's final heroism and sees him as an "extraordinary success."

Whose evaluation, then, of Jim is accurate? Jim's own, when he feels that he has finally found himself and thus dies willingly, with "a proud and unflinching glance"? Marlow's, when he sees Jim as a fallible creature who looks trustworthy but who fails—until the end—when an emergency arises? Stein's, when he says that a romantic like Jim has no choice but to follow his dream, even if it costs him his life? The French lieutenant's, when he refuses to judge Jim but ironically shows, by his own heroic example, Jim's weakness? Jewel's, when she calls Jim a traitor and refuses to forgive or understand him? The novel itself is puzzling, and Jim remains "inscrutable at heart." Yet it is important that we try to understand the novel and the character of Jim; for, indeed, "He is one of us."

Janet Wester

LORNA DOONE

Type of work: Novel
Author: R. D. Blackmore (1825-1900)
Type of plot: Historical romance
Time of plot: Late seventeenth century
Locale: England
First published: 1869

Secret agents, highwaymen, clannish marauders, and provincial farmers all figure against the background of wild moor country in this historical romance. Popular with Victorian readers, the book has endured as a simple, authentic tale of courage and love under stress.

The most memorable features of R. D. Blackmore's best novel, *Lorna Doone,* are its characterizations and its setting. The characters are drawn in the dramatic, often exaggerated fashion of the romantic tradition, with its larger-than-life heroes, heroines, and villains. John Ridd, who narrates the story, is a powerful figure, a giant of a man whose honesty, virtue, patience, and steadfastness match his great size and towering strength. His true love, Lorna Doone, is the epitome of the romantic heroine; she is mysterious and enchanting, but entirely unrealistic. Lorna grows up pure, shy, and virtuous—a priceless pearl of femininity by Victorian standards—in the coarse and isolated environment of a robbers' den, surrounded by a clan of thieves and ruthless cutthroats. Perhaps of necessity, Blackmore paints his heroine in wispy, shimmering pastels; at the close of the novel the reader still has no clear idea of her actual features. At the other end of the spectrum is the villainous Carver Doone, a figure unforgettable in his cruel, almost satanic nature. Perhaps the most vital force in *Lorna Doone,* however, is the Exmoor landscape. In soul-felt descriptions, Blackmore brings to life the wild moors, with their violent, stormy climate and harsh, forbidding countryside, as well as their magnificent and awesome beauty and loneliness.

The plot of *Lorna Doone* has its weak spots, such as the unnecessary and unconvincing conferral of knighthood on John Ridd, for whose impressive nature such an honor is trivial and extraneous; or the mediocre description of the Battle of Sedgemoor, which Blackmore borrowed from Macaulay. Overall, however, the narrative is filled with gripping excitement and told in a rugged, simple, and often lyrical prose. Some scenes in particular are unsurpassed, such as the wonderfully taut and realistic one in which John pits his strength and stubbornness against the fury of Tom Faggus' mare. In a different vein, but equally skillful, is John's description of his sorrow at Lorna's unexplained absence from their secret meeting place, a sorrow that spoils the natural beauty of the place in his eyes.

Ironically, *Lorna Doone* first became popular by accident; people bought the novel on the mistaken assumption—owing to a journalist's blunder—that it was about the Marquis of Lorna's marriage, which had captured public interest at the time. It was a propitious error, however, creating as it did the novel's first devoted reading audience, which has had its descendants in every succeeding generation.

LOST HORIZON

Type of work: Novel
Author: James Hilton (1900-1954)
Type of plot: Adventure romance
Time of plot: 1931
Locale: Tibet
First published: 1933

Shangri-La, the setting of this novel, has come to mean to many people a place of peace and contentment. Such was the Utopia James Hilton described in this philosophical romance, making it seem like a real place peopled by living beings rather than a land of impossible ideals.

James Hilton, in *Lost Horizon,* combines disillusioned pessimism with romantic escapism and thus captures the feelings of uncertainty and anxiety that pervaded Western society in the early 1930's. It is significant that the novel begins in Berlin where the twin specters of the period, the Great Depression and the rise to power of Adolf Hitler, loom vividly in the reader's mind. And, given the apparent collapse of this "rational" Anglo-American-European community, it is not surprising that a fiction writer should look to the "mysterious East" for an idealized and exotic sanctuary.

But it is also important that the hero of this quest, Hugh Conway, although jaded by his experiences, still embodies basic "Western" virtues—a strong sense of purpose, personal loyalty, a rigid "fair play" ethic, and efficiency, especially during moments of crisis. Thus, Hilton gives us the best of both worlds. On the intellectual level, he postulates a synthesis of "Eastern moderation" and "Western activism"; on the emotional level, he confronts the complexities and tensions of the times with a hopeful vision that shows the best in the Western tradition surviving, even if the worst destroys itself.

Hilton's small group of involuntary explorers is well chosen, if not deeply characterized. They are all—even Conway—characteristic Western "types" and the qualities they represent can, to a considerable extent, account for the state of the modern world.

Miss Brinklow stands for Western missionary zeal, albeit in a rather benign and comical form. Of the four she is the most easily recognized stereotype—the righteous, moralistic, spinster lady who, having no personal life of her own, tries to interfere with everyone else's. Hilton's treatment of the type is, however, gently ironical rather than sharply satirical; Miss Brinklow is likeable, sincere, and feisty, rather than priggish and icy. Her plans to convert and animate the Tibetan peasants is taken seriously by no one but herself. But the implications of her actions are not so amusing; such missionary fervor in souls less benevolent than Miss Brinklow's leads, of course, to violence and oppression.

Henry Barnard, the American financier, suggests the pragmatic, greedy, opportunistic side of Western culture. Personally he is a most engaging character—affable, entertaining, adaptable, easygoing, and levelheaded. And he is also a wanted criminal. Circumstances and bad luck, he insists, caught up with him and forced him into defensive monetary manipulations; he is a fugitive by accident; a victim, himself—the classic rationalization of the "white collar" criminal.

Both Miss Brinklow and Barnard, however, are easily distracted in Shangri-La and their vices indulged harmlessly. Presumably they will eventually outgrow their particular Western preoccupations and achieve that detached serenity characteristic in the Valley of the Blue Moon. The third member of the party, Captain Mallinson, is another matter.

Mallinson is young, passionate, idealistic, and loyal. He is, perhaps, even more admirable as an individual—and more dangerous as a character type. A product of an upper-class British gentleman's education, Mallinson firmly believes in all the "ideals" of his country and class: honor, common sense, patriotism, and a hard distinction between "right" and "wrong"—with "rightness" residing in the upper-class English view of life. Because he saw Conway behaving "heroically" in the Baskal evacuation, he idealizes him and then, as Conway "adjusts" to the new situation, he berates him for not living up to that idealization. Mallinson is the one member of the party who is so Westernized that he cannot fit into Shangri-La for even a short time. To him, life in the Lamasery is "unhealthy and unclean . . . hateful . . . filthy." Mallinson feels that anything he cannot understand or relate to is wrong and deserves destruction. "God," he tells Conway, "I'd give a good deal to fly over with a load of bombs!" Mallinson's idealism and passion, coupled with his narrowness of vision, make him the most potentially dangerous of the group.

Thus, all three are people who are personally likable and admirable, but who embody qualities which, if pursued to their logical and probable conclusions, will bring devastation upon themselves and the civilization they so admire and seek to serve.

But Conway, too, represents a characteristic failing in Western society. Although he is not destructive, he contributes nothing toward averting the impending chaos. Clearly he embodies the best qualities of the cultivated Westerner. He is intelligent, sensitive, tolerant, sympathetic, courageous when he has to be, and resourceful. But he is also without any direction or purpose. For all of his obvious knowledge and talent, he has wandered aimlessly from one minor diplomatic post to another, never much caring where he has been or where he is headed, only hoping for a few incidental pleasures along the way. "Label me '1914-18,' " he tells the High Lama, "I used up most of my passion and energies during the years I've mentioned . . . the chief thing I've asked from the world since then is to leave me alone." Thus,

Conway represents the potential leader who understands the world and has the capacities at least to attempt to deal with it, but whose will has been stultified by the traumas and complexities of the times. The underlying question of the book is whether or not Conway will find in Shangri-La the will and purpose that he needs.

The answer to that question and the center of the novel lies in the series of interviews between Conway and the High Lama, Father Perrault. In these scenes the history and nature of Shangri-La are explored, and its "mission" is presented to Conway. For his part, he must measure his own values, experiences, and apathy against the "doctrines" presented by the High Lama.

In spite of the Tibetan trappings, Shangri-La is a very Western establishment. All of the high officials and prime movers have been transplanted Europeans, especially Father Perrault, once a Capuchin friar, and his practical right hand man, Henschell, an Austrian soldier. The central philosophy is the Aristotelian "golden mean" and the underlying assumption is the same one Bernard Shaw preaches in *Back to Methuselah*: if human life can just be extended long enough, men will outlive the passions and extremes that lead to destruction. Thus, the purpose of Shangri-La is survival: "We may pray to outlive the doom that gathers around on every side," Perrault tells Conway. "Then, my son, when the strong have devoured each other, the Christian ethic may at last be fulfilled, and the meek shall inherit the earth."

Because he has apparently already achieved a state of "passionlessness" and because he possesses the "Western" capacities of sympathy, intelligence, and efficiency, Conway is the logical choice as Perrault's successor. The old man tells him that and then promptly dies. Almost immediately thereafter, Mallinson proposes an "escape" back to "civilization" and Conway is forced to the climactic decision of the novel.

In spite of his irritating behavior, Conway likes Mallinson, to some extent identifies with him, and, because of Mallinson's idealization, feels a responsibility toward the younger man. When Conway learns that Lo-Tsen will accompany them and that she and Mallinson are romantically attracted, his feelings and ideas about Shangri-La are shaken. He respects honest, youthful passion and is not too old to feel some of it himself—especially with regard to the "untouchable" Lo-Tsen. At the logical level, Mallinson casts real doubts on the High Lama's story. He dismisses Conway's references to the girl's age as absurd and Lo-Tsen's willingness to leave the Valley supports the young man's analysis. In summary, all Conway "felt was that he liked Mallinson and must help him; he was doomed, like millions, to flee wisdom and be a hero."

Thus, the rational hero acts, finally, on impulse; the passionless spectator acts out of feeling. Such reversals are, of course, not unusual in the best writing and may be a sign of complexity and stature in a character. Or they may represent an easy way to solve a difficult plot dilemma. Whether or not the reader can accept such a fast and facile resolution is a matter of individual taste and judgment.

What is most obvious about *Lost Horizon,* however, is that in it James Hilton created a new mythical kingdom, an exotic retreat to serenity and moderation, perfectly suited to the frenzied and bombarded sensibilities of the modern man.

LOST ILLUSIONS

Type of work: Novel
Author: Honoré de Balzac (1799-1850)
Type of plot: Naturalism
Time of plot: Early nineteenth century
Locale: Angoulême, France
First published in three parts: 1837, 1839, 1843

This longest of Balzac's novels is a study of a hero too innocent even to understand the machinations of his enemies. The book is perhaps the high point of the author's Scenes of Country Life *sequence of novels.*

One of the most popular of Balzac's novels and one of his greatest achievements, *Lost Illusions* has been read by countless generations, and its hero, Lucien Chardon, has been identified with by many of these readers. The book is a prototype of the tale of the inexperienced, ambitious young man who goes to the city to make his fortune, dividing his energies between literary and social pursuits. As in all Balzac novels, *place* is very important in *Lost Illusions*. The locations of the action, such as the Séchard printing shop, are meticulously described; it is evident that Balzac felt that surroundings play a strong influence on people.

No author, except Dickens, can match Balzac for the vividness with which he describes his characters. The portrait of old Séchard is a masterpiece, and the character is one of the most true-to-life in Balzac's vast gallery. Balzac shrewdly exposes the peasant miserliness and pettiness of the illiterate old man, who prides himself on his ability to cheat his own son, and has no conception of humane attitudes. David's reactions, his inner shame instead of anger toward his father, are sensitively portrayed. But the character of Lucien dominates the novel.

Akin to Eugène de Rastignac in *Le Père Goriot* (1835) and Julien Sorel in Stendhal's *The Red and the Black* (1830), the supreme opportunist in French literature, Lucien possesses a naïveté foreign to both of those ambitious young men. Although he is willing to use the love of a rich older woman to advance his fortunes, he first convinces himself that he loves her. Despite his follies, there is something likable about this country boy with the pretty face and pretensions to greatness. Although he always means well, Lucien compromises again and again, sacrificing family and friends to his ambition; yet he is never malicious, and the reader wishes him well, even while acknowledging his defective morality. The contrast between Lucien and his friend David is at the heart of the book. David, loyal and humble, is basically a realist, while Lucien builds his life on dreams. The irony of Balzac's tale lies in the fact that the virtuous suffer and the deceitful and ruthless prosper. By the end of the book, even Lucien has lost some of his illusions, but not all of them, as the sequel, *A Distinguished Provincial at Paris*, shows.

A LOST LADY

Type of work: Novel
Author: Willa Cather (1873-1947)
Type of plot: Regional realism
Time of plot: Late nineteenth century
Locale: Nebraska
First published: 1923

Marked by a studied attention to form, this novel achieves an epic-like tone, a characteristic derived from the theme as well as from the viewpoint of the novel. The book expresses admiration for the builders who opened the West, and captures the personalities of many women of those generations.

Willa Cather was the last of a generation of writers who lived through the passing of the old frontier, who saw at first hand the region of the homesteader transformed into a countryside of tidy farms and small towns; and she found in the primitive virtues of the pioneer experience her own values as an artist. The West, the past—one was the physical background of her best work, the other its spiritual climate. Miss Cather thought of the novel as an instrument of culture, not a vehicle for social reportage or character-mongering, an art worth a lifetime's effort and devotion. Coming at the end of an era, she tried to recapture a past that existed largely in memory, a past which was innocent and romantic and heroic. That was her aim and her achievement, and what she had to say she said with honesty and simplicity, with moral subtlety and stylistic evocation.

A Lost Lady is the first example in Miss Cather's writing of what she called the novel *démeublé,* fiction stripped of all furnishings to leave the scene bare for the play of emotions. Her method is well illustrated in the scene in which young Niel suffers his disillusionment in Marian Forrester. The whole passage is built upon the symbol of the wild roses which Niel picks early in the morning to place on Marian's windowsill so that she will find them when she opens the blinds of her bedroom. As he bends to place the flowers he hears beyond the closed blinds a woman's laugh: "impatient, indulgent, teasing, eager," and then a man's "like a yawn." Niel flees and throws the roses in the mud where cattle can trample them. The brief bloom of his worship of Mrs. Forrester is gone like the transient beauty of the flowers. From now on, Marian Forrester will be his lost lady. Captain Forrester serves in the novel as a symbol of the past and Ivy Peters as a symbol of the degraded present with its materialism and the loss of the old values of honesty and love and the enjoyment of the beauty in nature. Marian's turning from the Captain to Ivy symbolizes her own degradation.

THE LOST WEEKEND

Type of work: Novel
Author: Charles Jackson (1903-1968)
Type of plot: Psychological melodrama
Time of plot: Twentieth century
Locale: New York City
First published: 1944

Although The Lost Weekend *is in some respects more a case history than a novel, it is nevertheless a vivid and convincing story of a maladjusted personality. Jackson shows considerable insight into alcoholism as a social problem without destroying the personal quality of his hero's experience or the desperation of his struggle.*

In *The Lost Weekend,* Charles Jackson immediately poses the problem of the novel: why does an artistic, intelligent man destroy himself through alcoholism? In a moment of self-realization, Don admits to himself that the excuses he uses for drinking are rationalizations. Temporarily recognizing himself as a drunkard, he realizes that he has reached the point where one drink is too many and dozens not enough; yet he continues to drink.

Jackson attempts no major analysis of Don, but there are definite undertones of psychological problems; for example, latent homosexuality is suggested. In college Don is dropped from his fraternity for writing an overly emotional hero letter; and in adulthood his latent feelings are instantly discerned by Bim, a homosexual orderly in the alcoholic ward who whispers that he "knows" Don.

Don vacillates between self-love and self-hatred. As a boy he had admired tragic writers who had burned themselves out early. During the first stage of his spree, he recalls this and outlines an elaborate story to be called "In a Glass," but he soon sees with desperate clarity that he lacks both the talent and the will to write. Tellingly, Don's favorite modern author is Fitzgerald; he dwells upon Fitzgerald's wasted ability.

Mirror imagery is dominant. Don is fascinated by his face and wonders how others see him. As a boy he would stare into the mirror to see if his writing experiences had changed him. During the "long weekend" he sees himself many times, both through his own eyes, and by imagining how he appears to others. Thursday he sees himself in the mirror at Sam's bar as a well-dressed, sophisticated, fascinating man, but when released from the hospital on Monday, he studies his ruined face with fear and disgust. The only escape from the stranger in the mirror is drink, and the downward spiral continues.

LOVE FOR LOVE

Type of work: Drama
Author: William Congreve (1670-1729)
Type of plot: Comedy of manners
Time of plot: Seventeenth century
Locale: London
First presented: 1695

Generally considered one of Congreve's finest plays, Love for Love *is marked by a simple but not particularly original plot. Any defects in the play are overbalanced by the clever and amusing dialogue and by the several pairs of well-conceived and contrasting characters.*

Comedy was a form particularly suited to the Restoration temperament, and the comedies of the period were much superior to the tragedies. One of the most successful comedies of the Restoration stage was *Love for Love,* which established Congreve's reputation as a playwright of the front rank. The brilliance of the comedy in the play is of a hard, unfeeling sort, but it scintillates in its easy, rapier-like dialogue and its swaggering pace. It is clearly a descendant of Ben Jonson's comedy of humors of half a century before; there is the same tendency to caricature, the same labeling of characters by significant surnames, and the same method of parading the characters across the stage in a series of striking but loosely connected scenes. The action is rather confused, but, although the play is difficult to read, it works well on the stage, and is often very funny.

Of all of the Restoration writers of comedy, Congreve was the most skilled dramatic technician and the greatest wit. He probably possessed the finest sense of style, although his satire was not as cutting as that of Wycherley, or his touch as light as that of Etherage or Farquhar. *Love for Love,* like most of the Restoration comedies, is filled with coxcombs and coquettes, men about town, dupes, and fools, all busily involved in a tangle of intrigues, both financial and sexual in motivation. Ostensibly, the author's purpose is to satirize fashionable folly, but it often appears that he is more interested in titillating the audience with suggestive lines and situations. *Love for Love* and Congreve's other comedies provoked anger and even outrage among the Puritans, who considered the freedom of the Restoration stage scandalously immoral.

Love for Love is interesting also because it reflects the popular interests of the day, such as the fad of chocolate houses as meeting places and the interest in astrology. Congreve's witty dialogue makes frequent references to fashionable places and pastimes, allusions which must have drawn amused recognition from the audiences. But, despite the moral tacked on at the ending of the play, his real interest was in the juxtaposing of suggestive situations with dialogue at once shocking and delicately phrased. The speeches in *Love for Love* possess a precision and modulation of tone that compensate for any structural defects and occasional lapses of taste. The message of the play, if it has one beneath the layers of wit and satire and suggestive dialogue, might be found in the lovers' fear that disillusion inevitably follows too easy a fruition.

LOVE IN A WOOD

Type of work: Drama
Author: William Wycherley (1640-1716)
Type of plot: Comedy of manners
Time of plot: Seventeenth century
Locale: London
First presented: 1671

The first of three satiric comedies, Love in a Wood *shows brilliantly the genius of Wycherley, who gained insight as an intimate in society on both sides of the Channel. This play gained for him the favor of the king and the love of the king's mistress, the Duchess of Cleveland.*

As Wycherley uses the phrase, "in a wood" means "confused"; such a description might apply as well to the audience and readers of this play as to the characters in it. By the end, we are faced with no less than five marriages, one accomplished and four in prospect. The unusually large quantity of couples, the complicated intrigues they indulge in, and the various unravelings that are required, keep the play bustling with physical and dramatic movement; but it is a movement less controlled than in the playwright's later masterpieces, *The Country Wife* and *The Plain Dealer.*

The play contains many of the motifs of deception that were to become standard in Restoration comedy: disguises, mistaken identity, hiding, and overheard and misleading conversations, all of which create a confusion between appearance and reality. Valentine, for instance, hears an apparently compromising report of Christina and concludes her to be unfaithful; Gripe frantically attempts to maintain the pretense of Puritan piety and respectability; Sir Simon poses as a clerk, and then discovers to his consternation that Martha refuses to believe he is a knight. Critics have pointed out that Wycherley uses the metaphor of light and darkness to dramatize social reality and inner reality; it is significant that most of the crucial revelations take place in the darkness, where truth can safely come out.

The characters, also, are standard types: a fool, a hypocrite, a fop, a lecherous widow, and a wench, as well as a set of "realistic" lovers and a set of "ideal" lovers. The former characters comprise the "low" plot, the latter characters, the "high" plot (which is based on Calderón's *Mañanas de Abril y Mayo*). Wycherley skillfully uses Mrs. Joyner, on the one hand, and Vincent, on the other, to serve as go-betweens for the various characters and to lend coherence to the multitudinous strands of the action. Of course, Mrs. Joyner, the functionary of the low plot, helps only to increase the confusion, in accordance with the dictates of her financial interest; Vincent, on the other hand, with an earnest regard for the truth, does his best to clear up the misunderstandings. The high plot characters profit by the unraveling, while the low plot characters, despite the prospect of their marriages, only succeed in duping themselves or in making the best of a bad bargain.

Like other Restoration comedies, *Love in a Wood* creates a highly realistic and immediate sense of contemporary London: scenes unfold in places like Mulberry Garden and St. James's Park, and the dialogue is peppered with contemporary allusions and jokes. And like other comic dramatists of the period, Wycherley treats love as a battle between the sexes (metaphors of war and hunting abound), with women usually having the upper hand. But Wycherley is distinctive in his caustic wit and his cynical attitude toward human relationships. Aggression, lust, greed, and mistrust seem to be the main drives governing behavior. Dissimulation is taken as the norm; and so the complicated intrigues of the plot are as much an indication of the necessary condition of life as of the development of a comic drama. The marriages of the low plot characters are motivated by either financial interest (and in the case of Sir Simon and Lady Flippant, a mistaken view of financial interest) or revenge. Lydia and Ranger seem to be on firmer ground, but the jealousy of the one and the philandering of the other are, despite Ranger's protestations of reform, not very reassuring. Only the marriage between Valentine and Christina, based on genuine love and honesty, seems to have any hopeful prospects; but that one (note the names of the characters) seems too idealized to be very credible in this setting. The exception only proves Wycherley's rule about love and marriage in Restoration London.

LOVE'S LABOUR'S LOST

Type of work: Drama
Author: William Shakespeare (1564-1616)
Type of plot: Comedy of manners
Time of plot: Sixteenth century
Locale: Navarre, Spain
First presented: c. 1594

An early play, Love's Labour's Lost *shows neither the perfection of plot nor the fineness of characterization which distinguish Shakespeare's later plays; nevertheless, the work benefits from its clever dialogue and tone of good humor. A romantic exhaltation of love, the play is also an early comedy of manners in which the ladies try to teach the young noblemen the value of sincerity and faithfulness to vows.*

The central theme of *Love's Labour's Lost* is, in large terms, the conflict between flesh and spirit. This is a perennial theme; it can be found in all Western literatures, from the Greeks to the present day. In this play it takes the form of a conflict between love and learning, or more exactly, between love and the abuses of language, with "word" understood as vow as well as communication.

This play, like *Two Gentlemen of Verona,* foreshadows Shakespeare's "problem," or "dark" comedies, for, in this case, there is no character who understands the problem at hand. The king and his friends are too easily drawn from their vows, however absurd these were in the first place. Yet, the ladies are too cutting in their words, and too harsh in their demands when they insist that the men live in a hermitage for a whole year. The girls, at that point, are being in their turn "too spiritual."

Learning at this point in history was largely a matter of studying Latin texts, so one can easily conceive of the problem of love versus learning as one kind of language abuse. Holofernes and Armado falsify language with their pedantry, quite obviously. But so do the king and his men, with their vows, and with their misguided addresses (the letters and the pretense of being Russians), to the girls. The girls receive the addresses, which are almost pure "painted rhetoric," applicable to anyone, with scorn that is again false rhetoric. All the characters have, in a sense, "been to a feast of language and stolen the scrapes." The result of this abuse is the characters' isolation from one another at the end of the play.

LOVING

Type of work: Novel
Author: Henry Green (Henry Vincent York, 1905-   )
Type of plot: Domestic comedy
Time of plot: World War II
Locale: Eire
First published: 1945

Because of the qualities of depth and perception in his writing, Green's novels have never enjoyed a wide popular audience, and are better known to other writers than to the reading public. In Loving, *Green combines modern novelistic techniques with Dickensian humor and subtle social criticism as he offers a picture of the servants' world below stairs in an old mansion in Ireland.*

Henry Green's romantic comedies are in the tradition established in England by Shakespeare and pursued, at least in the novel, by Jane Austen and E. M. Forster. Within that tradition there are two distinct directions: one such as we discover in *A Midsummer Night's Dream,* which reveals the characters proceeding through confusion and lust to purification and stasis; and the other such as we find in *The Tempest,* which shows the actors in disorganization and sensuality, but developing toward love and action: that is, toward engagement with the real world. In short, one element in the tradition celebrates a romantic Eden, while the other recognizes the necessity of abandoning utopia for reality. *Loving* is a type of the latter mode.

Indeed a comparison between Green's novel and *The Tempest* is enlightening. Like Prospero, Charley Raunce is secluded on an island, Ireland. In the middle of a World War, he discovers himself in the midst of plenty and peace. And like Shakespeare's magician, he controls the destiny of the island's inhabitants—or at least of Mrs. Tennant's servants. His temptation is to remain among luxury and pleasure, secure from the deprivations and dangers in England.

Yet it is partly the enervation produced by safety and ease that forces Raunce to reconsider his position. More than that, however, he realizes that his love for Edith cannot grow in such a hothouse atmosphere. If they remain in Ireland their relationship will pall and at last disintegrate. Like Prospero, who perceives that in order to save the love of Miranda and Ferdinand he must give up his powers and return to Milan, Raunce must turn from stasis and take himself and Edith to England. *Loving* is a comedy of adult love that can only flower in actuality.

THE LOWER DEPTHS

Type of work: Drama
Author: Maxim Gorky (Aleksei Maksimovich Peshkov, 1868-1936)
Type of plot: Naturalism
Time of plot: Late nineteenth century
Locale: Russia
First presented: 1902

Considered the best of Gorky's plays and one of the most vital of Russia's dramatic pieces, this drama was pure naturalism in its day, but to modern taste it appears more romantic. The play helps to explain the causes leading to the Russian Revolution of 1917.

Maxim Gorky's exceptionally well-crafted play, *The Lower Depths,* is a transitional piece between the nineteenth century literary masters (Dostoevski, Tolstoy, Chekhov, for example) and such twentieth century writers as Blok, Bulgakov, Mayakovsky, to name but a few. As such, it fortuitously shares in the best of both worlds: the play is constructed with a nineteenth century eye toward dramatic structure while it treats contemporary socio-political themes. Among the most important of these themes is the issue of freedom versus slavery, a frequent topic of conversation—implicit or explicit—among the denizens of *The Lower Depths,* a cellar-like rooming house accommodating a varied group of inhabitants. Also threading its way through the play is the naturalistic assumption about predestination, forcing us to ask—without really expecting an answer—was the Actor foredoomed to alcoholism, was Anna actually destined to die of tuberculosis, leaving her husband Kleshtch penniless because of medical and burial expenses, and was Satine the only one who recognized how low *The Lower Depths* were? Many more such questions arise, but all serve only to illustrate the essential slavery of the characters to the lower depths of the socio-economic system and their lack of freedom to rise above it.

Even the poetic imagery in the play reinforces this theme, for the imagery revolves around references to light and dark, clean and dirty. The interior of the cellar rooming house, for example, is dark, but ideas and hopes are light. Conventional associations of good with light or white, and bad with dark or black abound. The conventional system even gets turned topsy-turvy when the Actor begins to view death by suicide as a hope for his salvation, so that death is not "black" but "white." Yet, throughout the play, dark or black retains its traditional connotation of "no hope" and doom.

Gorky's use of light-dark imagery is particularly evident as it is amalgamated into another especially effective literary device which he uses most strikingly—the device called "foreshadowing" or "prescience," a subtle hint or prophecy of events to manifest themselves in the future. Anna's death, for example, is predicted in Act I, although she does not die until the end of Act II. The Actor's death is suggested in the middle of Act III, but he does not commit suicide until the end of Act IV. Natasha likewise foresees an apocalyptic doom in Act III which does not come to pass until Act IV. In fact, the Actor senses his own fate at the beginning of Act IV although it does not occur until the end of that act—an ironic fulfillment of an apparently foreordained destiny. In the resolution of this precisely structured play, only Luka and Satine go unaccounted for; the rest play out their roles as though programmed by a computer. Yet, the impact is undeniable: the two escapees do not really escape, because they bear responsibility for the fate of others; and the victims survive spiritually—despite death or other devastation—as reminders of the inexorable workings of the socio-economic system. The end has been prophesized. In effect, Gorky only worked out the details, but those details were sufficiently compelling to support a revolution and to sustain a remarkable play.

LOYALTIES

Type of work: Drama
Author: John Galsworthy (1867-1933)
Type of plot: Social criticism
Time of plot: Early 1920's
Locale: London
First presented: 1922

One of the first plays to deal honestly and openly with the problem of anti-Semitism, Loyalties *displays Galsworthy's usual craftsmanship. The author takes such pains to deal fairly with both sides of the question that he comes close to destroying his own thesis.*

In an early essay on dramatic theory, John Galsworthy stated that the playwright's best and most honest approach is to present to his audience the true picture of life as he sees it, without fear or favor, and let the audience draw its own conclusions. Few of his plays follow that dictum as completely and effectively as *Loyalties*. Indeed, he has so balanced his sympathies that anyone searching the play for vindication of a particular viewpoint—such as an attack on anti-Semitism—is certain to be disappointed. *Loyalties* is not about prejudice as such; it is, as the title implies, about "loyalties"—their nature, their effects, and their excesses.

What is the line, the playwright asks, between "prejudices" and "loyalties"? To what extent is loyalty to a set or class or group or profession a necessary social virtue? And at what point do these same loyalties become questionable, even dangerous? Using the rarefied atmosphere of cultivated upper-class British society in the 1920's, Galsworthy subtly explores these questions in all their complexity and ambiguity, while at the same time telling a powerful personal story of wasted talent and inadvertent self-destruction.

Galsworthy chooses to focus his conflict on anti-Semitism because the ambiguous position of the Jew in upper-class English society makes him the perfect catalyst for a play in which all of the "loyalties" present in such a group are to be tested. Because of his money and social contacts, Ferdinand De Levis, associates with the group, but, because of his race, he is barely tolerated by it. When he accuses Ronald Dancy, one of the most accepted and well-liked members of the set, the thin veneer of courtesy dissolves and the group's latent prejudices quickly become overt. For his own part, De Levis is probably hypersensitive in his assumption that all reaction against his claims are racially motivated.

But it is unwise to overemphasize the anti-Semitic aspect of the play. Most of the characters are decent and, under pressure, do the honest thing. They are simply trying to keep faith with their own particular set. The problem is that, in one character's words, "loyalties cut up against each other." De Levis' intensity in pursuit of the thief is not due to the money itself, but to the vindication of what he feels to be a racial insult. Charles Winsor is loyal to his idea of hospitality and reacts strongly when he feels it affronted. General Canynge is loyal to his military *esprit de corps* ethic and so finds it impossible to believe that Dancy, a good soldier, could be a thief. Margaret Orme and Major Colford are loyal to feelings of friendship. Ricardos is loyal to his daughter. Old Twisden is loyal to his concept of the lawyer's obligation to truth and justice. And, finally, Mabel Dancy is loyal to her husband in spite of what she learns about him. Clearly, the loyalties are not bad in themselves, but, given the momentum of the situation, some of them take on wrong and dangerous aspects.

At the center of these conflicting loyalties is the character who is both the villain and the victim in the play, Captain Ronald Dancy. He is a colorful mixture of arrogant snob and likeable daredevil. The negative aspects of his character are most evident at the beginning of the play when he is brash, snide, and overtly anti-Semitic. But later on Dancy exhibits many positive qualities: personal charm, courage, devotion and loyalty toward his wife, and a strong sense of honor. His real misfortune is to be a natural born soldier thrust into a peaceful world and a trivial social class. The pressure of needing money to settle accounts with his previous mistress, the feeling that he had been cheated by De Levis, and the need for an adventure, all push Dancy to his daring, dangerous crime. And, when he is found out, his honor demands his life as expiation; "only a pistol keeps faith," his suicide note explains. But Galsworthy, speaking through Margaret Orme, makes the final comment: "Keeps faith! We've all done that. It's not enough."

LUCIEN LEUWEN

Type of work: Novel
Author: Stendhal (Marie-Henri Beyle, 1783-1842)
Type of plot: Psychological romance
Time of plot: The 1830's
Locale: France
First published: 1894

Published posthumously, Lucien Leuwen *is a long, unfinished work divided into two novels,* The Green Huntsman *and* The Telegraph. *In it, Stendhal gives a subtle, penetrating analysis of a young commoner in the difficult days after the revolution of 1830.*

Lucien Leuwen is an exceptionally long (though unfinished) and exceptionally brilliant, complex novel. It successfully integrates the life of an individual, for whom the novel is named, with the historical and institutional life of French society. Containing a vast panorama of major and minor characters, many of whom were modeled on the functionaries of Louis Philippe's regime, the novel also offers penetrating psychological and social analysis. In a sense, *Lucien Leuwen* resembles Stendhal's other major works: a young man, unable to bear the hypocrisy of the society in which he finds himself, is forced to grow, rebel, and compromise all at the same time. *Lucien Leuwen* is especially interesting because of the personality and situation of the major character and because of the setting into which he is born.

Lucien Leuwen is a decent fellow, with democratic ideals and a heart in the right place, who must either become dishonest, or be wholly isolated. In the army he is forced to "think right" (that is, stop thinking and start cultivating the local aristocrats), and in the service of the Minister of the Interior Lucien "plays the game." Indeed, his father's only worry is that Lucien will not be crooked enough for the life of politics. However, Lucien proves himself capable of carrying out all sorts of dishonest political tricks. In one scene, the local population is so enraged at his spying and attempted subversion of their election that they throw mud in his face and cry that now "his soul is on his face."

The government of Louis Philippe was run by the bankers; and the king himself—as well as his closest associates—was perpetually engaged in the most dishonest financial manipulations. It is this corruption, and not merely middle-class blandness, that suffused French society and French officialdom, which Stendhal exposes with utter ruthlessness. Lucien's father, who is one of these bankers, offers his son opportunity and a position against which Lucien finally rebels. After the father died, and the second part of the novel was completed, Stendhal's notes indicated that he would have had Lucien travel to Rome to be united with his first love; this third part, however, was never written. But completed or not, *Lucien Leuwen* remains a superb portrait of personal rebellion, compromise, and sacrifice.

THE LUSIADS

Type of work: Poem
Author: Luis Vaz de Camoëns (1524?-1580)
Type of plot: Epic
Time of plot: Fifteenth century
Locale: Europe, Africa, and Asia
First published: 1572

This epic poem was the product of a man of action during a period of great national activity, at a time when the national spirit of Portugal had reached a high point. In the epic tradition, the poem finds the gods of Olympus siding for and against the Portuguese heroes.

The Lusiads is one of the world's noted epics. It is dedicated to Portugal, while its author, Luis de Camoëns, is regarded as a symbol of that country. A poem of distant enterprise, one of whose themes is "man against the sea," *The Lusiads* also contains a fund of historic, geographic, cultural, and scientific information. It presents a panorama of interesting personalities, such as kings, navigators, *conquistadores,* missioners, and Asian monarchs. The poem is thus much more than a glorification of Vasco de Gama's discovery of India and more than a jingoistic puffing-up of Portugal's sixteenth century conquests in Asia, Africa, and Brazil.

Camoëns selected da Gama's 1497-1499 voyage only as the literary fulcrum of his work. This voyage united East and West in time and space, but it was used merely to tell the real story—that of the "Lusiads," or the men of Portugal. These men founded a new nation in Spain's northwest corner, following the battle of Ourique in 1139, when they placed five blue shields on their flag in the form of a cross. Celebrating Christ's five wounds and/or the five Moorish kinglings killed at Ourique, this symbol was carried southward in an anti-Islamic crusade until Portugal's continental limits were reached in 1252. Thus, from the start, Camoëns' poem has balance and continuity because all the leading figures of Portugal's history share its pages. No element was missing for Camoëns to write his epic, for Portugal's epic was achieved at home and, after 1415, abroad by kings, counselors, princes, saints, and all the heroes capable of conceiving, molding, and effecting a titanic enterprise. The common man, however, is its truest hero, for Camoëns wrote "I sing the noble Lusitanian breast," thus making an entire people his collective hero, an example predating the concept of the unknown soldier of World War I.

After the Moorish wars were completed Portugal was blessed by key "Lusiads" such as the scholarly King Diniz, who consolidated the new country by peopling southern Portugal, planting pine forests to build ships, developing agriculture, and founding Coimbra University. By 1415 Portugal was a compact, military nation on Europe's western edge with a martial aristocracy and hardy peasantry of Celtic-Swabian stock that unblushingly believed in the superiority of its religion, culture, and race. A geographic outpost of Europe, fanatically Christian, Portugal launched its ships into the uncharted seas, "never before navigated," ending medieval geography and rolling back the "Sea of Darkness." Its tiny caravels and galleons were commanded by Knights of Christ clad in chain mail, bearing the symbol of the Sacred Heart, and carrying huge, two-handed swords, since Camoëns' epic had as its stated purpose the destruction of Islam at its distance sources.

Having rounded the Cape of Good Hope and discovered India in 1497-1499, Portugal's *conquistadores* continued the traditional Spanish-Portuguese vendetta against "the Moors" throughout the Indian Ocean. *The Lusiads* exults in their killing, burning, and looting as they took the spice trade from "the obscene Ismaelites." They tried to capture Mecca and Medina so as to ransom the Holy Sepulcher in Jerusalem; they conquered most of the keys to the Indian Ocean; and reached China seven years before Cortez reached Mexico. They seized and destroyed what they believed was the Dalada, or Holy Tooth of Buddha, and they plundered the tombs of the emperors of China, but their missioners evangelized from interior Brazil to Japan. At the height of Portuguese Empire, Camoëns flag of "five azures in a cross designed" flew in Brazil's sertão, many regions of Africa including the interior Congo, the coasts of Arabia, Persia, Malaya, parts of Indonesia, and over countless islands. It has been said that the empire of Camoëns' poem comprised thirty-two foreign kingdoms, 433 overseas garrison towns, and many isolated fortresses, even though Portugal itself comprised less than one percent of Europe's land area and had perhaps one million people.

The Lusiads has been translated into many languages. It was written during Camoëns' seventeen years as a private soldier in Asia, where research opportunities were scant; yet, it is filled with mythological allusions, some of which are so obscure that professional classicists have to consult their texts in order to explain them. The astronomy of *The Lusiads,* for example, is accurate despite sixteenth century limitations, while Camoëns' descriptions of the eternal correlation of sea and sky, of the ocean's surface, and of weather conditions has been praised by such men as the German naturalist Von Humboldt in his "Kosmos." The most diverse elements enter into the complex structure of *The Lusiads,* including the flora and religions of India's subcontinent. The poem's nautical aspects have also been praised, often by professional seamen. Camoëns also intentionally archived elements of phonetics, grammar, spelling, and meter, for which reason his poem has been called simultaneously a poem and a museum. The poem's thought soars above its polished surfaces, or even its complex symbolism. Camoëns was a religious writer, who must be considered a poet of the Counter-Reformation, and who depicted the great *conquistadores* Almeida and Albuquerque as missionaries who carried war to pagan lands. Camoëns was a person of unusual piety, and has been likened to "a Christian poet at the foot of the Cross of Calvary."

His deepest admiration is reserved for the fanatic young King Sebastian of Portugal, the so-called "Portuguese Quijote," who died on a rash crusade against Islam in Africa's interior, and whom Camoëns considered the perfect epitome of a "Lusiad."

Camoëns also expressed his views on individual behavior, exalting virtues such as honesty, selflessness, and intrepidity in death. His heroes were always heroes of duty and honor, and he felt that death was happier than birth because there was one safe port—"to believe in Christ." He pilloried jealousy, greed, selfishness, cruelty (except against Infidels), and materialism, and it has been said that *The Lusiads* is written in letters of gold on a whiteness of marble, as Portugal's epitaph and testament.

The Lusiads remains a bond of unity between the peoples of the Portuguese world, whether in Continental Portugal itself, on the adjacent islands of Madeira and the Azores, or in Brazil, Angola, Mozambique, Macau, Timor, and even the enclave of Goa, lost to India in 1961. Camoëns' subtle influence on national behavior paterns is visible not only in "the unpleasing portraits of the poet that grace the walls of Portuguese taverns," as Aubrey Bell stated, but because he is studied in the class rooms of Portugal, its colonies, and Brazil. His memory, not that of a great king of warrior, was used as a symbol of nationality when Portugal recovered its independence from Spain in 1640. D. G. Dalgado wrote: "There is no country in which a poet is more honored; and no country pays a greater homage to any of its national poets than Portugal does to Camoëns." Thus, the greatest influence of *The Lusiads* was felt after its author's death, and the epic remains a living force today wherever its language is spoken.

William Freitas

LYSISTRATA

Type of work: Drama
Author: Aristophanes (c. 448-385 B.C.)
Type of plot: Utopian comedy
Time of plot: Fifth century B.C.
Locale: Athens
First presented: 411 B.C.

Lysistrata *is based on a highly comic assumption, probably ancient even in the time of Aristophanes, that is as impossible as it is comic; but the idea that women might coerce their men into laying down their weapons produced a bawdy and delightful work of art.*

Lysistrata is the most frequently produced Greek drama in the modern theater. Reasons for its current vogue are not hard to find, for the play deals openly with sex, feminism, and pacifism—all major preoccupations of America in the late 1960's and early 1970's. A popular slogan of our time, "Make Love, Not War," sums up perfectly Aristophanes' attitude in this comedy. Our era has largely taken up *Lysistrata* for its ideology, rather than for its intrinsic value as a play. Yet it does provide some amusing, and bawdily skeptical, entertainment.

By contrast with other of Aristophanes' plays on similar themes, *Lysistrata* seems rather thin in imagination. Undoubtedly the basic assumption of the comedy—that women could achieve peace and governmental reform through sexual abstinence—was an ancient idea even in Aristophanes' time. *The Acharnians* and *The Peace* present novel, if bizarre, methods of achieving peace, while *The Thesmophoriazusae* and *The Ecclesiazusae* show women in a funnier, more satirical light. However, modern audiences as a rule appreciate directness and simplicity, and do not object to a lack of originality in many instances; but they would probably dislike a satirical treatment of Lysistrata, the heroine, who is both a militant feminist and pacifist. The play seems eminently suited to contemporary tastes and interests.

In structure the drama is smooth and straightforward. First the problem is presented: the women are sick of having their husbands absent because of the Peloponnesian War. The solution is that they avoid sex with their husbands, but at the same time tease them, until the men decide to settle the war from sheer frustration. Out of that solution everything else follows—the women capture the treasury; the old men try to force the women into submission; when force fails the two sides hold an inconclusive debate in which the magistrate, a chief warmonger, is first decked out like a woman and then as a corpse by hostile females; then the women begin to defect from their oath of chastity; after a desperate effort Lysistrata whips the females into shape; and the men agree to seek peace. When negotiation fails between the Athenians and the Spartans, the diplomats are tricked into a peace settlement through feasting and drinking. Given the basic idea, almost all of this action is predictable. If it amuses, it is never surprising enough to produce laughter. Perhaps the best, and most comic idea in the play is that diplomats should never negotiate when they are sober. Cleverness and greed are inimical to peace, while drink and festivity promote good will.

Sex is a traditional subject for comedy, and particularly the battle of the sexes. In fact, Greek comedy evolved in part from phallic farce, and there are phallic jokes in *Lysistrata,* although this element is not prominent. The implicit humor of the play's central idea rests in the belief of Aristophanes and his audience that the Athenian women were inveterate tipplers and lechers. Of course, the audience consisted largely of men, to whom the idea of women taking over the affairs of state would have seemed irresistibly comic. The slapstick and banter between the chorus of old men and the chorus of women simply restate the age-old contest between male and female. The male chorus puts the matter succinctly when it says, in effect, "We can't live with 'em, and we can't live without 'em."

Yet *Lysistrata* carries a more important theme than sexuality, which is merely shown as a weapon to bring about peace. At the time this play was first produced in 411 B.C., Athens had been through twenty hard years of war with Sparta, and the end of this conflict was still seven years in the future. The seriousness of the war is brought out very forcefully when Lysistrata tells the magistrate that sons have perished in battle, and that many young women will never find mates because of this. The fact that the chorus consists of old men underscores the point that many Athenian youths had died in the Peloponnesian War. Here the drama becomes absolutely serious and reveals Aristophanes' true feelings about the war with no trace of buffoonery. The dramatist clearly regards Lysistrata as something of a heroine and not a butt for humor. When men have failed so badly to govern the affairs of the city, he says, it's time for the women to take over. But all the while Aristophanes and his audience are fully aware of the weaknesses of women. So in essence, the playwright is scolding the Athenian men by telling them that if they cannot put an end to the war in twenty years, they might as well give up.

Today the play is presented on stage or in print as straight drama, entirely spoken. The truth is that *Lysistrata* was originally presented as a musical comedy, in song, with choreography, colorful costumes, and masks. The actors were all male, as in the Shakespeare theater. This type of presentation tended to soften the strength of Aristophanes biting wit, and it gave the play an air of spectacle, of festivity. Aristophanes had the keen comic wit of a Bernard Shaw, but it was employed in a different medium and style, and used for opposite social ends.

James Weigel, Jr.

THE MABINOGION

Type of work: Tales
Author: Unknown
Type of plots: Heroic romances
Time of plots: The Middle Ages
Locale: Arthurian Britain, mainly Wales
First transcribed: Twelfth and thirteenth centuries; first translation published, 1838-1849

This collection of Welsh tales is among the finest examples of medieval literature, representing the best of Celtic culture. The world they disclose is one of great heroes, black villains, incomparable battles, women of great beauty, magnificent splendor, wretched squalor, chivalric romance, and harsh brutality.

Without the eleven stories which were gathered together and given the title *The Mabinogion*—a reservoir of Celtic folklore themes and motifs—the course of medieval literature, specifically that of Arthurian romance, and indeed European imaginative literature in general would not now possess their incomparable richness and character. These few tales, with a long oral tradition before they were written down, perhaps in the twelfth or thirteenth century, furnish some of the best known characters and motifs of European romance. Contrary to what one might expect, these are not crude stories from which more sophisticated Welsh tales came down to us. They have unity, assurance of style, skillful dialogue, accurate delineation of character, rich color, and a perspective of life that is noble. Their author, or innumerable authors, were artists well trained in nuances and subtleties of language. No one, of course, has ever doubted that the Welsh were skilled storytellers. So, we know, were the Bretons and Icelandic bards. And their talent has left indelible impressions upon Western literature. *The Mabinogion,* in particular, has contributed significant and ancient folkloric themes as well as some of the earliest lore of Britain.

Certain tales in this collection, because of their literary sophistication and possible contribution to the corpus of Arthurian romance, deserve close analysis: "Kilhwch and Olwen," "The Dream of Rhonabwy" and the three prose romances: "Owain," "Gerint," and "Peredur."

The unknown author of "Kilhwch and Olwen," one of the most artistic and enthusiastic contributors in *The Mabinogion,* creates a world of magic, color, and vigorous action. He narrates the story of the Celtic hero, Kilhwch, who seeks a giant's daughter for his wife. The plot is a typical mytho-heroic quest, with a list of forty tasks Kilhwch must accomplish before he wins Ysbaddaden's daughter, Olwen. The tasks (quest) are not so important as the assemblage of attendant persons to Kilhwch, which include his cousin Arthur, the latter's wife Gwenhwyfar (Guinevere), Bedwyr (Bedevere), and Cel (Kay). These form a nucleus for the later Arthurian Round Table Fellowship. Appearing here, too, is the giant herdsman, a familiar motif in folklore, one to surface in romances of the French Chrétien de Troyes.

An important contribution to medieval romance generally is that richness of color that vibrates and almost bursts prismatically in the Welsh narrative. Olwen wears a robe of flame-red silk and necklace of red gold set with pearls and rubies. The author states her hair was yellower "than the flower of the broom," her cheeks redder "than the reddest foxgloves." Wherever she walks, white flowers spring up behind her. Kilhwch himself rides with two greyhounds in collars of red gold; his purple mantle has a red-gold apple in each corner.

"The Dream of Rhonabwy," one of the early dream visions in Celtic literature, lacks such movement and character description but has more realism. The dream deals with Arthur's battles against the Saxons; the main incident is the game played between Arthur and Owain with its conflict between the former's men and the latter's ravens. Norman-French themes combine with older Irish and Welsh ones here with possible foreshadowing of Morgain la Fée (Modron), a shape-shifting figure who weaves her way through various Continental romances bringing magic birds, healing plasters, rings, and curative waters to innumerable heroes in time of need.

The importance of the three prose romances in *The Mabinogion,* ones which do not belong to the four Branches, lies in their connection with three similar works by Chrétien de Troyes. Much critical debate has been carried on between the Celticists, those who feel Welsh tradition underlies the spread of Arthurian material on the Continent, and the Continentalists, who assert that the latter influenced Welsh stories. As Gwen Jones notes, opinion is swinging toward the Celticists because of evidence from linguistics, comparative folklore, and methods of composition in the Middle Ages. At any rate, parallels between "Owain," "Peredur," and "Gerint" on the one hand, and Chrétien's similar verse romances on the other, are considerable; perhaps the Welsh authors and the French romancer worked from a lost common source.

The characters in the three Welsh tales may lack depth and the actions themselves may be insufficiently motivated, but Owain, Gerint, and Peredur partake of adventures which are entertaining. If the narratives lack the meaning and skillful joining of incident found in Chrétien's poems, this seems purposeful rather than due to bungling artistry. Besides, many of the tales in *The Mabinogion* are probably retellings of material whose origins may have been forgotten, if indeed they were ever known. Bits of ancient Irish stories, Norman-French fragments and archaic traditions in Welsh make up their subject matter; the Welsh tellers contributed the color and vigor of action. The audience must have loved this excess color in garments, tapestries, ornaments, and armor, and the innumerable battles and adventures, whether these were smoothly connected or not. Cohesive unity was not the author's or authors' intent as it was that of Chrétien de Troyes.

The familiar world of "hunting, fighting, shape-shifting and magic" is there; so is the "emperour" Arthur presiding over a court rich with armor and jewels, beautiful ladies and brave knights. The nebulous, unidentified sixth century "battle leader," as the Latin chronicler Nennius described him, may have been only a local chieftain leading somewhat limited skirmishes in southwest Britain. But now in *The Mabinogion* he returns to literature a powerful and glorious king. He presides over an extensive court, and important kings from all over the Western world come to pay him homage.

Whether he lived or not, this is the hero England needed and will always remember. And the Welsh tales of *The Mabinogion* helped immeasurably in clothing him and his famous knights with colorful splendor, regardless of possible influences from other sources such as Geoffrey of Monmouth's *History of the Kings of Britain,* Chrétien's narrative poems, or accounts lost in the mists of much earlier periods.

Muriel B. Ingham

MACBETH

Type of work: Drama
Author: William Shakespeare (1564-1616)
Type of plot: Romantic tragedy
Time of plot: Eleventh century
Locale: Scotland
First presented: 1606

This shortest of Shakespeare's four major tragedies was written to be performed for King James I and was designed to appeal to the monarch's fascination with witchcraft and supernatural phenomena. The play explores the nature of ambition and the complexities of moral responsibility through the story of a nobleman driven to murder at the instigation of his power-hungry wife. Macbeth's doom is fixed at this first evil act, after which he descends deeper and deeper into degradation in an attempt to conceal the crime and guarantee the invulnerability of his new position of power.

Not only is *Macbeth* by far the shortest of Shakespeare's great tragedies but it is also anomalous in several structural respects. Like *Othello,* and very few other Shakespearean plays, *Macbeth* is without the complications of a sub-plot. Consequently, the action moves forward in a swift and inexorable rush. More significantly, the climax, the murder of Duncan, takes place very early in the play. The result is that attention is focused on the manifold consequences of the crime rather than on the ambiguities or moral dilemmas which precede or occasion it.

Thus, the play is not like *Othello,* where the hero commits murder only after long plotting by the villain, nor is it like *Hamlet,* where the hero spends most of the play in moral indecision. It is more like *King Lear,* where destructive action flows from the central premise of the division of the kingdom. But *Macbeth* is much different from *King Lear* in the way that it does not raise the monumental, cosmic questions of good and evil in nature; instead it explores the moral and psychological effects of evil in the life of one man. For all the power and prominence of Lady Macbeth, the drama remains essentially the story of the lord, who commits regicide and thereby enmeshes himself in a complex web of consequences.

When Macbeth first enters, he is far from the villain whose experiences the play subsequently describes. He has just returned from a military success that has covered him with glory in defense of the crown. He is rewarded by the grateful Duncan, with preferment as Thane of Cawdor. This excellence and honor, which initially qualify him for the role of hero, ironically intensify the horror of the murder Macbeth soon commits.

His fall is rapid and his crime is more clearly a sin than is usually the case in tragedy. It is not mitigated by mixed motives or insufficient knowledge. Moreover, the sin is regicide, an action viewed by the Renaissance as exceptionally foul since it struck at God's representative on earth. The sin is so boldly offensive that many have tried to find extenuation in the impetus given Macbeth by the witches. However, the witches do not control behavior in the play. They are symbolic of evil and prescient of crimes which are to come, but they neither encourage nor facilitate Macbeth's actions. They are merely a poignant reminder of the ambition which is already within Macbeth. Indeed, when he discusses the witches' prophecy with Lady Macbeth, it is clear that the possibility has been discussed before.

Nor can we shift responsibility to Lady Macbeth despite her mannish goading of her husband. In one, perhaps amoral, way, she is merely acting out the role of the good wife, encouraging her husband to do what she believes is in his best interests. In any case, she is rather a catalyst and supporter; she does not make the grim decision for Macbeth and he never tries to lay the blame on her.

When Macbeth proceeds on his bloody course, there is little extenuation in his brief failure of nerve. He is an ambitious man, overpowered by his high aspirations. Nevertheless, we view Macbeth with much sympathy. Despite the clear-cut evil of his actions, we never feel the distaste we deserve for villains such as Iago or Cornwall, perhaps because Macbeth is not evil incarnate, but a human being who has sinned, no matter how serious the transgression. In addition, we are as much affected by what Macbeth says about his actions as by the deeds themselves. Both substance and setting emphasize the great evil, but Macbeth does not go about his foul business easily. He knows what he is doing, but his agonizing reflections show a man increasingly out of control of his own moral destiny.

Although Lady Macbeth demonstrated greater courage and resolution at the time of the murder of Duncan, it is she who falls victim to the physical manifestations of remorse and literally dies of guilt. Macbeth, who starts more tentatively, becomes stronger, or perhaps more inured, as he faces the consequences of his initial crime. The play examines the effects of evil on Macbeth's character and on his subsequent moral behavior. The later murders flow naturally out of the first. Evil breeds evil in that, to protect himself and consolidate his position, Macbeth is almost forced to murder again. Successively, he kills Banquo, attempts to murder Fleance, and brutally exterminates Macduff's family. As his crimes increase, Macbeth's freedom seems to decrease, but his moral responsibility does not. His actions become more cold-blooded as his options disappear. His growing resolution and steadfastness in a precarious predicament are admirable, but his specific actions are repugnant.

Shakespeare does not allow Macbeth any convenient moral excuses. The dramatist is aware of the notion, from contemporary faculty psychology, of the dominant inclination. The idea is that any action performed makes it more likely that the person will perform other such actions. The operation of this phenomenon is apparent as, in the face of complications, Macbeth finds it increasingly easier to rise to the gruesome occasion. However, the dominant inclination never becomes a total determinant of behavior, so Macbeth is left without the excuse of loss of free will. But it does become ever more difficult to break the chain of events which are rushing him towards moral and physical destruction.

As he degenerates, he becomes more deluded about his invulnerability and more emboldened. What he gains in will and confidence is counterbalanced and eventually toppled by the iniquitous weight of the events he set in motion and felt he had to perpetuate. When he dies, as we knew all along he must, he seems almost to be released from the imprisonment of his own evil.

Edward E. Foster